OXFORD STUDIES IN DEMOCRATIZATION

Series editor: Laurence Whitehead

....

DEMOCRATIC CONSOLIDATION
IN EASTERN EUROPE

SIMON FRASER UNIVERSITY
W.A.C. BENNETT LIBRARY

OXFORD STUDIES IN DEMOCRATIZATION

Series editor: Laurence Whitehead

· · · · · · · · · · · · · · · · ·

Oxford Studies in Democratization is a series for scholars and students of comparative politics and related disciplines. Volumes will concentrate on the comparative study of the democratization processes that accompanied the decline and termination of the cold war. The geographical focus of the series will primarily be Latin America, the Caribbean, Southern and Eastern Europe, and relevant experiences in Africa and Asia.

OTHER BOOKS IN THE SERIES

Democratic Consolidation in Eastern Europe

Volume I
Institutional Engineering

....

JAN ZIELONKA

OXFORD

UNIVERSITY PRESS

OXFORD

UNIVERSITY PRESS

Great Clarendon Street, Oxford OX2 6DP

Oxford University Press is a department of the University of Oxford.
It furthers the University's objective of excellence in research, scholarship,
and education by publishing worldwide in

Oxford New York

Athens Auckland Bangkok Bogotá Buenos Aires Calcutta
Cape Town Chennai Dar es Salaam Delhi Florence Hong Kong Istanbul
Karachi Kuala Lumpur Madrid Melbourne Mexico City Mumbai
Nairobi Paris São Paulo Shanghai Singapore Taipei Tokyo Toronto Warsaw

and associated companies in Berlin Ibadan

Oxford is a registered trade mark of Oxford University Press
in the UK and certain other countries

Published in the United States
by Oxford University Press Inc., New York

British Library Cataloguing in Publication Data

Data available

Library of Congress Cataloging in Publication Data

Democratic consolidation in Eastern Europe / Jan Zielonka, editor.
p. cm. — (Oxford studies in democratization)
Includes bibliographical references and index.
Contents: v. 1. Institutional engineering
1. Democratization—Europe, Eastern. 2. Democratization—Former Soviet republics.
3. Europe, Eastern—Politics and government—1989– 4. Former Soviet republics—Politics
and government. 5. Constitutional history—Europe, Eastern. 6. Constitutional
history—Former Soviet republics. I. Zielonka, Jan, 1955– II. Series.

JN96.A58 D43 2001 320.94′091717—dc21 00–046509
ISBN 0-19-924167-8
ISBN 0-19-924408-1 (pbk)

1 3 5 7 9 10 8 6 4 2

Typeset by Graphicraft Limited, Hong Kong
Printed by T. J. International Ltd.,
Padstow, Cornwall

....

Preface

....

This study of constitutional processes in thirteen post-communist states is one of three books prepared within the Project on Democratic Consolidation in Eastern Europe. The project has been sponsored by the European University Institute in Florence and its Research Council. The two other volumes in the series deal with (a) international and transnational factors involved in democratic consolidation, and (b) civil society and democratic orientations within Eastern Europe. The aim of the project is to contrast a set of democracy theories with empirical evidence accumulated in Eastern Europe over the last ten years. We try to avoid complex debates about definitions, methods, and the uses and misuses of comparative research. Instead we try to establish what has really happened in the region, and which of the existing theories have proved helpful in explaining these developments. Each volume starts with a presentation of conceptual and comparative frameworks, followed by in-depth analyses of the individual countries undergoing democratic consolidation.

I am especially grateful to the European University Institute and its Research Council for their generous financial support and intellectual leadership. Individual members of the Research Council such as Roeland In't Veld, Pierre Hassner, Johan Olsen, Vincent Wright, and Fritz Scharpf gave me the initial encouragement to undertake this ambitious project and guided me through its successive stages. I am also indebted to my co-editors of the two other volumes, Dieter Fuchs, Ronald Inglehart, Hans-Dieter Klingemann, and Alex Pravda, who provided important bridges between the project's three distinct parts. Special thanks go to Nida Gelazis who has made the most valuable organizational and editorial contribution to this volume, and to Alexandra George who has done the final polishing and prepared the book for publication. Excellent secretarial assistance was provided by Dorothea Detring. Above all I am indebted to the authors of the individual chapters for all the effort, talent, persistence, and devotion invested in successive drafts of their contributions.

Finally, I would like to thank Dominic Byatt from Oxford University Press for his willingness to take on this large publishing project and for ensuring its smooth accomplishment.

J. Z.

Contents

List of Figures

....

List of Tables

....

··

List of Contributors

··

KLAUS VON BEYME is Professor of Political Science at the University of Heidelberg.

MIRO CERAR is Assistant Professor at the Law Faculty of the University of Ljubljana and adviser on constitutional issues to the National Assembly of the Republic of Slovenia.

ROBERT ELGIE is Senior Lecturer in European Politics at the University of Nottingham.

GADIS GADZHIEV is a justice of the Constitutional Court of the Russian Federation and Professor at Moscow University.

VENELIN I. GANEV is a Visiting Fellow at the Helen Kellogg Institute for International Studies, University of Notre Dame.

NIDA GELAZIS is a Research Associate at the Robert Schuman Centre, the European University Institute in Florence.

PETR KOPECKÝ is a Lecturer in the Department of Politics at Sheffield University.

ALEXANDER LUKASHUK is a researcher and Director of the Belarus Service at Radio Free Europe/Radio Liberty in Prague.

DARINA MALOVÁ is Professor of Political Science at Comenius University, Bratislava.

LEONARDO MORLINO is Professor of Political Science at the University of Florence.

VELLO PETTAI is Lecturer in Political Science at the University of Tartu.

WOJCIECH SADURSKI is Professor of Legal Theory and Philosophy of Law at the European University Institute in Florence.

ADOLF SPRUDZS is the Foreign Law Librarian and Lecturer in Legal Bibliography, Emeritus, at the D'Angelo Law Library, the University of Chicago.

ISTVAN SZIKINGER is Staff Attorney at the Constitutional and Legislative Policy Institute in Budapest.

RENATE WEBER is Lecturer in International Human Rights at the National School for Political Science and Administration in Bucharest.

KATARYNA WOLCZUK is Lecturer at the Centre for Russian and East European Studies, the University of Birmingham.

MIROSŁAW WYRZYKOWSKI is Professor of Law at Warsaw University.

JAN ZIELONKA is Professor of Social and Political Sciences at the European University Institute in Florence.

PART I

Institutional Engineering in a Comparative Perspective

Institutional Engineering and Transition to Democracy

Klaus von Beyme

The enlightened neo-institutionalism of the 1980s brought institutions back into political science. Institutionalism or 'Grandpa's political science' had been supplanted by the competing paradigms of behaviouralism and neo-Marxism. These bitter enemies agreed on one point: institutions are only a framework to study the behaviour of actors. Yet even the neo-institutionalists still conceived of institutions in a rather instrumental way, as channels for political actors.[1]

It was left to the palaeo-institutionalists to reintroduce holistic considerations of institutional engineering. 'Grandpa's political science', with its tired discussions of the virtues of parliamentary or presidential government, enjoyed a renaissance. Some of these palaeo-institutionalists, such as the Italian Giovanni Sartori, belonged to the conservative resistance against the 'behavioural revolt'. They had long defended the study of politics as such against the creeping sociologization of political science. In France it was unnecessary to 'defend politics', since the institutionalist bias of political science there had never been abandoned. The consequences of the neglect of institutions in political science were clearest in Germany. In the 1960s, when Germany pondered the introduction of a British-style plurality electoral law, the electoral commission included three social scientists. By the 1970s, in the Enquete-commission for constitutional reform, only one political scientist was represented. Political science had left constitutional engineering to lawyers.

---

[1] See Renate Mayntz and Fritz W. Scharpf (eds.), *Gesellschaftliche Selbstregelung und politische Steuerung* (Frankfurt: Campus, 1995), 44.

Constitutional engineering involves the rationalistic bias that good constitutions can be designed. Leftist rational-choice neo-institutionalists, such as Jon Elster, insist that the consequences of constitutional change can hardly be predicted.[2] He is thus interested in promoting justice rather than speculating about solving problems efficiently. Non-normatively oriented analysts, meanwhile, distrusted 'good institutions' and instead proposed to educate good citizens in 'civil religion' to participate in a civil society. They neglected, however, the basic truth that such a programme also requires institutions (even 'good institutions') since state-run educational efforts may be prone to abuse of power.

The established democracies have institutions that are used by their citizens in a routinized way without asking for their legitimization.[3] Nevertheless, some institutions have to be protected by state measures and appeals to the people. This is true, for instance, of the electoral system when participation approaches the 50 per cent threshold and puts the democratic majority principle into question. Institutional engineering was thus not a concept invented for the new wave of transitions from dictatorship to democracy. It was rather a concept for the transition from democracy to democracy at a time when a consolidated democracy was in crisis.

Contemporary Italy is one case. Some scholars began asking whether Italy ever met the criteria for consolidation before 1994, when the old system was shaken without major resistance on the part of the established forces. French history provides other instances. In the nineteenth century a British citizen who wanted to buy the French Constitution received this answer from a bookstore owner: 'Sorry, we don't sell periodical literature.' The stability of consolidated democracy after the Second World War has obscured the fact that stability is the exception rather than the rule in constitutional history.[4]

---

[2] See Jon Elster and Rune Slagstad (eds.), *Constitutionalism and Democracy* (Cambridge: Cambridge University Press, 1988).

[3] See Roland L. Jesperson, 'Institutions, Institutional Effects and Institutionalism', in Walter W. Powell and Paul J. DiMaggio (eds.), *The New Institutionalism in Organizational Analysis* (Chicago: University of Chicago Press, 1991), 143–63.

[4] Institutional engineering in Western Europe is used all the time because of the European Union. In Germany one-fifth of all laws are the result of an impulse from Brussels—quite frequently involving the Constitution. There is not yet a European constitution, which would render national constitutional engineering

After the war, the European democracies were fairly similar variations of parliamentarism—including France before 1957. France introduced a semi-presidential system in 1958 and, ever since, systems in crisis—such as Austria and Finland—have also turned to constitutional engineering (in particular strengthening the popularly elected president) to resolve problems of political instability. In most European countries the democratic crisis is spreading, as evidenced by the decline of party identification and voter participation, fractionalization of the party system, and the alienation of citizens from what they call the 'political class'. In Italy alone, confidence in institutions is at the all-time low of 32 per cent.[5] Constitutional engineering seems to be the way out.

Given this model, Eastern Europe was unable to import foreign institutions. The concept of constitutional engineering is neutral on the question of whether constitutional provisions develop via *diffusion* and import from other countries, or spring up as *functional equivalents* because constitutional engineers in different countries have to solve similar problems. Ruslan Chasbulatov, as chair of the parliament in opposition to President Yeltsin, lectured deputies on their three choices: presidential, semi-presidential, and parliamentary. The result of the constitution-making process in Russia was nevertheless a rather original combination of all three, anchored in the semi-presidential system.[6]

Institutional engineering in Western Europe concerns four democratic institutions:

- the constitution as a whole;
- the discovery of the semi-presidential system;
- the search for a new electoral law that renders efficient majorities;
- the use of plebiscitarian instruments to overcome the crisis of the representative system.

obsolete and reduce constitutional adaptation to judicial review from Luxembourg. Quite a number of experts warn us that the longer a European constitution is postponed, the more complicated it will be to agree on one. See, for instance, Dieter Grimm, *Braucht Europa eine Verfassung?* (Munich: Carl Friedrich von Siemens-Stiftung, 1994).

[5] See Ola Listhaug and Mati Wiberg, 'Confidence in Political and Private Institutions', in Hans-Dieter Klingemann and Dieter Fuchs (eds.), *Citizens and the State* (New York: Oxford University Press, 1995), 298–322.

[6] See Klaus von Beyme, *America as a Model* (New York: St Martin's Press, 1987), 33 ff.

Constitutional engineering

Constitutional engineering in the transition from democracy to democracy has been rare. It happens most frequently when constitutions are federalized (Canada, Belgium), and when monarchies are adapted to modern parliamentary practice (Sweden 1971 and 1973). There is only one notable case of a transition from one type of regime (parliamentary) to another (semi-presidential)—France in 1958. In most other cases, institutional engineering has occurred without replacing the entire constitutional system.

Constitutions contain the meta-rules of a system that are accepted by all groups supporting the regime. The fourth wave of democratization in Europe, after 1989, led to a paradoxical situation: the meta-rules had to be fixed, though they were not yet consolidated and agreed upon by all of the relevant political forces of the transitional regimes. The written constitution, more so than in previous transitions, remained a promise for the future. What Schmitter called the partial regimes of the constitutional systems hardly developed: the party system took shape, but the system of interest groups remained underdeveloped.[7]

In the transition from communist dictatorship to democracy there was more institutional continuity than in processes of transition from fascist or right-wing dictatorships to democracy. Communist institutions after 1989 survived in many parts of Eastern Europe, especially those where transition was bargained for in a corporatist way (Poland and Hungary). In countries where a peaceful transition occurred, some institutions were already revitalized and democratized in the late 1980s. Then, in a second constitutional revitalization, the institutions of a market economy were added to the constitutional system.

Constitution-making is a power struggle, a fact clearly evident in Western Europe in the post-war years and in the 1970s, as well as in Eastern Europe in the early 1980s. Some of the old concepts, like perceiving parliamentary government as government by assembly, became an instrument for the hard-line communists to extend their power base. Sometimes the new presidential office antagonized floating parliamentary majorities, as in Poland and Russia.

---

[7] See Philippe Schmitter, 'Interest Systems and Consolidation of Democracy', in G. Marks and L. Diamond (eds.), *Reexamining Democracy* (London: Sage, 1992), 156–81.

Another paradox was evident: the more democratic the majority of the citizens pushing the regime to concede to the opposition was, the less radical was the constitutional innovation in the first phase of the transition. Countries with a clear *ruptura* were in the position to impose constitutional ideas, either by the new democratic forum (Czechoslovakia, Lithuania) or through the efforts of reform communists who remained in power during the first period of transition (Romania, Bulgaria, Albania, Serbia). A new constitution in the latter cases did not necessarily mean a new constitutional system. Where new states were created because of the disintegration of multiethnic regimes, such as in the Baltic states or in the successor states of Yugoslavia, the incentives to create a new constitution were great. Only Lithuania and Latvia revived their pre-communist constitutions in order to emphasize the continuity of their statehood, which perished through Soviet annexation.

Models of Constitutional Consolidation

Four models of constitutional consolidation were developed in Eastern Europe:

1. According to the Austrian example of 1945, the pre-authoritarian constitution could be reintroduced, as in Lithuania and Latvia. This road indicated continuity and denounced the Soviet period as a violent intermezzo.
2. Corporatist revolutions tend to amend the constitution if it contains enough provisions to please the bourgeois elements in the country, as was the case in the constitutions of the 1950s in Eastern Europe. In Hungary, Article 2.1 of the 1949 Constitution emphasized the values of bourgeois democracy as well as democratic socialism. In Albania, a substantially amended version of the 1976 Constitution was accepted as a draft because the debate on the 1991 Constitution was long and agreement was tenuous.
3. A third group went the normal route of working on a completely new constitutional draft. This happened mostly when one group had a hegemonic position—the Civic Forum in Czechoslovakia or the communists in Romania and Bulgaria (until 1991).
4. In some cases no agreement was reached, as in Poland in 1992. As a result, the 'Little Constitution' was adopted as a

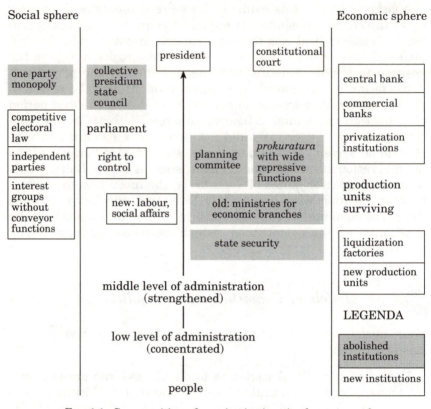

Fig. 1.1. *Superposition of new institutions in the process of constitutional engineering*

provisional constitution regulating the cooperation of the three branches of power. This situation resembled the French Third Republic, which in 1875 created three different constitutional laws but no integrated constitution. Article 77 of the Polish Little Constitution indicated which parts of the old socialist Constitution were still valid.

The Polish Constitution was accepted in May 1997 by a small majority of 52.71 per cent. Parliament had suspended the normal requirement that participation of 50 per cent of all eligible voters was required to validate a referendum's results, and indeed only 42.8 per cent of the electorate took part. The enemies of the new Constitution threatened to appeal to the Constitutional Court. Gdańsk, the east, and the south voted against the

Constitution, and to a great extent the Catholic Church remained sceptical. So the question arises whether or not Poland actually stuck to the model of 'non-agreement' in constitution-making.

The first compromise of 1992 weakened some of the president's powers and reserved for the parliament certain rights of co-determination through the possibility of a constructive vote of confidence (Art. 66.4). The president was not ready to accept this compromise and contributed to the destabilization of the government in order to impose himself as an arbiter. Before Prime Minister Hanna Suchocka was toppled in spring 1993, President Lech Wałęsa had negotiated with the Solidarity group and other foes of the prime minister. Solidarity consequently threatened strikes. This never went as far as the mobilization of the miners in Romania, who tried to oust Prime Minister Petr Roman. Suchocka made it clear, however, that these extra-parliamentary means weakened parliamentary democracy in Poland.

The experiences with Wałęsa had some impact on the framers of the 1997 Constitution. The presidential veto can now be overruled by three-fifths of all deputies (rather than the two-thirds required by the interim Constitution). Presidential influence on nominations of the most important ministers has been diminished. The president's budgetary veto—which had been abused by Wałęsa—was abolished altogether.

Most new constitutions combined Western democratic principles with indigenous national traditions. Russia called itself a 'democratic federative constitutional state with a republican form of government'. The 'social state' of previous versions was downgraded to a catalogue of 'declaration of state goals' (Art. 7 of the Russian Constitution). The principle of federalism, in contrast, was upgraded as debate continued. Originally, three 'Subjects of the Russian Federation' (Daghastan, Mordvinia, and the North Ossetian Republic) used the characterization 'socialist republic'. In the final version of the 1993 Russian Constitution, all socialist remnants had disappeared, though in the codification of the new economic system many concessions were made to the old *nomenklatura*. The parliamentary draft of the Russian Constitution contained an article on 'social market economy'. It disappeared and was downgraded to a more neutral reference to different forms of property (Art. 8.2 of the Russian Constitution). Article 9.3 of the 1992 draft Constitution emphasized a 'social partnership', but this was sacrificed in search of a compromise between reformers and hard-liners. In some respects, there was no harm done, and overblown promises were usually omitted. Sometimes the new formula sounded like an adaptation of communist constitutional articles. 'Social partnership' is reminiscent of the old 'socialist community' which hardly improved the liberty of Soviet citizens.

In Hungary, the result of constitutional bargaining proclaimed a 'peaceful political transition to a legal state which realizes a multi-party system' (preamble to the Hungarian Constitution). The 'social market economy' was accepted in many East European countries. In Germany it had been a propaganda slogan since Erhard, and remained such until it was introduced into the State Treaty with the GDR that ultimately led to German reunification (Art. 1.3, 11). Even the principles of the magic quadrangle of economic goals of the state (full employment, anti-inflation policy, balanced state budget, and balanced foreign trade) earned constitutional importance. The formula 'social and democratic legal state' in the German Basic Law spread in the third wave of democratization after the Second World War (Spain 1978, Art. 1).

The self-images of the transitional regimes, as they were manifested in the new constitutions, were sometimes very vague. They included 'political pluralism' (Art. 1 of the Romanian Constitution or the 'parliamentary system of government' in Art. 1.1 of the Bulgarian Constitution) and even the catchword 'civil society' (which appears in the preambles of the 1992 Lithuanian Constitution and the Slovenian Constitution). Most states were so insecure of their continuity they made lengthy references to history. Lithuania hinted that its state tradition began 'many centuries ago'. Slovakia invoked the 'cultural heritage of Cyril and Methodius' and the 'historic bequest of the Grand Moravian Empire'. Croatia even inserted a historical list of all the sovereign decisions made by the Croatian estates (which operated within other empires).

The separation of Church and state was emphasized in many constitutions. This was not generally understood as an attack on the freedom to worship, as it had been in the early days of the liacist movements. The privileged mention of the 'traditional religion of the Republic' in the Bulgarian Constitution (Art. 13.3) was hardly compatible with the state's religious neutrality. Russia emphasized the secular character of the state more than others (Art. 14 of the Russian Constitution). No religion was to be imposed by the state. Religion in this respect was treated on equal footing with ideologies (Art. 13.2 of the Russian Constitution). The invocation of almighty God in the Polish draft Constitution was not unique among Catholic states (most outspoken were the Irish constitutions of 1937 and 1972, preamble). The culture of preambles even in modern liacist cultures has a threefold function: to sketch in a ceremonial language the basic principles of the system, to integrate citizens, and to mention hopes for the future. In Eastern Europe, where it was necessary both to promote the integration of citizens and to offer hope where the prospects for the future were dim, this kind of verbal integration flourished.

Much attention was devoted to preventing the recurrence of totalitarianism. Most abuses of the communist system were forbidden, such as forced labour, censorship (Art. 28.3 of the Russian Constitution, Art. 1 of the 1992 Slovene Constitution), and the death penalty (Art. 15.3 of the Slovak Constitution). 'The right to live' (Art. 28 of the Bulgarian Constitution, Art. 20 of the Russian Constitution) logically entails outlawing capital punishment. Russia, however, was not in a hurry to implement this stipulation. The 'right to live' was limited by the addition that the death penalty is possible until its abolition by a federal law.

The reaction to totalitarian dangers allowed truisms into constitutions, such as outlawing regulations that limit immigration and emigration of citizens (Art. 36 of the Estonian Constitution, Art. 27 of the Russian Constitution), forbidding deportation (Art. 36.2 of the Russian Constitution), torture (Art. 21 of the Russian Constitution), medical experiments on people (Art. 18.1–2 of the Estonian Constitution), or collecting data on citizens' private lives (Art. 45.1 of the August 1993 Russian Constitution). (It did not strengthen confidence in the new legal state when this last provision disappeared at the last minute.) In some countries the deprivation of citizenship was outlawed. Only Poland had a provision that allowed the president to deprive someone of citizenship (Art. 41 of the Little Constitution).

Other truisms reflecting good intentions included the sentence: 'unpublished laws are not applied' (Art. 15.3 of the Russian Constitution). One can imagine that this was meant to be a barrier against the Russian practice of governing by *ukazy*, but in a legal state this provision is superfluous. Contradictions and limitations of granted rights also hinder citizens' trust in the legal state. In Russia (Art. 55.2) it was ruled that human and citizens' rights should not be diminished by state activities. But the catalogues of exceptions invite some misgivings. Not only 'moral reasons, health, and the rights and interests of other persons', but even 'the defence of the country and the security of the state' could justify curbing human rights (Art. 55.3). 'State security' was surely one of the most abused notions under communist rule.

Following the German example, the constitutionality of political parties entered some of the budding democracies' constitutions (Art. 149.5 of the Bulgarian Constitution, Art. 48.3 of the Estonian Constitution, and Art. 5 of the Polish Little Constitution). In the Russian Constitution (Art. 13.5), social organizations are also included. In most of the countries, constitutional courts were developed, though only in a few cases were courts directly entrusted with decisions on the constitutional status of parties. In many countries the democratic status of interest groups was regulated. Mandatory membership in mass organizations was outlawed in Russia. Originally this provision was limited to the trade unions (draft 1992, Art. 29). Yeltsin's December 1993 Constitution postulates the right to quit any mass organization (Art. 30.2).

In most constitutions the protection of private property was new. In some countries state ownership of mines was protected (Yugoslavia, Art. 73). Certain rights regarding agricultural land were preserved in the constitutions of some of the successor states of Yugoslavia.

Government stability was a concern in many constitutions—as it had been after 1945 when the new democratic regimes first 'rationalized' the parliamentary system. In Bulgaria (Art. 99) and Hungary (Art. 33.3) the president is subject to certain rules of consultation. The Swedish constitutional reform of 1971 first introduced this kind of provision because the Riksdag majority distrusted the heir to the throne. The distrust was due to concern not so much about his democratic intentions, but rather about his intellectual abilities to handle difficult procedures of coalition-building. Although many constitutions preserved plebiscitarian elements of the former socialist constitutions, excesses of communist-manipulated democracy such as recalling deputies (Art. 6 of the Little Constitution) or the imperative mandate for deputies (Art. 67 of the Bulgarian Constitution) were forbidden.

The most important criterion for testing for the democratic convictions of the founding fathers of the new regimes was the treatment of ethnic minorities. Declarations of the 'multinational people' (preamble of the Russian Constitution) or invocations of the 'democratic tradition of nation-building' (Yugoslav Constitution, Art. 4) resemble—in their grandiosity and vagueness—the rhetoric of the old regime. The Russian Constitution caused concern in its (Art. 1.2) differentiation between the notions of 'Russian' (*russkij*, ethnic meaning) and *rossiskij* (legal meaning), but in the end declared the two terms synonymous. The treatment of different languages was the most important part of ethnic relations. Sometimes a state language was fixed (Art. 3 of the Bulgarian Constitution, Art. 14 of the Lithuanian Constitution). In Russia (Art. 26.2 of the Constitution) the right to speak one's native language was granted for all ethnic groups. But a language of the state (Art. 68.1), territorial languages of the republics aside, was written into the Constitution. The most curious provision was found in Yugoslavia. After forty years of propaganda promoting the integration of the Serbo-Croatian language, the Constitution under Serbian dominance restricted the notion of 'Serbian' to two dialects written in the Cyrillic alphabet.

State languages can also be found in Western constitutions. Spain's Constitution (Art. 3.3) mentions the right and duty to know and use the state language. In Bulgaria (Art. 36.2–3) this was formulated as a 'duty to learn' Bulgarian, in line with the tradition of the Bulgarization of Turkish names in the 1980s. More trustworthy was the Slovak formulation (Art. 32) which did not impose a duty, but only mentioned the right of the ethnic minorities to learn the state language. Apparently those countries that were fairly ethnically homogeneous could afford to be most liberal —such as Hungary. No one should draw conclusions from the text of the Constitution about the social reality of ethnic politics. But it is noteworthy that the degree of liberalism and pluralism in most cases is already visible in the constitutions. Most important are the regulations on ethnic relations in laws supporting affirmative action. The Czech Republic and Hungary were most generous in this respect by granting ethnic minorities financial and organizational assistance.

In many cases, remnants of the old system are found in the descriptions of social rights and citizens' duties in the constitutions. Poland (1952/92, Art. 69) declared a right to recreation and leisure and promised to support the creative intelligentsia (Art. 77). Hardly any constitution went so far as the Constitution of the *Land* Sachsen-Anhalt in 1946, which incorporated the 'right of youth to pleasure'—a fairly ridiculous variation of the old principle of the 'pursuit of happiness'.

The constitution-making process in East Germany was initiated before March 1990, and the round-table discussion on a new democratic constitution at the time was more realistic than that of other ex-communist countries in stating that social rights are basically meaningless in areas where the democratic state is unable to control the creation of such goods as housing or work. As in the West, environmental protection was the door where unrealistic formulations entered the constitution. 'Everyone has a right to a sound environment' (Art. 44 of the Slovak Constitution) raises many expectations that cannot be satisfied. German leftist analysts, therefore, renounced writing into the Constitution everything under the sun that is good and desirable.[8] Nevertheless, this precedent did not prevent other constitution makers from promising a 'human demographic policy' (Russian constitutional draft 1992, Art. 8).

The 'duties of citizens' remained in many constitutions. The duty to pay taxes was emphasized much more than in communist regimes (Art. 53 of the Romanian Constitution, Art. 57 of the Russian Constitution). Military service (Art. 59.3 of the Russian Constitution) is mentioned as a duty, in combination with the right to choose civilian service instead. Some declarations, however, came close to older communist formulas. In other cases, the state handed over part of its responsibilities to its citizens by imposing on them the duty to preserve historical and cultural monuments (Art. 43). The constitutional sections dealing with the duties of citizens are certainly the most patronizing aspects of the new regimes.

Western analysts should be fair: as products of compromise, constitutions are hardly ever without contradictions. Universal declarations are often found next to state interventions on behalf of very specialized interests such as 'agriculture in the mountains' (Art. 23 of the Swiss Constitution). The more protracted the constitution-making process, as in Russia or Poland, the greater the contradictions in the constitutional system.

The Semi-presidential System

Constitutions are declarations about the distribution of power, and institutional engineering means the channelling of power through constitution-making. The search for good institutions has led—in both the East and the West—to a positive re-evaluation of hybrids, such as the semi-presidential system, and electoral laws that offer a bonus to majorities without being majoritarian. In both cases, loose talk of 'mixed systems' is widespread. But in fact, the German electoral system is no more a 'mixed type' than the French system is semi-presidential. The former is but a variation of the proportional system, while the latter is basically a subtype of parliamentary

---

[8] See Bernd Guggenberger et al., *Eine Verfassung für Deutschland* (Munich: Hanser, 1991).

regimes. Some authors try to create an independent type,[9] but a more rigorous examination shows that the French system is closer to a parliamentary regime than to an authentic presidential system.[10] There is a huge range of variation in presidential powers of presidents in semi-presidential systems. In some countries, such as France, the presidency is much stronger than provided for in the constitution; in others, such as Finland or Iceland, it is *de facto* weaker than provided for by the constitution. This relative power position may even vary over time. Even in the true presidential system of the United States, it was accurate at different times to speak of 'congressional government' or the 'imperial presidency'.[11]

Constitutional engineering in Italy has led to a debate in which Sartori's dictum that mixed types are better than pure types is widely accepted.[12] The Italian example discredited institutional engineering, however, because leading figures, such as Berlusconi, changed their opinions several times while calling on experts at every turn. Most absurd was the discussion on popularly elected prime ministers. Israel has elected one for the first time, and given the disintegration of the peace process that followed, its example offers no great hope. Thus far no West European system has introduced a semi-presidential system in a recent crisis. But it is noteworthy that public opinion polls show in most countries that the majority of people favour the popular election of presidents, thus advocating a semi-presidential system without knowing it.

At a March 1997 hearing of the subcommittee on 'form of government' of the parliamentary committee on constitutional reform, Sartori advocated the French version of a semi-presidential system with two rounds of voting—on the condition that the requirement for absolute majority was facilitated by a bipolar party system. But what he failed to make clear was that this system prevents the creation of a bipolar system because the president does not rely on a political party to the same extent that a parliamentary prime minister does.

[9] See Horst Bahro and Ernst Weser, 'Das Semipräsidentielle System: "Bastard" oder Regierungsform suigeneris?', *Zeitschrift für Parlamentsfragen*, 3 (1995), 471–85.

[10] See Winfried Steffani, 'Semi-Präsidentialismus: Ein selbständiger Systemtyp? Zur Unterscheidung von Legislative und Parlament', *Zeitschrift für Parlamentsfragen*, H4 (1995), 621–41.

[11] See von Beyme, *America as a Model*.

[12] Giovanni Sartori, *Comparative Constitutional Engineering* (Houndmills: Macmillan, 1994), 136 ff.

TABLE 1.1. *Modes of transition and governmental systems*

Erosion		Collapse		Continuity of elites (sometimes combined with the foundation of an independent state)	
Semi-presidential	Parliamentary	Semi-presidential	Parliamentary	Semi-presidential	Parliamentary
Poland	Hungary	Lithuania	Czech Rep. Slovakia	Russia Belarus Ukraine Romania Croatia Serbia	Bulgaria Latvia Slovenia

This plebiscitarian mood—reinforced in some cases by demagogic leaders who hoped to have easier access to power by popular vote —has created many semi-presidential systems in Eastern Europe. Some authors try to subdivide presidential-parliamentary and parliamentary-presidential systems.[13] This is, however, hardly convincing. Croatia or Serbia, according to their constitutions, would belong to those semi-presidential systems with a preponderance of parliament, but even a superficial observer will not confound the legal regulation with the *de facto* powers of Franjo Tudjman or Slobodan Milosevic.

More important is the question of the correlation between the path of transition and the type of regime. This is difficult to detect. Both regimes occur in all three types of transitions. Only the type 'continuity of elites' shows a preponderance of semi-presidential systems. Whereas the new or old elites used constitutional engineering in order to manipulate the electoral law in their favour, tinkering with regime type has not yet occurred. There has been no transition from parliamentary system to semi-presidentialism or the other way around. Even the two former communist systems that declined by erosion and negotiated revolution and kept parts of the constitution open to change—namely Poland and Hungary—are not likely to change the system, having agreed on a final constitutional settlement. The Polish case showed how difficult it was to reach a minimal consensus on the Constitution of 1997.

[13] Wolfgang Merkel et al. (eds.), *Gesellschaftliche Selbstregelung und politische Steuerung* (Frankfurt: Campus, 1996), 84.

Semi-presidential systems in the former Soviet Union are either disguised dictatorships or—in the case of the four predominantly Slavic republics—anocracies dominated by presidents. Parliament in no case is an effective counterweight to presidential power. In Belarus and Kazakhstan, parliament has been degraded to a kind of presidential legislative staff. The constitutions are made 'by the tailor for the tailor'.[14] Powers in hiring and firing ministers, dissolution of parliament, active and veto functions (decrees and ukazocracy) in legislation, and a substantial influence in amending the constitutions made presidents almost invulnerable to parliamentary activities. Certain by-institutions, such as the security council, have been dubbed 'the new politburo', since they enjoy power without responsibility.

Electoral Laws

Transitions to democracy were frequently combined with a new electoral law. After the first wave of democratization in this century, after 1918, the transition was accompanied by a transition to or a restoration of proportional electoral systems. Also, most institutional engineering after consolidation in Western democracies concerned variations of the proportional system. In the 1990s only two exceptions to this rule can be found:

New Zealand changed from the British plurality voting system to a personalized proportional system similar to the German model. A new sensitivity towards minorities—especially the Maori— contributed to this reform.[15]

Italy changed from the proportional system to a variation of a majoritarian system. This case is important because it was not a question of fairness, as it was in New Zealand, but of a deep crisis in the parliamentary system. The electoral reform of August 1993 was oriented towards the referendum of April 1993. The electoral reform seemed to enjoy high legitimacy, since 82.7 per cent of the voters had endorsed it. In both chambers, three-quarters of the seats were distributed according to plurality vote in single-member districts and one-quarter as a proportional compensation.

[14] See Jon Elster, 'Afterword: The Making of Post-communist Presidencies', in Ray Taras (ed.), *Post-communist Presidencies* (Cambridge: Cambridge University Press, 1997), 225–38.

[15] Stephan Ingh, 'Electoral Reform in New Zealand', *Journal of Legislative Studies* (1995), 76–92.

This rescued some minor groups. The expectation that the new system would usher out the corrupt old political class was not realized. Not a bipolar, but rather a tripolar system developed. The electoral alliances that were admitted prevented the system from realizing the idea of a direct investiture in the executive by the voters. Regional fragmentation of the party system increased, especially in the north where the Lega Nord dominated. The centre was reduced but it survived.[16]

Experts had long resisted fundamental electoral reform. Norberto Bobbio once argued that it was unfair to force the two venerable parties that participated in the *risorgimento*, the Liberals and the Republicans, to disappear through electoral engineering. The minor reform of 1993 forced several small groups to disappear. It brought even the formerly leading party, the Christian Democrats, to the brink of ruin. But they survived and, renewed as the Popolari, won 11.1 per cent in 1994. The 'éternel marais du centrisme' denounced by Duverger in the Third and Fourth Republics has not yet completely dried out.

The reform as a first attempt at institutional engineering proved to be half-hearted. 'Maggioritario ma non troppo',[17] two Italian political scientists have dubbed it. The Partito Democratico della Sinistra (PDS), the Lega Nord, and the Christian Democrats (PPI) demanded the absolute majority voting system with two rounds according to the French model in the Fifth Republic. Conservative analysts, on the contrary, opposed the majoritarian tendencies in the country and called the half-measure an 'act of violence' alien to Italian political culture.[18] The limits of institutional engineering were visible: the reforms were to be established by popular will, while experts in electoral engineering wanted a radical reform that was difficult to explain to the voters. Democratic legitimization of a reform threatened to fail because the matter was too complicated for simple yes-or-no answers by voters.

The logically consistent formula was not visible because electoral engineering was used to calculate advantages for various political groups and parties. Sartori—*il grande vecchio* of political science—had, like many other professors of political science, a chance to participate in a daily scholarly debate in the newspapers. He cautiously

[16] Norbert Freund, 'Wahlsystemreform in Italien', in I. Halbband (ed.), *Jahrbuch fur Politik*, vol. v (Baden-Baden: Nomos, 1995), 43–65.

[17] Stefano Bartolini and Roberto D'Alimonte (eds.), *Maggioritario ma non troppo* (Bologna: Il Mulino, 1995).

[18] Angelico Panebianco, 'Alternanza a rischio regime', *Corriere della sera* (24 Jan. 1994), 1, 9.

advocated the French system with two rounds. But his caveat was that the French system is acceptable only when it succeeds in structuring the party system. In many statements in the debate there was a criticism of the old *partitocrazia*, combined with the fear that Italian parties under a French electoral formula might be reduced to their French analogues. Electoral engineering was hardly able to predict the consequences of an electoral reform, especially when it was linked with the introduction of a semi-presidential system.

West European experiences with electoral engineering showed that the effects of changes of the electoral formula are hard to calculate. For decades the Germans were told that Hitler could have been avoided with a British electoral law. In recent years, retrospective scenarios made it appear more likely that the Nazis would have seized power even earlier under plurality vote.[19] The French socialists had denounced for two decades the French majoritarian system as detrimental to the left; then in 1981 Mitterrand discovered that the Gaullist formula benefited his Parti Socialiste (PS) once it reached a certain threshold of political support. In power, Mitterrand hoped to defend the PS position by a proportional electoral law, and thereby doomed France to return to its old formula. The French manipulation of electoral law did not serve as a warning for Italy. Italian experience with the former *legge truffa* should have made the country sceptical, but from time to time, the pseudo-rational arguments of constitutional engineers appeal to those who seek to escape from crisis.

In Eastern Europe the engineers of the new constitutions and electoral laws were on still shakier ground for their predictions. Most Eastern European countries have introduced variations on the proportional electoral system, combined with majority-building capacities. Three variations of proportional and combined electoral laws were introduced by the constitutional engineers:

- a personalized proportional law of the German type in which the result in single-member constituencies has little impact on the distribution of seats;
- the parallel system (the Germans first debated the abstract type under the misleading name of 'Grabesystem') which was first introduced in Mexico and later became popular because of Japanese experiments. It is characterized by a parallel distribution of one part of parliamentary seats by majoritarian and the other one by proportional provisions. In Eastern

---

[19] Jürgen Falter, *Hitler's Wahler* (Munich: Beck, 1991).

TABLE 1.2. *Modes of transition and electoral system*

Erosion	Collapse	Continuity of elites including foundation of independent states
Poland[a]	Czech Republic[a]	Russia[b]
Hungary[c]	Slovakia[a]	Ukraine[d]
	GDR	Romania[a]
	Lithuania[b]	Croatia[b]
		Serbia[a]
		Bulgaria[a]
		Slovenia[a]
		Latvia[a]
		Belarus[d]
		Albania[c]

[a] Proportional system in multi-member constituencies.
[b] Parallel system.
[c] Compensatory.
[d] Absolute majority voting.

Europe the constitutional engineers in Croatia, Lithuania, and Russia employed it;

• compensatory electoral systems that also involve a combination of majoritarian and proportional provisions. But in contrast to the parallel system, mandates won on the majority principle are not counted.

'Institutional engineering' concerns the power considerations involved in the creation of electoral laws. The type of transition had a limited influence on the choice of electoral laws (see Table 1.2). Generally speaking, where the old elites remained strong, they tried to stick to the majoritarian electoral system which predominated during communism.

Institutional engineers, exploiting the absolute majority system to strengthen their positions of power, frequently failed. The system succeeded in guaranteeing representativeness and participation, but failed to create a concentrated party system. This occurred due either to declining trust in communist parties, or to disintegration of the forum-type parties when the new forces chose to stabilize their power by employing an old electoral formula. The result was new compromises between the camps, most frequently hybrids of systems, combining majoritarian and proportional elements. In many cases the elements of the electoral law were not fully compatible. They were less the result of a logical system than an accident of momentary power relations between the parties.

Institutional engineering in Eastern Europe took place on a large scale. Out of nineteen countries, nine voted on the basis of a majoritarian system during the first elections. Eight of those have since changed the system for the second election: four created a combined system and two a proportional system. Among those countries that began with combined and proportional systems, five attempts at institutional engineering have been carried through. The institutional freezing hypothesis, according to which institutional engineers must succeed at once or not at all, was not confirmed. Sartori proposed another explanation for the reform pessimism: political scientists are incapable of giving adequate policy advice. Many criticisms of new electoral systems begin from conventional wisdom and make quite simple assumptions about causality. Most of the hypotheses on the impact of an independent variable (the electoral law) on a dependent variable (the party system) were mistaken in the case of Eastern Europe. Institutional engineers refer to intervening variables such as 'political culture' and 'cleavage structure in society' to explain the failures of prediction.

Another intervening variable was the choice of the governmental system. Since Lijphart it has been discussed whether in transitions to democracy the combination of semi-presidential systems with proportional electoral law or with combined systems do not create the worst of all possible worlds. This assumption was plausible under Wałęsa's presidency in Poland, but after some corrections were made to the proportional system it became less obvious. It seems to be less true in countries where the continuity of old elites (Romania until 1996) was unshaken and presidents had enough manipulative power to overcome the restraints of the institutional engineers.

Scepticism about institutional engineering spread among some experts. They withdrew to the position of circular causality relations among the variables and to less rigorous demands of simultaneous maximization of all the three functions of electoral systems. Venerable truisms were revived: electoral formulas create the desired function of stabilizing party systems only when the developmental differences in the country are not too alarming.[20] In spite of an equalizing 'social imperialism' of the communist

---

[20] Dieter Nohlen, *Wahlrecht und Parteiensystem* (Opladen: Leske & Budrich, 1990).

federations, the collapse of the planned economy left the budding democracies with enormous regional imbalances.

Plebiscitarian Decision-Making

When democracies enter a stage of crisis, political elites rediscover their electorates, and the call for plebiscitarian participation rings out. Even in highly anti-plebiscitarian systems, such as Germany, two-thirds of the electors favour plebiscitarian co-determination in the legislative process. German elites, however, remain stubbornly opposed to any concession in that direction because they partly believe the old myth that the Weimar Republic declined because of abuses of plebiscitarian instruments.[21]

Institutional engineers are often unconvinced that plebiscitarian instruments will improve democracy because:

- parties and parliaments are further weakened;
- votes in a referendum are interpreted as a vote of no confidence against the government consulting the voters. The opposite can happen as well: as in the case of Norway, where twice victors in a referendum were defeated in subsequent elections;[22]
- frequent referenda strengthen powerful interest groups which mobilize their interests;
- referenda simplify the complexity of political decisions to yes-or-no questions.

Again, Italy is the best test case of this sort of institutional engineering. Since 1970, twenty-six referenda have been voted on by the people, among them important questions, such as divorce (1974) and abortion (1981), and questions of minor importance, such as limitations on hunting (1990), or the abolition of the Ministry of Tourism (1993). Italian voters countered the traumatic Weimar experiences and decided moderately. Only in the case of public party finance (1993) did a great majority vote against the status quo occur. New social movements use the referendum against the established parties, as Italy experienced when the Christian Democrats' proposal on abortion was voted down (1981). Sometimes individuals

---

[21] Otmar Jung, 'Direkte Demokratie: Forschungsstand und Aufhaben', *Zeitschrift für Parlamentsfragen* (1990), 491–504.

[22] Mario Caciagli and Pier Vincenco Uleri (eds.), *Democrazie e referendum* (Bari: Laterza, 1994).

organizing committees win broad support. The referendum on the electoral system in 1993 heralded the end of the old republic and showed that strengthening one institution through institutional engineering may weaken another—in this case the political parties.

Even leftist thinkers did not consider referenda to be an instrument of democratization—except in situations of crisis or deadlock. Rather they recommended more participation from the subsystems. Plebiscitarian instruments as a way out of deadlock in democracies are dangerous. They are nevertheless preferable to a *coup d'état*, although they are tantamount to a legitimized coup. Decisions by popular vote are most dangerous when they yield very narrow margins of victory and defeat. The 1995 direct election of the Polish president invited attempts to invalidate the elections via the constitutional courts; Quebec decided by a tiny majority to stay within Canada; and the Danes and French accepted, without impressive majorities, the Maastricht treaties. The call for participation instead of representation has rarely proved to be the way out of a crisis.

There were two broad responses to the crisis of the 1990s: Italy chose the plebiscitarian road without very convincing results. Germany followed its purely representative concept and did not even accept a referendum for endorsing the Constitution after re-unification. Instead, the elites in West Germany tried to win over the constituency via financial transfers. They 'bought' legitimization instead of mobilizing acceptance through broader participation.

The institutional engineers in Eastern Europe had no trouble preserving this 'socialist achievement' in their constitutions, thus the possibility of calling referenda is included in most of the post-communist regimes. Fortunately, it has been used rarely. When it has been (by Russia in 1993 or by Belarus in 1996) it has had a highly manipulative character. Moreover conflicts between parliamentary majorities and presidents in both cases have undermined the legitimacy of the referenda.

Conclusion

Institutional and constitutional engineering is a concept that grew out of the revival of an enlightened institutionalism. The concept of institutional engineering was developed to describe transitions from democracy to democracy. It showed that changes were usually made within narrow limits. Rarely did systems change from one regime type to another or change a majoritarian electoral law to strict proportionalism. Changes were usually made from the middle ground by combining majoritarian and proportional systems, or through arrangements that remained within the proportional system but seemed to guarantee a strengthening of the relative majority parties.

Institutional engineering as a response to the crisis of Western democracies was accompanied by the largest wave of transition to democracy in history: almost overnight two dozen countries attempted to democratize. A peculiar constellation of old and new elites led the way through the tricky process of compromise between old and new forces and old and new institutions. Institutional engineering was hamstrung when opposing sides failed to find an agreement, leaving countries such as Poland or Hungary without a final constitutional solution. This need not be a burden in the future. The French Third Republic survived sixty-five years (1875–1940) in a similar situation.

In the third wave of democratization, the old assumptions that institutional change must be completed in the initial stage have been falsified. A greater volatility of voters and a weaker party system than in previous transitional regimes have left more room for manœuvre to institutional engineers. This was at least quite obvious in the realm of electoral laws.

Institutional engineering in Eastern Europe, however, showed that the progressive intention to make democracy work combined with the concept of plebiscitarian decision-making is always in danger of being abused. Changes that hinder democracy may always be adopted, even under the guise of 'democratic institutions', such as the application of referenda. Belarus is a latent danger everywhere.

2

Constitutions and Constitution-Building: A Comparative Perspective

Robert Elgie and Jan Zielonka

Constitution-building is often seen as 'the hour of lawyers'. Yet the chapters of this book describing the political bargaining and deal-making of the constitution-building process suggest that it is also the hour of politicians.[1] Constitution-building is a pre-eminently political act.[2] It is perhaps the quintessential political act, by which countries make choices concerning the most fundamental concepts in political life: power and authority; representation and legitimacy; liberty and equality. As such, constitution-building is also an essentially conflictual process. It crystallizes contending political forces, and is often marked by intense political bargaining and log-rolling. Constitution-building is also a regime-defining process. The short-term significance of the process is the demarcation of the present from the past and the promise of a better future. Its medium- and long-term significance is equally considerable, since it defines the formal rules of the political game and acts as a power-map[3] to be used for navigating through future political struggles. The chapters to follow confirm the thesis that constitution-building represents the essence of politics.[4]

---

[1] The expression 'the hour of lawyers' was used in Ralf Dahrendorf, *Reflections on the Revolution in Europe* (London: Chatto & Windus, 1990), 79.

[2] Daniel J. Elazar, 'Constitution-Making: The Pre-eminently Political Act', in K. G. Banting and R. Simeon (eds.), *Redesigning the State: The Politics of Constitutional Change in Industrial Nations* (Toronto: University of Toronto Press, 1985), 232–48.

[3] Ivo Duchacek, *Power Maps: Comparative Politics of Constitutions* (Santa Barbara, Calif.: ABC-Clio, 1973).

[4] Keith G. Banting and Richard Simeon, 'Introduction: The Politics of Constitutional Change', in *Redesigning the State*, 1–29.

This chapter examines the nature of constitutions and the constitution-building process by focusing on some of the most important choices that constitution builders face. It is divided into four main sections. The first section explores the complex relationship between democracy and constitutionalism. The second section identifies two major constitutional types, and considers whether or not constitution builders should adopt a codified constitution. The third section addresses the timetable for constitution-building and the execution of political power, including the limits imposed on democratically elected parliaments. Although constitutions could not independently ensure a smooth democracy-building process, they proved indispensable in structuring the new governments, spelling out a catalogue of basic rights, and legitimizing newly acquired self-rule—and in some cases an entirely new state. In fact, even the most imperfect constitutions (in terms of both substance and adoption procedures) have been a crucial asset to democratic consolidation.

Constitutional Brakes on Democracy

The relationship between democracy and constitutions is neither simple nor straightforward. Constitutions are basically about constraining the power of democratically elected parliamentary majorities.[5] As Vernor Bogdanor put it: 'Codified constitutions are, after all, valued as a means to the end of limiting governmental power; and, in a democracy, limiting also the power of the people to whom government is responsible.'[6] Constitutions impose a tight corset on the citizenry, taking away some power from the people and putting it into the hands of constitutional framers and constitutional courts. Generations of political analysts have struggled with the questions that this dilemma implies: can a true demo-

---

[5] Not to mention the fact that constitutions do not go hand in hand with democracy. Most existing states have written constitutions, but only some (about one-third) are democratic. All countries discussed in this book adopted new constitutions in the communist period, yet none of them could be called democracies before 1989. In fact, constitutions were consciously used by the ruling elites to suppress the rise of independent forms of expression in the 1980s. Democrats, the elite argued, violated the constitutional norm about the leading role of the Communist Party. *Dura lex sed lex* (i.e. hard law but law) was their argument. See Jan Zielonka, *Political Ideas in Contemporary Poland* (Aldershot: Avebury, 1989), 119–57.

[6] Vernor Bogdanor, 'Introduction', in Vernor Bogdanor (ed.), *Constitutions in Democratic Politics* (Aldershot: Gower, 1988), 3.

cracy serve three different masters: the voters, the framers, and the courts? Why should the people accept restrictions that have been codified in a past context and by a past generation? Why should unelected judges have the power to strike down legislation adopted by the representatives of the people? Is democracy compromised if a (small) minority of members of parliament (MPs) can prevent any changes in a constitution? Is there not a clear conflict between popular participation and constitutional constraints? In short, are not all constitutions inherently anti-democratic?[7]

Those in favour of constitutional restrictions and the division of power principle have presented three major arguments. First, they have argued in favour of the so-called 'deliberative' type of democracy as opposed to a 'voluntaristic' one.[8] On this view, constitutions prevent a tiny majority-of-the-day from revamping the entire constitutional system. Not only is the tyranny of the majority thus restricted, but also the spontaneous, passionate, and voluntary behaviour of the *demos* is tamed. Constitutions force the people and their representatives to engage in a complex deliberative process by imposing numerous procedural hurdles, require the state to gain broad public support for its ideas by making constitutional amendments difficult to adopt, and guard against the easy denial of certain individual rights. Is it possible to conceive of a democracy where voting rights, freedom of speech, and other political rights could easily be suspended?

Second, it has been argued that by taking some power away from ordinary parliaments and putting it into the hands of constitutional framers and courts, constitutions ensure that the representatives of the people cannot easily betray their electorates. Elected officials have a tendency to invoke the name of the people to legitimize the pursuit of their own interests. But dividing constitutional prerogatives between different agents creates a mechanism

---

[7] See for example Jean Jacques Rousseau, 'Sur le gouvernment de Pologne' and 'Du contrat social' (I. 7 and III. 18), in *Œuvres complètes*, vol. iii, ed. Bernard Gagnebin and Marcel Raymond (Paris: Pléiade, 1964), 262–3; John Locke, *Two Treatises of Government*, ed. Peter Laslett (New York: Mentor, 1965), book II, 348–443; Stephen Holmes, 'Precommitment and the Paradox of Democracy', in Jon Elster and Rune Slagstad (eds.), *Constitutionalism and Democracy* (Cambridge: Cambridge University Press, 1988), 195–240; and Wojciech Sadurski, 'Konstytucyjna Kwadratura Kola? Przyczynek do teorii liberalnego konstytucjonalizmu', *Civitas*, 1/1 (1997), 37–70.

[8] This distinction has been made in Stephen Holmes, 'Constitutionalism', in Seymour Martin Lipset (ed.), *The Encyclopedia of Democracy* (Washington: Congressional Quarterly, 1995), i. 300.

by which institutions check one another and allows voters more easily to monitor the behaviour of their representatives.

Finally, it has been pointed out that constitutions create the rules of the game that enable democracy to function effectively, rather than fall prey to paralysis or chaos. Ineffective democracy brings no justice to the people. Therefore, by clarifying prerogatives of different institutions and spelling out decision-making procedures, constitutions create the stability and predictability necessary for the democratic system, and prevent partisan interests from misusing democratic institutions.

These arguments have prevailed in all Western democracies. Constitutions are not about incapacitating the people, it is argued, but about helping the people to organize politically in a deliberative and predictable manner. Constitutional restraints are not about preventing 'true' democracy, but about strengthening it.

However, in the early stages of democratic transition in Eastern Europe, arguments against placing constitutional constraints on the *demos* gained credibility because of at least three important factors. First, the democratic legitimacy of constitution framers and constitutional courts was initially weak. Constitutional framers were either 'reformed' communists, controlling constitutional assemblies on the eve of the transition period, or unelected political elites participating in semi-secret round-table talks that produced semi-legitimate constitutional compromises. Institutions of constitutional judicial review had no precedent in these countries, and the judicial system as a whole had no tradition of independence. At the early stage of transition, constitutional courts were composed of small groups of political appointees; and many constitutional judges fell victim to political manipulation or even tried to use the court as a springboard for their own political ambitions. Most notably, the chairman of the Russian Constitutional Court, Valery Zorkin, was repeatedly embroiled in open political battles that cast doubt on the independence and neutrality of the Court.[9]

Second, after a long period of communist dictatorship, there was intense public pressure to let the people decide their own fate without any constitutional restrictions. In Russia, most notably, Andrei

---

[9] See Robert Sharlet, 'Chief Justice as Judicial Politician', *East European Constitutional Review*, 2 (Spring 1993), 32–7; or Vladimir Orlov, 'Qui prodest?', *Moscow News*, 12 Mar. 1993 (No. 11). For a more comprehensive review of the first years of constitutional courts in Eastern Europe see Herman Schwartz, 'The New East European Constitutional Courts', *Michigan Journal of International Law*, 13 (Summer 1992), 741–85.

Sakharov and other dissidents hailed the slogan: 'all power to the soviets' (that is, parliamentary assemblies elected by the people).[10] Even in the most 'Western' countries of the region, the belief that power should rest in the hands of voters and their parliamentary representatives was very strong. Describing the Hungarian situation, András Sajó asserted that 'Constitutionality is easily misunderstood as being a problem of majority will.' Similarly, on the eve of Poland's transition Andrzej Rapaczynski observed:

Polish views usually yield the following reasoning: all legitimate political power flows from the people. The depository and embodiment of the people's own sovereignty is the national legislature, chosen in universal, equal, direct, secret, and proportional elections. Therefore, the parliament, as the most direct representative of the people, reflecting the principal voices of the nation, should be the supreme organ of the government, and determine the policy of the nation.[11]

Clearly in this absolute, if not 'fundamentalist', concept of democracy there was little sympathy for constitutional constraints or the division of power principle.

Finally, the early post-communist experience in some countries suggests that it is the majority that needs protection from manipulation by elites, rather than the other way around. In other words, the possibility of 'minority tyranny' proved to be a greater danger than the alleged 'tyranny' of passionate and voluntaristic majorities.[12] For instance, in Czechoslovakia as few as thirty Slovak MPs

---

[10] See Andrei Sakharov, 'All Power to the Soviets', *XX Century and Peace* (Moscow), 8 (1989), 9–12.

[11] See András Sajó, 'The Roundtable Talks in Hungary', in Jon Elster (ed.), *The Roundtable Talks and the Breakdown of Communism* (Chicago: Chicago University Press, 1996), 92. Also Andrzej Rapaczynski, 'Constitutional Politics in Poland: A Report on the Constitutional Committee of the Polish Parliament', in A. E. Dick Howard (ed.), *Constitution Making in Eastern Europe* (Washington: Woodrow Wilson Center Press, 1993), 118. For Rapaczynski this quest for the absolute and unconstrained power of the people is characteristic of societies that 'fought hard for freedom to air their true convictions', but Wiktor Osiatynski also adds: 'Poland has never had a strong tradition of constitutionalism that limited parliamentary authority. . . . There is not even a national consensus about the fundamental values of constitutionalism.' See Wiktor Osiatynski, 'Perspectives on the Current Constitutional Situation in Poland', in Douglas Greenberg et al. (eds.), *Constitutionalism and Democracy: Transitions in the Contemporary World* (Oxford: Oxford University Press, 1993), 319.

[12] Julio Faundez has drawn a similar lesson from the Third World experience: 'It must be noted that the failure of democracy in most Third World countries, and in others as well, is not often brought about by the reckless behaviour of political majorities acting through legislative bodies. On the contrary, the histories of these

in the Chamber of Nations were able to paralyse the entire parliamentary decision-making process.[13] This subsequently led to
the Czech–Slovak split, orchestrated by a small political elite in
Bratislava and Prague, despite the fact that in 1991–2 a majority
of the electorate opposed splitting Czechoslovakia.

In the end, however, all the countries in the region adopted
constitutional restrictions on their *demos* and created powerful
constitutional courts. Why? Certainly the successful Western constitutional experience played a part here.[14] Despite their restrictive features, Western constitutions secured rather than undermined
democracy, and there was clearly no appetite in Eastern Europe
for democratic experiments. But the most important explanation
is to be found elsewhere: the post-communist countries in transition could not function properly without drafting and adopting new
constitutions. This brings us to the next crucial issue, the apparent indispensability of constitutions in Eastern Europe.

Constitutional Compulsion

In principle, democracy can flourish without a written constitution.[15]
For example, the constitution of the United Kingdom is embodied

countries suggest that, more often than not, it is the majority of citizens who need
protection from political elites who consistently frustrate democratic demands in
order to protect their interests. Sadly, the negative conception of constitutionalism
is often used as ideological cover to legitimize such behaviour.' See Julio Faundez,
'Constitutionalism: A Timely Revival', in Greenberg et al. (eds.), *Constitutionalism and Democracy*, 358.

[13] See David M. Olson, 'The New Parliaments of New Democracies: The
Experience of the Federal Assembly of the Czech and Slovak Federal Republic',
Budapest Papers of Democratic Transition, 24, Hungarian Center for Democracy
Studies Foundation (1992), 7–8.

[14] In fact, with the exception of New Zealand, all former British colonies have
deviated from the Westminster model and have established their own codified constitutional documents, of which the most notable example is, of course, the 1787
Constitution of the United States of America. Indeed, the US Constitution has itself
been exported at various times in some form or another to a number of South
American and South-East Asian countries. Elsewhere, European countries that
democratized in the post-Second World War period, such as Germany and Italy,
as well as those that democratized in the late 1970s, such as Portugal and Spain,
again chose to adopt codified rather than uncodified constitutions.

[15] In fact, as K. C. Wheare pointed out some decades ago, the term 'constitution' is used in two different senses. See K. C. Wheare, *Modern Constitutions* (London:
Oxford University Press, 1966), 1. First, the term is used in a broad sense to describe
'the whole system of government of a country', the collection of rules which establish

not in a single document but in a series of statutes and conventions of political practice which date back to 1297.[16] These statutes include the Acts of Union, which establish the geographical boundaries of the state; the 1701 Act of Settlement, which regulates the procedures for monarchical succession; the 1911 and 1949 Parliament Acts, which set out the relationship between the House of Commons and the House of Lords; and the 1972 European Communities Act, which indicates the status of European law in relation to domestic law. It is certainly the case that various aspects of British constitutional law are contained in certain official documents, such as the Official Revised Edition of the statutes in force, published by Her Majesty's Stationery Office,[17] but there is still no single overarching constitutional document in which the British constitution is to be found. The same is true for both New Zealand and Israel. In New Zealand, the 1990 Bill of Rights Act is 'rapidly becoming quasi-constitutional in character'[18] since it allows courts to overrule acts of parliament if they breach the rights contained in the bill. In Israel, the Scroll of Independence has already been given a similar status by the courts.[19]

The advantages of having an uncodified constitution are twofold. First, it may help to smooth the process of democratic transition. In Israel, opposing forces sought to gain control of the political system during the period of state foundation. These forces were

and regulate or govern the government. Some of these rules will be the result of organic laws and formal decrees and, as such, will have a legal status. Others will be the product of 'usages, understandings, customs, or conventions' and, accordingly, will be extra-legal in nature. Both types of rules, though, will shape elite political behaviour and so both will form the framework within which the government of a country takes place. Secondly, the term is also used in a narrower sense to refer to 'a selection of the legal rules which govern the government of [a] country and which have been embodied in a document'. In this sense, Wheare's use of the term closely resembles Finer's subsequent and classic definition of a constitution as a 'code of rules which aspires to regulate the allocation of functions, powers and duties among the various agencies and officers of government, and define the relationship between these and the public'. See S. E. Finer, *Five Constitutions* (London: Penguin, 1979), 15.

[16] S. E. Finer, Vernon Bogdanor, and Bernard Rudden, *Comparing Constitutions* (Oxford: Clarendon Press, 1995), 41.

[17] Ibid.

[18] Cheryl Saunders, 'Evolution and Adaptation of the British Constitutional System', in Joachim Jens Hesse and Nevil Johnson (eds.), *Constitutional Policy and Change in Europe* (Oxford: Oxford University Press, 1995), 68–94.

[19] Daniel J. Elazar, 'Constitution-Making: The Pre-eminently Political Act', in Banting and Simeon (eds.), *Redesigning the State*, 238.

unable to agree on a constitutional document, and their continuing disagreement threatened to compromise the security of the regime. In this context, the adoption of an uncodified constitution, in the form of David Ben-Gurion's proposal that each new legislature (Knesset) would, in effect, have the status of a constituent assembly, represented a compromise that helped to consolidate the democratic process.[20] Secondly, and more generally, it might be argued that an uncodified constitution allows countries to respond to changing social, economic, and political circumstances with a minimum of fuss. Arguably, uncodified constitutions provide the necessary degree of flexibility by allowing decision makers to engage in incremental constitutional reform, thus protecting the general integrity of the system while still permitting selected aspects of that system to be subject to change.

Both of the above arguments could in theory apply to Eastern Europe. In fact, the wisdom of adopting a new constitution has been questioned in most of the countries discussed here, and especially in Poland and Hungary. For instance, as András Sajó and Vera Losonci pointed out, many leading Hungarian politicians seemed to believe that the unwritten Hungarian constitution—a fragmentary system of medieval laws and liberal legislation which was politically repealed after 1920—reflected a genuinely liberal, constitutional, and democratic tradition.[21] However, this book clearly shows that the new democracies in the region could hardly afford not to have new written constitutions. This was true in the first instance because all of these states inherited communist constitutions. Although these constitutions contained numerous undemocratic provisions, they also contained some basic rules for politics and government. Abolishing these rules without creating new ones

---

[20] That said, it has also been argued that the lack of a written constitution in Israel made it easier for religious groups of Orthodox Jews to restrict various individual rights of Israeli citizens. See Bruce Ackerman, *The Future of Liberal Revolution* (New Haven: Yale University Press, 1992), 63–5.

[21] See András Sajó and Vera Losonci, 'Rule of Law in East Central Europe: Is the Emperor's New Suit a Straitjacket?', in Greenberg et al. (eds.), *Constitutionalism and Democracy*, 323. For the discussion of Poland see, e.g., Agnieszka Nogal, 'Nowoczesne panstwo a konstytucja', *Civitas*, 1/1 (1997), 253. The argument here is that even if countries in the region have chosen to adopt codified rather than uncodified constitutions, it should be appreciated that there was a choice to be made between the two. It should not be felt that an uncodified constitution is simply the product of either a unique Westminster-style system of government or an equally unique set of Israeli circumstances and, hence, that a codified constitution is appropriate for all other countries. Instead, evidence suggests that a codified constitution is an option rather than a requirement for good government.

would have led to paralysis and chaos. In fact, merely amending the old constitutions proved insufficient, as was made vividly clear in the Russian case.[22] (Although when Hungary revised 90 per cent of the old Constitution rather than adopting an entirely new constitutional draft, chaos was avoided.) In all of these countries, the adoption of a new constitution was seen as a crucial symbolic break with the communist legacy. (Although such a break was not necessarily welcomed by the majority of local elites; in Belarus most notably.) Finally, in new states, a new constitution was seen as a major and indispensable step in their process of state building. (Although in the Latvian case the 'new' Constitution was in fact the old one, originally adopted in 1922 and reinstated in 1992.)

Thus constitutions became, to use Bruce Ackerman's words, 'central symbols of revolutionary achievement', and 'the center of an enlightened kind of patriotism'.[23] Writing and adopting constitutions presented the new democratic forces with an opportunity to articulate fundamental principles and mobilize broad public support. It also allowed them to fix the rules of the institutional power struggle which, after all, was detrimental to government stability and threatened local elites with political extinction.[24] Adopting a new constitution was seen as a test for democratic maturity; and in most of the cases discussed here, it also became a test of mature independent statehood.

Of course, the establishment of a codified constitution did not necessarily bring about a fundamental change in the overall way in which Eastern European societies were governed. Nor did it always result in a democratic system. As Pogany accurately observed, in the post-communist context 'constitution-making, the formal act of drafting or revising a constitution, does not lead automatically to constitutional transformation'.[25] Yet this book clearly

[22] The Soviet Constitution was amended more than 300 times and the legality of some of the amendments could easily be questioned. In the early 1990s it was virtually impossible to know what the legal rules actually were. See e.g. Boris N. Toporin, 'Problems of Constitutional Reform in the Former USSR', *Coexistence*, 30 (Mar. 1993), 1–15. See also comments of Sergei Shakhrai in *East European Constitutional Review*, 2 (Spring 1993), 22.

[23] Ackerman, *The Future of Liberal Revolution*, 61.

[24] Constitutional chaos implied that political actors had to operate in a very uncertain and volatile environment and therefore there was an incentive to fix the rules of political competition and to impose a division of power principle that would 'disperse' and 'constrain' the absolute power of the people which could easily fall prey to political manipulation.

[25] Istvan Pogany, 'Constitution Making or Constitutional Transformation in Post-communist Societies', *Political Studies*, 44/3 (1996), 589.

shows that Eastern European countries in transition had neither the luxury of avoiding the constitution-making process, nor the option of an uncodified constitution. But the question remains: does *any* sort of constitution legitimize a new regime and produce a workable democratic system? And what is more important: the process or the product of constitution building?

The Process of Constitution Building

Philippe Schmitter distinguishes between the process and the product of constitution building.[26] The process is the means by which the constitution is drafted and adopted, while the product is the constitution itself. Arguably, the process is at least as important as the product. The process creates the immediate conditions in which the product then operates. If the process is consensual and legitimate, then it is likely that the product will be too. By the same token, if the process is conflictual and chaotic, then chances are that the product will reflect this as well. At least as much attention, then, should be paid to the constitution-building process as to its ultimate product. Three aspects of the constitution-building process seem especially relevant for the success of democratic consolidation. They concern how long it takes to prepare the constitution, who takes part in the constitution-drafting process, and how the final constitutional document is adopted. In the following section, the issues surrounding each of these sets of choices are examined.

The time-frame of constitution building

Whether constitutions are produced quickly or after long deliberation, the length of the process does not always correspond with the intentions of the framers. It is certainly true that the exigencies of the political system can erase any hope for a swift constitutional revolution and transform that desire into a protracted constitutional bargaining game. But despite the difficulties of controlling it, the length of the constitutional process seems to influence the product in terms of democratic consolidation.

---

[26] Philippe Schmitter, '"Process" not "Product" Engineering in the Consolidation of Democracy', paper delivered at the Conference on Democratic Consolidation in Eastern Europe, Florence, European University Institute (24–5 Jan. 1997).

The length of the constitution-building process has varied across countries, and within the same country at different historical moments. For example, although the Third French Republic was formally proclaimed in 1870, the country's basic constitutional law was not adopted until 1875. Similarly, the slow reconstruction of post-war West Germany's political system meant that the country's Basic Law was adopted in May 1949, four years after the end of the Second World War. By contrast, work on the Constitution of the Fifth French Republic began in June 1958 and was completed the following September. In Eastern Europe it took Bulgarians only twelve months to draft and adopt their new Constitution, while nearly eight years passed before Poland did the same.

There are various reasons why constitution-building sometimes turns out to be a relatively quick process, and there are several arguments suggesting that a quick process is better than a slow process. McWhinney makes the general argument that codified constitutions almost invariably occur 'in or immediately after a period of great public excitement and resultant public euphoria when it is relatively easy to build a certain climate of popular political consensus'.[27] Thus, quick constitutional settlements tend to occur when either exhilarating or traumatic political events bring about constitutional consensus. In addition, such settlements tend to occur when countries decide simply to reinstate a former constitution (sometimes with slight amendments), as in Latvia. In this case, there is less work for constitution builders to do, and the constitution-building process can be completed relatively quickly. Against this backdrop, Schmitter argues that constitution building in newly democratized states should be completed as quickly as possible: '"The sooner the better" should be the motto,' because '[t]he longer actors hesitate in this effort, the more they will be capable of evaluating how specific institutional arrangements can affect them and the greater the difficulty they will have in coming up with "fair" rules that all can agree to'.[28] In other words, newly democratized states are characterized by a process of institutional learning and it is better, according to Schmitter, to agree on a constitution before excessive competition and potentially irreconcilable political interests are clearly formulated and consolidated.

However, the experience of some Western European countries in transition suggest that a long constitution-building process

---

[27] Edward McWhinney, *Constitution-Making: Principles, Process, Practice* (Toronto: University of Toronto Press, 1981), 15.
[28] Schmitter, '"Process" not "Product" Engineering', 8.

is not necessarily disadvantageous. Recently, for example, the Constitutional Review Group in Ireland was given a year to formulate proposals for constitutional change which were then to be considered for an indeterminate period by a special parliamentary committee. Similarly, in Italy the reconsideration of the First Republic's Constitution has been long and reform has occurred incrementally. But can newly democratized states indulge in such a lengthy process? In principle, there is reason to believe that a protracted constitution-building process may have certain advantages for new democracies as well. A successful, long-standing, and widely accepted constitution tangibly represents the compromise reached between contending political interests in a country. Arguably, the best way to reach such a settlement is through a long constitution-building process, allowing for an iterated sequence of constitutional bargaining. If a common accord can be reached, then competing parties will find it more difficult to rescind parts of the agreement at a later date.

There is also an intermediate option between the extremes of a long and drawn-out constitution-building process. New democracies may benefit considerably from quickly adopting an interim constitution while work continues on a permanent constitution.[29] While this option does not require that a complete set of constitutional rules be adopted at the outset (especially if there is profound disagreement as to the nature of those rules), it is essential that certain rules of democratic accountability be put swiftly in place. Consequently, an interim constitution may facilitate implementation of the institutional changes required by rapidly shifting circumstances, and ease the way towards a compromise on specific constitutional arrangements.

The examples offered in this book indicate that a lengthy constitutionalization process does not necessarily result in permanent constitutional deadlock, let alone in total democratic breakdown. For example, Hungarians are still working on a new constitution, Poles adopted one only in 1997, as did the Ukrainians in 1996. Despite that, democracy now seems secure in Hungary, Poland, and probably also in Ukraine. In other words, if elites exercise self-restraint, adopting a constitution becomes less urgent. Nevertheless, in all three countries, an interim constitution proved indispensable. The 1989 constitutional amendments in Hungary amounted to a new interim constitution, as did Poland's 1992

---

[29] Stephen Holmes, 'Back to the Drawing Board', *East European Constitutional Review*, 2/1 (Winter 1993), 21–5.

'Little Constitution', and Ukraine's 1994 'Law on Power'. While it is hard to deny the beneficial effects of these interim constitutions, after their adoption the momentum to draft a permanent constitution dwindled. Moreover, a lengthy constitutional process failed to produce more consensus on the constitutional draft than was the case in countries that experienced a brief constitution-building period. Indeed, Schmitter's fear that a lengthy process increases the difficulty of reaching a broad constitutional consensus seems to be confirmed by the cases of Ukraine, Hungary, and Poland.

The Eastern and Central European experience also shows that 'quick-fix' constitutions (that is, constitutions adopted in a relatively brief period) proved to be remarkably effective, durable, and beneficial. The speed with which Bulgaria, Romania, and Lithuania adopted their constitutions has often been criticized. However, one can hardly imagine that the ongoing institutional power struggles occurring in these countries would have been curbed by postponing the adoption of a new constitution. On the contrary, these countries clearly benefited from their constitutions which specified the roles of various institutions, established clear rules for political bargaining, and set up a workable balance of political power. We will return to this issue somewhat later.

Constitutional framers

There have been many different types of constitutional framers throughout the history of democracy. Are some types of framers able to enjoy a greater degree of political legitimacy than others? And, by the same token, are they able to produce a more durable and workable constitution? Do certain types of framers tend to prefer certain types of constitutional outcomes? Is it axiomatic, as Jon Elster once put it, that 'any creator will try to control his creature'?[30]

In principle, we can distinguish between four basic types of constitutional framers:

1. Special Constitutional Convention (such as the American Constitutional Convention of 1787 or the German Parliamentary Council of 1948);
2. Sovereign Constituent Assembly (such as the Weimar Assembly of 1918 or the French Constituent Assembly of 1945);

---

[30] Jon Elster, 'Constitution-Making in Eastern Europe: Rebuilding the Boat in the Open Sea', *Public Administration*, 71 (Spring–Summer 1993), 169–217.

3. Ordinary Legislature (such as the Spanish 'Constituent' Parliament of 1977); and
4. Executive (such as Napoleon Bonaparte's governments of 1799, 1802, and 1804, the French Ministry of Justice in 1958, or President Menem's government of Argentina in 1994).[31]

According to Ackerman, the American model of a special constitutional convention provides constitutions with the highest degree of political legitimization. It also prevents the dangers of endless constitutional tinkering and the mixing of constitutional law with ordinary legislation (which is bound to happen when parliament drafts the constitution).[32] Andrew Arato, on the other hand, argued that the American model is superior only in theory, since it is virtually impossible to imitate this model under cultural and institutional circumstances different from those of eighteenth-century America. For Arato, parliamentary constitution-making is the second-best option, while constitutions framed by the executive are usually illegitimate and potentially authoritarian, despite the apparent success of the French Fifth Republic.[33]

Developments in Eastern Europe seem to support Arato's argument. Plans to call a special constitutional convention were seriously considered only in Russia (something Ackerman implicitly recommended), yet the Constitution was ultimately drafted by President Boris Yeltsin. Also, the 1996 Belarusian Constitution (officially labelled an amendment to the 1994 Constitution) was drafted by President Aleksander Lukashenka. A sovereign constituent assembly was employed only in Bulgaria and Romania, but in both cases the assemblies were dominated by ex-communists, which damaged their legitimacy somewhat. (The new Bulgarian Constitution was accepted only after fifty delegates walked out of the constitutional assembly.) In all other cases, the ordinary parliament was given the task of framing the basic law; and the legitimacy of these constitutions varies from country to country depending on many different factors. But despite criticism by those not involved in constitution-drafting and despite dramatic changes to the parliamentary party composition, none of the constitutions

[31] Our typology is based on a similar typology made by Andrew Arato. However, Arato talks about five different constitution-making models and not about four types of framers. He also provides a sound justification for this typology, which can also be applied to the typology provided in this chapter. See Andrew Arato, 'Forms of Constitution Making and Theories of Democracy', *Cordozo Law Review*, 17 (Dec. 1995), 197–201.

[32] Ackerman, *The Future of Liberal Revolution*, 51–60.

[33] Arato, 'Forms of Constitution Making', 231.

framed by ordinary parliaments has been repealed, even where critics won successive elections. Thus, the East European experience does not provide sufficient evidence to claim that certain types of constitutional framers are likely to generate a special kind of political legitimacy.

There is, however, sufficient evidence to claim that framers tend to adopt constitutional solutions to suit their own institutional interests. Yeltsin's Constitution established a truly super-presidential system, as did Lukashenka's 1996 constitutional 'amendment'. At the same time, parliamentary framers in other countries of the region created constitutions with strong parliamentary powers and relatively weak executives. Only the 1994 Constitution prepared by the Belarusian parliament envisaged strengthening executive powers at the expense of the legislative branch, but one should keep in mind that about 70 per cent of Belarusian MPs simultaneously worked in the executive branch. Ultimately, this draft was still unable to satisfy the president's thirst for power, which led to the 1996 constitutional amendment.

In addition, this book suggests focusing not only on formal institutional framers, but also on individuals and informal groups involved in the constitution-drafting process. Constitutional expert groups were created in most Eastern European countries to help formulate constitutional drafts. Although none of these groups took centre stage, as did the 1996 Constitutional Review Group in Ireland or the 1992 Vedel Committee in France, they presented the framers with alternative constitutional solutions and translated chaotic political interests into an organized legal framework. In Bulgaria and Hungary, for instance, the Roundtable Talks conducted between the democratic opposition and the communist government also led to some important decisions about the future constitutional order.[34] In a way, they represented an Eastern European version of the Spanish Pacts of Moncloa, the 1977 multi-party agreement that outlined the constitutional framework of the post-Franco democracy.[35]

---

[34] Although in Hungary the Roundtable Talks ruled out drafting a lasting constitution, while in Bulgaria the Roundtable agreed that the future Constituent Assembly would have the legitimacy to decide all the issues discussed at the Roundtable and limited itself to suggesting some minor constitutional amendments required for conducting free and fair elections to such an assembly. See chapters of András Sajó and Rumyana Kolarova and Dimitr Dimitrov in Elster (ed.), *The Roundtable Talks and the Breakdown of Communism*, 92, 199.

[35] See e.g. José María Maravall, *The Transition to Democracy in Spain* (London: Croom Helm, 1982), 42–4.

Referendum as a legitimizing strategy

It is often asserted that constitutions require a special kind of popular legitimacy, transcending that of ordinary legislation. On this view, it is not enough that the constitution is drafted by a 'legitimate' assembly following 'legitimate' procedures, but the final decision on the basic law of the country should be made directly by the constituents themselves. This argument prevailed in many countries. For example, in Western Europe referenda were held to ratify the 1937 Irish Constitution, the 1946 Italian Constitution, the 1946 and 1958 French Fourth and Fifth Republics' constitutions, amendments to the Danish Constitution in 1953, and the 1978 Spanish Constitution. However, many other constitutions have been adopted by the vote of a parliamentary or constituent assembly. Such voting may also be extended to the local level in federal states, as in the case of the US Constitution, which was adopted at the Constitutional Convention of September 1787, and later ratified by the state legislatures. Similarly, the 1949 West German Constitution was ratified by the Federal Parliamentary Council only after over two-thirds of the *Land* assemblies voted in favour of the draft. More often than not, however, constitutional reform comes about as a result of a vote in the national parliament or constituent assembly alone, as recently seen in Belgium, where constitutional reforms were brought about by votes in the national legislature.

A comparison of these two ratification procedures does not suggest that constitutions backed by plebiscites fare better than those without them. The Federal Republic of Germany's Basic Law, for instance, has proved to be a strong and durable pillar of democracy though it was never subjected to a plebiscite, whereas the 1946 French Constitution did not last, even though it was adopted by referendum.[36]

In the context of Eastern European democratization, the referendum issue has been fiercely debated, though in a slightly different manner. The major question was: do the revolutionary circumstances of Eastern Europe create a greater 'demand' for a constitutional referendum? Supporters of referenda insist that it is not enough that the revolutionary elite reach a constitutional compromise.

---

[36] In fact, French citizens were not only allowed to ratify the Constitution in a referendum, they were also consulted in advance on the primary decision of whether to draft a new constitution or reinstate the Constitution of the Third French Republic. Nevertheless, the Constitution survived only twelve years amidst severe criticism and recrimination.

Unlike normal legislation, a constitution needs to win a direct mandate from the people, without which the 'constitutionalization of the revolution' cannot occur.[37] Opponents of referenda insist that the revolutionary circumstances of Eastern Europe leave referenda susceptible to abuse. Because the situation is highly unstable and the political culture is underdeveloped, referenda fail to provide constitutions with the desired legitimacy, and create fertile ground for demagoguery. As Merkel argued, the circumstances of Eastern Europe are 'miles away from that kind of conceptual structure of public discourse which lifts referendum out of manipulative ratification into the higher sphere of "deliberative politics," called for by Jürgen Habermas'.[38] The examples presented in this book seem to support the latter argument.

The most striking case of manipulating constitutional referenda occurred in Belarus. The 1996 referendum was organized by the president in clear violation of the 1994 Constitution and over the opposition of both the parliament and the Constitutional Court.[39] The procedures, form, and substance of the referendum were imposed by the president, who also enjoyed a total monopoly over the mass media. In Russia, the referendum endorsing President Yeltsin's constitutional draft was probably the only way to keep democratic hopes alive in Russia after the violent clash between parliament and the president in September 1993. That said, the referendum could hardly claim to be a truly popular mandate, since the opposition was silenced by the president's tanks. Constitutional referenda in Romania, Estonia, Lithuania, and Poland were less controversial, but even there serious legitimacy problems surfaced. In Lithuania, for instance, there were only twelve days for public discussion of the constitutional draft between its approval by parliament and the referendum. In Poland, the referendum's legitimizing 'blessing' was also undermined by the fact that only 24 per cent of all eligible voters voted in favour of the

[37] See especially Ackerman, *The Future of Liberal Revolution*, 15, 53–4.

[38] Wolfgang Merkel, 'Institutions and Democratic Consolidation in East Central Europe', Estudio/Working Paper 86 (Madrid: Instituto Juan March de Estudios e Investigationes, 1996), 26. The work Merkel refers to is Jürgen Habermas, *Faktizität und Geltung* (Frankfurt am Main: Suhrkamp, 1992), 367 and ff.

[39] Since parliament was unwilling to accept the constitutional amendments of President Lukashenka, the president convened an ad hoc popular assembly, the All-Belarusian People's Meeting, to decide on the referendum. Although the assembly was not envisioned by either the 1994 Constitution or any other ordinary law, it obediently endorsed the president's idea. See 'Constitutional Watch', *East European Constitutional Review*, 4 (Fall 1996), 5.

constitution.[40] In short, referenda in Eastern Europe provided new constitutions with little popular legitimization, and in some cases they proved to be a tool of political manipulation.

The Product of Constitution Building

If constitution builders face a bewildering set of choices concerning the constitutionalization process, then they face even more bewildering options concerning what kind of regime they want to constitutionalize. The framers must decide whether or not to include a charter of rights in the constitution. They must choose the most appropriate balance of power arrangement between central and sub-central units of government, and ascertain whether it is best to establish a federal, unitary, or intermediate system of territorial government. They must agree upon the best relationship among the units of government at the central level and the degree to which the powers of the executive, legislative, and judicial branches of government should be separated. They must distribute responsibilities among the individual units of government at the central level and decide, for example, whether to create a bicameral or unicameral legislature. They also need to select the most fitting electoral system, choosing between a proportional system and a majoritarian system, or settle on some form of mixed system.

When making these choices, constitution builders are clearly motivated by their short- and long-term political interests. Constitution builders do not conduct their business behind some sort of 'veil of ignorance'. They have supporters to reward, enemies to stymie, principles to defend, and prejudices to express. Consequently, the final constitutional document may be a masterpiece of common sense or a patchwork of compromise; it may be a brief statement of fundamental political principles or a long-winded recitation of almost every conceivable goal, aspiration, and political desire.

Politics aside, analysts have been trying to cope with one fundamental question: do certain constitutional products guarantee better prospects for democratic consolidation? The choice between presidentialism and parliamentarism has probably been the most fiercely debated. Juan Linz forcefully advanced the virtues of

---

[40] Amidst widespread calls for a boycott of Poland's constitutional referendum the turnout was only 42%, and resulted in 57% of voters approving the Constitution and 43% rejecting it. See *RFE/RL Newsline*, 74/II (16 July 1997).

parliamentarism in contrast to the perils of presidentialism,[41] whereas Shugart and Carey insisted that properly crafted presidential or premier-presidential forms of government can overcome the traditional disadvantages of presidential regimes.[42] So far, experience has made the holes in both arguments visible. Critics of the presidential system were proved right in their claim that it creates a syndrome of 'dual legitimacy' that generates political deadlock. Moreover, the mutual independence of presidents and parliaments has tended to fuel rivalries detrimental to both institutions. Presidents have done much to frustrate the development of healthy party systems in the region, while failing to provide the most lauded benefit of presidentialism: strong and effective government. That said, presidentialism in Eastern Europe has not produced the 'winner-take-all' syndrome which proved so damaging in certain Latin American countries. In fact, almost all presidents in the region have found it necessary to engage in troublesome give-and-take negotiations with both government and opposition parties in parliament. Nor has presidentialism in Eastern Europe produced a two-bloc system with cabinets composed solely of members of the governing party. Most Eastern European presidents are not linked to any single political party, and in some countries they are even legally obliged to abandon party membership before assuming office. The region's presidents have indeed shown a plebiscitarian penchant for calling referenda, but often this was more a sign of impotence vis-à-vis parliaments than an indication of dictatorial tendencies.[43] Some presidents indeed have tried to obtain more power or invoke emergency authority, but parliamentary leaders have done the same. Post-communist politics has often resembled a zero-sum game, but parliaments have been as responsible for this as presidents.

[41] See Juan J. Linz, 'The Perils of Presidentialism', *Journal of Democracy*, 1/1 (1990), 51–69, and 'The Virtues of Parliamentarism', *Journal of Democracy*, 1/4 (1990), 84–91.

[42] Matthew Soberg Shugart and John M. Carey, *Presidents and Assemblies: Constitutional Design and Electoral Dynamics* (Cambridge: Cambridge University Press, 1992), 273–87.

[43] Consider for instance, President Václav Havel's unsuccessful 1992 effort to call a referendum on the future of the Czech and Slovak Federal Republic or President Boris Yeltsin's successful 1993 effort to hold a referendum on the merit of his reforms and the need for new elections. For a more detailed argument see Jan Zielonka, 'New Institutions in the Old East Bloc', in Larry Diamond and Marc F. Plattner (eds.), *The Global Resurgence of Democracy*, 2nd edn. (Baltimore: Johns Hopkins University Press, 1996), 217–19.

More important in our context is that the actual functioning of presidents and parliaments has not always corresponded to the constitutionalized solution. For instance, President Sali Berisha was able to impose dictatorial rule over Albania regardless of his relatively weak formal powers, while President Michal Kováč of Slovakia has never been able to utilize fully his formal powers vis-à-vis the parliamentary cabinet of Prime Minister Vladimír Mečiar.[44] The latter case also shows that parliamentarism can also degenerate into semi-dictatorship. As Merkel rightly asserted:

The apparent power of the parliament over the executive is actually the power of the parliamentary majority over the government. The parliament in turn is controlled by the government through increasing party discipline. Majority parties instrumentalize the executive and legislative branches for their own interests. The rigid domination of a majority in parliament, the colonization of the justice and public administrations, the cleansing of the public media and the intimidation of the private media through Meciar's left–right-coalition show the miniscule autonomy that constitutional organs and constitutional norms enjoy vis-à-vis the winning electoral majority in the Slovak Republic.[45]

The debate among constitutional analysts about which electoral system most favours the development of democracy has also proved inconclusive when applied to Eastern Europe. Several countries in the region decided not to deal with the electoral system in their constitutions, and none of them opted for British-style plurality elections. Both 'weak' and 'strong' proportional representation (PR) systems are employed in Eastern Europe, but a clear-cut correlation between the choice of electoral system and the overall progress of democracy has not yet emerged. In other words, countries with strong (if not extreme) PR systems have not necessarily fared worse than those with weak PR systems. Clearly, factors other than electoral systems have had significant impact on democratic progress in the region.

Complex aggregate models for the 'optimal' constitutional product proved even more difficult to apply to Eastern Europe. For instance, Arend Lijphart's preference for a 'consensus' as opposed to 'majoritarian' democratic system is being severely tested in

---

[44] As Darina Malová points out in her chapter, President Kováč has never taken part in cabinet meetings, and only once tried to solicit a cabinet report, but failed to obtain it.

[45] Merkel, 'Institutions and Democratic Consolidation', 35–6.

Slovakia, which meets most of Lijphart's criteria for consensus democracy.[46]

All this does not suggest that there are absolutely no guidelines for constitution builders to follow, but only that we are not close to the 'hyperrational ideal' for designing institutions envisaged by Claus Offe.[47] What is right for one country might not be right for another. Moreover, what is right for one set of countries, such as established West European democracies, might not be right for another set of countries, such as the newly democratized East European regimes. In short, the transferability of set constitutional rules collides with the complexity of particularistic political cultures. Moreover, basic concepts, such as the notion of presidentialism, suffer from epistemological confusion. Different writers use the same term to mean different things. For example, Russia is frequently classed as an example of a presidential regime, yet in a number of key respects it deviates from the prototypical US model. So, arguments suggesting that particular forms of government are better than others often suffer from conceptual ambiguity.[48] Even when such ambiguity is absent, arguments about the advantages and disadvantages of particular concepts are often normatively laden. As Pippa Norris has shown, 'irresolvable value conflicts' underpin arguments about the respective advantages and disadvantages of majoritarian versus PR electoral systems.[49] Those who argue for one simply have a different vision of representative democracy from those who argue for the other.

It would be wrong to assume, however, that constitutional framers can choose different types of constitutional products without any implications. For example, the choice of a strong PR electoral system over a weak PR will always imply more parliamentary fragmentation undermining the efficiency of democratic

[46] Ibid. 40. For the original argument see Arend Lijphart, 'Democratic Political Systems: Types, Cases, Causes, and Consequences', *Journal of Theoretical Politics*, 1 (1989), 33–48. Also, Arend Lijphart, *Democracies* (New Haven: Yale University Press, 1984), esp. 3–9.

[47] Claus Offe, 'Designing Institutions in East European Transitions', in Robert E. Goodin (ed.), *The Theory of Institutional Design* (Cambridge: Cambridge University Press, 1996), 225.

[48] Robert Elgie, 'The Classification of Democratic Regime Types: Conceptual Ambiguity and Contestable Assumptions', *European Journal of Political Research*, 33 (1988), 219–38.

[49] Pippa Norris, 'Choosing Electoral Systems: Proportional, Majoritarian and Mixed Systems', *International Political Science Review*, 18/3 (1997), 311.

work. On the other hand, the choice of a weak PR system will undermine the principle of democratic representation, because many voters will end up with no parliamentary representation. More crucially, this book bears witness to the fact that constitutions that fail to establish clear rules of the institutional game and the unequivocal separation of powers will not contribute to democratic consolidation.

Conclusions: Do Constitutions Matter?

Although all but one of the countries discussed in this book have managed to adopt a new constitution, the state of democracy varies widely. Does this mean that wrong constitutional choices were made in some countries? Or perhaps that adopting a new constitution does not really matter? This book leaves little doubt that constitutions by themselves cannot produce a workable democracy. Constitutions are one tool among many for democracy builders to use (or abuse) with greater or less skill.

That said, in the countries considered here, constitutions performed at least three basic functions.[50] First, they provided all countries with a charter for government by spelling out who their officials are, how they are chosen, their terms in office, how authority is divided among them. It is difficult to imagine how institutional power struggles could have been curbed had adopting new constitutions been postponed.

Second, constitutions provided Eastern European countries with charters of fundamental rights. Since some of these rights were not even recognized by the communist legal system while others were formally recognized but notoriously abused, constitutions catalogued these rights and set up mechanisms for their protection.

Third, constitutions have provided Eastern European countries with the symbolic opportunity to express popular aspirations for free, democratic, and sovereign statehood. Since most of the countries analysed here are historically new or quasi-new creations, the adoption of constitutions with broad support was a way to manifest independent and mature self-rule. In most countries, new constitutions also became symbolic expressions of their European and Western credentials.

[50] This cryptic typology is based on Walter F. Murphy, 'Constitutions, Constitutionalism, and Democracy', in Greenberg et al. (eds.), *Constitutionalism and Democracy*, 8–9.

Of course, individual constitutions have fulfilled these functions with varying degrees of success. In principle, the more partisan the constitutional process and unbalanced the constitutional outcome, the less a constitution affected the democratic process. Yet this book also suggests that even imperfect constitutions, in terms of substance and adoption procedures, managed to curb the ongoing institutional power struggle and created legal and political conditions in which democracy had a chance to assert itself. Even the 1993 Russian Constitution, imperfect as it may be, proved an asset to Russia's very fragile democracy. Likewise the hastily adopted constitutions in Lithuania, Bulgaria, and Romania contributed to democratic development there. Meanwhile, the staggered constitutional process in Poland and Hungary did not make democratic consolidation any easier.

Have some constitutional models improved democracy in Eastern Europe more than others? The answer provided by this book is neither clear nor straightforward. First of all, this book confirms Finer's thesis that 'different historical contexts generated different preoccupations: different preoccupations have generated different emphases.'[51] Second, this book confirms that a constitution is not, to cite Julio Faundez, an 'intellectual commodity that can be used to sell, impose, or transplant political models'.[52] What works for some countries does not necessarily work for others, and it is therefore difficult to construct a general constitutional model. Third, this book shows that there are clear limits to constitutional engineering. Constitutions are products of complex political bargaining and the final product of this bargaining tends to resemble a hybrid that only partially corresponds with an original design or model. Fourth, although some constitutional solutions proved to work better than others, they were not necessarily the products of constitutional engineering, but resulted from cultural, economic, and social factors characteristic of a given country at a given time.

Constitutions proved indispensable in the process of democratic consolidation in Eastern Europe. The constitution-making proved to be more important than the varieties of constitutional products offered. Although constitutions are not always treated as sacred, they have become an important reference point for all political decisions: in this region, violating the constitution is no longer a costless practice.

[51] Finer, *Five Constitutions*, 22.

[52] Julio Faundez, 'Constitutionalism: A Timely Revival', in Greenberg et al. (eds.), *Constitutionalism and Democracy*, 358.

·······················
3
·······················

Constitutional Design and Problems of Implementation in Southern and Eastern Europe

Leonardo Morlino

A traditional theme of political philosophy has been identifying the 'optimal government', that is, defining what is considered to be the best polity. Since Plato's Republic this question has remained at the core of political philosophy.[1] With the process of democratization, first in southern Europe and Latin America and more recently in Eastern Europe and other areas of the world, this question has become crucial for political elites as well. Attempts to answer this question often lead to heated, lengthy debates on choosing the constitutional structures for these countries. But really to understand the democratic outcome in a given country, one must explore how the constitutional design was implemented. Implementation is a key institutional aspect in the multifaceted process of democratic consolidation.[2]

Nevertheless, despite its salience the implementation of constitutional norms has been overshadowed by the 'best design' question.

This chapter was partially written during my stay at Nuffield College, Oxford, as Jemolo Fellow, in spring 1998. I gratefully acknowledge my debt to Laurence Whitehead and Vincent Wright for giving me the opportunity of working in what is, from my perspective, a quiet and at the same time stimulating institution. Some of the data were collected with the precious help of Alessandro Chiaramonte and Catia Chierici. I warmly thank both of them.

[1] Several years ago, Bobbio suggested that historically the central, recurring themes of political philosophy have been: (1) what is the best government? (2) What are the bases of political obligation? (3) What is the nature of politics? And (4) the analysis of political language. Norberto Bobbio, 'Considerazioni sulla filosofia politica', *Rivista italiana di scienza politica*, 1/2 (1971), 367–80.

[2] See Leonardo Morlino, *Democracy between Consolidation and Crisis: Parties, Groups and Citizens in Southern Europe* (Oxford: Oxford University Press, 1998).

Throughout this period of democratization, political scientists rightly have been much more interested in the problems of creating a polity. Indeed, the focus has been on the same questions with which the political elites in new democracies have been grappling. Consequently, some of these political scientists assumed the role of 'counsellor to the king'. In Klaus von Beyme's chapter in this volume, he recalls the main aspects of the related political science debate by referring to Giovanni Sartori, who coined the term 'constitutional engineering', and to other scholars who have also been important in this field, such as Juan Linz and Arend Lijphart. Recently, attention has also been focused on the reasons behind certain constitutional choices,[3] the salience of the modes of constitution-making,[4] or the environment in which constitution-making takes place.[5] But creating an analytical framework for studying the implementation of constitutional norms has been avoided, largely because it is difficult to organize the many problems related to this issue. Therefore, I will attempt to deal directly with this issue, cognizant that this is a tentative exploration into an empirical minefield.[6] As suggested by the first section, this study's aim is to isolate the key guiding concepts for analysing constitutional designs and their implementation. In the second section I will explore the main aspects of constitutional design and the related problems of implementation as they affect the consolidation process with reference to southern Europe. Next, I will present the constitutional designs of the main Eastern European countries and identify certain problems with design implementation.[7] Finally, some tentative conclusions will be drawn from the empirical material in the

[3] See Arend Lijphart, 'Democratization and Constitutional Choices in Czecho-Slovakia, Hungary and Poland', *Journal of Theoretical Politics*, 4/2 (1992), 207–23.

[4] See esp. Jon Elster, 'Ways of Constitutional Making', in Axel Hadenius (ed.), *Democracy's Victory and Crisis* (Cambridge: Cambridge University Press, 1997), 123–42.

[5] Juan J. Linz and Alfred Stepan, *Problems of Democratic Transition and Consolidation: Southern Europe, South America and Post-communist Europe* (Baltimore: Johns Hopkins University Press, 1996), 81–3.

[6] On the problems and difficulties of implementation see Jeffrey L. Pressman and Aaron Wildavski, *Implementation*, 3rd edn. (Berkeley and Los Angeles: University of California Press, 1984).

[7] The constitutions of these and other Eastern European countries are analysed more closely in the following chapters of this book. One of the earliest and best analyses of democratic consolidation in these countries is in K. Dawisha and B. Parrott (eds.), *The Consolidation of Democracy in East-Central Europe* (Cambridge: Cambridge University Press, 1997), but see also part IV of the important work by Linz and Stepan, *Problems of Democratic Transition and Consolidation*.

first two sections with reference to the patterns of implementation. The question of the best design will be conclusively answered.

The Uses and Misuses of Comparative Studies

Immediately, two key questions deserve to be addressed: does a comparison between southern and Eastern European democracies in terms of constitutional design and implementation make sense? And if so, what are the basic conceptual guidelines of this analysis? First, to address the methodological issue, the comparison is between two groups of countries, all of which are considered to be more or less stable democracies at the end of the 1990s. These countries can be divided into two groups. The first group comprises the four southern European countries Italy (where a democratic regime was installed in the late 1940s), Spain, Portugal, and Greece (where democracies were installed in the 1970s). The second group includes ten Eastern European countries that embraced democracy in the 1990s. The first five, the Czech Republic, Estonia, Hungary, Poland, and Slovenia, were admitted for consideration in the first round of EU enlargement, while for the remaining five, Bulgaria, Latvia, Lithuania, Romania, and Slovakia, EU accession negotiations have been postponed. Except for Slovakia, all of these countries are defined as 'free' by the 1997 and 1998 Nation in Transit Surveys.[8] Slovakia is defined as 'partly free' in 1997, and 'free' in 1998. Consequently it can be safely included in this analysis, not only because of its application to enter the EU.

Although obviously important, a few other Eastern European countries were not included in this analysis, such as Albania, Belarus, Russia, Ukraine, and the other successor states of Yugoslavia (that is, Croatia or Macedonia). These countries were rated as either 'partly free' (that is, on the border between democracy and non-democracy) or 'not free' (that is non-democratic) by the survey cited above. For instance, Albania is still in the midst of an uncertain transition, Belarus can be defined as having consolidated an authoritarian regime, while the remaining countries—Croatia included—are on the border in terms of established civil and polit-

---

[8] See table 4 in Adrian Karatnycky, Alexander Motyl, and Boris Shor (eds.), *Nations in Transit 1997: Civil Society, Democracy and Markets in East Central Europe and the Newly Independent States* (New Brunswick NJ: Transaction Publishers, 1997); and the only table in Adrian Karatnycky, 'The Decline of Illiberal Democracy: The 1998 Freedom House Survey', *Journal of Democracy*, 10/1 (1999), 112–25, esp. 124–5.

ical rights or have only very recently installed their democratic institutions (Ukraine held its first competitive elections in 1994,[9] but it cannot yet be defined as democratic).[10]

Even after narrowing the scope of this analysis, the differences between the remaining fourteen countries create several problems. In the four[11] southern European cases democratization replaced authoritarianism, while in the ten other countries democratization replaced mobilizing authoritarianisms or post-totalitarian regimes.[12] Continuity problems are not at the core of this analysis and, therefore, the difference can be overlooked.[13] However, two other factors cannot be glossed over. In all Eastern European countries, political transition has been intertwined with the transition to an open market economy. Moreover, in six of the ten countries borders have changed, due either to secession or to the creation of a new state. These countries include the three Baltic states (Estonia, Latvia, and Lithuania), Slovenia, the Czech Republic, and Slovakia. These basic differences comprise what Claus Offe dubbed Eastern Europe's three simultaneous transitions.[14] Another difference concerns the international environment. The Cold War of the 1950s, the persistent bipolar international system of the 1970s, and the fundamental changes that followed the fall of the Berlin Wall, German unification, and the end of the bipolar system in the early 1990s have had a unique effect on each wave of democratization. Thus, in addition to analysing constitutional implementation of these different waves of democratization, a review of the important international factors will also be attempted. Finally, there is a staggering difference between the richness of

[9] Charles R. Wise and Trevor L. Brown, 'The Consolidation of Democracy in Ukraine', *Democratization*, 5/1 (1998), 105–37.

[10] Karatnycky, Motyl, and Shor (eds.), *Nations in Transit 1997* is very detailed on most political and economic aspects.

[11] Five, if Italy's two periods of change are considered.

[12] For more on these notions, see Juan J. Linz, 'Totalitarian and Authoritarian Regimes', in Fred I. Greenstein and Nelson W. Polsby (eds.), *Handbook of Political Science*, Macropolitical Theory 3 (Reading, Mass.: Addison-Wesley Publishing Co., 1975) and also Leonardo Morlino, 'Authoritarianisms', in Anton Bebler and Jim Seroca (eds.), *Contemporary Political Systems: Classifications and Typologies* (Boulder, Colo.: Lynne Rienner Publishers, 1990). More recently, Linz and Stepan, *Problems of Democratic Transition and Consolidation*, 40–85, developed theoretically the typological analysis and that of implications of the previous non-democratic regime for transition and consolidation.

[13] Linz and Stepan, *Problems of Democratic Transition and Consolidation*.

[14] Claus Offe, 'Capitalism by Democratic Design? Democratic Theory Facing the Triple Transition in East Central Europe', *Social Research*, 59/4 (1991), 865–92.

collected data and research done in southern Europe and those on the ten Eastern European countries. Thus, there are strong empirical constraints on the kind of comparison and analysis that is possible. But despite these many contrasts, a meaningful comparison can be justified provided that the theoretical focus is well defined and clearly limited.

Leaving the problems of comparison aside, the next task is to set up the key guiding concepts of this analysis. First of all, the notion of constitutional design is straightforward and widely accepted[15] as encompassing the set of governing institutions—such as head of state, cabinet, and parliament—and their interrelationships, the modes and levels of centralization and decentralization, and the electoral system. These five dimensions encompass the main constitutional choices and decisions that characterize every democracy.[16] Moreover, since I am concentrating on how these choices are applied, it is important to distinguish between the two main modes of implementation. First, constitutional implementation may consist of the adoption of other laws to fulfil constitutional norms. Second, it may be as simple as the direct enactment of a constitutional norm—for example, the creation of the parliament as conceived by the constitution. Be it one or the other, focusing on implementation implies, above all, checking whether or not the new rules have created a system that aims at (*a*) shaping preferences and positions existing in and expressed by society, or (*b*) mirroring these preferences to have a better expression of social values and interests. More precisely, constitutional design can be analysed along a continuum between an extremely manipulative and a completely neutral design. Extreme manipulative design characterizes governing institutions that strongly shape the expressions of civil society, such as mediation structures (primarily parties and interest groups) and the political behaviour of citizens. A neutral design indicates a set of governing institutions that mirrors civil society as much as possible. Certain kinds of regimes, such as a presidential system, an executive-dominated parliament, a unitary

---

[15] See the chapter by von Beyme in this book.

[16] In his two models of democracy, Arend Lijphart, *Democracies* (New Haven: Yale University Press, 1984) also analyses the written/unwritten constitution and adoption of direct democratic devices. Both of these dimensions are overlooked here: the first one is not relevant for all the cases studied here; the second is salient in one or two cases (and when necessary it will be mentioned). On the basic choices of constitutional design see also Matthew S. Shugart and John M. Carey, *Presidents and Assemblies: Constitutional Design and Electoral Dynamics* (Cambridge: Cambridge University Press, 1992), 1–15.

state, or a majoritarian electoral system, create strongly manipulative constitutional systems. Meanwhile, a head of state elected by parliament, a parliament-dominated executive, federal systems, and highly proportional electoral systems create more neutral constitutional systems. A manipulative design creates artificial parliamentary majorities, raises in different ways the thresholds for representation, limits the number of parties, may make parties more cohesive, and may achieve a greater control over represented interests. On the contrary, a neutral design mirrors society, though such systems are also unavoidably vulnerable to exploitation and manipulation by party actors. When applied to empirical examples, majoritarian constitutional designs and manipulative designs, on the one hand, and consensual designs and neutral designs, on the other, usually overlap. Nevertheless, there is a basic analytical difference between these two categorizations. The manipulative/neutral dimension emphasizes the actual impact of constitutional design on society, as it is implemented. In addition, some cases may prove that a consensual system can have a manipulative impact or a majoritarian system can have a neutral impact. For example, a combination of an overall consensual constitutional design with manipulative results is conceivable where a mixed electoral system simply distorts parliamentary party size[17] or where specific parliamentary rules strongly shape legislative activity at the expense of the participation of all political forces in the actual decision-making process. By the same token, a majoritarian design may actually have a neutral impact where a majoritarian force fully dominates the political arena.[18]

Thus, the role of party leaders and party systems in the study of constitutional design cannot be ignored. These actors are heavily instrumental in the actual implementation of constitutional design. Accordingly, a basic assumption of this analysis is that the connection between constitutional design and party systems is at the core of constitutional implementation. In fact, party leaders are the actors making the constitutional choices and implementing them in the various political roles they play. Thus, in order to implement constitutional design it is necessary for political actors to have a

[17] This was the case in Italy after the approval of a new electoral system in 1993 (see Leonardo Morlino, '1997: Is There an Impact? And Where is it? Electoral Reform and the Party System in Italy', *South European Society and Politics*, 2/3 (1998), 103–31.

[18] Needless to say, in the long term a majoritarian design may undermine and eventually change the dominance of a party. On the problems related to party dominance see Morlino, *Democracy between Consolidation and Crisis*.

stable, structured political arena where the players and the game are defined and known, that is, a stabilized, structured party system. Consequently, how the implementation takes place simultaneously depends on the institutional design and the characteristics and stability of the party system. The argument, then, that the salience of parties and party systems in southern Europe is not paralleled in Eastern Europe does not hold. Certain studies have shown that although public trust in parties is low, parties are nevertheless very salient actors in the new Eastern European democracies.[19]

In this study, the party system will be the key factor that interacts with constitutional design. There are three important variables that should be considered when evaluating the party system: the stability of the party system, the organizational structure of parties, and the fragmentation of the party system. The underlying reasoning is that unstable, barely structured or unstructured, and fragmented party systems are weak, and consequently they are more susceptible to conditioning and shaping by manipulative institutions. A bi-partisan system, a predominantly one-party system, or a limited multi-party, stable, and organizationally structured party system, is more difficult to condition or influence.[20] More precisely, when the implementation of constitutional design is analysed and its connection to the party system is explored, the adaptation and appropriateness of the constitutional system can be determined.

The implementation of a constitutional design may involve either weaker or stronger constitutional adaptation. This includes: simply not implementing and consequently freezing constitutional rules; partially implementing them; totally or partially repealing

---

[19] See e.g. Matthew Wyman, Stephen White, Bill Miller, and Paul Heywood, 'The Place of Party in Post-communist Europe', *Party Politics*, 1/4 (1995), 535–48; and Richard Rose, 'Mobilizing Demobilized Voters in Post-communist Societies', *Party Politics*, 1/4 (1995), 549–64.

[20] This is a simple way of framing the problem of institutionalization of parties and party systems. For a more developed empirical analysis and theoretical justification for the adoption of these variables see Morlino, *Democracy between Consolidation and Crisis*, ch. 2. In his analysis of Latin American party systems Scott Mainwaring follows a parallel approach by considering: stability in patterns of interparty competition, party roots in society, legitimacy of parties and elections, party organization (see recently Scott Mainwaring, 'Party Systems in the Third Wave', *Journal of Democracy*, 9/3 (1998), 67–81).

Here, the availability of some data and not of others suggested this simpler approach with the additional consideration that in an European setting the legitimacy of parties and elections is not really questioned by a significant share of the population and consequently the variable can be ignored. On this see again Morlino, *Democracy between Consolidation and Crisis*, ch. 3.

them; and totally or partially changing constitutional norms. Adaptation takes place when party leaders respond to perceived values and interests—including their own—by shaping 'neutrally designed' institutions. From this perspective, the main consequence of constitutional adaptation is achieving a stronger consistency between constitutional rules and the attitudes, beliefs, positions, and mutual strengths of party actors. After democratic institutions are installed, attitudes and strengths of the parties in power very often begin to diverge from those of the constitution makers. That is, the party or the coalition of parties that create the democratic regime often lose power and other actors are left to implement the rules. This is usually due to dramatic events—changes in the relationships between political actors, changes in the political strength of certain actors in subsequent elections, or the change in political focus from democracy building to coping with real, day-to-day problems. The adaptation allowed by a neutral design is mainly achieved during the first moments of implementation, when governing elites and groups impose their visions of how institutions ought to work, even by repealing or transforming the rules so that they better conform to their own values, interests, and goals. Thus, adaptation can be studied by examining the relationship between institutions and rules, on the one hand, and the party system, on the other. Besides, it is important to remember that a neutral design is the most probable choice where leaders and parties are distant or very distant from one another, that is, they are polarized. This implies that adaptation is most likely to occur following a partial or total change of governing parties.

Constitutional appropriateness is the opposite mode of constitutional implementation. Unlike neutral design, manipulative design constrains parties through institutions and rules. Appropriateness is the notion introduced by March and Olsen[21] and is adopted here to describe constitutional implementation in which party leaders cannot act freely within the institutions, but must adapt to them. From this perspective, the key question party leaders face is determining the most appropriate action and strategy for achieving their goals, provided that a given rule exists and must be implemented. The legally appropriate action is very often ultimately declared by the Constitutional Court. The Court performs a fundamental role, particularly when actors conflict

---

[21] James G. March and Johan P. Olsen, *Rediscovering Institutions: The Organizational Basis of Politics* (New York: Free Press and Collier Macmillan Publishers, 1989).

over the rules. Establishing a system of appropriateness means that routines and interpretations emerge with time, depending on the regime's stability and the ability to constrain, shape, or reshape the party system. The key element that offers the possibility for an implementation characterized by appropriateness is the existence of a basically established legal system, that is, when authorities and citizens comply with the rules. If there is no legal framework, manipulative constitutional design will be either circumvented or ignored. Consequently, establishing constitutional appropriateness is not possible, and consolidation is improbable.

On the whole, a neutral design coupled with a stable, limited, and/or structured party system is implemented by adaptation, whereas a manipulative design with an unstable, fragmented, and/or an unstructured party system is implemented by appropriateness. These two possibilities are complemented by two other hypotheses (see Fig. 3.1). For lack of a better word, the situation where neutral designs and unstable, fragmented, and/or unstructured party systems coexist will be called 'balance'. In a balance situation, weaknesses, uncertain results, and fluidity predominate in the political arena. In the situation where manipulative design is coupled

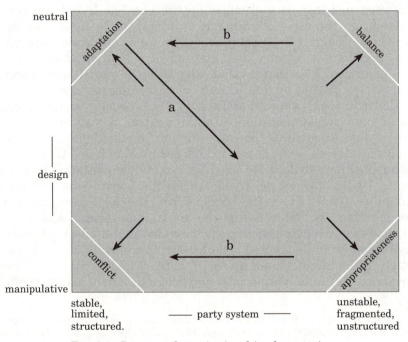

Fig. 3.1. *Patterns of constitutional implementation*

with a strong party system and where the rule of law has been established and the constitution cannot be ignored 'conflict' is inevitable. Conflict may be open or latent, but it is deeply embedded in this combination of factors. When there is either very poor or no rule of law the situation is much more confused, but basically even a manipulative design is 'manipulated' and adapted to the will of party leaders.

In Fig. 3.1, the four short arrows point to four extreme possibilities, and three additional options for how to cope in each situation are offered. The four extreme 'corner' hypotheses could be complemented by intermediate possibilities. These additional possibilities may occur, for example, first, when no choice between manipulative and neutral design is made because the two different goals of efficacy and representation are pursued simultaneously and/or the party system is neither completely stable nor completely unstable, but in an indeterminate position. Second, there is also the possibility that as the constitution is being implemented, the rules may still be changing—either increasing or decreasing the level of neutrality. Third, it is even more probable that the stability, fragmentation, and structure of the party system will change. In Fig. 3.1 the longer a arrow points to a hypothesis that seems to illustrate the recent changes in Italy, while the b arrows better indicate the recurring process of consolidation where implementation of constitutional design is complemented by the stabilization of the party system. Of course, in terms of changing patterns of implementation, several other possibilities are worthy of speculation, but the most empirically meaningful seem to be those indicated above.[22]

In terms of tracking the changing patterns of implementation, another salient factor is time. If the constitutional process is long, drafting and approving a constitution may go hand in hand with the stabilization and structuration of the party system, and even its 'natural' fragmentation or defragmentation. If the constitutional process is short, new rules create the problem of establishing

---

[22] From a methodological point of view the question 'what causes what' could be addressed. On the ground of the previous statements, the simplest reply is: when the constitutional choices are made and the implementation is at stake, manipulative design affects party system and party system affects neutral design. However, intermediate, ambiguous empirical situations are more common. In this whole perspective, the question of what is the independent variable can also be better formulated: both party system and constitutional design have to be considered as independent and dependent variables to control more precisely 'what causes what'.

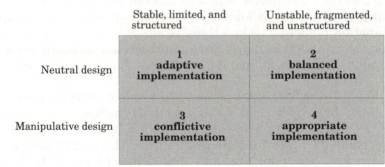

FIG. 3.2. *What type of implementation?*

constitutional appropriateness in a fluid party system. Constitutional choices almost always precede the period of party stabilization and structuration. Consequently, the actual question is: once the constitution is approved, is the party system going to stabilize, and, if so, how long does this process take? These questions suggest the following hypotheses: (1) the sooner the party system is stabilized, the stronger the party system will be, and the more neutral the constitutional design; the higher the possibility for adaptation rather than appropriateness. (2) The sooner the organizational structure is formed, the stronger the party system will be, and the more neutral the constitutional design; the higher the possibility of implementation by appropriateness. (3) The less fragmented the system is (and consequently the smaller the number of parties), and the more neutral the constitutional design; the higher the possibility for adaptative implementation. Of course, a set of intermediate empirical hypotheses could also be developed, above all when adaptation and appropriateness are more or less limited and partial.

In Fig. 3.2, the four 'corner' possibilities from Fig. 3.1 are simplified into four types of implementation. The adaptive (1) and the appropriate (4) implementations are 'pure' types of implementation, while the remaining two are intermediate types. In the second cell, neutral design and unstable party system balance each other with uncertain, unpredictable results, and basically no consolidation of any sort. In the third type, where strong, manipulative design confronts a strong party system, accommodation usually results as party leaders impose their interpretations of the institutional structure. In this last type, consolidation is achieved.

Nevertheless, implementation is not simply contingent on the type of constitutional design and party system. Legislation that develops constitutional rules is a key element in the process of democratic consolidation as well as the gradual establishment of the rule of law. Specific attention might also be paid to Constitutional Courts and their role in defining how and which rules are implemented, or what legacies of the previous regime are compatible with the new democratic regime, what the political role performed by the judiciary is, or, to the extent that parties try, how they attempt to influence the judiciary. But although these (and others) may be important factors in the process, the theoretical framework set up above is specifically devoted to the types of implementation (adaptation, appropriateness) and how they relate to the party system. Limiting the factors involved follows through with the main goal of the chapter, which is to check whether this framework is useful in comparing the transitions of both sets of countries. If the theoretical framework is successful, then the conclusions may allow us to speculate about the future developments in Eastern Europe on the basis of the longer experience of southern Europe in the process of democratic consolidation.

The Experience of Southern Europe

The installation of constitutional design symbolically ends when parliament approves the constitutional charter, as was the case in Italy (December 1947), Greece (June 1975), Portugal (April 1976), and Spain (October 1978). Moreover, in Italy a new phase of institutional engineering began in 1993 after the referendum amending the electoral law was approved, and continued in 1997 with the proposals for constitutional amendments by a two-chamber parliamentary committee, which were debated on the floor in 1998. But simply making choices about what type of regime to install and adopting constitutions is only the first step. After constitutions are approved by parliament, further legitimacy is often acquired through referenda. In Spain, citizens expressed their support for the new regime by approving its basic democratic institutions in the 6 December 1978 referendum. The presence of other powerful actors, such as the military, may also block full implementation of constitutionalized choices. A good example is Portugal, where the minimal requirements for democracy were met only after civilian control of the army was formally stated in the constitutional reform of October 1982. Therefore Portugal had been a hybrid polity during the period between constitutional adoption in 1976 and 1982. Although pluralism was achieved, the different factions of the army—as a consequence of the coup on 25 April 1974—still controlled the open, competitive interplay between civilian actors within institutions. Therefore, in Portugal, partial consolidation began and overlapped with the creation of additional—but key—elements to complete the democratic installation. Thus, I will begin by reviewing constitutional choices and consolidation of each institution in all four countries, beginning with the head of state, then evaluating the relationships between cabinet and parliament, local and central powers, and finally categorizing the electoral system.[23]

The head of state

Although the head of the state in Greece and Italy has always been elected by parliament, the power balance has changed over the years. In Portugal, where the head of state is directly elected, the role of this office has also changed as part of the demilitarization process. In Spain, the monarchy also has had a key moment with the attempted *coup d'état* in 1981, when the king was able to stop the army and thus gain definitive legitimacy.

The 1975 Greek Constitution was approved without the vote of the socialist PASOK party opposition. PASOK opposed the so-called 'superpowers' granted to the head of state in the Constitution, which made the office resemble the French presidency, except that the Greek head of state is not directly elected.[24] The constitutional amendments adopted by the PASOK government in 1985–6 and the pro-socialist president, Khristos Sartzetakis, amended most of chapter 2, section B, part 3, of the Greek Constitution concerning the powers of the head of state.[25] Basically,

---

[23] Guy Hermet wrote one of the very few comparative analyses of the Spanish and Portuguese constitutions. Guy Hermet, 'Emerging from Dictatorship: The Role of the Constitution in Spain (1978) and Portugal (1976)', in Vernon Bogdanor (ed.), *Constitutions in Democratic Politics* (Aldershot: Gower, 1988), 256–73.

[24] This was also emphasized by the president of the committee that drafted the Constitution and was immediately elected head of state (on 20 June 1975). See also, Constantine D. Tsatsos, 'Making the Constitution of Greece', in Robert A. Goldwin and Art Kaufman (eds.), *Constitution Makers and Constitution Making: The Experience of Eight Nations* (Washington: American Enterprise Institute for Public Policy Research, 1988), 69–93, esp. 75.

[25] In particular the following articles were changed: 32 (paras. 1, 4), 35 (1, 2, 3), 37 (2, 3, 4), 38, 41 (1, 2, 4), 42, 44 (2, 3), 47 (3), and 48. At the same time, Art. 39, which had created the Council of the Republic, and Art. 43.3 were repealed.

the head's discretionary powers regarding the dismissal of cabinet, calling and chairing cabinet meetings, and issuing bills on the organization of the state were repealed. The powers of appointing the prime minister, dissolving parliament, calling referenda on national issues, granting amnesty, and declaring a 'state of siege' were transferred to the parliamentary majority and, consequently, to the prime minister.[26]

In Portugal, the 1982 constitutional amendment resulted from a long political debate and was more complex and substantial than the Greek case. The 1982 amendment shifted the prime minister's political responsibility from the president to parliament, while maintaining the president's power to dissolve parliament and appoint and dismiss the prime minister. In addition, the Council of Revolution was abolished and the Council of State, the Constitutional Court, and the Superior Council of National Defence were created. The amendments gave the president (who was still directly elected) a different autonomous power of guarantee. At the same time, the addition of other norms[27] strengthened the role of the assembly vis-à-vis the president. The new constitutional arrangement gave the prime minister a central role by making the PM dependent on the assembly for votes of confidence, and thus able to circumvent the president with the support of the majority

---

The Council of the Republic was formed by the head of state, the former presidents of the republic, the prime minister, the former prime minister, the speaker of parliament, the leader of the opposition. It never met between 1975 and 1985, except once to define more precisely the functioning of the Council. As a matter of fact, its task of controlling the head of state became superfluous when the powers of that office were restricted. At the same time, ten years after the democratic installation, the critical advisory role it could perform appeared useless. Finally, this body was not able to establish any political role for itself. For the Constitutional Charter see H. Oberdoff (ed.), *Les Constitutions de l'Europe des Douze* (Paris: La Documentation Française, 1992), 163 ff.; for a balanced appraisal of the 1975 Constitution in terms of continuity–discontinuity in Greek institutional history and the impact of the 1986 revision see also N. Diamandouros, 'Politics and Constitutionalism in Greece: The 1975 Constitution in Historical Perspective', in R. Gunther (ed.), *Politics, Society, and Democracy: Comparative Studies: Essays in Honor of Juan J. Linz* (Boulder, Colo.: Westview Press, 1995), 279–96.

[26] From a juridical perspective, a good, thorough analysis of such a revision is conducted by Virginia Perifanaki Rotolo, *L'evoluzione della forma di governo in Grecia* (Padua: CEDAM, 1989). For a cursory analysis see also Dimitrios K. Katsoudas, 'The Constitutional Framework', in Kevin Featherstone and Dimitrios K. Katsoudas (eds.), *Political Change in Greece* (London: Croom Helm, 1987), 14–33.

[27] See, for example, the enlargement of legislative competence for the parliament (Arts. 167–8) or the transfer of competence on emergency state and siege state to the same body.

in parliament.[28] These new rules were put to the test after the army was stripped of political influence in 1985 and, most importantly, after 1987 when the Social Democratic Party gained a majority in parliament. This is a good example of how institutional engineering is a key step in the longer-term adaptive process, when higher institutional consistency is gained through the expulsion of an independent military power allowing political parties to acquire a decisive role in politics. In other words, a representative body (parliament) expelled an unelected body (the army) from the institutional structure and simultaneously weakened the president by giving parliament control over the prime minister and dissolving the Council of Revolution—an institution constitutionally linked to the president.[29] The second step in the adaptive process came after the Social Democrats gained a strong parliamentary majority, when the already weakened powers of the president were largely 'disactivated'.[30]

In Spain, the king has maintained a neutral role of democratic guarantee, which was particularly evident during the attempted military *coup d'état* in 1981. The king's firm, prompt action effectively toppled the coup attempt. In Italy, the president's stronger role was seen during the 1992–4 transitional period when two

---

[28] The revision of 1982 leaves the president without autonomous powers in governmental activity, and also his power of dismissing the prime minister (Art. 198/2) and his veto powers (Art. 139) are limited and the range of discretion narrowed.

[29] Therefore, such a constitutional revision put an end to the anomaly of the military political presence in the Portuguese Constitution and, since 1982, Portugal can be considered to be a democracy rather than a democratic hybrid.

[30] This is common in semi-presidentialism. See how Maurice Duverger sketches this model: Maurice Duverger, 'A New Political System Model: Semi-Presidential Government', *European Journal of Political Research*, 8/2 (1980), 165–87; and the successive analysis by Giovanni Sartori, *Comparative Constitutional Engineering: An Inquiry into Structures, Incentives, and Outcomes* (London: Macmillan, 1994), 121–40. Let it be also recalled here that the Portuguese president maintains less power vis-à-vis the French president; basically, even when he could be supported by a parliamentary majority, the president has no autonomous power of legislative initiative (that is, he is not the head of the executive as in France). It is also interesting to stress how a semi-presidential arrangement has weaker constraints than others. The main side effect of this is the variability in the actual working of this institution in connection with the personality or the political strategies of the president. For example, Mario Soares, elected twice in 1986 and 1991, has performed his role in a different way during the two terms, being much more 'interventionist' during the second term, when the party leadership was stronger than before. This goes against the analysis that political scientists usually suggest. On the presidency of Soares, see the excellent article by Manuel Braga da Cruz, 'O Presidente da República na génese e evolução do sistema de governo português', *Análise social*, 29 (1994), 125–6, 237–65.

cabinets, one presided over by Giuliano Amato and the other by Carlo Azeglio Ciampi, were appointed by President Oscar Luigi Scalfaro without the clear prior support of a parliamentary majority. Disagreements, conflicts, and above all the breakdown of traditional parties (such as the Christian Democrats and Socialist Party) gave the president an opportunity to perform a more substantial political role.

The parliament

The Italian assembly is composed of two chambers with the same powers and elected by similar laws, that is, it is a symmetrical and congruent parliament.[31] This design survived the changes made to the electoral laws of both chambers. By contrast, the bicameral Spanish parliament is neither symmetrical nor congruent, since only the lower chamber has legislative power. Greece and Portugal have unicameral assemblies. In all four countries, the relationship between the cabinet and the parliament has been problematic. Italy is the most extreme case of parliamentary dominance, where MPs often intervene in the law-making process by changing the government's legislative proposals despite the fact that they belong to the same party.[32] In the early 1990s, the role of parliament became even more relevant, at least until 1996 when Romano Prodi's cabinet was appointed to office.

In Portugal, two distinct phases in the cabinet–parliament relationship emerge. Since the early 1980s the representative role of parliament has been predominant, with legislative output even higher than the government's. This was the result of a routine in which the incumbent parties preferred negotiating laws in parliament rather than rubber-stamping government initiatives.[33] But, after the 1987 government gained efficacy in the parliamentary decision-making process, the government's legislative role prevailed. The social democratic majority elected in 1987 and 1991 accounts for this change.

Although to different degrees, Spain and Greece have achieved fairly similar patterns of executive dominance. In both states, the

[31] See Lijphart, *Democracies*.

[32] See M. Morisi, *Le leggi del consenso: partiti e interessi nei parlamenti della Prima Repubblica* (Messina: Rubbettino, 1992), 36 ff.

[33] Manuel Braga da Cruz and Antunes M. Lobo, 'Parlamento, partidos e governo: acerca da institucionalizaçao politica', in Baptista M. Coelho, *Portugal: o sistema politico e constitucional 1974–1987* (Lisbon: Instituto de Ciencias Sociais-Universidade de Lisboa, 1989).

majority of laws passed by parliament originate in the government. In Greece, however, the role of parliamentary members was
strengthened through the practice of the majority and opposition
parties proposing amendments to bills. This was the only way for
parliament to counter the otherwise overwhelming dominance of
the government vis-à-vis the Voulì. Often, these amendments have
nothing in common with the discussed bill, which results in the
approval of catch-all laws. Although there is no such practice in
Spain, the government controls parliamentary activities primarily through party discipline. Several rules in the parliamentary
standing orders grant strong privileges to the governmental parties
in parliament.[34]

The cabinet and prime minister

If properly understood and cautiously approached,[35] the duration
of a cabinet may usefully indicate the relative stability of the relationship between cabinet and parliament. As an indicator of the
extent to which cabinet controls the legislature, cabinet turnovers
can reveal precise patterns. The clearest case is Portugal,[36] where
six cabinets were formed within the first two years of the new regime
(1974–6), that is, a new cabinet was formed every four months. In
the second period (1976–81) there were seven: a new cabinet every
twelve months; while in the most recent period (1981–95) cabinets
changed once every three years (34.2 months). Similar stable patterns were immediately established in Spain and Greece. Spain has
had nine cabinets in the twenty-one years since Franco's death, or
seven cabinets in nineteen years, one every three years or so (32.6
months), if the transitional cabinets are excluded. In the past
fourteen years the cabinet changed only as often as parliamentary
elections were held, though a few important reshuffles were made.
In Greece, if the first two transitional cabinets are excluded,
eleven new cabinets were formed in twenty-one years, with their
duration very close to that of Spain.[37] The opposite pattern of

[34] As for the data on which this analysis is grounded, see Morlino, *Democracy
between Consolidation and Crisis*, ch. 2.
[35] Let it be recalled how the change of cabinet is a traditional indicator, and
about it there is a large literature beginning at least with the analyses on cabinet
instability in Weimar Germany and other countries during the 1920s and 1930s.
[36] See Morlino, *Democracy between Consolidation and Crisis*, table 2.3.
[37] A more precise analysis of the actual working and dynamics of weak executives is in Kleomenis S. Koutsoukis, 'Cabinet Decision Making in the Hellenic Republic
1974–1992', in Michael Laver and Kenneth A. Shepsle (eds.), *Cabinet Ministers*

parliamentary dominance is apparent in post-1953 Italy, setting a record with fifty-five cabinets in forty-three years.

Briefly put, in Spain such patterns of stability and executive dominance are accounted for by the limited number of parties, the constructive no-confidence vote (Art. 113 of the Constitutional Charter), and other norms embedded in the Constitution and the standing orders of the Cortes. In fact, Spain's only irregular cabinet change occurred after the resignation of Adolfo Suárez at the end of January 1981, when there were problems in the governing party Unión de Centro Democrático (UCD). The UCD virtually disappeared within a year, which was as much a problem of delegitimization as of democratic institutions. A month-long power vacuum followed, which culminated with the previously mentioned attempted *coup d'état* on 23 February 1981. Greece has had even fewer parties, despite the absence of constitutional norms strengthening the cabinet.[38] Therefore, cabinet changes in Greece are an even more meaningful indicator of executive dominance. Between 1989 and 1990, four short cabinets were created amidst corruption scandals, strong ideological party conflicts, and serious economic problems. In the Portuguese case, the six transitional cabinets within the first two years simply mirror the dynamics of the Movement of Armed Forces (MAF)—which launched the coup in April 1974 and dismantled the authoritarian regime. But

---

and Parliamentary Government (Cambridge: Cambridge University Press, 1994), 270–82. Spain follows similar lines that characterize a chancellor democracy; for example, in the autonomy of ministers in their fields and the coordination only with the prime minister when economic resources are not involved or the bills suggested by the minister do not affect the competence of other ministers.

[38] Mainly, the requisite of the absolute majority of all MPs to approve a motion of no confidence vis-à-vis the absolute majority of present MPs (Art. 84.6). The Portuguese Constitution follows the same lines as the Greek in this case. In fact Arts. 195.4 and 198.1 f. require the absolute majority of MPs 'em efectividade de funçoes' to reject a governmental programme or to approve a motion of no confidence. The expression 'effectively incumbent MPs' may only be understood within the constitutional tradition of Portugal. In any case, it is fully equivalent to the Greek requirement of all MPs also as a consequence of a curious constitutional routine established in Portugal. The MPs who cannot participate in a parliamentary session, even if temporarily, e.g. for a day, appoint a substitute. Such appointments are recurring, so that at any moment all MPs are effectively incumbent or in office. For a thoughtful analysis of this routine and the related data see W. C. Opello, 'Portugal's Parliament: An Organizational Analysis of Legislative Performance', *Legislative Studies Quarterly*, 11 (Sept. 1986), 295–8. In all three countries the parliamentary standing orders (the texts are published by *Diario da Republica* for Portugal and the *Official Bulletins* for the other two countries) basically confirm the constitutional norms.

conflicts between parties were also evident. Therefore, stability came after the party agreement that brought about the 1982 constitutional revision and the expulsion of the army from politics.[39]

Local and central powers

Although both the Portuguese and Greek constitutions create a unitary state, decentralization has been at the core of Portuguese political debates in the late 1990s, and some decisions promoting decentralization have been implemented in Greece. But the most interesting and controversial problems dealing with centralization have surfaced in the other two countries.

In Spain, the process of decentralization began slowly due to title VIII of the Constitution, which presented different routes to autonomy,[40] and set up complex mechanisms. The installation of pre-autonomies began in 1979 and ended in 1983, when all statutes were approved, the first elections were held in the seventeen regions (1980–3), and unicameral parliaments, executives, presidents, and high courts were set up. Nevertheless, installation was uneven: while it was possible to see the beginnings of consolidation in some regions (Catalonia, Basque Country, and Galicia), other regions lagged behind. In terms of patterns and more precise indicators of consolidation, a few aspects should be mentioned. First, the declaration of the partial unconstitutionality of the 'Organic Law for the Harmonization of Autonomy Process' (LOAPA)[41] in August 1983 meant at least the 'freezing' of asymmetric regions, where powers and competence were allocated differently—even among the three 'historical regions' with deeper traditions and different languages and cultures. Second, the

---

[39] An additional analysis of cabinet change from different perspective would be possible and useful. As a meaningful indicator of consolidation and crisis, however, the above considerations should be enough.

[40] For details, see Jesús Leguina Villa, 'Las Comunidades Autónomas', in Eduardo García de Enterria and Alberto Predieri (eds.), *La Constitución española de 1978* (Madrid: Editorial Civitas, 1982), 727–80; Juan Maldonado Gago, 'La organización territorial del estado', in Paloma Román Marugán (ed.), *Sistema político español* (Madrid: McGraw-Hill, 1995), 53–66.

[41] The law was approved in 1982 to implement a 'acto autonómico' reached by the Socialists and the then incumbent party, the Unión de Centro Democrático (UCD) (see below). On the LOAPA see Andrés De Blas Guerrero, 'Estado de las autonomías y transición política', in Ramón Cotarelo (ed.), *Transición política y consolidación democrática en España (1975–1986)* (Madrid: Centro de Investigaciones Sociológicas, 1992), 105–19.

devolution of power, one of the most important indicators in this process, was very slow. In fact, by June 1985, 300,000 function-aries of the central government had been transferred to the regions and by the end of that year 'all but a few regional governments had received the full measure of competencies granted to them by their Statutes of Autonomy'.[42] That same year a law for financing the autonomous regions was approved. But even as recently as February 1992, another 132,000 civil servants moved to the regions,[43] in 1993 several additional tasks were transferred to the regions, and in 1994 a new system for transferring financial resources to regions came into effect.[44] Thus, although the core of the process took place in the mid-1980s, it has dragged on for more than a decade. This is also clear from the role played by the Constitutional Court in the LOAPA case and hundreds of other conflicts raised by the central versus the regional government and vice versa.[45] By 1993, such legal conflicts had sharply declined. Curiously enough, throughout this period such conflicts were com-plemented by several agreements between the central government and regional leaders or between leaders of national and regional parties, and above all by hundreds of intergovernmental commit-tees created especially for the negotiated devolution of power. By the mid-1990s, in any case, the issue had not yet been settled. Basque terrorism and radical separatist demands continue to keep the process open.[46]

[42] As G. Shabad recalls, 'After Autonomy: The Dynamics of Regionalism in Spain', in S. G. Payne (ed.), *The Politics of Democratic Spain* (Chicago: Council of Foreign Relations, 1986), 112.

[43] This figure is indirectly suggested by Paul Heywood, who gives a number of 432,186 functionaries who had 'changed masters' between 1982 and 1992, with another 40,000 new recruits still at the regional level. Paul Heywood, *The Government and Politics of Spain* (London: Macmillan, 1995), 156.

[44] As suggested by *El País* (see *Anuario*, 1995), the share of expenditures decided by the regional governments is still growing: actually it tripled in the twelve years 1983–95.

[45] During the 1981–93 period the conflicts between the central government and Communidades Autónomas show the following trend: 49 (1981), 51 (1982), 68 (1983), 101 (1984), 131 (1985), 96 (1986), 101 (1987), 92 (1988), 60 (1989), 32 (1990), 18 (1991), 32 (1992), 12 (1993). See M. Sanches de Dios, 'El poder judicial y la jurisdición constituencial', in P. Román Marugán (ed.), *Sistema politico español* (Madrid: McGraw-Hill, 1995), 154.

[46] Even the recent electoral results with the partial victory of the rightist party and the need to form a cabinet with the support of regional parties opened again the process of the allocation of powers and related resources between the centre and the main represented peripheries.

In Italy, contrary to constitutional stipulations, implementation of a regional governing system was frozen until 1970. During the initial stages of consolidation, policies were geared towards creating a unitary state. But decentralization was one of the immediate effects of the crisis that exploded in the late 1960s. By the mid-1970s, there was a slow transfer of power to the fifteen new governing institutions and their elected and bureaucratic bodies. From the mid-1980s social and political demands called for additional decentralization, and in some cases more radical struggles for independence and secession emerged. Moreover, decentralization became a key issue in the political debate and was not only included in the political programmes of local organizations, such as the Northern League, but was also adopted by centre and leftist parties. The constitutional amendments drafted by the two-chamber parliamentary committee reflected these changing sentiments by proposing federalism and stronger decentralization. Articles 56 to 63 of the 1997 draft stipulate that new regional 'statutes', electoral laws, and tax systems will be decided at the regional level. Despite these initiatives by the parliamentary committee, the draft 'passed away' due to the inability to come to an agreement on the floor between the parties of the governmental majority and the opposition.

The 'rules of the game'

Both Spain and Portugal have proportional electoral systems, characterized by either fairly small or small constituencies. In Spain, where the threshold is 3 per cent, regional parties with strong local roots are not punished by the electoral system. In Greece, the proportional system is coupled with very high thresholds; however, its main characteristic is that it has been changed several times, but always strongly limiting fragmentation.[47] Until 1993, the Italian proportional system made no attempt to constrain party fragmentation. The electoral law had to be amended after the 1993 referendum, following a powerful direct appeal from the discontented electorate. The parliament approved new electoral laws for the lower chamber and Senate by early August 1993.[48] These

[47] For details, see Morlino, *Democracy between Consolidation and Crisis*.
[48] Let it be remembered that in spite of the opposite indications of some governmental parties, a previous referendum in June 1992 had approved the abolition of casting more than one preference vote on the electoral ballot, in this way changing a fairly important aspect of Italian proportional representation.

new laws created a mixed system, with national elections partially majoritarian.[49]

What Outcomes, and Which Implementation?

First, a quick summary of the established arrangements in each dimension is helpful. Portugal, Spain, and Greece have become semi-parliamentarian regimes or 'chancellor' democracies, that is, regimes in which the role of the prime minister and cabinet prevails vis-à-vis the assembly. In a sense, all three regimes are either largely or partially majoritarian, and thus either largely manipulative (Greece) or partially manipulative (Spain and Portugal). The process of adaptation/appropriateness was particularly relevant in Greece and Portugal. Over time, the prime minister in Greece has become more important than the head of state, especially after 1985. The ambiguous constitutional roles of the prime minister and the head of state were neutralized by the one-party cabinets, created through a reinforced PR system. In Portugal, after the 1982 constitutional amendment, the depoliticization of the army after 1986, and most importantly the establishment of a predominant party system after 1987, a semi-chancellor democracy was implemented through the direct election of the head of state and the proportional electoral system.

---

[49] In contrast with the relatively pure proportional representation system used over the preceding four decades, the new law allocates three-quarters of the seats in both houses on the basis of a plurality (single-member) electoral system. The remaining quarter of the seats are allocated on the basis of proportional representation to partly compensate those parties that did not receive representation on the first (plurality) segment. In Senate elections the voter has one vote to cast, and a party that elects a senator through the single member/majority segment of the ballot has the votes that were cast for its victorious candidate subtracted from its total in the calculations of seats to be allocated in the proportional representation segment. In elections for the Chamber of Deputies the voter has two votes; one for the single-member constituency. The remainder following this subtraction is the basis upon which the allocation of the proportional representation seats is calculated. In addition to the majoritarian biases inherent in all single-member district systems, a 4 per cent minimum nationwide vote is established by law as a prerequisite for receiving representation through the PR segment for the Chamber of Deputies; for the Senate, there is no legal threshold, but since the allocation of PR seats is calculated at the regional level, there is a *de facto* threshold of about 10 per cent (actually, it can be either much lower or much higher) of votes cast for receiving PR seats. The proportional-representation segment of the vote softens the impact of the plurality system somewhat.

In Italy, the highly proportional system was meant to be 'neutral', simply reflecting the cleavages and conflicts existing in society by granting parliamentary representation to every relevant political force. A different choice might have implied further radicalization and the disruption of the regime. Similarly, the decision-making process at the centre also aimed at being 'neutral'. Namely, both the rules of decision-making and the established routines gave parliament strong influence over the cabinet.[50] Parliament is composed of two chambers which are almost perfectly symmetrical and congruent.[51] Thus, in Italy a highly parliamentary regime was established and consolidated. Yet the prominent role of the Christian Democratic Party meant that it worked much like a semi-parliamentary regime or as a chancellor democracy before 1953. But later, it turned into a true parliamentary democracy with proportional representation and a key role for both chambers. The new electoral system adopted in 1993 seems to have opened the way for the creation of a new democratic arrangement in which party elites promoted a bipolar party system that is weak and unstable. After the failure of an ad hoc parliamentary committee and its constitutional project in 1998,[52] the demand for constitutional change remained undelivered and is still pending especially in terms of strengthening regionalization.

Decentralization is a salient aspect only in the case of Spain. The other three countries are unitary states, though limited decentralization was implemented in Italy after 1970. On the whole, Spanish 'autonomous communities' basically weakened majoritarian rule due to the combination of semi-parliamentarism and the electoral system, and it contributes to a more neutral design. In Italy, if some form of federalism is approved, it will probably be the country's most significant constitutional amendment. Again, this design is often associated with a multi-centred, non-majoritarian model.

Thus, first of all, Italy shows how the party factor can influence how constitutional rules actually work. In other countries institutional differences influence the consistency of semi-parliamentary regimes. For instance, the Portuguese president's constitutional role

[50] This possibility became a reality when the dominant role of Christian Democracy lost some of its strength in the late 1950s.

[51] See Lijphart, *Democracies*, for the notion of symmetry in terms of equal legislative powers of the two chambers and congruence with reference to a similar representative basis.

[52] See Giovanni Sartori, *Un'occasione mancata? Intervista sulle riforme costituzionali*, ed. Leonardo Morlino (Bari: Laterza, 1998).

of counterbalancing power vis-à-vis the prime minister means that the president could again become a powerful actor in a transformed party system, while in Greece and Spain, for different reasons, this possibility is either non-existent or very low. The ability to reduce the fractionalization of the party system by amending the electoral law has been more successful in Greece than in the other three countries, and again the difference should be stressed. The Italian PR system was an insignificant factor in the first legislative assembly when the Christian Democrats were dominant, but later it allowed a growth of fragmentation that was maintained during the decades that followed.

As should be evident, different outcomes are the result of different ways of implementing a constitutional design and in this the party system plays a key role. The stability of the party system can be calculated from the decline of electoral volatility[53] and, above all, by the index of party fragmentation. In Italy following a decline in fragmentation in 1948 (from 0.79 to 0.66) the configuration of the party system remained stable, within 0.74–0.76 for about twenty years (1953–72).[54] After 1972, the index wavered and peaked at 0.84 in the period between 1992 and 1996. In Greece, the index has been relatively frozen at 0.61–0.63 since 1981, though it dropped to 0.60 in November 1989 during the second election in the same year, and unexpectedly jumped in 1996 to 0.67. Spain and Portugal have been relatively more volatile. Except for a ten-point difference in Spain between 1979 and 1982, and a thirteen-point difference in Portugal between 1985 and 1987, the difference in the index of party fractionalization from one election to the next ranged between 1 and 4 points.[55]

---

[53] See Morlino, *Democracy between Consolidation and Crisis*.

[54] Ibid., table 2.11.

[55] Ibid., table 2.11. PF is calculated on the basis of votes received by each party. If the same calculus is done with reference to the seats (the seat fractionalization) and a difference is made with vote fractionalization, this is only useful to point out more clearly the impact of the electoral law, with particular regard to Greece. In fact, only in this country does a distinct impact emerge: the adaptation of the voting behaviour has a clearly decreasing trend. A stronger 'reinforced' PR brings about a declining gap between votes and seats. In all other cases the picture is basically the same as that suggested by table 2.11. In Greece between 1974 and 1990 there is a consistent reduction of the difference among the two indexes: −18 (1974), −16 (1977), −11 (1981), −8 (1985), −4 (June 1989 and November 1989), −4 (1990). This trend supports the hypothesis of the gradual adaptation of the electorate for a 'useful' vote. Of course, the index of seat fractionalization is lower than the other index because of the reductive impact of the electoral law.

An analysis of the 'effective' number of parties (ENP) creates a similar picture. In Italy there was a virtual freezing of the party system, followed by a strong growth between 1992 (3.5) and 1996 (7.6). An even stronger stabilization took place in Greece following the adoption of a more manipulative electoral law: there was some growth, an ENP of 2.6, only in 1996. Meanwhile, Portugal has had a much more recent stabilization, and Spain's remains the most unstable. The dramatic changes that occurred there in 1982 are mirrored in the record low number of Spanish parties (from 4.2 in 1979 to 2.9 in 1982). In the second half of the decade the situation became more stable, but the difference between Spain and Italy or Greece is still striking. In Portugal the political changes of 1985 are reflected in the ENP, and again there was a subsequent stabilization and a clear reduction in the number of parties in 1987, 1991, and 1995: from 4.2 to 2.2, and then to 2.5.

The main cleavage present in all four countries is the common class division which, particularly in complex modern societies such as Italy and Spain, is no longer particularly meaningful in shaping the political arena. As suggested by several surveys, only a left–right split persists in these countries, coupled with a value dimension and a partisan, organizational dimension. Spain and Italy in the 1990s both have a centre–periphery conflict as well, and in Spain this conflict has an added ethnic component. The environment is an issue in Italy, though it is not very strong. Religious cleavages have disappeared from the Italian, Portuguese, and Greek political arenas, though religion has some salience in Spain. On the whole, analysing social cleavages is not useful for understanding the basis of party system stability and fragmentation in the four countries.

Because of the very low threshold and the high proportionality of the Italian electoral law, the party system that first took shape in the 1948 second general elections was highly fragmented. But at the end of the century the picture has changed: the system has stabilized and extreme multipartism has been in place for decades. At the same time there is a strongly organizational structure. Therefore, on the whole, the benefits of increased structuration and stability outweigh the cost of fragmentation.

The new party system of Portugal in the 1970s and early 1980s was characterized by limited multipartism, with a fairly strong, but gradually declining Communist Party. In the mid-1980s, however, a basic restructuring of the party system took place with a noteworthy organizational development.[56] The change was initiated by

---

[56] See Morlino, *Democracy between Consolidation and Crisis*.

an attempt to build a new party, the Democratic Renewal Party (PRD), led by the former President Ramalho Eanes. The failure of this attempt contributed to the triumph of the Social Democratic Party (PSD) in the 1987 elections. The absolute majority of parliamentary seats won by PSD marked a shift to a predominant-party system, which remained in place after the 1991 elections, when an absolute majority was again installed. Change came in 1995, when the Socialists won a plurality, formed a cabinet, won the presidency in 1996, and a bipolar system was more clearly established.

The party systems of Spain and Greece took shape quickly. In the case of Spain, the establishment of a dominant party system with the Spanish Worker Socialist Party (PSOE) after the 1982 elections, and until 1993, left some problems within the party system unresolved. These problems included restructuring the right wing (after the breakdown in 1981–2 of the Unión de Centro Democrático), the uncertain role and establishment of regional parties, and the internal divisions within the Communist Party (which split into three different parties in the 1980s). Thus stabilization of the system was not followed by the stabilization of its components—that is the parties themselves.

In Greece, the centre is the area that was eventually destroyed by the stabilization of a bipolar pattern of competition between Nea Dimokratia and the socialist PASOK. But after the 1981 elections, largely won by PASOK, a party system with the strong dominance of the incumbent party seemed to be established until the 1989 elections. On the whole, the initial impact of the electoral threshold and the simple development of competition were to allow few, well-defined parties to dominate the political arena and to prevent the entrance of new forces. The Greek party system achieved a definite structure of party competition, a competitive logic, and a certain degree of stability. At the end of the 1980s, the electoral dominance of PASOK was fading: the three elections held between 1989 and 1990 mirror this change. Later, a few splits took place. The first one concerned Nea Dimokratia and the formation of the Political Spring (POLAN) in 1993,[57] due to serious disagreements with the external and domestic policies of Prime Minister Konstantin Mitsotakis's cabinet. The second one affected PASOK in 1995 with the formation of the Democratic Social Movement (DIKKI). There was even a division in the extreme left between the communists and the Synaspismos. As a result, PASOK was voted back into power after the October 1993 elections, characterized by

[57] The new party Politike Anoixe (Political Spring) garnered 4.9% and ten seats in 1993.

a high TEV score (17.7),[58] but it also won the 1996 election despite a split within the party. After 1989, alternation seemed to become a key aspect of Greek democracy when PASOK was again replaced by Nea Dimokratia. Despite name changes, reshaping, and splits, in all three countries a shift from a dominant party system to a limited bipolar multipartism was not preceded or followed by a change within the main parties. Popular Alliance-Popular Party (AP-PP) and Socialists in Spain, Social Democrats and Socialists in Portugal, and PASOK and Nea Dimokratia in Greece were still the main actors in the political arena at the end of the 1990s.

The opposite situation emerged in Italy in the early 1990s with the change in the electoral law (see above) and, above all, with the formation of important new parties and the splintering or disappearance of old ones. Change occurred in two key phases in 1991 and 1994, but the apparent beginning of the change can be traced back to the end of the 1980s, when local lists flourished. The left was the first segment of the political continuum to undergo a crisis and a profound transformation.[59] In the case of the Italian Communist Party (PCI), this slow, gradual process came to a head with the fall of the Berlin Wall in November 1989. A new party was created in February 1991 with a new name, the Democratic Party of the Left (PDS).[60] The old Christian Democracy and Socialist Party split and its traditional junior partners (Liberals, Republicans, and Social Democrats) disappeared almost completely. Some of its leaders emigrated to the new Forza Italia (Go Italy!) and other new tiny parties that belong to one of the two electoral coalitions that competed in the 1994 and 1996 elections.

---

[58] See Morlino, *Democracy between Consolidation and Crisis*, Fig. 2.3.

[59] But the process of democratic integration of the PCI had at least two previous key moments: in 1973, with the so-called strategy of the 'historical compromise', aiming at the formation of an alliance with Catholic forces and even with a Catholic party, Christian Democracy (DC); and in 1978–9, when the PCI supported Andreotti's cabinet during a difficult period of terrorist attacks. Later, democratic integration advanced and the party held important internal debates that gradually changed its identity. But the objective presence of the USSR on the international scene with its traditional links with the party was still seen by some as a possible anti-democratic point of reference for communists and a cause for fear. The disintegration of the USSR and subsequent fall of the Berlin Wall heralded the final stage of this break-up. As a consequence, on the one hand, anti-communism no longer had good reason to exist; on the other hand, that break-up was also the definitive answer to the old internal debate on 'real socialism'; the communist alternative had been made bankrupt. A new artificial form of anti-communism was rebuilt by Forza Italia in the 1994 electoral campaign—and it also survived later on.

[60] See Carlo Baccetti, *Il PDS: verso un nuovo modello di partito?* (Bologna: Il Mulino, 1997).

Here, the most important aspect to recall is that there were anti-cipated reactions, and changes, to the electoral system. They mainly concerned the partial change of constitutional design. This also had a profound impact in a context of mobilization, fragmenta-tion, and ongoing party destructuration.

What can we conclude from this analysis of southern Europe? Italy is a model case of a neutral design coupled with a strongly stabilized party system, which was organizationally highly struc-tured when the design began to be implemented. Consequently, Italy has followed an adaptive implementation pattern. Greece is also a model case of manipulative design with a strong, stable, and highly structured party system. The initial mode of implementation was adaptation, indicated by the constitutional revision of the mid-1980s, but later appropriateness with manipulation of party electoral strengths in a bipolar system emerged. Consequently, this Greek implementation can be defined as conflictive. The other two cases have produced less obvious patterns. Nevertheless, in Spain a quasi-manipulative design is complemented by an unstable party system in the first years of democratic establishment and con-solidation. Thus, eventually, the rules played a dominant, shaping role—even to the point of manipulation—and allowed regional issues to become important. Thus manipulative constitutional design with high consensus at the same time develops a pattern of constitutional appropriateness. Finally, Portugal may be defined as a case of balanced implementation because of the late stabilization of the party system, but also late implementation of constitutional design with its most manipulative feature—the semi-presidential arrangement—worked in a consensual way by giving a role to the political opposition and manufacturing an apparently stable bipolar system. Fig. 3.3 summarizes the entire analysis by placing each case in one of the four cells. A fifth case has been mentioned above and can be added: Italy after 1992. The additional party fragmentation, the organizational destructuration, and the partial destabilization of the party system were complemented by the change of the electoral laws and demand for constitutional reform. Given the situation of the party system and the anticipated reac-tions to the change of electoral system at a country level, appro-priateness seems to have been the main path followed in this second Italian transition (see also Fig. 3.1). It is very likely that this pattern will be confirmed if some constitutional reform is approved and implemented.

The four main patterns of implementation may be further deciphered by considering some other more precise aspects of the process. For instance, the adaptive implementation of the Italian

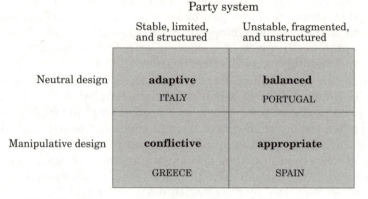

Fig. 3.3. *What types of implementation in southern Europe?*

case can be characterized by two main elements. First, the implementation of some key rules was postponed by either open or implicit decisions of party leaders who considered those rules no longer suitable to their strategies. Also, it is important to look at the limited and partial implementation of other key rules that did not have constitutional status (see, for example, the important agrarian reform). The balanced Portuguese implementation included periods when certain constitutional and regular laws were repealed or revised (as in 1982 and 1989). The slowness of the process, the late stabilization of the party system, and the influence of the head of the state in the early years of consolidation are important additional characteristics. The conflictive Greek implementation is better described as the establishment of routines that have acquired constitutional saliency, with massive approval of delegation laws that give a sort of 'absolute' power to the prime minister (who is also the party leader) by strengthening the chancellor democracy through informal rules. The appropriateness of the Spanish case is unique in two elements. First, the overdevelopment of some institutional aspects with progressively growing decentralization was unique, as was the role played by the Constitutional Court in this issue. Secondly, the interplay of certain sets of constitutional laws and other rules had important effects on the regime as a whole, such as the internal electoral rules within the main parties vis-à-vis the electoral law, or the standing orders of parliament vis-à-vis the constitutionalized role of the prime minister.

The modes of implementation through adaptation or appropriateness give a fairly precise idea of the process. But moving beyond explaining why certain constitutional choices were made, the type and development of the party system, the type of consolidation processes (adaptation, appropriateness, or intermediate types), and the democratic outcomes, the important lesson to be drawn here is the salient connection between constitutional design and the party system.

In both Italy and Portugal, there is a relevant problem in the adaptation of constitutional design during consolidation. The main reason for this is that the coalition of partisan actors, unions, and (in Portugal) sectors of the army was central in beginning the process of consolidation during the phase of transition. In Italy, the Communist Party participated in the drafting of the Constitutional Charter and a Communist leader also chaired the Constituent Assembly; but later the Communists were isolated and they also took different attitudes vis-à-vis the regime they helped to build. The main consequence was adaptation by freezing, as mentioned above. In Portugal, the *coup d'état* and the Constitution had the army at the core of the political arena. When the role of the army gradually became secondary and some agreement was reached by civilian leaders, basic adaptation with repeals and changes, that is, with the necessary revision, was simply unavoidable, but also balanced by existing rules.

Depending on the period considered, the different constitutional designs in Italy and Portugal can be seen to have had profound adaptive changes to that design. In Italy, the same design gave way to a chancellor democracy when Christian Democracy (DC) had a dominant role until 1953, and gradually turned into a parliamentary democracy when the party role of DC was weakened and smaller parties, such as the Liberals, Republicans, Social Democrats, and later Socialists, gained importance. Likewise the semi-presidential system in Portugal was working as such during the first years of party instability and became largely ineffective when the Social Democrats acquired a dominant position in the party system and in the country between 1987 and 1995. During those years it worked in a way that was closer to a chancellor democracy with a strong prime minister and only an opposition role played by the Socialist president. Later, with the stabilization of bipolarization, this formula for a strong prime minister was further strengthened when the Socialists gained both the premiership and presidency of the republic.

In Greece, the initial ambiguities of constitutional norms were superseded by the reductive action of the electoral system and the integration of Socialists into the new regime, which confirms its categorization as a conflictive implementation. The outcome of the electoral laws was the creation of a chancellor democracy, while the effects of integrating the Socialists were seen when the Constitution was amended in the mid-1980s.

Spain had the fewest problems with appropriate implementation. Nevertheless, the combined effects of an electoral system that accommodates local (i.e. regional) parties and weakens the governmental party, the Socialists (which have depended on the support of regional parties in parliament since 1993), have been the development of regionalization and a strong decentralization.

On the whole, in each of the four countries, institutions have set constraints, increased expectations, and forced political actors as well as bureaucrats to consider the appropriateness of their actions in terms of constitutional norms. Thus, the double-edged influence is empirically confirmed: on one side, party elites hope for constitutional adaptation, while on the other, constitutional norms dictate the appropriateness of the actions of political elites. At this point the question is how these conclusions about the processes of consolidation in southern Europe can be meaningfully exported to Eastern Europe.

The Problem from an Eastern Perspective

A systematic, qualitative analysis of Eastern European countries paralleling that of southern Europe is made partially irrelevant by the subsequent chapters specifically devoted to each of these countries. Moreover, in terms of depth, it is impossible to replicate the southern European study due to the substantially shorter time-span of the consolidation process in Eastern Europe. But, in defence of my project, it should be emphasized that none of the ten East European countries has had such a difficult and uncertain transition to democracy as Portugal.[61] Prima facie, general directions and goals of political change were much more definite, at least in the beginning. It has even been confirmed by the European Union's initiation of accession agreements with these countries that, since the beginning of the transition period in each of these ten countries in the early 1990s, no threats of crisis and of the breakdown of recently installed of democratic regimes remain.

---

[61] Nor did the army have an important role in the transitions. Of course, in all countries the role of the army had to be redefined in a more or less successful way. Especially on Hungary and Romania see Zoltan Barany, 'Democratic Consolidation and the Military: The East European Experience', *Comparative Politics*, 30/1 (1997), 21–44, esp. 31–9.

On the whole, the key aspects of constitution-making are pace, timing, modes, and the agencies of constitution-drafting. In fact, the timing and pace of transition were precise and quick. If the formation of a body bringing together all political forces, the so-called 'round tables', is taken as the symbolic start of each transition, the process began first in five countries between February 1989 and January 1990: Poland in February, Hungary in June, Czechoslovakia in November, Bulgaria and Romania in January. In contrast, Romania's transition began not at a bargaining table, but after the bloody December of 1989. Those countries that had problems attaining independence and secession followed in 1990 (Slovenia) and 1991 after the attempted coup in Russia (Estonia, Latvia, and Lithuania). If, then, the approval of a constitution is the *terminus ad quem* of transition which overlaps with the beginning of democratic installation, the previous rank order is reversed: the three Baltic countries and Slovenia completed the transitions at a quicker pace: each had adopted a new constitution within less than one year. Hungary can be included in that group as well. The remaining countries were slower in adopting their new constitutions: Bulgaria, twenty months; Romania, almost two years; the Czech Republic and Slovakia, close to four years; and if the approval of the 1997 Constitution is considered, Poland waited almost eight years (although it did approve the so-called 'Little Constitution' in 1992). The explanation of the beginning is simply related to the breakdown of the USSR and the domino effect that followed. The rate of change, also in comparison with southern Europe, is mainly explained by the acquired legitimacy of liberal democratic patterns among domestic political elites and people, and at the same time by the extent of the conflicts on what kind of democracy, state, and economic system to install. But in none of these countries, in contrast with Italy in the late 1940s or Portugal, was there a basically different anti-liberal-democratic power base: even important nationalist forces in Eastern Europe supported a democratic institutional arrangement. Besides, the modes of constitution-making with regard to the agencies of transition do not appear to be a relevant explanation for the time and pace of change. Perhaps the long Bulgarian transition might be seen to be related to the fact that the Constitution was drafted by an elected constitutional assembly. However, other transitions in which the constitution was drafted by a state institution and adopted without a referendum were also long, such as the Polish case. Furthermore, this second one is the most recurring mode of drafting the constitution: in addition to Poland, the Czech

Republic, Hungary, Latvia, Slovakia, and Slovenia followed this path.[62] Romania, Lithuania, and Poland are the only countries considered here where the constitution was further legitimized by a referendum.

To a great extent, the variables associated with constitutional adoption depend on elite choices, political traditions, and other idiosyncratic elements. This has been the analysis of other authors as well, even if they do not say it explicitly. As with southern Europe, the focus must be on consolidation and therefore primarily on how specific, democratic constitutional rules are implemented. The analysis of implementation presupposes the previous or contemporaneous establishment of the rule of law. Here, a basic difference has to be drawn between two sets of countries: those in which the rule of law is more deeply embedded, at least in relative terms, and those in which the weight of the rule of law is more doubtful and flawed by persistent corruption and a weaker guarantee of basic rights. This analysis shares the official point of view of the European Union, formally expressed in the 'Commission Opinion' in July 1997.[63] At the end of the 1990s, the Czech Republic, Hungary, Poland, Slovenia, and also Estonia (despite some problems with Russian-speakers), are more stable democracies with a relatively more effective rule of law. In the opinion of the EU, the other five countries are clearly in a different position. Although it has been observed since July 1997, Bulgaria still has not completed the actual guarantee of basic rights for all people as shown by police brutality and the intrusiveness of the intelligence service. Latvia

---

[62] See Wolfgang Merkel, 'The Consolidation of Post-autocratic Regimes: A Multilevel Model', paper given at IPSA XVII World Congress, Seoul (17–21 Aug. 1997).

[63] See Commission Opinion on Bulgaria's Application for Membership of the European Union, Brussels, 15 July 1996; Commission Opinion on Czech Republic's Application for Membership of the European Union, Brussels, 15 July 1996; Commission Opinion on Estonia's Application for Membership of the European Union, Brussels, 15 July 1996; Commission Opinion on Hungary's Application for Membership of the European Union, Brussels, 15 July 1996; Commission Opinion on Latvia's Application for Membership of the European Union, Brussels, 15 July 1996; Commission Opinion on Lithuania's Application for Membership of the European Union, Brussels, 15 July 1996; Commission Opinion on Poland's Application for Membership of the European Union, Brussels, 15 July 1996; Commission Opinion on Romania's Application for Membership of the European Union, Brussels, 15 July 1996; Commission Opinion on Slovakia's Application for Membership of the European Union, Brussels, 15 July 1996; Commission Opinion on Slovenia's Application for Membership of the European Union, Brussels, 15 July 1996.

has relevant problems in guaranteeing integration and basic rights of Russian-speaking minorities. While Lithuania does not suffer from the grave minority problems of Latvia or Estonia, full protection of other basic rights is still lacking, and, more importantly, the country continues to struggle to balance the establishment of a fully functioning market economy while also maintaining a wide social safety-net. In Romania and Slovakia corruption, poorer guarantees of basic rights for all citizens (especially minorities), and generally weaker establishment of the rule of law characterize their limited consolidation. But the theoretical framework, suggested in the first section of this chapter and the empirical comparison with southern Europe, takes for granted the establishment of the rule of law as the key element in understanding which kind of constitutional implementation is carried out in the countries evaluated. In other words, how can appropriateness be possible without the establishment of the rule of law? This is an additional question to which the empirical analysis of the second set of Eastern European countries must reply. But this is also an additional justification for dealing separately with the two groups of countries.

Although reference to the specific country chapters is crucial for understanding specific problems and outcomes of transition, Table 3.1 presents a basic but systematic review of the constitutional designs of the five most consolidated countries: the Czech Republic, Estonia, Hungary, Poland, and Slovenia. It also points to some important trends. First, parliamentary design is the prevalent regime type. Even in the countries where semi-presidential arrangements are indicated by the direct election of the head of the state, such as Slovenia, the well-balanced power distribution and institutional interrelation show that the president's role is rather weak, thus confirming the dominant parliamentary design. There are, however, two countries that stand apart. Hungary is a typical chancellor democracy with a strong prime minister, though its function greatly relies on the party system. Poland is closest to creating a semi-presidential design, and the 1997 Constitution confirms this.[64] With regard to the executive–assembly relationship, the limited time elapsed since the instalment of the Constitution does not allow the formulation of established routines. However, in Hungary and Poland the cabinet dominance is, first of all, embedded in the

---

[64] Among the several analyses that at this point have been published on the constitutions of these countries in addition to the charters, see the Italian contributions of Sergio Bartole, *Riforme costituzionali nell'Europa centro-orientale*, (Bologna: Il Mulino, 1993), and Stefano Ceccanti, *La forma di governo parlamentare in trasformazione* (Bologna: Il Mulino, 1997).

TABLE 3.1. *Constitutional designs: the most consolidated countries*

Dimension	Czech Rep.	Estonia	Hungary	Poland	Slovenia
Head of state					
Elected by	parliament	parliament, but by electoral college at third ballot	parliament	citizens	citizens
Powers	participation in cabinet meetings limited power to dissolve the assembly appoints 15 judges of the Constitutional Court limited veto power head of the armed forces	first two choices in nominating prime minister limited power to dissolve the assembly limited veto power initiate amendments to the Constitution	symbolic power limited power to dissolve the assembly	veto power power to dissolve the assembly call referenda head of the armed forces	symbolic power power to dissolve the assembly nominates judges to the Constitutional Court
Parliament					
Chambers	two	one	one	two	one
seats	200 and 61 asymmetric and incongruent	101	386	460 and 100 asymmetric and incongruent	90 a National Council, 40 members, partially elected, represents socio-economic interest, professional circles, local authorities, has legislative initiative only

Powers	legislative (LC)	legislative ultimate authority over key political decisions call referenda	legislative elects members of the Constitutional Court power of dissolving local representative bodies	legislative (LC) dismiss the president (two-thirds majority vote)	legislative (LC) bill is passed after 3 readings call referenda
Executive/ legislative Cabinet	(1996) three-party minority coalition (ODS, ODA, KDU-CSL)	(1992) three-party coalition (FA, Mod., ERSP) (1995) two-party coalition (KMU, REF Party) (1997) one-party minority (KMU)	(1990–4) three-party coalition (MDF, FKDP, KDNP) (1994) two-party coalition (MSZP, SzDSz)	(1993) two-party coalition (SLD, PSL) and independents (1997) two-party coalition (AWS, UW)	(1990–2) three-party coalition (LDS, SKD, SDS) (1992–6) grand coalition based on LDS and SKD (1996) two-party coalition (LDS, SKD) and independents
Prime minister	appointed by head of state	elected by the head of state and endorsed by parliament	elected by parliament	appointed by head of state	elected by parliament
Powers	vote of confidence motion of no confidence (no fewer than 50 MPs, absolute majority vote)	motion of no confidence (one-fifth of MPs)	constructive vote of no confidence vote of confidence	constructive vote of no confidence vote of confidence	autonomous regulatory power of government constructive vote of no confidence

TABLE 3.1. (*cont'd*)

Dimension	Czech Rep.	Estonia	Hungary	Poland	Slovenia
Local government					
Territorial units	municipalities, lands, and regions are possible but not implemented	cities, towns, and rural municipalities	counties, cities, towns, villages, and the capital	49 voivodships and municipalities	municipalities
Elected by	councils, citizens	councils, citizens	councils, citizens	regional assemblies at voivodship level elected by municipal councils, citizens	councils, citizens
Powers	depend on the state for two-thirds of resources only if necessary state can interfere to protect law and only by means of specific laws	budget autonomy and tax-raising powers supervision to be established by law	resources from state budget have the same rights, but different duties determined by law laws on local govt. require two-thirds of MPs local governments can turn to the Constitutional	85% of resources from state budget government supervises local self-government local referenda	state subsidizes most of local functions state supervises performance of local governments

Note: LC = lower chamber.

constitutional rules, whereas a more equal relationship characterizes the Czech Republic and Estonia. An in-between position,
though closer to the second two countries, is taken by Slovenia in
which strong regulatory powers are given to the government.[65]

From the theoretical perspective proposed here, it is very important to understand whether, on the whole, the constitutional
design frames a manipulative institutional arrangement or a
neutral one, or if the outcome is mixed. This cannot be evaluated
before the electoral system is included in the equation. Table 3.3
systematically reviews the main components of each electoral
system. Consistent with the previous analysis, Hungary and Poland
stand apart from the other countries. In fact, Hungary has a mixed,
complex system with three tiers: a majoritarian component for more
than 40 per cent of all seats, a proportional one at the regional level,
and a national single district from which 20 per cent of seats are
allocated (see Table 3.3). Poland has a second chamber elected
through a plurality and the less proportional formula for the lower
chamber. The result is a very high index of disproportionality
(35.1), which is much higher than in Great Britain (6.2) or France
(12.3).[66] Estonia and Slovenia have similar proportional systems in
terms of district size, two-tier system, and proportional formulas.
Finally, the Czech Republic's lower chamber is elected through
a highly proportional system, complemented by the majoritarian
system used to create the Senate.

From the electoral systems and institutional arrangements, the
Czech Republic, Estonia, and Slovenia can be considered to have
neutral designs, with some variation among them. For instance,
Slovenia's system includes the strong autonomous regulatory
power of the executive. In Estonia, there is the possibility of an
alternative body electing the president when there is insufficient support for a single candidate in parliament. In the Czech
Republic, the bicameral legislature is asymmetrical since the
Senate is elected through a majority system but has no legislative
powers. In contrast, Poland has a manipulative design: a semi-
presidential arrangement, characterized by a Senate which is elected
through a plurality system and a predominantly centralized state.
Hungary seems to be right in the middle: a mixed parliamentary
system with a strong German-type prime minister complements a

[65] For an appraisal of presidential powers of all countries analysed here (and
others) see Timothy Frye, 'A Politics of Institutional Choice: Post-communist
Presidencies', *Comparative Political Studies*, 30/5 (1997), 523–52.

[66] Linz and Stepan, *Problems of Democratic Transition and Consolidation*, 290.

mixed electoral system. But it is precisely this arrangement which creates a strong manipulative impact, as is the case in Germany.[67]

Table 3.2 reviews the institutional designs of the other five countries: Bulgaria, Latvia, Lithuania, Romania, and Slovakia. Among these, three have parliamentary designs (Bulgaria, Latvia, and Slovakia), with few mechanisms to strengthen the position of the cabinet vis-à-vis the parliament, such as the no-confidence vote. Despite the direct double-ballot election of the Bulgarian head of state it cannot be considered a semi-presidential one. In fact, the president's powers are basically symbolic and the prime minister is elected by parliament to countervail the possibility that the elected president could command greater influence at the mass, visible level.[68] The two other countries, Lithuania and Romania, are semi-presidential systems where the elected head of state can chair cabinet meetings, thus becoming the real leader of executive power. But it is nonetheless important to distinguish Lithuania as more decentralized than Romania. Thus, if the focus is more specifically on executive–assembly relationships, Bulgaria, Latvia, and Slovakia have achieved an equilibrium between the two powers, although higher parliamentary decisional efficacy is obvious in all three countries. In Lithuania and Romania, the attempt to build a stronger executive is apparent, though its strength may change with the incumbent majority in parliament.

By incorporating electoral systems into this analysis, a more thorough evaluation of the five constitutional designs is possible. Table 3.3 shows that Lithuania has a mixed system, which is half majoritarian and half proportional with a 5 per cent threshold for parties and 7 per cent for coalitions, which acts as a disincentive for party alliances. The remaining four countries chose a proportional system. Slovakia has the relatively most proportional system combined with large districts (the average seat per district is 37.5) and a threshold that acts as a disincentive for electoral coalitions (up to 10 per cent). Latvia is in second place, with smaller districts (20 seats each) and a national threshold of 5 per cent. Romania

---

[67] Germany, Great Britain, and Spain are three of the most important European cases of 'chancellor democracy', characterized by a strongly majoritarian and manipulative institutional arrangement. In fact, it has none of the weaknesses that semi-presidentialism may have when there is political heterogeneity between the president and the parliamentary majority, and the president is compelled to a coalition. In this perspective the French example during both the Mitterrand and Chirac presidencies is very telling.

[68] See the chapter by Darina Malová in this volume for a discussion of the election of the president in Slovakia.

TABLE 3.2. *Constitutional designs: the least consolidated countries*

Dimension	Bulgaria	Latvia	Lithuania	Romania	Slovakia
Head of state					
Elected by	citizens	parliament	citizens	citizens	citizens
Powers	limited power to dissolve the assembly; limited veto power; schedules elections for parliament and for bodies of local self-government; appoints 4 out of 12 judges to the Constitutional Court; head of the armed forces	limited power to dissolve the assembly through a referendum; presides over extraordinary cabinet meetings; head of the armed forces	limited power to dissolve the assembly; strong role in international affairs; legislative initiative	limited power to dissolve the assembly; limited participation in cabinet meetings; appoints 3 out of 9 judges to the Constitutional Court; head of the armed forces; call referenda	limited power to dissolve the assembly; limited veto power; appoints 10 out of 10 judges to the Constitutional Court from among 20 parliamentary-nominated candidates; call referenda
Parliament					
Chambers	one	one	one	two	one
Seats	240; asymmetric and incongruent	100	141 (92), 137 (96)	328 (+ 15 for minorities) and 143; asymmetric and incongruent	150

TABLE 3.2. (*cont'd*)

Dimension	Bulgaria	Latvia	Lithuania	Romania	Slovakia
Powers	legislative appoints 4 out of 12 judges of the Constitutional Courts call referenda	legislative dismisses the president (two-thirds of MPs) elects 3 out of 7 judges of the Constitutional Court call referenda (one-third of MPs)	legislative appoints judges to the Constitutional Court announces local government elections call referenda	legislative (LC and Senate) two-thirds of parliament can overturn Constitutional Court rulings	legislative can dismiss the president elects chairman and deputy chairman of Supreme Court and Constitutional Court and judges
Executive/ legislative Cabinet	(1991) technocrats, supported by parties (1995) three-party coalition (BSP, BANU, ECO) and independents (1997) one party (UFD)	(1993) two-party coalition (LW, LFU) and small groups (1994) three-party coalition (LW, HP, Economists) (1995) non-partisan grand coalition	(1992) one party (LDLP) and small groups (1996) two-party coalition (HU/LC, LKPD) (1997) two-party coalition (LK, LKPD)	(1990) one party and independents (1992) three-party coalition (NDSF, ADP, neo-communist) (1996) three-party coalition (CDR, UDS, UDMR)	(1992) two-party coalition (HZDS, SNS) (1994) four-party coalition (SDL, NDP, DUS, KDH) (1994) three-party coalition (HZDS, SNS, ZRS)
Prime minister	elected by parliament on proposal by head of state	appointed by head of state	appointed by head of state upon confidence vote in parliament	appointed by head of state	appointed by head of state

Powers	vote of confidence motion of no confidence (one-fifth or more of MPs and majority to pass)	vote of no confidence	vote of no confidence (majority of half of all MPs)	vote of confidence motion of censure (majority of LC and Senate)	vote of confidence motion of censure
Local govt. Territorial units	regions and municipalities	districts and metropolitan, urban, and rural municipalities	counties and municipalities	counties, towns, municipalities, communes	regions, districts, municipalities
Elected by	mayors—municipal councils; councils—citizens; regional governor—appointed by Council of Ministers	councils—citizens	councils—citizens	mayors—citizens; councils—citizens	mayors—citizens; councils—citizens
Powers	resources largely dependent on state budget; borders of administrative territorial units determined by the president on a motion from the Council of Ministers; local referendum	resources dependent on state budget (change expected)	parliament can introduce direct administration on local government; large autonomy and financial independence	prefects appointed by government in each county; limited autonomous financial resources, mostly dependent on state budget (change expected); local referendum	autonomous financial resources and share of national tax revenue

Note: LC = lower chamber.

TABLE 3.3. *Electoral systems of ten Eastern European countries*

Countries	Electoral system	Number of votes	Assembly size	Tiers	Electoral formula	Number of seats	Number of districts	Average district magnitude	Legal threshold (%)
Bulgaria	List-PR	1	240		D'Hondt	240	31	7.7	4 nat.
Czech Republic (LC)	List-PR	1	200		LR-Droop	200	8	25.0	5–7–11 nat.[a]
Czech Republic (UC)	Majority	1	81		Majority-runoff	81	81	1.0	
Estonia	Two-tier list-PR	1	101	PR-regional PR-national	Hare Modified d'Hondt	101 (–)[b] rem.[b]	11 1	9.2 (–)	5 nat.
Hungary	Mixed	2	386	MG PR-regional PR-national	Majority-plurality Droop LR-Hare	176 152 (–)[c] 58.0 (+)[c]	176 20 1	1.0 7.6 (–) 58 (+)	5 nat. 5 nat.
Latvia	List-PR	1	100		Saint-Lagüe	100	5	20.0	5 nat.
Lithuania	Mixed	2	141	MG PR-national	Majority-run-off LR-Droop	71 70	71 1	1.0 70.0	5–7 nat.[d]
Poland (LC)	Two-tier list-PR	2	460	PR-regional PR-national	D'Hondt D'Hondt	391 69	52 1	7.5 69.0	5–8 nat.[e] 7 nat.

Poland (UC)	1	Plurality	100	Plurality	100	49	2.0	
Romania (LC)	1	List-PR	328 (+)f	LR-Hare	328	42	7.8	3 nat.
Romania (UC)	1	List-PR	143	LR-Hare	143	42	3.4	3 nat.
Slovakia	1	List-PR	150	LR-Droop	150	4	37.5	5–7–10 nat.g
Slovenia	1	Two-tier list-PR	88 (+2)h	PR-regional / PR-national	Hare / D'Hondt	88 (–)b / rem.b	8 / 1	11.0 (–)

Notes: LC = lower chamber; UC = upper chamber; rem. = remainder seats.

a The three thresholds are for single parties (5%), for coalitions of two or three parties (7%), for coalitions of four parties (11%), respectively.

b Seats not assigned at the regional level are distributed as national 'compensation mandates'.

c The application of Droop quota at the regional level leads to some seats being 'carried over' into the national level. The national level's 58 seats (plus any unallocated regional seats) are allotted to political parties according to 'scrap votes', i.e. those cast for previously unsuccessful MG-candidates or regional lists.

d The two thresholds are for single parties (5%) and joint lists of two or more parties (7%) respectively.

e The two thresholds are for single parties (5%) and coalitions of two or more parties (8%) respectively.

f Plus members representing ethnic minorities (currently 15).

g The three thresholds are for single parties (5%), for coalitions of two or three or four parties (7%), for coalitions of three or four parties (10%), respectively.

h Plus two members representing Hungarian and Italian ethnic minorities (elected in two single-member constituencies).

Sources: Inter-Parliamentary Union, *Chronicle of Parliamentary Elections and Development* (Geneva, various issues).

Neutral	Manipulative
Czech Republic Estonia Slovenia	Hungary Poland
Bulgaria Latvia Slovakia	Lithuania Romania

FIG. 3.4. *Constitutional designs in Eastern Europe*

follows with even smaller districts (7.8 seats per district in the lower chamber and 3.4 in the upper chamber) but with slightly lower thresholds. Bulgaria is very close to Romania, but the small district size (7.7 seats) is compounded by the d'Hondt formula, the least proportional of all proportional formulas. The overall evaluation, then, is that Lithuania chose the most manipulative design, combining semi-presidentialism with a mixed electoral system; Romania also has a manipulative design through semi-presidentialism, but its electoral system softens the extent of manipulation. The other three countries have fairly neutral designs.

Fig. 3.4 summarizes the evaluation of all ten countries by showing a slight prevalence of neutral designs, as was expected. In comparison to Figs. 3.1 or 3.2, one might anticipate that at least the poor adherence to the rule of law in Lithuania and Romania may pose a problem for democracy there, since relatively manipulative designs rely heavily on a commitment to the rule of law to work effectively. The irony, then, is that the two countries in which it is more difficult to implement strong rules are at the same time those that decided to create and implement stronger rules. But what about the other countries? To answer this question, the connections between the central actors of transition must be explored. As suggested by Fig. 3.1, this means an analysis of the parties and, above all, the party systems of these countries.

The salient features of party systems are the party stability, extent of fragmentation, and forms and extent of rooting in civil society. The data available for measuring these features are not completely satisfying, though they do give some basic information. However, since there is less information than on southern Europe, a few additional qualifications must be added. The general evaluation of party stability and electoral volatility (TEV) is essential, but of course, only decreasing volatility or a rating equal to or below

25 per cent indicates stabilization or stability of parties. For an evaluation of fragmentation, as done with southern Europe, the Rae index of vote fragmentation (VF) is the best available measure. In this case decreasing figures or a figure under or equal to 0.80 coupled with moderate fragmentation are considered to indicate stabilization. In fact, relatively high fragmentation is a destabilizing feature by itself: the sheer number of parties creates the basis for higher mobility, probability of change, and fluidity in the political arena. Given the salience of this aspect, seat fragmentation or the 'effective' number of parties is also an important index. Moreover, it provides additional information. Here the impact of the electoral system can also be evaluated if seen in comparison with VF, where decreasing figures or a figure around 3.0 correspond with a moderate fragmentation of parliamentary parties and together with a low TEV provide some general indication on establishment of the party system and its possible rooting in civil society. From this last point of view, the stronger continuity of the ex-communist parties shows a solid party structuration, although one in which personalistic, clientelist links and habits are maintained after four decades and more. Of course, when available, additional information on party organization and survey data on established party identities would give more weight to this analysis. An overall evaluation of the type of party systems could also be useful, above all if complemented by information on the active cleavages. Class cleavage in Eastern Europe today means the generic, ambiguous persistence of left–right differences, the existence of pro- and anti-market views, the pro- and anti-private enterprise,[69] in addition to such cleavages as have either disappeared or are fading in Western and southern Europe, such as the urban–rural cleavage or religious cleavages; these are even more interesting than the cleavage between ethnic minority and nationalistic parties.

Table 3.4 offers a glimpse of the party systems of the first group of countries. In these countries, all parties are financially supported by public funds, which is essential to their existence. Lewis and Gortat,[70] for example, stress the enormous importance of financial

---

[69] The class cleavage cannot, of course, be conceived in these cases as 'a traditional class conflict between workers and owners'. In Eastern Europe it cannot be expected to find aspects of this kind (see Jon Elster, Claus Offe, and Ulrich K. Preuss with Frank Boenker, Ulrike Goetting, and Friedbert W. Rueb, *Institutional Design in Post-communist Societies: Rebuilding the Ship at Sea* (Cambridge: Cambridge University Press, 1998), 136.

[70] Paul G. Lewis and Radzislawa Gortat, 'Modes of Party Development and Questions of State Dependence in Poland', *Party Politics*, 1/4 (1995), 599–608.

TABLE 3.4. *The party system: the most consolidated countries*

Party system	Czech Rep.	Estonia	Hungary	Poland	Slovenia
TEV	20.25 (96–92) 18.00 (98–96)	44.60 (95–92)	26.23 (94–90) 31.40 (98–94)	50.30 (93–91) 46.90 (97–93)	25.70 (96–92)
VF	0.88 (92) 0.82 (96) 0.79 (98)	0.89 (92) 0.83 (95)	0.86 (90) 0.82 (94) 0.79 (98)	0.91 (91) 0.91 (93) 0.79 (97)	0.88 (92) 0.85 (96)
ENP	4.80 (92) 4.10 (96) 3.70 (98)	5.90 (92) 4.20 (95)	3.80 (90) 2.90 (94) 3.40 (98)	9.80 (91) 3.90 (93) 2.90 (97)	6.60 (92) 5.50 (96)
Type	Multipartism	Multipartism	Multipartism	Multipartism	Multipartism
Main cleavages	Class Religion Ethnic	Class Rural/urban Ethnic	Class Religion Urban/rural	Class Rural/urban Ethnic Religion	Class Religion
Continuity/survival (% of seats)	Weak (KSCM95—10.3)	Strong (KMU95—40.6)[a]	Very strong/strong (HSP94—54)[a] (HSP98—35)	Strong (SLD93—37; 91–13,5 PSL93—29; 91–10,8)[a]	Fairly strong (ZLSD92—15,6)[b]

Notes: TEV = total electoral volatility; VF = vote fractionalization; ENP = effective number of parties.

[a] In the first phase, there is a much weaker continuity with the old Communist Party.

[b] In the first phase, there is a stronger continuity with the survival of the old Communist Party.

support for Polish parties. Despite this, party support is not deeply rooted in society or well developed. Hungary is the case for which an evaluation of relatively higher stability and lower fragmentation is the most plausible. This situation arises from the presence of a predominant party until mid-1990 and a clear bipolarization later, low and decreasing fragmentation, and from some extent of continuity vis-à-vis the previous regime, above all until the end of 1990s, due to skilful leadership and the weakness of all other parties. The TEV is nearest to the threshold for stabilization (26 per cent), but higher in the change from predominant party system to bipolarized pluralism; and party identification is relatively lower than that of other countries in 1990–1 (51 per cent).[71] Party identification became one of the highest in Eastern Europe[72] four years later. Moreover, in 1995, one year after elections, 69 per cent were stand-patters, and would vote for the same party.[73] Still on the positive side, as the landslide victory of 1994 displayed, in early 1990s the dominant party (HSP) was able to achieve a stable identity, define links with social groups (particularly with the post-communist union federation[74]), and establish a membership list of about 30,000.[75] However, on the whole, the new democratic parties do not have developed roots. Grilli[76] provides some evidence on total party membership between 1988 and 1992. If reliable, a total of about 200,000 members in all parties is a very low figure, confirmed by a membership rate of 2.5.[77] To understand better the significance of this number, the high average membership rate in Italy during the 1950s and 1960s was 18.2 and in Spain the lowest average membership in the 1970s and 1980s was 4.2.[78] Finally,

[71] See Linz and Stepan, *Problems of Democratic Transition and Consolidation*, 283.

[72] See Richard Rose and William Mishler, 'Negative and Positive Party Identification in Post-communist Countries', unpublished paper (1998), fig. 1.

[73] Gabor Toka, 'Political Parties and Democratic Consolidation in East Central Europe', *Studies in Public Policy*, 279 (Glasgow: Centre for the Study of Public Policy, University of Strathclyde, 1997), table 5.

[74] See Michael Waller, 'Adaptation of the Former Communist Parties of East-Central Europe: A Case of Social-Democratization', *Party Politics*, 1/4 (1995), 473–90, esp. 483.

[75] See Attila Ágh, 'Partial Consolidation of the East European Central Parties: The Case of Hungarian Socialist Party', *Party Politics*, 1/4 (1995), 491–514.

[76] Pietro Grilli, *Da uno a molti: democratizzazione e rinascita dei partiti in Europa Orientale* (Bologna: Il Mulino, 1997).

[77] Kenneth Ka-Lok Chan, 'Party System Evolution and Democratic Consolidation in Post-communist Poland', ECPR Joint Sessions of Workshops (Warwick: University of Warwick, 23–8 Mar. 1998), table 5.

[78] For a detailed analysis of this topic in southern Europe, see Morlino, *Democracy between Consolidation and Crisis*, ch. 4.

popular dissatisfaction,[79] generated by the drastic decision to manage the economic crisis, made rooting parties in civil society difficult—the incumbent party included. Thus, in the mid-1990s, the Hungarian party system still seems one of the most stable systems with decisively low fragmentation. But, as in the case of Spain during the 1980s, its stability stems from the weakness of other new parties, and not from its ability to develop widespread support and solid roots. Consequently, it is no wonder that in 1998 there was a change to multipartism, which makes Hungary similar to post-1996 Spain.

Poland belongs to the same category: evident, clear, decreasing trends in all three measures and continuity of the ex-communist party account for this conclusion (Table 3.4). But the additional element that influences this outcome is the bipolarization of the party system which is stabilizing in itself, and consistent with the high negative identification in 1995, higher even than that of Hungary: 90 per cent versus 70 per cent.[80] Additional data confirm, however, the weak party base: low party identification;[81] a membership rate of 1.5; a very low trust in parties (net trust equal to −64);[82] the percentage of stand-patters between April 1994 and December 1995 decreasing from 73 per cent to 49 per cent;[83] a low, but stabilized party membership between 1991 and 1995 with a total of about 240,000 members.[84] These data cover different, probably less optimistic realities. On the whole, the two ex-communist parties (the Democratic Left Alliance and the Polish Peasant Party) have gained considerable durability, some articulated organization, and links with unions, associations, and youth organizations. At the same time, the political heirs of the Solidarity movement which formed AWS, won the last elections, and became the main incumbent party have been trying to turn a composite, diversified movement into some kind of more cohesive party. Despite the

[79] See Attila Ágh, ' "Bringing the Government Back in": Governmental Stability and Democratization in Hungary', *Budapest Papers on Democratic Transition* (Budapest: Hungarian Center for Democracy, 1998).

[80] The interesting notion of negative identification is the conceptualization of the survey answer to the following question: 'Now please put a cross by the names of all those parties that you would never vote for' (see Rose and Mishler, 'Negative and Positive Party Identification', fig. 1). A stability due to negative attitudes is of course different from and weaker than a positive identification.

[81] See Linz and Stepan, *Problems of Democratic Transition and Consolidation*, 283.

[82] Ka-Lok Chan, 'Party System Evolution', table 5.

[83] Toka, 'Political Parties and Democratic Consolidation', table 5.

[84] See Lewis and Gortat, 'Modes of Party Development'.

several splinter groups within the party, the personal divisions, and opposing concepts of the meaning of the Solidarity revolution,[85] the glue for maintaining incumbency—above all, if protracted—is the party's connections with unions and the unavoidable, growing salience of the parliamentary party. In this way the base has been laid for stronger stability and lower fragmentation, which parallels the Hungarian case. On the whole, although more defined characteristics of the Polish system continue to emerge, the path undertaken seems to lead in the direction of democratic and party stabilization.[86]

Among the three remaining countries, the Czech Republic has the lowest TEV and decreasing VF and ENP during the whole decade. Although the weak continuity with the past suggests weak party roots, the stand-patters just before 1996 election are close to 60 per cent.[87] Moreover, a high electoral turnout is complemented by a quick stabilization of voter preferences even by 1992,[88] the highest percentage of committed party supporters, a higher membership rate than in other Eastern European countries—even higher than that of Spain, if the ex-communist party is considered (6.4)— and a low percentage of anti-party non-voters.[89] Thus, keeping in mind that the ENP and the structuration expected in Eastern European countries should not be measured against those of southern Europe, the Czech Republic can safely be placed in the same cell as Hungary and Poland. However, in contrast with Hungary and Poland, the main Czech party, the Civic Democratic Party (CDP), is centralized by its strong leadership and shows an apparent growth of membership. The same may be said for at least one other Czech party, the Communist Party of Bohemia and Moravia (CPBM), which is the successor party of the communists. From this perspective, the party system in which new and old parties are stable and coexist is particular to the Czech Republic's deeper stabilization, despite the relatively high but decreasing vote fragmentation.[90]

[85] See Ka-Lok Chan, 'Party System Evolution', 6–7.

[86] See also Alexander Smolar, 'Poland's Emerging Party Systems', *Journal of Democracy*, 9/2 (1998), 22–33.

[87] Toka, 'Political Parties and Democratic Consolidation', table 5.

[88] See Petr Kopecki, 'Developing Party Organization in East-Central Europe: What Type of Party is Likely to Emerge', *Party Politics*, 1/4 (1995), 515–34, fig. 1.

[89] See Ka-Lok Chan, 'Party System Evolution', 21.

[90] See Kopecki, 'Developing Party Organization', and more recently Steven Saxonberg, 'A New Phase in Czech Politics', *Journal of Democracy*, 10/1 (1999), 96–111.

The high vote fragmentation and very high ENP, complemented by very low positive and negative identification (22 per cent and 54 per cent, respectively),[91] and the lowest trust for parties among all political institutions (see Cerar in this book), suggest the opposite trend has occurred in Slovenia. Its relatively low TEV and continuity with the past do not make up for the other two key aspects. Slovenia, in fact, has the highest VF and ENP of all other countries, except Latvia. This is also the case in Estonia, where the effects of a very high VF and ENP, close to those of Slovenia, are compounded by a higher TEV. Consequently, after the 1995 elections party stability is low, despite the continuity pointed out by the vote cast and the seats gained by VF and ENP by the ex-communist party (40.6 per cent) in 1995.

Another classic pattern of party stabilization is through deep-rooted cleavages that structure political space and related competition.[92] Simply by looking at which parties get votes, the main cleavages may be seen in Table 3.4 for the five countries.[93] More meaningfully, the survey analysis conducted by other authors[94] gives an even rosier picture in terms of the stabilization of the ideological base of competition. In fact, in addition to being fairly ethnically homogeneous and economically advanced relative to other countries, the societies in the Czech Republic, Hungary, and Poland display important socio-economic cleavages, complemented by salient religious cleavages.[95] In Estonia the problem of state-

---

[91] Rose and Mishler, 'Negative and Positive Party Identification', fig. 1.

[92] See Seymour M. Lipset and Stein Rokkan (eds.), *Party Systems and Voter Alignments: Cross-national Perspective* (London: Collier-Macmillan, 1967).

[93] For an early analysis in terms of cleavages and related continuities of party systems in Eastern Europe, see Maurizio Cotta, 'Building Party Systems after the Dictatorships: The East European Cases in a Comparative Perspective', in Geoffrey Pridham and Tatu Vanhanen (eds*.), Democratization in Eastern Europe: Domestic and International Perspective* (London: Routledge, 1994), 99–127. See also Maurizio Cotta, 'Structuring the New Party Systems after Dictatorship: Coalitions, Alliances, Fusions, and Splits during the Transition and Post-transition Stages', in Geoffrey Pridham and Paul G. Lewis (eds.), *Stabilizing Fragile Democracies: Comparing New Party Systems in Southern and Eastern Europe* (London: Routledge, 1996), 69–99.

[94] See Stephen Whitefield and Geoffrey Evans, 'Electoral Politics in Eastern Europe: Social and Ideological Influences on Partisanship in Post-communist Societies', in John Higley, Jan Pakulski, and Wlodzimierz Welokowski (eds.), *Post-communist Elites and Democracy in Eastern Europe* (London: Macmillan, 1998), 226–50. Also Geoffrey Evans and Stephen Whitefield, 'Identifying the Bases of Party Competition in Eastern Europe', *British Journal of Political Science*, 23/3 (1993), 521–48.

[95] See Evans and Whitefield, 'Identifying the Bases of Party Competition', esp. 236, table 12.2.

building came first, which strongly correlates with socio-economic issues. Thus, in these four countries there is a high stabilization of competitive space. Slovenia too has problems with state-building, but competing parties are mobilized around two traditional basic cleavages: socio-economic and religious differences. This would push toward the previous optimistic direction in terms of stabilization of competition, but no additional empirical research supports this conclusion.

Table 3.5 illustrates the situation in the other five countries. Bulgaria has the greatest stability problem, which is also mirrored by cabinet instability and widespread corruption. This is also confirmed by the analysis of Higley et al.[96] on the Bulgarian fragmented elites and their effects on stability. However, a bi-partisan system and the consequent bipolarization of the system and the lowest, decreasing VF and ENP in combination with the proportional electoral system point to a relatively more limited party system. The sheer number of elections in Bulgaria—four at the national level in seven years—shows the beginning of the habituation process,[97] which is a key aspect of consolidation. It cannot be forgotten, however, that electoral mobilization may reflect social protest, as happened in early 1997,[98] and therefore may portend future instability. Karasimeonov[99] had already indicated that the 1994 elections 'stabilized [the] party landscape', and on the whole this is confirmed by the 1997 elections. Therefore, despite an overall weaker stabilization, Bulgaria fits into the same cell as the Czech Republic, Hungary, and Poland. A similar evaluation can be made of the Romanian party system, based on various consistent features: the decrease in all three indices; a strong continuity with the past with FNS, which later split; a relatively higher party identification (64 per cent) in 1991 (even higher than that of Hungary and Czechoslovakia);[100] the highest positive and negative identification in 1995 (41 per cent vis-à-vis 95 per cent);[101] alternation in government incumbency; and public financing of political parties.

[96] John Higley, Jan Pakulski, and Wlodzimierz Welokowski, 'Introduction: Elite Change and Democratic Regimes in Eastern Europe', in Higley, Pakulski, and Welokowski (eds.), *Postcommunist Elites*, 1–33, 14 ff.

[97] Dankwart Rustow, 'Transition to Democracy: Toward a Dynamic Model', *Comparative Politics*, 2 (1970), 337–63.

[98] See Nadege Ragaru, 'Démocratie et représentation politique en Bulgarie', *Les Cahiers du CERI*, 19 (Paris, 1998).

[99] Georgi Karasimeonov, 'Parliamentary Elections of 1994 and the Development of the Bulgarian Party System', *Party Politics*, 1/4 (1995), 579–88, 586.

[100] See Linz and Stepan, *Problems of Democratic Transition and Consolidation*, 283.

[101] See Rose and Mishler, 'Negative and Positive Party Identification', fig. 1.

TABLE 3.5. *The party system: the least consolidated countries*

Party system	Bulgaria	Latvia	Lithuania	Romania	Slovakia
TEV	20.80 (91–90) 19.00 (94–91) 34.60 (97–94)	50.30 (95–93)	25.70 (96–92)	47.30 (92–90) 15.50 (96–92)	26.00 (94–92) 38.70 (98–94)
VF	0.64 (90) 0.76 (91) 0.74 (94) 0.67 (97)	0.84 (93) 0.90 (95)	0.76 (92) 0.88 (96)	0.55 (90) 0.86 (92) 0.84 (96)	0.82 (92) 0.83 (94) 0.81 (98)
ENP	2.40 (90) 2.40 (91) 2.70 (94) 2.50 (97)	5.00 (93) 7.60 (95)	2.50 (92) 2.70 (96)	2.10 (90) 4.70 (92) 3.90 (96)	3.20 (92) 4.50 (94) 4.70 (98)
Type	Twopartism (electoral cartels)	Multipartism	Twopartism	Multipartism	Multipartism
Main cleavages	Class Urban/rural Ethnic	Class Urban/rural (Ethnic)	Class (Ethnic)	Class Ethnic	Class Religion Ethnic
Continuity/survival (% of seats)	Strong (BSP91—44.2)[a]	Very weak	Very strong (LDLP92—56.6) (LDLP96—9.8)[a]	Fairly strong (FNS90—69.9) (FNS92—13 + NDSF92—35.7)[a]	Fairly strong (PDL92—19.3) (PDL94—12)[a]

Notes: TEV = total electoral volatility; VF = vote fractionalization; ENP = effective number of parties.

[a] In the first phase, there is a stronger continuity with the survival of the old Communist Party. In Romania the FNS split into two parties.

Moreover, the fact that other more personal links might account for party strength does not undermine the overall evaluation. On the contrary, eventually it may strengthen it.

Latvia definitely belongs to the category of unstable, fragmented, and unstructured party systems: the three main indices consistently point to this conclusion, with an ever-growing ENP. In addition, the lack of public funding for parties dooms the party system to remain unstable for some time and it brings about the formation of coalitions of factions or movements[102] rather than stable parties. Also, of all three Baltic states, Latvia probably has the most serious ethnic problems with the Russian-speaking population. Moreover, 'the government's ability to protect the right to organize in the private sector is weak'.[103] In Lithuania the manipulative impact of the electoral system (see Table 3.3) can be seen in the gap existing between the very high VF and the low ENP. The electoral system is not likely to be responsible for the weakening of the ex-communist party, support for which fell from 56.6 per cent in 1992 to 9.8 per cent in 1996. However, the highly manipulative design, compounded by changing incumbency and alternation, does not help either party rooting or stabilization of the party system.

Slovakia is the most intriguing case. The evaluation of the EU is very clear: it is a country with poor political stability (see the European Commission Report 1997). The evaluation of Karatnycky et al.[104] is even more negative: in their survey, Slovakia scored 2 on political rights, 4 on civil liberties, and was given a status of 'partly free', all of which define a transitional polity rather than a consolidated democracy. The analysis of Higley et al.[105] on the Slovakian fragmented elites and the consequent instability is consistent with the two previous analyses. These evaluations are also clearly supported by the increasing trend displayed by the two main indexes. A higher VF and stronger increase of ENP (Table 3.5) with a proportional electoral system that mirrors the partisan changes in the polity (see Table 3.3) suggest instability. Increasing polarization in the relationships between political elites[106] points to the outcome. The ex-communist party is weaker in 1994 than

---

[102] See Linz and Stepan, *Problems of Democratic Transition and Consolidation*, 409.

[103] Karatnycky, Motyl, and Shor (eds.), *Nations in Transit 1997*, 235.

[104] Ibid. 338.

[105] In Higley, Pakulski, and Welokowski (eds.), *Postcommunist Elites*, 14 ff.

[106] Gordon Wightman and Sona Szomolanyi, 'Parties and Society in Slovakia', *Party Politics*, 1/4 (1995), 609–18, at 616.

Stable, limited, and/or structured	Unstable, fragmented, and/or unstructured
Czech Republic Hungary Poland	Estonia Slovenia
Bulgaria Romania	Latvia Lithuania Slovakia

Fig. 3.5. *Party systems in the Eastern European consolidations*

in 1992 and is politically marginal with 12 per cent of seats. Moreover, in addition to a high turnout—which may not be really salient—there are other important aspects. They include: a membership rate higher than in Poland or Hungary (3.1,[107] although this figure excludes the Movement for a Democratic Slovakia which won with 35 per cent of votes); a higher percentage of committed party supporters than in Hungary or Poland (29 per cent vis-à-vis 14 per cent and 15 per cent); a lower percentage of anti-party no-voters than Hungary (25 per cent versus 42 per cent);[108] and finally, a growing percentage of stand-patters (from 61 per cent in November 1993 to 79 per cent in July 1995 and 77 per cent in April 1996).[109] These are not decisive features which could change the overall evaluation. However, at least they show the existence of a possible changing situation, and something actually happened after the 1998 elections, when a stronger bipolarization emerged with the Slovak Democratic Coalition (26.3 per cent of votes and 28 per cent of seats) which came very close to the Movement for Democratic Slovakia (27 per cent of votes and 29 per cent of seats). All in all, if the high ENP is also emphasized, Slovakia has still to be placed in the right column of Fig. 3.5.

Table 3.5 presents the main party cleavages in this second group of countries. Whitefield and Evans[110] stress the strength of the ethnic cleavage in Lithuania, but also in Bulgaria and Slovakia. In Bulgaria, Romania, and Slovakia the main cleavage

---

[107] Ka-Lok Chan, 'Party System Evolution', table 5.   [108] Ibid.

[109] That is, to clarify, in 1996 more than two-thirds of those interviewed declared that they maintained the same voting preference as they had expressed in the 1994 elections.

[110] Whitefield and Evans, 'Electoral Politics in Eastern Europe'.

Party system

	Stable, limited, and structured	Unstable, fragmented, and unstructured
Neutral design	**adaptive** Czech Republic Bulgaria	**balanced** Estonia Solvenia Latvia Slovakia
Manipulative design	**conflictive** Hungary Poland Romania	**appropriate** Lithuania

FIG 3.6. *What implementations in Eastern Europe?*

is the socio-economic,[111] though in the first two countries attitudes toward a market economy and political liberalism are intertwined because the transition to a fully-fledged democracy appears far from being concluded. In Slovakia, economic issues and attitudes towards the West are distinct from social and political attitudes 'arguably because the transition has gone further'.[112] The interesting point of this cleavage analysis is that a stabilizing trend seems to be unfolding in Slovakia, which is only tentatively supported by the empirical analysis of the ground of partisan indicators discussed above.

If Fig. 3.4 and Fig. 3.5 are compared, the result can be seen in Fig. 3.6, which deserves to be discussed to check its empirical plausibility. The first consideration to point out is that most of the cases can be categorized as either of the two intermediate types (see Fig. 3.2). In contrast with southern Europe, where each case occupied one of the four cells, in Eastern Europe seven out of ten cases belong in the balanced or conflictive implementation cells. Second, in Lithuania an implementation characterized by appropriateness means that the constitutional traditions of the country, with specific reference to the 1938 presidential constitution, are important in determining the constitutional choices and their

[111] Ibid. 16: 'an association of economic, social and political liberalism and attitudes to the West.'
[112] Ibid.

subsequent implementation by a weak party system. Moreover, how basic and socio-economic rights will be implemented will be decisive for evaluating existing institutions. From this perspective, a telling example is the University of Vilnius's case against the Ministry of Finance (see Gelazis in this book). The point remains that basic rights of minorities are not fully protected yet. Consequently, a greater degree of appropriateness would be helpful.

Despite the differences that characterize the Czech Republic and Bulgaria, party elites and the party system are at the centre of consolidation and implementation in both countries. Both countries suggest that within adaptive implementation the third important component is the relationship between rules and the party system, and the Constitutional Court is bound to have a limited role. The Czech Court has the power of prior control of drafted bills, but a president elected by parties appoints the fifteen judges of the Court. In Bulgaria, party cartels can block the action of the Court and thus allow the freezing of part of the Constitution—for example, those articles concerning social rights or other basic rights.[113]

In the conflictive pattern of implementation consolidation can create stronger results depending on the stability of parties and institutionalization structure. In fact, the term 'conflictive' simply indicates the *possibility* for conflict between party leaders and institutional actors. Both in Hungary and in Poland, however, conflict actually took place. In Hungary, attempts were made to freeze a few constitutional norms and delay their implementation (see Szikinger in this book). Poland suffered from open conflicts between the president and party leaders in the government. At a higher level, the rule of law is very important also in this type of implementation: strong manipulative norms need a well-established rule of law to be implemented in an arena where stable, strong actors, party leaders, dominate. But this is very difficult to achieve in a country such as Hungary, where there is no autonomous constitutional tradition. Thus, despite some attempt by the Constitutional Court, this implementation is likely to turn into an adaptive implementation. This is reflected in the fact that

---

[113] For an early analysis of the Bulgarian Court and the Czechoslovak one, see Herman Shwartz, 'The New East European Constitutional Courts', in A. E. Dick Howard (ed.), *Constitution Making in Eastern Europe* (Washington: Woodrow Wilson Center Press, 1993), 163–207, esp. 189–94. On the role of these key institutions see also Sergio Bartole, 'Le nuove democrazie dell'Europa centro-orientale alle loro prime prove', in Sergio Bartole and Pietro Grilli di Cortona (eds.), *Transizione e consolidamento democratico nell'Europa Centro-Orientale: elites, istituzioni e partiti* (Turin: Giappichelli, 1998), 191–203, esp. 200–3 and below.

the Hungarian Constitution was amended nine times in 1990.[114] This is even more apparent in Romania where there is no control of constitutional conformity and the government enjoys an enormous number of law delegations; it is not surprising that almost one-third of all legislation originates from government party leaders. Consequently, on the whole, the Romanian implementation type is a conflictive one, but closer to the adaptive pattern.

The last group of countries is the most interesting: neutral design and weak actors beg the question: how is it possible to implement the constitution and achieve some extent of consolidation? All four countries that fit into the balanced implementation complement idiosyncratic modes and a recurring aspect, with the partial exception of Latvia. In Estonia uncertainties, such as that of the actual role of the head of the state, are overcome by political accommodations among party elites. In Slovakia additional informal rules—for example, enforcing party discipline, a very relevant aspect in the parliamentary decision-making process—are developed to move closer to an adaptive implementation where stronger parties are central. In Slovenia, an incomplete constitution, in which several thematic areas are omitted and which is heavily dependent on the subsequent laws for its implementation (see Cerar in this book), leaves the door wide open for an adaptive path where economic interests could more easily emerge if supported by public trust.[115] Finally, in Latvia political life is polarized by the problems of citizenship and integration of Russian-speaking 'minorities', which actually make up almost half of the population (around 42 per cent). Consequently, neutral design and weak actors may be a positive combination for allowing consolidation to proceed. The recurring aspect in these countries, except for Latvia where it was created later in 1995, is the key role of a third factor between rules and the party system—the Constitutional Court. This role has already emerged in some other cases. Here, however, it is systematically present and for obvious reasons: the political vacuum left by neutral design and weak parties in a democratic context, where none can openly challenge the new democratic regime, is taken over by the necessary, institutional support of the primacy of rules. Whether courts are successful or not is a different story, but the opportunity for a central role emerges very clearly and can be exploited.

[114] See Ágh, 'Bringing the Government Back in'.

[115] In six surveys done each year from 1991 to 1996, Cerar shows how banks and large companies are the actors with the highest trust in Slovenian society, whereas not only parties, but also all other political and administrative institutions, show a strongly negative trend.

Concluding Remarks

The analyses of southern and Eastern Europe were developed along the same dimensions, but the longer time-span of the southern European democracies unavoidably brings about problems in comparing the outcomes of both analyses. Nevertheless, several conclusions may be drawn. First, the establishment of the rule of law is at the core of all patterns of implementation. This is most relevant in the appropriate implementation practised in Spain, but also strongly concerns all countries under consideration here. In Spain an appropriate implementation has been the outcome of the role played by a few political leaders vis-à-vis a related set of rules that were implemented and maintained. In a few Eastern European countries the task of developing an appropriate implementation is taken by the Constitutional Court. Above all, the cases of balanced implementation give a strong, empirical support for this assertion, because the uncertainties of the rule of law, the lack of constitutional traditions, and the lack of strong political actors leave much room for other actors to emerge. In southern Europe the Court had no such role: in Italy, for example, it was created at the end of the consolidation phase in the late 1950s.

Second, both the southern and the Eastern European cases suggest that among the variables that shape a weak party system are a high or medium–high 'effective' number of parties, the stability of party supply, above all at the electoral level, and an underdeveloped party organization. That is, an adaptive implementation is possible with a low 'effective' number of parties, which may be even more salient than the electoral fragmentation. In fact, in the long term, as suggested by the case of Greece,[116] VF and ENP tend to converge because the mechanical impact is complemented by the psychological impact of the electoral system. In this perspective the conclusion is that the electorate may not be rational or strategic, but rather voters do not like to waste their votes. Moreover, Greece shows that this gradually happens when wasted votes become obvious after two or three elections.

The timing of stabilization and defragmentation of the party system, on the one hand, and the implementation of a constitution, on the other, are less salient than expected. In fact, once the constitutional decisions are made, in most cases the two sub-processes unfold in a parallel way. In addition, the kind of design that is

---

[116] See above and Morlino, *Democracy between Consolidation and Crisis*.

approved eventually appears to be much more important than the timing. Therefore, the hypotheses put forward at the beginning of this chapter can be reworded without the inclusion of timing, but with the key addition of the role of the constitutional court. Thus, adaptation and appropriateness are the two main patterns of constitutional implementation while balance and conflict are the intermediate patterns. The pattern followed depends on the combination of neutral or manipulative constitutional design and electoral stabilization, the number of parties, and the development of party organization. Moreover, when there is a balanced implementation, a third actor, the Constitutional Court, is likely to become the pivotal actor in the democratic arena, and this may increase the extent of appropriateness in the process of implementation. Although speculatively one could think of other 'third actors' in these countries, the Constitutional Court is the most obvious third actor because of the salience of the problem of legality and the related necessity of building a tradition of guaranteeing individual rights in the process of democratic consolidation.

The more precise modes of implementation, which were evident in the four southern European cases, are less obvious in Eastern Europe. Except when constitutional norms were frozen and implementation was delayed in some cases of adaptive implementation, other recurring modes did not emerge. Here, a closer qualitative analysis would help and undoubtedly open the way to a rich repertoire. However, the main reason for difference remains in the longer time-frame of the analysis of southern Europe. In this sense the trend and unfolding of the process is enormously more evident and defined in those countries. For Eastern Europe, some speculation would also be possible in terms of prevailing modes of implementation as the process unfolds.

To return to the puzzle addressed in the first lines of this chapter: what has this analysis brought to the debate around determining the best constitutional design? Within the theoretical perspective developed here, the best theoretical design is not a philosophical abstraction or the result of an analysis in terms of efficiency,[117] but the specific outcome of complementing political realities with elites' choices. A manipulative design—be it majoritarian or quasi-majoritarian—is the best design if consciously chosen by democratic elites without a strong party system, and appropriately implemented.

---

[117] This is, for example, the direction interestingly developed by Miroslav Novak, 'Is There One Best "Model of Democracy"', *Czech Sociological Review*, 5/2 (1997), 131–57.

A neutral design—be it consensual or quasi-consensual—is the best one if a strong, democratic party system exists, although deep internal division may result. A manipulative design compounded by a strong party system is risky because of the potential for conflict and polarization. Only in the long term, after such challenges are overcome, can this combination prove stabilizing. When compounded by a weak party system, a neutral design is never desirable because of the unavoidable political distortion caused by giving a strong political role to the magistracy, such as the Constitutional Court. But as mentioned before, this design may also prove viable in the long term when appropriateness has been affirmed and the magistracy has become much less politicized.

PART II

Institutional Engineering in a National Perspective

....

4

....

Estonia: Positive and Negative Institutional Engineering

Vello Pettai

Estonia's adoption of a new constitution in June 1992 was one of the fastest institutional transformations of post-communist Eastern Europe.[1] However, the ten-month transition itself did not come easily. It began in August 1991 with a 'miracle compromise' between the country's two main political forces at the time, the Supreme Council and the Congress of Estonia, to convene a Constitutional Assembly. It was slowed in early 1992 for several months as debates raged over such things as direct presidential elections and the political rights of former communist officials. And it ended with one group of Estonian politicians still adamantly calling for an alternative solution, the resurrection of a semi-presidentialist and fairly authoritarian Constitution from 1938.

Yet, despite all these perturbations, the process of political change in Estonia during 1991–2 remained on the whole steady. The rapid decision to create a Constitutional Assembly and the comprehensiveness of the new Basic Law both evidenced a desire to structure the new politics of independence as effectively and securely as possible. In the years since, this 'positive' work of Estonia's framers has paid off in the consolidation of a parliamentary democracy. All of the major institutions of Estonia's new political system have been tested, and each has proved its initial viability. However, political determination in terms of institution-building can

The author would like thank Rein Taagepera, Rein Ruutsoo, and Jan Zielonka for helpful materials, comments, and ideas used in this paper.

[1] For a comparative list of countries and the time it took for each to adopt new institutional arrangements, see Joel Hellman, 'Constitutions and Economic Reform in the Post-communist Transitions', *East European Constitutional Review*, 5 (Winter 1996), 56.

also be a mixed virtue, especially when 'engineering' is applied to such domains as citizenship. In Estonia's case, the 'negative' engineering of this issue through restrictive citizenship laws created a population of some 340,000 mostly Russian 'non-citizens' out of a total population of 1.5 million. The policy resulted in a fair amount of political tension, including a major crisis in the summer of 1993. Although, since then, some positive steps have been taken to ameliorate the situation, this aspect of institutional change will still take time to consolidate.

This chapter will begin by outlining Estonia's road to a new constitution and political system in 1991–2. It will then offer an assessment of the new institutions at work since 1992. Most importantly, it will argue that despite constant conflicts and fiery debates, the constitution-making process was essential for creating a basis for democratic consolidation. Though the challenges still posed by the integration of so many non-citizens remains an issue, the stability of the overarching political structure should provide a sufficient backdrop against which this transition, too, can eventually take place.

Seizing the Opportunity

On the eve of the 19 August 1991 Moscow putsch, Estonia was severely divided politically, and seemingly nowhere near ready to undertake the solemn and consensus-obliging task of constitution-making. Ever since Estonia had begun pushing actively for independence in 1989, two fundamentally different conceptions of independence had been competing against each other, splitting the country's political society down the middle. The Estonian Popular Front, which since 1988 had been Estonia's leading political organization, favoured a more flexible approach to independence, one that would work within existing institutions and be oriented toward making a fresh start politically once independence was achieved. To this end, the Front took part in elections for the Soviet Congress of People's Deputies in March 1989 as well as in local elections in Estonia later that year. Next, the Front set its sights on capturing the republic's Supreme Council (or parliament), where it won a plurality of seats in March 1990. This victory set the stage for the adoption of a moderately toned declaration of transitional independence on 30 March. The statement was in contrast to Lithuania's categorical declaration of independence, and thus was characteristic of the Front's philosophy of gradualism and consensus.

Opposed to this broad and conciliatory strategy was a movement called the Citizens' Committees, launched in February 1989 by a group of more dissident-based politicians and intellectuals. The Committees' approach to politics was more radical and uncompromising. They demanded rapid change and dismissed all attempts at continuing to work with the 'dying Soviet empire'. But the Committees were much more than a mere nationalist outbidder of the Popular Front. They had an equally tangible vision of independence of their own. The Committees argued that because Estonia had been illegally occupied and annexed by the Soviet Union in 1940, none of the political institutions created by Moscow could be accepted or legitimized in any way. Any dealings with them, the Committees asserted, would be tantamount to dealing with an illegal occupier. Instead, the Committees maintained that power had to go back to those people from whom it had been taken in 1940, namely the citizens of the inter-war republic and their descendants. In line with this strategy, the Committees began registering such citizens and their descendants in the summer of 1989. After initial opposition, the Popular Front also endorsed the Committees' efforts in early 1990, though in general the Front appeared more interested in taming the Committees and their ideas rather than pushing the same agenda. In February 1990, after the Committees had registered over 600,000 citizens, nationwide elections were held for a special 499-member Congress of Estonia. In March, the Congress met in Tallinn to debate ways of 'restoring' the Republic of Estonia and its citizenry.

The Congress generated much initial enthusiasm because its message was straightforward: the Soviet occupation was illegal and Estonia must therefore demand the unconditional restoration of its independence from the Soviet occupier. The claim for immediate independence was given additional credence by the fact that for fifty years the West had refused to recognize the Baltic states' incorporation into the Soviet Union. Thus it seemed that international law also expressly called for Estonia's freedom. Finally, if the country continued to exist legally through *de jure* recognition, there was no need to get caught up in the morass of 'secession' from the Soviet Union, as the Kremlin demanded and the Popular Front had initially been willing to accept. Such a course of action was, according to Congress leaders, even dangerous for the cause of true independence and could have resulted in Soviet satellite status for the country. Thus, throughout 1990 and 1991 the Congress of Estonia continued to meet, and although its clout began to diminish as the independence struggle dragged on, it remained a kind of

shadow parliament to the Supreme Council and a bulwark against
any attempts to move toward a 'second' or 'third' republic in disregard of the first.[2]

Although the Supreme Council held the *de facto* reigns of power,
it could not completely ignore the political pressure and moral weight
of the Congress or seek to act unilaterally even in this tense situation. On the first day of the Moscow putsch (19 August), therefore, the Supreme Council adopted only three simple statements:
one denouncing the putsch and calling on the world not to recognize it; a second authorizing a special Extraordinary Defence
Council to run the republic if the Supreme Council were prevented
from gathering; and a third calling on the people of Estonia to remain
calm and to resist Soviet forces peacefully if necessary. The
Council remained firm on the goal of independence, but it was not
until the second day of the coup (20 August) that the politicians
seriously began working on an independence declaration.

Published recollections by participants on all sides of those 'two
decisive days on Toompea Hill' in Tallinn show just how precarious the decision-making over independence was at that time.[3] On
the morning of 20 August, leaders in the Supreme Council decided
to invite members of the Congress for a meeting to discuss ideas
about what a declaration of independence should say. On the one
hand, some members of the Supreme Council had already argued
that the parliament should automatically declare itself a *Taastav
Kogu* (or constitution-making body) and proceed with drafting a
new constitution. During a meeting with Congress members, these
Council members even put forward a draft resolution to this effect.
For the Congress leaders, however, this proposal was an anathema,
since they saw it as another attempt by the Council (as an ex-Soviet
institution) to usurp all power. Congress leaders therefore maintained that a constitution-making body could only be created after
new elections in a *de facto* independent Estonia. Finally, during a
second tense, closed-door meeting that evening, the deputy speaker
of the Council and a moderate leader of the Popular Front, Marju

[2] In fact, as early as May 1990, the Congress threatened to assume full legislative
power in the republic (including over the Supreme Council) if its principles were
not followed by the existing authorities. Although realistically the Congress had
no executive means to back up such a usurpation of power, the warning did threaten
a major split in Estonian politics.

[3] 20. augusti klubi ja Riigikogu Kantselei, *Kaks otsustavat päeva Toompeal
(19.–20. august 1991)* (Two Decisive Days on Toompea) (Tallinn: Eesti Entsüklo-
peediakirjastus, 1996).

Lauristin, came up with the ultimate compromise: instead of creating a Taastav Kogu unilaterally through the Council or postponing its establishment until new elections could be held, she proposed that the two organizations (the Council and the Congress) themselves form a joint Constitutional Assembly, authorized to draft a 'bi-partisan' basic law for later adoption by popular referendum. The Assembly would contain an equal number of members from both sides, and as a result would hopefully bring much-needed unity to the upcoming task of state consolidation.

The final proposal was accepted by leaders of both the Congress and the Council, although some dissenting voices were heard on both sides.[4] Also opposed to the deal were, naturally, the Supreme Council's twenty-seven Russian-speaking, pro-Soviet deputies. While a few of these deputies were present in the parliamentary chamber on 20 August and sought to cooperate with Estonian leaders, most stayed away and apparently welcomed the attempted putsch as a long-awaited restoration of Soviet order.[5] When the final vote on independence was held in parliament, the pro-Soviet deputies announced that they would not participate and were listed as 'not present'.

Later that evening, the Council and the Congress further agreed that Estonia would not request *new* diplomatic recognition from the international community after its independence was achieved, but rather that it would insist on the 'restoration' of diplomatic ties broken after the 1940 Soviet occupation.[6] This was a victory for the Congress of Estonia. Lastly, it is interesting to note that, according to several observers, another reason for the compromise's success was the fact that the chief proponent of a 'new republic' (as well as the chief adversary of the Congress), Prime Minister Edgar Savisaar, had not participated in the negotiations.[7] Savisaar had been in Sweden during the first day of the coup, and had made it back to Estonia (via Finland) by the night of 19 August. On 20 August he was apparently more involved in overseeing Estonia's defences and organizing a Popular Front rally against the coup than in following the negotiations between the Congress and the Council. His only influence on these talks appears to have been through his justice minister Jüri Raidla, who put forth the failed proposal to declare the Supreme Council to be a new Taastav Kogu.

---

[4] See Ülo Uluolts, ibid. 125–8.   [5] See Viktor Andrejev, ibid. 83–4.
[6] On this point, see Mart Laar, ibid. 106–7.
[7] Lauri Vahtre, *Vabanemine* (Emancipation) (Tallinn: IM Meedia, 1996), 101. Also Vardo Rumessen in *Kaks otsustavat päeva Toompeal*, 120.

Thereafter, it is not clear why Savisaar did not intervene in the talks in favour of a more Council-dominated declaration, since any revival of the Congress's influence in politics through its inclusion in a Constitutional Assembly was clearly against his interests. In any case, the final draft was completed without him; and when the declaration was passed on 20 August at 11.02 p.m. Savisaar, sitting in the prime minister's loge in the parliamentary chamber, reportedly showed little elation, although he did vote for it.[8]

Thus the Supreme Council's historic 'Resolution on the National Independence of Estonia' was adopted by a margin of 69 to 0.[9] Within two days, Iceland became the first country to restore diplomatic relations with the Republic of Estonia, while the Russian Federation (where Boris Yeltsin's pro-democracy forces had also resisted the putsch attempt) recognized Estonia's independence on 24 August. Soon afterwards, Estonia's renewed statehood was universally recognized, and the country eventually became a member of the United Nations and other international organizations.

Constitutional Engineering Begins

The 20 August declaration broke a major impasse in Estonian domestic politics, while also greatly advancing the task of state-building. The moment for compromise had been seized and an opportunity for decisive moves gained. But the Council and the Congress remained wary of each other, and throughout the seven-month term of the Constitutional Assembly relentless jockeying persisted.[10] The first controversy concerned the size of the new Assembly. The Congress, having a total of 499 members, favoured a larger Assembly of 80 representatives—40 from the Congress and

---

[8] Vahtre, *Vabanemine*, 103; and Rumessen, in *Kaks otsustavat päeva Toompeal*, 121. Savisaar also declined to include his reflections from 19 and 20 August in the book *Kaks otsustavat päeva Toompeal*.

[9] For complete text, see Advig Kiris (ed.), *Restoration of the Independence of the Republic of Estonia: Selection of Legal Acts (1988–1991)* (Tallinn: Ministry of Foreign Affairs of the Republic of Estonia and Estonian Institute for Information, 1991).

[10] For an excellent participant's account of the stage-by-stage work of the Assembly, see Rein Taagepera, 'Estonia's Constitutional Assembly, 1991–1992', *Journal of Baltic Studies*, 25 (1994), 211–32. A complete collection of the minutes of the Assembly was published in 1997. See Viljar Peep (ed.), *Põhiseadus ja Põhiseaduse Assamblee, koguteos* (The Constitution and the Constitutional Assembly, the Complete Work) (Tallinn: Eesti Vabariigi Justiitsministeerium, 1997).

40 from the Council. The Supreme Council, meanwhile, supported a smaller body of only 40 members (20+20). The difference of opinion between the two bodies arose largely because members of the part-time Congress generally had more time to spare and thus were more eager to get involved, while members of the full-time Council were preoccupied with their existing commitments and thus more cautious about additional work.[11] On 3 September, the Supreme Council split the difference by adopting a decision to create a Constitutional Assembly of 60 members—30 from each representative body.[12] In an additional move, however, the Council sought to reassert some of its authority vis-à-vis the Congress by unilaterally laying down some ground rules for the Assembly. In a decision on the 'tasks and procedures of the Constitutional Assembly', the Council decided that the Assembly's first session would not be opened jointly by the leaders of the Council and the Congress, but by the chairman of the Supreme Council alone (meaning Arnold Rüütel, who would lead the Assembly until it chose a permanent speaker[13]). The Council further set a rigorous 15 November deadline by which the Assembly (meeting only on Fridays and Saturdays) was obliged to submit a draft constitution only to the Supreme Council. Again the Congress was slighted. Thirdly, the Council reserved the right to decide whether to put any constitutional draft to a national referendum.

As one member of the Assembly has noted, this remained the most serious question throughout the constitution-making process: how much would the Council go back on the 'bi-partisan' and seemingly binding status of the Assembly, in order to change the draft Constitution to its own liking before it was put to a referendum?[14] This fear turned out to be justified. Very early in the Assembly's term a widespread impression emerged that Congress members had begun to dominate the discussions.[15] This was partly

[11] Taagepera, 'Estonia's Constitutional Assembly', 216–17. Also, Heinrich Schneider (ed.), *Taasvabanenud Eesti põhiseaduse eellugu* (The Antecedent Story behind Re-emancipated Estonia's Constitution) (Tartu: Juura, 1997).

[12] 'Eesti Vabariigi Ülemnõukogu Otsus Põhiseadusliku Assamblee valimistest' [Decision of the Supreme Council of the Republic of Estonia on Elections to the Constitutional Assembly], 3 Sept. 1991. *Riigi Teataja* (1991), 30/356.

[13] 'Eesti Vabariigi Ülemnõukogu Otsus Eesti Vabariigi Põhiseadusliku Assamblee tööülesannetest ja töökorraldusest' [Decision of the Supreme Council of the Republic of Estonia on the Tasks and Procedures of the Constitutional Assembly of the Republic of Estonia], 3 Sept. 1991. *Riigi Teataja* (1991), 30/357.

[14] Taagepera, 'Estonia's Constitutional Assembly', 218, 225, 226.

[15] Kalle Muuli, 'Põhiseaduslik Assamblee on järjepidevuslaste päralt', *Postimees* (9 Sept. 1991).

because many members elected from the Supreme Council were often too busy with their other legislative duties.[16] Thus, many in the Supreme Council looked forward to the opportunity of overcoming this disadvantage when the draft Constitution was sent to the Council for approval. Ultimately, the most serious *ex post* meddling was thwarted. Still, supporters of the Council were able to include a point reiterating the fact that the Assembly did not have any legislative powers. This clarification was meant to prevent any attempts by the Assembly to declare itself the new parliament of the country.[17] In return, the resolution guaranteed that financial support for the Assembly would be provided by the Supreme Council's chancellery. This would deter any bureaucratic obstruction of the Assembly's work. Lastly, the Assembly was empowered to make decisions based on a simple majority of those voting. This was meant to speed up the Assembly's work and not make it hostage to the one-third(!) or so members of the Assembly who routinely did not show up to the meetings.[18]

Engineering Citizenship

The revival of the Congress of Estonia's political fortunes after the failed Soviet coup extended far beyond gaining an equal voice in the Constitutional Assembly. By October 1991, the debate over citizenship issues also began tilting in its favour, that is toward the exclusion of Soviet-era immigrants from automatic citizenship in the restored republic. The Congress's legal-restorationist logic claimed that only those who had been citizens of the pre-war Estonian state and their descendants should have the right to automatic citizenship once statehood was renewed. In the Congress's opinion, all residents who arrived during the illegal occupation could

---

[16] These people served Monday to Thursday in the Supreme Council and then Friday and Saturday in the Assembly, while the Congress-based delegates served only in the Assembly.

[17] Taagepera, 'Estonia's Constitutional Assembly', 217–18.

[18] Average attendance according to Taagepera was 62%. One of the persistent no-shows was Lennart Meri, the foreign minister at the time, but also later the first president under the new Constitution. Six of the seven Russian members of the Assembly (elected via the Supreme Council) were also frequent absentees. For additional commentary (including number of oral interventions per participant), see Rein Taagepera, 'Constitution-Making in Estonia', paper prepared for the Conference on the Design of Constitutions, University of California, Irvine (10–12 June 1993).

(should and would) be made subject to special naturalization procedures, based on specific language and residency requirements. This had been the Congress's position ever since it started registering citizens for its movement in 1989,[19] and throughout 1990 most Estonian politicians seemed to agree with it, although few outside the Congress were vocal about it. During early 1991, however, the Congress's influence on citizenship weakened, as the prolonged independence struggle with Moscow prompted many Estonians to begin believing that some compromise with local Russians would be needed. In March, Estonia held its plebiscite on independence with all residents (citizens and non-citizens) participating. This seemed to legitimize the rights of all residents to eventual automatic citizenship. In early August, the Popular Front even approved a citizenship policy very close to the so-called 'zero-option' of blanket citizenship for all. Yet, when the Soviet coup collapsed with such farcical speed and Estonia regained its independence within the space of a few days, the political tide shifted back to more uncompromising positions and the zero-option dropped completely from view. A more exclusionary solution became dominant.

The final decision on citizenship by the Supreme Council did not come until 6 November. In the meantime, there were widespread debates over the equity and morality of denying automatic citizenship to so many Soviet-era immigrants. Most ominous, of course, was the fact that under this principle some 90 per cent of Estonia's 500,000-strong Russian-speaking minority would be declared non-citizens. Back in 1945, Estonia had been over 95 per cent Estonian. In the following decades, however, waves of mostly Slavic immigrants reduced the Estonian share of the population to just 61.5 per cent by 1989, while the percentage of Russians grew to 29. Thus, although technically not based on ethnic criteria, the restrictive citizenship principle would nonetheless have serious ethno-political consequences in terms of disenfranchising most of Estonia's Russian-speaking minority. This result was obviously favourable to many Estonian nationalists, and in some debates the citizenship policy was as forcibly argued in ethnic terms as it was in legal ones. But the exclusionary policy also had a legitimate basis in international law, given the illegality of the Soviet occupation —something that Estonian politicians would cling to and cite

[19] The movement also registered 'citizenship applicants' during its campaign (some 30,000 in all) among those who supported Estonian independence, but were not technically citizens of the inter-war republic. These people were later allowed to elect non-voting representatives to the Congress.

repeatedly when accusations were later made (either from Moscow or more obliquely from the West) that the law was exclusionary.[20]

From the point of view of constitution-making, therefore, the early 'engineering' of the citizenship issue meant that the Assembly would now be crafting a political system that, at least for the next decade or so, would be dominated and run by Estonians. This consequence did not, of course, blind the framers to the need to take into account the anomalies which would arise from such a large population of minority non-citizens. Many articles in the future Constitution would indeed explicitly address this issue. At the same time, the situation certainly kept the Assembly from having to think about engineering institutions in, say, a consociational way in order to facilitate power-sharing with the Russians. The subsequent process was in fact more akin to writing a constitution for a homogeneous nation-state than for the multiethnic republic that the country actually was.[21]

Parliamentarism versus Presidentialism

Because the Constitutional Assembly had been issued from two representative bodies, its orientation in constitution-making was naturally parliamentarist. Had, for example, popular elections been held for an Assembly, the Estonian public at large would probably have supported a more presidential or semi-presidential system. In Estonia's political history there were two elements which favoured some kind of presidentialism. The first was very recent and arose from institutional precedent. Since the beginning of Estonia's political mobilization in 1988, Arnold Rüütel, the chairman of

[20] The 6 Nov. Supreme Council resolution merely laid down the principle of automatic citizenship exclusively for inter-war citizens and their descendants. A later law, passed on 26 Feb. 1992, established definitive naturalization requirements to include a two-year period of residency, a language test, and a one-year waiting period. In true restorationist style, these requirements were even drawn from an earlier Estonian statute from 1938. 'Candidates' for citizenship who had registered with the Citizens' Committees before 1990 were granted citizenship without the language requirement.

[21] This circumstance also probably discouraged most of the seven Russians elected to the Constitutional Assembly through the Supreme Council from actively participating in the constitution-drafting process. After all, many of them had in November 1991 been declared non-citizens, although they were not as a result stripped of their mandates. Secondly, the Russians' lax participation in the Assembly was also a result of language. The Assembly proceedings were conducted exclusively in Estonian, which most of the Russians did not speak.

the Estonian Supreme Soviet (and later Supreme Council), had played a pseudo-presidential role during Estonia's fight for independence. He had been the one to go before Mikhail Gorbachev and the USSR Supreme Soviet Presidium in November 1988 to defend Estonia's declaration of sovereignty; he had served as the republic's *de facto* head of state when meeting with world leaders in 1990 and 1991; and he had also maintained a popular image among average Estonians, who grew to like having one person personify the country's political leadership. Thus, as in all of the republics of the former Soviet Union, where the institutional structure was universally made up of a Supreme Soviet and its chairman, in Estonia too the preconditions for presidentialism were present.

Secondly, during Estonia's first independence period from 1920 to 1940, an initially super-parliamentary system (created by the 1920 Constitution) eventually gave way in 1934 to an authoritarian dictatorship ruled by Konstantin Päts. Päts eventually installed himself as president through a new constitution in 1938. Although Päts's regime was eminently non-democratic (including political arrests and censorship), his image as a president who brought stability to a Depression-ridden and increasingly besieged country satisfied most Estonians in the late 1930s, and did not look half bad to many Estonians in the early 1990s.

The Constitutional Assembly therefore faced both of these legacies; and when it began accepting initial drafts with which to work in late September, three of the five proposals presented were presidentialist in nature. The first was a draft prepared by a team of prominent lawyers led by Justice Minister Jüri Raidla. Its essence was largely presidential, although it claimed to be a mixture of presidentialism and parliamentarism.[22] Next, a strongly presidentialist draft was presented by Ando Leps, also a lawyer and member of the Supreme Council. Leps's version drew from the 1938 Constitution, which in its original form became the third proposal submitted by a small group of Congress of Estonia members. Fourth on the list was a parliamentarist draft submitted by a minor politician, Kalle Kulbok. And lastly, a parliamentarist draft was submitted by Jüri Adams, a member of the Congress of Estonia and leader of the Estonian National Independence Party (ENIP).[23]

[22] Taagepera, 'Estonia's Constitutional Assembly', 222; Vahtre, *Vabanemine*, 111–12.
[23] What was surprising about Adams was that in terms of education he had only a forester's degree and no formal training in law; but he went on to serve as a respected member of the Riigikogu (parliament) and even as minister of justice during 1994–5.

In his proposal, Adams took the approach of mending the 1920 super-parliamentarist Constitution with some more balanced provisions.[24] When four of the five proposals were voted on in succession on 11 October (Kulbok withdrew his at the last minute), it was Adams's parliamentarist draft that came out on top and which would be used by the Assembly as the basis for its further deliberations.[25] As Taagepera noted, 'The choice of [this] starting draft set the scene for an essentially parliamentary outcome.'[26]

The Assembly's First Draft

During the next two months of deliberations, the Adams draft underwent extensive revision. In particular, the original draft was very vague on the exact duties and powers of the legislature, government, and president. (It spent more time detailing how these office holders were to be elected.) The Assembly thus went to work in committee, looking at individual sections of the Adams draft. Each of the seven committees was allowed to hold hearings with as many as three foreign experts, invited via the Council of Europe as well as individually from the United States to review the draft. (These advisers were almost all specialists in constitutional law; only a few were political scientists.) By the arrival of the original mid-November deadline set by the Supreme Council, the Assembly was still nowhere near done with its work.[27] A redaction committee was set up on 8 November to begin unifying the various chapters of the draft emerging from each committee. Nevertheless, it would still take the Assembly over a month to proceed through the final reading of the draft and release it to the public on 21 December.[28]

In this all-important first draft, the powers of the legislature, government, and president were spelled out in greater detail, often listing (as in the case of the president) as many as eighteen precise prerogatives and duties. These sections would greatly help to

[24] Jüri Adams, 'Eesti Vabariigi Põhiseadus, Eelnõu', in Schneider, *Taasvabanenud Eesti Põhiseaduse eellugu*, 268.

[25] 'Hääletamine Põhiseaduslikus Assamblees', *Nädalaleht* (26 Oct. 1991).

[26] Taagepera, 'Estonia's Constitutional Assembly', 223–4.

[27] Taagepera notes that this was one moment where some Assembly members feared that the Council might try to pull the plug on it by using the Assembly's failure to make the deadline as a pretext. This however did not happen. Ibid. 225. Also, Rein Taagepera, 'Mida ÜN peaks PA-ga peale hakkama', *Rahva Hääl* (16 Nov. 1991).

[28] 'Eesti Vabariigi Põhiseadus, Eelnõu', *Rahva Hääl* (21 Dec. 1991).

flesh out the new structure of power. At the same time, where the Adams draft had been specific, the new version left many procedures open for subsequent laws to regulate. These issues included, very importantly, the precise electoral formulas to be used for the *Riigikogu* (parliament) as well its procedural rules for decision-making. The new draft also lowered the majority necessary for a parliamentary override of a presidential veto from a two-thirds majority of all parliamentary members to a simple majority of votes.

Social rights, interestingly enough, do not appear to have drawn much attention during the constitutional debates. In part, this was due to the legacy of Soviet socialism, which many liberal-minded Estonians did not remember fondly. At the same time, there was a small group of Social Democrats in the Assembly who, in their discussion of welfare issues, often found common cause with the many Estonian nationalists who favoured state support for Estonian families and Estonian culture.[29] The Adams draft (largely influenced by the nationalist ENIP) was a mixture of social conservatism and nationalist welfare. Article 27 of the draft proclaimed, 'Care for the needy shall rest first and foremost with the members of [one's] family,' while the next paragraph stated, 'The state shall be obliged to organize assistance in cases of old age, physical disability, or loss or absence of a wage-earner.'[30] Article 25 stated, 'Every person shall have the right and obligation to find employment,' but again the next phrase read, 'The state shall assist in the finding of employment.' Finally, Article 21 conferred the primary responsibility for child-rearing and education on parents, but state schools were also guaranteed. Many of these contradictions were pared away in committee, but the 21 December draft still contained many broad promises and guarantees.

A consistent element in Adams's and all of the subsequent drafts was the degree of concessions made to the country's large Russian-speaking and non-citizen populations. Some 30 per cent of Estonia's Russian-speakers were concentrated in the north-east, in the cities of Narva, Kohtla-Järve, and Sillamäe, where they made up as much as 95 per cent of the population. Thus, special language and participation arrangements had to be made for these areas. In the Assembly's first draft, Article 29 stipulated that in areas where minorities represented over half of the population, the language of that minority could also be used in local administration alongside

---

[29] Personal communication by Rein Ruutsoo, member of the Constitutional Assembly, 30 Oct. 1996.

[30] Adams, 'Eesti Vabariigi Põhiseadus, Eelnõu', 4–5.

Estonian. Article 28 guaranteed everyone's right to preserve their nationality (or ethnicity) as well as promising the right of cultural autonomy for minority ethnic groups. The Adams draft allowed non-citizens to vote in local elections, a practice almost unheard of in the rest of the world. Although this provision was stated more vaguely in the 21 December draft, the principle was ultimately clearly enshrined in the final version (Art. 156).

Public Discussion of the First Draft

By mid-December 1991, the public thought it high time that something concrete be released. During the three months the Assembly had been operating, relatively little had been reported about its deliberations or progress.[31] This vacuum allowed many proponents of a presidential system as well as opponents of the Assembly in general to take public pot shots at the body. The public discussion that ensued after the release of the Assembly's draft raised two main issues. The first was a call to rename the head of state *president* instead of *riigivanem* (state elder) as the Assembly had drafted it. This change eventually went through. The second and more controversial issue was the draft's stipulation that the president be elected by the Riigikogu. This decision was, of course, in step with normal practice in parliamentary systems; but most Estonians, who wanted to feel they had direct input in electing their leaders, favoured a popular election. A poll taken in late January–early February 1992 showed that nearly 75 per cent of those surveyed supported direct presidential elections.[32] Many opponents of the Assembly also insisted that a popularly elected president would be a 'balancing' factor in the division of powers and would add an element of 'personal responsibility' to government. In an effort to counter such sentiments, some Assembly members, such as Marju Lauristin, sought to explain why a popularly elected president would be dangerous for Estonia.[33] Lauristin noted that the only reason a directly elected president functioned well in certain countries, such as France or the United States, was because disciplined political

[31] Indeed, one of the more extensive sources of information about the Assembly's work came from the émigré participant Rein Taagepera, who published four local newspaper articles on the topic while visiting Estonia in November 1991.

[32] EKE Ariko, 'Rahvas ei taha loobuda õigusest valida presidenti', *Postimees* (12 Feb. 1992).

[33] Marju Lauristin, 'Riigivõimu küsimus', *Postimees* (3 Jan. 1992); Vello Saatpalu, 'Riigipea valimine', *Rahva Hääl* (29 Feb. 1992).

parties served to filter out uncertain candidates before they reached the ballot. In Estonia's case, direct presidential elections without such parties would only serve to divide society. Moreover, echoing classic political science arguments against presidentialism, Lauristin recalled that in a parliamentary system the executive (or prime minister) can always be removed quickly through a no-confidence vote. But an unpopular, but directly elected, president would be able to maintain his or her popular mandate until the end of the term—creating a dangerous situation of competing sovereignties between the president and parliament.

In mid-January, the Assembly formed a new committee to sort through the proposed changes. At that time, another brief attempt was made to disband the Assembly, but this was neutralized when the Assembly agreed to cooperate more fully with a pro-presidential 'expert group' headed by the Justice Minister Jüri Raidla.[34] Finally, on 14 February, the Assembly passed its final version of the draft Constitution by a margin of 32 to 3 (with 6 abstentions), and the document was officially submitted to the Supreme Council (and later also to the Congress of Estonia) for consideration.

Rounding the Constitutional Corners

Although the new constitutional draft was fairly comprehensive in scope, a number of issues remained relating to its immediate implementation, which the Assembly deemed wise to codify in a separate document. As a result, another special Assembly committee was formed in January to work on an 'implementation law' for the Constitution, which would regulate these transitional issues, but which would thereafter no longer be a permanent part of the text. For example, the implementation law stated that the first term of the new Riigikogu would last a maximum of three years (as opposed to the future term of four years), while the first president's term would be scaled down to four years (instead of five). Both of these modifications were meant to facilitate a gradual habituation to the new system. Second, for the three years following its adoption, constitutional amendments could be made by relaxed majorities in the Riigikogu or by popular initiative (though ultimately, neither of these methods was used). Overall, these and other provisions proved a good way for making compromises on some of the more controversial issues, particularly the mode of presidential

---

[34] Taagepera, 'Estonia's Constitutional Assembly', 225–6.

election. In late February, the Assembly succumbed to public pressure and agreed to allow a one-time direct election of the president in 1992. The Assembly stipulated, however, that the winner had to garner at least 50 per cent plus one votes in order to be elected. If no candidate gained such a majority, then the final choice from among the top two vote getters would go to the newly elected Riigikogu.

Lastly, Estonia's constitutional debate could not pass without facing the issue of post-communist lustration. On the one hand, the Assembly had already agreed to an 'oath of conscience' which would be required of all persons seeking elected and appointed office in Estonia (whether national or local) up to 31 December 2000 (Arts. 6 and 7 in the implementation law). This oath would specify that the candidate had never been a member of any foreign security service nor participated in the active persecution of fellow citizens. Yet in mid-February, as the implementation law was being completed, a group of seven members of the Assembly submitted an emergency appeal calling for the inclusion of a more specific lustration clause in the law. The proposed 'paragraph 8' would have explicitly prevented top communist officials from running for local or national office as well as from serving in local or national government posts until 31 December 2000. The ban would have specifically affected those people who actively served the Communist Party, i.e. all its functionaries, all members of the Estonian Communist Party Bureau, all city and regional Party secretaries, and all national, regional, and city secretaries of the Estonian Komsomol. After heated debates, the Assembly decided that the issue was too political for a constitution-making body to decide, and recommended to the Supreme Council that paragraph 8 be included as a separate question on the final constitutional referendum ballot. The implementation law was passed by the Assembly on 28 February, by a margin of 28 to 3.

When the draft Constitution came before the Supreme Council in mid-March, opponents of the Assembly had another opportunity to challenge the draft. Although the Council decided graciously to treat the draft as an integrated text and only to vote on it as a whole, it first indulged in the pleasure of returning it to the Assembly, claiming that it 'lacked consensus among the Estonian people'.[35] In the month that followed, many minor changes in wording were made to the Assembly's draft, but by and large little was changed. The president was given the right to appeal to

[35] Cited ibid. 226.

the Constitutional Review Chamber of the Supreme Court if his veto was overridden by parliament, but the presidential election process was left unaltered. As a result, several press articles reappeared attacking the Assembly's draft and claiming that the people had been left powerless and deprived of the right to elect their leaders.[36] Other opponents called for a new round of 'public discussion' over the draft. The Assembly, however, reaffirmed its support for the document and concluded its final session on 10 April (albeit with only twenty-four members present).

The Supreme Council thus relented on 20 April 1992 and voted to forward the draft constitution to a referendum, although the implementation law would be delayed for another three weeks. During this period, the lustration 'paragraph 8' was conveniently dropped, although it is not exactly clear how.[37] Instead, a new (and completely unrelated) referendum question appeared asking voters if the 5,000 or so non-citizens who had applied for citizenship by 5 June 1992 should be allowed to vote on an exceptional basis in the upcoming presidential and parliamentary elections. In the Supreme Council, many Popular Front deputies had wanted to include this concession to non-citizens directly in the implementation law. However, nationalist deputies were able to force it onto the referendum ballot. Meanwhile, the Council also agreed to mandate new Riigikogu elections by 27 September 1992 at the latest, which eased fears that the Council might seek to prolong its mandate indefinitely. Lastly, the Council declared the referendum date to be 28 June 1992, in advance of which the complete draft of the Constitution would be published again in both Estonian- and Russian-language newspapers.

The conclusion of Estonia's ten-month constitution-making enterprise came after the draft was approved by an overwhelming 91.2 per cent of the votes cast. Still, in the run-up to the referendum, last-minute opposition continued to be heard from one vociferous group of Estonian politicians, who insisted that only a return to the 1938 Constitution could be considered legal and just. Calling themselves 'Restitution', the mavericks (including the respected physicist Endel Lippmaa) attempted a last-ditch campaign

---

[36] Andrus Ristkok, 'Võimulolijatele võimutäius', *Rahva Hääl* (7 Apr. 1992). Also a group of lawyers allied with Supreme Council chairman Arnold Rüütel voiced their 'expert' opinion. 'Eksperdid põhiseaduse eelnõust', *Rahva Hääl* (22 Apr. 1992).

[37] Neither Taagepera nor Vahtre provides any clue. Nor does Jüri Adams in a lengthy newspaper article published in May. Jüri Adams, 'Põhiseaduse eelnõu saatus Ülemnõukogus', *Postimees* (20 May 1992).

for a 'no' vote in the referendum; but, as the results showed, few people took them to heart. The outcome of the second referendum question on special voting rights for citizenship applicants was much closer; this initiative failed 53 per cent to 47 per cent. Right-wing parties and members of the Congress of Estonia campaigned against it, while many moderate Estonian politicians simply avoided taking a public stand.

New Institutions at Work

Fundamental rights and duties

After the 28 June referendum, Estonia now had 15 chapters, 168 articles, and some 6,669 words of Constitution to live by.[38] In its final form, in fact, the document's structure differed remarkably little from the original draft proposed by Jüri Adams, though its content had been significantly expanded along the way. Chapter 2, for example, on fundamental rights, liberties, and duties was now greatly expanded, totalling forty-seven full articles. Its most important provisions proclaimed the equality of all persons before the law as well as their right to protection under the law. Article 14 states that the enforcement of all rights and liberties shall be the duty of the legislative, executive, and judicial powers, as well as of local government. Article 15, in turn, guarantees that 'everyone has the right to appeal to a court of law if his or her rights or liberties have been violated'. Relating to criminal rights, Article 21 safeguards an individual's right to be told immediately the reason for his or her detainment by the authorities as well as to be informed of his or her legal rights.[39] It also explicitly forbids the detention of anyone for more than forty-eight hours without a court order. The Constitution also guarantees the presumption of innocence and outlaws double jeopardy. Article 32 guarantees the inviolability of property, while a separate article (Art. 33) enforces the sanctity of a person's home from unlawful intrusion or search.

---

[38] For the authoritative English-language translation of the 1992 Constitution, see *Estonian Legislation in Translation/Legal Acts of Estonia*, 1 (Jan. 1996). A similar translation is available via the Estonian Government's official web page, http://www.riik.ee/engno/index.html. For additional commentary on the functioning of the Estonian Constitution, see the articles by Merusk, Schneider, Narits, and Roosma in *Juridica International*, 3 (1998).

[39] The article adds that this information must be supplied to the individual 'in the language and manner which he or she understands', thus ensuring Russian-language speakers equal protection under the law.

Three articles (34–6) deal with freedom of movement, including the right of all individuals to enter and exit Estonia as well as to choose freely their place of residence. These provisions clearly reflect left-over antipathy toward the Soviet system of tightly regulated exit visas for travel abroad as well as *propiski* (or local registration) for internal migration.

Social welfare rights

Social welfare rights in the new Constitution were in general left fairly vague. Article 27, for example, declares that 'The family, being fundamental for the preservation and growth of the nation, and as the basis for society, shall be protected by the state.' Article 28 also pledges that 'Everyone shall have the right to health care.' However, the only explicit right to welfare benefits is given to families with many children, and the disabled. The elderly, individuals without providers, those unable to work, and the needy are all listed as entitled to state assistance, but the extent of that assistance is to be 'determined by law'. This provision has obviously given legislators and the government a fair amount of leeway in drawing up the state budget each year, especially during the two years of economic shock therapy that immediately followed the adoption of the Constitution. Although most Estonians seemed resigned to the belt-tightening, it was also clear that even those opposed to the hardship could find little recourse in the Constitution. Finally, education is also a guaranteed right in the basic law, but the document obliges state and local governments merely to 'maintain the necessary number of educational institutions . . . [i]n order to make education available'.

Judicial and constitutional review

The principle of judicial review is codified in Article 15 of the Constitution:

Everyone whose case is being tried by a court of law shall be entitled to demand any pertinent law, other legal act or procedure to be declared unconstitutional. The courts shall observe the Constitution and shall declare as unconstitutional any law, other legal act or procedure which violates the rights and liberties laid down in the Constitution or which is otherwise in conflict with the Constitution.

The task of arbitrating the constitutionality of laws rests with the Constitutional Review Chamber of the Supreme Court, set up in early 1993. The Chamber is a five-member subdivision of the seventeen-member Supreme Court. According to the Constitution, cases may be referred to the Chamber on appeal either by the lower courts, the president, or the legal chancellor.[40] For example, any time a lower court declares a law unconstitutional, the decision is automatically appealed to the Constitutional Review Chamber. In the president's case, the head of state can appeal only after his veto has been overridden by the Riigikogu. Lastly, the legal chancellor can appeal a case only after he has issued a warning to the institution that has acted unconstitutionally and that body has refused to comply. Already by mid-1994, each of these three appeal mechanisms had been tried out; and by early 2000 over forty cases had actually been heard. For instance, the legal chancellor had contested the constitutionality of local autonomy referenda held in the northeastern towns of Sillamäe and Narva in July 1993 and won. Several lower courts had challenged the validity of parliamentary laws and government decrees. And the president had appealed several overturned vetoes. Still, no case had yet been brought to trial specifically involving social welfare rights.

The president

Regarding the main branches of government, the Constitution ended up pitting the Riigikogu against a relatively weak, but by no means powerless president. Among the twenty powers and duties given to the president in Article 78 is the important job of nominating a candidate for prime minister, subject to approval by the Riigikogu. If the Riigikogu rejects the president's choice twice, and is thereafter unable to approve its own candidate, the president must then dissolve parliament and call for new elections.[41] In addition, the president has the responsibility to nominate other candidates for top state positions, including the chairman of the Supreme Court, the state controller, the legal chancellor, and the commander of the armed forces during peacetime. All of these nominees must be confirmed by parliament. Finally, the president serves as the 'Supreme Commander of Estonia's national defence'

[40] The legal chancellor serves the function of an independent ombudsman, monitoring the legal conduct of state officials as well as the constitutionality of laws passed by the national parliament and local municipal councils. He may also hear complaints from citizens about government services, but does not have the power to investigate administrative abuse or injustices.

[41] Art. 89. The president must also dissolve parliament if the latter is unable to pass a national budget within two months after the beginning of the fiscal year.

with the right to declare states of emergency in cases of foreign aggression or natural disaster.

Thus, the institution of president was not entirely toothless, and in 1992 the nation got in Lennart Meri a fairly brazen office holder, eager to set precedents and determine the full scope of his powers. On 20 September 1992, the special one-time popular presidential election took place alongside the Riigikogu elections. The favourite in the race, Supreme Council chairman Arnold Rüütel, was blocked from reaching the 50 per cent+1 majority he was hoping to gain by three other candidates. (He garnered only 41.5 per cent of the vote.) He and the second place finisher, Lennart Meri, were then referred to the new Riigikogu, where the right-of-centre majority opted for Meri, even though the latter had won only 29.5 per cent of the popular vote.

During his two terms in office, Meri used his powers under Article 107 of the Constitution to veto over two dozen laws. On eight occasions he was overridden by a simple majority in parliament, and appealed to the Constitutional Review Chamber. In seven of those eight cases Meri won.[42] In January 1994, the president had a brief stand-off with Prime Minister Mart Laar, when Meri delayed the appointment of several government ministers nominated by Laar in a cabinet reshuffle. The Constitution states that the president shall 'appoint and recall members of the Government' as proposed by the prime minister (Art. 78, para. 10), but there is no requirement defining when the president needs to do this. Through this foot-dragging strategy, Meri tried to exert leverage over the government. Eventually, however, he confirmed the ministers. In international affairs, Meri was avid to play his role as head of state, since he had served as foreign minister from 1990 to 1992. When meeting with foreign leaders, he often conducted what seemed to be his own foreign policy, leading to frequent conflicts with the Foreign Ministry. The most vivid example of this came in August 1994, when Meri led a freestyle negotiation with Russia over the final withdrawal of Russian troops from Estonia. In that deal, Meri conceded the right of retired Soviet military personnel to stay in Estonia, a move which the government had opposed adamantly. From 1995 to 1996, Meri also haggled with the government over the appointment of several ambassadors.

As for the president's relations with parliament, the new Constitution appeared to be working out as intended with some

---

[42] Not surprisingly, one of the laws Meri contested was the President of the Republic Act passed by the Riigikogu in May 1994.

occasional, but generally healthy, friction. Observers noted that during his first term President Meri may well have been careful not to alienate the Riigikogu excessively, since the latter would eventually decide his re-election. When presidential elections came up again in August 1996, Meri was given a warning about his behaviour when he failed to muster the two-thirds majority in the Riigikogu required for his re-election to a second term. It was Meri's rival from 1992, Arnold Rüütel, who this time thwarted the president by securing the support of thirty-two mostly rural deputies who steadfastly voted against Meri in the three rounds of voting. This forced the convening of an electoral college that would decide the issue. In accordance with the Constitution, 273 representatives from all of Estonia's local governments were convened. Two rounds of voting in this body finally resulted in the re-election of Meri and the start of a full five-year term.[43]

The parliament

The Riigikogu's institutionalization process began with its first election in September 1992. The Constitution requires that the 101-member parliament be elected through free elections based 'on the principle of proportionality'. While this clearly hints at some kind of proportional electoral system, the exact details and formulas of this process were left out of the Constitution and are now found in a separate Riigikogu Electoral Law first adopted in April 1992. This law, too, became an object of political engineering, since there was latent tension among Estonia's politicians regarding electoral rules. One camp favoured a system that would encourage more personality-centred voting, while another preferred a system promoting party lists. In the end, a mixture of the two principles was created, which was more a mess than a functional compromise. Nevertheless, with three elections now having been held under this system, a sort of institutional inertia had set in and the system was unlikely to be changed soon. The exact procedures involve voters voting for individual candidates, who run either as independents or as members of a party or coalition. Vote-counting and seat distribution occurs based on a three-tiered system of aggregation. At the first, or district level, individual candidates are elected when they surpass the necessary vote quota for the district. At the

---

[43] For a complete account of the presidential election, see 'Estonia' under the Constitutional Watch section of the *East European Constitutional Review*, 5 (Fall 1996).

next level, additional mandates are awarded to parties, based on the total votes in each district cast for a party through the individual candidates running under its name. Finally, all remaining seats are divided proportionally based on each party's national vote total using a modified d'Hondt formula and national candidate lists supplied by each party or coalition.[44]

In the September 1992 elections, when the system was first employed, a fairly representative parliament resulted, with a total of nine parties or electoral blocs elected.[45] A right-of-centre coalition led by Prime Minister Mart Laar took office and survived for two years until Laar was dismissed by a no-confidence vote. Since parliamentary elections were right around the corner, a caretaker government was installed which led the country until the March 1995 elections. Since the electoral system was not significantly changed, the second elections saw the number of victorious parties and coalitions increase only slightly to ten. A centre-left government took power under the leadership of Tiit Vähi of the Coalition Party. Yet eight months later Estonia faced one of its most serious government crises, when the interior minister and leader of the Centre Party, Edgar Savisaar, was accused of having secretly taped conversations with other Estonian politicians. Although Savisaar vehemently denied the allegations, President Meri ultimately dismissed Savisaar (at Vähi's request), based on the Constitution (Art. 78, para. 10). This move also pushed Savisaar's party out of the government coalition, forcing Prime Minister Vähi to turn to the liberal Reform Party in order to form a new cabinet in November. Yet this government lasted only one year and in February 1997 Vähi was himself replaced by his Coalition Party colleague Mart Siimann. Siimann unsuccessfully tried to rebuild a majority coalition with either the Reform or Centre parties, but finally settled for a simple minority government with some rural party allies. This team survived until March 1999, when Estonia's third parliamentary

[44] In the modified Estonian version of the d'Hondt formula, the usual series of divisors (1, 2, 3, etc.) is raised to the power of 0.9. There is also an electoral threshold of 5% for parties and coalitions to participate in the third seat distribution level. For further specifications, see Vello Pettai and Marcus Kreuzer, 'Party Politics in the Baltic States: Social Bases and Institutional Context', *East European Politics and Societies*, 13 (1999), 148–89.

[45] The only major distortion to come about involved one émigré Estonian, Jüri Toomepuu, who polled nearly 17,000 votes in his district and ended up bringing into parliament on his coat-tails other candidates who won as few as 51 votes. For an account of the 1992 elections, see Vello Pettai, 'Estonia: Old Maps and New Roads', *Journal of Democracy*, 4 (1993), 117–25.

elections brought the right wing back into power, including Mart Laar once again as prime minister.

Having experienced a total of seven different cabinet changes during a period of just seven years, government stability in Estonia was still relatively weak. However, this problem seemed less to do with any constitutional deficiencies and more to do with endemic political in-fighting and lack of compromise. Greater party institutionalization and less fragmentation in parliament would be the real answers to these difficulties, but these changes would take more time to achieve.

Local government

The task of getting local governments on their feet began with the first municipal elections held in October 1993. The very first article of the chapter on local authorities in the Constitution designates local governments as the main organizers of local life and services (Art. 154). It gives them the explicit right to levy and collect local taxes (primarily property taxes) in order to help fund independent local budgets (Art. 157). In addition, many of the country's national tax laws (such as the personal income tax) automatically allocate part of the proceeds to local governments. By 1996, most towns seemed to be making do, although many rural communities considered merging in order to increase their tax base. In October 1996 and October 1999, Estonia held its second and third sets of local elections, which passed smoothly.

Non-citizens and minorities

With the adoption of Estonia's first citizenship laws in 1991 and 1992, the country created for itself an unprecedented legal cleavage between citizens and non-citizens, more or less mirroring the ethnic cleavage between Estonians and Russian-speakers. By early 1997, this situation had only slowly begun to stabilize, thanks to the passage of additional legislative acts and the enactment of various special provisions in the Constitution. As a first step in May 1993, the Riigikogu passed a law detailing the exact language requirements for naturalization. With this, the legal process of integrating non-citizens could begin. The criteria were set at relatively moderate levels;[46] however, even these proved difficult to master for many Russian-speakers who had never

---

[46] The language requirement assumed an Estonian vocabulary of around 1,500 words, which was tested in both oral and written form.

learned Estonian. In the summer of 1993, a further crisis erupted when the Riigikogu attempted to pass an Aliens Act to regulate the legal status of non-citizens. The act evoked widespread protests among non-citizens, who feared that the government (under the guise of a reregistration of non-citizens) would try to take away their permanent residency status. The turmoil prompted the north-eastern towns of Narva and Sillamäe to hold local autonomy referenda in July, although these were later nullified by the Constitutional Review Chamber. The tension eventually subsided only after the Riigikogu amended the law, though by this time much public confidence in the government among non-citizens had been lost.

The October 1993 local elections helped to recoup some of this mistrust, when non-citizens participated actively in the elections based on the provisions included in the Constitution.[47] In Tallinn, for example, Russian parties won nearly 40 per cent of the seats, while in other cities minorities were equally well represented. In the parliamentary elections in March 1995, two Russian parties (the United People's Party and the Russian Party) posted even more gains, breaking into the previously 100 per cent ethnic Estonian parliament by winning six seats in the assembly. Furthermore, in 1995 and 1996 the process of issuing new residency permits for non-citizens was completed, although the naturalization rate remained sluggish. By October 1996, only 83,500 people had been naturalized, and of these only half had actually taken the full language and culture exam.[48] Moreover, a new citizenship law passed in January 1995 raised the naturalization requirements to include a civics exam in Estonian. This change appeared to slow down the process even further. Thus, by mid-1997 some 340,000 people were still listed as permanent residents in Estonia. Of these, some 90,000 were registered as Russian Federation citizens, but the rest remain stateless persons.[49]

---

[47] Art. 156 allows all permanent residents in Estonia to vote in local elections. The only requirement is that they pre-register with local election officials approximately one month before the poll.

[48] Many applicants received citizenship under simplified terms if they were ethnic Estonian or had registered as 'citizenship applicants' with the Congress of Estonia back in 1989 and 1990. The total number of naturalized citizens is taken from 'Estonia Today, Citizenship Statistics: An Update as of 1 October, 1996', information sheet released by the Estonian Ministry of Foreign Affairs, 20 Oct. 1996. The number of applicants who actually took language exams is based on personal communications from the National Language Board and the Citizenship and Migration Board.

[49] In 1996, Estonia also began issuing aliens' passports to stateless persons, so that they could travel freely.

In the 1992 Constitution specific reference was made in Article 9, paragraph 1 to the constitutional guarantees of non-citizens: 'The rights, liberties and duties of everyone and all persons, as listed in the Constitution, shall be equal for Estonian citizens as well as for citizens of foreign states and stateless persons who are present in Estonia.' This article would serve as a blanket protection for all non-citizens. However, some rights in the Constitution are qualified by the phrase 'unless otherwise determined by law'. This stipulation was included in the right to receive state welfare benefits (Art. 28), the right to pursue a profession or job of one's choice (Art. 29), the right to engage freely in entrepreneurship (Art. 31), the right to own all types of property (Art. 32), and the right to receive government information about oneself (Art. 44). In addition, Article 48 restricts membership in political parties to citizens. Article 30, meanwhile, also limits employment in the civil service to citizens, although it also states that exceptions can be made in this provision. Thus when, in January 1995, the Riigikogu passed the Civil Service Act, which reiterated the citizenship requirement for national and local government employees, it also allowed some non-citizens, who were employed either in law enforcement, in the state revenue service, or in rescue services, the right to continue working for three to five years. Other non-citizen employees, however, would be terminated by February 1996. In late 1995, the Riigikogu extended this deadline to February 1997, since, as one government minister noted, the earlier date would have affected at least 2,400 people in north-eastern Estonia alone.[50] Still, it was inevitable that the citizenship requirement for government jobs would lead to a certain number of dismissals.

In Estonia's courts, relatively few challenges have arisen regarding the country's citizenship policy as a whole or individual decisions on naturalization or residency permits.[51] However, in October 1996 one major precedent was set when a Tallinn district court overturned the expulsion of a Russian Federation citizen, Pyotr Rozhok, after he had been accused by the Estonian government of political subversion. Rozhok, a member of Vladimir Zhirinovsky's Liberal Democratic Party, was thrown out of Estonia in March 1995 by the Citizenship and Immigration Board. But, following an appeal by Rozhok, the court ruled that the Board had not followed due procedure and as a result ordered that Rozhok be allowed to return to Estonia.

---

[50] 'Riigikogu muutis avaliku teenistuse seadust', *Päevaleht* (21 Dec. 1995).

[51] For example, similar non-citizens' groups in Latvia have waged constant court battles with the Latvian Department of Immigration and Citizenship.

Conclusion

In a September 1996 report to parliament, Estonia's legal chancellor, Eerik-Juhan Truuväli, noted that the initial phase of constitutional consolidation had more or less been completed.[52] Most of the essential laws enumerated or alluded to in the Constitution had been passed. With most of the basic structures in place, he said, the next stage would consist of certain important modifications. In preparation for that next stage, the Estonian government formed an expert commission in mid-1996 to begin reviewing various suggestions for constitutional amendments. The commission completed its report in 1998 and called mostly for a number of technical modifications (including a clearer delineation of powers between the president and prime minister in cases of national defence). At the same time, the commission also suggested that debate be reopened as to whether the president should be chosen by popular election. In December 1999 the new right-of-centre majority in parliament agreed to undertake a major initiative to amend the Constitution during its elected term. While the leaders of this effort hoped to adopt many of the technical amendments through a special four-fifths majority vote in parliament (based on Art. 166 of the Constitution), they also recognized that the more political issues would have to be decided by referendum, which most likely would not be possible before 2001.

Thus, eight years after Estonia's politicians had scrambled desperately to restore their unity in the face of a reactionary Soviet putsch, the results of their leap into a Constitutional Assembly seemed on the whole to be gratifying. As one of the architects of that 'miracle compromise', Marju Lauristin, later reflected:

I am convinced that the support that was expressed during that memorable late-night vote in favour of the so-called 'third way', which would become the Constitutional Assembly, was in fact a wholly successful compromise between two hitherto seemingly irreconcilable trajectories [i.e. the Supreme Council and the Congress of Estonia], which, in turn, guaranteed both the continuity of legal authority and its legitimacy, while also allowing for the radical renovation of the [Estonian] state's constitutional foundation in line with the democratic principles of the late 20th century.[53]

Of course, the final verdict on this 'radical renovation' will come only decades into the future. But Estonia's political evolution

---

[52] Enno Tammer, 'Õiguskantsler pahandas seadusandjaga', *Postimees* (26 Sept. 1996).

[53] 20. augusti klubi ja Riigikogu Kantselei, *Kaks otsustavat päeva Toompeal*, 81.

since 1991 had indeed entailed a 'radical' transformation, one very much imbued with the principle of constitutional and institutional engineering. Beginning with the very creation of the Constitutional Assembly, attention was focused on how institutions could be structured through incentives and deterrents to produce reasonable and balanced effects. Debates over presidentialism, post-communist lustration, and legal protections all revolved around how these issues could be best resolved within the context of Estonia's current needs and political traditions.[54] In a somewhat negative sense, Estonia's constitutional framers also applied this institutional engineering to the domain of citizenship. Here a balance was sought in that the socio-economic rights of non-citizens were generally not curtailed, even though their political power was effectively eliminated. The nationalistic design behind this move no doubt cast a shadow over its legitimacy. Nonetheless, the legal arguments and procedures used to resolve it also provided some basis for the country to 'grow out' of the problem, given time.

These two aspects of what might be called 'positive' and 'negative' engineering were Estonia's main accomplishments as it sought to secure its statehood through economic development, European integration, and social progress. The over-complicated Riigikogu electoral law and the difficult presidential elections of 1996 indicated that not all the newly engineered institutions worked perfectly. These problems suggested the conclusion that, although compromise was necessary, existing institutions were often second-best alternatives. Still, given the risks Estonia took in trying to produce such a comprehensive system all at once, the results were more than satisfactory.

[54] See Rein Taagepera, 'Mida sisaldab PA põhiseaduse projekt', *Rahva Hääl* (20 Nov. 1991).

5

Rebuilding Democracy in Latvia: Overcoming a Dual Legacy

Adolf Sprudzs

Compared to other post-communist states, constitutional engineering has been extremely difficult in Latvia. In 1990, Latvian democratizers simply reinstated the 1922 Latvian Constitution with a few minor amendments, as a logical legal step in Latvia's struggle for independence from the USSR. This was significant because it expressed Latvia's right to self-determination by lifting the yoke of Soviet occupation and re-establishing its formerly democratic nation-state. The Constitution's readoption enhanced the legitimacy of the new regime and had a stabilizing effect on the newly independent state. When the Baltic 'singing revolutions' helped bring about the collapse of the Soviet empire,[1] Latvia still had the necessary elements for once again becoming an independent state —territory, population, and state power. However, in 1990 the social environment was quite different from that of the 1920s and 1930s.[2] Thus, there was a price to pay for high legitimacy and quick stabilization: Latvia had to grapple with the problems of two historical legacies—those of the inter-war independence period and the Soviet era. Although lauded as Latvia's golden past, the inter-war democracy had many problems, some of which stemmed directly from the institutional structure embodied in the 1922 Constitution. In addition to creating an inherently unstable government,

---

[1] See Nils R. Muiznieks, 'The Influence of the Baltic Popular Movements on the Process of Soviet Disintegration', *Europe-Asia Studies*, 47 (1995), 3–25.

[2] See Juris Dreifelds, *Latvia in Transition* (New York: Cambridge University Press, 1996); and Rasma Karklins, *Ethnopolitics and Transition to Democracy: The Collapse of the USSR and Latvia* (Baltimore: Johns Hopkins University Press, 1994).

the Constitution contained several gaps: sections on basic rights and local government had been skipped because there was no consensus at the time of constitution-drafting. Thus, the quick fix of readopting the 1922 Constitution actually exacerbated institutional engineering and slowed down democratic consolidation. But the Soviet legacy left perhaps the largest barrier to easy reinstitution of the 1922 Constitution. After post-Second World War war casualties, executions, deportations, and emigration, and after communist-period immigration to Latvia by non-Latvian nationals, the population drastically changed from the relatively homogeneous nation-state of the inter-war period. In 1989, only 52 per cent of the population residing in Latvia were Latvian nationals. Thus the re-established Latvian nation-state could not simply restart where it left off in 1940, but was forced to contend with a myriad of old and new concerns.

Inter-war Legacies

Latvian leaders' decision to retain the 1922 Constitution rather than drafting a new one reflected their efforts to emphasize the legal continuity of the Latvian state. The period of pre-war Latvian independence from 1918 to 1940, the fact that the Soviet annexation of Latvia had not been recognized *de jure* by the Western powers, and the generation of multiethnic citizens of Latvia who remembered those years with affection and personal attachment were very important elements influencing the decision to *restore* the independent Republic of Latvia. The full reinstatement of the 1922 *Satversme* (Constitution of Latvia) was therefore seen as a logical legal consequence. The weight given to this argument during the independence struggle gave the transitional government's leaders little incentive to scrap the old Constitution and convene a constitutional convention, which was sure to divide further a country already grappling with the problems associated with re-establishing its sovereignty.

This step was not unique to Latvia. Similarly, Lithuanian reformers saw the importance of reinstating the 1938 Constitution for the purpose of establishing legal continuity with the previous independent, democratic state. But in Lithuania, the 1938 Constitution was revived for only one hour, before it was replaced by the temporary Basic Law, based in large part on the Soviet Constitution. Latvian leaders took another path, stubbornly denouncing the communist regime, and choosing what seemed to be a lesser evil—the 1922 Constitution. Another reason to keep the 1922 Constitution may stem from the fact that it set up a parliamentary regime which appealed to the framers—the Supreme Council and, later, the 1993 Saeima. But regardless of the motivation behind the decision, the reality that followed was that Latvia of the 1990s was forced to revisit the contentious, unstable period of its inter-war democracy.

Latvia proclaimed its independence on 18 November 1918, in the aftermath of the First World War.[3] After a war of liberation to free the country from German and Russian domination, reconstruction of the war-ravaged land began in 1920. A peace treaty between Latvia and Soviet Russia was finally concluded on 11 August 1920, in which Russia recognized the independence and sovereignty of the Latvian state and 'forever' renounced all sovereign rights over the Latvian people and territory.[4] After Latvia was recognized *de jure* by the Allies and admitted to the League of Nations in 1921, building democratic institutions finally became the young nation's priority. The first general elections, by secret ballot and held according to a proportional system, were held in April 1920 to elect the *Satversmes Sapulce* (Constituent Assembly). The twenty-four political parties and groups participating in the elections presented fifty-seven candidate lists,[5] representing citizens of Latvia as defined by the 23 August 1919 Law on Citizenship.[6] These elections created the 150-member Satversmes Sapulce. The Social Democrats and the Farmers' Union became the major forces in the newly elected Assembly, along with a good representation from the eastern province of Latvia—Latgale—as well as representatives of all the major minority groups.[7] The Satversmes Sapulce convened its first session on 1 May 1920, and performed the duties of the highest state organ for more than two years

---

[3] For a concise, modern, and well-written history of Latvia and the Latvians, see Andrejs Plakans, *The Latvians; A Short History* (Stanford, Calif.: Hoover Institution Press, 1995); for quarterly updates on constitutional politics in Eastern Europe, including Latvia, see the section 'Constitution Watch' in the *East European Constitutional Review*, published by the University of Chicago Law School and the Central European University since 1992.

[4] *League of Nations Treaty Series* (*LNTS*), ii (1920–1921), 212–31.

[5] A. Svabe (ed.), *Latvju Enciklopedija* (*LE*), 3 vols. (Stockholm: Tris Zvaigznes, 1953–5), s.v. 'Satversmes sapulce' [Constituent Assembly], iii. 2252.

[6] Ibid., s.v. 'Pavalstnieciba' [Citizenship], ii. 1883–1884.   [7] Ibid., iii. 2252.

while drafting the text of the *Satversme*, the Constitution of Latvia, which was passed on 15 February 1922, and came into effect on 7 November 1922.[8]

The Satversme proclaimed that 'Latvia shall be an independent democratic Republic' and declared that 'the sovereign power of the Latvian State shall belong to the People of Latvia'.[9] The Constitution dealt mainly with the organization of the state and the formation, rights and duties of its constitutional organs—the unicameral Saeima (parliament), the president, the Cabinet of Ministers, and the courts of justice. The proposal to include a second part dealing with rights and duties of citizens was discussed and debated by the Assembly, but no agreement was achieved and these matters were not included in the final text.[10] Perhaps because of its quasi-legislative function, the Constituent Assembly's Constitution created a parliamentary government in Latvia. The 100-member Saeima elects the president to a three-year term. The president, in turn, nominates a prime minister to assemble a cabinet and, with Saeima approval, to serve as head of the government.

The Nazi–Soviet Pact on Non-aggression of 23 August 1939, with its secret protocols, sealed the fate of Poland and the Baltic states and unleashed the Second World War. Estonia, Latvia, and Lithuania were coerced to sign Pacts of Mutual Assistance with the USSR in early October 1939, permitting the establishment of Soviet military bases on their territories, being assured in Article V of the Pact (for Latvia) that 'The carrying into effect of the present pact must in no way affect the sovereign rights of the contracting parties, in particular their political structure, their economic and social system, and their military measures.'[11] Nevertheless, eight months later, in June 1940, the Baltic states

---

[8] The full text of the 1922 Satversme [Constitution of Latvia] in English is available in *Jahrbuch des öffentlichen Rechts der Gegenwart*, 44 (1996), 417–23 and other sources, e.g. Martin Scheinin (ed.), *International Human Rights Norms in the Nordic and Baltic Countries* (The Hague: Martinus Nijhoff, 1996), 97–104; The International Institute for Democracy [Strasbourg] Council of Europe Press (ed.), *The Rebirth of Democracy* [twelve constitutions of Central and Eastern Europe] (Strasbourg: International Institute for Democracy [Strasbourg] Council of Europe Press, 1995), Latvia at 259–74.

[9] Constitution of the Republic of Latvia, 1922, Arts. 1 and 2.

[10] Svabe (ed.), *Latvju Enciklopedija*, s.v. 'Valsts iekarta' [State Organization], iii. 2583.

[11] Dr Alfred Bilmanis (compiler), *Latvian–Russian Relations: Documents* (Washington: Latvian Legation, 1944), 198–9, at 199.

were occupied by the Red Army, and in early August 1940 forcibly incorporated into the USSR.[12]

Legalizing Independence and Fostering Regime Stability

In their battle against Soviet power during the Gorbachev era, Latvian leaders based the legitimacy of their independence movement on the illegal nature of the Soviet annexation of Latvia. Leaders used provisions of Soviet law adopted in response to international non-recognition of the annexation—although it was never meant to have anything but decorative effect. According to these provisions, they argued that the Latvian state had never ceased to exist, and called for an end to Soviet occupation. Although neither the limits of the newly found freedom of expression nor the toleration level of the new political activity were known at the time, Mikhail Gorbachev's glasnost and perestroika policies brought forth courageous 'calendar demonstrations' in Latvia in the late 1980s. These demonstrations gained momentum and support, slowly lifting long-standing fears of the repressive system. Latvians eagerly joined forces with their Baltic neighbours to begin the struggle for independence and sovereignty lost fifty years earlier.[13]

---

[12] See William J. H. Hough, III, 'The Annexation of the Baltic States and its Effects of the Development of Law Prohibiting Forcible Seizure of Territory', *New York Law School Journal of International and Comparative Law*, 6 (1985), 301–533; for relevant documents see 'Forcible Occupation of the Baltic States and their Incorporation into the Soviet Union', in *Foreign Relations of the United States: Diplomatic Papers, 1940* (Washington: GPO, 1959), 357–444; important investigation and collection of documents and testimony on the Baltic case was performed in 1953 and 1954 by a US House Select Committee to Investigate Communist Aggression and the Forced Incorporation of the Baltic States into the USSR, under the chairmanship of Charles J. Kersten, which also published a very thorough and comprehensive report, including the following conclusion: 'The evidence is overwhelming and conclusive that Estonia, Latvia, and Lithuania were forcibly occupied and illegally annexed by the U.S.S.R. Any claims by the U.S.S.R. that the elections conducted by them in July 1940 were free and voluntary or that the resolutions adopted by the resulting parliaments petitioning for recognition as a Soviet Republic were legal are false and without foundation in fact'—see *Third Interim Report of the Select Committee on Communist Aggression*, 83rd Congress, 2nd Session (Washington: GPO, 1954), 8; reprinted as *Baltic States: A Study of their Origin and National Development, their Seizure and Incorporation into the USSR* (Buffalo: William S. Hein & Co., 1972).

[13] For a collection of expert discussions in English, French, and German of political and legal developments in the Baltic states, see Adolf Sprudzs (ed.), *The Baltic Path to Independence: An International Reader of Selected Articles* (Buffalo:

Following the highly visible but diffuse protest activities, an effort was made to coordinate the work of dissidents, folklore ensembles, the Helsinki '86 group, the Latvian Environmental Protection Club, and the Latvian National Independence Movement, by creating an umbrella organization, the People's Front (PF), in June 1988. PF united these early activists with influential Latvian writers, artists, intellectuals, and progressive Communist Party reformers and quickly became the leading force in the struggle for Latvian independence.

After the first multi-party elections to the Latvian Supreme Council, held in March and April 1990, PF garnered a two-thirds majority in the Assembly. At its first session, held on 4 May 1990, the new anti-communist majority adopted the declaration 'On the Renewal of the Independence of the Republic of Latvia'.[14] Next, the Assembly restored the validity of the 1922 Latvian Constitution, but suspended it, with the exception of Articles 1, 2, 3, and 6, 'until the adoption of new wording of the Constitution'.[15] Nevertheless, these parliamentary decisions had only a symbolic value at that time, since political power was still in the hands of the centralized Soviet institutions. It took more than a year of dangerous tension, confrontation, and even casualties before the Soviet grip on Latvia finally loosened after the Moscow putsch. The Latvian Supreme Council quickly took advantage of the confusion and passed a resolution on 21 August 1991, 'To declare Latvia as an independent, democratic republic, in which the sovereign power of the Latvian State belongs to the people of Latvia and its sovereign state status is determined by the Republic of Latvia's Constitution of 15 February 1922.' At the same time, the Supreme Council also declared that 'Until the time when the occupation and annexation of Latvia is liquidated and the Saeima of the Republic of Latvia

---

William S. Hein & Co., 1994). For a participant's story of the events in Latvia, see Olgerts Eglitis, *Nonviolent Action in the Liberation of Latvia*, Monograph Series 5 (Cambridge, Mass.: Albert Einstein Institution, 1993).

[14] For the text of this declaration as read by Deputy Apsitis of the Editorial Commission on a BBC 7 May 1990 broadcast, see Adolf Sprudzs, 'The Rule of Law and the Baltic States', in *Bibliothek und Recht—international: Libraries and Law—International: Festschrift Ralph Lansky*, vii (Hamburg: Arbeitsgemeinschaft für juristiches Bibliotheks und Dokumentationswesen, 1991), at 231–41.

[15] Ibid. 237–41, at 239. Art. 1: Latvia is an independent democratic republic. Art. 2: The sovereign power of the state of Latvia belongs to the people of Latvia. Art. 3: The territory of the state of Latvia, within the boundaries determined by international treaties, consists of Vidzeme, Latgale, Kurzeme, and Zemgale. Art. 6: The Saeima is elected by universal, equal, direct, secret, and proportional ballot.

is convened, supreme power is to be executed exclusively by the Supreme Council of the Republic of Latvia. Only the laws and institutions of the supreme power are legally in effect in the territory of the Republic of Latvia.'[16] During the week that followed, the independence of Latvia, Estonia, and Lithuania was recognized by the Russian Federation, Ukraine, Belarus, Georgia, and the European Community nations, followed by the United States on 2 September, and the USSR on 4 September. By 17 September 1991, Latvia took its seat at the United Nations and finally gained international recognition as an independent state *de facto* and *de jure*.[17]

The 1922 Constitution: A Difficult Fit

Latvia's quick reinstatement of the 1922 Constitution has been generally recognized as a stabilizing factor internally—preventing potential conflicts between different branches of state power—and has also been a positive element for Latvia's image abroad. But fifty years had left substantial, irreversible differences between inter-war and post-communist Latvia. The territory and resident population had changed, which raised issues of security, citizenship, and legitimacy. At the same time, the problems with the inter-war Constitution had never been resolved—which only exacerbated problems with democratic consolidation and regime stability.

While the territory of Latvia (based on the peace treaty of 1920 with Russia and on post-First World War border settlements with Latvia's other neighbours) was otherwise intact, one district was missing. The district of Abrene in the province of Latgale, comprising about 3 per cent of the pre-1940 Latvia, had been annexed in 1944 to the territory of the Russian Soviet Federative Socialist Republic (RSFSR).[18] Apart from this still unresolved dispute, in which Russia strangely claims that the 1920 peace treaty 'lost its force in 1940 when Latvia became part of the USSR',[19] and some border control problems, Latvia has resumed exercising sovereign powers over its territory. Russian troops which had 'controlled about 850 military facilities including large areas of land and many buildings throughout Latvia',[20] were pulled out by 31 August 1994, in accordance with

[16] *Jahrbuch des öffentlichen Rechts der Gegenwart*, 44 (1996), 395.

[17] Plakans, *The Latvians*, 183.

[18] See Dietrich A. Loeber, 'The Russian–Latvian Territorial Dispute over Abrene: A Legacy from the Times of Soviet Rule', *Parker School Journal of East European Law*, 2 (1995), 537–59.

[19] Ibid. 537, 549–53.   [20] Dreifelds, *Latvia in Transition*, 172.

the Treaty on Russian Troop Withdrawal signed in Moscow on 30 April 1994.[21] The remaining active Russian military presence at the Skrunda early-warning radar station continued until 1 September 1998. The dismantling of the station was scheduled before 29 February 2000 and took place ahead of schedule in late 1999.[22]

But much more divisive and contentious was the issue of citizenship. In the initial stages of the independence movement, it was necessary to work according to Soviet rules. Thus, at the first multi-party elections to the Supreme Council, held in March/April 1990, all Soviet citizens residing in Latvia were able to participate in elections. Despite the fact that only around half the population were ethnic Latvians, a pro-independence Council was elected and the independence aspirations were supported by many non-Latvians. Nevertheless, after independence, political factions that had previously cooperated in the PF were now competing with each other politically. In this environment of political competition, coupled with resentment of the Soviet occupation, the issue of recreating a homogeneous nation-state and strictly defining Latvian citizenship emerged.

Population losses in Latvia from 1940 to mid-1945 were tremendous. From an estimated total population of 2 million in 1939, war casualties, executions, deportations, and emigration had reduced the population to about 1.4 million in 1945.[23] Post-Second World War Soviet reprisals, guerrilla warfare, forced collectivization of agriculture with mass deportations of Latvian farmers in 1949, and the influx of Russian administrators and workers further changed the demographic situation. In 1959, the percentage of Latvians had dropped to 62 per cent, by 1979 to 53.7 per cent, and by 1989 had reached its all-time low of 52 per cent.[24] The Russian share of the population in 1989 was 34 per cent; Belarusians 4.5 per cent; Ukrainians 3.5 per cent; Poles 2.3 per cent; and Lithuanians 1.3 per cent.[25] Large-scale migration was systematically implemented as part of the general Russification policy which not only encouraged immigration by offering incentives such as preferential treatment for housing and social services, but also 'discriminated against local cultures and languages and favored the Russian

---

[21] See the Latvian text of this treaty and related agreements in *Latvijas Republikas Saeimas un Ministru Kabineta Zinotajs*, 2/25 (1995), 166–97.

[22] *LRSMK Zinotajs* (1995) 2: 187.   [23] Plakans, *The Latvians*, 152.

[24] *The Baltic States: A Reference Book* (Tallin: Estonian Encyclopedia Publishers, 1991), 92.

[25] Ibid.

language and the Russian-speaking population'.[26] By the mid-1980s, fears that the Latvian nation had reached a point of danger were widespread, as was the belief that the country 'was moving inexorably toward that point where national dissolution and extinction could become irreversible'.[27]

In preparation for the first democratic elections of the newly independent Latvia, the Supreme Council adopted its 'Resolution on the Renewal of the Republic of Latvia's Citizens' Rights and Fundamental Principles of Naturalization' on 15 October 1991, which restored Latvian citizenship to those who were citizens of Latvia on 17 June 1940, and their descendants, and established fundamental principles for granting Latvian citizenship through naturalization.[28] In dealing with one of these principles, that is, 'whether political integration into Latvia had to be a precondition for Latvian citizenship', the Supreme Council

decided that political integration was a necessary precondition, that only people who identified with the independent state of Latvia and its democratic form of government could be offered citizenship. Thus the requirements for naturalized citizenship reflected this logic by encouraging potential citizens to become integrated into Latvia through residence, acquiring basic Latvian language proficiency, acquiring basic knowledge of Latvia's constitution, renouncing competing citizenship, and taking a loyalty oath.[29]

The Supreme Council did not, however, enact any measures for citizenship through naturalization because of the prevailing opinion that as a transitional body, elected by an electorate which included non-Latvian nationals (and therefore, according to their qualifications, non-citizens of Latvia), it did not have the required legal authority under the 1922 Constitution.[30] This argument did not prevent the Council from adopting the law 'On Registration of Residents' on 17 December 1991, requiring all residents of the Republic of Latvia to register and receive a personal identification number, also enabling those who could prove their Latvian citizenship by appropriate documentation to restore their status as such. This law defined who could participate in the 1993 elections to the Saeima.

---

[26] See Steven Woehrel, 'Russians in the Baltic States', *Current Politics and Economics of Russia*, 4 (1996), 127–41, at 128.

[27] Ibid. 50.

[28] See Inese Birzniece, 'Latvia's Citizenship Law: The Politics of Choosing an Identity', *American Foreign Policy Interests* (Dec. 1995), 10–20, at 11–12.

[29] Ibid. 15.   [30] Ibid.

Despite its insistence on not adopting a citizenship law, the question of Latvian citizenship was a subject of heated debate in the Supreme Council, as well as in the press. Proposals ranged from granting automatic citizenship to all current permanent residents of Latvia, the so-called 'zero-option', to much more restrictive policies of limiting Latvian citizenship only to those who had it before Soviet occupation and their descendants. The central position was taken by one proposal for extending naturalization to selected non-citizens who could be politically integrated over a period of time, so that the majority status of the Latvian nation would not be endangered by massive absorption of non-Latvians. The 'zero-option' was supported by political activists in the Russian-speaking immigrant groups and by those who feared an ethnic polarization, while it was opposed by those who thought the independent Republic of Latvia was the only instrument that could save and preserve the Latvian nation, its language, and ancient culture.

In the period before the Saeima was elected, registration of residents of Latvia continued, establishing at the same time the community of the 'people of Latvia', who, as the authentic citizens of Latvia at the time of the election, would have the right to elect the fifth Saeima, thus being connected legally and symbolically to the pre-war democratic Republic of Latvia. The combined results of the registration of residents showed that on 6 October 1994, 38 per cent of ethnic Russians residing in Latvia (285,314) registered as Latvian citizens; the total number of Latvian citizens (1.75 million of 2.48 million residents) constituting 71 per cent, with 724,000 or 29 per cent of Latvia's residents being non-citizens. The three largest ethnic groups of non-citizens, according to the 1994 data, were 466,000 or 64 per cent Russians, 86,000 or 11 per cent Belarusians, and 63,000 or 8.7 per cent Ukrainians. Almost half of the non-citizens (356,000) of Latvia lived in Riga, the capital of Latvia.[31]

Five different draft citizenship bills were considered by the Saeima immediately after elections. By 23 September 1993, three of those bills were sent to the Saeima Legal Committee, for analysis and recommendations. On 23 November 1993, a plenary debate took place, and in a secret ballot the Saeima voted to adopt (with 53 votes in favour, 28 votes against, and 6 abstentions) the Legal Committee's recommended draft law which had been proposed by the government coalition of Latvia's Way and the Farmers'

---

[31] See Inese Birzniece, 'Latvia's Citizenship Law: The Politics of Choosing an Identity', *American Foreign Policy Interests* (Dec. 1995), 16.

Union.[32] After the first reading, the draft law on citizenship was sent by the Saeima to the Council of Europe and the CSCE (now the OSCE) for review and comments by their legal experts. As a result of subsequent comments from these and other sources some changes were made, and the revised text was adopted after the third reading by the Saeima on 21 June 1994, and sent to the president for promulgation. However, President Guntis Ulmanis returned the law to the Saeima seven days later for reconsideration of several points, including proposed percentage quotas[33] (opposed by international experts). The Saeima reviewed and eliminated the quotas and passed the amended bill again on 22 July 1994, which was promulgated by the president on 11 August 1994.[34] Some amendments were made on 16 March 1995, exempting certain categories of people from the naturalization process, thus significantly reducing the number of naturalization applications received.[35]

Although simply passing the law 'On Citizenship' did not satisfy all parties involved, it at least provided a *modus vivendi* for dealing with the situation. It might be said that the restrictive citizenship policy adopted by the Saeima created another problem: resolving the status of aliens in Latvia. The long-awaited law 'On the Status of Former USSR Citizens Who Do Not Have Citizenship of Latvia or Any Other State' was enacted on 12 April 1995, giving 'legal status (equivalent to permanent resident status) to most noncitizens (former Soviet citizens) residing in Latvia (as of 1 July 1992) but who were born in or entered Latvia after 17 June 1940, if they do not have Russian citizenship or that of any other State. Such persons will be entitled to receive a Republic of Latvia passport, which will be a valid travel document giving the holder the right to reenter Latvia without a visa. The law also includes demobilized Soviet/Russian armed forces personnel and their family members if they were demobilized before 28 January 1992 (the same date as that cited in the Latvia–Russia troop withdrawal agreements signed on 30 April 1994).'[36]

Academic discussions held in late 1995 and early 1996 on the subject of developing a political nation in Latvia, the national

---

[32] Ibid. 16–18.

[33] The government set quotas for the naturalization of non-citizens which would be calculated 'to ensure the development of Latvia as a single community state'. See 'Constitution Watch: Latvia', *East European Constitutional Review*, 3/2 (Spring 1994), 12.

[34] Birzniece, 'Latvia's Citizenship Law', 18–19; Latvian text in *LRSMK Zinotaajs*, 17 (1994), 1499–509.

[35] Birzniece, 'Latvia's Citizenship Law', 18–19.   [36] Ibid.

processes in Latvia, and the political nation and ethnological strategy in Latvia reveal a gradual liberalization of the concept of citizenship.[37] Comparisons were drawn from the experience of developing a political nation in the USA, which called for the need to integrate all Latvian residents on the basis of tolerance and respect of democratic principles and practice.[38] One of the concluding thoughts was that 'The issue of the emergence of a political nation is linked to the consolidation of a new national identity and Latvia's progress towards a modern European society.'[39] It was also agreed that a political nation could be multicultural and multiethnic (as in Latvia) but needed consensus on independence of the state and basic democratic values. Latvian and non-Latvian views have grown closer during the last few years in these matters. The existing differences of views and convictions will continue for a long time but mutual tolerance seems to be improving, dictated by the realization that no dramatic changes or miracles are forthcoming (such as the willingness of the more developed nations in the West to help Latvia by accepting as immigrants a portion of those Soviet-era settlers who would like to leave Latvia). Many of those Russians and their descendants who are Latvian citizens have ties to Latvia which in some cases go back several centuries. Many others are related to Latvians through mixed marriages[40] and long-standing friendships. Others were born in Latvia and consider Latvia their homeland. These and similar factors explain the fact that despite the recognized cultural differences, Latvians and non-Latvians have managed to overcome various provocations by extremists on both sides and are gradually moving towards a democratic and civil territorial community in which the rule of law and mutual respect is not the exception but the accepted norm.

A clear example of this trend was given by the results of the 1998 referendum on changes to the citizenship law. After much

[37] See 'Politiskas nacijas veidosanas Latvija' (Forming a Political Nation in Latvia), in *Latvijas Zinatnu Akademijas Vestis* (texts of seven lectures), 11/12 (1995), 38–48; and *Newsletter of the Latvian Center for Human Rights and Ethnic Studies*, 7 (Mar. 1996), 10–12.

[38] Discussed by historian Dr Leo Dribins in the 1995 seminar, ibid.

[39] Ibid. 48.

[40] See Iveta Pavlina, 'Ethniski jauktas laulibas Latvija' (Ethnically Mixed Marriages in Latvia), in *Latvijas Zinatnu Akademijas Vestis—A* [Humanities/Letonica: Ethnography], 11/12 (1995), 55–60. The author establishes, among other things, that in the former USSR Latvia was in the first place with the number of mixed marriages; that every fourth marriage in Latvia is a mixed marriage, that every third Russian and every fifth Latvian is marrying a partner of a different ethnic group—see 55, 56, etc.

pressure from within and outside Latvia, the Saeima passed several amendments to the citizenship law on 22 June 1998. The amendments significantly liberalized the policy by discarding the so-called 'windows' system (which differentiated non-citizens by age and gave each age group a different time-frame for applying for citizenship) and granting automatic citizenship to children born in Latvia after 1991. After the law's passage, an opposition group headed by the Fatherland and Freedom Party (FFP) put into motion Article 72 of the Constitution which requires the president to suspend promulgation of the law pending the outcome of signature collection in support of a referendum on the amendments.[41] FFP succeeded in collecting the necessary signatures and the referendum was scheduled to coincide with parliamentary elections of 3 October. As a result, the citizenship issue again became the pawn of competing political parties, which incorporated their opinion of the referendum into their political campaigns. The results of the referendum were close, but the amendments to the law were upheld: out of the 73 per cent of eligible voters participating in elections, 53 per cent voted in favour of the law. It is hoped that the results of the referendum will influence future policies in terms of furthering liberalization and integration of non-Latvian citizens and residents. However, in July 1999 the Saeima approved a new language law favouring Latvian. This met with the disapproval of the OSCE, was eventually sent back to parliament by President Vaira Vike-Freiberga, was watered down, and was reapproved despite FFP opposition. Nevertheless, the incident suggests that further pressures on citizenship and language rules could surface.

Overcoming the Obstacles to Institutional Engineering

Parliament, government, and the presidency

Even without the territorial and demographic changes in Latvia, the 1922 Satversme itself has been responsible for inhibiting progress towards democratic consolidation. Post-communist Latvian leaders recognized that a major flaw in the inter-war republic's political system was the fractionalizing effect of the electoral system. The combination of the electoral law and the strong parliamentary system inherent in the Constitution recreated the instability of the 1920s and stymied measures to overcome these weaknesses.

[41] See 'Constitution Watch: Latvia', *East European Constitutional Review*, 7/3 (Summer 1998).

The electoral law of inter-war Latvia was very liberal, permitting small groups of citizens to form political parties and present candidates for elections. Because it was based on the proportional system of representation a multiplicity of political players were able to emerge. Intense bargaining and haggling between the many parties elected to parliament to build government coalitions was a regular feature of the process of forming governments, since the few major parties never gained a clear majority. Governments that were formed did not last very long. From 1922 to 1934, four parliamentary elections were held, while thirteen different cabinets were formed and dissolved during the same period.[42] There was growing discontent with the inefficient political process, aggravated by the difficulties of the worldwide economic crisis. As a result, an authoritarian regime was established on 15 May 1934 by Prime Minister Karlis Ulmanis, leader of the Farmers' Union, who dismissed the Saeima, suspended parts of the Constitution, established a 'Government of National Unity', and promised constitutional reform. World events, however, moved faster than Ulmanis's plans for a constitutionally better organized republic, and the Latvian government was eventually taken over by the USSR.

Nevertheless, the problems faced by the inter-war republic were still clear in the minds of the reformers elected to the Supreme Council in 1990. In preparation for the Saeima elections, the Council amended the Latvian Electoral Law of 9 June 1922, by increasing the threshold requirements from 2 to 4 per cent and extending voting rights to all citizens above the age of 18 (previously it had been 21).[43] These changes sought to reduce the influence of minor parties and increase the pool of citizens able to participate in elections.

Undeterred by the new threshold, 874 candidates representing 23 political parties, groups, and organizations competed for the 100 Saeima seats in the 5–6 June 1993 elections.[44] Eight parties gained seats in parliament. The largest number of seats—36—was won by Latvia's Way (LW), which was a coalition of major popular leaders in Latvian politics with prominent representatives from Latvian exile organizations and communities. A coalition minority government was formed by Valdis Birkavs (LW; formerly deputy

[42] Plakans, *The Latvians*, 127.

[43] *LRAPV Zinotajs*, 46–9 pos. 590 (1992), 2389–97, at 2389. After the Fifth Saeima was elected, it amended the Constitution in accord with the Supreme Council's electoral law changes. Art. 8 was changed on 27 Jan. 1994 to lower the voting age from 21 to 18.

[44] Plakans, *The Latvians*, 194; and Dzintra Bungs, 'Latvia's Transition to Independence Completed', *RFE/RL Research Report*, 3 (Jan. 1994), 96–8, at 96.

chairman of the Supreme Council) with the help of the Farmers' Union which had gained 12 deputies. Guntis Ulmanis (Farmers' Union; an economist and a grand-nephew of Karlis Ulmanis, the last president of pre-war Latvia) was elected president by the Saeima, and the generally popular former communist leader Anatolijs Gorbunovs (chairman of the Supreme Council and now one of the prominent leaders of LW) was elected the president of Saeima.[45] At its first session the fifth Saeima declared that the amended 1922 Constitution was now fully in force and operational.[46]

Although the creation of the LW coalition government went quite smoothly, creating the parliamentary majorities needed to pass bills was problematic. Debates on the floor were easily co-opted by various parties in the opposition, making important laws difficult to approve. Within one year of elections, the LW–FU coalition was breaking apart. After the failure of an FU-supported bill, two of the party's ministers resigned in protest of what they saw as betrayal by LW. The attempt to fill those ministerial posts led to protracted competition between several smaller parties promoting their own candidates in debates with the president and LW. The failure of this competition led to the resignation of LW Prime Minister Valdis Birkavs in the summer of 1994. By September, another weak coalition government was in place, but only after President Ulmanis's threats to dissolve parliament were heeded. Except for a few ministers' resignations, the government remained in place until the September 1995 elections.

Having rediscovered the divisiveness of the inter-war combination of electoral law and parliamentary politics, the Saeima again changed the electoral law prior to the 1995 elections. Raising the threshold from 4 to 5 per cent succeeded in shrinking the number of competing parties (twenty-three parties ran in 1993 while only nineteen competed in the 1995 elections). However, while only eight parties won seats in 1993, nine were able to enter parliament in 1995. Again, no single party dominated, but the perfectly even split between left and right, combined with a collective fear of extremist parties, prompted the formation of a grand coalition government consisting of seven parties and excluding only the pro-Russian Socialists and the populist People's Movement. This government quickly succumbed to the fate of previous coalitions, however, followed again by long political manoeuvring, bargaining, and coalition-building. Inability to impose coalition discipline was behind a reshuffle in mid-1997, and another long period of party negotiations and coalition-building followed the late 1998 general election,

[45] Plakans, *The Latvians*, 196. [46] *LRSMK Zinotajs*, 30 (1993), 1993.

while coalition fragility led to the downfall of yet another government in July 1999.

Discord between the governing coalitions and the various opposition factions has weakened the parliamentary regime and given the president power to moderate between these disputes. Formally, the president has limited powers. Formally, the Constitution empowers the president to convene the cabinet to address specific issues and to require the legislature to reconsider laws it has passed. The president has veto power (Art. 71), but it is limited and may be easily overturned by a vote in parliament. The Constitution, therefore, places clear limits to presidential power. However, in light of the fact that, since 1993, the average prime ministerial term has been only slightly more than one year, the president's role in maintaining stability has become crucial. While the president has the constitutional authority to propose dissolving the Saeima, exercising that authority is very risky. To dissolve the parliament, more than half of all voters in a special election must support the president's initiative; if they do not, the president must resign. No president has ever exercised this provision, though threats were issued every time coalition formation hit an impasse. The Constitution designates the president to be the head of the armed forces and authorizes him or her to appoint a commander-in-chief in time of war, to declare war in accordance with the decisions of the Saeima, and to appoint Latvia's diplomatic representatives. The president also presides over the National Security Council, which supervises intelligence operations and defence policy matters.

Article 72 of the Constitution gives power to one-third of all deputies to ask the president to suspend promulgation of a particular bill. Once promulgation of the bill is suspended, either a referendum on the law must be organized or the Saeima may vote on the bill once more, but this time there must be a qualified majority for the bill to pass.[47] This article has been invoked frequently in

[47] Art. 72 states 'The President of the State shall have the right to withhold the promulgation of a law for a period of two months. He shall postpone the promulgation at the request of not less than one-third of the Members of the Parliament. This right shall be exercised by the President of the State or by one-third of the Members of the Parliament within seven days of the adoption of the law by the Parliament. The law, the promulgation of which has been thus postponed, shall be submitted to a referendum, if not less than one-tenth of the electors so desire. Should such request not be formulated within the period of two months as mentioned above, the law shall be promulgated at the expiry of that period. The referendum shall not be taken, however, if the Parliament put this law to the vote once more and if then not less than three-fourths of all the members be in favour of its adoption.'

the struggle between majority and minority factions in parliament, with the outcome that important laws, such as the citizenship law, are not passed or their passage is delayed. The president, meanwhile, has assumed an important role intervening between rival factions, which has strengthened the visibility of this office and lent it more credibility than the parliament—which is at odds with the principles behind a parliamentary regime.

Latvia's first post-Soviet president, Guntis Ulmanis, expanded his influence beyond the institutional powers of the presidency by employing the 'bully pulpit of the presidency'. In addition to his role in persuading parliamentary forces to cooperate, he used his authority to force the Saeima to liberalize the citizenship law it passed in June 1994, which the international community had criticized. Utilizing the prestige of his office, he spoke out publicly and selectively on a few significant issues to prod the government and the Saeima in one direction or another. Ulmanis was a key figure in the struggle to liberalize laws concerning non-citizens, a position unpopular among many Latvian voters. His successor, émigré Vaira Vike-Freiberga, played a similar role in 1999 when she sent back to parliament a controversial law that was said to overly promote the Latvian language to the disadvantage of minorities.

Local government

Under the Soviet regime, 'Latvian local government had operated much as it did throughout the communist world, functioning essentially as an appendage of the central government and subject to the dictates of the communist party.'[48] It was a completely centralized system which had to be changed as quickly as possible, to keep pace with the massive movement toward independence. This process of change has been going on since the local elections of 1989 and 1994 as part of the constitutional reform and is continuing at the time of writing.[49] According to the present arrangements, there are in Latvia 600 territorial units which have local self-

[48] See John Greenwood, Richard Haslam, and Charlie Balsom, 'Local Democracy Building in Latvia', *Administration*, 42 (Summer 1994), 211–24, at 214.

[49] See Edvins Vanags, 'Development of Local Self-Government in Latvia', *Humanities and Social Sciences*, 1/2 (1994) [*Latvia* issue 'On the Way toward Democracy'], 38–48; for reforms and legislation in the period 1989–93 see Greenwood, Haslam, and Balsom, 'Local Democracy Building in Latvia'; for an analysis of the 1994 local election results, see Dzintra Bungs, 'Local Elections in Latvia: The Opposition Wins', *RFL/RL Research Report*, 3/28 (15 July 1994), 1–5; see also a general discussion of local self-government in Latvia and its possible reforms in *Pasvaldibas Latvija* (Self-government in Latvia), Politikas burtnicas 1

government: 26 districts and 7 major cities, with the districts sub-
divided into 492 rural communes and 69 district town territories.
Riga, the capital, has its own territorial arrangement with six administrative subdivisions.[50] Of the 600 territorial self-government
units, 406 have less than 2,000 inhabitants, including 157 local
government territories that even have less than 1,000 people.[51] Under
the centralized totalitarian system when everything was decided,
directed, and financed 'by the Center', this was workable and
'efficient'. Now there is a sort of 'tug-of-war' going on between
the various representatives of the local self-governments and the
central administration in Riga. Various government conceptions
and other reform proposals are being debated, all trying to find a
better distribution of rights, responsibilities, and financial sources.
The 1922 Constitution mentions local self-government only once—
in Article 25 which establishes the right of the Saeima to demand
data and explanations from ministers and local self-government
units. The prevailing view is that the local self-governments are
subordinated to the Cabinet of Ministers in the same way as all
the administrative agencies of central government.[52] This situation
seems to be in direct contradiction with the principles of the 1985
European Charter on Local Government. Reform has been debated
at length but has yet to be adopted and enforced.[53]

The courts

Legal reforms aiming in some measure toward a state that would
be based on the rule of law were initiated already in 1988. They
gradually became more assertive, even in the framework of the
USSR, and culminated in the Declaration of the Independence of

(Riga: Izdevejs Izglitiba, 1994); and a discussion of constitutional reform proposals to strengthen the rights of local self-government by Maris Pukis, 'Satversmes
grozijumu priekslikumi pasvaldibu tiesibu nostiprinasanai' (Proposals for Constitutional Reform to Strengthen Self-Government Rights), in *Satversmes reforma
Latvija: par un pret* [Constitutional Reform in Latvia: For and Against], Ekspertu
seminars (Riga, 1995) g. 15. junijs. (Riga: Sociali economisko petijumu instituts
'Latvija', 1995), at 75–86.

   [50] See *Pasvaldíbas Latvija*, 12.   [51] Ibid.
   [52] See Pukis, 'Satversmes grozijuma priekslikumi pasvaldibu tiesibu nostiprinasanai', 78.
   [53] The Cabinet of Ministers agreed in May 1996 on the local self-government
reform conception which aims at decentralization and projects more efficient
arrangement of territorial self-government units and their financial support.
There is opposition to government plans among representatives of local government and members of the Saeima.

Latvia on 4 May 1990.[54] The pace of reform legislation quickened, of course, after the collapse of the USSR in 1991. The Latvian legal community played a very important role in these developments. The judicial system as such was, however, as unprepared to assume an appropriate role in a democracy as were the other two branches of government, if not more so. A new Law on the Power of the Courts was adopted on 15 December 1992 by the Supreme Council of the Republic of Latvia,[55] establishing the principle and guarantee of independent courts of law and the inviolability of judges.[56] The judicial system of Latvia was subsequently reorganized into three levels of courts: the district courts or municipal courts, the regional courts, and the Supreme Court.[57] This reorganization affected the regular flow of court proceedings, dictated considerable changes in the positions and the number of judges and support personnel, and presented multiple difficulties. The shortage of fully qualified judges who would fulfil all the demands of the new democratic order, and would be committed to independent Latvia and its Constitution, has been difficult to overcome. A government report, covering August 1994 to August 1995, indicates that in the 39 district (or/and municipal) courts there were positions for 219 judges, of which 15 positions were still vacant and for an additional 11 places candidates were being considered; the five regional courts had 49 positions for judges, for which only 33 judges had been appointed and confirmed, with the worst situation in the eastern region of Latgale which still needed seven judges for its regional court.[58] To help improve the professional education quality of judges, a Judicial Training Centre was established in April 1995, in cooperation with and with the support of the Latvian Judges' Association,

[54] For a description and analysis of these early years of the struggle for the independence of Latvia by an important participant, see Talavs Jundzis, 'Tiesibu reformas un to loma Latvijas neatkaribas atjaunosana, 1988. gads–1990. gada 4. maijs', *Latvijas Vestures Instituta Zurnals*, 1 (1995), 121–42, and 2 (1995), 132–52, with a summary in English 'The Reforms of Law and their Role in the Resumption of Independence of Latvia' (1988–4 May 1990). Dr Jundzis was Latvian minister for defence, 1991–3.

[55] *LRAPV Zinotajs*, 1/2 (14 Jan. 1993), pos. 15, 74–104.

[56] For a brief analysis of this law see Gvido Zemribo, 'The Judicial Power of the Courts in Latvia', *Humanities and Social Sciences*, 1/2 (1994) [*Latvia* issue 'On the Way toward Democracy'], 29–37; now ambassador of Latvia to Denmark, Justice Zemribo was chief justice of the Latvian Supreme Court at the time and also chaired the commission that prepared the law.

[57] Ibid. 34–5.

[58] *Valdíbas darba gada parskats*—No 1994. gada augusta lidz 1995. gada augustam (Annual Work Survey of the Government, August 1994 to August 1995) (Riga, 1995), at 158–9.

the Central and East European Law Initiative of the American Bar Association, the Soros Foundation, and the United Nations Development Programme.[59] The Judicial Training Centre offers twelve-week professional courses for new judges, has presented a workshop on 'Judicial Independence and Separation of Powers' for government officials, and is offering assistance for a project to computerize Latvian courts. Judges appointed to the recently established regional courts[60] often have little, if any, of the experience necessary and appropriate for their new functions, which include the handling of appeals. The Judicial Training Centre has also offered training to such judges 'in areas such as appeals procedure, arbitral principles, civil procedure, and privatization',[61] and is helping slowly to raise the level of judiciary competence in Latvia. The higher courts have access to computers and the general availability of legal information is improving. Court housing facilities and adequate financial support for the courts in many cases are still problems waiting for solutions. Transition from the 'simplicity' of courts in the totalitarian past to a system that would be compatible with the principles and practices of a democratic state has proven to be (as elsewhere) very difficult, time-consuming, and complicated. Nevertheless, the Latvian government has chosen the difficult road to Europe, and, since the Declaration of Independence on 4 May 1990, has stated its adherence to fifty-one international conventions in the field of human rights, assuming various legal obligations implied in them.[62] Comparison and harmonization of the existing national legislation with these international obligations is now an urgent task, especially since 1995 when Latvia joined the Council of Europe and became an associate member of the European Communities, which, of course, involves additional legal duties. Of special significance is the European

[59] *Valdíbas darba gada parskats*—No 1994. gada augusta lidz 1995. gada augustam (Annual Work Survey of the Government, August 1994 to August 1995) (Riga, 1995); see also *ABA Central and East European Law Initiative* (1995 Annual Report), 21.

[60] According to the quoted Latvian government report, the five regional courts began their work on 31 Mar. 1995.

[61] See *ABA CEELI Update*, 6/2 (Summer 1996), 10.

[62] See Egils Levits, 'Cilvektiesibas un pamattiestbu normas un to juridiskais rangs Latvijas pasreizeja tiesibu sistema' [Human Rights and Basic Rights and their Legal Rank in the Present Legal System of Latvia], manuscript for an article forthcoming in *Juristu zurnals*; Hon. Egils Levits, now a judge from Latvia on the European Court of Human Rights, played an important role as a Western legal consultant during the struggle for the independence of Latvia, was the first Latvian ambassador to Germany, a minister of justice, and then again Latvia's ambassador to Austria, Switzerland, and Hungary.

Convention on Human Rights which Latvia has signed but not yet ratified. It is clear that judges of the Latvian court system must become familiar with this and other international agreements which impose specific legal obligations on Latvia, especially in the field of human rights, so that correct interpretations as well as methodology in court decisions are made. The beginning of formal membership negotiations with the EU in early 2000 can be expected to strengthen this trend.

Amending the Constitution

The difficulty in adopting regular laws was doubled when attempting to initiate constitutional reforms and re-engineer the imperfect inter-war institutions. Nevertheless, after many starts and stops, reformers finally succeeded in provoking consensus for change in light of government instability, parliament's loss of face in public opinion, and the overall effect these problems had on parliamentary strength. Constitutional amendments require three readings and support of a majority of at least two-thirds of all deputies (Art. 76). Article 78 stipulates that 'not less than one-tenth of the electors shall have the right to submit to the President of the State a fully elaborated scheme for the revision of the Constitution, or a Bill, which shall be submitted to the Parliament by the President. Should it not be accepted by the Parliament without substantial amendments, it shall be submitted to a referendum.'

Several amendment initiatives were put forward in spring 1997, following the most severe government crisis to date. The already highly polarized Saeima suffered further disruption from changing loyalties of independent deputies and maverick party members. Following the 1995 elections, over one-third of all MPs changed their party affiliation. At the time, party leaders had begun contemplating parliamentary dissolution and early elections.[63] These developments prompted parties first and foremost to amend those parts of the Constitution that seemed to contribute to the constant instability. Many proposals were submitted, but only ten survived the difficult amendment process. First, parliamentary and presidential terms were extended from three to four years (Arts. 10, 35, and 39) with the hope of counteracting the pressure for parties to campaign throughout their terms in office. Next, Article 11 was changed so

[63] 'Constitution Watch: Latvia', *East European Constitutional Review*, 6/2/3 (Spring/Summer 1997).

that elections would occur on one day instead of two and that date would be fixed and not open to debate in parliament. This amendment aimed at curbing voter apathy and excessive inter-party competition. After the Saeima's close brush with parliamentary dissolution, Articles 13 and 81 were changed to clarify the rules governing pre-term elections and extending the government's ability to adopt laws between Saeima sessions. Another response to the preceding coalition crisis (which was in part due to alleged corruption of MPs[64]) was to set limits on parliamentary immunity (Art. 30). The remaining amendments were somewhat less contentious, and seem to clarify murky constitutional wording (Art. 84 regarding judicial appointments and dismissals, Art. 45 specifying the president's right to grant amnesty and pardon, and Art. 37 changing minimum age and citizenship requirements for presidential candidates).

Rectifying the Rights Gap in the 1922 Constitution

Another major shortcoming of the 1922 Satversme was the missing second part on civil and political rights of individuals, on which the Constituent Assembly failed to agree in 1922. The need for this amendment to the Constitution was widely recognized in post-communist Latvia, and was the subject of heated debate among the public. Initially, however, the Supreme Council presumed that since it was a Soviet-era institution, it had no legal standing to amend the Constitution. Because of the perceived need to provide written guarantees of the rights of individuals and citizens, the Supreme Council instead adopted the 10 December 1991 law 'On the Rights and Responsibilities of Citizens and People'. Although the law was intended to be an effective supplement to the Constitution, it was actually only an ordinary law, and was easily superseded by later legislation.[65] The 1991 law clarified specific rights and obligations that are contained in numerous international treaties. It defined the primary obligation of the state as protection of the individual through the rights of individuals, including the rights of free speech and freedom of conscience,

---

[64] 'Constitution Watch: Latvia', *East European Constitutional Review*, 6/2/3 (Spring/Summer 1997).

[65] *LRAPV Zinotajs*, 415 (1991), 26 ff.; English text in *Jahrbuch des öffentlichen Rechts der Gegenwart*, 44 (1996), 395–8, and in Scheinin (ed.), *International Human Rights Norms in the Nordic and Baltic Countries*, 105–10.

equality before the law, the inviolability of the individual, and the right to fair and impartial judicial process. The law also protected economic rights, such as the right to private property, choice of profession, the right to strike, and certain legal protections. Prohibition of discrimination against or limitations to rights of national minorities and ethnic groups were also included. The law specifically granted all individuals—regardless of whether or not they are citizens—the right to seek redress through courts to defend their rights and interests and to seek compensation for illegal arrests or prosecutions. Under the law, citizens possess the rights to vote, to seek political office, to form political parties, to own land and natural resources, to leave Latvia and return freely, and to own registered firearms. In return, citizens were expected to be loyal to the Republic of Latvia, to defend their country's freedom and independence, and to defend the democratic order.

Although the intention of the law was to provide citizens and non-citizens with an extensive list of rights and duties, because it did not have the same status as the Constitution the question of whether and how these rights and duties can be enforced in court remained unanswered. The law itself did not prescribe a specific judicial avenue for enforcement.[66] If, however, 'review of normative enactments in administrative cases becomes an established competence of the Constitutional Court, it will mark a step forward in setting up a local procedure enabling individuals to base complaints on the Constitutional Act on the Rights and Obligations of Citizens and Persons or a prospective second part of the Constitution'.[67]

Such arguments eventually led to the creation of a new Latvian Constitutional Court by constitutional amendment (Art. 85, adopted on 12 June 1996). The Court consists of seven justices appointed to ten-year terms; three justices are nominated by the Saeima, two by the cabinet, and two by the Supreme Court. All appointments must be confirmed by the Saeima. Cases may be brought by the president, at least 20 Saeima deputies, the cabinet, the presidium of the Supreme Court, the prosecutor general, local governments, individual government ministers (in particular instances), the human rights agency, and the state audit board.

Nevertheless, even with the creation of the Constitutional Court, without a constitutional amendment to include human rights

[66] See Ineta Ziemele, 'Incorporation and Implementation of Human Rights in Latvia', in Scheinin (ed.), *International Human Rights Norms in the Nordic and Baltic Countries*, 73–110, at 78.

[67] Ibid. 89.

directly in the Constitution, the Court had no way of determining when rights concerns superseded other political decisions. In February 1997, a special committee in parliament was created, with representatives of seven political parties, to discuss and draft a constitutional amendment on including human rights in the basic law. The committee created a list of twenty-nine articles specifying citizens' rights and then published the draft amendment in newspapers to promote public debate. Once again, the issue of citizenship became the focal point of the debate. The Fatherland and Freedom Party (FFP) allied with the Movement for the National Independence of Latvia (MNIL) to limit the state's responsibility for and free movement of non-citizen residents in Latvia. In March 1998, these two parties submitted an alternative amendment draft including these limitations, along with the demand that the primacy of the Latvian language be included in the Constitution. Since no amendment could be made without the cooperation of these two parties, concessions were made to accommodate some of their requests. The amendment initiative was further spurred by the looming parliamentary elections in October 1998—it was generally believed that if the amendment were not adopted by the sixth Saeima, adoption of the important human rights amendment would be postponed indefinitely.

Almost immediately after elections, the outgoing Saeima adopted four constitutional amendments accompanying the addition of section 8, which included twenty-seven new articles addressing human rights. The first four amendments reflect the political deal struck between opposing party groups to enable the adoption of the section 8. Article 4 now clearly states that Latvian is the official language of the country and the provision that determines amendment procedures (Art. 77) now includes Article 4 in the group of constitutional articles that require a national referendum before they can be amended. Article 82 now lists the type of courts existing in Latvia. Previously, it stated that 'all citizens shall be equal before the law and the courts', but now this phrase has been altered and moved to Article 91, which states that 'all persons shall be equal before the law and the courts. Human rights shall be implemented without any discrimination.'

Among the 'Basic Human Rights' listed in section 8 are the freedom of thought, expression, conscience, religious affiliation, association, education, choice of profession, provision for social guarantees, and stipulation of the right of minorities to preserve their cultural identity and language. There is a provision that anyone can defend their rights and legal interests in the courts, and when a court finds that rights have been encroached upon, the individual has the right to due compensation. The principle of the presumption of innocence is included. Every citizen of Latvia is entitled to vote and to be elected to office. It is stipulated that the Church is separated from the state. Article 116 allows the majority of these freedoms, including freedom of religion, to be restricted by law in order to protect other people's rights, the democratic set-up of the state, as well as the security and well-being of the whole society. Article 105 provides that the right to private property can also be restricted in accordance with the law. These new articles in addition to the newly created Constitutional Court have paved the way for judicial protection of human rights, which, although somewhat belated, has reinforced democratic consolidation in Latvia.

Conclusions

The initial period of the transition of all post-communist democracies has been marked by the emergence of numerous political parties, although only a few of them can really be considered similar to the traditional political parties as they are known in the West. Elections in the new democracies have been largely free and democratic, but these elections do not necessarily guarantee regime stability. Latvia's experience is a notable example, in which elections resulted in a divided parliament in which coalition governments were formed with great difficulty. The lesson gained from these transitions is that building a democratic society takes time, requires a lot of determination and effort, and is costly for most participants. Therefore, the fact that Latvia's period of institutional engineering was relatively long may have seemed frustrating to some, but at least one benefit of the protracted period was the high level of legitimacy enjoyed by the new regime.

High legitimacy is, after all, what has kept Latvia on the democracy-building track despite its many problems. The process of political self-definition is still continuing, and has affected the chances for stable long-term economic and political planning. Popular participation in the processes of government, while very active in the early years of independence and the 1993 parliamentary elections, has diminished considerably in the following years. Ordinary citizens have doubts as to the quality and trustworthiness of their political representatives and their mistrust and cynicism over the political process is widespread. The gap between the ruling elite and the population, if compared to the critical years of the struggle for independence, has widened significantly, despite the loudly professed declarations of equality and democracy. Rhetoric seems to dominate over the efforts to improve reality. While prosperity for a few has arrived with miraculous speed and abundance, the standard of living for a large majority of the population has declined dramatically. When the problem for many is simple survival, there is little inclination or time for acquiring knowledge about lofty principles of human rights, for the learning of democratic skills, or for participation in the building of civil society. Nevertheless, by passing necessary constitutional amendments, such as extending the parliamentary term and constitutionally incorporating human rights, the democratic regime has survived and has taken steps to reinforce parliamentary and government stability as well as to mend the gap between state and citizen.

Institutional Engineering in Lithuania: Stability through Compromise

Nida Gelazis

Lithuanian constitution drafters could have been following the advice of several constitutional scholars in the West who claimed that quickly adopting an amendable constitution is preferable to indefinitely wrangling over the details.[1] This is not to say that the Lithuanian Constitution was drafted in an environment of relative harmony, but that drafting and adopting a constitution, however imperfect, was ultimately valued more highly than postponing the process. In large part, the quick-fix Constitution was a result of Lithuania's postcolonial status: by legally legitimizing its independence from the USSR and clearly distinguishing itself from the NIS countries, Lithuania could make its way back to 'Europe'. This is observed in other post-communist states seceding from federal structures; not only the other two Baltic states, but also Slovakia and Slovenia saw adopting a new constitution quickly as the way to boost their legitimacy—and prove their democratic intentions— as independent states in the international community, in the hope of securing themselves from possible reannexation.

Deep political conflict during constitution-drafting is clear from the compromise inherent in the system that was adopted. After months of bickering, the presidential and the parliamentary blocs finally settled on a semi-presidential system. Other important but contentious decisions were postponed for the legislature to decide. But the compromise did not put the separation of powers principle in jeopardy. Though somewhat clumsy, the institutions are well balanced and, due to tinkering with the electoral laws, parliamentary

[1] See Jan Zielonka, 'The New Institutions in the Old East Bloc', *Journal of Democracy*, 5/2 (Apr. 1994), 88.

majorities were formed rather easily and no major power struggles between institutions have ensued.

The quick fix also meant that regime creation was an elite decision. Public debate of the draft was remarkably limited and brief and referendum participants were basically expected to vote for any draft that was put before them.[2] This elite hoped that the draft's legitimacy would come from the process of its creation, namely, the expert committees set up to develop a Lithuanian constitutional tradition from the three (basically irreconcilable) inter-war constitutions. This legitimacy would seem rather weak, given that the inter-war 'democracy' in Lithuania—with its aversion to liberalism and propensity towards fascism—was hardly a model for the new post-communist state to follow. Yet in the absence of a guiding state interest or consolidated civil society, hearkening back to Lithuania's 'golden past' was a tool for concealing individual preferences and partisan interests.[3] And in picking and choosing from the various institutional models available, the new institutional system created by the 1992 Constitution has no resemblance to any of the inter-war regimes. One positive outcome of focusing on the structures of the inter-war state was the lesson learned regarding balance of powers. The compromise eventually reached between the parliamentarist and presidentialist blocs did not jeopardize the stability of the system created and power balance was the priority.

Although the short-term benefits of a quick adoption seem quite clear, the medium-term situation is less favourable. The combination of vague popular consent for the general principles of the constitution and the facility with which constitutional laws can be changed has led to a situation in which politicians easily succumb to populist tendencies. While the legitimacy of the Constitution has rarely been questioned since its adoption and the peaceful transfer of power from one party to another has followed each election, the Constitution has not adequately addressed perhaps the most important goal of the transition. Stephen Holmes has identified this as 'the creation of a government that can pursue effective reforms

---

[2] See 'Constitution Watch', *East European Constitutional Review*, 1/1 (Spring 1992), 5.

[3] '[D]esigners of institutions shy away from accepting responsibility in public for what they are really doing, and that they tend to hide instead behind the often rather fictive notion of imitation or transplantation.' See Claus Offe, 'Designing Institutions in East European Transitions', in Robert E. Goodin (ed.), *The Theory of Institutional Design* (Cambridge: Cambridge University Press, 1996), 213.

while retaining public confidence and remaining democratically accountable'.[4] In Lithuania, democratic accountability will come not only with adequate legislation but also with the development of an active civil society which develops and articulates social interests and goals of the state.

Lithuania's 'Legal Path'

The adoption of the 1992 Constitution represented the penultimate step in what Vytautas Landsbergis has often called Lithuania's 'legal path to independence'.[5] The 'legal path' was chosen not only because of its peaceful, democratic qualities that were believed to be necessary to gain Western sympathy and support. It might be argued that this method was not chosen at all, but was in fact the only hope for independence. Current MP and former Constitutional Court justice Stasys Staciokas recalled that the 'legal path' was born out of the realization that Moscow was more inclined to give in to requests supported by legal reasoning.[6] Therefore, by persuading Soviet legal experts and communist bureaucrats to enter its ranks, the Sajudis Popular Front was able effectively to force its independence goals using routine procedures and tactics to extract services from the central government in Moscow.[7] With this in mind, the sequence of events leading to the adoption of the Basic Law in 1990 can be seen as deliberate and tactical.

After Mikhail Gorbachev's introduction of the glasnost pro-gramme the Sajudis Popular Front was created. By deleting Article 6 (which granted the Lithuanian Communist Party primacy) from the LSSR Constitution, the Supreme Soviet opened the door for Sajudis members to run for office in what became the first multi-party elections of December 1989. When Gorbachev visited Vilnius in January 1990 and met with the new Sajudis majority in the

---

[4] Stephen Holmes, 'Back to the Drawing Board', *East European Constitutional Review*, 2/1 (Winter 1993), 23.

[5] Lecture by Vytautas Landsbergis, 'Chechnya's Secession from Russia', given at the University of Chicago Law School (Feb. 1995).

[6] Interview with Stasys Staciokas, Vilnius, Oct. 1996.

[7] See Algis Krupavicius, 'Pokomonistine Transformacija ir Lietuvos Partijos' (The Postcommunist Transformation and Lithuania's Parties), in Algis Krupavicius, Povilas Gaidys, Kestutis Masiulis, et al. (eds.), *Politines Partijos Lietuvoje* (Political Parties in Lithuania) (Vilnius: Litterae Universitatis, 1996), 41.

Supreme Council, he also adopted legal tactics when attempting to slow down the independence process. Gorbachev promised to consider amendments to the USSR Constitution that would allow the eventual secession of Soviet republics from the USSR. But Sajudis leaders found another way. By arguing that Lithuania's inclusion in the USSR Constitution was the result of a secret pact between Hitler and Stalin (which had long been declared illegal by the international community) Sajudis leaders asserted that the Soviet Constitution did not apply to Lithuania, and any amendments made to the Soviet Constitution would be irrelevant.[8] This led the way for the Sajudis majority in the Supreme Council to pass the declaration of independence on 11 March 1990. In order formally to bridge the fifty-year gap between the internationally recognized constitutional democracy that existed during the inter-war period, Sajudis leaders immediately reinstated the 1938 Constitution (the last of three constitutions adopted during the twenty-two-year inter-war independence period).[9] There were two reasons why the symbolic readoption of the pre-Second World War Constitution was important. First, after its declaration of independence, no influential Western democracy acknowledged the Republic of Lithuania. Therefore, Lithuanian leaders continued to work as they had, making sure that no legal loophole remained which Moscow might find to draw Lithuania back into its net. Secondly, by cooperating with the Sajudis movement, the Lithuanian Communist Party had not lost its public credibility or democratic viability and therefore might have insisted on retaining the Soviet Constitution as the basis for an independent 'Lithuanian Soviet Republic'. Sajudis needed to assure the West that it was determined to create a liberal democracy in Lithuania. Less than one hour after the reinstallation of the 1938 Constitution, the Supreme Soviet adopted the Provisional Basic Law, which served as an interim constitution for nearly two years. In an effort to avoid calling new elections and to maintain the stability of the current government, the Basic Law resembled the Lithuanian Soviet Constitution in its provisions concerning institutions and power structures.

---

[8] Lieven's account of the events in 1990 reflects the dissonance over the viability of this tactic for gaining independence among the Lithuanian elite as well as their miscalculation in terms of gaining immediate international support for this course of action: Anatol Lieven, *The Baltic Revolution: Estonia, Latvia, and Lithuania and the Path to Independence* (New Haven: Yale University Press, 1993), 230–44.

[9] See 'Constitution Watch: Lithuania', *East European Constitutional Review*, 1/1 (Spring 1992), 5.

Drafting the Constitution

As early as 7 November 1990 the presidium of the Supreme Council formed a special Constitutional Committee to come up with a 'constitutional concept' which was to serve as the basis for future constitutional drafts and debates. Besides inviting Supreme Council deputies, the presidium also brought in legal specialists from outside the legislature and Soviet judiciary to participate in the Committee. Attendance lists include deputies, representatives of the Procuracy, the Cabinet of Ministers, intellectuals from universities and research organizations, and other members of the judiciary. Although a 31 December 1990 deadline was given by the presidium, the document produced by the working group, called the 'concept sketch', was finally presented to the Supreme Council on 25 April 1991.

The sketch not only served as the blueprint for future constitutional drafts, but also foreshadowed which constitutional issues would be the most contentious during parliamentary debate. The Committee members attempted to produce a single constitutional concept from the three constitutions adopted during the inter-war period. This was a formidable task considering that the 1922 Constitution created a strong parliamentary system, while the 1938 Constitution was a Lithuanian version of fascism.[10] The problems associated with readopting either alternative were obvious to most participants, but a viable compromise initially seemed to elude everyone.

Lithuania's Inter-war Constitutional Tradition

The 1922 Constitution granted the Seimas extensive powers. Besides being the sole law-making body in the government, the parliament was required to ratify nearly all international treaties, as well as declare war or peace. The Seimas was given the right to elect the president and control the Cabinet of Ministers, as well as the opportunity to dismiss either by a two-thirds vote. In contrast to other parliamentary systems, the president could dissolve

---

[10] For a description of Lithuanian anti-liberal thought in the inter-war period, see Leonas Sabaliunas, *Lithuania in Crisis: Nationalism to Communism 1939–1940* (Bloomington: Indiana University Press, 1972), esp. 32–4.

the parliament but was required to resign as soon as a new assembly was elected. Although the president was given decree power,
all presidential acts required the countersignature of the prime
minister. The Seimas's monopoly of power was absolute, and
since no provision had been made for arbitration of disagreements
between the branches of power, the inherently suicidal regime toppled quickly.

The next inter-war Constitution was adopted in 1928 with the
condition that it would be in force for a ten-year trial period before
needing to be ratified by parliament.[11] To a great extent, the 1928
Constitution resembled its predecessor, with a few changes added.
The president was given legislative power in between Seimas
sessions, without the condition that the parliament should ratify
those laws once its session reconvened. This Constitution also created a vehicle for arbitrating disagreements between the branches
by holding referenda to resolve contentious issues. The combination of giving the president legislative power in the absence of the
Seimas and the ten-year trial period resulted in an extraordinary
regime: for the next eight years, the president ruled, in line with
the Constitution, not only by fulfilling the duties given to the president but, since he never called parliamentary elections, by performing the duties of the parliament as well. Not surprisingly,
when the Seimas was finally elected, the Constitution was quickly
thrown out.

In what was probably an effort to constitutionalize a *fait accompli*,
the 1938 Constitution formally instituted a presidential system.[12]
Like the 1928 Constitution, the new Constitution extended the terms
of both the Seimas and the president from three years to five. The
directly elected president had the right to dissolve the parliament,
but the Seimas could dismiss neither the president nor the cabinet. The Seimas and the president were given legislative powers,
but all Seimas laws needed to be promulgated or vetoed by the
president. Referenda were employed once again to arbitrate disagreements between the branches as well as to ratify constitutional
amendments. In order to institute a certain amount of longevity
to this basic law, more complicated amendment procedures were
adopted.

[11] See Leonas Sabaliunas, *Lithuania in Crisis: Nationalism to Communism
1939–1940* (Bloomington: Indiana University Press, 1972).
[12] Ibid. 34.

The Constitutional Concept Sketch

The tenacity displayed during Lithuania's fight for independence was once again displayed by the Committee in attempting to fulfil Sajudis's promise of reinstating inter-war 'democracy'. Despite the unfeasible task of meshing the three constitutions of Lithuania's 'golden past' the Constitutional Committee was committed to producing the missing link of the country's constitutional evolution. With all the options it had to choose from, the Committee decided to create an essentially parliamentary system, but stressed the importance of checking the Seimas's power. In those instances where no consensus was reached in the Committee, the sketch included alternative projects next to the contested articles. The Seimas was deemed the sole legislative power, responsible for adopting the tax code and state budget, and creating local administrative territory units. It would hold a vote of confidence in the president's choice for prime minister and cabinet, as well as other president-appointed offices.

The Seimas could be comprised of 99 or 141 deputies, for a term of either four or five years.[13] No provisions to dissolve the Seimas were included. A Seimas-elected president was offered as an alternative project to a directly elected head of state, although the sketch did include a provision to allow the Seimas to impeach the president. The president was given the power to appoint the prime minister, promulgate or veto Seimas-adopted laws, call Seimas sessions, deal with foreign policy issues with the help of the foreign minister, declare states of emergency (with Seimas approval), and decree power with approval from the prime minister.[14] The Cabinet of Ministers was put under the control of the Seimas.[15] Like the 1938 Constitution, the Committee's sketch included complicated constitutional amendment procedures, requiring that a referendum be held in order to change certain articles.[16]

The Committee's most drastic departure from the inter-war constitutions was in its chapter on the judiciary.[17] Throughout the inter-war period, the courts were seen as secondary to the task of governing. The thought that the courts could arbitrate during

---

[13] See 6–7 of 'Lietuvos Respublikos Konstitucija: Koncepcijos Metmenys' (The Constitution of the Republic of Lithuania: Conceptual Sketch) (7 Nov. 1990), available from the archives of the Lithuanian Seimas.

[14] Ibid. 8.   [15] Ibid. 10.   [16] Ibid. 12.   [17] Ibid. 11–12.

conflicts between the other branches had never before been considered. The sketch created the institution of a constitutional court,
consisting of nine judges, for the sole purpose of guaranteeing that
the president, cabinet, parliament, and other courts would correctly
implement the Constitution.

When the Committee presented its concept sketch to the
Supreme Council in April 1991, many articles were vague and incomplete. However, it is impossible to dismiss the document entirely.
First, it is important to note that a parliamentary system was
favored by a committee that was not purely comprised of Council
deputies. Second, the Constitutional Court as well as the new importance given to the judiciary in general were preserved in the final
constitutional draft. Finally, no matter how superficial the link to
the past was, the references to the inter-war constitutions were
symbolically important as an instrument to push through the
quick adoption of a new constitution.[18]

Two Constitutional Drafts

Eight months passed after the conceptual sketch was delivered
to the Supreme Council and the Constitutional Commission was
formed. Although the Supreme Council successfully led the country through the Soviet economic blockade and Soviet tank attacks,
it never learned to function effectively as a parliament. The newness of democracy, the inexperience of the deputies, and the splintering of Sajudis completely stalled the work of the Supreme Council. Nearly all of the time during Council sessions was allotted
to discussing and amending the standing orders. Questions of
accountability for economic reform measures would invariably end
in the resignation of the prime minister—subsequently the office

[18] Offe, 'Designing Institutions'. Offe asserts that 'it does not help the viability
and operative success of newly designed institutions if they are perceived by
others as actually being newly designed. The designer, if seen as such, will
unavoidably come under the suspicion of trying to impose his partisan interest or
normative point of view upon the broader community, and that suspicion alone,
unjustified though it may be in some cases, may invalidate the recognition and
respect of the new institution and prevent it from unfolding its socializing function. It is as if the man-made and hence contingent nature of institutional change
must be denied and artificially "forgotten." Otherwise, the example of the designer
will invite others to attempt a different design, the consequence being an overload
of contingency, complexity, and uncertainty which contradicts the essence of what
we mean by an institution' (at 214).

changed hands three times in less than two years. After two years of institutional chaos, the Supreme Council finally addressed the need to adopt a new constitution. On 11 February 1992 the Supreme Council adopted the law 'On Constitution Drafting' which instituted a strict schedule for the adoption of a constitution. The Council created the Constitutional Commission, which was empowered to draft a constitution according to the conceptual sketch. The Commission's draft was to be presented to the Council by the end of March, then debated, amended, and adopted by October 1992.

While the Constitutional Commission worked to meet its deadline, newly formed non-parliamentary parties (most prominently the Liberal Party) and the Sajudis Popular Front, which had lost most of its support in the Council, coordinated their efforts to participate in the constitution-drafting process. At first, Sajudis hoped to influence the process by organizing a referendum on its draft amendment to the Provisional Basic Law. The amendment would have created the office of the president. The proposed law envisioned a directly elected president who would serve a five-year term. Presidential candidates were required to be between 40 and 65 years of age, Lithuanian 'by blood', and to have lived in Lithuania for at least the last ten years.[19] The amendment would also have given the president broad powers to dissolve the government and the Supreme Council, as well as to stop any government decree he or she deemed unconstitutional. The purpose of this referendum was twofold. First, Sajudis hoped to automatically increase the power of its leader Vytautas Landsbergis over the renegade Supreme Council deputies. Second, with a majority of citizens voting in favour of a strong presidency, Sajudis would have gained leverage in adopting a more presidential constitution than envisioned by either the conceptual sketch or the Commission's constitutional draft. The referendum failed due to low voter turnout, but since those who did vote clearly favoured the proposal, Sajudis felt that enough voters had voiced their opinion to require the Commission's draft to be changed. After the failure of the referendum, Sajudis urged support for the Liberal Party's draft Constitution, which it quickly renamed the Sajudis draft. In a final assault on

---

[19] The last requirement was aimed at shutting out Second World War Lithuanian émigrés from elections. As was later demonstrated by Valdas Adamkus's successful bid for the presidency in 1997, émigré leaders are seen by the public as legitimate candidates, 'unsoiled' by the Soviet past, and therefore quite popular as political leaders.

the Council, Sajudis collected signatures calling for its dissolution. Although two years remained in its term, the Supreme Council voted to call pre-term elections, which were held simultaneously with the constitutional referendum.

Remarkably, the Commission's draft was substantially altered during the summer of 1992 in an effort to comply with some of the Sajudis draft's articles. With only twelve days remaining before the 25 October elections, Council members voted to adopt the constitutional draft. During the final debates, which were held during an extraordinary session, almost every deputy voiced bitter resentment at the way in which the draft had been created and debated. Despite these reservations and unresolved created, deputies representing various opposing factions conceded that this was the best chance for adopting a constitution in the near future and, since the Council of Europe requires it of its members, Lithuania needed to adopt a constitution as soon as possible.[20] The draft was adopted by the Council on 13 October 1992, but hardly any time remained for public debate. Voters had a chance to familiarize themselves with the draft only when it was printed in the daily newspapers. Finally, on 25 October 1992, the Constitution was approved by 56.7 per cent of the electorate.

The 1992 Constitution

The Lithuanian Constitution could be categorized as a quick-fix constitution, not only because the decision to adopt it seemed rather spontaneous, but also because it represents a compromise between two major rival forces in the first democratically elected Supreme Soviet. The indecision of this period coupled with the demand that a constitution be quickly adopted resulted in a constitution that is neither strictly parliamentary nor presidential, an electoral system that is neither strictly proportional nor single-candidate majoritarian. Lithuanian constitution drafters dutifully incorporated internationally prescribed norms into the draft, but failed decisively to engineer a new institutional structure that would match the needs of the country—or for that matter even argue convincingly what the needs of the country are. Perhaps what has been created is the ultimate stop-gap[21] constitution: one in which nearly all alternatives

---

[20] See Parliamentary Record, *Lietuvos Respublikos Auksciausia Taryba*, first call, sixth session (12 Oct. 1992), 65.

[21] Holmes, 'Back to the Drawing Board'.

are present, and for which, after a few years of testing and institutional learning on the part of politicians, the advantages of one form of government over the other may become clear. Presumably, by that time, a constitutional amendment could be adopted to favour one or another institutional system. But in order to promote stability (another element the inter-war constitutions lacked) the drafters developed challenging amendment procedures, making the Lithuanian Constitution rather difficult to change.

Although the constitution drafters caved in to Sajudis demands that the president's powers be expanded, the Seimas of the 1992 Constitution does not have decreased powers in comparison with the Seimas of the Commission's draft. In the final draft, the president was simply given limited power to check the Seimas. For example, the first article in the Seimas chapter of the Commission's draft referred to the Seimas as the 'highest representative and sole legislative branch of power, which is accountable only to the nation'.[22] No such article exists in the present Constitution and it therefore more closely resembles a traditional European parliamentary system, where the president and parliament are made to cooperate by instituting checks on each branch's power. It has been argued that such a system of 'mutual dependence'[23] helps create a more stable system. Since the Constitution's adoption, the Seimas has been quite cooperative with the president, but the reasons for that have more to do with the majority party in parliament than with institutional structure.

In 1993, after voting in the ex-communist Lithuanian Democratic Labour Party (LDLP) majority in the Seimas, voters chose Algirdas Brazauskas as president. In line with Article 83 of the Constitution, Brazauskas formally suspended his activities in the LDLP by resigning as the party's head. Despite his break with the party, Brazauskas very rarely conflicted with the Seimas majority, and the presidency maintained a low profile during contentious parliamentary debates. He used his right to veto parliamentary decisions sparingly: out of nearly 1,000 laws that had been passed between 1993 and 1996, Brazauskas vetoed only 23. And although an absolute majority vote by the Seimas may overturn a presidential veto, in 17 of the 23 cases, the LDLP majority chose

---

[22] Art. 56 of the Commission's draft constitution.

[23] See Alfred Stepan and Cindy Skach, 'Constitutional Frameworks and Democratic Consolidation: Parliamentarism versus Presidentialism', *World Politics*, 46/1 (Oct. 1993), 1–22.

to add the president's changes to the vetoed laws before passing them once again.[24]

The first time Brazauskas stepped in to try to stabilize the government was during the bank crisis in the winter of 1995. When it was exposed that Prime Minister Adolfas Slezevicius had retrieved his deposit from a bank a day before the activity of the bank was suspended, several ministers resigned in protest at the PM's behaviour. When Brazauskas advised Slezevicius to resign, the prime minister did not obey, but waited for support from his party in parliament. Only when the LDLP could not salvage the situation did Slezevicius finally quit his position.[25]

Having lost party support after the 1996 parliamentary elections, when the right-wing Homeland Union-Conservatives of Lithuania (HU-CL) replaced LDLP's Seimas majority, Brazauskas's influence became increasingly imperceptible. Although the HU-CL is one of the offshoots of the Sajudis party, any previous commitment to a strong presidency its members may have had disappeared when they took over the Seimas. Once again, Brazauskas's compliance with the Seimas had little to do with constitutionalized powers of the president but was more a result of party politics.

Electoral Laws

The question of what type of electoral formula to adopt in 1992 was just as contentious as choosing a parliamentary or presidential system. Since the 1922 Seimas was elected through a purely proportional system and the 1938 assembly through a first-past-the-post multi-district scheme, the 1992 Council chose to compromise again. Consequently seventy Seimas deputies are elected by a single-district proportional system, while the remaining seventy-one are directly elected in separate electoral districts. If after the first round of elections no single candidate garners support from

[24] After the 1996 parliamentary elections (in which the LDLP lost substantially to the right-wing parties) President Brazauskas's ability to influence legislation dropped significantly. In the nine months remaining prior to presidential elections, Brazauskas vetoed eight laws, all of which vetoes were quickly overturned by the parliament. See Alvidas Lukosaitis, 'Parlamentas ir Parlamentarizmas Nepriklausomoje Lietuvoje. 1918–1940 ir 1990–1997 m.', in Algis Krupavicius (ed.), *Seimo Rinkimai '96: treciasis 'atmetimas'* (Elections to the Seimas '96: The Third 'Round') (Vilnius: Tverme, 1998), 25.

[25] See 'Constitution Watch: Lithuania', *East European Constitutional Review*, 5/1 (Winter 1996), 14–16.

at least 50 per cent+1 of the electorate, a second round is held between the top two candidates. For the proportional half of elections, parties must submit lists of their candidates, and seats are distributed to those parties who receive at least 4 per cent of the vote. For parties representing ethnic minorities, this threshold was reduced to 2 per cent.[26]

In preparation for the 1996 Seimas elections, several amendments were made to the 1992 electoral law. The changes reflect an intention by the Seimas to reduce the number of political parties in the future, but also exhibits the low public sympathy for minority rights. The threshold was increased to 5 per cent for all parties (including ethnic minority parties) and 7 per cent for two-party coalitions. State campaign funding, previously offered to all registered political parties, is now issued only to parties that hold seats in parliament. Campaign financing limits were also increased from 140,000 lits to 700,000 lits.[27] Despite these efforts, the number of parties represented in the 1996 Seimas did not decrease. Although smaller parties did not win as many seats as they had in the past, one or sometimes two representatives were able to enter parliament through the multi-district direct elections. The sole representative of an ethnic minority was directly elected by a predominantly Polish district outside Vilnius.

Political Parties

Most of the strong political parties active today have gained their popularity through links to parties of the past. The most obvious example is the LDLP, which has clear ties to the Lithuanian Communist Party. Before he was voted into the presidency, Algirdas Brazauskas was the head of the LDLP. Before Lithuanian independence, Brazauskas had been the first secretary of the Lithuanian Communist Party (LCP). Like many communist leaders, Brazauskas actively participated in the Sajudis movement. As the head of the LCP, Brazauskas took credit for being the first national communist party leader in the USSR to break off from the Moscow party centre—a move that was subsequently copied by Communist Party branches throughout the USSR. By actively

---

[26] For an in-depth study of the 1992 electoral law and electoral outcomes, see Terry D. Clark, 'The Lithuanian Political Party System: A Case Study of Democratic Consolidation', *East European Politics and Societies*, 9/1 (Winter 1995), 41–62.

[27] The lit is pegged to the US dollar at a 4 : 1 ratio.

participating in the independence movement, the communists were able to maintain their legitimacy as a political party. Support for the LDLP in the 1992 Seimas elections came from diverse social sectors. Using the old LCP networks, the LDLP was able to garner support from already organized groups, such as unions and communal farms, in what was otherwise an unconsolidated civil society. With the Sajudis movement continuing to splinter into new political parties and an inexperienced parliament floundering on policy decisions, the LDLP was seen by many as a better alternative.

Between 1992 and 1996, the opposition worked towards destroying the LDLP's credibility by accusing party members of corruption and incompetence. Insinuations were easy to make since many communist leaders seemed to make enormous profits from the transition to liberal democracy. The absence of conflict of interest laws early on meant that the predominant strategy for success in business was through politics, since government officials and business tycoons worked together to cash in on privatization while promising government aid to the unemployed and destitute. When Prime Minister Adolfas Slezevicius was found to have withdrawn his investment in a bank days before it was closed by the central bank, the single act effectively proved all previous insinuations of LDLP corruption to be true. LDLP made a pitiful showing in the 1996 elections, winning only 12 of its previous 70 seats in the Seimas.

The big winners in the 1996 elections were parties with clear ties to the Sajudis movement. Among those parties, the HU-CL is the party that most closely resembles Sajudis and the views of its celebrated leader, Vytautas Landsbergis. Its rhetoric borders on nationalist populism—the HU-CL prides itself on its struggle to maintain a moral, Catholic society while adopting traditionally social democratic economic principles. It hopes to soften the blow of painful economic reform by fostering sentiments of national unity and sacrifice for Lithuania.

Three other Sajudis offshoots are the Christian Democrats, Social Democrats, and the Centre Union. The first two are reincarnated parties from the inter-war period. The Christian Democrats have formed a coalition with the HU-CL and will probably be the most influential of the minority parties, even though their politics do not differ strongly from the other two. Parties prey on public confusion and the result is a party system committed to promoting individual candidates instead of clearly stated ideological convictions. Parties with clearly stated political ideologies and economic policies, like the Liberal Party, have never been able to win enough seats in parliament to make a difference.

The Constitutional Court and Basic Rights

The second favourite vehicle of the parliamentary opposition besides referenda is petitioning the Constitutional Court. Often the cases brought to the Court have been petitions by groups of minority MPs to review legislation passed by the majority in parliament.

Social and economic rights occupy a prominent space in the Lithuanian Constitution. Just as they had been in the inter-war constitutions, basic rights and freedoms are listed before all the government institutions. Beginning with Article 6 ('The Constitution shall be an integral and directly applicable statue, every person may defend his or her rights on the basis of the Constitution') the Constitution dedicates three chapters to citizens' rights and the state's obligation to help citizens realize them. The Constitution also demands that certain socio-economic rights be provided by the state. For example, Article 39: 'The state shall take care of families bringing up children, render them support'; Article 41: 'secondary, vocational, and higher schools shall be free of charge in public schools'; Article 42: 'support for culture and science, Lithuanian history, art, and other cultural monuments and objects'; Article 45: 'the state shall support ethnic communities'; Article 52 'the state guarantees the right of citizens to old age and disability pension, as well as to social assistance in the event of unemployment, sickness, widowhood, loss of breadwinner, and other cases provided by law'; Article 53: 'the state shall take care of people's health and shall guarantee medical aid and services in the event of sickness. The procedure for providing medical aid to citizens free of charge at state medical facilities shall be established by law'; and Article 54: 'the state shall protect the environment.' Each of the articles listed put demands on the state budget to realize citizens' rights to a prescribed standard of living.

Debates on how these requirements would be met in an economically devastated country, or even why they should be included in the Constitution, were not apparent before its adoption. Perhaps the inclusion of these articles was thought necessary by drafters in order to convince the public that the state would not abandon its commitment to citizen's basic needs under a democratic regime. After all, the Constitution's first test was its adoption by referendum. But the absence of public debates prior to the referendum and the remarkably few cases brought to trial for violations of these rights lead to the conclusion that most citizens are not aware that these rights exist or how to go about defending their rights in court.

One instance in which constitutionalized rights have been publicly challenged occurred in June 1995, when Health Minister Antanas Vinkus came to parliament complaining that only a pitiful part of the budget-allocated funds had actually been delivered to the Ministry of Health.[28] Basing his argument on Article 53, he complained that the Constitution had been violated because the Ministry of Health did not have enough money to ensure that proper health care was offered to Lithuanian citizens or to pay medical staff their meagre wages. Because it did not receive all of the money allocated to the Ministry in the state budget, medical equipment and drugs were purchased from firms on credit. This sent the Ministry deeper into debt, since interest accrued on credit is high and was never taken into account when the state budget was adopted. He predicted that the situation would undoubtedly raise the prices of hospital stays and services. At the time patients were required to pay 4–5 lits per day, while the actual cost swallowed by the hospitals came up to an average of 700 lits per day on each patient. Vinkus reported that citizens were required not only to pay for hospital stays (albeit at extremely low rates) but also to buy their own pharmaceuticals without any aid from the government. Eventually, the Seimas responded by adopting a law which organized a national health insurance scheme, to which employed citizens were required to contribute each month. The new system came into effect on 1 January 1997.

In another highly publicized case, Vilnius University sued the Finance Ministry in 1996 for not issuing money to the university promised in the budget. Although the university operates independently from the state, thus far the budget has allocated money to it every year. VU based its arguments on Article 41 of the Constitution, which guarantees that education will be provided free of charge. Without forwarding the question to the Constitutional Court (Art. 106 allows courts to forward cases involving constitutional questions to the Constitutional Court for deliberation before the lower court makes its final decision) the Vilnius district court decided in favour of Vilnius University and required the Finance Ministry to turn over the outstanding payment. It is important to note that Vilnius University did not bring up the argument that the funding was insufficient to provide higher education free of charge. Although all public schools and universities suffer from insufficient funding, no such case has ever been brought to court.

[28] See *Lietuvos Respublikos Auksciausia Taryba* (June 1995).

Amending the Constitution

During parliamentary debates on the adoption of the Constitution, the only point on which all the factions were able to agree was that the constitutional draft was imperfect. Time and again supporters of the Constitution begged sceptics to look beyond the draft's shortcomings and vote for the draft just so that Lithuania would not lose its place in line for EU membership.[29]

Since its adoption in 1992, proposals to amend the Lithuanian Constitution have generally fallen into three categories: (1) amendments proposed by government institutions either to fix perceived constitutional mistakes or to supplement unclear or incomplete institutional arrangements, (2) politically motivated amendments to pass alternative provisions which failed to be adopted in 1992, and (3) constitutional amendments demanded by international organizations, primarily by the EU association agreement and its protocols.

The first category of amendment proposals stems from government institutions that believe the constitutional provisions concerning their particular branch of power to be either completely inadequate or contradictory. According to Arturas Paulauskas (general prosecutor until 1992 and deputy prosecutor 1993–6), Article 118 is poorly formulated because the framers of the Constitution (parliament) could not clearly conceptualize the function of the Procuracy.[30] Article 118 of the Constitution states that the 'procedure for the appointment of public prosecutors and judges and their status shall be established by law'. Because no decisions were made initially about the status of the Procuracy, the prosecutors' terms in office, and their comprehensive list of duties, Paulauskas argues that the office of the prosecutor is unstable and overburdened with work. In practice, the effect of an inadequately drafted constitutional blueprint for the institution is clear—the staggering backlog of cases has made it impossible for prosecutors to bring suspected criminals to trial quickly. Many cases are tabled for years, which, when coupled with the only recently repealed law on

---

[29] *Lietuvos Respublikos Auksciausia Taryba*, first call, sixth session (12 Oct. 1992), 65.

[30] See 'Konstitucija ir Prokuraturos Statusas Teisingumo Sistemoje' (The Constitution and the Status of the Procuracy in the Judicial System), in *Lietuvos Respublikos Konstitucija: Tiesioginis Taikymas ir Nuosavybes Teisiu Apsauga* (The Constitution of the Republic of Lithuania: Direct Effect and Protection of Property Rights), conference report (Vilnius: Teise, 1994), 13.

pre-trial detention, means that many people are imprisoned for years before their cases can be tried in court. Moreover one of its functions, investigating civil servants' activities for infractions of human rights or corruption, has been also given to the Seimas ombudsman (Art. 73). Therefore the two institutions have been left to figure out for themselves where their powers and responsibilities lie. Citizens with gripes about civil servants are more likely to bring their complaints to local prosecutors, and not to the Seimas ombudsman.

Former Supreme Court chairman Mindaugas Losys argues that Article 61 of the Constitution (which gives MPs the right to submit enquiries to the prime minister, ministers, and other state institutions elected by the Seimas) could allow parliament to question a decision of a judge in a specific case. Therefore because the Supreme Court and the Court of Appeals justices are appointed by the Seimas, Article 61 could be used to justify Seimas interference in the activities of the Court, which is prohibited by Article 114. Already, judges have been brought before Seimas committees to be reviewed for allegations of bribe-taking and corruption. But interference in specific cases before the Court has also been undertaken by certain MPs. Intimidation by Seimas members was particularly evident during the Vytas Lingys murder trial in 1992. Within six months, Boris Dekanidze, one of the leaders of the notorious organized crime gang 'Vilnius Brigade', was arrested, charged, tried, and executed for ordering the murder of journalist Lingys. The case against Dekanidze consisted almost solely of the testimony of the hit man, who escaped the death penalty through plea bargaining. Most legal experts in the country agree that the chances that an innocent man was convicted are quite high. However, little public sympathy exists for the known mafia leader, and the public outcry against the Lingys murder was seen by judges and MPs as a great opportunity to demonstrate publicly their commitment to fighting organized crime.[31]

These two problems, along with the right to 'free' health care and education, are occasionally debated, but no steps have yet been taken to initiate constitutional amendments. An important reason is that little support can be gathered for more freedom of the judiciary. Apathy does not only stem from years of mistrust of the courts in the USSR. Despite arguments put forth in favour of maintaining some influence on courts in order to fight corruption, citizens

---

[31] See 'Constitution Watch: Lithuania', *East European Constitutional Review*, 4/1 (Winter 1995), 16–18.

and parliamentary deputies alike believe that there are more important things to worry about than the freedom of the court. Thus, judges' complaints go unheeded in the Seimas, which is the only government branch that may initiate constitutional amendments (Art. 147).

Since the adoption of the Constitution, several issues which had been contentious in the Constitutional Commission have been revisited by certain political groups. Halfway through its term, the LDLP majority in the Seimas proposed amending Article 55 and shrinking the size of parliament from 141 to 79 deputies. This had been one of the alternative projects in the Constitutional Committee's conceptual sketch. LDLP argued that cutting the size of parliament would save money for the state. After the proposal failed to gain the support of the opposition in parliament, the issue was brought up again in an independent referendum campaign organized by a small group of popular television personalities and politicians. The referendum attempt failed to gather enough voters' signatures and was also dropped. While an argument of saving money for the republic at its own expense might be remarkable by any parliament, the LDLP's motives could have been questionable. The state is already 'saving money' by allowing MPs to serve as cabinet ministers simultaneously. To shrink the Seimas might further shrink the pool of influential political actors, not to mention the representativeness of the government. This issue does not appear to be a priority for the new HU-CL and Christian Democrat Seimas.

Thus far, of all the complaints about the Constitution, the Seimas has responded only to the plight of municipal officials. Although proposals to extend municipal council terms came up during constitution-drafting, at the time arguments for strict centralized control seemed to be more salient. Even before the communist regime, Lithuania had always been a centralized state— an authoritative voice had always come from the capital, in the form of parliamentary legislation and budget decisions, governors appointed by the president, or directives. In line with tradition, local governments under the 1992 Constitution are not strong. Although the centralized state structure was deemed necessary due to Lithuania's small size, at least one other reason exists for keeping the provinces weak. During the independence movement, regions populated by ethnic Poles began using Sajudis arguments to promote their reannexation to Poland. Unfortunately the right to self-determination was reserved for ethnic Lithuanians and their demands were promptly denied. The current chapter on local government not only limits the influence local government can have on the centre, but also prohibits citizens from creating effective representative bodies. In 1995, the LDLP proposed extending the two-year terms of local councils to three or four years. Although the LDLP was unable to garner enough support to amend Article 119 before the summer 1995 elections, after the Homeland Union-Lithuanian Conservatives (HU-CL) won the majority of local council seats, they helped pass the constitutional amendment to extend the term to three years in summer and autumn 1996.

By far the most successful argument for amending the Constitution has been a direct request by the EU. The very first amendment proposal was to allow foreigners to purchase land in Lithuania. LDLP hoped to take advantage of the easier amendment procedures allowed for changes to Article 47. According to Article 153, during the first year of the Constitution amendments to certain articles, including Article 47, required only one reading and only three-fifths support in Parliament. LDLP tried to pass its amendment just as the special regulations were about to expire on 19 October 1993. The attempt ultimately failed, but debates continued for another three years. Lithuania's small size and aggressive neighbours allowed nationalists repeatedly to win debates in favour of closing the doors to foreign investment. However, once the land issue became the primary constitutional barrier to association membership in the EU, the opposition agreed to cooperate with the LDLP majority in drafting an agreeable amendment. The revamped Article 47, which was finally adopted on 20 June 1996, shamelessly allowed the sale of non-agricultural land to foreign citizens from the EU and G-24 member countries only. The law seems good enough to fulfil Lithuania's obligations to the association agreement, but ethnic minority representatives in Lithuania, particularly the Poles, strongly oppose the recent amendment.

Conclusions

Despite the contention surrounding the 1992 Constitution prior to its adoption, the moment it was approved by referendum, the questions surrounding the legitimacy of the drafters and the process were instantly dropped and the new Basic Law was embraced by all political actors. It seems clear that the regime has been further stabilized by the electoral laws, which consistently allow one party to gain a decisive majority in parliament. This majority allows legislation to be easily coordinated with the work of the government ministries, which submit draft laws to parliament for its rubber stamp. The peaceful and smooth transition from one majority to the other through free and fair elections shows that democratic consolidation has occurred in Lithuania.[32] Given the level of conflict within the Supreme Council prior to the 1992 referendum, it seems clear that without the quick adoption of the Constitution, consolidation might have been substantially postponed. Although some scholars have questioned the importance of acting quickly,[33] in Lithuania's case early constitutionalization was inextricably linked with forging its statehood and distinguishing itself from other (non-Baltic) former Soviet satellite states.

Further democratization, however, cannot be assured by the Constitution alone. Charles Gati correctly, I think, remarked that 'Most people in the postcommunist world have already made a choice between order and freedom, and their choice was order.'[34] The Lithuanian institutions have heartily accepted the power granted them by the people, and have enjoyed a relatively stable environment in which to operate. Lithuania's bid to enter the European Union now means that it must push through necessary reforms to meet the EU's obligatory criteria for admission. These forces effectively increase the distance between the people and the state, while leaving little tolerance for deliberation and debate on important issues. The identification of social interests and openness of state decision-making is needed if Lithuania's consolidated democracy is to thrive.

[32] See Guiseppe di Palma, *To Craft Democracies: An Essay on Democratic Transition* (Berkeley and Los Angeles: University of California Press, 1990).

[33] Holmes, 'Back to the Drawing Board'.

[34] Charles Gati, 'If Not Democracy, What? Leaders, Laggards, and Losers in the Postcommunist World', in Michael Mendelbaum (ed.), *Post-communism: Four Perspectives* (New York: Council on Foreign Relations, 1996), 169.

Bulgaria: The (Ir)Relevance of Post-communist Constitutionalism

Venelin I. Ganev

Hardly anyone would dispute the claim that a constitution is the most monumental product of institutional engineering. This consensus, however, dissolves when the impact of constitutionalism on the life of a polity is put under scrutiny. Those who belittle the social impact of constitutions may argue that their significance is trivial, though they have no counterfactual arguments substantiating their claims. Conversely, proponents of fundamental laws may emphasize the close correlation between functioning constitutional mechanisms and benevolent features of communal life, such as peace, stability, and the protection of minorities. These arguments are vulnerable to the charge that they disregard the other factors that may have determined the workings of political institutions.[1]

Prudence demands that every effort to gauge the impact of a constitution be prefaced by the candid admission that such pursuits are tainted by a fairly high degree of speculation. Thus, the most adequate strategy for evaluating the significance of institutional engineering in the post-communist world is to resist the lure of 'either/or' explanatory frameworks and engage in a more sustained effort to delimit spheres of relative success from domains of lingering failures. A closer look at institutional engineering in post-communist Bulgaria might prove helpful in this respect. In the aftermath of an intense period of restructuring of all political institutions, Bulgaria emerged as a consolidated democracy chronically incapable of coping with its social problems or improving

---

[1] For a revealing exchange on this issue, see the challenging arguments of Robert A. Dahl in *A Preface to Democratic Theory* (Chicago: University of Chicago Press, 1956), the quotation is on 135; and the response of M. J. C. Vile, *Constitutionalism and Separation of Powers* (Oxford: Clarendon Press, 1967), 303–12.

its level of economic prosperity. The study to follow will examine the kaleidoscopic ways in which institutional engineering reflects the enduring dilemmas of post-communism. The evidence of this enquiry can only be tentative and inconclusive; but perhaps it will help delineate the limits of constitutionalism as a political project unfolding in a post-communist setting.

Constitutional Choices

As the euphoria of 1989 began to recede, the task of laying down the constitutional basis of the democratic order became the horizon of political thought and action in Eastern Europe. Right from the start political elites—communist and non-communist alike—faced an imposing dilemma: should they proceed quickly with the adoption of a new constitution? Or should they postpone this immense endeavour until the seismic effects of 'the transition' had calmed enough to allow the 'shared vision' of a good constitutional polity to emerge? The former strategy augments the risk that the final product of their collective effort will look more like the hastily scribbled notes of a passionate amateur than the masterpiece of a clairvoyant genius. On the other hand, temporizing may usher in a protracted period of tinkering with an all-but-defunct institutional framework, and eventually foreclose the 'constitutional option' altogether. Apparently Bulgarian political elites spent precious little time plumbing the depths of this conundrum. Almost unanimously and without hesitation they committed themselves to the task of creating and promulgating a new constitution. Bulgaria, then, may serve as a case study of the benefits and disadvantages of a quick-fix constitution, since only twenty months after the palace coup deposing communist dictator Todor Zhivkov (10 November 1989) a new basic law went into effect (13 July 1991).

Consensus on the decision to hold general elections to the Great National Assembly (empowered to adopt a new constitution) was reached during the Roundtable Talks, held between communist officials and representatives of the democratic opposition in January–April 1990.[2] At this early stage, Bulgaria's experiments with institution-building were limited. Attaining a measure of trust and opening up channels of communication between old and new

---

[2] On the Roundtable Talks, see Rumyana Kolarova and Dimiter Dimitrov, 'The Round Table Talks in Bulgaria', in Jon Elster (ed.), *The Roundtable Talks and the Breakdown of Communism* (Chicago: University of Chicago Press, 1996), 178–213.

elites overshadowed concerns about enshrining particular institutional models into a permanent legal framework. Even though the Roundtable Talks precipitated the passage of important amendments to the communist Constitution, the widely shared perception was that none of the existing political institutions was legitimate enough to be entrusted with the task of constitution-making. More basic reform was thus delayed until such time as a popularly elected assembly could be called.

The elections (held on 10 and 17 June 1990) were won by the party of the ex-communists (who renamed themselves the 'Bulgarian Socialist Party' or BSP), who garnered 217 seats in the 400-member Great National Assembly. The other seats were distributed among the major opposition parties, the Union of the Democratic Forces (UDF), with 144 deputies, the party of ethnic Turks, the Movement for Rights and Freedoms (MRF), with 23, and the Bulgarian Agrarian National Union (BANU), with 16). The Assembly clearly possessed 'upstream legitimacy', since it was created in a legitimate way.[3] But with time it became clear that this legitimacy suffered from the Assembly's double mandate: to finalize the text of the Constitution, and to pass ordinary legislation. As the country began to slide into economic and social crisis, the legitimacy of the constitution-making process was adversely affected. The public reasoned that if a group of politicians are incapable of solving the problems of normal politics, there is no cause to expect that they will fare better when confronted with the challenges of constitutional politics. In the short run this functional duality turned out to be as perilous a threat to the legitimacy of the new Constitution as the fact that it was adopted by an assembly dominated by unrepentant ex-communists.

The festering problems of the Great National Assembly were further exacerbated when it became clear that work on the constitutional text had been consigned to the periphery of the parliamentary work. Rather than perfecting the *métier* of institutional engineering, the parliamentary majority indulged in the pleasures of incumbency.

The sluggish work of the Assembly provoked a group of thirty-nine opposition MPs to boycott the Assembly and begin a hunger strike, demanding that a deadline for the adoption of the Constitution be set. This rebellious act succeeded in spurring neo-communist elites into action, but at a high price. It aggravated

---

[3] See Jon Elster, 'Constitutionalism in Eastern Europe: Rebuilding the Boat in Open Sea', *Public Administration*, 71 (1993), 178.

tensions within the UDF, which soon thereafter split into three factions. The most radical faction remained implacably hostile to the new Constitution and refused to sign it, whereas the two moderate factions continued their work along with the ex-communists and successfully brought it to fruition in July 1991. The 'solution' came fairly quickly; it remained to be seen what it would 'fix'.

The Constitution was not endorsed by a popular vote, although interesting stories unfolded regarding its ratification. First, a referendum was scheduled, in order to forestall the allegations of monarchists that any constitution which did not heed popular opinion on the issue of monarchy would be illegitimate. Later, for reasons which remain obscure to this day, the referendum was called off. When the Constitution was finally adopted with the requisite two-thirds majority, President Zhelyu Zhelev refused to sign it.

The new Constitution forcefully corroborates the hypothesis that parliaments that possess the 'pouvoir constituant' usually ensure a strong role for parliament in newly adopted fundamental laws.[4] Article 1 proclaims that Bulgaria is a 'republic with a parliamentary form of government'. Despite the fact that parliament has to share the distinction of 'representing the people' with a popularly elected president, its supremacy is guaranteed by the Basic Law. 'Policy-making' falls squarely within the domain of parliament and the government: the president does not have the power to appoint ministers, cannot introduce draft legislation, and has a weak veto (the veto may be overridden by an absolute majority vote in parliament). At the same time, the president does possess some potential power: the authority to make strategic appointments (ambassadors, four of the twelve Constitutional Court justices, several members of the board of directors of the National Bank, high-ranking military officers, etc.), guaranteed access to the national electronic media, and regular contact with foreign dignitaries and opinion makers. The president cannot be dismissed by parliament (although the president may be impeached by the Constitutional Court pursuant to a motion filed with the Court by no less than two-thirds of all deputies, Art. 103), and parliament can be dismissed by the president only if it fails in three successive attempts to install a government (Art. 99). How exactly this potential power is realized depends upon the character and personality of incumbent presidents, and the strategies employed by political actors leading the other major political institutions. But

---

[4] Ibid. 192.

it is indisputable that fears of possible ascendancy of 'an imperial presidency' are ungrounded.[5]

The Constitutional Court consists of twelve members (the president, the National Assembly, and the assembly of the judges of the Supreme Court of Cassation and the Supreme Administrative Court each appoint four of the justices, Art. 147), and has the power to invalidate laws that contradict the Constitution (Art. 151 in conjunction with Art. 149).

The new Constitution departs radically from its communist predecessor of 1971. Virtually the entire institutional edifice has been refashioned. No signs of what J. Samuel Valenzuela has labelled 'perverse institutionalization' (building into the constitution undemocratic elements such as 'reserved domains' exempt from democratic policy-making, or subordination of elected officials to non-elected elites)[6] can be detected in it. The office of the vice-president seems to be the only vestige of the past to survive the constitution-making process. This office was established in April 1990, i.e. when the old Constitution was amended by the last all-communist parliament in the aftermath of the Roundtable Talks agreements. Its strategic potential became visible in July 1990, when BSP-backed President Petar Mladenov resigned, and the leader of the opposition, Zhelyu Zhelev, was elected president. In a gesture of goodwill (or in accordance with the terms of a secret deal) Zhelev picked Atanas Semerdzhiev, a respected general and member of the moderate faction in BSP, as his vice-president. In 1992 Zhelev ran, and was re-elected, on the same ticket with the famous Bulgarian dissident and poet Blaga Dimitrova. A year later, Dimitrova resigned from office over Zhelev's political quarrels with his UDF partners, and the vice-president's office remained vacant for the rest of Zhelev's term. Bulgaria is the only East European country with a vice-president, and it is plausible to assume that this institution was preserved in the new Constitution simply because it was already 'there'.

Even though the Constitution does not envisage a specific electoral system, proportional representation (PR) has become an

---

[5] For more on the Bulgarian presidency, see Venelin I. Ganev, 'Bulgaria', in Robert Elgie (ed.), *Semi-presidentialism in Europe* (Oxford: Oxford University Press, 1999), 124–49.

[6] J. Samuel Valenzuela, 'Democratic Consolidation in Post-transitional Settings: Notion, Process and Facilitating Conditions', in Scott Mainwaring, Guillermo O'Donnell, and J. Samuel Valenzuela (eds.), *Issues in Democratic Consolidation: The New South-American Democracies in Comparative Perspective* (Notre Dame: University of Notre Dame Press, 1992), 62–7.

basic component of Bulgarian political life. After a brief experiment with a mixed electoral system (deployed during the 1990 elections to the Great National Assembly), Bulgarian political elites opted for a system of proportional representation, with a 4 per cent threshold and a distribution of seats calculated by a version of the d'Hondt method.

Several attempts to amend the Constitution have been undertaken so far, all without success. In 1994, for example, when Prime Minister Ljuben Berov resigned, none of the three parliamentary factions controlled enough votes to elect a new government, and the danger that the deputies would fail to elect a new prime minister in three successive ballots loomed large. President Zhelev promptly announced that if no prime minister was elected he would dismiss parliament, schedule new elections, and appoint a caretaker government, as mandated by the Constitution. At that point, party leaders realized that the Constitution does not contain any provisions regarding parliamentary control during the interim period between governments. In addition to the obvious risks stemming from unbridled executive power, some deputies were haunted by the prospect that for several weeks they would be deprived of their parliamentary immunity and hence exposed to corruption investigations. A proposed amendment establishing some forms of parliamentary control and declaring that all deputies would retain their immunity was passed on a first reading (constitutional amendments are passed by a three-quarters majority of all deputies on three readings held on three different days, Art. 155). Subsequently, however, support for the project began to unravel, and no further steps were taken prior to the dissolution of parliament.

Occasionally leaders of the ex-communist BSP voiced their displeasure with the constitutional arrangements regarding judicial independence and private property. More specifically, they alleged that the courts 'do not follow the will of the people' and that constitutional guarantees of private property inhibit salutary governmental action. But these complaints were never synthesized into legislative initiatives or placed on the parliament's agenda.

Finally, during the second half of his presidency President Zhelev repeatedly expressed the view that Bulgaria should become a 'presidential republic' and that the constitutionally delineated domain of presidential prerogatives should be expanded. This rhetoric, however, did not crystallize into concrete proposals and to this day the concept of 'presidential republic', while still floating in the air, remains murky and ambiguous. Even though some constitutional changes might be necessary if Bulgaria is to join the

European Union (for example, the text which bars foreigners from acquiring ownership of land may have to be lifted), both party leaders and the citizenry at large seem to share the perception that ambitious projects to revamp the Constitution are likely to generate marginal benefits at best, while levying incalculable costs on society as a whole.

Does the fact that a 'quick-fix' constitution worked in Bulgaria authenticate the intrinsic superiority of this strategy, or is Bulgaria's relative success simply the result of a constellation of haphazard events? Those who espouse the latter view may refer to at least one, albeit extremely important, conjunctural factor: the results of the first general and the first presidential elections held under the new Constitution. The UDF faction and incumbent president Zhelyu Zhelev, who won these elections, had boycotted the work on the new Constitution and had refused to endorse it. Only months after instigating mass protest against the adoption of the Basic Law, the UDF elites found themselves victorious in elections organized under the auspices of the Constitution, and in control of all the major institutions it created: parliament, the presidency, and the cabinet. In this situation, their previous claim that a communist-sponsored constitution stands in the way of democracy (or rather 'democrats') became a non sequitur.

Those who prefer the quick-fix solution in principle, however, also may invoke the Bulgarian case. It injected a welcome amount of stability and predictability into a turbulent and volatile environment. Cooperative work on a constitution which fixes the rules of elite competition can serve as what Guiseppe di Palma has called 'a shortcut to habituation'. In other words, the quick-fix constitution may stimulate 'democratic' behaviour in a conflict-ridden milieu and engender a minimum of respect among elites that previously shared nothing but mutual animosity.[7] Indeed, immediately after the passage of the Constitution, one of the potentially most significant elements of the quick-fix solution was achieved: it ensured a peaceful transition of power.

Through the institutionalizing of a comprehensive set of incentives for elite behaviour, the framers brought a civilized 'closure' to burgeoning controversies over alternative constitutional 'models', controversies that are in principle insoluble. As analysts have pointed out, 'arguments for or against a presidential or parliamentary system are inconclusive, while the need for some kind of stable

---

[7] Guiseppe di Palma, *To Craft Democracies* (Berkeley and Los Angeles: University of California Press, 1990), 87.

constitutional order is urgent'.[8] The perception that there are rules and procedures to be followed precedes the realization that the presidency is too weak, or that the Constitutional Court is too strong. Even a tentative and conditional acceptance of a new rule forces elites to surrender the hubris inherent in the search of 'the great defects' of the constitutional text, and to accept the idea that the constitution contains provisions that lend themselves to conflicting interpretations, ambiguities which need clarification, and lacunae which must be 'bridged' by conventions forged in the course of institutionalized elite interaction. In retrospect, even the opponents of the constitution recognize, however begrudgingly, that this first episode in large-scale institutional engineering was an indispensable step towards democratic consolidation.

Constitutional Practices

Did the healthy seeds of the quick-fix solution blossom into a 'mature' Bulgarian constitutionalism? Did institutional engineering in Bulgaria engender a 'developed' political culture? These are, I would argue, questions *mal posées*. They presuppose that emerging political practices in Eastern Europe follow a preordained path from nothingness to a hypothetical state of 'full maturity' and that it is therefore warranted to describe and evaluate them from the abstract vantage point of a 'genuine Western democracy'. Accordingly, the inchoate post-communist political systems are either celebrated as 'moving towards' the Western model, or sternly dismissed as 'stunted' democracies. And almost invariably, Bulgaria falls into that second category—an allegedly hopeless case of a Balkan country in which attempts to construct democratic institutions are doomed to crash on the rocky shores of recalcitrant illiberal culture.[9]

This approach displays numerous shortcomings (its clearly discernible teleological overtones being the most disturbing), but in this context its most conspicuous defect is its tendency to evaluate political systems on the basis of what they lack.[10] Thus the task of

[8] Jan Zielonka, 'New Institutions in the Old Eastern Bloc', in Larry Diamond and Marc F. Plattner (eds.), *The Global Resurgence of Democracy* (Baltimore: Johns Hopkins University Press, 1996), 224.

[9] See, for example, the passages on Bulgaria in Claus Offe, *Varieties of Transition* (Cambridge, Mass: MIT Press, 1996).

[10] See Guillermo O'Donnell, 'Illusions about Consolidation', *Journal of Democracy*, 7/2 (Apr. 1996), 39.

furnishing a cogent description and meaningful interpretation of features that those systems do display is blithely neglected. If the Bulgarian system is found to 'fall short' of the 'Western model', should we then conclude that the country is drowning in an impenetrable 'Balkan' chaos? If Bulgarian political institutions compare negatively when gauged against the performance of their Western counterparts, are they to be dismissed as constitutional accoutrements devoid of substance? If political practices do not live up to 'liberal expectations', should they be shrugged off as 'new wine in old wineskins'? The evidence strongly suggests that the answer to all these questions should be in the negative. At least several important 'rules of the game' have been firmly established; the process of democratic inclusion is underway; and institutional engineering has created 'spaces' of norm-patterned interaction where a new type of political discourse has begun to gel.

Rules and Procedures

At least so far, Bulgaria has been spared one specific type of political turmoil, namely institutional chaos. Although the expression 'war of institutions' is currently in vogue in the country and figures prominently in the self-serving rhetoric of failed politicians, as a description of the mode of contention among various political authorities it is untenable. In fact, disputes over jurisdiction, expansionist institutional strategies, and truculent usurpation of authority are rare occurrences. The subjects of vehement criticism are the ineffective policies of respective institutions, and not these institutions' authority to enact these policies. And sometimes the 'war' is in fact nothing more than the principle of separation of powers in action, as for example when the Constitutional Court declares legislation unconstitutional or parliament overturns presidential vetoes.

On several occasions the leaders of the BSP unleashed egregious attempts to tip the institutional balance in their favour, but so far these campaigns have been successfully stalled by the judiciary. For example, in 1995 the BSP-dominated parliament sought to curtail the president's prerogative to appoint ambassadors by incorporating into its standing orders the requirement that all candidates for an ambassadorship be subjected to 'hearings' and 'approval' by the parliamentary Committee on Foreign Relations. Upon an appeal filed by the president, the Constitutional Court declared this norm void.[11] Similarly, in 1996 parliament declared that the president can only appoint the chairpersons of the Supreme Court of Cassation and the Supreme Administrative Court if the respective decree is countersigned by the Minister of Justice. The Court invalidated this provision as well.[12] The Court has also protected the integrity of parliamentary power by thwarting the government's attempt to raise taxes by decree.[13]

Obviously, a grudging respect for rules and procedures does not in itself bespeak a willingness to cooperate on policy-making. Nonetheless, the rules of the game have so far kept the vituperative skirmishes between politicians from degenerating into a 'bare-knuckles' brawl between institutions. A corollary of the aforementioned developments is the ascendance of an independent judiciary. Arguably the greatest success of the young Bulgarian democracy, judicial independence would have remained a utopian dream had it not been for the establishment of a Constitutional Court and the entrenchment of the principle of irremovability of judges in the Constitution. During their ill-conceived campaign to remonopolize political power in 1993–6, the ex-communists resorted to a variety of techniques to 'cleanse' the judiciary. The 'Law on Judicial Power', passed in 1994, marked the summit of the ex-communists' endeavour to settle accounts with their perceived opponents on the bench. The major objective of the law was to introduce retroactively new eligibility requirements for the country's top judges (needless to say, these requirements were crafted in such a way as to eliminate all judges appointed after 1989) and to dismiss immediately all those who did not qualify. The Constitutional Court declared all provisions establishing the retroactive force of the new law unconstitutional, and struck down a text allowing parliament to dismiss judges 'if their behaviour undermines the prestige of judicial power'. Thus this campaign of the ex-communists came to naught, and the integrity of the judicial system was maintained.[14] In 1996, the BSP decided to wield 'the power of the purse' by slashing financing for the judicial system.

[11] Decision 4/95, published in *Reshenija i opredelenija na Konstitutsionnija Sud na Republica Bulgaria 1995* [Decisions and Resolutions of the Constitutional Court of Republic of Bulgaria] (Sofia: Akademichno izdatelstvo, 1996), 49.

[12] Decision 13/96, published in *State Gazette*, 66/1996.

[13] Decision 3/96, published in *State Gazette*, 14/1996.

[14] For a detailed discussion of these developments, see Venelin I. Ganev, 'Judicial Independence and Post-totalitarian Politics', *Parker School of Law Journal of International Law*, 3/2 (1996), 224 and *passim*.

This amendment was protested by the president and invalidated by the Court.[15]

The prolonged battles surrounding the judicial branch brought into focus another 'engineered' aspect of Bulgarian politics: the imposition of limits on majority tyranny. Needless to say, one of the paramount objectives of each constitution is the containment of despotic majorities, and so far in Bulgaria autocratic aspirations have been successfully tamed. First and foremost this observation holds true in the case of the ex-communists' effort to bar the party of ethnic Turks (MRF) from the national political process, an incident which will be discussed in more detail below. But the saliency of this observation is illustrated by the aborted effort to launch a 'lustration' campaign in Bulgaria. After the opposition won the 1991 parliamentary elections, it passed three consecutive laws imposing various restrictions on the rights of former high-ranking communist officials. The first legislative act, the amendments to the 'Banks and Credits Law', established a five-year ban on appointments of a restricted number of former party functionaries (members of the Central Committee of the Bulgarian Communist Party and secret service agents) to the boards of directors of Bulgarian banks. The second law, an amendment to the 'Pensions Law', declared that time spent on the payroll of the Communist Party and its satellite organizations would not count as employment for the purposes of the pension law. The third law rendered certain members of the *nomenklatura* ineligible for elective positions in Bulgarian universities and other academic institutions (it should be emphasized that all of them kept their tenure and were allowed to continue teaching). Immediately upon their passage these laws were appealed the Constitutional Court, which invalidated the first two; the third was repealed soon thereafter. No legislative initiatives to launch policies that smack of *de jure* discrimination have been undertaken since then.

The taming of potentially despotic majorities in parliament contributed to a general respect for individual rights. At present Bulgaria is a country in which there are no political prisoners and no arbitrary arrests, freedom of speech is respected, freedom of association is vigorously exercised, an independent press is largely accessible, and freedom of religion is guaranteed.[16] Social

[15] Decision 17/96, published in *State Gazette*, 88/1996.

[16] This is not to say, of course, that instances of human rights violations do not occur. The point is, rather, that such abhorrent phenomena—for example, violations of prisoners' rights—do not occur in the proportion and frequency which would substantiate the claim that Bulgarian political practices are 'exceptionally bad' and

rights, however, are consigned to the attic of the constitutional edifice. Bulgaria often cannot provide its citizens with bread, electricity, and central heating, not to mention medical care, timely and consistent payment of pensions, or a clean environment.

This situation is not the intended result of institutional design (allegedly under the auspices of strict monetarism), but in fact runs contrary to the explicit intentions of Bulgarian politicians. When designing a system of constitutional rights, Otto Kirchheimer has argued, framers may resort to one of two strategies: either 'make concessions' and 'reach a compromise' which lends itself to an unambiguous and coherent regulation, or simply amalgamate the wishes of all politicians and create 'a unique linking and acknowledgment of the most varied value systems'.[17] The Bulgarian constitution makers took the second path—and with astonishing zeal at that. As a result, Bulgarian citizens are 'blessed' with an array of rights about which most other nations can only dream. In addition to all classical political rights Bulgarian citizens are entitled to: state assistance in the upbringing of their children (Art. 47.1), the right to work (Art. 48.1), healthy and non-hazardous working conditions, guaranteed minimal pay, rest, and leave of absence (Art. 48.5), the right to strike (Art. 50), social security and welfare aid (Art. 51.1), unemployment benefits (Art. 51.2), free medical care (Art. 52), education (Art. 53), the right to avail themselves of national and universal cultural values and develop their own culture in accordance with their ethnic self-identification (Art. 54), the right to a healthy and favourable environment (Art. 55). The only contentious issue was whether or not to include the term 'social' in the preamble of the Constitution (where Bulgaria is defined as 'a democratic, law-governed, and social state'). Those who favoured the term argued that 'the social component' is indispensable if Bulgaria is to style itself as a modern 'democracy', while those who opposed it maintained that it would serve only as a pretext for maintaining an intrusive state in an autonomous civil society. Ultimately, the text was included in the Constitution, but its impact is impossible to gauge. At any rate, it is hard to find

therefore stand apart from more 'normal' forms of human rights violations observable in other countries. See Venelin I. Ganev, 'Prisoners' Rights, Public Services and Institutional Collapse in Bulgaria', *East European Constitutional Review*, 4/4 (1995), 76.

[17] Otto Kirchheimer, 'Weimar—and What Then? An Analysis of a Constitution', in *Politics, Law and Social Change: Selected Essays of Otto Kirchheimer* (New York: Columbia University Press, 1969), 53–4.

any evidence that it has actually shaped social and economic policies.

Though the secondary role of social rights mirrors economic realities, not constitutional design, the tendency to marginalize these rights is reinforced by two additional factors. The first factor is institutional. Even though Article 5.2 declares that 'the provisions of the Constitution shall apply directly', Bulgarian citizens are not allowed to initiate the procedure of judicial review (this prerogative belongs to one-fifth of the deputies, the president, the Council of Ministers, the Supreme Court of Cassation, the Supreme Administrative Court, and the chief prosecutor, Art. 150). This means that the Court is prevented from developing a body of jurisprudence addressing specifically the problem of 'socio-economic rights'. Theoretically this process may be undertaken by the chief prosecutor, who may assume the functions of an ombudsman, but at present he is under no pressure to do so.

The second factor is jurisprudential. The practice of the Bulgarian Court has shown that the specific domain of socio-economic rights is hard to delineate for a very particular reason: often the actions (or inaction) that violate socio-economic rights also contravene general constitutional principles, and as a rule judges prefer to invoke precisely these principles when deciding constitutional cases. For example, denial of the right to work may also constitute a breach of the principle of equality, while tampering with pension rights may amount to retroactive imposition of duties. This raises the question whether all these rights have a 'content' that is not reducible to or completely overlapping with basic constitutional principles. A political problem compounds the jurisprudential one. Plaintiffs in such cases are politicians who resort to sweeping claims when framing their petitions, which dovetails nicely with the justices' desire to stay 'on stable ground' when declaring legislation unconstitutional. Therefore this dimension of constitutional adjudication remains minimally developed, and what is particularly murky is how potential conflicts regarding the rights of private individuals will be handled.

In sum, at this point socio-economic rights seem to be doubly irrelevant in Bulgaria. They do not impose a burden on politicians, who easily disregard them when designing and financing policies. And they are not a potent source of 'special frustration' pulsating independently of the overall disillusionment with the stark neosocialist economic reality which slowly began to improve only in 1997.

The foregoing analysis of institutionalized interaction, judicial independence, and constraints on majority tyranny warrants the conclusion that—to invoke the conceptual armoury forged by Giovanni Sartori—while the existence of consensus about absolute values is debatable and a consensus at the 'policy level' is at times impossible to reach, 'consensus on regime level', or procedural consensus, is a fact of life in contemporary Bulgaria.[18] It is utterly misleading, then, to insist that Bulgarian politics is 'marked by deep divisions'.[19] To expect it to be otherwise would be pitifully naive; to overdramatize this fact would be to indulge in journalistic sensationalism. The genuinely intriguing thing is that, whether due to a tentative commitment or a careful cost–benefit analysis, the norms of the Constitution have played their assigned role of a scaffolding around which new institutional practices coalesce.

Extended Participation

Institutional engineering in the post-communist environment was driven by the pragmatic self-interest of political elites. But even the most cynical observers would find it difficult to deny that these self-interested actions were meshed with strong democratic values. One example is the political inclusion of various hitherto marginalized and repressed groups. One of the greatest achievements of Bulgarian democracy in the 1990s is the opening of the national democratic process to the sizeable Turkish minority. First and foremost this process was made possible by the tolerant and cooperative behaviour of Bulgarians and ethnic Turks—political leaders and ordinary citizens alike. But it was fortified and 'constitutionalized' by an independent judiciary which 'engineered' it into existence.[20]

Of course, anyone who addresses this issue should feel compelled to comment on the most publicized provision of the new Bulgarian Constitution, namely Article 11.4, prohibiting the formation of political parties 'on an ethnic basis'. This is clearly a discriminatory measure targeted at the Turkish minority. Immediately upon the adoption of the new Constitution, a group of nationalist MPs affiliated with the ex-Communist Party asked the Constitutional

[18] See Giovanni Sartori, *The Theory of Democracy Revisited,* vol. i (Chatham: Chatham House, 1987), 90–1.

[19] For a specimen of this kind of writing, Stefan Krause, 'Problems Remain Unsolved as Government Stumbles Onward', *Transition* (23 Aug. 1996).

[20] For more on this process, Rumyana Kolarova, 'Tacit Agreements in the Bulgarian Transition to Democracy: Minority Rights and Constitutionalism', *University of Chicago Law School Roundtable* (1993), 23–53.

Court to declare the party of ethnic Turks unconstitutional. In a landmark decision, the Court affirmed the constitutionality of the MRF. Since this ruling was issued, at least three Turkish parties as well as a dozen Roma and Macedonian parties have been duly registered and allowed to participate in the political process.[21] Thus, those who hastily argued that the reasoning of the Court is 'tenuous and fragile'[22] were proven wrong: the decision in effect blocked the attempt to ban ethnic parties.

In 1995, the courts staved off another BSP attempt to encroach upon the electoral rights of ethnic Turks in the ethnically mixed south-east region of Kurdzhali. The 1995 mayoral election in the region was won by an ethnic Turk, whereupon the BSP-backed candidate filed a suit alleging electoral fraud. The district court ruled in his favour. MRF appealed to the Supreme Court, the ruling of the lower court was overturned, and the original election results were confirmed. Several days later the ethnic Turk who had been elected originally assumed office without further incident.

In short, Bulgarian political practices have made it possible for previously excluded minorities to reclaim their right to participate in the national political process and to claim judicial protection when their rights are violated. It may very well be true that political institutions, among which one must count the institution of judicial review, are yet to enter the stage of 'full maturity'. But it can hardly be denied that they have created compelling incentives that regulate the behaviour of political elites and 'lead to outcomes similar to those that would occur in other democratic settings'.[23]

New Political Discourse

The effort to construct democratic institutions and structure political behaviour has produced yet another tangible effect: the emergence of a new type of political discourse. Political institutions provide the framework within which party elites jockey for rhetorical power. Gradually, arguments derived from 'the Constitution'

---

[21] There seems to be some confusion about the constitutional status of 'a party of the Roma' which allegedly has been denied registration (as reported by L. Troxel, 'Bulgaria's Gypsies: Numerically Strong, Politically Weak', *RFE/RL Research Report*, 1/10 (6 Mar. 1992). This is an error: after a consultation with the leading human rights organization, the Helsinki Committee, I was able to determine that no such event took place. I wish to thank Ionko Grozev for clarifying this point.

[22] See Elster, 'Constitutionalism in Eastern Europe', 200.

[23] Barbara Geddes, 'Initiation of New Democracies: Institutions in Eastern Europe and Latin America', in Arend Lijphart and Carlos Weisman (eds.), *Institutional Design in New Democracies* (Boulder, Colo.: Westview Press, 1996), 35.

suffused the rhetoric—if not the thinking—of these party elites. The catch-phrases of the communist era—'the will of the people', 'the socialist ideal', 'immediate redress for past injustices', and 'national integrity'—were supplanted by claims anchored in various interpretations of the constitutional text.

An example may illustrate this argument. In the summer of 1996, the BSP nominated Georgi Pirinski as its presidential candidate. Pirinski was born in New York in 1948 and hence became an American citizen. Doubts arose, therefore, whether he met the constitutionally established requirement that the president be 'a Bulgarian citizen by birth' (Art. 93.2),[24] and the issue was brought before the Constitutional Court. Right from the beginning, this problem became enmeshed in two competing discourses. According to the BSP and its satellites, the question was whether or not Pirinski is 'a true Bulgarian'. Consequently, the Court was admonished by the ex-communists to refrain from 'frivolous interpretations' and to take into consideration Pirinski's 'identity' and 'ethnicity'. Conversely, those who detected a constitutional problem with Pirinski's candidacy pointed out that the issue of contention is not his 'Bulgarianness' or 'ethnic identity', but whether he became a citizen by birth or by naturalization. The former argument was rooted in general conceptions about ethnicity, identity, and history, while the latter invoked problems pertaining to eligibility, legally established types of Bulgarian citizenship, and the possible retroactive effect of citizenship laws.

Not surprisingly, the Court employed the second type of language. Without referring to Pirinski by name, the justices ruled that whether or not an individual becomes a citizen 'by birth' should be determined in accordance with the citizenship law in force at the time of birth. In 1948, when Pirinski was born, the communist-sponsored citizenship law provided that children of Bulgarians living abroad did not acquire Bulgarian citizenship by birth if they obtained automatically the citizenship of their birthplace (the

---

[24] This convoluted text reflects the preferences of political opponents who sought to bar potential rivals from the presidential elections scheduled to be held only months after the adoption of the Constitution. The 'citizenship by birth clause' was included at the behest of the anti-communist opposition, which sought the elimination of Andrei Lukanov, a prominent communist who was born in Moscow and held Soviet citizenship before becoming a naturalized Bulgarian citizen. In return, the opposition consented to the inclusion of two additional eligibility requirements: that the candidate must be at least 40 years old (which disqualified Konstantin Trenchev, the influential leader of the 'Podkrepa' trade union), and that he or she must have resided in Bulgaria for at least five years prior to the elections (which rendered ineligible the last Bulgarian tsar, Simeon, who lives in exile in Spain).

intention was to deny Bulgarian citizenship to the children of political emigrants). On the basis of this interpretation, the Electoral Commission concluded that in 1948 Pirinski had acquired American citizenship by birth, and therefore he did not become a Bulgarian citizen by birth but by naturalization. Thus he was declared ineligible to run for the presidency. Upon appeal, this decision was unanimously affirmed by the Supreme Court. Even though the BSP propaganda machine unleashed a vicious blast of vitriolic attacks against the courts, the decision was accepted by the public as an authoritative interpretation of an awkward constitutional provision. Consensus has emerged that the decision shed light on a constitutional technicality that has no bearing upon questions of 'personal identity' or 'ethnicity'.

The foregoing analysis shows that 'institutional engineering' has made a difference in Bulgaria. Whether or not changes in political practices qualify as a 'genuine adoption of Western paradigms' is a question that is likely to be kept on the agenda by Western writers who need highly 'stylized' cases to construct 'models' purporting to map the different routes taken by the former communist countries, or by Central European scholars in whose self-congratulatory analysis countries like Bulgaria are assigned the role of inveterate 'laggards', incapacitated by inborn defects.[25] The fact that changes have transpired, however, is indisputable. As a response to the palpable threat of chaos and arbitrary rule, institutional engineering was successful to the extent that it bolstered rule-governed elite behaviour, predictable patterns of institutional interaction, and respect for rights. As a specifically democratic endeavour, the effort to cement the institutional basis of communal life promoted inclusion and ethnic peace. Finally, the functioning of major political institutions engendered a new political discourse that helped diffuse disruptive conflicts between irreconcilable world views, and thus contributed towards the 'normalization' of highly charged controversies.

Institutional Engineering and Political Crisis

As a political project, institutional engineering is geared towards creating an enduring, stable framework facilitating rule-governed

---

[25] For the latest foray into this odd genre see Tim Snyder and Milada Anna Vachudová, 'Are Transitions Transitory? Two Types of Political Change in Eastern Europe since 1989', *East European Politics and Societies*, 11/1 (1997), 1–36.

elite interaction. Inevitably, however, this framework is exposed to the vicissitudes of turbulent post-communist politics. Coping with acute crisis is one of the most formidable challenges confronting political institutions, and thus far the Bulgarian political system has displayed impressive resilience in times of trouble. A survey of the resolution of the political crisis of December 1996–January 1997 will yield ample evidence to support this claim.

On 21 December 1996, after almost two years in office, the government of BSP chairman Zhan Videnov resigned. By all accounts, this was the most corrupt, inefficient, and inept government, not only in post-1989 Bulgaria but possibly in the entire region. In the aftermath of the 1994 general elections, when the BSP reaffirmed its iron grip on the executive branch, Bulgaria was still considered a fairly stable country with problems more akin to the reformist dilemmas of the Czech Republic than to the travails plaguing Romania. By the end of 1996, Bulgaria had become the poorest country in Europe, with an average monthly salary of $12 and an average monthly pension of $4.[26] The country's grain was shipped abroad by BSP-affiliated 'trading companies' which pocketed hefty profits while the country was thrown into a disastrous grain shortage. BSP-appointed 'bank managers' siphoned millions of citizens' bank deposits into private accounts in foreign banks and then disappeared abroad. Inflation reached 320 per cent in 1996, GNP shrank by 9 per cent, and nothing could stop the national currency's free fall.

Against the backdrop of these catastrophic failures, Videnov's resignation was widely perceived as an implicit admission of guilt and a token of the BSP's willingness to take a new direction. Very soon, however, these hopes began to dissipate. The BSP confidently blamed all disasters on the opposition (which had been out of power since October 1992) and reiterated its determination to continue its rule. This arrogant behaviour by politically bankrupt party leaders finally pushed the limits of popular patience and mighty waves of popular protest spread throughout the country. After years of lethargic 'muddling through', Bulgaria found itself engulfed by a potentially explosive crisis.

Given the focus of this paper, however, I will concentrate exclusively on the functioning of political institutions during these crucial days and show how political conflict was resolved in various institutional settings. The Constitution (Art. 99) establishes the following procedure for solving governmental crisis. Upon

---

[26] See for more data *Democratsija* (31 Jan. 1997).

consultations with all parliamentary groups, the president bestows the mandate to form a government on a prime minister designate, who is nominated by the largest parliamentary party (in the 1996 case, the BSP). Should the prime minister designate fail to complete this task within seven days after being nominated, the mandate is passed on to a prime minister designate nominated by the second-largest party (in this case, the UDF). Should the second prime minister designate fail to accomplish his or her mission within seven days, the task of forming a cabinet is entrusted to a prime minister designate nominated by one of the smaller parliamentary parties (in this case, the People's Union, the MRF, or the Bulgarian Business Block—a populist party). If an agreement is not finalized within seven days, the president appoints a caretaker government, dismisses the National Assembly, and schedules new elections. Given the configuration of forces in December 1996, and specifically the opposition's determination to avoid forming a government that would have to abide by the whims of a BSP-controlled parliament, two outcomes were possible: either a new BSP government, or general elections. Consequently, hundreds of thousands of men and women took part in the daily anti-BSP rallies, demanding that the ruling party give up its mandate to form a government and call elections.

With the intensification of popular protest, two lines of conflict became increasingly visible. The first divide pitted the BSP against everyone else. Most of the BSP leaders, including the infamous Videnov himself, claimed that since their party had a majority in parliament (125 of the 240 seats), it should be allowed to proceed with the formation of a new government. This contention was countered by the forceful claim that if the BSP installed a new government, popular discontent would assume unmanageable proportions. In institutional terms, this conflict pitted the BSP-controlled parliament and cabinet against the presidency, an institution occupied by Zhelyu Zhelev until the end of his term on 21 January 1997, and by Petar Stoyanov (who dealt a crushing defeat to his BSP opponent Ivan Marazov in the November 1996 presidential elections) thereafter. On 8 January 1997, the BSP nominated Interior Minister Nikolay Dobrev as prime minister designate and demanded that he be given a mandate to form a government. Outgoing President Zhelev declined to issue the requisite decree, arguing that since Stoyanov would have to work with the new government, only he possessed the prerogative to confer a mandate. Immediately upon assuming office Stoyanov, an ardent BSP opponent, pledged to fulfil his duty and give a mandate to Dobrev, though personally convinced that the scheduling of new elections was the only viable alternative to total political collapse. On 29 January, Dobrev was presented with a presidential decree authorizing him to form a new government. At this point all institutional hurdles to the formation of a new BSP government were cleared; in anticipation of Dobrev's decision, the interaction between the major political institutions (president, parliament, and government) came to a halt.

In this context, the second line of conflict acquired a special significance: the friction between hard-liners and moderates within the BSP. There were signs that while the majority of BSP leaders were adamantly opposed to any compromise and were prepared to resort to bloody reprisals in order to quell popular protest, an influential minority, led by Dobrev himself, was leaning towards a peaceful solution, inevitably amounting to refusing to form a government. On several occasions the collective leadership of the BSP urged Dobrev to present the line-up of his cabinet to parliament, but he procrastinated, obviously wary of destructive consequences.

The conundrum with which conciliatory politicians had to grapple was how to resolve both conflicts simultaneously without relying on the regular channels of institutional interaction (which were blocked by intransigent BSP hard-liners), and how to draw a veil of legitimacy over an outcome that radicals within the BSP were likely to declare 'non-binding'.

As it turned out, the framers of the Bulgarian Constitution had 'engineered' an alternative institutional site that was brilliantly deployed by President Stoyanov and Prime Minister designate Dobrev to diffuse the impending crisis. Article 100.3 of the Constitution provides that the president presides over a Consultative National Security Council (hereafter 'the Council'), an entity lacking clearly defined prerogatives and constitutional status. On 4 February 1997, after a preliminary meeting with Dobrev (whose mandate to form a government was to expire at midnight the same day), the president summoned the Council and invited all leading politicians in the country (including Videnov and several of his ministers) to take part in it. After deliberations lasting several hours, and despite Videnov's obdurate protest, the Council issued a resolution announcing that the BSP would decline to form a government, that none of the other parliamentary factions would use their mandates for that purpose, and that new general elections would be held in April.

In the past, the Council had been used as a forum where political leaders would exchange views about alleviating looming strife, but it had never served as a decision-making body issuing resolutions regarding the function of other political institutions. In this case, however, the Council's resolution in effect triggered the dissolution of parliament and the formation of a caretaker government appointed by the president. With the benefit of hindsight one may assert that this was a brilliant success: further public protests were cancelled, the caretaker government turned out to be a spectacular success, and the hard-liners suffered a defeat in the intra-party settling of scores within the BSP.

Any generalizations based on this dramatic episode may be far-fetched and unwarranted: it would be ridiculous to assert that peaceful resolution was 'built into' the constitutional design, and there is no guarantee that in the future destabilizing incidents will continue to be peacefully resolved within the same constitutional framework. But several conclusions about the beneficial impact of institutional engineering in Bulgaria may be tentatively offered.

As designed in the Constitution, the procedure for installing a new government—granting a mandate to a single individual who must comply with a pre-set deadline (seven days)—accomplished two objectives coveted by traditional institutional craftsmen. First, it precluded the possibility of a protracted gridlock: parliamentary forces are pressured either to install a new government or accept the dissolution of the National Assembly. The other beneficial impact is more intangible and elusive. By entrusting the momentous decision to a single individual (as opposed to a collective entity like a parliamentary faction or a party's governing body) the framers of the Bulgarian institution sought to counter the strategic calculations inherent in group decision-making with the considerations of an individual who would be held accountable for his or her actions. At least in the case of Dobrev, this insight in political psychology worked quite well: as he pointed out during his press conference on the evening of 4 February, his conduct was motivated first and foremost by his personal determination not to stain his hands with blood. Certainly, no institutional arrangement would pacify an unscrupulous would-be dictator. Nevertheless, forcing the option of stepping down or resorting to massive use of violence against unarmed civilians does seem to create an incentive to negotiate among politicians at least minimally disturbed by the prospect of bloodshed.

The Constitution also 'engineered' an alternative institutional setting where authoritative decisions may be reached when the 'normal' decision-making becomes impossible. The Council did not act as an 'emergency committee' that arrogates to itself 'extraordinary powers'.[27] Rather, its intervention was regarded by all participants, including the BSP, as a legitimate mode of operation by a constitutionally established body whose function is conducive to the continuation of the normal political process. It should also be underlined that the decision reached by various political actors was not a 'pact' in the sense defined by O'Donnell and Schmitter, namely 'an explicit, but not always publicly explicated or justified agreement among a select set of actors which seeks to define (or better, to re-define) rules governing the exercise of power'.[28] The resolution of the Council was presented to the public as a fully transparent act of a state institution resolving a particular conflict without redefining any rules pertaining to the exercise of power. The institutional potential inherent in the Constitution was utilized with a view to furthering the democratic process.

Finally, existing political institutions proved capable of sustaining a balance between adversarial and consensual elements in the decision-making process. Without a doubt, the resolution of the Council reflects the preferences of the anti-communist opposition and does attest in many respects to the political defeat of the BSP. And yet, virtually all rivals made it clear that a decision endorsed by the BSP carries much greater weight and legitimacy. There was a sustained effort on the part of President Stoyanov to cajole Dobrev and to obtain his signature under the resolution of the Council; and when the prime minister designate finally lent his support to this strategy, virtually all leaders of the opposition praised him as a man of integrity and a responsible politician. Thus the defeat of the BSP was perceived as a victory of collective reason, a victory in which the trustworthy BSP leaders participated. Conversely, the conspicuous failure of the hard-liners within the BSP was perceived as a triumph of the spirit of constitutionalism over a neo-Stalinist clique bent on subverting the principles underpinning the constitutional process.

During the January 1997 crisis, the edifice of Bulgarian constitutionalism trembled mightily but did not yield. Mass protest was 'absorbed' by the system without any negative consequences for the institutional framework and without transgressions of constitutional principles. The millions of citizens who were willing to get rid

[27] On the question of emergency powers and post-communist constitutionalism, see Venelin I. Ganev, 'Emergency Powers in the New East-European Constitutions', *American Journal of Comparative Law* (1997).

[28] See Guillermo O'Donnell and Philippe Schmitter, *Transitions from Authoritarian Rule: Tentative Conclusions about Uncertain Democracies* (Baltimore: Johns Hopkins University Press, 1986), 37.

of a thoroughly discredited government used their constitutional rights to do so. And politicians who were willing to resolve these conflicts in a peaceful manner had the requisite institutional instruments at their disposal. What started out as a cacophony of despair ended like a carefully orchestrated symphony of hope.

In Lieu of a Conclusion: The Limits of Post-communist Institutional Engineering

If institutional building has exerted such a positive effect on Bulgarian democracy, then why did Bulgaria under Videnov earn the dubious distinction of being 'the worst managed state in Europe'?[29] Why was Bulgarian society trapped for years in an abyss of intractable socio-economic problems? Why are the lives of so many Bulgarians of all ages and occupations marred by misery and hopelessness?

There are two alternative ways of approaching these questions. One would be to reject out of hand the very idea that Bulgarian politics displays some of the features attributed to 'true democracies' and to disparage the notion that Bulgarian political institutions are anything more than embellishments upon a moribund constitutional body. The other approach would be to acknowledge a paradox: political institutions were successfully installed and do function in accord with pre-fixed rules, and yet Bulgarian society proved vulnerable to a series of excruciating crises. The former answer offers all the certainty and complacent satisfaction inherent in one-dimensional, logical, simple explanatory schemes; the latter invites us to plunge into an array of complex puzzles.

To recognize these puzzles—and I see no reason why they should not be recognized—means to start thinking of institutional engineering as a multifaceted social project. In other words, bad governance does not necessarily result from fatal flaws in institutional design—it is a large-scale initiative that bounces off and meshes with a multitude of factors at work within a concrete social environment. Explanations for the peculiar ways in which these factors affect and subvert the 'engineered' institutional landscape converge on the question of the limits of institutional engineering in a post-communist environment.

Obviously, all relevant aspects of this problem cannot even be hinted at here, and the summary to follow will simply flag several issues illuminating the (ir)relevance of constitutionalism in the post-1989 period. Construed as an effort to structure the behaviour

---

[29] *New York Times* (28 Oct. 1996), 4.

of political elites, institutional engineering may create powerful incentives for maintaining non-violent forms of elite rivalry. Rather quickly, the motley crew of Bulgarian party leaders were transformed into a Schumpeterian political class[30] that, for all its penchant for 'transgressions', is well aware of the 'rules of the game'.

What institutional engineering has yet to create, however, is an incentive to govern, to bring into being forms of elite behaviour informed by the belief that the benefits of a prolonged incumbency may accrue if the needs of specific groups in society are reasonably met and the supply of public goods and services is kept at a satisfactory level. In contrast to political systems where such incentives exist, in Bulgaria the rule-structured, 'constitutional' behaviour of elites is either the prelude to or an element of looting of state resources. In no other type of state is such a high percentage of the national wealth concentrated in the hands of elected officials as in post-communist states. Understandably, then, the incentive to follow rules and refrain from disruptive behaviour vis-à-vis one's fellow politicians is superimposed on a web of opportunities shaping the conduct of incumbents. Foremost among these is the opportunity to strike it rich during a period of chaotic privatization, license private banks operating with state money, and create a discretionary regime for granting tax exemptions.

If and when constitutions take root, they do seem to fend off the eventuality that 'striking crimes' perpetrated by authoritarian leaders will shake the foundations of political order; all the same, they are no cure for the 'smaller vices' which Tocqueville detested and which today have become a permanent fixture of post-communist politics: rent-seeking, insouciance, corruption, neglect of vital societal needs, shortsightedness, rapacious profiteering.[31] If, having made the first step, Bulgaria follows a preordained trajectory from authoritarian repression to elite cooperation to democratic consolidation to positive-sum bargaining and ultimately to efficient policy-making, it remains to be seen when this last stage will commence. If there is no such uplifting trajectory, then hope should be pinned on not-yet-invented mechanisms for societal pressure and incentives for self-monitoring among post-communist elites. Until then, the incentive to govern will be dwarfed by other incentives luring those who inhabit Bulgaria's engineered political institutions.

[30] 'The democratic method is that institutional arrangement for arriving at political decisions in which individuals acquire the power to decide by means of a competitive struggle for the people's vote': Joseph Schumpeter, *Capitalism, Socialism and Democracy* (New York: Harper Colophon Books, 1975), 269.

[31] On 'striking crimes' and 'smaller vices' see Alexis de Tocqueville, *Recollections* (New Brunswick, NJ: Transaction Publishers, 1992), 5.

Conceived as a strategy for regulating interactions between institutions, political engineering may accomplish the venerable task of imposing order. Parliamentarians keen on usurping chunks of presidential power may expect that the Court will strike down their laws, and ministers disregarding laws may be brought to court by ordinary citizens. But while this constraining function has been robustly displayed in Bulgarian political practices, the 'enabling' elements inherent in the constitutional edifice have remained inoperative.[32] Constitutions are sculpted to enhance the capacity of the political system to respond to public demands. So far this coveted process has not transpired in Bulgaria, and, once again, its absence is traceable to the peculiarities of the post-communist political condition.

After 1989 a process of decomposition and disintegration of bureaucratic structures gained momentum. This development stripped state institutions of their penetrative ability and rendered 'positive' action impossible. Institutions would wage their garden-variety wars over policies, in strict compliance with the Constitution: and when all controversies were finally cleared, politicians invariably would discover that they were bereft of qualified bureaucratic manpower and did not command sufficient logistical resources to deliver on their promises. Moreover, ensuring a regular flow of 'feed-back' information has never been a priority for bureaucrats trained under socialism;[33] and newly established executive agencies by definition lack what Evans and Rue-schemeyer have aptly called 'noninstitutional sources of cohesion of the bureaucratic apparatus', i.e. commitment on the part of newly appointed functionaries to a work ethic and professional stand-ards conducive to efficient, corruption-free modes of running the respective institution.[34] As a master plan for reforming the polit-ical institution of a former dictatorship, Bulgarian constitu-tionalism is a stunning success. As a stratagem for replacing an overblown and unresponsive system of government with a set of efficient institutional tools employed in the pursuit of good

[32] For the distinction between 'inhibitive' and 'enabling' elements of institution building, see Stephen Holmes, 'Constitutionalism', in Seymor M. Lipset (ed.), *The Encyclopedia of Democracy*, vol. i (Washington: Congressional Quarterly, 1995), 302.

[33] See Tony Verheijn, *Constitutional Pillars for New Democracies: The Cases of Bulgaria and Romania* (Leiden: Leiden University Press, 1995), 31.

[34] See Peter B. Evans and Dietrich Rueschemeyer, 'The State and Economic Transformation: Towards an Analysis of the Conditions Underlying Effective Inter-vention', in Theda Skocpol et al. (eds.), *Bringing the State Back in* (Cambridge: Cambridge University Press, 1985), 59.

policies, it has been a miserable failure. With the fragments of surviving communist institutions unusable and the newly inaugurated agencies still underconstructed, the effort to solidify the institutional basis of 'positive' state intervention is bound to be futile.

Finally, institutional engineering seeks to recast the relations between state and society. In this sphere accomplishments blend with disappointments. The people have been granted all basic democratic rights and are growing accustomed to taking their grievances to independent courts. The system of political representation is efficient, but displays primarily a *negative efficiency*, a term I use (borrowing from Shugart and Carey[35]) to denote the ability of elections to serve as a means for voters to get rid of incumbents. Institutional engineering has allayed nagging preoccupations with the possible recrudescence of abusive state practices at a time when societal expectations about state assistance remain high and unfulfilled. Apparently, something is lacking in the mixture of voters' rage and judicial oversight if mechanisms for effective control over politicians are to be brought into being. And it is clear that in a post-communist setting the 'extra' effort needed to solve collective action problems or to perfect 'the art of association' will not be forthcoming. During the long years of communism and in the daze of the first 'post' years, the citizenry have definitely learned how to get by; what they still have not mastered is the ability to 'get by' together. While a corrupt state can only be monitored by powerful social actors, under post-communism these actors are likely to be complicit with the state in various corrupt schemes. Designed to revitalize democratic institutions, constitutional engineering may be fully successful only if it energizes society at large, a formidable task that no quick-fix solution can resolve.

Thus the survey of the various dimensions of institutional engineering in Bulgaria amplifies the case for a more subtle analysis of the peculiar ways in which a post-communist context tolerates both elite constraints and elite irresponsibility, institutionalization of governance and endurance of corruption, democratic control and democratic debility. One may only wish that in light of such evidence, abstract discussions of the putative benefits inherent in different constitutional models will be supplemented by a more rigorous discussion of the limits of post-communist institutional engineering as a social project.

---

[35] For descriptions of the positive aspects of 'efficiency' see Matthew Shugart and John M. Carey, *Presidents and Assemblies* (Cambridge: Cambridge University Press, 1992), 7 and *passim*.

Constitutionalism as a Vehicle for Democratic Consolidation in Romania

Renate Weber

On the basis of the inter-war democratic initiatives as well as of the communist regime, Romania could hardly be described as having a constitutional tradition. In fact, the 1923 Constitution was quite advanced, since it proclaimed the separation of powers and the supremacy of the fundamental law, and guaranteed fundamental rights. However, none of these regimes developed a tradition of *observing* their constitutions. This was true of the inter-war regime, but was most obvious during the communist regime, which implicitly denied written rules and tolerated frequent abuses perpetrated by the political leadership and its secret police.

With such a poor record of constitutionalism in Romania, it might seem questionable whether the post-communist constitution could have a significant impact on democratic consolidation. After all, why pay attention to something that has been ignored for so long? Yet in 1990 and 1991, the constitutionalization process was the main focus of the National Salvation Front (NSF). At the time, the new political elite fought hard to ensure that the new fundamental law would express mainly their interests. But with little experience in constitution drafting or institutional engineering, the political elite created a constitutional regime that left plenty of room to manœuvre. For instance, the Constitution's vague wording allows flexible interpretation and the imprecision of the functions of constitutional institutions opens the possibility to alter their power and authority through ordinary legislation. Moreover, the NSF was harshly criticized for the political monopoly it created for itself and therefore the legitimacy of the Constitution adopted in 1991 is open to question.

Thus, in the case of Romania, the result of constitution drafting is ambiguous. The Constitution concentrates political power in the executive branch, but this has not prevented the president and the government from exceeding even those limits on their power. Necessary political reforms have been adopted through governmental 'emergency ordinances' whose confirmation by parliament may be delayed for two to three years. But even these necessary reforms have sometimes been revoked by the Constitutional Court, which ruled the free-handed use of the emergency procedures provision by the executive unconstitutional. Thus, on the one hand, non-observance of the Constitution, its letter, its spirit, and its guarantees—as imperfect as they are—has been one of the characteristics of the post-communist regime. But, to a very large extent, it is also true that the Constitution permits the shift of political power through free and fair elections. Somewhat paradoxically, the weaknesses of the current Constitution have played an important role in society at large, raising awareness about the necessity of several constitutional amendments which could transform the Romanian Constitution into a reliable basis for democracy in the country.

National Salvation Front: Revolution or Communist Party Replacement?

During the last years of the communist regime the political and economic climate in Romania was particularly harsh. No economic reforms were initiated, the state was the sole owner of industry, the main landowner, and the only legal entity entitled to conduct international trade. Politically, Romania's communist dictatorship was characterized by the overwhelming control of the Communist Party. Even though formally the state and party structures were separate, all political decisions were made by the communist leadership. Moreover, unlike other communist countries in Central and Eastern Europe, Romania did not have an active political opposition to the communist regime. Although there were several outspoken dissidents, their public support was in fact absent since the only non-governmental organizations that operated at the time were Communist Party offshoots. Dissident organizations such as Solidarity in Poland, Charta 77 in Czechoslovakia, or Ecoglasnost in Bulgaria simply did not exist in Romania.

Therefore, when Ceauşescu was defeated in December 1989, there was no pre-existing political or civic organization ready to fill the political vacuum. In response, the National Salvation Front was created on an *ad hoc* basis from a heterogeneous group of dissidents and Communist Party members, but with no guiding ideology. The creation of the NSF was announced by Ion Iliescu, a well-known Communist Party personality, after Ceauşescu's flight from Bucharest.[1] Its main purpose was temporarily to take control of the government while new elections were organized. On the evening of 22 December 1989, the Council of the NSF issued its first 'Statement to the Country' which proclaimed that 'In this crucial moment we have decided to organize ourselves in the National Salvation Front which relies on the Romanian army and which gathers all the healthy forces of the country, regardless of their nationality, and the groupings which bravely stood up for the defense of freedom and dignity during the totalitarian dictatorship.' The communiqué also announced the dissolution of Ceauşescu's power structures, the dismissal of the government, and the termination of the activity of the State Council (the regulatory body between the meetings of the Great National Assembly whose power was merely to endorse all decisions).

To avoid potential chaos the statement declared that 'the state is thus taken over by the Council of the National Salvation Front . . . All the ministries and central institutions, within their current frame, will continue their normal activity but will be subordinated to the National Salvation Front in order to ensure normal economic and social life. Within the country local, municipal and county councils of the National Salvation Front will be organized as organs of the local power.' The statement also contained a ten-point programme for the democratic development of the country and a list of individuals chosen to be members of this new power structure, the Council.

---

[1] The revolutionary events began in the city of Timisoara on 15 Dec. 1989, when a group of people surrounded the house of a Hungarian priest, Laszlo Tökes, to oppose his eviction. In the following days several industries went on strike and the population of Timisoara demonstrated against Ceauşescu. The response of the army and of the secret police (even now the bloody events have not been officially clarified) was violent and several people were killed. Ceauşescu presented the events as a result of an international plot against the Romanian communist state and ordered a demonstration in Bucharest to be held as proof of his popular support. After demonstrators began chanting in protest against Ceauşescu, the demonstration was officially stopped and participants were chased away by police. Nevertheless, a few hundred demonstrators remained in the main streets of Bucharest, throughout the afternoon and night of 21 Dec., demanding Ceauşescu's resignation and freedom. The reprisal was savagely carried out by the Securitate (the Romanian intelligence service), the army, and the police. Most demonstrators were arrested, severely beaten, and several were even tortured and killed. The next day, hundreds of thousands of protesters filled the streets of Bucharest and by noon Ceauşescu had fled the city.

Despite its efforts at bringing order to the revolution, the NSF was harshly criticized because of its composition and its course of action. The first criticism stemmed from the fact that the basis on which the members of the NSF had been chosen remains shady. Ion Iliescu had always claimed that the 'revolutionaries' who were present either at the television station or in other hot spots (such as the Communist Party headquarters) suggested nominees for membership in the Front. To the first thirty names announced on 22 December 1989, more were added in the following days, with the final number of members amounting to 145. Only a few names on that list (less than ten) were those of famous dissidents and their presence was perceived as necessary to give legitimacy to the whole structure. The others on the list were individuals who had held leading positions in the Communist Party (and were repudiated by Ceauşescu) and their supporters.

In a book on parliamentary law, two judges of the Constitutional Court (who were also members of the Constitutional Drafting Committee) assert that the only criterion for the creation of the National Salvation Front was 'direct participation in the victory of the December 1989 Revolution'.[2] They also state that '[f]rom the beginning the Front was conceived as a mass movement precursory to a multiparty system, unifying various political and spiritual tendencies'.[3] In their opinion '[a]ccordingly, the Front created its state structure, also as a precursor of the future state, by means of establishing the Council of the National Salvation Front which had united representatives of all patriotic forces of the country, belonging to all social levels, all nationalities, thus having the role of the supreme organ of state power.'[4] But others contend that the few dissidents who were designated as members of the NSF were merely window dressing, since the real power within the organization belonged to Iliescu and his team—that is individuals connected to either the Communist Party or the Securitate (the former secret police). Therefore the post-Ceauşescu political leadership was perceived by some as a sort of continuation, if not of the previous regime, at least of a part of the communist leadership,[5] and the legislation

---

[2] Mihai Constantinescu and Ioan Muraru, *Drept parlamentar* [Parliamentary Law] (Bucharest: Gramar, 1994), 10.

[3] Ibid.   [4] Ibid.

[5] From the very beginning and until now many journalists have expressed this view. Some national newspapers—such as *Romania libera, Cotidianul, Ziua*—have constantly considered the new leadership of the country as being 'crypto-communist' or 'neo-communist'. Some political scientists and historians have also shared this view. In an interview published by the review *22* in its issue No. 45

adopted under its influence was considered to protect the interests of its members.

The second criticism of the NSF was that although the Front was created as an *ad interim* organization and pledged to renounce its leadership after democratic elections, after only one month it transformed itself into a political party. The NSF's announcement to run for elections (which it had the sole authority to organize) raised various concerns regarding the new party's impartiality in the process and many began to question the Front's commitment to democracy. Shortly after this announcement almost all of the dissidents left the NSF, and many of those who joined the 'new' political party were former high-ranking Communist Party officials.

Following the 'statement' several legal acts, including constitutional norms, were adopted. All were presented as having a provisional character, and would be in force only until the adoption of the new Constitution. The first was the Decree-Law No. 2 of 27 December 1989 on the establishment, the structure, and the functions of the Council of the National Salvation Front and its local councils. The governing programme of the Council mentioned as such several options: a multi-party system; a democratic and pluralistic system of government; separation of powers; free elections; equality of rights regardless of one's ethnicity; the right to be elected as Romania's president for only one or maximum two mandates; freedom of the press; freedom of religion. According to these new regulations the Council of the Front was the only legislative authority, entitled to issue 'decree-laws'. By 9 February 1990 over 80 decree-laws had been issued by the Council touching upon a wide range of economic, social, and political issues.

The structure and broad powers of the Council of the National Salvation Front were meant to allow it to govern the country

from November 1996, the well-known historian Serban Papacostea, a member of the Romanian Academy and director of the Nicolae Iorga History Institute, declared: 'The period opened in December 1989 by Ceauşescu's overthrow, and which will cease with the current president's retirement from his head of state position, will be known by history as the final stage of the Soviet-communist regime in Romania, initiated in March 1945 by the Petru Groza government. Two prevailing and interdependent characteristics relate to this final stage and to the person who represents it: at the international level an absolute devotion toward the Soviet Union and its hegemonic system in Central-Eastern Europe; at the domestic level an effort to safeguard the essence of the communist regime, to reduce to minimum— imposed by the new historical trends—the concessions for political and economical freedoms, to maintain control over the power procedures in all the domains of the social-political life.'

peacefully in a chaotic and conflict-ridden political atmosphere until democratic elections were held. Thus, the Front's foot-dragging in announcing the election date and its decision to become a political party that would participate in the elections was considered to be a re-creation of a communist-style party state. After the Front announced its intention to run for election on 23 January 1990, several demonstrations took place in Bucharest organized by the Independent Group for Democracy. These demonstrations were relatively small, but it became obvious that more people supported the Group's ideas. Encouraged by the show of support for demo-cratic principles, several traditional and newly created political parties organized a large demonstration on 28 January 1990. Frightened by the large number of people who were expected to participate in this demonstration in front of the government headquarters, the NSF organized a counter-demonstration. Late in the afternoon, a clash between the participants of the two demonstrations became inevitable. Under this tremendous pres-sure, that evening Iliescu invited the political leaders of main political parties to negotiations. An agreement was reached which created a new institution, the Provisional Council for National Unity (PCNU).

The PCNU was formally established by Decree-Law No. 81 of 9 February 1990 and included representatives of many political parties. The main goal of the 253-member Council was to adopt Decree-Law No. 92 of 14 March 1990 on parliamentary and pres-idential elections. This act had a significant impact on the country's constitutional development since it defined the new state institu-tions by creating a bicameral parliament and the office of the pres-ident. Regarding the elections, the law adopted the PR system, a decision which, at that time, clearly brought an advantage to the NSF since it was the largest and the most popular party. The new parliament would act both as a legislative body and as a Constitutional Assembly, having as a mandate the adoption of a new constitution in the following two years. Regarding the election of the president, it is clear that the semi-presidential system cre-ated by Decree-Law No. 92 was tailor made to suit Iliescu. The NSF needed Iliescu as a strong president, elected directly by the people, with clear prerogatives. Due to the fact that Iliescu had been presented by the largest part of the media, mainly the television, as the leader of the revolution against the Ceauşescu regime as well as the same media's portrayal of him as the peace maker in the post-revolutionary period, he was the most popular candidate in the country.[6] Ultimately, the institutional choices made by the Constitutional Assembly turned out remarkably similar to those of Decree-Law No. 92 in terms of the structure and powers of the parliament and the president, which is quite understandable given that the same group of people who had taken power in December 1989 also won the May 1990 elections.

The Framers of the New Constitution

The 20 May 1990 elections brought the National Salvation Front an absolute victory. The fact that the NSF won almost 70 per cent of the parliamentary seats meant that it had the power to adopt the new Constitution unilaterally (two-thirds of the Assembly), since both houses of parliament were deemed by Decree-Law No. 92 to be the Constituent Assembly. Probably any political party with such a large proportion of votes would take advantage of the situation to impose its own interests on the new Constitution, and the NSF was no exception. Nevertheless, the Front did express a certain amount of openness by adopting relatively democratic principles and ideas in the new Constitution, although less because of a deep commitment to democracy than to improve the public perception— both within Romania and internationally—of the Iliescu regime as a continuation of the former communist state.

The adoption procedure had three stages:[7] the adoption of the theses regarding the future Constitution (a sort of pre-draft); the adoption of the draft Constitution; the approval of the Constitution by means of a referendum. Conducting constitution-drafting in stages was meant to open the drafting procedure to public debate. Thus, the first act of the Constitutional Assembly was to appoint a Drafting Committee to issue the theses for the new Constitution. Three different pre-drafts were issued and published in newspapers, but the debates that followed were rather weak. Most journalists emphasized only political aspects of the

---

[6] Although a free media emerged immediately after 22 Dec. 1989, and in 1990 there were hundreds of newspapers everywhere in the country, they covered only a very small percentage of the population. In many places, specially in the countryside or in small towns, where the vast majority of the population lived, the television (the state one which was the only one at that time) was the only channel of information. Therefore, whatever was presented by the television was considered by a very large number of people as the truth.

[7] See Ion Deleanu, *Drept constitutional si institutii politice* [Constitutional Law and Political Institutions] (Bucharest: Europa Nova, 1996), 93–6.

choices. Newspaper articles dealt primarily with the form of government (that is, the establishment of a republic or monarchy), the powers of the president, the establishment of a Constitutional Court. The debates clearly showed the lack of understanding of democracy and constitutionalism, not only among the public at large, but also among lawyers and politicians. Those who were more acquainted with the issues were involved either in the drafting process or in the debates in the Assembly. No bar association was ever involved in commenting on the drafts and, at that time, no non-governmental association was in a position to possess sufficient expertise to analyse the draft constitution. Thus, few legal experts were involved in the public debate.[8]

In addition to the debates over the Committee's drafts, several articles published in *România liberă* (*Free Romania*) emphasized the possibility of reinstating the 1923 Constitution, which at the time of its adoption was considered to be among the most democratic in Europe. But the main drive behind this campaign was the lack of trust in the Constitutional Assembly, due to its composition.[9] The strong parliamentary majority held by the NSF gave way to fears that the party of the president would simply adopt measures that would enable it to prolong its tenure in parliament.[10] At the same time, the configuration of the Assembly and its strong ties to the communist-era institutions meant that the police, prosecutors, and the military courts could put pressure on the NSF to preserve the privileges granted to these institutions under the previous regime.

The three drafts were extensively discussed by the Drafting Committee and other representatives of the parliament as well as with legal and constitutional experts from the Council of Europe, the USA (mainly American Bar Association), and several European countries. Several good provisions of the Constitution were

[8] See Lucian Mihai, 'De ce nu voi vota pentru aceasta Constitutie' [Why I Shall not Vote for This Constitution], in *România liberă*, 14572/538–14577/543 (Nov.–Dec. 1991). See also Dan Ciobanu, 'Aplicarea normelor de drept international de catre instantele judecatoresti romane, in lumina anteproiectului de Constitutie' [The Enforcement of the International Law Norms by Romanian Courts as Reflected in the Pre-draft Constitution], *Dreptul* [Law], 7–8 (1991).

[9] After the 1990 elections the Christian Democrat National Peasant Party and the National Liberal Party, the two main forces of the opposition at that time, shared less than 10%.

[10] For a broad picture on the third running of President Iliescu for another presidential mandate—considered to be the third one, but decided by the Constitutional Court to be the second 'constitutional' one, see *Revista romana de drepturile omului*, 13 (1996).

accepted as a result of these discussions. Within the government at the time, the ideological climate was not favourable to individualism and liberalism. Throughout its history Romanian politics has taken a paternalistic approach. The head of state has always been considered to be the most important person involved in decision-making, regardless of the head-of-state's institution's legal capacity. This was a legacy of the communist regime, which particularly in Romania was favourable to such an approach, and Ceauşescu's regime took this tendency to the limit. Another factor that contributed to state paternalism was the weakness of civil society. During communism all associations, such as women's organizations, youth groups, and trade unions, had been created and controlled by the Communist Party.[11]

This combination of factors—the lack of understanding of constitutionalism, the traditional paternalism of the state, and the absence of civil society organizations—led to the adoption of a constitution through a process driven by symbolism rather than by concrete issues. The political leadership waged this symbolic campaign primarily through the public media. At the time, the state controlled public television and radio and they were both used by the Front to manipulate public opinion. The message presented to the public by the state media was that rejecting the Constitution —either by the Constitutional Assembly or by the people through the referendum—would be siding with an 'international conspiracy' against Romania. With this political backdrop, the Constitution was adopted by the Constitutional Assembly on 21 November 1991 and entered into force after being confirmed by a national referendum held on 8 December 1991.

---

[11] What happened after December 1989 was that an old law, No. 21/1924, which had never been abolished, was reinforced and has become the legal frame for the newly emerging civil society. A few thousand non-governmental (non-profit) organizations have been created. For several years they were considered as anti-governmental structures, 'paid by foreign forces', thus being perceived as a threat to national security. Yet, due to all those meetings with foreign experts and under the influence of the European Convention on Human Rights, Art. 37 of the Constitution makes it quite clear that 'Citizens may freely associate into political parties, trade unions and other forms of association', the prohibition concerning only 'secret associations'. But the framers of the Constitution had no intention at all of enhancing the NGO sector and no privileges were granted to associations, foundations, etc. It was Law No. 137/1995 on environment protection which, for the first time (and uniquely until now), stipulates the right of a NGO to stand in justice in its own name but in the interest of another: 'NGOs have the right to take court action with a view to preserving the environment, irrespective of who suffered the prejudice' (Art. 86).

A Few Constitutional Choices

In Romania the question of whether or not the Constitution would be adopted quickly was not an issue in itself. On the contrary, ever since the December 1989 revolution, everyone had hoped that adopting a new fundamental law would be a step towards stability. Any reluctance was only due to the composition of the Assembly and the monopoly of power enjoyed by Iliescu which allowed certain constitutional choices to be made which put the democratic transition in jeopardy. The quick adoption of the Constitution and the difficulty of predicting constitutional outcomes led to a constitution riddled with vague wording and contradictory elements. The result was, therefore, not instant stability as had been hoped, but a prolonged period of democratic consolidation. A review of the debates preceding the adoption of the Constitution and the result of the adopted Constitution in practice reveals that the intentions of the articles adopted were seldom realized in practice and instead of changing the Constitution, the Romanian political elite manipulated constitutional provisions to suit their political goals.

Separation of powers

One of the casualties of the fast-track constitution-drafting in Romania was the principle of separation of powers. Several legal acts adopted after the overthrow of the communist regime expressly mentioned the separation of powers as the foundation of the country's democratic evolution. However the 1991 Constitution does not contain any specific provision on this principle, 'although during the debates within the Constitutional Assembly and outside it this principle was regarded as a possible remedy against the constitutional infringements made by the communist political regime'.[12] The Constitution does not refer to 'powers' but to 'authorities' of each institution, though it does not refer at all to 'separation'. Nevertheless, many of the constitutional experts who were members of the Drafting Committee assert that the principle of separation of powers still applies. They argue that separation of powers is inherent in the cooperative character of the activity of each institution,[13] and that the most important thing is to have the

---

[12] Deleanu, *Drept constitutional si institutii politice*, 92.
[13] Ibid. 92–100. See also Ioan Muraru, *Drept constitutional si institutii politice* [Constitutional Law and Political Institutions] (Bucharest: Editura ACTAMI, 1995), 14–26.

principle at work. In this light 'one could understand the position of our Constitutional Assembly who did not mention the principle of separation of powers in the fundamental law, but it has organized the authorities according to its requirements'.[14]

Yet some observers have criticized this solution harshly. The principle of separation of powers was included in the December 1989 'Statement to the Country', which also laid the foundation for the creation of the Constitutional Assembly. Thus, it was argued that by excluding the principle implicitly from the Constitution, the Assembly acted illegally.[15] Lucian Mihai asserts that 'it is possible that from a scientific point of view the principle of separation of powers is wrong and the theory of "state authorities" is correct. But the Statement of December 22, 1989 did not express a scientific opinion, but the aspiration of the insurgents, that is, of the revolutionaries. The adoption of a Constitution is not a scientific endeavour but a political decision framing the desire of the governed people.'[16]

Further investigation into the institutional structure set up by the Constitution and its practical outcome reveals that democratic consolidation has suffered in the absence of a clear adoption of the principle and the unclear provisions regarding institutional competence in the Constitution. Problems related to separation of powers are particularly clear in the judiciary as well as in the delegation of legislative competence from the parliament to the government. I will focus on these specific issues below.

Presidentialism vs. parliamentarism

Experts have indicated that parliamentary governments tend to bring greater stability to new democracies than presidential regimes due to the emphasis in parliamentary systems on institutional cooperation rather than competition. But due to the strong role of the president in appointing the government and the weakness of the parliamentary opposition, the stability of the government has hardly been the problem. Yet the consequences for democracy building have been rather negative.

---

[14] Genoveva Vrabie, *Organizarea politico-etatica a Romaniei* (Romania's Political and State Structure) (Bucharest: Virginia Editura, 1995), 27.

[15] Lucian Mihai, 'Separarea puterilor in stat: propuneri de modificare a Constitutiei' [Separation of State Powers: Proposals to Amend the Constitution], *Revista romana de drepturile omului*, 2 (1993). In July 1998 Lucian Mihai was appointed as a judge to the Constitutional Court; immediately afterwards he was elected as its president for the next three years.

[16] Ibid.

The Constitutional Assembly opted for a semi-presidential form of government. According to Article 58 (1) of the Constitution, 'the Parliament is the supreme representative body of the Romanian people and the sole legislative authority of the State'. Both parliament and the president are directly elected. In order to understand to what extent this was a real constitutional option for the state or whether it was simply a constitutional solution to extend Iliescu's power, we must recall the events in Romania after December 1989. At that time, Ion Iliescu became the most important political personality in the country and he exercised his power in all decisions on domestic or foreign affairs. Despite the creation of a new government and prime minister, it was never denied that Iliescu had the final word in all decisions made within the economic, social, and political spheres. Moreover, there were several instances in which he succeeded in imposing his own opinions over those of different members of the government. Therefore, the general impression from the broad powers given to the president in the constitutional provisions clearly reveals that the office was meant for Iliescu.

The president has the power to promulgate laws according to Article 77, can return a law to parliament for reconsideration (only once), as well as send any bill to the Constitutional Court to have its constitutionality confirmed. Accordingly, the president may address messages to parliament (Art. 88); consult with the government on urgent extremely important matters (Art. 86); participate in and preside over government meetings (Art. 87); and is entitled to organize referenda on matters of national interest (Art. 90). In terms of the president's function in selecting, appointing, and revoking public authorities, the president has the power to dissolve parliament (Art. 89); to designate a candidate for the office of prime minister; and to appoint and dismiss certain members of the government (Art. 85). The president also plays a role in controlling the function of other institutions by 'guarding the observance of the Constitution and the proper functioning of the public authorities' and acting as 'a mediator between the Powers in the State, as well as between the State and society' (Art. 80.2). The president appoints judges (Art. 124) as well as three of the Constitutional Court justices (Art. 140—the others are appointed three by the Senate and three by the Chamber of Deputies). In terms of national security, the president is not only the commander-in-chief of the armed forces but also presides over the Supreme Council of National Defence (Art. 92).

Perhaps the most controversial power granted to the president by the Constitution is found in Article 94 (c), which states that the president has the power 'to make appointments to public offices under the terms provided by law'. This is to say that presidential powers are not limited to the constitutional framework, but may be extended by means of a law which has a totally different procedure of adoption from the Constitution. This provision is regarded as dangerous because it opens a path for legal abuses which can enormously increase the controlling powers of the president without being unconstitutional.

But the legal—including the constitutional—provisions which determine presidential powers are not the only issue here. The real issue is how this constitutional framework can be used—or abused—by the president, and how the president has subverted institutional arrangements to control decision-making through informal means. In terms of the president's strong political role, little changed after Iliescu lost power to Emil Constantinescu in the 1996 elections. President Constantinescu inherited a *de jure* and *de facto* situation which he did not want to challenge. While the use of informal mechanisms is difficult to trace, certain incidents reveal that the most important decisions in the country have been made not through constitutionalized structures, but by behind-closed-doors agreements between the political elite. For instance, after his resignation from the post of prime minister, Victor Ciorbea publicly stated that Emil Constantinescu had asked him to dampen the pace of the economic reform, in order to allay fears that the trade unions' demonstrations would negatively affect the nation's image during the 1997 NATO summit. Moreover, in December 1999 President Constantinescu dismissed Prime Minister Radu Vasile, a procedure which went far beyond his constitutional powers since it is only parliament which is entitled through a no-confidence vote to dismiss the government, prime minister included.[17]

It is interesting to note that with a couple of exceptions neither Iliescu nor Constantinescu have ever used the presidential prerogative to take part in meetings of the government. Instead of acting

---

[17] What concretely happened was that more than half of the ministers resigned while the rest of the government expressed their solidarity with this gesture. The president considered that in this situation the prime minister no longer had a government to rule over and therefore was no longer able to exercise his function. The president dismissed him. This procedure was followed by harsh criticism on behalf of opposition parties and political analysts as well. For several days the president and the Christian Democrat National Peasant Party (to which the prime minister belonged) negotiated with Radu Vasile for his resignation, and although the presidential decree on dismissal was never cancelled the resignation was accepted by the president. The parliament was not involved in either of these two legal activities.

openly, they have both preferred to make use of informal solutions for influencing the decision-making process. One possible explanation for the president's reliance on informal means is the constitutional provision forbidding the president from maintaining party membership after election to the post. Ion Iliescu—who ran twice on behalf of the Party of Social Democracy in Romania—thought that by acting behind the scenes, he could convince the electorate of his politically unbiased position.

The delegation of powers from parliament to the government

In addition to the presidents' efforts, the government has engaged in its own project for amassing power by stretching the limits of Article 114 of the Constitution which allows the government to adopt legislation by issuing emergency ordinances.[18] The use of this procedure implies that an ordinance enters into force and has legal consequence before being endorsed by parliament. Parliament may overturn these ordinances, but this creates other problems regarding the legal stability of the country. When parliament overturns an ordinance, a legal vacuum ensues, which forces the Assembly either to legislate a replacement law quickly, or to leave the legal gap until there is sufficient time to consider the issues in depth. In November 1996, more than one-third of all laws had been adopted by the government through this procedure. The opposition severely reproached the abuse of this procedure which was perceived as a means to avoid parliamentary debates. Moreover, in 1996 the government issued 'emergency orders' in the field of organic laws (most notably by passing a law on political parties and a law on tax exemptions). But in the face of this constitutional violation, surprisingly enough, all the parliamentary parties accepted this procedure, due to the fact that the parliamentary term was coming to an end. Thus, although these laws may be checked in terms of their compliance with the Constitution, in practice this

[18] Art. 114 stipulates: '(1) Parliament may pass a special law enabling the Government to issue orders in fields outside the scope of organic laws. (2) The enabling law shall compulsorily establish the field and the date up to which orders can be issued. (3) If the enabling law so requests, orders shall be submitted to Parliament for approval, according to the legislative procedure, until expiration of the enabling term. Non-compliance with the term entails discontinuation of effectiveness of the order. (4) In exceptional cases, the Government may adopt emergency orders, which shall come into force only after their submission to Parliament for approval. If Parliament does not sit in a session, it shall obligatorily be convened. (5) Orders shall be approved or rejected by a law which must also contain the orders that ceased to be effective in accordance with para (3).'

has not been done regularly, and when it has, the process takes place months (even years) after the statutory orders actually come into force and have legal effect. After the 1996 elections, the new government abused its right to issue emergency orders: in one year it issued approximately 100 emergency orders, in domains regulated either by ordinary laws or by organic laws and in spite of the fact that several parliamentary parties expressed their protest.

In June 1998 the Constitutional Court was asked to decide on a case regarding the constitutionality of an emergency ordinance amending the law on public administration. The Court decided that the emergency order was unconstitutional because it was adopted while the country was not in an 'exceptional situation', required by the Constitution, though it avoided giving an opinion on the fact that the domain of local administration is regulated by organic law. As a result, the government appointed in 1998 halted the use of emergency ordinances. Perhaps if a specific provision on the separation of power had been included in the fundamental law, the Constitutional Court could have ruled that the use of the 'emergency ordinances procedure' is against the letter of the Constitution as well.

Bicameralism

Abuse of power by both the president and the government is partly caused and allowed to continue by the weakness of the parliament and its bicameral structure. The option for a bicameral parliament, originally introduced by the post-revolutionary NSF regime, was generally justified because it was the 'Romanian tradition'.[19] Indeed, the 1923 Constitution had established a bicameral parliament but at the time there were clear differences between the two chambers. Today the two chambers are elected in an identical way and both have identical competence. Their differences are rather circumstantial: the number of the members (the Senate has approximately one-third of the number of the Chamber of Deputies) and the size of the constituency they represent (a senator's represents more than double that of a deputy's); the age allowing someone to become a MP (35 for the Senate as opposed to 23 for the Chamber of Deputies). At the same time, 'In case of vacancy in the office of the President, if the President's term should be suspended, or if the President is temporarily incapable of

---

[19] Mihai Constantinescu, Ion Deleanu, Antonie Iorgovan, Ioan Muraru, Florin Vasilescu, and Ioan Vida, *Constitutia Romaniei: comentata si adnotata* [The Constitution of Romania] (Bucharest: Regia autonoma 'Monitorul Oficial', 1992), 136.

exercising this power, the duties of the President shall devolve, in this order, on the President of the Senate or the President of the Chamber of Deputies' (Art. 97). The Senate has the competence to appoint the advocate of the people. Minorities can be represented ex officio only in the Chamber of Deputies.

In order to become law, bills must be passed by a majority in both parliamentary chambers and then promulgated by the president. Bills may originate in government or either chamber and then passed to the other which may either adopt the law or make amendments to the bill. In case an amendment is made to the original bill, a mediation commission of the two chambers must approve the final version (or the plenary of the entire parliament in case of failures) before it is passed on to the president. The result of this institutional arrangement has meant that debating and adopting a law by each chamber has considerably lowered the pace of law-making. To make matters worse, there has been little coordination of the chambers' activities, and instead the chambers compete with one another for the final word on particular pieces of legislation. There were several instances when after a law was adopted by one chamber it was sent to the other, where it took months or even several years before the bill was adopted by the second chamber.

Perhaps the most troubling problem related to elections is the absence of an independent and permanent body organizing and supervising elections. Since 1990, Romania has held parliamentary and presidential elections three times and local elections twice and each time a new ad hoc Central Electoral Bureau or local county bureaux were created. Their methods of regulation has varied, but have been consistently unclear and have even overstepped the boundaries of their competence by actually changing laws. After each election, these ad hoc bodies have been dismissed, which has made it difficult for allegations of political bias and other abuses of power to be properly investigated.

The electoral system has also had a strange impact on the work of the parliament. The Constitution states that political parties have no right to revoke MPs for any reason and that only the electorate have the possibility of sanctioning the acts of any MP through their vote in subsequent elections.[20] However, this is

[20] The Constitution states, in Art. 66, that '(1) In the exercise of their mandate, Deputies and Senators shall be in the service of the people; (2) Any imperative mandate shall be null.' For the constitutional debate on this issue see Renate Weber, 'Curtea Constitutionala versus Parlamentul Romaniei' [The Constitutional Court vs. the Romanian Parliament], *Revista romana de drepturile omului*, 5 (1994) and Decision No. 44/1993 of the Constitutional Court.

more true in theory than in practice since the electoral system envisages a proportional system based on party lists with no possibility for indicating a preferential vote to a particular candidate on the lists. Thus, the party ultimately exercises control over its members since it alone decides the membership and order of its candidate list.

The rules regarding which parties are entitled to put forward candidate lists in elections have been amended in an effort to streamline the political spectrum. The first act regulating party formation was the Decree-Law No. 8 of 31 December 1989, according to which a political party could be created with as few as 251 members. At the time, 250 parties were created and registered. As might be expected, the number of parties has decreased with time, but is still fairly large. Party formation has actually been encouraged by the low, 3 per cent threshold required to gain entry into parliament.

The new law on political parties, adopted in April 1996, requires at least 10,000 members in order to be registered. Moreover, these party members cannot all reside in one region, but must represent a broad geographical area.[21] Although all registered parties are entitled to financial support from the state budget, parliamentary parties are in a much better position to forward their interests when calculating the amount of these grants. At the same time, the law requires that voting procedures within parties be conducted by secret ballot and obliges the parties to discuss all their members' opinions. During discussions in the parliament voices were heard congratulating the MPs for 'imposing democracy in the internal life of political parties'.

As a result of the new law, less than fifty parties have been registered and although the 1996 parliamentary elections maintained the 3 per cent threshold, only nine parties were elected (six of them belonging to either of two coalitions). This outcome reveals that the attempt to limit the number of political parties was quite successful. However, it is too soon to say what will happen with those parties that have been left out of parliament.[22] Moreover, it is difficult to predict whether and how the parliamentary parties contribute to improving the country's evolution towards democracy and observance of the rule of law.

---

[21] This peculiar requirement was aimed at curbing the number of national minority-based parties.

[22] By the beginning of 2000—when elections were scheduled to take place—the amendment on the 5% threshold was still under discussion.

The judiciary

If the judiciary is to be the third power in the state and the only one without political affiliation, a country's legislation must be very clear in asserting and guaranteeing the independence of the judiciary. But in the Romanian judicial system, prosecutors, who are subordinated to government (minister of justice through Public Ministry), are also considered magistrates and appointed to the Superior Council of the Magistracy which decides upon 'promotion, transfer, and sanctions of judges' (Art. 124 of the Constitution). Thus, the Romanian Constitution has succeeded in having the judiciary controlled by the executive without an equal possibility for the judiciary to check the acts of the executive branch.[23] This power imbalance was further aggravated by Law No. 92/1992 on the judiciary (amended in 1997), which gives the minister of justice the possibility of controlling (through government inspectors) the professional activity of the judges.[24]

Although according to the Romanian Constitution 'Judges appointed by the President of Romania shall be irremovable, according to the law' (Art. 124), it took President Iliescu about three years to comply with this constitutional requirement. Concerning the judges of the Supreme Court, their situation is more complicated as they are irremovable, but their mandate lasts only six years before it must be renewed by the Superior Council of the Magistracy and they must be reappointed by the president.

Another means of ensuring the independence of judges is to pay them adequately. For several years, with the exception of those in the Supreme Court of Justice, judges had the same salary as any state bureaucrat and for a long time the Romanian parliament and government rejected the idea of increasing judges' salaries. For example, when the 1996 budget was under discussion, the minister of justice magnanimously declared before parliament that his budget was too ample since Romanian judges do not work for money, but for the benefit of the country. But despite these political overtures, in 1998 the government accepted the proposal to increase significantly judges' salaries. Currently, their situation is quite the

[23] See Mihai, 'Separarea puterilor in stat'.
[24] These provisions have been criticized by the Council of Europe Rapporteurs. For more details see Renate Weber, 'Memorandumul MAE: raportul Konig-Jansson' [The Memorandum of the Ministry of Foreign Affairs: The Konig-Jansson Report], *Revista romana de drepturile omului*, 5 (1994).

opposite of what it used to be and today the perception is that judges 'have too many privileges'.[25]

In response to the question raised above, regarding the effect of the absence from the Constitution of an explicit adoption of the separation of powers principle, it seems that there are several domains where this absence has been detrimental, mainly related to the judiciary and the justice system. This is clear in the case of the judiciary's independence, because it has resulted in the inclusion of prosecutors in the judiciary, although they are also part of the Public Ministry, which belongs to the executive branch. It was also the absence of this principle which allowed for the creation of the Superior Council of the Magistracy, consisting of magistrates (both judges and prosecutors), which, among other things, will play a role in the disciplinary council for judges. It is hard to imagine how an independent judiciary can work under such conditions. After the November 1996 elections a real war has begun—through mass media—between the general prosecutor of Romania and the minister of justice. The minister announced his intention to adopt fundamental changes within the judiciary, among which he would take effective control over the prosecutors. The general prosecutor has presented this as an attempt to impose political control over their activity. In July 1997 the new political leadership decided to amend the law on the judiciary, which led to strong debates within parliament. Among those opposing the amendments were the Superior Council of the Magistracy, whose members were appointed by Iliescu during his presidency and whose mandate was supposed to be cut short so as to allow its renewal as soon as possible.

The Constitutional Court

No one has ever questioned the necessity for constitutional control in Romania. But the debate over which institution should exercise this control was heated. The Romanian pre-communist tradition dictated giving the right of constitutional control to the Supreme Court. In fact, the Romanian Court's power to check constitutional compatibility of legislation and government acts was secured at a time when it was unusual to have constitutional control in

---

[25] Their salaries are calculated in a different way from the rest of state budget paid employees; they enjoy several additional sums (for loyalty, for working in a dusty environment, etc.); they have their own medical insurance system, clinics, and hospitals; a tough discussion is going on regarding a different pension system.

Europe. However, the 1991 Constitution reflects that constitution makers made a different choice[26] by establishing a politically and legally distinct body,[27] the Constitutional Court, which has been granted the right 'to adjudicate on the constitutionality of laws before promulgation' (Art. 144.a) as well as the right 'to decide on the exceptions brought to the Courts of law as to the unconstitutionality of laws and orders' (Art. 144.c).

While the constitutional articles regarding the Court seem to demonstrate its role in checking the power of the other institutions, other constitutional articles seem to diminish its role. For example, if a law is declared unconstitutional before promulgation it is returned to parliament for reconsideration (Art. 145). If, however, the law is passed again in both chambers by a two-thirds majority, the law is considered adopted and should be promulgated. The Constitution does not address this contradiction and the only reasonable explanation might be the fact that a two-thirds majority is sufficient to amend the Constitution. But since Article 147 requires a referendum to approve constitutional amendments, the conflict between Article 145 and Article 147 remains, and is not constitutionally resolved. Moreover, the officials entitled to petition the Court when they suspect that an unpromulgated law violates the Constitution are the president, the speaker of either chamber, the government, the Supreme Court of Justice, fifty deputies, or twenty-five senators. In practice, however, it has been very difficult to convince these officials to pay attention to the constitutionality of a law, and as a result several obviously unconstitutional laws have been passed.

Another problem is raised in Law No. 47/1992, which states in its Article 1 that the Constitutional Court is the only authority that has constitutional jurisdiction. This is indeed the case in regard to unpromulgated laws or promulgated laws by means of exception, as well as government ordinances by means of exception. It does not, however, apply to government decisions or other acts adopted by ministers or other public authorities which may be controlled only by the courts in cases brought before them.

In addition to the confusion surrounding the Constitutional Court's formal powers, the Court has damaged its own credibility through various unusual decisions. The procedure for appointing

---

[26] For a critical opinion see Adrian Vasiliu, 'Curtea Constitutionala, locul si rolul ei in statul de drept' (The Constitutional Court, Its Place and Role in Relation with the Rule of Law), *Revista romana de drepturile omului*, 2 (1993).

[27] According to the Constitution, the Constitutional Court is not part of the judiciary, but a distinct authority.

judges to the Court (three are appointed by the president; three by the Senate, and three by the Chamber of Deputies) seems to be clear in asserting their independence; but several allegations have been made about the political bias of the Court's decisions.[28] Moreover, several decisions of the Court have been rather odd. In one case the Court decided to launch a sort of extraordinary appeal against one of its own decisions.[29] More recently, the Court has held that it may not rule on any procedural inconsistencies of its own decisions, although the civil procedure code allows for this option, thus creating the impression that the Court is above the law.[30] In fact, following the example of other Romanian institutions, the Court's tendency to give itself more power than the Constitution provides has become obvious. In response, in 1997 the law on the Constitutional Court was amended such that all the cases brought before the Court would be decided by the plenary of the Court, thus curbing the Court's practice of deciding twice or even three times on the same issue.

The relationship between central and local power

The Romanian Constitution states in Article 119 that 'Public administration in territorial-administrative units is based on the principle of local autonomy and decentralization of public services.' But this provision has constantly been infringed, which supports the assertion that decentralization was pushed through by international actors, such as the Council of Europe, rather than by domestic commitments to the principle. Law No. 69 of 28 November 1991 on local administration (adopted only a few days before the Constitution) contradicts several principles laid down in the fundamental law. Once again, international pressure was necessary to convince parliament to amend this law, which it finally did in May 1996, just before the local elections. Nevertheless, this law has had a minimal impact on local administration, since it took parliament five to seven years to pass the necessary laws to support it, such as a law on local budgets, or principles on the taxes and other sources of income for local government.

---

[28] These allegations have been made in relation to some decisions, i.e. on the law regulating the restitution of nationalized houses; on President Iliescu's right to run for a third presidential mandate.

[29] See Renate Weber, 'O stranie decizie a Curtii Constitutionale' [An Odd Decision of the Constitutional Court], *Revista romana de drepturile omului*, 2 (1993).

[30] See *Revista romana de drepturile omului*, 13 (1996).

The reasons why Romania clings to centralization are, on the one hand, because of mentality, since centralization was the communist practice, and, on the other hand, because a centralized state is much easier to control. In its Recommendation 12 (1995) on local democracy in Romania, the Congress of Local and Regional Authorities of Europe (of the Council of Europe) was extremely critical of Romanian local administration and its relations with the central administration. The Congress noted all the legal 'weaknesses, gaps and imprecisions' together with 'a number of abuses—particularly on the part of certain prefects—in the application of Law No. 69 on local self-government, in connection with the suspension and dismissal of mayors, the provisions of the said Law leaving too much discretion to the administrative authorities'. Some of these criticisms were addressed in 1997 through an emergency order which amended the law on local public administration.[31] For a little over a year, the provisions of this emergency order were dutifully implemented. But, after June 1998, when the Constitutional Court struck down the use of emergency orders, the law was deemed unconstitutional and therefore was no longer in force. Only by the end of 1999 did parliament adopt the amendments required.

Special mention must be made in relation with the nationalist trends which have influenced some provisions of the Constitution. Both the Hungarian political party (the Democratic Alliance of Hungarians in Romania) and a nationalist-extremist party (the Party of Romanian National Unity) were represented in the Constitutional Assembly. At the same time another extremist party was created in the country and it was very vocal (the Great Romania Party). In the absence of an organized civil society, nationalistic discourse became a powerful rhetorical tool for parties to gain entry into the political sphere. The Constitution to a great extent satisfied this trend. For example, Article 1 proclaims Romania as a national state; Article 3 (4) states: 'No foreign populations may be displaced or colonized in the territory of the Romanian State' (a provision taken *tale quale* from the 1923 Constitution); Article 41 (2) stipulates that: 'Aliens and stateless persons may not acquire the right of property on land.' From the constitutional debates,[32] it is clear that these articles were driven by the paranoid illusion that Transylvania might be bought—piece by piece—by Hungarians from abroad.

[31] The financial aspects related to the competencies of local administration are still waiting to be regulated.

[32] The debates of the Constitutional Assembly were published in the *Official Gazette*, part III, in 1990 and 1991.

Several minority groups (the Hungarian group being the most vocal) have expressed their concern over these articles, which they consider to set up the basis for their assimilation by the Romanian majority. They also point to Article 4 (1) which declares 'The State foundation is laid on the unity of the Romanian people,' which in combination with the other articles seems to offer an opportunity for the exclusion of ethnic minorities from the political sphere. Yet constitutional protections of minorities are included in the Constitution. For instance, Article 6.1 declares: 'The State recognizes and guarantees the right of persons belonging to national minorities, to the preservation, development and expression of their ethnic, cultural, linguistic and religious identity'; Article 16.1 states: 'All citizens enjoy the rights and freedoms granted to them by the Constitution and other laws and have the duties laid down thereby'; Article 59.2 affirms: 'Organizations of citizens belonging to national minorities, which fail to obtain the number of votes for representation in Parliament, have the right to one Deputy seat each, under the terms of the electoral law.' That means that the Romanian Constitution does not merely recognize the national minorities but also accepts special measures to strengthen the affirmation of their identity.

But interpretations of the 'nationalist' articles in the Constitution do not seem to accommodate the rights of minorities.[33] For instance, no official institution, such as the parliament or the Constitutional Court, has expressed a view according to which 'the Romanian people' (as in Art. 4) or the 'nation' (as in Art. 1) would encompass all the citizens of the country, regardless of their nationality. On the contrary, in a book on the Romanian Constitution issued by six experts who were members of the Drafting Committee (all of them being at various moments judges of the Constitutional Court) we find:

The State is not merely the expression of an organized human community, 'anyone', always heterogeneous and fluctuating. This community is ever-lasting and distinct from other communities precisely through the specific and indestructible ties between its component members as well as through its own countenance, meaning its power to constitute a nation. Therefore the nation is not an exclusive ethnic or biological phenomenon.

---

[33] For a more detailed presentation see Renate Weber, 'The Protection of National Minorities in Romania: A Matter of Political Will and Wisdom', in Center for International Relations (ed.), *Law and Practice of Central European Countries in the Field of National Minorities Protection after 1989* (Warsaw: Center for International Relations, 1998).

It is a complex reality and the result of a long historical process having as its foundation the common ethnic origin, language, culture, religion, psychological characteristics, life, traditions, desires and above all the history and the aspiration to last on its territory.[34]

Moreover, in a footnote on the same subject, the authors assert that '[t]he concept of "human community" is the only compatible with the concept of "nation" because the syntagma "human community"—totally different from the notion "society"—expresses precisely the history of those composing the nation, the genealogical ties between the successive generations, and their members' willingness to live together.'[35]

For several decades the national minorities in Romania have enjoyed certain rights, such as the right to use their native language in administration and in courts and the right to be educated in their native language. Moreover, in the regions inhabited by minorities, the ability to speak both Romanian and the minority language was a condition of hiring staff in public administration and in courts. After 22 December 1989, however, contradicting the values declared by the initial statements, Romania lowered its own standard of minority rights protection. The Law No. 69/1991, on the local public administration, introduced the compulsory use of the official language (Romanian) in administration. It also contained a provision that seemed to comply with the right to use native languages, stating that 'Citizens belonging to national minorities can use their mother tongue orally or in writing when dealing with public administration authorities or using their services' (Art. 54/2). Unfortunately, in practice this provision was rendered inoperable by the next paragraph which lays down the circumstances under which this right can be exercised: 'Written documents and applications shall be accompanied by authorized translations in Romanian.' This procedure is extremely bureaucratic, difficult to comply with (particularly by monolingual minorities), expensive, and useless if in the end the administration's response is given in Romanian. The law also demanded the use of the official language by members of local or county councils during their sessions, even if all members belong to the same ethnic minority. The 1997 amendments—as well as the new version of the law—allow the use of the mother tongue in administration in those regions where persons belonging to national minorities comprise more than 20 per cent. Similar amendments are impossible in the case

---

[34] Constantinescu, et al., *Constitutia Romaniei*, 6–7.   [35] Ibid.

of the use of minority languages in courts, since the Constitution clearly states that the Romanian language is the only language of court proceedings; it is true that there is a right to an interpreter provided free of charge for minorities and foreigners, but only in penal cases.

Another domain in which rights standards traditionally enjoyed by minorities were lowered is education. Article 32 of the Constitution protects 'the rights of persons belonging to national minorities to learn their mother tongue and their right to be educated in this language'. The last paragraph mentions that 'the ways to exercise these rights shall be regulated by law'. The possibility of regulating this issue through a special law was interpreted in a restrictive way without bearing in mind the spirit of the Constitution. Therefore, several rights, such as the right to have exams in the native languages, were abolished.

After the 1996 elections several changes were made to Romania's policy towards ethnic minorities. For the first time in Romania's history a national minority party (the Democratic Alliance of Hungarians in Romania) was included in the government coalition, and granted ministerial and deputy ministerial positions. A strong endeavour was carried out in 1997 to amend the existing legislation to meet the minorities' requirements on using their native language. Both the Law on Public Administration and the Law on Education were changed by means of emergency ordinances. But once again, progress made through unconstitutional means proved useless for several years: the ordinance amending the Law on Local Public Administration was struck down by the June 1998 Constitutional Court decision, while the two years of parliamentary discussion on the ordinance amending the Law on Education revived the nationalistic rhetoric, particularly with regard to the existence of universities and faculties in minority languages as well as the study of Romanian history and geography in minorities' native languages. The law was finally promulgated in August 1999, in a form according to national minorities' requirements.

Rights, freedoms, and their constitutional guarantees

The entire Title II of the Constitution is dedicated to 'Fundamental rights, freedoms and duties' (Arts. 15–54). The Drafting Committee as well as the Constitutional Assembly were very proud of this chapter. However, while recognizing the importance of constitutionally regulating rights and freedoms, it is important to understand that 'the absence of constitutional guarantees represents the most significant common characteristic' of these provisions.[36] The Constitution lays down civil and political rights as well as economic and social rights. But it has no provision regarding their direct enforcement. It was the Constitutional Court which issued a decision mentioning the direct enforcement of constitutional rights, though Romanian courts are rather reluctant in applying the Constitution as such.[37] When analysing the constitutional guarantees of the rights and freedoms it is obvious that this issue did not really concern the framers. In line with the communist tradition, there has been a wide gap between the proclamation of rights on the one hand and their enforcement and surveillance on the other.

In addition to the aforementioned constitutional provisions, Articles 11 and 20 may also be included, because all the rights listed by the Universal Declaration, the two International Covenants,[38] and the European Convention[39] are part and parcel of domestic legislation. Their existence was beneficial for Romanian society although on only a few occasions were they invoked by parliament as well as by some courts. For example, in 1992, the Supreme Court of Justice based its decision on the restitution of a nationalized house on the Universal Declaration. Later, the Constitutional Court issued several decisions invoking provisions of the International Covenant on Economic, Social, and Cultural Rights,[40] of the International

---

[36] Lucian Mihai, 'Consideratii privind reglementarea drepturilor omului in Constitutia Romaniei din 1991', [observations on Human Rights Regulations under the 1991 Romanian Constitution] *Revista romana de drepturile omului*, 1 (1993), 8–16.

[37] In a recent decision, the Supreme Court of Justice itself considered against the text of the Constitution that a Constitutional Court decision issued by means of exception in a case brought before the Court is obligatory only in that unique case.

[38] They were ratified in 1974.

[39] The European Convention of Human Rights was ratified in 1994.

[40] By Decision No. 30/1994 the Court decided on the unconstitutionality of the law by which the deadline of renting contracts for living quarters had been extended. It had been stated that these provisions violated the right to own property, as the extension of contracts was decided without the owners' agreement. Even though the Constitution does not stipulate as such the right to housing, the Court regarded it as part of the broader right to decent living conditions stipulated in Art. 43. The Court invoked the provisions of Art. 25 of the Universal Declaration of Human Rights and of Article 11 in the International Covenant on Economic, Social, and Cultural Rights that mention the right to housing in the broader context of satisfactory living standards. The Court rejected the exception of unconstitutionality on grounds that extension of renting deadline was a legal policy measure compatible with the aggregate constitutional provisions. Another decision containing reference to the provisions of an international treaty was Decision

Covenant on Civil and Political Rights (or both),[41] and of the European Convention.[42]

In reference to socio-economic rights, few constitutional guarantees exist. It is true that the Constitution sets forth in Article 1.3 that 'Romania is a democratic and social State' but there are no mechanisms for indicating how this 'social character' is to be observed. In their book on the Romanian Constitution, six legal experts consider that

The 'social' attribute may be considered as a correction of classic liberal democracy, essentially political. The essence of liberal democracy is the 'freedom' but in the case of undeveloped countries 'freedom' tends to become

No. 114/1994 by which Art. 32 of Law No. 88/1993 was declared unconstitutional. According to its provisions, professors were not allowed to teach in a higher education institution above the limit established by law on the numbers of hours per week. The Court based its decision on the provisions of Art. 6 pt. 1 of the International Covenant on Economic, Social and Cultural Rights, according to which the right to work includes the person's right to earn their living by means of a job they choose or accept freely. Thus, the Constitutional Court ruled that 'People's right to work cannot be made the object of any limitation or restriction, each person being free to work as much as his/her physical or mental abilities—which that person alone can assess—allow him/her to.' At the same time, the Constitutional Court interpreted 'reasonable limitation of working hours' set forth in Art. 7 lit. d of the Covenant in the sense that it may by no means be the ground for restrictions to the right to work, but underlines the right of not imposing on one the duty to work beyond one's physical and mental abilities.

[41] By means of Decision No. 6/1993, the Constitutional Court ruled out as unconstitutional the provisions of Law No. 58/1992 that stipulated different taxes for three categories of persons (taxes were increased by 30% for incomes resulting from multiple sources). The Court invoked the provisions of Art. 26 of the International Covenant on Civil and Political Rights referring to non-discrimination, Art. 2.2 of the International Covenant on Economic, Social, and Cultural Rights, and Art. 14 of the European Convention on Human Rights.

[42] The Court declared the provisions of Art. 75.1 of the Labour Code unconstitutional by Decision No. 59/1994. According to these provisions, complaints filed against decisions to annul labour contracts as well as labour litigation relating to reintegration of managers in their former jobs were to be solved by the administrative body ranking higher in the hierarchy or by a collective leadership body. The Court referred to the violation of Art. 16 of the Constitution on non-discrimination and of Art. 21 on free access to justice and based its decisions on the provisions of Art. 6 pt. 1 of the European Convention, on the grounds that the administrative bodies that annulled the labour contract cannot represent an independent impartial tribunal, as the Convention requires. The Constitutional Court decided on the unconstitutionality of Art. 200.1 that used to punish by prison same-sex relations between consenting adults (Decision No. 81/1994). The Court invoked the provisions of Art. 8 of the European Convention, making reference to the case law of the Strasbourg European Court, more precisely to the *Dudgeon*, *Norris*, and *Modinas* cases.

a metaphor if it is not financially supported. On the other hand, for these countries, issuing a global development strategy and its implementation are indispensable. For these countries—and not only for them—the 'general interest' is above the individual interests, specific to liberalism.[43]

But what are the implications of this approach? Does it mean that political parties based on a liberal ideology—including the classical one which stresses the individualist approach—are to be banned? Does it mean that the Constitution itself determines which ideology and political approach the country must adopt? As yet, no one seems to have attempted to address this issue. But it seems that a silent consensus has been reached to consider this provision merely as rhetorical, and to ignore it.

However, due to its character as a 'social state', the Romanian state has, through its Constitution, a wide range of prerogatives, even obligations, in order to ensure the welfare of its citizens. Thus, according to Article 43.1, 'The State shall be bound to take measures of economic development and social protection, of a nature to ensure a decent living standard for its citizens.' The rights enjoyed by Romanian citizens range from 'the right to pensions, paid maternity leave, medical care in public health establishments, unemployment benefits and other forms of social care, as provided by law' (Art. 43.2) to Article 33.1, which mentions that 'The right to protection of health is guaranteed', while paragraph 2 specifies that 'The State shall be bound to take measures to ensure public hygiene and health.' In terms of work, the fundamental law no longer mentions a 'right to work', but instead 'The right to work cannot be restricted. Everyone has a free choice of profession and workplace' (Art. 38.1). The fact that all employees are entitled to 'the right to social protection and labour. The protecting measures concern safety and hygiene of work, working conditions for women and the young, the setting up of a minimum wage per economy, weekends, paid annual leave, work carried out under hard conditions, as well as other specific situations' is also recognized (Art. 38.2). In addition to this, the fundamental law also contains several articles related to the right of women to receive equal pay for equal work, to the protection of the handicapped, of children, and the young, general compulsory and free education at all levels, the right to associate (including trade unions), the right to strike, the collective labour contract, banning of forced labour, and others.

The most important question to be raised is whether all these provisions—and especially their development through ordinary

[43] Constantinescu et al., *Constitutia Romaniei*, 14.

legislation and through practice—will be capable of turning Romania into a welfare state or if they are the result of a backward mentality, according to which the state is omnipotent, omnipresent, and paternalistic. Thus far, the implementation of the Constitution's socio-economic guarantees is directly related to the political, economic, and social programme of the government—meaning of the ruling party (or coalition). Every year a budget on state social security is adopted but more and more the burden has been transferred from the state to companies. The result has been that approximately 40 per cent of the total labour force in Romania works 'on the black market'. Thus laws issued to protect employees (such as Law No. 83/1995, according to which employers are compelled to hire their employees by contract and to pay high social assistance funds) largely miss their targets. It has become clear that punishing wealthy companies does not mean encouraging the creation of new jobs, and therefore these laws will not do much to improve social protection. Needless to say, no one has ever been fined for non-observance of these regulations, thus confirming that such legislation does not mean very much.

One of the institutions given the mandate to protect human rights is the ombudsman (the advocate of the people). It is regulated in the Constitution within its second title 'Fundamental rights, freedoms and duties' and is thus regarded as a guarantee for the citizens to enjoy their rights and freedoms. But the Constitution is rather vague when describing the institution and its competence. Article 56.1 reads: 'The Advocate of the People shall exercise his power ex officio or upon request by persons aggrieved in their rights and freedoms, within limits established by law.' Article 55.1 also states that 'the organization and functioning of the Advocate of the People institution shall be regulated by an organic law.' Some authors have remarked that these constitutional provisions are too vague to allow us to realize how effective this institution will be.[44] It is worth mentioning that the Constitution did not recommend any deadline for such a law and the law was issued only in the spring of 1997—six years after the adoption of the Constitution. In his book on constitutional law and political institutions, Ion Deleanu, a member of the Drafting Committee and a former judge at the Constitutional Court, mentions that several ombudsmen from various countries have criticized the Romanian constitutional provisions for their ambiguity: the independence of

[44] Mihai, 'Consideratii privind reglementarea drepturilor omului in Constitutia Romaniei din 1991'.

the advocate of the people is neither explicit nor stressed enough; the competencies and their means of implementation are not defined, etc. But the author was confident that the law will make the necessary corrections.[45] Unfortunately the law did not make any such correction and up to the present time the institution is still quite invisible.

Conclusions

Several facts allow me to assert that the Constitution has played a positive role in democratic consolidation, while others make me more reluctant. Paradoxically, since its adoption the Constitution has been invoked all the time and observed by those who voted against it and has been violated mainly by those who voted in its favour in 1991. Thus, there is still a distinction to be made between legality and legal rhetoric. Many reproaches have been made concerning the imperfections of the Romanian Constitution. But the existence of an early Constitution, as imperfect as it is, has been perhaps the most important accomplishment of the Romanian revolution. Looking back and analysing the stages Romania has passed through, it is more and more obvious that the 1991 Constitution was the best that could be done. Given the political climate in 1994 or 1995, when nationalist-extremist parties were not only in parliament but also in the government and when the ruling party acted more and more in an authoritarian way, it seems clear that a more liberal constitution could not have been adopted.

Of course, the conflict between observance and violation of the Constitution, or the delay in implementing certain provisions (such as the effective local decentralization, the establishment of the ombudsman, or the law on referenda), has impeded the development of the country. However, society has learned the necessity of fighting to safeguard the Constitution and the democratic institutions it created. In terms of legal and political education this means a lot. For example when President Iliescu criticized the Romanian courts for their decision on the issue of nationalized houses, by stating that their role as judges is not to rule but to wait for parliamentary regulations, the public's view was that he had interfered with a domain which is not his, thus violating the Constitution. When, according to his wish, the general prosecutor launched extraordinary appeals against those court decisions and

[45] Deleanu, *Drept constitutional si institutii politice*, 185.

the Supreme Court admitted them, the reaction was not a lack of trust in the justice system, but an understanding of how important it is to respect the institutions and their independence. When President Constantinescu dismissed Prime Minister Vasile in 1999, criticism was made from a constitutional perspective. The fact that all these political gestures were unconstitutional was more and more clearly understood.

At the same time, the Constitution has imposed certain limits on government behaviour, through its—albeit imperfect—checks and balances system. This was the case in many decisions of the government which have been declared unconstitutional by the Constitutional Court. Most obviously, the Court's 1998 decision to restrict the use of emergency ordinances has paved the way for a new focus on constitutionality. Unfortunately, this lesson has come at a high price. Some of the government's ordinances, for instance the Law on Education, were quite progressive and it is questionable whether the lengthy and contentious process of parliamentary debates would result in similarly liberal laws. However, if the Romanian Constitution is to be observed not only in its letter but also in its spirit, which must be understood in its democratic dimension, the democratic evolution of the country will be secured.

9

Ukraine: Tormented Constitution-Making

Kataryna Wolczuk

In stable regimes, the institutional structure mediates actors' behaviour and determines policy outcomes in terms of who gets 'what, when, and how'. The collapse of communism reversed that relationship, and the primary role was assigned to elites, who reshuffled institutions and reassigned powers and responsibilities (something German constitutionalists refer to as *Kompetenzkompetenz*). As new constitutional frameworks are built, the distinction between the tools and outcomes of politics became blurred and confused. Because of the breakdown of the established pattern of politics, the post-communist world of politics can be best characterized as punctuated equilibrium.[1] To restore equilibrium, various paths have been pursued: a rapid revamp as in Bulgaria, or learning by trial and error as in Poland. However, constitution-making in Ukraine can be best conceptualized in terms of a Gramscian catastrophic equilibrium: a situation that arises when the old system has passed into posterity but the new one has yet to emerge. Ukraine's improvised and disrupted constitution-making left it suspended between the past and the future.

The first couple of years of independence was a period of institutional preservation rather than institutional engineering, and the delay was not spent deliberating the merits and perils of institutional templates.[2] Then, when constitution-making finally got under

[1] Stephen D. Krasner, 'Approaches to the State: Alternative Conceptions and Historical Dynamics', *Comparative Politics*, 16/2 (Jan. 1984), 242.

[2] Stephen Holmes argues that delaying constitutional choices and opting for stop-gap constitutions may well be advantageous as hasty solutions can be avoided, while the accumulated expertise leads to the mastering of constitutional choices. See Stephen Holmes, 'Conceptions of Democracy in the Draft Constitutions of Post-communist Countries', in Beverly Crawford (ed.), *Markets, States and Democracy: The Political Economy of Post-communist Transformation* (Boulder, Colo.: Westview Press, 1995), 71–80.

way, the final choices were made in a haphazard and improvised manner. Nevertheless, a precarious configuration of domestic and external factors allowed the Constitution to pass, albeit on the spur of the moment. The adoption was peaceful and respectful of the parameters of the 'improvised' legality, though not without tension. Ukraine adopted its new Constitution in June 1996, as the last to do so of the post-Soviet states.

The foregoing suggests two purposes for this chapter. First, it will explore the factors that contributed to an inability to decide on a constitutional framework, and highlight the circumstances in which the choices were finally made. Secondly, it will analyse the impact and functioning of the new Constitution. The short period of time since the passage of the Constitution makes an assessment of the extent to which norms have been routinized and internalized by political actors tentative and preliminary. Nevertheless, the analysis should reveal some of the shortcomings of the constitutional design, which up to a point can account for continuing institutional rivalry. At the same time, the prospects for democratic consolidation in Ukraine are still open.

Independence and Constitutional Choices

The disintegration of central Soviet structures and the shift of power to the republics inspired the creation of the Ukrainian presidency in July 1991. It was hoped that a presidency would enhance the self-governing capacity of the republic. At the republic level, the system was based on the Supreme Council (performing both legislative and some higher executive functions) and the Council of Ministers, headed by a chairperson, who named ministers and other top officials responsible for economic matters. Designed to promote supposed Soviet federalism, they were not capable of coping with the new burden of decision-making when power devolved to the republics. Thus, the purpose of the presidency was to strengthen the institutional resources of the republic. Much more important, however, was the external dimension. At the federal level, the presidency was symbolically to legitimize Ukrainian sovereignty against the old Soviet centre, and more particularly against the Gorbachev presidency (created in March 1990). Thus, the Ukrainian presidency was given sweeping powers 'to suspend the action of decisions of the executive power of the USSR on the territory of Ukraine if they contradicted the constitution and the laws of the

Ukrainian SSR'.[3] Since the president was to be popularly elected, his mass mandate was to strengthen local elites vis-à-vis Moscow.

At home, direct legitimacy could give the Ukrainian president an advantage over the still undemocratically elected parliament dominated by the state and economic bureaucracy. Thus, the popular legitimization of the head of the executive branch was circumscribed by a division of powers that gave the upper hand to parliament. The president (to be elected directly for five years in double-ballot elections) would have the right to form a government with parliamentary approval, to initiate the legislative process, and to veto legislation. However, a simple parliamentary majority would suffice to override the presidential veto, and the government would be required to resign in the event of a no-confidence vote. Furthermore, the parliamentary chairman retained the right to suspend decisions of the executive branch under certain circumstances. The president could not dissolve parliament and call for new elections if the government resigned. In essence, the presidency was an addendum to Soviet-era parliamentarism rather than a revision of it. Even if crudely grafted onto the system of soviets, the early presidential prerogatives opened the door for the gradual extension of the role of the president.

The reshuffling of institutions was originally intended to prepare the republic to compete with Moscow. Ukrainian independence, declared in August and confirmed by referendum in December 1991, would seem to change the context and scope of institutional reform dramatically. The demise of the Communist Party exposed the ill-defined, inefficient, and often purely decorative institutions of Ukraine. Swift constitutional reform was needed to transform decorative statehood into a coherent and efficient institutional edifice. There was a desperate need to define competences between legislature and executive and between centre and periphery. Yet once the inspiration of external restraint disappeared, political momentum for constitutional change dissipated.

The consequences of being divided between neighbouring empires over the centuries, followed by a communist iron hand ruling from Moscow, began to haunt newly independent Ukraine. The atomized society lacked the high degree of national unity and robust national identity which 'provides for consensus, for a

---

[3] Art. 7 of the 'Law on the Creation of the President of the Ukrainian Soviet Socialist Republic and Changes to the Constitution of UkrSSR', which was published in *Pravda Ukrainy* (1 Aug. 1991).

shared set of values and world views, and these in turn encourage the emergence of social institutions and democratic (or for that matter any other kind of) rules of the game'.[4] The passage to independence was animated by the self-interested members of the communist *nomenklatura*, who skilfully synthesized the ideology of national liberation provided by the democratic opposition with their own agenda of preserving power under new circumstances. The national democratic opposition was ultimately too weak to dictate the pace and direction of change. Instead, it ended up oscillating between acclaiming the ex-communists in their reincarnation as democratic state makers, and exposing their cynical manœuvres. Soon, however, this Janus-faced strategy of the national democrats backfired. Championing democracy, market reform, and national revival, while in and out of tandem with the ruling elites, the national democrats' incoherent stance contributed to a significant erosion of popular trust and the legitimacy of the goals they advocated, without achieving them.

The communist experience in Ukraine failed to provide sufficient incentives to bring about the immediate reform of the inherited Soviet institutional framework. With weak agencies of democratization, no power base for launching radical institutional reform existed. Because of the ambivalence towards the ancient regime and the high degree of continuity, there was no consensus on the extent to which the Soviet institutional order was delegitimized and consequently on whether and how it should be changed. The situation was exacerbated by the fact that there was no readily available model that Ukraine could adopt. The absence of a prolonged period of Ukrainian statehood deprived Ukraine of a historically legitimized template of government. In September 1991 the Soviet 1978 Constitution, after some mostly symbolic changes, was transformed into the Constitution of independent Ukraine. The resuscitation of the Soviet Constitution was intended to boost the procedural legitimacy of the 'old-new' regime.

The first president—Leonid Kravchuk—was elected on the same day the referendum was held. Throughout the eventful year of 1991, he had led the rapid transition to nationalism of Ukraine's communist elites. Understandably, once elected Kravchuk sought to clarify the powers of his ill-defined office. He resorted to state-building rhetoric to demand the strengthening of the executive branch as 'reforms were necessitated by the unresponsiveness

---

[4] Alexander J. Motyl, *Dilemmas of Independence: Ukraine after Totalitarianism* (New York: The Council on Foreign Relations, 1993), 71–2.

of the state agencies, especially at the local level, to the new demands posed by Ukrainian independence'.[5] In the first months of his term, he was granted additional prerogatives concerning political and economic reforms; his platform of the consolidation of statehood was not contested by any major political grouping. In particular, the pro-reform minority—the national democrats—had limited room for manœuvre. They found it difficult to dissociate themselves from Kravchuk's line of reasoning, as the legitimacy of the Ukrainian state had yet to be established.

Despite the existence of some parliamentary factions, the parliament—elected in March 1990—remained highly unstructured.[6] Over half of all the deputies—the former members of the CPU after its dissolution in August 1991—had no party affiliation. (As deputies could belong to more than one faction, precise numbers cannot be estimated as the factions' membership overlapped considerably.) Parliament, being rooted in the old system, was incapable of acting purposefully, let alone proposing a coherent reform package. Rather, as Motyl put it, it resembled a 'debating society . . . with half the people's deputies, those with Communist sympathies, arguing passionately for inaction, while the other half, those with democratic inclinations, argued just as passionately for action of any kind'.[7] Yet, running the state and managing the divorce from the Soviet economic space necessitated a multitude of decisions that had to be taken quickly, if the country was to prevent the approaching slide into economic disarray, which was just beginning. A remedy was found in the ad hoc granting of law-making powers first to the president and then to the government. Between November 1992 and May 1993, the Cabinet of Ministers headed by Prime Minister Kuchma had the extraordinary authority to adopt resolutions with the power of laws. However, the parliament stopped short of turning these emergency measures into more permanent arrangements; it merely temporarily delegated its prerogatives. In this flux, President Kravchuk's somewhat prevaricating style of leadership was not conducive to clarifying the 'rules of the game', despite his initial vigour. He quietly disengaged from direct leadership of the executive branch and focused on representative and highly visible functions concerning security and foreign affairs. Despite securing what would appear to be sufficient

---

[5] Roman Solchanyk, 'Ukraine: Political Reform and Political Change', *RFE/RL Research Report*, 1/21 (22 May 1992), 2.

[6] The national democrats' calls for the pre-term elections in 1992 were duly dismissed.

[7] Motyl, *Dilemmas of Independence*, 165.

prerogatives as head of the executive branch, Kravchuk hardly influenced policy-making (e.g. by initiating the legislative process or issuing decrees) apart from the half-hearted reform of central institutions, which involved setting up new ministries and consultative bodies. The majority of adopted laws—uncoordinated, random, and contradictory as they were—stemmed from the parliament's or the government's initiative. Having observed the initially rapid aggrandizement of the presidency, some authors argued that Ukraine was slipping into an authoritarian presidential regime by 1993.[8] However, Kravchuk's presidency was never strong enough to control political outcomes; parliamentary structures were not replaced with presidential ones; and, most importantly, Kravchuk did not gain control of the mechanism of his own accountability (as he lost the elections in 1994). Instead, Ukraine continued to suffer the consequences of an ill-defined hybrid system of Soviet parliamentarism with elements of presidentialism.

The catastrophic degradation of the economy motivated an emergency reshuffle of responsibilities: but proper constitution-drafting continued to languish, even though the concept of the new Constitution was adopted still under the Soviet Union in June 1991. That project envisaged a presidential republic based on the principle of a separation of powers combined with the existing system of soviets. On the basis of vague guidelines, two drafts were prepared in 1992 and 1993 by the unwieldy Constitutional Commission, whose membership had not changed since 1990. If the first draft leaned towards a stronger presidency, the second one reflected a more ambivalent stance (perhaps due to Kravchuk's indecisive style of leadership), vesting more authority in parliament. However, the Constitution, in contrast to issues such as relations with Russia, Crimean separatism, or nuclear weapons, did not attract the attention of elites. While other states were busy promulgating new constitutions, the ritualistic Soviet-style nationwide discussion and consultation of the draft Constitution in 1992–3 could hardly be taken as a sign of a commitment to constitution-making in Ukraine.[9]

This limited interest can be attributed to the fact that the chaotic machinery of government provided elites with ample

---

[8] See, for example, P. Roeder, 'Varieties in Post-communist Authoritarian Regimes', *Post-Soviet Affairs*, 10/1 (1994) and Paul Kubicek, 'Delegative Democracy in Russia and Ukraine', *Communist and Post-communist Studies*, 27/4 (1994), 423–41.

[9] As was proudly pointed out, about 47,000 comments and proposals were made, all of which the Constitutional Commission apparently considered.

opportunity for rent extraction from the semi-liberalized economy. In other words, the old guard resisted any delineation of authority which would restrict its ability to plunder. At the same time, domestic actors were not ready to make clear-cut institutional choices. The ruling, post-*nomenklatura* elite was not differentiated enough to seek specific institutional advantages and did not understand how various institutional arrangements could benefit its interests. Thus, the notion of maximizing interests by pursuing strategies to secure institutional advantages had limited resonance in Ukraine in the first two years of independence.

This reluctance to engage in institutional engineering and the shortage of risk-taking actors must be viewed in the wider context of the consolidation of Ukrainian statehood. Embarking on any delineation of authority would entail conflict and thus undermine the fragile foundation of statehood. Ukraine as an independent state was not consolidated enough to face instability. Thus, a public appearance of unity was to cover up Ukraine's regional, cultural, linguistic, and political cleavages. Conflict over institutions was not allowed to surface so as not to threaten or undermine the support of the Ukrainian elites for independence. Priority was given to asserting collective and territorial integrity through a mixture of anti-Russian and pro-European foreign policy measures and through the crafting of symbolic pillars of nationhood. Kravchuk stressed the need to protect the new fragile state against unnecessary shocks, and the slogan of 'national self-determination' became the sacred dogma for all political forces. Instead of 'democracy' or 'market economy', the buzzwords of the Ukrainian transition were 'statehood', 'sovereignty', 'nationhood'. Yet the state- and nation-building rhetoric starkly contrasted with the very limited institutional transformation taking place in the country.

By 1994, the necessary differentiation between the governing functions could be delayed no longer. Equilibrium had to be restored, as the desperate need for economic stabilization, aside from any transformation, meant that the difficult question of what kind of institutions Ukraine should be furnished with could no longer be postponed.

The Critical Juncture

The presidential and parliamentary elections of 1994 ended the period of the symbolic politics of unity and marked the earnest beginning of the structuralization of political life in Ukraine. The

principal confrontation, resulting from the genuine need for an effective and competent structure of government, took place.

As the symbolic consolidation around independence could not
conceal the heterogeneity and cleavages running within Ukrainian society and polity, the constitutional process exposed the sheer
number of issues that had to be dealt with. Even though the framing of constitutions in new states rarely reflects any sense of a
harmony among competing parties, reform requires at least broad
agreement in favour of change. In Ukraine this would have meant,
as a minimum, the rejection of the system of soviets based on the
principle of 'unity of power', something that did not sit easily with
the conception of a separation of powers. However, even this minim-
alist agenda for institutional reform was hardly shared universally.
Herein lies the explanation for the delay in the promulgation of
the Constitution after the 1994 elections.

The plurality electoral law disadvantaged political parties in
the first free parliamentary elections in 1994, and fewer than half
of all elected deputies had party affiliations.[10] Yet changes in the
parliamentary rules (streamlining the membership of factions)
facilitated a degree of structuralization of parliament and the emergence of three political blocs: the left, right, and centre. However,
the Ukrainian political spectrum was only crystallized and strong at
its antipodes. Both the left (communists, socialist factions) and the
right (*Rukh, Derzhavnist*) were essentially party-based, with deep
ideological commitments. In contrast, having no clear constituency
nor party affiliations, the centre, made up of such factions as
Yednist, Centre, Interregional Group, Independents, Social Market
Choice, and non-affiliated deputies, could be more precisely described
as consisting of left-centre-right politicians. Overall, the centre
avoided ideological clashes between the left and right, focusing on
more pragmatic (often economic) pursuits. Depending on the issue,
the centre could side with either the left or the right. No overall
sense of discipline, apart from the final vote on the Constitution,
was ever imposed on this bloc. At the same time, it comprised nearly
half of all deputies; the leftist bloc occupied something over
one-third of all seats, while the national democrats trailed with
under a quarter. As the fragmented centre could not become a

---

[10] Under the electoral law, it was easier for workers' collectives and voters' groups
to nominate candidates than it was for political parties. Also, the 50% threshold
of voter turnout had to be passed to elect a deputy and a successful candidate had
to obtain more than 50% of votes. Because of these strict requirements, many
seats were not filled in 1994 and were only gradually filled in numerous repeat
elections.

stabilizing and mediating actor in its own right, no clear majority and opposition emerged in parliament. While this amorphousness prevented a consensus in favour of reform, it did leave room for the type of manœuvre that eventually resulted in the adoption of the Constitution, against all the odds. It was Leonid Kuchma, the second president of Ukraine, who managed to wring a constitutional majority from the divided parliament. Under Kuchma, who in contrast to his predecessor championed economic and political reform, the presidency became a focal point of political innovation. Kuchma's risk-taking approach turned him into a mediator between the two incompatible visions—at the price of expanding the powers of the presidency.

After the 1994 elections, a new Constitutional Commission co-headed by President Kuchma and the left-wing chairman of the Supreme Council Oleksandr Moroz and consisting of forty-two members representing 'subjects with the right of legislative initiative' was created.[11] Its composition did not bode well for a rapid completion of the task, as the commission could hardly organize its work, let alone agree on the form of government. Yet President Kuchma was not willing to put up with the confused constitutional environment. He had already demonstrated his determination immediately after the election, in August 1994, when he asserted his authority by issuing two decrees (*ukazy*) which effectively made the executive branch at central and local levels accountable to the president. The *ukazy* indicated that the 1978 Constitution ceased to perform the organizing function and was no longer respected even nominally.

While the constitutional commission was entangled in ideological disputes, Kuchma proposed a more permanent solution to the constitutional crisis—'The Law on Power'. The law was to regulate executive–legislative relations until the new Constitution was ready. The initiative had three more narrowly political purposes. First, it was to counteract the left's proposed 'Law on Local Councils' of July 1994, which was designed to strengthen the system of soviets. With the Supreme Council as the highest state organ, the president would be deprived of any means of controlling the executive structure, and thereby limited to ceremonial functions. Secondly, the presidential 'Law on Power' would disguise

---

[11] The commission consisted of 15 representatives of the Supreme Council (proportionally representing the parliamentary factions), 15 representatives of the president, 1 representative of the Supreme Rada of Crimea, and 7 members from the judicial branch (Supreme, Arbitrary, Constitutional Courts, and Procuracy).

farreaching constitutional changes in favour of the presidency
as an 'ordinary' law, thereby neatly getting round the two-thirds'
requirement necessary to change the Constitution. Thirdly, it
would provide a precedent for the new Constitution, most notably
creating a presumption for a strong executive presidency.[12]

Once the draft was tabled in parliament, the centrists and right
factions faced a dilemma: to aid the strengthening of the pro-reform
president, or to guard parliamentary prerogatives. Although the
pro-reform forces opted to support the president, they still favoured
a power-sharing system based on a balance between the legislature and a strong yet accountable executive branch. Hence, Kuchma's
draft was amended, and presidential prerogatives were diluted. The
articles on the dissolution of parliament by the president and
impeachment of the president by parliament were dropped. Even
after those changes, the amended law mustered only a simple majority in May 1995, and it was evident that—despite Kuchma's hopes
—changes to the 1978 Constitution were necessary. Kuchma could
not expect the support of the left, which he needed for a constitutional majority. Facing its steady opposition, Kuchma, conscious of
his high popularity rating in contrast to that of the legislature,
resorted to his popular mandate and decreed a referendum on
confidence in both the president and parliament. Confrontation
was averted only by an extraordinary Constitutional Agreement
(*Konstytutsiynyi Dohovir*) between Kuchma and parliament, led by
its leftist chairman Oleksandr Moroz. The agreement stipulated
a suspension of certain sections of the 1978 Constitution and the
adoption of the amended 'Law on Power' for a year, until the new
Constitution was sanctioned in a nationwide referendum.

The *Dohovir* was only a momentary interval in the unfolding
conflict over power. It could not last as a substitute for a fully-fledged
constitution, as the communists along with some agrarians and
socialists denied its constitutionality on the grounds that it was
passed only by a simple majority; they were also outraged by
Kuchma's arm-twisting techniques, which they called proof of his
authoritarian inclinations. Yet, the *Dohovir* was not without its
significance—it set a precedent for the resolution of the political
conflict in Ukraine, and its one-year deadline mobilized all actors.

However, there were no signs of progress emanating from the
Constitutional Commission. To speed up the process, the task of

---

[12] Kataryna Wolczuk, 'The Politics of Constitution-Making in Ukraine', in Taras
Kuzio (ed.), *Contemporary Ukraine: Dynamics of Post-Soviet Transformation* (London: M. E. Sharpe, 1998).

drafting the basic draft was delegated to a working group of legal experts. This worked to the president's advantage as this group tended to favour the presidential point of view on executive–legislative relations. Yet, there was little time for such deliberations. Once the draft was ready, it was amended and accepted by the Constitutional Commission (though the communists voted against it), and submitted as an official draft to parliament in March 1996—even though it was not viewed by many as a masterpiece of constitutional engineering.[13]

The draft Constitution, as the president put it, was intended 'to end Soviet rule in Ukraine once and forever'.[14] It proposed a two-chamber legislature (*Natsionalni Zbory*): the House of Deputies was endowed with law-making and budget functions, while the upper chamber, the Senate, was allocated the authority to approve presidential candidates for top posts.[15] Most importantly, the president would have the right to issue decrees with the power of laws; to veto parliamentary bills (which could be overruled by a two-thirds majority in the House of Deputies); to dissolve the legislature (if the lower chamber rejected the programme of government twice within sixty days). In contrast, parliament could not easily veto presidential decrees.[16] It could however, impeach the president, although only through a cumbersome procedure involving the Constitutional Court. According to the draft, the Cabinet of Ministers would be approved by parliament and would exist for the duration of the president's term in office. The cabinet would not have the right of legislative initiative, which would be the prerogative of the president. Interestingly, although the draft envisaged an executive presidency, there was no attempt to abolish the post of prime minister and the Cabinet of Ministers. The president was not even named the head of state. This puzzling restraint can be explained by the reluctance of the president to take visible responsibility for the performance of the executive branch. The role of the cabinet was designed as an intermediate link in the chain of executive authority, which was ultimately to be headed by the president. Such an arrangement of relations between the president and prime minister was incorporated into the new Constitution, which

[13] It was published in *Uriadovyi Kurier* (21 Mar. 1996).

[14] Interview with Kuchma, Ukrainian TV (24 Nov. 1995).

[15] The Senate was to be directly elected. However, due to the weakness of the party system the successful candidates in direct elections tended to be local state officials, who according to the draft would have been appointed by the president.

[16] Only the ruling of the Constitutional Court—nominated by the Senate and president—could suspend presidential decrees.

allowed for the prime minister to be conveniently blamed for the dire state of the economy and unilaterally dismissed by the president.

Although both the specific provisions and the general spirit of autocratic rule in the draft sparked wide-ranging criticism across the political spectrum, there was relief amongst the right-centre factions that at least there was a complete draft to work on. Nevertheless, the communists were very critical of the draft and questioned the authority of the Constitutional Commission to prepare it.[17] In addition, they collected three million signatures in support of a referendum on the principles of the new Constitution, and tabled their own draft of the 'Constitution of the Ukrainian Soviet Socialist Republic' in parliament. According to their draft, power was to be vested in a vertical chain of people's councils with the Supreme Council being the highest state body. The Supreme Council would perform or delegate executive functions, and appoint judges and oversee the judiciary. The draft envisioned no presidency or constitutional court. The left's overarching objective was to preserve the Soviet system of power intact and it effectively advocated the Soviet system of *narodovladya* embedded in people's soviets as opposed to the system based on a separation of powers. The left claimed the presidency was an invitation to introduce a dictatorship.

In contrast, both the centre and the right allocated the president more than a figurehead role. It was soberly recognized that, in the short term at least, a parliamentary system was not an option for Ukraine. As Sartori pointed out 'parliamentary democracy cannot perform (in any of its varieties) unless it is served by *parliamentarily fit* parties, that is to say, parties that have been socialized (by failure, duration, and appropriate incentives) into being relatively cohesive or disciplined, into behaving, in opposition, as responsible opposition, and into playing, to some extent, a rule-guided fair game'.[18] It was evident that those pillars of parliamentarism were not present in Ukraine. For many, the aversion to parliamentarism stemmed from its connotations with the system of soviets, so close to the hearts of the left. A more radical departure was needed, such as a semi-presidential system, which was seen as necessary to clear away the remnants of Soviet institutions. And an executive presidency was deemed an indispensable solution to

---

[17] The communists argued that the working group consisted only of pro-presidential specialists and the communist representatives did not approve the final draft. See *Holos Ukrainy* (26 Dec. 1995).

[18] Giovanni Sartori, 'Neither Presidentialism nor Parliamentarism', in J. J. Linz and A. Valenzuela (eds.), *The Failure of Presidential Democracy*, vol. i (Baltimore: Johns Hopkins University Press, 1994), 112.

the crisis of ungovernability. At the same time, as no faction was ready to place the fate of the country in one person's hands, the power-sharing arrangement had to be crafted carefully. Setting up a more balanced machinery of government was the primary concern of the centrist factions. Some national democrats were more willing to sacrifice the power of parliament, in exchange for a favourable solution to the 'national question' in the Constitution.

During constitution-drafting a wide array of issues was contested, reaching far beyond the already complex issue of the delineation of authority. Constitution-making revealed a fundamental disagreement on the very basis of Ukrainian statehood. National democrats and communists differed not only in their view of the overall form of government, but also on the issues of sovereignty, territorial integrity, and nationhood. There was also no agreement on the extent to which the Constitution should become a nation-building instrument, asserting the 'national' nature of the polity. Thus, apart from dividing competences among the legislature, executive, and judicial branches and defining centre–periphery relations, the bones of contention included: the subject of the Constitution, 'the Ukrainian people' or 'the People of Ukraine'; national symbols (the anthem, emblem, flag); the state language; socio-economic guarantees; the status of private property; the status of the Crimean peninsula; the status of foreign military bases in Ukraine. Issues of language and symbols divided constitution-makers even more deeply than the delineation of powers, and evoked debilitating, passionate debates, which permeated constitution-making until the very end.

There were also external factors at play, in that the final stages of constitution-making coincided with the Russian presidential elections in 1996. It was clear that the communist faction was actively obstructing the process in anticipation of a Zyuganov victory and the subsequent revival of the communist cause across the post-Soviet space. For those who feared this possibility, constitution-making became a matter of consolidating sovereignty. Serhiy Holovatyi, the minister of justice, commented on the content of the draft: 'These are only details. Because, today, what concerns me the most is the problem of survival. And that very much depends on whether or not Ukraine will have its own constitution before the elections in Russia.'[19] The quick ratification of the Constitution had finally become the uttermost priority.

---

[19] *Ukrainian Weekly* (17 Mar. 1996).

Committed as they were to the passage of the Constitution, the centre-right parliamentary factions formed an informal conciliatory group aimed at changing the outline of the institutional framework, to make the draft 'passable' in parliament. This in particular meant a revision of the idea of the bicameral legislature (envisaged in the March draft) which evoked the most zealous resistance across the political spectrum.[20] They improved the system of 'checks and balances' in April and May 1996, though not to the extent of alienating the president, who, in the face of the leftist attempts to impede the ratification process, was a much-needed ally. As a result, an amended version—the so-called Syrota draft—was produced. Despite various tactics used by the left to control or hinder the debates, on 4 June 1996 the draft underwent its first reading; as expected, it obtained only a simple majority.[21] Recognizing that it would take something of a miracle to muster a two-thirds majority, the national democrats began to call for the president to subject the draft to a referendum.

Indeed, the final stimulus came from the president himself, though the manner in which this was achieved alienated even his allies in parliament. Kuchma re-emerged as the dominant force in the constitution-making, after finally losing patience with the volatile parliament, which amended 'his' earlier draft. On 26 June 1996 the president announced that with no prospect of the Constitution being adopted by the Supreme Council, a nationwide referendum voting on the March draft would be held in September 1996. In one fell swoop President Kuchma sidestepped the cumbersome compromises worked out within the Supreme Council (and agreed with him) over four months. The March draft was regarded by the centre-right deputies, even those allied with the president, as inferior to the already approved draft.[22]

---

[20] Apart from the Ukrainian Republican Party and its *Derzhavnist'* faction, the rest of the national democrats viewed the Senate as a step towards the federalization of Ukraine, and argued that in a unitary state there was no need for such regional representation.

[21] The most frequently used method for obstructing sessions (known as 'constructive destruction') was the refusal to register so that a quorum could not be reached. This was not only used by the left, as the right-wing factions resorted to it when they were not satisfied with the changes to the Constitution proposed by the left.

[22] There was a group of approximately forty deputies who consistently defended the presidential position, and effectively acted as a president's 'fifth column' in parliament. These deputies combined parliamentary mandates with posts in the executive branch at the central and local level, and were ultimately subordinated to the president. The new Constitution prohibited this practice.

The decree triggered frantic action on the part of the parliament to complete the ratification. This was undoubtedly motivated by the fact that, once the president set out on the path of confrontation, pre-term parliamentary elections after the referendum could not be ruled out. As a result, the parliament, led by the leftist chairman —Oleksandr Moroz, who until then had hindered the passage— began a non-stop debate and after a twenty-three-hour marathon of repetitious voting completed the task in a tense atmosphere in the morning of 28 June 1996. The constitutional majority of 301 was reached when 315 deputies voted in favour of the constitution, 36 against, 12 abstained. The left bloc, renowned for its voting discipline up till that point, splintered under pressure during the final night, as some of its more patriotically inclined members were successfully persuaded that some kind of constitution had to be adopted. The major bones of contention were 'national issues' (symbols, language, preamble), all of which were passionately debated until the very last minute. Institutional arrangements were not changed during that fateful night[23] (although as a token gesture to the left the Soviet-era title *Verkhovna Rada* was preserved), so that the parliament repeatedly voted on various issues, often coupling articles in a package to stimulate obstructive factions to compromise until a constitutional majority was mustered. Having achieved his main goal, the president congratulated the parliamentarians, apologizing for his tactics and retracting the threat of the referendum.

According to the Ukrainian Constitution, the unicameral parliament is the 'sole body of legislative power' (Art. 75), whereas the president is 'head of state' and 'guarantor of state sovereignty and territorial indivisibility of Ukraine, the observance of the Constitution of Ukraine and human and citizens' rights and freedoms' (Art. 102) and the Cabinet of Ministers is 'the highest body in the system of bodies of executive power' (Art. 113). The Supreme Council approves the prime minister proposed by the president (Art. 85.12) and can dismiss the cabinet in a no-confidence vote, although not within one year following the approval of its programme (Art. 87). The president, apart from the right to

---

[23] Although the institutional framework was not changed during the night, some attempts were made to do so. Prime Minister Pavlo Lazarenko and his entourage proposed a last-minute change requiring that the prime minister not only be appointed but also dismissed by the president with the consent of parliament. The idea was, as expected, favourably looked upon by the left. It was rejected as a recipe for constitutional deadlocks because it allowed the possibility of a prime minister remaining *in situ* despite his dismissal by the president.

appoint the prime minister with the agreement of the Supreme Council, was granted the rights: to appoint members of the Cabinet of Ministers and heads of central bodies of executive power proposed by the prime minister (Art. 106.10); to dismiss the prime minister and ministers unilaterally (Art. 106.9); to veto parliamentary bills, though the veto can be overridden by a two-thirds majority in parliament (Art. 94 and 106.30); and numerous appointive powers, e.g. one third of the Constitutional Court, the Council of the National Bank, prosecutor general, and other central executive organs (in most cases the consent of parliament is required). In the transitional provisions, the president was granted law-making authority on economic issues (not regulated by laws) for three years (which coincided with Kuchma's remaining term in office) on the condition that they are signed by the prime minister and that the draft laws are simultaneously submitted to parliament. Also, presidential draft laws are to be considered by parliament on a priority basis (Art. 93). Furthermore, the president can be removed only through a complex procedure of impeachment in the event of treason or some other crime (Art. 111). On the other hand, the president can only dissolve parliament if it cannot convene for thirty days during a plenary session (Art. 106.8). The Constitutional Court was given sole authority to interpret the Constitution. It comprises eighteen judges nominated for nine years; the president, parliament, and the Council of Judges appoint six judges each.

In principle, the Constitution created a presidential-parliamentary system, which is characterized by dual authority over the cabinet as both the president and parliament can dismiss it unilaterally.[24] Kuchma's initiative in constitution-making paid dividends, as parliament sanctioned a strong presidency (although not to the extent Kuchma had hoped). However sceptical parliament was of its own ability to overcome internal polarization and work constructively, it stopped short of relinquishing all strings of power to the president. Most importantly, the major lever of power—the right to dissolve parliament—was effectively denied to the president. While this was intended to protect parliament from any authoritarian leanings of the presidency, in practice it means that no effective instruments were provided to resolve potential deadlocks between the president and parliament. At the same time, as it soon became clear, few incentives for cooperation were built into the Constitution.

---

[24] For the classification of regimes with directly elected presidents see Matthew S. Shugart and John M. Carey, *Presidents and Assemblies: Constitutional Design and Electoral Dynamics* (Cambridge: Cambridge University Press, 1992).

Troubled Consolidation: Ukraine under the New Constitution

The purpose of this section is to survey the impact of the new constitutional framework in Ukraine on the executive–legislative relations. Due to the short span of time that the new fundamental law has been functioning in Ukraine in comparison to other post-communist states, any conclusion on its impact is preliminary at best. However, there are grounds to argue that the adopted constitutional design is one of the causes of, rather than a solution for, Ukraine's prolonged constitutional crisis.

The peaceful and lawful passage of the Constitution (despite troubled and prolonged constitution-making) and the evident ability to compromise is a creditworthy achievement which augurs well for the development of a consociational style of politics in Ukraine. From 1994, process was characterized by a degree of consensus on the key goal—the passage of the Constitution, which the dispute over specific constitutional provisions was not allowed to threaten. Despite this success at the level of process, the main questions about the constitutional product remain. Does it mark a breakthrough in Ukrainian politics, and can it constrain the debilitating clash over authority? The evidence thus far is not encouraging. Although the institutionalization of the machinery of government has been progressing, so far the Constitution has failed to provide a breakthrough and halt institutional rivalries. This can be attributed to several factors.

First, the circumstances under which the Constitution was adopted. During constitution-making the most important cleavage emerged between the left and 'the rest'. The former blocked the passage, while the centre-right together with the president worked on the draft. But this coalition was situational and short-lived. The anti-left pro-constitutional alliance splintered once its main objective was fulfilled. The adoption of the Constitution by parliament under the threat of referendum fuelled anti-presidential sentiments, and a different vector of conflict—along institutional lines—emerged. An anti-presidential majority, albeit fragile, began to emerge within parliament. In his determination to push through his draft, the president ignored his centre-right allies in parliament in the final days of the process, and his rashness later rebounded on him. The national democrats, content with the new constitutional national 'credentials' of Ukraine and wary of the president's authoritarian leanings, became less willing to side with him.

Secondly, the desperate need to compromise accounts for the lack of clarity of constitutional provisions, most importantly those regarding form of government. Given the scale of compromise, the sheer number of such interpretations should come as no surprise. Because of the number of laws that need to be adopted, the formal passage of the Constitution is only the first stage in the process of erecting an institutional edifice. As procedures to deal with future issues finally fall into place, shifting the conflict to the level of ordinary laws should in principle be less destabilizing. This, however, may not prove to be the case, especially when the actual content of constitutional norms is considered. In Ukraine, the adopted form of government—presidential-parliamentary—is more balanced than in many post-Soviet states (excluding the Baltic states). However, it creates the overlapping prerogatives of the president and the legislature over government. This feature of the system, as Shugart and Carrey argue, accounts for its propensity to generate conflict along president–legislature lines, while it fails to provide for any tension-defusing devices.[25] As this presidential-parliamentary system has to be further developed through ordinary legislation, there is an incentive to interpret the constitutional provisions in partisan ways.

The Constitution necessitated the adoption of forty-nine new laws on local government, state administration, the Constitutional Court, elections, political parties, etc. As law-making (apart from economic matters) remains the exclusive prerogative of parliament, this was used by parliament to assert its authority at the expense of the president and the Cabinet of Ministers. As the cabinet was simultaneously subordinated to the president and parliament, the latter was able to tip the balance in its own favour. In particular it attempted to clarify the structure of the executive branch by delineating the role of the president as the nominal head of state and the functions of the Cabinet of Ministers as the supreme executive organ dependent on a parliamentary majority. The wording of the Constitution became a guiding principle: as chairman of parliament Moroz emphasized, 'the president is the head of state' should imply that he is not the chief executive.[26] When two drafts of the 'Law on the Cabinet of Ministers' were tabled in parliament by the cabinet and the Parliamentary Commission on Legal Reform respectively, the latter draft was tabled for further

---

[25] See Matthew S. Shugart and John M. Carey, op.cit, ch. 4.
[26] *Zerkalo Nedeli* (27 July 1996).

consideration. According to the draft, the president was required to submit the candidate for prime minister for parliament's approval, agreed on earlier with both the speaker of parliament and the parliamentary groups and factions.[27] If the Supreme Council does not approve the presidential candidate then it is required to elect the prime minister by a two-thirds majority; if it fails the president can appoint the prime minister unilaterally.[28] Although the president can fire the prime minister, according to the draft, he must inform parliament of the reasons for this dismissal. As Volodymyr Stretovych, head of the Parliamentary Commission for Legal Reform explained: 'Drafting the law, we counted on the fact that in the future the prime minister will be a member of the parliamentary majority. Thus parliament must be told how the Prime Minister that it supports failed to execute his duties properly.'[29] Although that draft did not violate the constitution *per se*, it explicitly expanded its provisions by elaborating scenarios unanticipated by the fundamental law. The stress on the role of the parliamentary majority, absent in the Constitution itself, demonstrated an attempt to strengthen the parliamentary elements side of the presidential-parliamentary system fixed in the Constitution.

Yet President Kuchma was equally eager to expand the presidential side, and assert his position as that of chief executive. He issued two decrees 'On the Cabinet of Ministers' and 'On the Structure of the Presidential Administration' in December 1996. The first proposed a radical change to the existing structures by subordinating to the president the ministries of defence, internal affairs, and foreign affairs—which was explicitly in breach of the Constitution. Furthermore, the draft stipulated that the decisions of the chief, first adviser, and deputy head of the presidential administration were legally binding for the executive branch. As the presidential administration is a consultative organ appointed by the president with no legal powers, the president was aiming to limit the power of the prime minister and the cabinet by shifting authority to his immediate entourage.[30] As, at the same time, the Supreme Council had already adopted the law on the Cabinet of Ministers in the first reading, the decrees were clearly designed to

[27] The draft states that the Cabinet of Ministers consists of a prime minister, a first deputy prime minister, three deputy prime ministers and ministers, and it is not to exceed twenty-five people. The posts of minister without portfolio are excluded from the cabinet.

[28] *Ukraina Moloda* (25 Oct. 1996).   [29] *Ukrnews* (23 Jan. 1997).

[30] *Den* (20 Dec. 1996).

cause conflict. Indeed, they were criticized by the left, the centre, and even the national democrats.[31] The issue of control over the Cabinet of Ministers was not resolved by the parliament before the 1998 elections, and, together with the related question of the formation and role of parliamentary majority, erupted into a profound parliamentary crisis in January–February 2000.[32]

On several other occasions parliament demonstrated its new-found assertiveness after the passage of the Constitution, and organized opposition to presidential initiatives: it overrode presidential vetoes by constitutional majorities (something that hardly ever happened before the adoption of the Constitution), as in the cases of the 'Law on the Audit Chamber' and the 'Law on Privatisation'.[33] In particular, the 'Law on Local Self-Government' and the 'Law on State Administration' were meant to elaborate the vague sections of the Constitution, broaching the divisive question of the role of the executive branch in localities. The president returned the first of the two laws to parliament no fewer than three times before bowing to parliament's will and signing. Kuchma's veto of the second law was overturned, but he has yet to sign it.[34] At the same time, Kuchma complained that parliament violated constitutional Article 93, according to which 'Draft laws defined by the president of Ukraine may not be delayed, and are to be considered as a priority by the Supreme Council of Ukraine.' The president argued that parliament failed to discuss the majority of laws which he had forwarded to the legislature, and criticized parliament 'for a continuously low coefficient of effective work'.[35]

The unfolding president–legislature struggle immediately put a strain on the newly created Constitutional Court, as both the parliament and the president filed several cases against each other. A law on the Constitutional Court had been adopted despite its disputed Article 13, which stipulated the Court's exclusive prerogative to interpret the Constitution and laws, as well as determine the constitutionality of laws, presidential decrees, and acts of the

---

[31] *Den* (18 Dec. 1996).   [32] This is discussed below.

[33] Also, legislators elected Viktor Musiaka, a member of the 'Reforms' caucus, as deputy parliamentary speaker. Musyaka resigned as President Leonid Kuchma's representative in the legislature when Kuchma called a controversial referendum on the Constitution. Thus, his election acquired the symbolic significance of an anti-presidential move. See *Zerkalo Nedeli* (5 Oct. 1996).

[34] This resulted in legislative stalemate, as the Constitution does not specify the procedures to be implemented when the president fails to sign a law already passed in parliament.

[35] *Zerkalo Nedeli* (23 Nov. 1996).

Cabinet of Ministers. This provision—despite being based on the Constitution—was opposed by the leftist factions, because the right to interpret the Constitution was taken away from parliament, which—as they continue to argue—is the supreme authority in the country. The Constitutional Court has failed to rise above the president–parliamentary 'tug-of-war', and its first rulings can be interpreted as ambiguous at best, or overtly partisan at worst.[36] However, the Court has not had an easy start, as it has been put on the defensive by leftist parliamentarians who continue to question its constitutional powers and the reputed pro-presidential leanings of its members. It may be argued that the Constitutional Court has yet to earn the reputation of being an apolitical arbiter and for the time being ought to avoid confrontations with other branches of power. On the other hand, indecisive manœuvring has already undermined its credibility and reduced its capacity to resolve constitutional stalemates in the future.

During constitution-making, legislative–executive relations were drafted in a vacuum as a new electoral system had yet to be designed. Once the Constitution was in place, it was evident that whatever electoral system was chosen would strongly colour the institutions outlined in the fundamental law; this provided powerful incentives to use the new electoral law to engineer both short- and long-term advantages. The law on elections created the conditions for exceptional alliances, as both left- and right-wing factions (dominated by organized political parties) closed ranks behind the mixed system based on 50 per cent of seats elected on party lists and 50 per cent in one-mandate districts, claiming that it was indispensable to structure a party system in Ukraine. The projections based on public opinion polls showed that a mixed system would particularly benefit the left in the 1998 parliamentary elections, as they were the most likely to capitalize on the dire socio-economic situation. The non-party centre factions (such as the Constitutional Centre, Yednist', Independents) and non-affiliated deputies opposed the draft, only too well aware of their decreasing chances of re-election under such a system. They found an ally in the president, who argued that although in principle Ukraine needs such a progressive system, in practice there was no time to implement it. The president feared a victory of the left and the

---

[36] The first ruling was on the constitutionality of combining parliamentary mandates with posts in the executive branch, which cannot be held concurrently under the new Constitution. The Constitutional Court ruled that deputies who were still elected under the 1978 Constitution did not have to renounce one of their posts, despite the fact that the new Constitution explicitly prohibits such a possibility.

emergence of an even more obstructive parliament in the last year of his term (the presidential elections were held in the autumn of 1999). Also, in the longer term, the consolidation of the party system and structurization of parliament would decrease the need for such pronounced presidential elements in the Constitution. Such considerations prompted the president to propose prolonging the term of parliament and postponing the elections for a year (which would involve changes to the transitional provisions in the Constitution), in order, as he argued, to avoid the destabilizing effects of the electoral campaign for the economic reforms. The left and the right, despite their mutual animosity, were not to be deterred by the president's suggestion, and the law based on the mixed system was finally adopted in October 1997, and reluctantly signed by the president.

Amidst the executive–legislative battles, the economy continued to decline with gross implications for the living standards of the population. In the run-up to the 1998 parliamentary elections, the left was only too keen to exploit the dire state of the economy, and the incompetence and corruption of the government. In particular, the communists and socialists continuously referred to the socio-economic rights embedded in the Constitution. They stressed the 'unconstitutionality' of governmental policies, which by pursuing economic reforms infringed on the socio-economic welfare of the citizens. The Ukrainian Constitution, apart from listing human rights and political freedoms, is rich in 'positive' socio-economic rights such as the rights to 'personal development' (Art. 23), 'employment' (Art. 43), 'free education' (Art. 15), and a 'decent standard of living' (Art. 48). The Ukrainian constitution drafters, like their counterparts in the majority of post-communist states, found it difficult to abandon the rhetoric of 'developed socialism' (Art. 1 defines Ukraine as a social state). Although the constitutional norms follow the principle of 'direct action', which presumes their enforceability in courts, only the Constitutional Court can adjudicate the constitutionality of laws and other legal acts (although it is unclear whether acts of local self-government, which are most likely to deal with socio-economic rights, fall under the jurisdiction of the Constitutional Court). And although the 'Law on the Constitutional Court' envisages a special procedure for cases regarding constitutional freedoms and rights of individuals, these cannot be filed directly by citizens, but only by subjects that have the right of appeal to the Constitutional Court (the president, a group of forty-five deputies, the Supreme Court, the parliamentary ombudsman of human rights, the Supreme Council of the

Autonomous Republic of Crimea). This limitation, along with the prevailing legal culture and belief that the socio-economic pledges in the Constitution are merely a statement of intent rather than a legally enforceable right, means that the Constitutional Court has not been burdened with such issues. However, the glaring gap between the constitutional norms and the provision of socio-economic welfare has been readily exploited by the left to discredit the 'unaccountable' executive branch and to portray itself as the champion of 'social constitutionalism' in Ukraine.

The electoral cycle envisaged by the new Constitution consisted of the parliamentary (spring 1998) and presidential (autumn 1999) elections. The two elections had the cumulative effect of not only shifting the balance of power between competing political orientations, but also challenging the constitutional order itself. Despite being held under the new mixed electoral system, the 1998 parliamentary elections failed to deliver a breakthrough in the structurization of parliament. The left bloc emerged with a plurality (but not majority) of seats. Despite the fact that the centre swiftly organized itself into political parties prior to the election, divisions within the centre-right orientation prevented the emergence of a stable majority in the newly elected legislature. This was vividly demonstrated in the three-month marathon to elect the speaker of parliament, which culminated with the election of Oleksandr Tkachenko, one of the leaders of the Peasant Party of Ukraine. As all but one of the candidates who challenged Kuchma in the presidential race held parliamentary seats, the executive–legislative relations turned into a function of the electoral campaign. As the opposition to Kuchma was weakened by the split between the left and right, the incumbent secured another five-year term in office in a trade-off with the communist candidate Petro Symonenko, though only after grossly abusing state power and exploiting control over state-controlled media.

In the aftermath of his comfortable victory, Kuchma put the question of the revision of the constitutional division of power back on the agenda. Despite the appointment of the reformer Victor Yushchenko to the post of prime minister, Kuchma launched an assault on the legislature, on the grounds that its inability to form a majority supportive of the government was stalling the progress of economic reform in Ukraine. In January 2000 he decreed a nationwide referendum in April 2000 in which the population will be requested to approve a number of points: no confidence in the current parliament; the stripping of law makers of their immunity; the creation of an upper legislative chamber; a reduction in the size of the lower chamber from 450 to 300; and granting the president the right to disband the parliament if it does not form a majority within one month after the elections or approve the state budget within three months. The decree blatantly violated constitutional provisions, which required that any changes to the Constitution be approved in an elaborate procedure and sanctioned by a two-thirds, constitutional majority.

The decree galvanized the centre-right deputies into action; they proclaimed the formation of the parliamentary majority and attempted to vote to dismiss Tkachenko as parliamentary chairman. As the latter resisted by violating parliamentary rules, the majority (243 deputies from a 450-deputy house) walked out and assembled in a separate session in another building. After two weeks of parallel existence, the majority (by that time 259) took over the parliament building amidst skimishes with leftist deputies. Despite parliament's relaunch of its regular legislative work, the fate of the current parliament is far from secure; as of mid-February 2000, the president has not rescinded his decree. The ruptured *Verhkovna Rada* is an easy prey for the president, who stirs up popular support for his actions by anti-parliamentary, populist rhetoric about the need for decisive decision-making to reverse the country's staggering economic decline. In the referendum campaign, as in the run-up to the presidential elections, the president did not shy away from applying various informal means of pressure using his control of the state executive agencies. If Kuchma succeeds in increasing his formal powers after the referendum, the presidency will dominate the political landscape in Ukraine to the extent that the principles of power-sharing and checks and balances will become a constitutional fiction.

Conclusion

Following independence, Ukraine functioned without working constitutionally delineated institutions, procedures, rules, and routines for longer than any other post-communist state. Yet, while the polity was driven by aborted reforms and improvised encounters and the Ukrainian economy continued to be grossly mismanaged, the country has remained peaceful. There has been no destabilizing escalation of conflict or violence. Even though institutional reform proved a difficult and protracted experience, the type of presidential authoritarianism that emerged in neighbouring Belarus was avoided in Ukraine. Despite the overall aggrandizement of the

Ukrainian presidency, the institution did not turn into the bedrock of the Ukrainian institutional firmament. The excessive reliance on personalities, so very characteristic of the post-Soviet transformation (apart from the Baltic states), has not so far been written into the constitutional norms in Ukraine.

This outcome can be attributed to an unintended series of 'checks and balances', resulting from the multiple political cleavages that cut across institutions and political groupings. Even if Ukraine's body politic has been haunted by numerous phantoms (weak political parties, regional clans, corruption, clientelism, lack of accountability), the diffusion rather than concentration of power seems to be the trademark of Ukraine's transformation. Under such circumstances, prolonged catastrophic equilibrium and tormented constitution-making did not endanger the long-term prospects for democracy in Ukraine. Institutional reform was undertaken amidst fears of unpredictable consequences, which tended to impose last-minute restraint and underpinned the consensual passage of the new Constitution. And although the underlying compromise failed to find favour with the majority and fully satisfied only the few, the Constitution is more balanced than those found in many post-Soviet states.

At the same time, post-constitutional developments alert one to the fact that a relatively balanced constitutional delineation of authority will not necessarily end the political 'tug-of-war' and deliver an efficient policy-making mechanism. The post-constitutional presidential–parliamentary rivalry in Ukraine may be an inevitable final stage of any institutional delineation of authority that will abate once the rules are polished in constitutional practice. But it appears that the unsettled conflict along president–parliament lines is actually fuelled by the new Constitution that instituted a particular form of semi-presidential system based on dual legitimacy and overlapping competencies.

Four years after the passage of the new Constitution, Ukraine stands at crossroads. Either the constitutional framework will gradually evolve towards a more parliamentary system of government through the assertion of the parliamentary majority in constitutional practice. Or, if President Kuchma has his way, the system will be tilted in favour of the presidency. While the first route does not spell a quick-fix solution to the executive–legislative strife, it would enhance the role of the representative legislature, which, despite its polarized composition, is a powerful marker of democratization in Ukraine. The alternative means a gravitation toward the Belarus-Kazakh model, centred on a powerful presidency with a docile parliament in the background and no effective 'checks and balances'.

Democratic consolidation in constitutional terms is achieved when 'democracy becomes the only game in town', when all actors habitually resolve political conflicts according to the established constitutional norms.[37] Under conditions of a precarious balance and fearing an escalation of the crisis, Ukrainian elites may choose to cling to the new Constitution for better or for worse, especially as Ukraine's socio-economic transformation has hardly taken off and needs urgent attention.

[37] Juan J. Linz and Alfred Stepan, *Problems of Democratic Transition and Consolidation: Southern Europe, South America and Post-communist Europe* (Baltimore: Johns Hopkins University Press, 1996), 5.

Power Imbalance and Institutional Interests in Russian Constitutional Engineering

Gadis Gadzhiev

In Russia, the communist legacy has been at least as strong and pervasive as in the other post-communist countries of Central and Eastern Europe. In most countries of the region, this legacy has been tamed through patient bargaining and eventual compromise on the balance of powers, regime type, and other crucial choices necessary for building a strong foundation for democratic consolidation. However in Russia, compromise was never reached, important decisions regarding power-sharing were postponed, and as a result, a super-presidential regime was created, not through negotiations and compromise, but through brute force. Russia is the only post-communist country that experienced a military intervention *after* democratic elections had taken place. When tanks and police were sent to the White House in September 1993 to bar parliament from meeting, President Boris Yeltsin succeeded in ending the stalemate between competing branches of power, but the underlying causes of the conflict were hardly resolved. The roots of this conflict are found in the weakness of civil society and political party organization. Without organized interest groups or ideologically based political parties, elected representatives had—and continue to have—nothing on which to base their policies other than the pursuit of self-interested goals. Moreover, the institutionalized state structure that gave the president a monopoly of power only aggravated the accountability deficit and pushed civil society further from the decision-making process. Far from creating the basis for another revolution, one prognosis for Russia's 'incomplete democracy' seems to describe the situation well: 'the overthrow of democratic institutions appears less a threat than the persistence of [a] regime in which the populace expects elected governors to be dishonest and unaccountable, and elite behavior meets these expectations. Such an incomplete democracy can persist indefinitely, but it will be a "broken-backed" democracy that is inefficient and often ineffective, and supported by its citizens as a lesser evil rather than because it is good in itself."[1]

In the first part of this chapter, I will focus on how amending the 1978 Russian Constitution deteriorated into a power struggle between parliament and the president and how it affected constitutional engineering. Next, I will describe the institutional structure that resulted from the constitution-drafting process. Finally, I will demonstrate how the Russian Constitution, which set clear rules for the institutional game but without respect for the division of power principle, has contributed to state weakness. By concentrating power in the Russian presidency, the executive has become overburdened and the state ineffective.

Institutional Competition

The attempt by political forces participating in the constitutional process to promote their own interests is not surprising.[2] Usually, the constitutional balance of power between the legislative and executive is proportional to the willingness of the political forces involved in constitution drafting to compromise. In Russia, however, compromise during constitution drafting was eclipsed by excessive institutional competition. In post-communist countries, such power struggles were prevalent for at least three reasons; an institutional vacuum remained after the communist system was toppled, democratic elites targeted institutions while manœuvring for political clout, and, perhaps most importantly in the Russian case, there was an absence of strong parties and loyal constituencies.[3] In Russia, this combination of factors culminated in a stubborn fight for power between the legislature and the president. Institutional warfare was waged, figuratively speaking, on two fronts. At one level, political forces focused on amending the 1978 Soviet-era

---

[1] Richard Rose and Doh Chull Shin, 'Qualities of Incomplete Democracies: Russia, the Czech Republic, and Korea Compared', *Studies in Public Policy*, 302 (1998), 5.

[2] See Jon Elster, 'The Role of Institutional Interest in East European Constitution-Making', *East European Constitutional Review*, 5/1 (Winter 1996), 63–5.

[3] See Jan Zielonka, 'New Institutions in the Old East Bloc', *Journal of Democracy*, 5/2 (Apr. 1994), 88.

Russian Constitution while, at the other, both the parliament and the president organized their own committees to work on separate constitutional drafts concurrently. Thus the constitutional-drafting process in the formal legal sense was understood as the simultaneous process of amending the acting Constitution while working out drafts of a new one.[4] This process was one in which both sides resisted compromise and became the pretext for the bloody conflict in October 1993 and the imposition of a constitutional model which strongly favoured one side, the president.

The separation of powers had never been an important constitutional principle during the Soviet period. Throughout most of the Soviet era, in constitutional terms executive and legislative power had been fused, with the executive being part of the parliamentary structure. But in any case, in practice, even had there been a constitutional separation between legislative and executive power, this would have had no effect because of the position of the Party. With the Communist Party controlling every level of society, power concentration, not balance, was the engine behind institutional functioning at that time. This began to be seriously challenged only after Mikhail Gorbachev became head of the Party, and began the process of change which was ultimately to lead to the collapse of the system.

Three aspects of Gorbachev's changes are relevant to this issue. Two of these were introduced at the XIX Conference of the Party in mid-1988, and the third in 1990. At the Conference, Gorbachev declared that the Party must withdraw from playing a direct administrative role in Soviet life. While he assumed that it would continue to be a major player in the course of Soviet politics, the Party's role was no longer to involve direct administrative control of Soviet institutions. This decision was formalized with the removal of Article 6, which enshrined the Party's leading role in Soviet society, in March 1990. The second change was his announcement of a new parliamentary structure for the Soviet Union, consisting of a Congress of People's Deputies and a standing Supreme Soviet. These new legislative bodies, although a classic

---

[4] The remark about the constitutional process in the formal legal sense is connected with the following fact: Russian scientific literature differentiates between the constitutional process in its broad and narrow sense. The constitutional process in the broader sense means the reaching of civil consent in society on the primary principles of the state structure. In the narrow sense it is actually working out and adopting the Constitution. See V. B. Pastuchov, 'Formation of the Russian Statehood and Constitutional Process: Politological Aspects', *State and Law*, 2 (1993).

compromise,[5] did create a new legislative structure which was meant to be more closely linked to the populace at large than the former Soviet organs had been, and, in the light of the stated withdrawal of the Party from a direct administrative role, were meant to emerge as the leading parliamentary forum of the new political structure. Following the 1989 elections to the Congress, these bodies did become a very important arena of political life within the USSR. The third measure was introduced by Gorbachev in 1990 when he was worried about the weakening of the capacity of the centre to control events at lower levels. This was the establishment of an executive presidency which, although initially to be filled by election at the Congress, was to have very extensive powers. Had the Soviet system developed constitutionally along the lines implicit in Gorbachev's proposal, a formal separation of powers would have been the result.

Institutional change also came to the Russian Republic. Initially Russian leaders simply replicated the situation at the Soviet level. The existing parliamentary structure was replaced by a directly elected Congress of People's Deputies (without places set aside for the Party and other public organizations), which in turn was to form a smaller Supreme Soviet. Elections were held to the Congress in March 1990, and two months later Boris Yeltsin was elected to the post of chairman of the Supreme Soviet (effective head of state). On 24 May 1991 the position of president was formally established, and on 12 June Yeltsin was popularly elected to that post. These constitutional changes were meant both to bolster the Russian leadership in its continuing struggle with the Soviet centre and to make the constitutional structure consistent with the Declaration of State Sovereignty of the RSFSR (12 June 1990). But these changes were seen as a strictly interim measure; on 16 June 1990 the Russian Congress of People's Deputies established a Constitutional Commission whose task was to prepare a new constitution reflecting Russia's newly proclaimed sovereign status.

This initial attempt at institutional engineering was meant to weaken the centralization of the Soviet regime whereby the Soviet authorities dominated the republics. It was assumed that the establishment of a new institutional structure that was not based on the Party would enable both Soviet and Party control to be broken within Russia. The dominant idea was that the new democratic

---

[5] The compromise is reflected in the way that a certain number of seats were set aside for the Party and various public organizations and thereby shielded from running the electoral gauntlet, and that competitive elections were seen to be desirable but not mandatory.

governing system could easily emerge from the old one. As I. G. Shablinsky noted,[6] after decades of complete contempt for parliamentarism, and one-party control of the soviets, reformers thought it extremely important to promote the role of the parliament. It is important to stress that balancing powers between the legislative and executive bodies did not seem very significant at the time.[7] But the outcome indicates that simply bringing these institutions 'to life' was insufficient to guarantee the balance of power between institutions.

The institutional changes made in Russia in 1990 and 1991 created an extremely contradictory power arrangement. The establishment of a popularly elected president as the head of the executive effectively grafted the presidency onto a parliamentary system without making any clear division between the responsibilities of the two institutions. While the Congress was referred to as the 'supreme organ of state power' and the president as 'the supreme official and head of executive power', with the implication that the former was the chief policy-making body, by virtue of their direct election both had a popular mandate and Yeltsin's was more recent than that of the parliament. The distinction between the two institutions was further blurred by the Congress effectively passing much of its power on economic matters to the president in November 1991 (see below). Without clearly demarcated spheres of responsibility, with both the presidency and chairmanship of the Supreme Soviet occupied by people with growing personal and institutional ambitions (respectively Yeltsin and Ruslan Khasbulatov), and with the unity of the Russian elite coming under strain as a result of differences over (particularly economic) policy, conflict between the president and parliament became almost inevitable. Instead of emerging as either a presidential or parliamentary republic, the state began showing signs of both.

Conflicts between president and parliament emerged even before the USSR had collapsed. In the last months of 1991, the Supreme Soviet criticized government policies in a number of areas, opposed Yeltsin's action in appointing regional heads of administration in place of holding local elections, and reversed a number of Yeltsin's decrees, including those relating to the imposition of a state of emergency in Chechnya-Ingushetiya and the merger of the security ministries. In November, however, the parliament abrogated

---

[6] I. G. Shablinsky, 'The Constitutional Reforms in Russia and the Principle of the Separation of Powers', unpublished; author's abstract (Moscow: 1997), 22.

[7] *Izvestija* (25 Mar. 1991).

some of its power by granting to Yeltsin extraordinary powers for one year to introduce decrees designed to carry out economic reform measures without reference to parliament. Over the following year, relations between president and parliament deteriorated further. As economic reform bit home and popular living standards fell, sections within the parliament became increasingly critical of the president and his policies. But while Yeltsin refused to fortify ties with the deputies (thereby building upon the nucleus of support for him that existed in parliament) and while he continued to support economic change, relations deteriorated. The conflict between president and parliament, although characterized by a high level of rhetorical threat, was actually one in which both sides sought in practice to play by the newly emerging rules of the political game. As a result, the convocations of the Congress of People's Deputies, which had the power to change the Constitution and thereby fundamentally to affect the power of the president, became the site of major battles in this conflict.[8] But they were also the site of attempted compromises between the two parties as both institutions engaged in political bartering for power. At the Sixth Congress in April 1992, Yeltsin removed from ministerial posts two of his key supporters who were most associated with the economic reform policies to which the parliament was objecting (Burbulis and Shakhrai). Nevertheless, this apparent attempt at compromise failed to satisfy the parliament,[9] which maintained its criticism of the president and his policies. At the Seventh Congress in December 1992, at which Yeltsin's extraordinary powers came up for renewal, a compromise proposal was worked out between Yeltsin and Khasbulatov. Yeltsin's extraordinary powers would be continued for a year, in return for which the powers of the Supreme Soviet would be expanded by allowing it to confirm presidential nominees for prime minister and four key ministries (foreign, defence, security, and interior). But instead, Congress refused to accept this compromise, rejected Yeltsin's choice of Yegor Gaidar as prime minister, sought to bring the government under parliamentary, rather than presidential, control, and tried to insulate itself against dismissal by linking any attempt to dissolve the parliament with the automatic disappearance of the president's authority. This crisis was resolved, temporarily, through

[8] The course of the conflict has been outlined in many places. For one such account, see Richard Sakwa, *Russian Politics and Society* (London: Routledge, 1993), ch. 2.

[9] Indeed, it was as much an attempt to insulate them from the parliament as it was a peace offering; both took up advisory positions in Yeltsin's administration.

an agreement brokered by the head of the Constitutional Court, Valery Zorkin. Among other things this involved a popular referendum on a new constitution, the freezing of the pre-December president–parliament relationship, and no appointment of new Constitutional Court judges.

The compromise brokered by Zorkin did not last long and was formally rejected at the Eighth Congress in March 1993. At this meeting, the idea of a referendum was rejected, Yeltsin was stripped of many of the emergency powers he had been granted in November 1991 (including the right to issue decrees), and the government was given the right to submit legislation directly to parliament, independent of the president. These measures were not only a breach of the earlier agreement, but a significant diminution of presidential powers. Yeltsin now publicly declared the imposition of 'special rule' (an action which, had it been carried through, would have been unconstitutional) and that a referendum would be held in April as planned. This announcement persuaded the leadership of the Congress to go along with the referendum (while significantly changing the questions),[10] but it also led the Congress as a whole to introduce a series of measures further reducing presidential powers. In any event, when the referendum went ahead on 25 April, the result seemed to be a victory for Yeltsin: 58.7 per cent declared they had confidence in the president, 53 per cent approved of his economic policies, 49.5 per cent wanted early elections to the presidency, and 67.2 per cent wanted early parliamentary elections. Yeltsin now pushed on with the question of constitutional reform.

The issue of a new constitution had been in the air since the establishment of a Constitutional Commission by the First Congress of People's Deputies in June 1990. This body had produced a number of drafts for consideration, but none of them gained the support of major political actors. In addition, Yeltsin had set up his own commission, which in April 1993 produced a draft which, had it been introduced, would have inaugurated an openly presidential system. Any hope of reaching a compromise vanished when, in May 1993, the Constitutional Commission approved a draft constitution which removed the president as head of the executive branch and as commander-in-chief of the military. It also proposed granting the Supreme Soviet the right to cancel ministerial decrees. In my

---

[10] It also persuaded them to agree to early parliamentary and presidential elections, but this was rejected by the Congress as a whole, which also sought both to impeach Yeltsin and to remove Khasbulatov. Both moves failed.

opinion, it was this proposal (which would have completely obliterated the principle of separation of powers) that finally pushed the limits of the institutional competition between the president and parliament and eventually led to Yeltsin's dismissal of the Supreme Soviet by Decree 1400 (21 September 1993). In an attempt to garner Federation-wide support for his draft, in June 1993 President Yeltsin called a ten-day Constitutional Assembly to discuss and amend his draft. Conference participants included representatives of the local soviets, party leaders, and other representatives of prominent interest groups and politicians. Drafts were prepared by a range of bodies, including the parliament. Unable to reach a compromise, the Assembly failed to commit to a new draft by the end of the ten-day period and a smaller Conciliation Committee was established to hammer out the remaining details. Finally, on 12 July 1993, the Assembly was reconvened and a draft constitution based on both presidential and parliamentary drafts was approved. However this was overrun by Yeltsin's dismissal of the parliament.

Yeltsin justified the Decree 1400 by accusing the parliament of contributing to economic decay, using legislation as a means to gain power, and stalling the constitutional reform process. He also announced that parliamentary elections and a simultaneous constitutional referendum would be held on 11–12 December 1993.[11] Yeltsin's decree created a frightening stand-off, in which parliament continued to operate despite the decree until the president sent police to prohibit people from entering the White House. When parliamentary sympathizers turned to violence, the police and the army responded with force on 3–4 October and ended the conflict. With parliament out of the way and girded by strong public support, the president turned to his constitution-drafting team to work out a draft which would be presented at the December referendum. Thus, the final text of the Constitution and its separation of powers scheme was not the result of debate and compromise but rather a military trophy of the president.

Predictably, the only draft that had any influence on the draft Constitution presented to the referendum in December 1993 was that of the president, which not surprisingly formulated a regime in which the president and executive branch were dominant. The president's draft Constitution differed from the July Constitutional Assembly draft in a number of essential articles,

---

[11] Dwight Semler, 'The End of the First Russian Republic', *East European Constitutional Review*, 2/3:4/1 (Fall 1993/Winter 1994), 109.

particularly those dealing with the principle of separation of powers. For example, the presidential draft gave the president the power to define, in conformity with the Constitution and the federal laws, the primary direction of domestic and foreign policy and to determine the order of formation of the upper house of the Federal Assembly, the Federation Council. The history of the latter article is extremely interesting because it was silently and anonymously inserted after the debate on the draft was completed, sometime between 28 October and 4 November (the date that the Referendum Draft was published), and significantly changed the balance of powers in the regime. Article 96 of the Constitution now states that the means of formation of the Federation Council and the means of elections of deputies to the State Duma are established by federal law. Deputy Viktor Sheinis, an active participant in the constitutional process who witnessed the creation of both the initial draft Constitution and the July 1993 Conference draft, asserts that the issue of direct popular elections of Federation Council deputies had never arisen during public debates. Yet, in the final draft, the word 'election' was replaced by 'formation'. This change was made at the beginning of November—after the referendum campaign had already begun and after a number of meetings between the president and regional leaders as well as with members of the Constitutional Assembly.[12] When the voting in the referendum was tallied, it was announced that 58.43 per cent had supported the Constitution, on a turnout of 54.8 per cent.[13] This meant that, in effect, only 30.7 per cent of the total electorate voted for the Constitution, and it was rejected in seventeen republics and regions of the Federation. Thus although the Constitution was declared to be adopted, its narrow margin was hardly a ringing endorsement.

Evaluating the 1993 Russian Constitution

President and parliament

What type of regime did this process create in Russia? Although some observers have come to the conclusion, using somewhat

---

[12] Victor Sheinis, 'Capitulation of Parliamentarism', *Nesavisstmaya Newspaper* (25 Oct. 1995).

[13] However, it was later claimed that the turnout was actually below 50%. If so, the result would have been formally invalid. These claims have never been disproved, but nor have they been proved.

paradoxical methodology, that Russia is a parliamentary republic,[14] most more or less agree with Stephen Holmes, who considers Russia to be a super-presidential state.[15] But perhaps a more important question to explore is: how has this regime type affected Russian governance? V. A. Chetvernin concluded that the system of separation of powers established by the Russian Constitution cannot properly guarantee rights to freedom, security, and property. He asserts that this is the result of granting the president extensive legislative powers and because the mechanism of checks and balances between the legislative and executive powers works in favour of the latter.[16]

The constitution-drafting process offers hints about what kind of regime the framers were hoping to create. The 1958 Constitution of the French Republic is sure to have been used as a model while working out the Russian constitutional scheme. But contrary to the French model, Russia's weak parliament has insufficient constitutional means to moderate the actions of the president— clearly a direct consequence of the president's 'victory' in the constitutional power struggle.[17] Thus, as A. V. Butakov asserts, the constitutional status of the president of the Russian Federation relative to that of the legislative power considerably exceeds the corresponding status of the French president. Even in a classical presidential republic, such as the USA, the president is not granted the right to issue decrees, dismiss the Congress, or unilaterally hold referenda. In a mixed republic such as France, there is a clear logic of separation and balancing of powers. Therefore, even the French president's prerogatives are not as broad as those of the Russian president. Butakov's argument is that the Russian president's constitutional status in relation to the legislature represents the amalgamation of the American and the French separation of powers models. But in fact, the Russian president's

[14] B. Strashun, 'Paradoxical as it may Seem the Draft of the Constitutional Commission Presupposes a "presidential republic" and the Draft Constitution Conference the "Parliamentary One"', *Constitutional Conference*, N 1 (Aug. 1995).

[15] Stephen Holmes, 'Superpresidency and its Problems', *East European Constitutional Review*, 4 (Fall 1993).

[16] V. A. Chetvernin, 'Ideology of Rights of Man and Principles of Separation of Powers in the Constitution of the Russian Federation', V. A. Chetvernin (ed.), in *Collection of Articles on the Formation of the Constitutional State in the Post-totalitarian Russia* (Moscow: Institute of State and Law of the Russian Academy of Science, 1996), 24.

[17] N. N. Varlamova, 'The Russian Constitution Experience of Three-Dimensional Interpretation', in Chetvernin (ed.), *Collection of Articles*, 41.

powers exceed those of both models, thus ensuring the Russian president's dominant position vis-à-vis the Federal Assembly.[18]

According to the 1993 Russian Constitution, the president of Russia is head of state, responsible for guaranteeing constitutional rights and freedoms and defining the primary direction of internal and foreign policies. Moreover, the president coordinates the functioning of and interaction between state institutions (Art. 80 of the Constitution). Among his powers the president has the right to legislative initiative, to veto laws adopted by the Federal Assembly, to dismiss the State Duma under certain conditions, to announce elections to the Duma, and to issue decrees and directives as long as they comply with the Constitution and federal law.

In addition to its legislative activity, the Federal Assembly has the following functions: (*a*) budgeting and financing, (*b*) participation in the formation of government and other state institutions, and (*c*) general monitoring and oversight (chapter 5 of the Constitution). The parliament performs its monitoring function through various institutions of the chambers (such as the commission for investigating the events of October 1993), special deputies' question and answer sessions, and institutions, such as the Chamber of Accounts, which is responsible for monitoring the implementation of the federal budget.[19]

The Russian Constitution does not spell out how the two chambers of the Assembly are to be coordinated. There are no structures or committees to manage the operation of the Duma and Federation Council and there is no parliamentary president or high council to preside over the parliament as a whole. Despite the Federal Assembly being a 'state body', and thereby needing to have some kind of 'organizational unity', the only common denominator between the two chambers of parliament is their capacity to pass laws. Although they work together to this end, the two chambers of the Russian parliament do not consider themselves to be a single institution.

The formation of the two chambers occurs differently. Members of the Duma are elected to four-year terms directly by the people (Arts. 96 and 97 of the Constitution). The mechanism for forming the Federation Council is more complicated: the members of the

---

[18] A. S. Butakov, 'The Russian System of Separation of Powers', *Jurisprudence*, 1 (1997), 11.

[19] The membership and organizational structure of the Chamber of Accounts is determined by the federal legislators. The status of this institution is regulated by a federal law as of 11 Jan. 1995. Legislative Review of the Russian Federation, no. 3 (1995), art. 167.

upper house must hold simultaneously a position within a local governing body in the Russian Federation. Art. 95 reads: 'Two representatives from each entity of the Russian Federation enter into the Federation Council: one each from the representative and the executive branches of state power.' Thus, State Duma deputies' mandates are confined to four years, and can be further shortened if the president disbands the lower house earlier in accord with Articles 111 and 117 of the Constitution. In contrast, the mandates of Federation Council members are not specified in the Constitution and must be determined by the representative institutions of the various subjects of the Russian Federation. Since the president cannot disband the Federation Council and the mandate of the Council members depends on their mandate from the regions (which have their own election procedures), any change in the composition of the upper house occurs gradually and independently of Duma elections.[20] In the end, the Russian Constitution even envisages different sets of prerogatives for each of the chambers of the Federal Parliament (Arts. 102 and 103 of the Russian Constitution), and both chambers are governed by a separate set of standing orders.

Before the 1992 Federation Treaty was signed and incorporated into the 1993 Russian Constitution (with minor changes), the Russian Federation was built according to a national principle. The subjects of the Federation were simply the national republics, autonomous regions, and autonomous *okrug*. The Treaty has compounded the national principle with a territorial one, and as a result the Russian Federation comprises 21 republics (despite the fact that the Chechen government does not recognize its inclusion as a republic of the Federation), 6 *krai*, 49 regions, 2 cities with federal importance, 1 autonomous region, and 10 autonomous *okrug*. The influence of all these subjects of the Russian Federation on the relationship between the executive and legislative powers is to be exercised principally through the Federation Council. The formation of the Council was one of the decisions that was postponed until after the Constitution was adopted by referendum. As mentioned above, the ambiguity over the *formation* of the Council was due to the secret change of Article 96 prior to the constitutional referendum. The Federation Council consists of, ex officio, the leaders of the executive and representative (legislative) branches of the subjects of the Federation. Thus, the Council represents the

---

[20] A notable exception of this was only the first joint session of both chambers of the Russian parliament, as it is stipulated by the concluding and transitory ordinances of the Russian Constitution.

link between federal and regional governments. Instead of serving in a strictly legislative capacity, in principle it should act as a balance between the legislative focus of the Federal Assembly and the executive, and it is also responsible for the synchronization of federal and regional interests. It should therefore be an important stabilizing factor in the Federation.

Since its creation in 1993, the Federation Council has evolved politically. Initially, the head executives of the subjects of the federation were appointed directly by the president, but now they are elected directly by the citizens (only two republics are exceptions, Dagestan and Karachaevo-Cerkezia). This has had a clear effect on the separation of powers structure; instead of a Council of presidential appointees within the parliament, the Council has moved closer to becoming a truly representative body. Many Council members have become influential politicians in their own right, such as Yuri Luzhkov, the mayor of Moscow, or Alexander Lebed, the governor of the Krasnoyarsk *krai*. But, although it influences important decisions in Russia, the Council has been excluded at crucial moments. The civil war in Chechnya offers a vivid example of this. Although the Council must approve all major decisions concerning state security (declaration of a war by the president, the use of Federation military forces outside its borders, and declarations of martial law and state of emergency), the Council was completely excluded from decision-making on Chechnya; the intervention of Russian forces in Chechnya was not sanctioned by the Federation Council.[21] This serves not only to indicate the shortcomings of the Constitution's wording, but more importantly the stunning accountability deficit of Russia's elected representatives. While the elected Federation Council is left out of the decision-making process at crucial moments, other unelected bodies, in this case the Security Council, make important decisions while neither the legislature nor the president suffers from these decisions in subsequent elections. But it also shows the way in which the president is willing to tailor his actions in order to get around the Constitution; by refusing to declare a state of emergency in Chechnya, he was able to avoid triggering the constitutional need for Federation Council approval.

The Constitution also seeks to provide a means for the removal of the president, and this directly involves the parliament. Under certain circumstances (see below), the president has the power to dissolve the State Duma. But the parliament also has the power, indeed responsibility, to remove the president if that person is guilty

---

[21] Nor was the State Duma involved in this episode.

of treason or a 'grave crime' (undefined). If one-third of the members of the State Duma file a charge that the president is guilty of treason or a grave crime, the motion is adopted by two-thirds of the all Duma members, the Supreme Court confirms that there are elements of a crime in the president's actions, and the Constitutional Court affirms that the established procedure for filing such a charge has been observed, the Federation Council may, in a two-thirds majority vote of all members, remove the president from office. Such an impeachment procedure would be difficult to achieve, especially given that half of the members of the Federation Council hold executive positions similar to that of the president, but it is not inconsistent with impeachment procedures in some other presidential systems. However its difficulty is reflected in the fact that although a number of attempts have been made to begin impeachment proceedings—principally by the communists—none has got off the ground.

The outcome of the restructuring of the legislative branch has reflected the president's desire to weaken parliament. Lack of coordination between the chambers allows the president to pit one chamber against the other when needed, while loose wording of the powers of the legislature allows the president to ignore its prerogatives to influence important decisions, as was the case with the war in Chechnya. In other words: separating power *within* the parliament itself precludes the possibility of unification between the two chambers into a single political organ. The desire to weaken the parliament is also underscored by the logic of the political opposition in 1993. The upper chamber, which is a proponent of the interests of the various units of the federation, could have become an important balancing power against the vast prerogatives with which the president has been endowed. But under the existing Constitution, it cannot perform this role. Similarly the parliament's capacity to remove an errant president is difficult to put into practice.

President and government

One of the most important factors in the relationship between president and parliament is the status of the government. This was a critical element in the conflict prior to 1993, and it has remained a point of contention under the new constitutional regime. Indeed, for every society undergoing the transition from an authoritarian to a democratic political regime, the institutionalization of the relationship between the representative and executive branches of power is very important. The incorrect resolution of their relationship may lead to a constant competition between them, and, on such a basis, spur antagonism between the parliament and executive power, as occurred in Russia prior to 1993.[22] Thus the crucial question must be answered by constitution framers: is the government responsible to the parliament or the president? In Russia according to one observer, conflicting constitutional articles make this question difficult to answer. Article 83 of the Russian Constitution declares that the head of the government is appointed by the president with the consent of the State Duma and the government may be dismissed by a decision of the president. But Professor I. M. Entin considers the government to be under parliamentary control and politically responsible to it for its actions.[23] This thesis rests on the provision that the Duma must approve the prime ministerial candidate. However it is clear that the Duma's approval of the candidate for prime minister is not a necessary condition for forming the government. If the president presents the candidate for prime minister to parliament and the Duma rejects this candidate three times, the president then appoints the rejected candidate as prime minister, dismisses the Duma, and calls pre-term elections (Art. 111.4 of the Constitution). Moreover, the president is not simply 'able' to dismiss the Duma in this case but 'must' dismiss it. Imagine this scenario: the newly elected president proposes an obviously unsuitable candidate for the post of prime minister. After this candidate is rejected three times, the president dismisses the Duma. If, after elections, the constituency selects a Duma almost identical to the previous parliament, and the new Duma twice issues a vote of no confidence in the government within three months, then the president (according to Art. 117.3 of the Constitution) is compelled either to dismiss the government or to dissolve the Duma once again. However, the president cannot dismiss the Duma according to Article 117 for one year following its election (Art. 109.3 of the Constitution). But if the Constitutional Court were petitioned to rule on these contradictory articles, and decided on the supremacy of Article 117.3, then theoretically, the president could

[22] Edvard Ozhiganov, 'The Institutionalisation of the Relationship between the Executive and Representative Branches of Power and the Political Regime in the Russian Federation', in *President–Government–Executive Power: The Russian Model* (Moscow: Centre of Constitutional Researches of Moscow Public Fund, 1997), 41.

[23] I. M. Entin, *Separation of Powers: Experience of Modern States* (Moscow: Literature of Law, 1995), 173.

govern without the legislative branch for up to three and a half years.

This issue of the approval of the prime ministerial nominee has been the major point of contention between the parliament and president since 1993, even given the strength of anti-Yeltsin sentiment in the Dumas elected in both 1993 and 1996. In part this is because of the way in which the president's economic reform agenda was significantly moderated after the December 1993 elections and his governments have, over time, become even less radical in their composition than that of early 1992. Perhaps the most striking case of conflict occurred in 1998, when Yeltsin sacked his prime minister Viktor Chernomyrdin and, after some casting around, presented the Duma with the nomination of Sergei Kirienko. A little-known technocrat with no political base, Kirienko was not a popular choice. He was rejected twice by the Duma before it finally approved his nomination, more in fear of the threat of election than enthusiasm for his candidacy. However with the outbreak of the Russian financial crisis in late summer, Yeltsin sacked Kirienko and nominated former Prime Minister Chernomyrdin. However the Duma twice rejected Chernomyrdin's nomination, and this time, instead of presenting his nominee a third time and thereby forcing the issue, Yeltsin nominated a compromise candidate, Yevgeny Primakov. What this episode showed is that although the power in appointment is weighted in favour of the president, if the parliament holds its nerve it can prevent an appointment with which it disagrees.

Relations between the president and the government have frequently been characterized by Russian analysts as 'strong president—weak government'. The president can dismiss the prime minister, take decisions on the resignation of the government, appoint and dismiss the deputy prime ministers and federal ministers, preside at the sessions of the government (though the president is not the head of the government formally), and can repeal government decrees and regulations if they contradict the Constitution, federal law, or presidential decrees. But at the same time, it is necessary to take into consideration that, according to Article 114 of the Constitution, it is the government that implements financial, credit, and monetary policy, as well as a uniform state policy in the field of culture, science, education, health services, social security, and ecology. Consequently, the government in Russia is not necessarily so weak.

However the government's responsibility to draft the state budget, which can cause conflict with the president, can also produce problems in the relationship with the parliament. Article 114 stipulates that the government submits the budget to the Duma, which in turn votes on it after debate and review. After the Duma votes on the budget law, it must be sent to the Federation Council for approval (Art. 106 of the Constitution). Similarly, federal taxes must also be approved by both the Duma and the Federation Council. Thus, every year the approval of the budget invites contentious opposition between the government and parliament. Institutional competition is only aggravated by party competition; parliament has been dominated by the left-wing and populist parties, which predictably block the passage of a budget drafted by a liberal government. In the case of a very strong polarization in the executive and legislative branches of power, the likelihood of which has been increased by the activist role Yeltsin has generally sought to play, the government is severely constrained in its capacity to adopt a realistic budget. It cannot deal with the everyday problems because it has no political support from either of the two chambers of parliament. Thus, in order to adopt a realistic budget, an important informal practice has been instituted, and has gained quasi-constitutional importance: the president routinely appoints a representative from an influential political faction in the Duma to the post of minister of finance. It is thus clear that the government sits between president and parliament and the balance here remains fluid, even within the position of basic presidential primacy.

President and Constitutional Court

The fourth component of this power balance at the apex of the Russian state structure is the Constitutional Court. There had been no constitutional court during the Soviet period; the Court for the Russian Republic was established in October 1991. Despite fears among many that the new Court would be simply a bystander with no role to play, it was quite an influential institution prior to its closure at the time of the 1993 crisis. Among the tricky issues that came before it were the challenge to Yeltsin's banning of the CPSU and the confiscation of its property, Yeltsin's attempt to merge the security agencies in late 1991, and the status of the March 1992 Tatarstan referendum. But its most important role was played out through its chairman Valery Zorkin. With both parliament and president trying to play within the accepted rules of political life during their 1992–3 conflict (at least until September 1993), the Constitutional Court was called in on a number of occasions to adjudicate between the parties. More importantly, as noted above, Zorkin played an active role in brokering an agreement between Yeltsin and his opponents at the end of 1992. However in playing a high profile role, and often seeming to favour the parliamentary side in the dispute, Zorkin incurred the wrath of the president, and when the Court met and declared Yeltsin's decree suspending the Constitution unconstitutional, Yeltsin suspended the Court.

The 1993 Constitution allocates to the president a number of important powers in relation to the judiciary. The president suggests candidates for the posts of judges of the Constitutional Court, the Supreme Court, and the Superior Arbitration Court for confirmation by the Federation Council. Single-handedly, the president appoints judges to all other district and federal courts. Article 125.2 of the Constitution allows the president, one-fifth of the members of the Federation Council or deputies of the State Duma, the government, the Supreme Court and Supreme Arbitration Court, and local legislatures and executives to petition the Constitutional Court to rule on the constitutionality of federal laws, normative acts of the president, the Federation Council, State Duma, and the government; republican constitutions, local charters, as well as laws and other normative acts; agreements between government branches and between the federal and local governments; and international agreements of the Russian Federation that have not entered into force. Individual citizens may also petition the court in cases involving the constitutionality of decisions regarding constitutionally guaranteed rights and freedoms (Art. 125.4 of the Constitution). Finally, if the president is accused of treason or any other crime which calls for impeachment, the Court possesses the important role of ruling on the constitutionality of procedural compliance in the case (Art. 125.7).

The Russian Constitutional Court has been instrumental not only in interpreting the confusing and contradictory labyrinth of constitutional principles, but also in clarifying the fluctuating goals of the state as well as the constant power struggles between government branches (see Art. 125.3 of the Constitution). In fact, through several of its decisions, the Constitutional Court has further strengthened presidential powers. One such case (Decision of the Constitutional Court of 31 July 1995) concerned verifying the constitutionality of presidential decrees restoring constitutional legality in the territory of the Chechen Republic. In its ruling, the Constitutional Court agreed that the Constitution allows the president additional covert powers.[24] In another Court decision

---

[24] *Bulletin of the Constitutional Court of the Russian Federation*, 5 (1995), 11.

(22 April 1996), regarding the interpretation of Article 107 of the Constitution, the Court upheld the president's attempt to return federal laws to the Chambers of the Federal Assembly for amendment and stated that such action was within the presidential veto powers contained in the Constitution. In the opinion of the Constitutional Court, if the procedure for adopting federal laws is transgressed in the legislative process, the president has the right to return a law to the corresponding chamber, pointing out the specific breaches of procedure. In this case, the law cannot be considered 'adopted' in the sense of Article 107.1 of the Constitution, and not returning it for reconsideration would not be a violation of Article 107.3 of the Constitution.[25]

The Constitutional Court has also been very active in one area of the Constitution which has been significant in all of the post-communist countries, that of socio-economic rights. At the very beginning of the constitution-drafting process, the Constitutional Commission was determined to include a list of social rights, believing that unless the Constitution contained such rights its adoption would be delayed. It is the responsibility of the Court to ensure that all citizens' constitutional rights are observed throughout the country, and since its re-establishment in February 1995,[26] the Court has handled more disputes concerning economic and social rights than civil or political rights. This seems consistent with the experience of other post-communist states, such as Hungary, Poland, and Belarus.

Social rights form the majority of all constitutional rights. They include social security in old age, in case of sickness, disability, loss of a breadwinner, child-rearing, and other cases established by law (Art. 39.1), the right to a guaranteed minimum level of remuneration for labour (Art. 7.2), the right to protection against unemployment (Art. 37.3), the right to state support for maternity, childhood, and family (Art. 7.2), the right of needy citizens to receive free or affordable housing (Art. 40.3), and the right to health protection and medical care—including free medical care in state and municipal health institutions (Art. 41). Russian doctrine considers that social rights should uphold the humanitarian values of equality, social justice, and humanism. Consequently, social rights in Russia have not been limited to meeting the needs of the elderly or disabled citizens or those otherwise in need, but have been a

---

[25] *Bulletin of the Constitutional Court of the Russian Federation*, 3 (1996), 10.

[26] Although legislation establishing the Court was adopted in mid-1994 the final judge was not appointed, and therefore the Court could not begin work, until Feb. 1995.

means of restitution, of righting past wrongs, as well. This is most clearly reflected in the way in which these rights have been used to extend aid and protection to citizens who have suffered from political repression, were victims of the 1957 nuclear plant explosion, participated in rescue missions after the Chernobyl nuclear plant explosion, as well as to ethnic groups that suffered from Stalin's repression. For example, the Constitutional Court, reviewing the constitutionality of the law 'On Rehabilitation of Victims of Political Repression' of 1991, found that its goals are to rehabilitate victims of political repression, and decided to enforce payments for (within current financial constraints) compensation of property and moral damages.

This expansive understanding of socio-economic rights in Russia originates from the ideals of socialism. Currently, however, the state is dedicated to building a free market economy. It is not clear that, with the shrinkage of the state that many leading decision makers see as essential for the growth of a market economy, the state will be able to sustain such an expansive view. The more cases that are brought successfully to the Court based upon the results of state negligence or direct state action, the less able the state will be to meet its obligations under the law. This tension is one which will need to be worked out quickly.

Constitutional Amendments

The introduction of the president's Constitution in which the president dominates all aspects of government did not resolve the power struggle between competing institutions. In fact the existing inequality between state institutions has only heightened the animosity between them, leading some members of the parliament at times to call for the restoration of a parliamentary political system. It has also led to attempts to reform the Constitution. On 21 June 1995, the State Duma approved three draft laws with a qualified majority vote to amend the Federal Constitution. The first draft law (to amend Arts. 83 and 103 of the Constitution) expanded the number of cabinet members and their appointments that were to be approved by the State Duma. Parliamentarians hoped to gain the right to approve the president's appointment of the deputy heads of government, the minister of foreign affairs, defence, interior, and the directors of the foreign investigation and the federal investigation services. The second bill envisaged changing Articles 103 and 117 of the Constitution. This draft concerned the individual members of the Russian cabinet, who could be held personally responsible for their decisions and actions by allowing the Duma to recall cabinet members with a qualified majority vote. At the same time, the procedure of recalling ministers would restrict the president from freely disbanding parliament. The third draft law introduced changes in Articles 101, 102 and 103 of the Constitution, which would have organized committees for parliamentary supervision in both chambers of the federal parliament, primarily aimed at investigating the work of the federal institutions of the executive. But these amendments were ultimately dismissed when the Federation Council, fearing a possible strengthening of the powers of the lower house of parliament, revoked all three draft amendments.

Following the period of severe financial crisis in 1998, the blatant institutional power imbalance was blamed for the country's troubles, and the focus returned to amending the Constitution. Somewhat surprisingly, the Federation Council was the initiator of the proposed constitutional changes, targeting the very same articles of the Constitution which the Duma's amendment project addressed, though the power was to be shifted from the Duma to the Council. According to these draft amendments, the appointment of the prime minister would be approved by Federation Council, on the basis of the argument that the regional governors are responsible for securing and disbursing the state budget. The Federation Council also argued that the financial crisis was a direct result of the Duma's ultimate approval of the president's weak candidate, Sergei Kirienko. Prior to his appointment, the president proposed the same candidate three times to the Duma even though it was obvious that he lacked sufficient political support. The fact that the Duma finally *did* approve Kirienko, the Council argued, reflected the Assembly's fear of being dissolved by presidential decree. Since the president cannot disband the Federation Council, the upper house reasoned it should exercise the important check on the president and therefore approve prime minister candidates. Unfortunately, though perhaps not surprisingly, these draft amendments were not approved by the State Duma.

The final, and most surprising, initiative for amending the Constitution came from the president himself, after failing to gain Duma approval of his candidate for prime minister. Although successive efforts to amend the separation of power structure have failed, after Sergei Kirienko's dismissal and the president's inability to gain the Duma's support for Viktor Chernomyrdin a political deal was cut between the president and the parliament. The political agreement, announced by the president on 7 September 1998 and which will continue to be in effect until the end of this Duma's term, outlines the procedure by which the Duma and the president will begin monthly consultations on amending the Constitution. The agreement stipulates that these amendments must envisage, in particular, broadening the powers and controlling functions of both chambers of the federal parliament, broadening the powers of the government, and introducing consultations between the executive and legislature. The document also addresses the problem of adopting a federal law on the constitutional assembly. In the month following the agreement, the changes proposed included additions to the federal constitutional law 'On the Russian Federation Government' to direct more power to both chambers of parliament in terms of forming the cabinet and checking the work of the government, while simultaneously extending the power of the prime minister. Although the president will still appoint and dismiss the prime minister, prior consultations with parliament have been envisaged.

Conclusion

The 1993 Russian Constitution has created a striking power imbalance between state institutions in which none of the other government branches can check the actions of the president. However, the extensive powers and responsibilities concentrated in the hands of the president evidently exceeded the strength and ability of that office. To counter this problem, President Yeltsin has built up an enormous and largely unaccountable presidential administration. Unelected bodies brought into the decision-making process, such as the Security Council, have been responsible for some of the most damaging political decisions, such as undertaking military action in Chechnya. Heavily reliant on the dynamism and health of one man, continually confronted by the hostility of the frustrated parliament, submerged by the weight of the problems facing the country, and lacking any powerful partners in rudimentary civil society, the super-presidential system has been unable to foster the development of a stable and vigorous democracy. In the initial years after the adoption of the 1993 Constitution, it was possible to argue that the Russian super-presidential state, however imbalanced and ineffective, was still better than the pre-1993 constitutional chaos. It was possible to argue that President Yeltsin, despite his obvious shortcomings, was at heart a true democrat reluctant to misuse his enormous powers. However, in the autumn of 1998, it became clear that the era of Yeltsin was coming to an end and the system created in 1993 presents a major threat to democracy-building in Russia. This system has been virtually helpless in coping with the severe financial crisis that brought Russia to the brink of economic bankruptcy. Yeltsin's poor health has prevented him from conducting the daily business of running the country and forced a *de facto* delegation of his power to various other bodies.[27] Moreover, the prospect that the vast powers of the president may be misused by a less democratically inclined successor to Yeltsin became realistic and frightening. President Yeltsin recognized the gravity of the situation and promised to elaborate some major constitutional changes. The scope and speed of these changes is difficult to predict. But one important conclusion of this chapter is certainly justified: a constitution creating a striking power imbalance between the major branches of government is detrimental to democracy. Had President Yeltsin been more generous in constitutionally delegating power to parliament after his 'victory' in the violent contest of September 1993, efforts to build a workable democracy in Russia might have been realized to a greater extent.

The resultant power imbalance is the main reason that the state has grown weak, since the executive has become excessively overburdened and the state ineffective.

Such construction of the Constitution envisages that a president with enormous powers invested in him should work effectively and, without doubt, be committed to liberal values. This idea, incarnated in the Constitution, turned out to be rather risky. A president with poor health has created quite a different situation, with those close to him becoming a hub of decision-making, and other branches of power cannot balance this potentially illegal centre of power. It is good, of course, if those surrounding an unhealthy president are devoted to the idea of observing the Constitution. But what if something quite different happens and those surrounding the not-quite-capable president start to ignore constitutional provisions?

The Constitution must include mechanisms that envisage the most incredible and sometimes unexpected situations, yet it is possible that the Russian Constitution does not envisage everything. Article 92 (part 2) stipulates that the president of the Russian Federation shall cease to exercise his powers before the end of his term in the event of his persistent inability, for health reasons, to

---

[27] See John Thornhill, 'Yeltsin Gives up Day-to-Day Government of Russia', *Financial Times* (29 Oct. 1998).

carry out the powers invested in him, or impeachment. Due to health reasons, President Yeltsin announced his voluntary resignation on the last day of the twentieth century. It was a courageous decision testifying to the fact that Boris Yeltsin understood his responsibilities to the people. But it could be envisaged that another president would not act similarly. What then is the procedure for terminating a president's authority in the event of his persistent inability to carry out the powers invested in him?

The president of Russia, Prime Minister Vladimir Putin, probably considers that the main goal is to strengthen state power. It is difficult to say whether this main political idea of acting president is based on his recognition and acknowledgement of the imbalance between the branches of power, as thus far he has not made any such statements. But there is still the fact that all his public statements address the necessity of strengthening state power. And even military actions in Chechnya are explained in terms of overcoming the weakness of state bodies and restoring their powers throughout the whole territory of the Russian Federation.

Some statements of Vladimir Putin on the strengthening of state regulation of economic processes have also attracted attention. Behind such political statements one usually finds a hidden desire to return to a centralized planned economy. Putin emphasises the fact that, in his belief, strengthening the state's position in the economy simply means creating stable conditions for the effective functioning of market. Addressing whether it is mistaken to say that the state has unreasonably retired from economy, Putin said that the state must not interfere (as it did previously) in the economy through the restoration of direct planning. Rather, it must adopt laws and rules concerning the functioning of the market that are simple and intelligible enough for everybody to understand. Strengthening of the state means that the state must ensure observance of established legal provisions. The state must be careful to ensure that these rules are applied equally to everybody, and the rules must be observed by all participants of the market.

Finally, one other statement by the new political leader of Russia deserves special attention: that just courts must be a central link in the mechanism for securing democracy and ensuring conditions that will force Russia forward in the new millennium.

Constitutionalism in Belarus:
A False Start

Alexander Lukashuk

From all accounts, the constitutionalization process has failed to contribute to democratic consolidation in Belarus. Whereas all the other post-communist states have adopted constitutions that have had a clear affect on the political process, Belarus's Constitution is, at best, an occasionally used tool for manipulation by the country's autocratic president Aliaksandar Lukashenka. But the fact that the Constitution remains at the centre of the struggle between President Lukashenka (who maintains that the Constitution approved by the November 1996 referendum is the sole foundation of law in the country) and the democratic opposition (which considers the Constitution drafted by the president illegal and the new legislative body, the National Assembly, illegitimate) at least shows that the Constitution cannot be ignored. Moreover, a closer look at the constitution-drafting process reveals that certain choices (and omissions) laid the foundation for the current undemocratic regime.

Promising Signs

In the late 1980s and early 1990s, Gorbachev's glasnost policy had a strange impact on the Soviet public. There was something religious in the way people read newspapers and watched television. The general belief was that words themselves, if strung along in the right sequence, had the power to set things right. This was particularly true if the words were contained in a constitution. The public longing for a new constitutional testament could not be ignored by any political force. Belarus, it seemed at the time, was no exception.

Despite the revolutionary spirit, the electoral laws allowed democrats to win only about 12 per cent of parliamentary seats, while the Communist Party maintained control of up to 80 per cent of the parliament (or 274 out of 345 of MPs). The remaining seats were taken by independent candidates. One of the top Communist Party officers, Mikalai Dzemiantsei, was appointed as chairman of the Supreme Soviet (parliament). The real power in the country still belonged to the first secretary of the Communist Party Central Committee, Anatol Malafeeu. The departments of the Central Committee paralleled the structure of the Council of Ministers, and through these institutions the Party controlled all appointments to the executive, judicial, and economic state organs. This Soviet governing system, in which all important decisions were first to be approved by the Party, functioned in Belarus until August 1991. After the Moscow putsch in September 1991, the Party was banned and Dzemiantsei was forced to resign.

Initial work on a new constitution began in May 1990 at the very first session of the newly elected Supreme Soviet of the then Belarusian Soviet Socialist Republic. On 27 July 1990, at the conclusion of the first session, deputies partially cancelled the old Constitution by adopting the Declaration of State Sovereignty. One year later, after the 1991 communist putsch, the Declaration was given the status of constitutional law. This 'interim Constitution' played an instrumental role in Belarus's independence from the USSR, serving as a foundation for many of the laws, decrees, and decisions that were adopted during the next three years. Adherence to the Constitution's guidelines was the subject of heated parliamentary debates.

The Supreme Soviet declared full sovereignty and independence of Belarus, confirmed the superiority of the national legislation over that of the Soviet Union, and declared its foreign policy independent from Moscow. The text of the Declaration defended the Belarusian language, demanded compensation for the victims of Chernobyl,[1] banned foreign military bases on the territory of Belarus, and demanded Belarus's share of Soviet gold, diamonds, and hard currency reserves. In terms of institutions, the Declaration

---

[1] References to the Chernobyl nuclear reactor disaster were powerful tools for the mobilization of anti-Soviet sentiments among the population, particularly after glasnost and the new information that was published (years too late) about the disaster. See Kathleen J. Mihalisko, 'Belarus: Retreat to Authoritarianism', in Karen Dawisha and Bruce Parrott (eds.), *Democratic Changes and Authoritarian Reactions in Russia, Ukraine, Belarus, and Moldova* (Cambridge: Cambridge University Press, 1997), 238.

envisaged establishing a National Bank and an independent financial system, national tax and custom agencies, and separate armed forces, police, and security agencies which were to be subordinated to the Supreme Soviet. Establishing the rule of law was declared to be the goal of the state and division of powers was declared the most important principle of the rule of law. For the first time two major goals of the foreign policy were put down: to eliminate nuclear weapons and to seek the status of neutrality.[2]

Before August 1991, however, the Declaration had limited practical impact. It was adopted when the communists were still in power and the communist leadership of the republic never took its stipulations seriously. The opposition regarded the Declaration as its victory, but due to its limited representation in parliament, it could do little to speed things up in terms of its implementation. Only the final article of the Declaration, which stated the goal of adopting a new constitution, was ever initiated. In July 1990 the Supreme Soviet created a Constitutional Commission, with the chairman of the Supreme Soviet, Mikalai Dzemiantsei, as its head.[3] Seventy-four deputies and legal experts were invited to participate in the Commission. No specific rules or strict procedures were outlined regarding the procedure for adopting the constitution. The Commission's task was simply to produce the draft according to the guidelines in the Declaration of Sovereignty. It was understood that the Commission's draft could be adopted like any other law—after two parliamentary readings.

The Constitutional Commission submitted its first constitutional draft to the Supreme Soviet in November 1991. The assembly approved the draft after the first reading and submitted it to a nationwide debate. The text was published in four newspapers, with a total circulation of more than 1,000,000. With the USSR at the point of disintegration, the draft Constitution was instrumental for democracy-building and psychologically reassuring to the population. The country seemed ready to reclaim its status as an independent state.

For the first time in Belarusian history a basic element of democracy—the division of legislative, executive, and judicial

---

[2] The first goal was achieved in 1996 when the last Russian nuclear missiles were withdrawn from Belarus; the latter was buried in April 1993, when the Supreme Soviet approved Belarus's inclusion in a CIS collective security agreement. See *RFE/RL Research Report*, N 17 (1993), 24.

[3] In September 1992 he was replaced by the new speaker Stanislau Shushkevich; in between the Commission worked under the leadership of deputy speaker Vasil Shaladonau.

powers—had been included in the country's constitutional draft. Belarus was to be a mixed parliamentary-presidential republic, in which the parliament was to be a professional body. Parliament's exclusive powers included adopting, amending, and interpreting the Constitution and laws, calling referenda and elections, and approving the state budget and levying taxes. It was to elect the prime minister and approve other key government ministers. The draft introduced the institution of a constitutional court, and the parliament was to control all the appointments in the judicial branch. The prosecutor general and the head of the National Bank were also to be approved by the parliament.

That first draft introduced a made-to-order president according to the classic communist pattern in which the executive could accumulate as much power as possible but remain unaccountable. The president was proclaimed head of state and head of the executive. The president was to name a candidate for this position, with appointment and dismissal subject to a vote of parliament. The president was given the right to ban strikes.[4] The president was to be directly elected by secret ballot and to serve a five-year term. The draft did not give the president the right to dismiss or suspend the parliament, although the parliament could impeach the president.

The draft guaranteed all the basic rights and freedoms provided by the Universal Declaration of Human Rights. Although many of these rights had been mentioned in the previous Soviet constitutions, the difference in the new draft was the absence of communist phraseology which was used in the past to render these freedoms worthless. Certain statements included in the draft were clearly prompted by the desire to ensure that past criminal conduct of the totalitarian state could not be repeated. However, many basic rights required the enactment of special laws in order to become binding. Thus, the draft did not restrict the ability of parliament to legislate away many constitutional rights and privileges.[5]

After the draft's publication, over 6,000 people inundated the Commission with their ideas for additions, amendments, and corrections to the document. The social democratic 'Hramada' Party submitted its own draft of an entirely different constitution. To a certain degree, the public debate generated by the draft actually benefited the process of democratic consolidation in Belarus. It lifted

---

[4] This regulation was prompted by a mass strike in the spring of 1991 which alarmed the authorities.

[5] This is exactly what has been happening in Belarus since 1996 when the president started to run the country by decrees, abolishing or suspending constitutional provisions.

many taboos and stimulated further discussion of explosive issues which communist glasnost assiduously avoided, such as the role of the Communist Party, the establishment of a multi-party system, the right to private ownership, and the division of powers. However, the debate had shown that human rights and freedoms were a priority neither for the legislators nor for the public. There had been little discussion on this part of the draft. Immediately after discussing the draft the parliament adopted a law on criminal investigation which made it fairly easy to violate the right to privacy, the inviolability of the home, and the secrecy of correspondence.

An Attempt to Jump over the Abyss

After the August 1991 putsch, Stanislau Shushkevich was elected chairman of the Supreme Soviet, the Communist Party was banned, and its property was confiscated. Unfortunately, those were the only changes that occurred in Belarus. The democratic parliamentary opposition tried to initiate immediate parliamentary elections, in accordance with the Constitution. Speaker Shushkevich first supported the idea, but later inexplicably dropped the initiative from the agenda. The moment was lost and urgent political changes were put off indefinitely. The communist *nomenklatura* fully preserved its control of the judicial and legislative branches.

In the spring of 1992, worried by the absence of reform and threats to Belarusian sovereignty, the opposition, primarily the Belarusian Popular Front (BPF), an anti-communist, strongly pro-independence organization, started a national campaign to conduct a referendum on early parliamentary elections. BPF saw early elections as one way to break the political impasse in the Supreme Soviet. More than 442,000 people signed a petition in support of the referendum (the minimum required by the law was 350,000) which was subsequently validated by the country's Central Electoral Commission. In the course of a month, the Supreme Soviet was to set a date for the referendum. Instead, parliament ignored the petition and its deputies took a half-year vacation, giving the communist forces ample time to regroup.

During parliament's summer recess, the government assumed a legislative role by issuing numerous decrees and adopting long-term decisions of a political nature. For example, due to the absence of laws on information and freedom of expression, the government became co-owner of nine mass media publications, effectively controlling more than 80 per cent of the press and fully controlling national radio and television. Cabinet officials also took an active role in organizing political forces that would act as loyal supporters of the government. During the summer, a number of communist-oriented public organizations formed an umbrella coalition known as the Coordination Committee, chaired by a senior government official.

The reaction of the presidium of the Supreme Soviet to this usurpation of the parliamentary prerogatives was one of muted irritation; by then, the chairman of the Council of Ministers, Viachaslau Kebich, was too strong to be confronted.

At the end of the year when the Supreme Soviet returned from its long vacation, it moved to ban the referendum on early elections. By a majority vote, parliament turned down the request to hold a referendum on the grounds that organizers had participated in 'gross violations of the law' while obtaining supporters' signatures, though this allegation was never verified in court. There was no immediate negative reaction by the public, and the BPF failed to find an adequate response to this decision. In the eyes of the BPF, parliament's decision drove home the glaring fact that working within the parameters of democratic procedure would not succeed in Belarus. Moreover, given the unreformed legislature, the ineffective state-owned economy, and the total absence of privatization, the segment of the population previously involved in social issues suddenly became uninterested in political activity, leaving the BPF with little or no political base from which to garner support.

Adopting the New Constitution

Though the Constitution was approved in the first reading in 1991, its final adoption was delayed by two and a half years. In August 1992, a new draft was published. Some 100 articles (of a total of 165) were corrected and several other suggestions were offered. The most vocal debates and opposing views were about the statements concerning the foundations of the constitutional order, citizens' rights, the parliament, the presidency, and local self-government. In the second draft the communist term 'Supreme Soviet' was replaced by the historic Belarusian term 'Soym', the number of deputies was cut in half in comparison with the existing Supreme Soviet, to 160, and the term of office for MPs was reduced by one year, to four. Overall, the list of powers of the Soym and its chairman was shorter than that of the Supreme Soviet;

the missing prerogatives had been transferred to the president and to the government.

The distribution of powers in the second draft corresponded to the new balance of powers in Belarus at that time. With the Communist Party banned, the presidency was no longer a coveted and guaranteed position for its leader. The real power was in hands of the executive, and the draft shifted some of the constitutional rights from the parliament and president to the prime minister. If the first draft granted the president executive powers, for example, the second draft created a figurehead president, who would have had a small number of ceremonial duties. The prime minister was given wider control over the cabinet and was declared the commander-in-chief of the armed forces. According to the first draft, it was the parliament that took decisions on state loans and foreign credits and on granting aid to foreign powers; now those were the sole responsibility of the government. The second draft granted the government two additional rights absent in the first variant: the right to veto decisions taken by local soviets if they contradict national laws and the ability to initiate the procedure for amending the Constitution. The second draft simultaneously stripped the Constitutional Court of the latter right. Thus, the executive, by far the strongest institution during the constitution-drafting period, attempted to acquire constitutional authority formerly held by the legislative and judicial branches.

In the absence of clear adoption procedures, technically the Supreme Soviet could have adopted a new constitution after the second reading. But the adoption of a new constitution was hindered not so much by controversy over various drafts or inability to reach compromise on crucial issues as it was by the parliament itself. After the publication of the second draft in 1992, the Commission produced more than twenty-five versions of the text. Moreover, long debates over specific articles went to naught since parliament repeatedly failed to assemble the required quorum. Thus, the constitutional debate lost its impetus and the parliament's legendary indecisiveness was widely ridiculed. The image and legitimacy of the future Constitution was tarnished even before it was adopted.

Having to sift through two dozen constitutional drafts proved to be a daunting task. After lengthy debates in the spring and summer of 1993, parliamentarians could not even agree whether or not to name the document 'The Constitution of the Republic of Belarus'. The name of the parliament itself was changing constantly—one day, it was to be called the 'Supreme Soviet', the next day 'Soym' sounded better, then 'National Assembly' was considered, followed by 'Supreme Council', and finally 'Supreme Soviet' seemed to sound the best of all. The size of the legislature fluctuated between 360 and 160 seats. Unable to decide whether the parliament should be a professional body (that is, one in which deputies work on a regular full-time basis), members coined the following final version of Article 92; 'A deputy of the Supreme Soviet exercises his powers in the Supreme Soviet on a professional basis but, if he so chooses, without severing his ties with production activity or office service.' It should not be surprising that, at the time this article was written, about 70 per cent of deputies also worked in the executive branch.

The most heated arguments concerned issues of power—the presidency, the prerogatives of the parliament and the government, and dominion of local administrations. The fourth constitutional draft, for example, considered in the spring of 1993, had eight different versions of a chapter on local self-government. The presidency was introduced in 1991 in the very first draft, written under the guidance of the Communist Party which at the time was still in power. This idea took various forms in subsequent versions, disappearing in some drafts and reappearing in others. Six months before the Constitution was adopted, in June 1993, a vote was taken in order to establish some clear guidelines for the Constitutional Commission: 147 deputies voted in favour of a strong president, 101 voted for a weak president, and 130 voted against introducing this office at all. There were only 288 deputies present during the vote. The outcome reveals that up to 90 deputies voted simultaneously for two or three mutually exclusive options.[6]

The most adamant opponents to establishing a presidency were the parliamentary opposition, the BPF, and the chairman of the Supreme Soviet. BPF leader Zianon Pazniak and speaker Stanislau Shushkevich were both quite popular at the time; indeed, each stood a good chance of being elected president. Shushkevich maintained that a presidency should not be introduced in the republic for at least another three years. During this period, he asserted, the parliament should shape up and help strengthen existing democratic institutions. Pazniak, for his part, claimed that a presidency would lead to dictatorship. He felt that Belarusian society in its present condition would be unable to counterbalance any possible totalitarian encroachments by a president. The deteriorating economy and Russia's imperialistic interest in

[6] See *East European Constitutional Review* (Fall 1993/Winter 1994), 61.

Belarus, in his view, also argued against the introduction of a presidency.

Unfortunately, these arguments stood little chance of acceptance. First of all, by no means were the arguments against establishing a presidency in Belarus convincing. Economic, legal, and administrative chaos required a strong state and a strong executive.[7] Although orthodox communists contemptuously branded the notion of a presidency 'a bourgeois invention', there still existed a pervasive traditional belief in the merits of one strong leader. All the while, the process of power consolidation was continuing; Prime Minister Viachaslau Kebich was acting in an increasingly president like manner by issuing decrees and signing international agreements without consulting parliament.

This development fully satisfied the parliamentary majority whose main goal was to protect itself from change and prolong members' terms in office.[8] Prosecution demands notwithstanding, the Supreme Soviet has never lifted immunity for deputies who have committed crimes. Deputies took great care to protect their personal interests. Many obtained free apartments, bought cars and consumer goods at reduced prices, and received food parcels in times of scarcity (1990–1). In order to avoid setting a precedent concerning early resignation from the Supreme Soviet, the majority voted to preserve the powers of one deputy who emigrated from Belarus and became the citizen of another country. By this time, the Supreme Soviet had become a major source of anti-parliamentarism in Belarus. According to numerous polls, voters in Belarus neither relied on nor respected the Supreme Soviet as an institution. Conditions were ripe for the emergence of a strong leader.

Meanwhile, the constitution-drafting process was coming to an end. The first head of the Constitutional Commission, Mikalai Dzemiantsei, lost power after the communist *coup d'état* but no one was appointed in his place. The next speaker of the parliament, Stanislau Shushkevich, presided over numerous debates on the draft Constitution but was dismissed two weeks before its adoption.

---

[7] For an argument for strengthening post-communist states, see Stephen Holmes, 'Cultural Legacies or State Collapse? Probing the Postcommunist Dilemma', in Michael Mendelbaum (ed.), *Post-communism: Four Perspectives* (New York: Council on Foreign Relations, 1996), esp. 51–68.

[8] The parliamentary pledge of 1992 to hold early elections in 1994 was brushed aside. The opposition was too weak to force the majority to stick to their promises and the power broker, Viachaslau Kebich, was happy with the loyal parliament. Deputies were sure that if he won the presidential election there would be no unpleasant surprises for them.

Shushkevich's successor, Miachyslaw Hryb (a former police general), used an iron fist to adopt the Constitution; first by instituting a secret ballot, forbidding absentee voting, and extending the vote for three days until a sufficient quorum had voted. Only under these extraordinary conditions was it possible to pass the new Constitution on 15 March 1994.

The New Constitution

The preamble of the 1994 Constitution begins with the words 'We, the people of the Republic of Belarus . . .' and ends with a reference to a referendum as a means for amending the Constitution; the draft represented an attempt to create a fundamental democratic framework which provided for a full range of freedoms and a basis for a state ruled by law. Article 1 described Belarus as a unitary, democratic, social state based on the rule of law. Article 2 declared the individual to be of supreme importance to society and the state. According to Article 3, the people were the sole source of state power in the republic; they were to exercise their power directly and through representative bodies. Article 4 stipulated that democracy was to be exercised on the basis of a variety of political institutions, ideologies, and views. The most important in terms of establishing democratic foundations for further development of Belarus was Article 6 (separation of powers): 'The State shall rely on the principle of dividing power into legislative, executive, and judicial power. State bodies, within the limits of their powers, shall be independent. They shall cooperate among themselves and check and counterbalance one another.' Nevertheless, these laudable objectives were never implemented in Belarus.

The parliament

The Constitution declared the Supreme Soviet (parliament) the highest representative, standing, and sole legislative body of state power. Two hundred and sixty deputies were to be elected by direct vote (majoritarial system) for the term of five years. The Supreme Soviet was to call national referenda; adopt and amend the Constitution; adopt laws and resolutions and monitor their implementation; provide interpretation of the Constitution and laws; call regular elections of deputies of the Supreme Council and local councils of deputies as well as presidential elections; form the Central Commission on Elections and National Referenda; elect the

Constitutional Court, the Supreme Court, the Supreme Economic Court, the procurator general, and the chairman and the council of the Supervisory Authority as well as the chairman and members of the board of the National Bank; determine the guidelines of the domestic and foreign policy; approve the national budget, set national taxes and dues, and monitor the issue of money. The parliament had also the right to ratify and denounce international treaties; adopt decisions on amnesty; determine military doctrine; declare war and conclude peace; institute state awards, ranks, and titles. Laws and resolutions of the Supreme Soviet were to be adopted provided that a majority of elected deputies had voted for them; adopted laws should be sent to the president for signature within ten days of their adoption. If vetoed by the president, the bill should be again approved by two-thirds of the elected deputies to become a law.

The presidency

Warnings notwithstanding, deputies introduced a rather strong presidency: the president was declared the head of state and the executive. The president was to be elected directly by the citizens for the term of five years. Article 100 specified powers and responsibility of the new office. The president was to: (1) protect the sovereignty, national security, and territorial integrity of Belarus and safeguard political and economic stability and the respect of civil rights and liberties; (2) manage the system of bodies of executive power and ensure their cooperation with the representative bodies; (3) set up and abolish ministries, state committees, and other central bodies of administration; (4) appoint and dismiss, with the consent of the Supreme Soviet, the prime minister, his or her deputies, ministers of foreign affairs, finance, defence, internal affairs, and the chairman of the KGB; appoint and dismiss other members of the Cabinet of Ministers as well as accept their resignations; (5) introduce to the Supreme Soviet candidates for election for the post of chairman of the Constitutional Court, chairman of the Supreme Court, chairman of the Supreme Economic Court, chairman of the board of the National Bank; (6) annually present reports on the state of the nation; (7) appoint judges, other than those whose election fell within the competence of the Supreme Soviet; (8) represent the state in relations with other countries and international organizations; (9) in the event of necessity declare a state of emergency and submit the decision to the Supreme Soviet for approval within three days; (10) have the right to defer a strike or suspend it; (11) sign laws and have the right to return them with objections to the Supreme Council for further discussion and a second vote. The president was also declared head of the Security Council and the commander-in-chief of the armed forces; he had a number of other duties which he was supposed to execute by issuing decrees and edicts.

The Constitution also specified the procedure of removing the president from office. One of the following three reasons was deemed necessary for this: violation of the Constitution, crime, or inability to discharge duties because of state of health. The issue was to be raised by the Supreme Soviet and approved by the Constitutional Court; the president's powers were to be transferred to the speaker of the parliament. The president, on the contrary, had no right to dissolve the parliament.

The courts

Specifics of the judicial system in Belarus were determined not by the Constitution but by the law. The Constitution laid out basic principles of administering justice: independence of judges, collegiality, and publicity. The adversarial proceedings and equality of the parties involved in the trial as well as the right to appeal formed the basis of administering justice. The Constitution did not mention jury trial (still absent in Belarus).

The most important instrument of the rule of law in the republic was the Constitutional Court. Eleven judges were to be elected by the parliament for the term of eleven years. The Court could act either at its own discretion or on the recommendation of the president, the speaker of the parliament, its standing committees, or no fewer than seventy deputies, the Supreme Court, the Supreme Economic Court, or the procurator general. The Constitutional Court was to produce rulings on: the conformity of laws, international agreements, and other obligations of Belarus to the Constitution and international law; the conformity of edicts of the president, ordinances of the Cabinet of Ministers, and orders of the Supreme Court, the Supreme Economic Court, and the procurator general that are of a proscriptive nature to the Constitution, the laws, and instruments of international law ratified by Belarus. The Court could also submit proposals to the parliament for amendments and addenda to the Constitution and laws. Such proposals were subject to compulsory consideration by the parliament. The Constitutional Court made rulings by a simple majority of votes of the full complement of judges; its findings were final and not subject to appeal or protest. Laws and edicts, international agreements, and other obligations deemed to be unconstitutional were declared to have no legal force in Belarus.

The office of the procurator general was the second most important legal supervising body in the country. The head of the office was to be elected by and subordinated to the parliament. The procuracy overviewed implementation of the laws by the executive bodies, enterprises, non-government organizations, and citizens. The procurator's office also supervised investigation of crimes and conformity to the law of judicial decisions; procurators could conduct preliminary enquiries and support public prosecutions in the courts.

Basic rights

Safeguarding the rights and liberties of citizens was declared the supreme goal of the state. All were equal before the law and entitled, without discrimination, to equal protection of their rights and legitimate interests. Restriction of personal rights and liberties was permitted only in the instances specified in law, in the interest of national security, public order, the protection of the morals and health of the population, as well as rights and liberties of other persons. The Constitution preserved the death penalty. The Constitution introduced presumption of innocence; no one was to be forced to give evidence or provide explanations against himself, members of his family, or close relations. Evidence obtained in violation of the law had no legal force.

The Constitution guaranteed privacy, secrecy of communication, the inviolability of the home, freedom of movement, and freedom of thoughts and beliefs and their free expression. An important provision banned monopolization of the mass media and censorship. Citizens were guaranteed the right to receive, store, and disseminate complete, reliable, and timely information on the activities of state bodies and public associations, on political, economic, and international life, and on the state of the environment. The freedom to hold assemblies, rallies, street marches, demonstrations, and pickets as well as freedom of association were complemented with guarantees of direct democracy (right to vote and to be elected, to participate in referenda, to equal access to any post in state bodies).

In general, the chapter on human rights and freedoms followed those of the Universal Declaration of Human Rights. It turned out, however, that the ease and unanimity with which this chapter was adopted belied the fact that constitution makers did not really consider it important. Most of them considered the issue of human rights nothing more than part of the necessary popular rhetoric, the *comme il faut* language of the new time. The concept of 'human rights' had no practical meaning and could not be enforced in court. Many essential rights required the enactment of special laws. In Belarus's practice this requirement very soon degraded to presidential decrees and even regulations of city councils and other branches of the executive. Courts have always ruled in favour of the authorities on such issues. The same has been true for social and economic rights. Although the text was scattered with references to their guarantee, in most cases the language came directly from the Soviet Constitution. No one seemed to examine the cost of these guarantees; no one seemed to notice that they were unworkable.[9]

The Failure of Made-to-Order Presidency

The country's first presidential elections took place in June and July of 1994. The law requires that a candidate secure the support of seventy deputies or collect signatures of at least 100,000 voters in a period of two weeks. The campaign itself lasted one month. The parliamentary majority fully expected that this role would be assumed by their leader, Prime Minister Kebich. But as Poland's ill-fated General Wojciech Jaruzelski once remarked, 'The presidential system is a kind of lottery.' The experience of Poland, Hungary, and Bulgaria readily proved that all too often a presidency tailored for one man ends up being occupied by another. In Belarus, the position was ultimately taken by a parliamentarian who personified all the characteristics of the republic's Supreme Soviet—incompetence, populism, inconsistency, hatred of democracy, and utter disrespect for the law.

Out of twenty-four possible contenders, six were registered as candidates: Prime Minister Viachaslau Kebich; leader of the parlia-

---

[9] For example 'Citizens of the Republic of Belarus shall be guaranteed the right to work as the worthiest means of an individual's self-assertion, that is, the right to choose a profession, type of occupation, and work in accordance with one's vocation, capabilities, education, and vocational training, and having regard to social needs, and the right to healthy and safe working conditions. Employees shall be entitled to remuneration for the work they have done in accordance with the quantity, quality, and social significance of such work.' Or one more example: 'Citizens of the Republic of Belarus shall be entitled to housing.'

mentary opposition Zianon Pazniak; MP Aliaksandar Lukashenka; former speaker Stanislau Shushkevich; Belarus Communist Party secretary Vasil Novikau; and finally, the leader of the Agrarian Union, Aliaksandar Dubko. Kebich's team was unanimously accused of unfair play. Since most of the media in Belarus is state owned, the prime minister enjoyed a great advantage over other candidates in terms of coverage. Furthermore, just before election day, the government stopped the presses of the republic's only independent weekly (*Svaboda*). Two liberally oriented programmes on state radio were also silenced and their producers fired. Kebich's opponents, therefore, had great difficulty in reaching their audience.

Viachaslau Kebich, who based his campaign on rapprochement with Russia, was heavily favoured by Moscow. On the eve of the elections, Russian President Boris Yeltsin met Kebich and pledged his support to the candidate. Before the second round, Russian Premier Viktor Chernomyrdin visited Kebich in Minsk and the two leaders signed a number of economic agreements. Finally, the Russian Orthodox Church also exhorted the faithful to cast their ballots in favour of Kebich.

Despite many abuses, it is safe to say that the voting on 23 June was the freest ever conducted in Belarus's short experience with democracy. The prime minister's biased television campaign actually backfired on him. The main issue for nearly all voters was the economy which, in the absence of reforms, had gone into free fall. In a classic protest vote, people fed up with old-guard rule snubbed Viachaslau Kebich (who received 17.4 per cent of the total vote) in favour of Aliaksandar Lukashenka (who won the election with 45.1 per cent of all votes). Zianon Pazniak wound up with 12.9 per cent of the vote, Stanislau Shushkevich with 9.9 per cent, Aliaksandar Dubko with 6 per cent, and Vasil Novikau with 4.6 per cent.

Lukashenka rose to fame as head of the parliament's anti-corruption commission. He threatened to expose and 'send corrupt [government] officials to the Himalayas', and to 'return to the people that which was taken away from them'. His vocal criticism of the government won him massive support from a citizenry whose average monthly salary was less than $20 in an inflationary climate of 40 per cent (spring 1994). The Belarusian electorate rejected a candidate of the old communist *nomenklatura* only to elect another figure of the exact same ilk. In the 10 July second round of voting, Lukashenka won a landslide victory, polling 80.1 per cent of the total vote. Kebich got even less than in the first tour—only 14.2 per cent.

Lukashenka's Peculiar Presidency

Technically, Lukashenka won the presidential campaign on an anti-corruption platform. This was ironic as there really were no corrupt 'new Belarusians' around that were capable of forming a rigid opposition in order to protect their interests. Unlike in Russia, Belarus missed the phase of *nomenklatura* liberalization. Belarusian *nomenklatura* did not have a chance to amass fortunes sufficient to form a class of owners. There were no export quotas for oil, gas, or metal to make quick millions because the country had no similar natural resources. The most popular get-rich-quick scheme in Belarus consisted of obtaining cheap credits from state-owned banks and building a dacha. These new dachas were built around cities and close to the roads; they were easy to see and easy to hate by the electorate. Lukashenka's promise to confiscate these malignant examples of conspicuous consumption (although he never fulfilled it) won him hundreds of thousands of votes from the country's rank and file.

When Lukashenka became the legitimate head of state, the *nomenklatura* accepted him with no resistance. Their entire well-being was connected to their positions inside the system—and Lukashenka was just another figure on top. In fact, even key figures from the previous administration who supported Prime Minister Viachaslau Kebich and campaigned strongly against Lukashenka defected to the president's side after the election. An act of contrition was all that was required of them to retain their coveted posts. Some even rose in the hierarchy. Even former Premier Kebich, after swearing his loyalty, was awarded a seat in Lukashenka's hand-picked parliament and given a lucrative pension 'in recognition of his contributions to the state'. Conversely, the young ambitious politicians who opposed the old *nomenklatura* and helped Lukashenka achieve victory were required to quit soon after the election since their views were not compatible with the policies that prevailed. Some of them retired voluntarily, others were fired, while some became prominent opposition figures.

The phenomenon of Lukashenka's rise was made possible by the total lack of reform in Belarus in the first years after the demise of the USSR. The Belarusian Supreme Soviet of the time was the Eastern and Central European champion in terms of longevity. While Poland and the Czech Republic held one parliamentary election after another, and even political reporters could not cope with the ever-changing names of prime ministers in Eastern European countries, the political landscape of Belarus remained unchanged. The boast of stability was the main argument in dealing with European organizations and foreign investors; maintaining stability was the main goal and achievement of the government.

What was 'achieved' was not so much stability as stagnation. Minsk looked more and more like the land that time forgot: no new advertising, no new companies, no tourists. The dearth of economic reforms led to huge state debts incurred by having to support collective farms and the military-industrial complex, which was high-tech but useless. The suffocating social atmosphere held too little oxygen to allow for the development of political parties. Self-government did not take shape and the few non-governmental organizations that did exist depended solely on foreign grants for their survival. The only new thing was the Constitution itself—it may be argued whether it was not enough or too late, but it was doomed to fail in a society with no significant social group strong enough and interested in backing the constitutionally agreed balance of power.

The very Constitution that introduced a presidency to the republic became the first president's first victim. Aliaksandar Lukashenka said in a public address in October 1995; 'Constitution how we understand it means that there are three branches of power; legislative, executive, and judicial. And all these branches grow on the tree of the presidency.' Lukashenka founded this interpretation of constitutionalism by manipulating Article 100 which specified presidential powers. The article stipulated that the president 'shall adopt measures to ensure political and economic stability'. In the president's interpretation those lines overrode all other constitutional requirements and gave him an absolute carte blanche to reign and to rule at his will. The central government, executives in the regions, and the courts willingly sided with the president.

In the spring of 1995, Lukashenka demanded the right to dissolve the parliament. In May, a referendum was conducted to determine the republic's official language, state symbols, and extent of economic integration with Russia. The question of the president's right to dissolve parliament was also considered but its results were to be deemed non-binding. Still, over three-quarters of the 64 per cent that voted chose to afford Lukashenka such a right.

Lukashenka enjoyed far greater support than any other political figure. Nobody seemed to mind that he was gradually acquiring much more power than was allowable under the Constitution. The public appeal of the Supreme Soviet issued on 25 October 1995 summarized the year of the presidency in the following way: 'Statements of the leader of the nation about his unwillingness to obey the constitution and the law, his disrespect and insult of other branches of power, first of all of the Supreme Soviet, his promises to introduce "direct presidential rule" show that the process of damaging the foundations of law and civic stability has begun. The president grossly violates constitutional rights of citizens, extinguishes all expressions of free thought and criticism in his address.'

After three unsuccessful attempts, a new Supreme Soviet of Belarus was finally elected in December 1995. A total of 197 deputies (of a possible 260) were elected. The Agrarian Party won 47 seats, the Communist Party 45, the Civic Party 15, and the Social Democrats 9. The remainder of the elected deputies were registered as independents. Sixty-three of the 197 newly elected deputies were employed in executive bodies of state power, 38 in agriculture, 35 in industry, and 22 were lawyers.

Not a single candidate from the main opposition party, the BPF, was elected. Several appeals concerning possible violations of voting procedure were rejected by the Central Electoral Commission. The Council of Europe issued a statement that 'the repeat elections, like the first and second rounds held in May and June, suffered from limited freedom of media, unsatisfactory access of candidates to them, and a crucial absence of political debate before the elections'. The Council's report did however stipulate that in view of existing electoral legislation and the political situation in the country, the elections may be considered to have been free and fair.

The success of the campaign depended on turnout. The Constitutional Court approved a previous parliamentary decision to decrease the turnout barrier from 59 per cent to 25 per cent. A week before the elections, however, under fierce pressure by the president, the Court amended its position and clarified that this norm be applied only in the next parliamentary elections of 2001. 'The Constitutional Court genuflected before the executive,' claimed the independent press. On 10 December, however, turnout was 52.9 per cent and the parliament was elected.

The first session was held on 9 January 1996. The deputies formed six factions, each of which was based on party affiliation. The pro-presidential faction 'Accord' had 59 members; the agrarian faction, 47; the communists, 44; the liberal democratic 'Civic Action' faction, 18; and the social democratic 'Labour Union' faction, 15. The 57-year-old leader of the Agrarian Party, Siamion Sharetsky, was elected chairman of the Supreme Soviet. Of his three deputies, one was a communist, the second a member of the pro-presidential 'Accord' group, and the third a liberal democrat.

Parliamentary deputies created a total of fifteen commissions and introduced several procedural changes. Deputies agreed to meet at plenary sessions only once or twice a week; the rest of the time would be spent working in commissions and factions. It was deemed that this would increase effectiveness. Many deputies, however, felt that the new procedure would actually hamper political debate and render individual deputies (who were elected in constituencies but not by party lists) indistinguishable from one another. The new parliament, like its predecessor, was semiprofessional.

Division of power remained the main constitutional problem in Belarus. Many believed that the new parliament was better organized than the previous one and thus better equipped to resist any dictatorial intentions the president might have. Alas, from the outset, the new parliament had to deal with the old problem of restricted access to mass media. No sooner did deputies elect a new speaker than they discovered his phone was being bugged by the president's security force.

Ignoring the fact that sixty-three seats in the parliament remained vacant, the president announced that there would be no further parliamentary elections due to financial problems. Local government elections were conducted at the same time as parliamentary elections but failed in most cities and towns. The territories in question, where approximately 70 per cent of the population resides, were governed solely by presidential nominees.

The relationship between the president and the Constitutional Court remained extremely tense. The Court proved to be the only force in the republic which was at least to some degree capable of defending and maintaining the balance of powers. In its annual address, the Court declared that the state of constitutional legality in Belarus was unsatisfactory. In 1995, the Court examined 14 presidential decrees and ruled 11 of them illegal. In spite of this, on 29 January 1996, the president issued still another decree—this one obliging government and local authorities to carry out all his previous decrees and disregard the rulings of the Constitutional Court.

Pressure on the Court continued to escalate in 1996 until the president proposed to eliminate this institution altogether. Parliamentary speaker Siamion Sharetsky, however, publicly opposed the idea of disbanding the Court. 'The republic must have a body that can control the implementation of fundamental law by all branches of government,' declared Sharetsky. At the same time, however, the speaker requested that the Court suspend hearings on several cases launched at the initiative of the previous parliament.

The Opposition

This conciliatory approach at the expense of the law did not work well. The political season of 1996 in Belarus started with a rally in support of the Constitution. Fourteen political parties and five civic groups formed what became known as the Movement in Support of the Constitution. Parliamentarians and party leaders joined forces to demand support and respect for the rule of law and the decisions of the Constitutional Court. For a while it seemed as though the Constitution might function as a common rallying point for the multitude of diverse political forces. As it turned out, however, that demonstration was the last peaceful one of its kind.

Minsk became the setting for five other major anti-government gatherings in the tens of thousands. Authorities crushed these protests with brutal force. Leaders of the opposition were forced to flee the country and hundreds of people were arrested. In order to legitimize the crackdown on dissent, government authorities issued a number of rulings restricting various constitutional freedoms. The municipal court of Minsk ruled that picketing of government buildings is a form of demonstration and therefore requires prior written permit from the city council. The court based its decision on Soviet-era legislation adopted six years before the Constitution.

The majority of the new parliament at this time was still demonstrating its loyalty to the president. In May 1996, the Supreme Soviet convened to approve a number of nominations made by Lukashenka to key positions. Especially significant was the appointment of Valyantsin Ahalets as the republic's new minister of the interior: it was, after all, Ahalets who was largely responsible for the use of force to disperse peaceful demonstrations. When asked at the parliament whether he would adhere to the Constitution if appointed, the general said that he would follow the orders of the president. When the same question was asked again, Ahalets repeated his answer. Nonetheless, he was approved by an absolute majority.

Despite a number of conciliatory gestures, president and new parliament were soon at odds. Lukashenka infringed constantly on parliament's prerogatives by appointing his nominees to positions which required parliamentary approval; in July he took away the parliamentary newspaper *Narodnaya hazeta* from the Supreme

Soviet and reorganized it into a closed joint-stock company, with 75 per cent of shares becoming state property.

By July, the president was blaming parliament for undermining his policies, and parliament was blaming the president for violating the Constitution. Lukashenka announced he would present a new economic programme along with a new constitution in September. Since he did not expect parliament to accept either of his proposals, the president said he would call a referendum on them.

The second half of the year saw Belarus in the throes of acute constitutional fever. The country was offered a choice of three possible versions of the Constitution—the one proposed by the president, the variant submitted by parliament, and the original version of the Constitution adopted in 1994. The president suggested the following four questions for the referendum: (1) do you agree that Belarusian Independence Day should be celebrated on 3 July—the day the republic was liberated from German occupation in the Great Patriotic War? (2) Do you agree that the Republic of Belarus should adopt as its constitution the version accepted in 1994 but which includes those changes and additions proposed by President Lukashenka? (3) Are you in favour of the free and unrestricted sale and purchase of land? (4) Do you support the delegalization of the death penalty in the Republic of Belarus? The first two questions were pronounced binding, the third and fourth were consultative. The second question entailed several drastic changes to the current Constitution. It called for reducing the number of deputies and making parliament a bicameral legislature, with a third of the members of the upper house appointed by the president himself; extending the presidential term from five to seven years; changing the methods of designating judges to the Constitutional Court, so that six out of eleven would be appointed by the president, including the chief justice; giving the president the right to set election dates and appoint Central Election Commission officials; giving the president the right to call parliamentary sessions, and dissolve parliament; amending the Constitution so that the president could be removed from his post only in the event of high treason; and giving anyone who had served as president a senatorial seat for life. No mention was made of what would happen to the currently elected 199 deputies in the smaller new legislature.

Lukashenka suggested the referendum be held on 7 November, the anniversary of the communist revolution of 1917. By law, the parliament could neither veto nor amend any questions that the president proposed for a referendum unless they contradicted the law 'On the Referendum'; however, only the legislative branch had the right to appoint the date for a national plebiscite. Thus, it was the date issue that became the first point of contention between the president and parliament.

Seven political parties joined forces in an effort to preserve the Constitution. They initiated a number of their own questions for the referendum in order to counteract those set forth by the president. The Supreme Soviet voted to hold the referendum on 26 November; it was agreed that another round of local as well as parliamentary elections would also be held on that date, inasmuch as sixty-one seats of the Supreme Soviet remained vacant. The parliament also added three additional questions to the referendum bulletin: (1) Are you in favour of the Constitution of 1994 which changes and additions proposed by the members of the communist and agrarian factions of the Supreme Soviet? (2) Are you in favour of having constituents directly elect the leaders of their local executive bodies? (3) Do you agree that all branches of power should be financed openly and exclusively from the state budget?

The alternative draft was submitted by communists and agrarians and supported by parliamentary liberals. The most important difference between the alternative draft and the 1994 Constitution was that chapter 4—'President of the Republic of Belarus'—was omitted completely in the parliament's version; thus, the presidency was to have been abolished. Accordingly, presidential powers and responsibilities were distributed among the other branches of the government.

According to the constitutional law of 1994, only the Supreme Soviet has the power to adopt a new constitution; a referendum may deal only with changes and additions. The two texts proposed for the referendum were rather new constitutions than amendments. Hence, parliamentary speaker Siamion Sharetsky appealed to the Constitutional Court to review the decision of the Supreme Soviet. Upon deliberation, the Court refused to analyse either of the two drafts. Instead, it appealed to the president and the parliament to withdraw their proposals and cancel the referendum altogether. The Court said that Belarus 'is a young state and such hasty and ill-thought out moves can only worsen the political situation'.

This 'zero-option'—as it became known—was in a way supported by Russian President Boris Yeltsin. On 30 September, Yeltsin urged Lukashenka to compromise in his confrontation with parliament (events in Belarus started to resemble those in October 1993 in Moscow; a reminder far from pleasant for Boris Yeltsin).

At the same time Yeltsin called speaker Sharetsky and warned him 'not to mess with the president'. One of the main Russian political actors at the time, secretary of the Security Committee General Alexander Lebed openly supported President Lukashenka. Russian ultra-nationalist Vladimir Zhirinovsky also hastened to side with the Belarusian president. The influential mayor of Moscow, Yuri Luzhkov, lent his support too.

The chairman of the Constitutional Court warned parliament of the dangers of dictatorship should the new Constitution be supported in a referendum. 'Tomorrow we will have a totalitarian regime in the centre of Europe—complete with a castrated parliament and Constitutional court,' said Valery Tsikhinia. The judge likened the president's plan to a 'legal Chernobyl'. Tsikhinia added that Lukashenka's constitutional project had sharply divided the nation into two camps, and implored the president to withdraw his proposal in the interest of peace and stability. In an effort to woo the electorate, Lukashenka issued a series of decrees increasing pensions, student stipends, aid to families with many children, and child support. Enterprises were also ordered to pay workers all back wages owed, and prices of energy, transport, medicine, and several consumer goods, including milk and bread, were to remain regulated until the end of the year.

While Lukashenka was generously distributing state funds in bonuses to the electorate, he banned funding for the by-elections. His justification was that he had promised the Belarusian people that neither the referendum nor elections would be financed from the country's budget, but only from 'voluntary' contributions deposited into a referendum fund. The official mass media were waging a massive pro-presidential campaign.[10] The presidential appointees, among them ministers, judges, and generals, were sent to the regions to supervise the campaign.

The parliament appointed its member, the well-known lawyer Viktor Hanchar, head of the Central Electoral Commission and hoped the Commission would be able to secure fair voting. However, the Commission had no control of what was going on. Its bank account was empty; local authorities bluntly ignored all its demands. According to the law, voting could start two weeks prior to the designated date. On the second day of the early voting, chairman of the Commission Viktor Hanchar announced that he would not

---

[10] The coverage on state-controlled television was totally pro-Lukashenka. According to the monitors of the European Union, out of 2,178 minutes devoted to the referendum, 1,970 favoured the president. The rest of the time was neutral between the sides.

validate the results of the referendum because of gross violations of the procedure. He said the Electoral Commission did not know how many ballot slips were printed—a key figure used in election fraud—because the slips had been printed by the president's administration and sent directly to local authorities. On 15 November, the president fired Hanchar during a live television broadcast. The next day police forced him out of office.

Parliamentarians began raising the issue of initiating impeachment proceedings against the president. Under the Constitution, the president might be impeached if at least seventy deputies signed a petition to start proceedings, and two-thirds of the elected legislature voted for the executive's removal. More than seventy signatures were collected and the petition was sent to the Constitutional Court.

It was at this moment that the balance of power seemed to tilt toward the legislative branch. The president's men started to panic and began to exert pressure on deputies of the Supreme Soviet and judges of the Constitutional Court. Some deputies rescinded their signatures, then returned them only to rescind them once again. Three days before the referendum, the Constitutional Court began its deliberations concerning the petition. It was at this time that a delegation from Moscow consisting of Prime Minister Viktor Chernomyrdin and Duma leaders Genadij Seleznev and Yegor Stroev arrived in Minsk. It should be noted that it was not just Lukashenka who sought Moscow's support. Certain members of the Belarusian parliament's opposition had also travelled to Moscow and found sympathy from democratically oriented Russian politicians. These opposition members, of course, assured their supporters in Moscow that Belarus and Russia would remain everlasting friends. The Russian-mediated negotiations between President Lukashenka on one side and parliamentary speaker Sharetsky and Constitutional Court chairman Tsikhinia on the other, dragged on for hours into the night. The following morning, a compromise agreement was finally signed. Lukashenka agreed that the referendum's results would be consultative rather than binding; parliament agreed to halt impeachment proceedings. The chairman of the Constitutional Court added his signature to those of the president and the speaker.

The compromise agreement blatantly violated the Constitution and existing laws and clearly favoured the president. Sharetsky and Tsikhinia, both elderly men in their sixties, could not tolerate the physical demands of the negotiations and caved in under pressure from the Russian delegation and the president. The signed compromise agreement is testimony to the fact that Belarus's most qualified and experienced law-makers felt it reasonable to violate existing law. In fact, the focal point of the night-long negotiations was the Constitution. Sharetsky and Tsikhinia assisted President Lukashenka in dismantling this document.

Now only technical considerations remained. The president won some time by delaying the thread of impeachment. (Constitutional Court Justice Mikhail Pastukhou later declared that the agreement made it impossible for the Court to consider impeachment proceedings against the president.) A significant number of parliamentarians who supported the president voted against the agreement on his request. In response, Lukashenka accused the parliament of sabotaging the agreement and declared that referendum results would after all be binding, and not merely consultative. Moscow nervously looked on as the Belarusian president went back on his word, but this time chose to stay out of the situation. The referendum was conducted on the following Sunday. International organizations chose not to send monitors since they considered the referendum illegal. Civilian monitors who noted thousands of violations during the first few hours of voting alone quickly decided it was pointless to continue and stopped their monitoring efforts. The following Monday morning brought few surprises: it was announced that over 70 per cent of the Belarusian electorate had voted to adopt the president's Constitution and support him in all his other propositions.

Conclusion

The rest is history regarding what is now called 'the worst authoritarian regime' in Eastern Europe. The international community has not recognized the referendum or the subsequent constitutional changes. The president prolonged his term in office by two years, disbanded the Supreme Soviet, and created a hand-picked bicameral parliament instead. The opposition protests were crushed and many political activists had to flee the country, the speaker of the Supreme Soviet Sharetsky included. Belarus's Soviet-style economy is in deep crisis, human rights and freedom of press are severely limited. The OSCE had to send a permanent monitoring group to Belarus in order to find ways out of the political crisis. Relations with the West are worse than during the Cold War; integration with Russia questions the very sovereignty of Belarus.

The fall of constitutionalism in Belarus was caused by several factors: a weakened national identity, the absence of economic reforms during the first five years of independence, a frozen internal political process, state monopoly of the electronic media, and Russia's heavy economic and political support of the authoritarian Belarusian authorities. None of these factors were gone by the year 2000, and the current status is likely to be preserved in the near future.

12

The Czech Republic: From the Burden of the Old Federal Constitution to the Constitutional Horse Trading among Political Parties

Petr Kopecký

The Czech Constitution was adopted with remarkable consensus by parliament on 16 December 1992, and was widely accepted as a good foundation for the country's political system. The past, especially the last three years of the Czechoslovak Federation, was important during the debates preceding the Constitution's adoption in at least two respects. First, the Constitution was drafted and agreed upon within the institutional structure of the communist Czechoslovak Federation. Some of these institutions, like the Czech National Council and the Charter of Fundamental Rights and Freedoms, were actually incorporated into the new Constitution. Other institutions, such as the suddenly redundant Federal Assembly, directly influenced the shape of the new Constitution. Second, it proved difficult for the constitution framers to forget the three years of tiresome bargaining on a new constitution for the Federation. For example, the debates on the division of powers in the Czech Constitution were influenced by the experience of the president during the last years of the Federation. Simply put, the freedom of the framers was circumscribed by the past, and this paper aims to show how and to what effect. I will focus on the impact of the legacies of the past, and show how the nature of bargaining becomes more predictable when the domestic political actors involved in constitution-drafting provide a stable set of opinions

This chapter partly draws on my *Parliaments in the Czech and Slovak Republics: Party Competition and Parliamentary Institutionalization* (London: Ashgate, 2001 forthcoming).

and motivations from which a compromise is forged. In order to demonstrate these points, the chapter is divided into three parts. The first examines the key elements of the constitution-making process in the Czechoslovak Federation between 1989 and 1992. It will explain the crucial constitutional decisions made during the Roundtable negotiations and show how that particular legacy combined with the volatile nature of transition politics resulted in the split of Czechoslovakia. The second part concentrates on the process of drafting the new Constitution for the Czech Republic at the end of 1992. The final part discusses the effects of the Constitution on the newly democratic Czech Republic.

From the Velvet Revolution to the Velvet Split: Constitutional Bargaining of 1989 to 1992

The year 1989, which saw the implosion of the communist bloc, was a pivotal year for Eastern Europe. The sweeping reforms of that year, however, should not obscure the fact that the regime change in each East European country proceeded according to the path set by its own internal developments. Unlike in Hungary and Poland, where changes were negotiated between the reformed-communist leadership and the opposition over a period of several months, the Czechoslovak communist regime clung to power until confronted with mass protest, and even then capitulated only after initial attempts to squelch demonstrators failed. On 17 November 1989, police brutally repressed a student demonstration on the streets of Prague. The popular reaction was immediate and Prague was flooded by thousands of demonstrators. Within the course of a few days, the protests spread throughout the country, and on 24 November the Communist Party leadership resigned en bloc. Using the existing links between dissident activists, students, actors, and intellectuals critical of the regime, the opposition was able to organize itself amazingly quickly to direct the revolutionary momentum to bringing an end to the communist regime. The democratizers established two umbrella organizations—Civic Forum (OF) in the Czech lands and Public against Violence (VPN) in Slovakia—which encompassed a wide variety of groups, many of which were rooted in the opposition movements that had developed in the preceding decades. Both movements began negotiations with the communist government to surrender its monopoly of power, more or less simultaneously in Prague and Bratislava.

The first problem facing the opposition was how to implement the envisaged reforms. The decision was made at the Roundtable Talks (which began in November 1989) to work with the existing parliament, 'purified' of its most discredited members. The 'purification' was carried out through the precedent in federal law which, ironically, had been used in 1968 to force reformers out of parliament.[1] The key feature of this rediscovered procedure was to abandon the practice of using by-elections to fill vacant seats in parliament, and instead allow (for a limited period of time) alternative candidates to be nominated by political parties and social organizations, together with the OF and VPN.[2] Accordingly, the Federal Assembly (and somewhat later the national and local councils) engaged in a self-cleansing process, whereby about one-third to one-half of MPs in federal, national, and local assemblies were replaced by candidates supported by the anti-communist opposition.

Concurrently, the decision was made to form a new government that would reflect the changing balance of forces. The first attempt, under the leadership of Ladislav Adamec—the last chairman of the communist-led federal government—was unsuccessful. The proposed ratio of fifteen communist ministers to five opposition ministers was unacceptable to the opposition which, backed by a massive demonstration in Prague, demanded more drastic changes in the composition of government. Adamec resigned on 8 December 1989 and two days later a new government was installed under the leadership of Marian Čalfa, and dubbed the 'Government of National Understanding'. With a majority of its members nominated by the OF and VPN, the Government of National Understanding functioned largely unchanged until the 1990 elections. The reconstruction of the Czech and Slovak republican governments followed shortly afterwards, under the direction of the OF in the Czech Republic and the VPN in Slovakia.

Finally, the decision was made to elect a new president. The incumbent president—Gustav Husák—was for many the symbol of communist repression following the 1968 Prague Spring. In accord with the Roundtable agreements, he abdicated on 10 December 1989, immediately after approving the Čalfa government. The debates

[1] See Zdeněk Jičínský, *Československý parlament v polistopadovém vývoji* (Post-November Czechoslovak Parliament) (Prague: NADAS-AFGH, 1993); Jon Elster, 'Transition, Constitution-Making and Separation of Czechoslovakia', *European Journal of Sociology*, 36 (1995), 105–34.

[2] Jičínský, *Československý parlament v polistopadovém vývoji*, 60.

within OF and VPN on a presidential candidate were numerous, producing two strong candidates: Václav Havel and Alexander Dubček.[3] Both obviously enjoyed moral authority as dissidents against the old regime, but unlike Havel, Dubček was also a symbol of Czech-Slovak coexistence. In the end, and in spite of his partial reluctance to accept the post, Havel was chosen as the only common candidate of the OF and VPN, particularly for his crucial role in the Roundtable negotiations. Dubček assumed the post as chairman of the Federal Assembly which, after the first round of recomposition, elected Havel as president of Czechoslovakia. The election took place on 29 December 1989 in a nearly unanimous vote, and three days later Havel delivered his first New Year's address. The much-celebrated figure of the Czechoslovak Velvet Revolution thus became the head of state, symbolizing the irreversibility of the reforms launched just a few weeks before.

An interesting fact regarding the presidential election was the proposal to change the existing communist Constitution to allow the direct election of the president.[4] The proposal came from the Communist Party in the hope that its candidate—former federal prime minister Ladislav Adamec—would garner more popular support than the little-known dissident Václav Havel. However, both the OF and VPN insisted on the Federal Assembly electing the president, partly because they were sure to win due to the dissident majority in the newly 'lustrated' parliament, and partly because a deal had already been struck between the opposition and the Communist Party that the president would be Czech and non-partisan while the prime minister would be Slovak. In other words, the opposition insisted on keeping with the procedure embodied in the communist Constitution.

This brings us on to the second problem the opposition had to solve: choosing a strategy for institution-building; the sequence, timing, and nature of constitutional reform. The three new institutional pillars—the president, the Federal Assembly, and the federal government, together with the prominent opposition leaders in the OF and VPN during the Roundtable Talks, were able to push through a number of profound changes to the country's institutional design. The Communist Party, surprised by the sudden collapse of its regime and under continuous pressure from the 'street', was in a state of disarray, unable to mount any serious resistance to the opposition. Virtually all proposed changes initiated by the opposition met no

---

[3] Jičínský, *Československý parlament v polistopadovém vývoji*, 66.
[4] See ibid. 56, 68–9.

resistance from the debunked rulers, and when the Communist Party attempted to force its issues onto the agenda, it was defeated by the tenacious opposition. Moreover, by 1989, a draft federal constitution had already been written by a group of Czech dissident lawyers, grouped around Pavel Rychetský, which could have served as an interim, if not a final constitutional formula.[5] However, the protagonists of the Velvet Revolution decided to continue working under the communist Constitution, with slight adjustments removing its most unacceptable provisions.

The strategy chosen by the dissidents aimed at avoiding radical steps in favour of a conciliatory approach. The spirit of unbroken legality and incrementalism became the norm, precluding the swift reform of existing institutions. There were three principal reasons behind this strategy. First, the sudden and total collapse of communist power was not perceived as such at the time. It was difficult to imagine that the conservative Czechoslovak communist leaders would surrender without resistance—something which encouraged moderation on the part of the opposition. Second, regardless of the overall consensus within the opposition, its representatives were constrained by the respect for Slovak sovereignty. The 1968 Constitution gave far-reaching powers to Slovakia's political representatives, who jealously guarded that which was perceived to be an important achievement in the long-standing debates between Czechs and Slovaks. And since the ultimate goal of the opposition was to remain united, no further steps were taken to push through radical constitutional amendments.[6] Third, as Stanger argues, Havel did not seem to have believed initially that adopting a new constitution belonged at the top of the movement's list of priorities.[7] Neither the restructured Federal Assembly nor the opposition leaders felt they held enough legitimacy to adopt substantial constitutional changes. This position was unchallenged by dissidents who, because of their commitment to what might be called 'anti-political politics', tended to undervalue formal rules and postponed constitutional changes until after the June 1990 elections.

Thus, despite the fact that neither the OF nor the VPN was particularly keen on the communist Constitution,[8] its legal framework

---

[5] See Allison K. Stanger, 'The Price of Velvet: Constitutional Politics and the Demise of the Czechoslovak Federation', in Michael Kraus and Allison K. Stanger (eds.), *Irreconcilable Differences? Explaining Czechoslovakia's Dissolution* (Boulder, Colo.: Rowman & Littlefield, forthcoming 2000), 137–62.

[6] See Elster, 'Transition, Constitution-Making'.

[7] See Stanger, 'The Price of Velvet'.

[8] See Jičínský, *Československý parlament v polistopadovém vývoji*, 25.

was adopted in order to provide rules of the game according to which a new constitution could be drafted. The articles giving the leading role of the Communist Party, creating the National Front as the official umbrella for all organizations, and enshrining Marxism-Leninism as the official state ideology were removed from the communist Constitution, while the provisions governing the balance of power between different institutions, as well as the overall federal arrangement, remained basically intact. Also, as an integral part of the constitutional reform strategy, the terms of the newly elected MPs and the president were shortened. Instead of serving regular four-year parliamentary terms and a five-year presidential term, the president, the Federal Assembly, and the Czech and Slovak National Councils would serve for only two years, during which time a new constitution was to be promulgated. The driving force behind the shortened terms was the belief that the 1990 elections would represent a plebiscite against the old regime, rather than a true expression of pluralism. Structured political forces were expected to develop later, and so it seemed desirable to allow the first, status quo parliament to serve only a two-year term. The idea was endorsed strongly by Havel as well, since he was reluctant to serve a full four-year term at that time.

Another important change was to the electoral system. The communist-era majoritarian electoral system was replaced by the proportional system that had been used in the inter-war republic (1918–39). This was the first time that a reference to the First Republic had been explicitly made in the context of reshaping the institutional structure of the country. But this did not prevent the decision from being controversial. On the one hand, the PR system was favoured by the Slovak representatives (VPN) and the existing political parties (including the communists) because of the advantages it gives to smaller parties. The OF, on the other hand, was heavily split on the issue. Havel and some of his associates in particular argued for a majoritarian system that would allow for the selection of independent candidates and marginalize the role of political parties.[9]

The law that was eventually adopted reflected a compromise, but obviously favoured the first group more than Havel. He and his followers were persuaded eventually that the PR system offered increased probability that a complete party spectrum would be represented in parliament—something deemed desirable at a time

---

[9] See Jičínský, *Československý parlament v polistopadovém vývoji*, 99–101; Elster, 'Transition, Constitution-Making'.

when new organizations were only beginning to spring up. Under a majoritarian system, it was argued, the OF and VPN would be able to exploit their dominant positions and win all the parliamentary seats.[10] Moreover, the new electoral law was considered to be only temporary (that is, used only during the first free elections), which fostered Havel's later attempts to push through an alternative electoral system. As Federation president, Havel tabled a new electoral law for the 1992 elections as part of a broader package of constitutional amendments presented to the Federal Assembly in December 1991. However, this proposal, together with the package as a whole, was rejected in the Federal Assembly. Thus, the 27 February 1990 electoral law was used in Czechoslovak federal elections, as well as in the Czech Republic, with no fundamental changes.

The decision to carry on with the old communist Constitution, shorten the parliamentary and presidential terms to two years, and adopt a new electoral law were hallmarks of the hectic transition period. In terms of the institutional structure, there was more continuity than real change in this period, but we can now move on to look more closely at how the outcomes of the first round of constitutional bargaining were, indeed, extremely important in the events following the June 1990 elections. Judging retrospectively and referring particularly to the federal arrangement, Elster notes that the 1968 Constitution may be 'a unique example of a text that came to life only after death—after the abolition of the regime whose affairs it was supposed to regulate'.[11] Furthermore, reflecting on the shortened parliamentary terms, he argues that it was an unfortunate decision, partly because valuable time was lost by campaigning before the next elections and partly because the compression of the time horizon carried the risk of political overheating.

Constitutional Bargaining: 1990 to 1992

The Federal Assembly and the Czech and Slovak National Councils were elected in the first free elections on 8–9 June 1990, with a mandate to adopt a new constitution. The landslide victory of both opposition movements made it possible to create an

---

[10] Jičínský, *Československý parlament v polistopadovém vývoji*.
[11] Elster, 'Transition, Constitution-Making', 109.

OF-VPN government coalition which, together with the Slovak Christian Democrats, controlled 98 seats in the 150-member Chamber of People, and 102 seats in the 150-member Chamber of Nations. The 5 per cent electoral threshold prohibited sixteen parties, movements, and coalitions from entering the parliament, so that besides the OF and VPN, seven other political movements succeeded in gaining parliamentary seats. The Communist Party, with only 47 seats, was in a clearly secondary position. The situation was more or less mirrored in the National Councils: although the victory of the VPN in Slovakia was not as overwhelming as that of the OF in the Czech Republic, only four parties gained representation in the Czech Republic, while in Slovakia (in part due to a lower threshold) seven parties, movements, and coalitions entered parliament. The Federal Assembly re-elected Havel as president on 5 July 1990.

While significant advances were made in social and economic restructuring, political developments in Czechoslovakia after 1989 became dominated by a shift towards division which culminated in the split of Czechoslovakia at the beginning of 1993. The successful cooperation forged when laying down the basis for a market economy was not carried over when attempting to solve the protracted disputes about the division of powers between the Federation and the republics, and about the relations between the government, parliament, and the president. An examination of Czechoslovak federalism, emphasizing the constitutionally determined parliamentary structure, and an examination of the parties and party system formation, emphasizing the nature of politics underlying institutional structures, should help explain the process that led to the division of Czechoslovakia.

The complex institutional structure of Czechoslovakia was inherited from the 1968 Constitution and clearly reflected an attempt to quell conflicts between Czech and Slovak nationals through a number of institutional devices. As indicated above, the Constitution established Czechoslovakia as a federal state, consisting of two separate republics. The national and linguistic boundaries coincided. Both the Czech and Slovak republics had separate unicameral legislative assemblies called National Councils, and both republics had their own national governments. Each republic acquired a relatively high degree of autonomy to run its affairs within its jurisdiction. Education and cultural affairs in particular were exclusively the republic's domain. The above-mentioned constitutional act on power-sharing, passed in 1990, extended the areas of autonomous jurisdiction even further including, for example, a provision that the Central Bank governor would alternate annually between a Czech and a Slovak.[12]

The federal government depended on the support of the bicameral Federal Assembly. The Chamber of People was elected through a PR system and, due to the difference in population size of the two republics, had approximately twice as many Czechs as Slovaks. The Chamber of Nations had an equal representation from each nation: 75 MPs were elected by the Czechs and 75 by the Slovaks. Despite the difference in composition, the chambers had basically symmetrical powers. Legislation had to be passed by both chambers, according to two sets of parliamentary rules. Article 40 of the federal Constitution stipulated that a quorum of an absolute majority of both chambers was required to take a valid vote on regular legislation. For certain categories of legislation listed in Article 44 (including budgetary and currency issues, foreign economic relations, and citizenship), majority rule was prohibited, meaning that each of the two national sections of the Chamber of Nations voted separately and a majority of all elected members had to be obtained in both sections of the Chamber of Nations as well as in the Chamber of People to adopt a bill. This voting procedure, known as the 'ban on majoritization', granted veto power to the national representations in the Federal Assembly on a significant number of legislative acts. Moreover, adopting the federal Constitution, referendum initiatives, and declarations of war required the support of a three-fifths majority of all the members of the House of People and each of the two sections of the Chamber of Nations. This left a rather small number (thirty) of deputies with an effective veto power in the Federal Assembly.

If classified, the constitutional formula in the Czech and Slovak Federal Republic provided for a textbook example of a consociational system of institutions.[13] The government was a grand coalition of political leaders from both national segments, the principle of proportionality was embodied both in the electoral system and in the distribution of important administrative posts, both republics enjoyed relative autonomy to manage internal affairs, and there was a strong minority veto in the Federal Assembly.

[12] Elster, 'Transition, Constitution-making', 109.

[13] For definition see Arend Lijphart, *Democracy in Plural Societies: A Comparative Exploration* (New Haven: Yale University Press, 1977); Arend Lijphart, 'Democratization and Constitutional Choices in Czecho-Slovakia, Hungary and Poland 1989–1991', *Journal of Theoretical Politics*, 4/2 (1992), 207–23; and Karen Henderson, 'Czechoslovakia: The Failure of Consensus Politics and the Break-up of the Federation', *Regional and Federal Studies*, 5/2 (1995), 111–33.

TABLE 12.1. *Key constitutional and institutional proposals between June 1990 and June 1992*

Date	Proposal	Origin	Content	Result
December 1990	competence law	MPs	amendment to the existing division of power between republics	accepted
February 1991	constitutional court	president	introduce constitutional court	accepted
July 1991	referendum	president	introduce referendum	accepted
November 1991	voting procedure	MPs	changing of voting procedure in the Federal Assembly —lifting the ban on majority voting	defeated
January 1992	'five points' presidential proposal	president	change of electoral system; increase of presidential powers to rule by decree, and to dissolve Federal Assembly; change to the rules on referendum	defeated

Nevertheless, for various reasons this system was unacceptable to both Czech and Slovak political elites, not least because they were committed to different constitutional proposals. As Table 12.1 demonstrates, several draft constitutions were tabled between 1990 and 1992, but none enjoyed much success. Therefore, we need to understand exactly why in a consociational system—which theoretically provides stable democracy in a segmented society—Czechs and Slovaks opted to divide the Federation rather than find a compromise between the constitutional drafts.

It was not so much the institutional system that was responsible for the break-up of Czechoslovakia, but rather the combination of the institutional structure of the 1968 Constitution and the volatile pattern of post-communist politics.[14] The power-sharing system embodied in the 1968 Constitution could hardly survive the stress from the rapidly changing political landscape. High voter volatility is a characteristic feature of the post-communist transition.[15] In contrast with the early periods of democratization in Europe, Eastern European voters were not loyal to any pre-existing party and did not have a strong feeling of social responsibility. Such an open electoral market, it has been argued, is likely to encourage competitive behaviour between political elites, and hence potentially destabilize the conduct of democratic politics.[16] As Geddes puts it: 'In contemporary Eastern Europe, almost all votes are up for grabs . . . [which] . . . not only increases the stakes and unpredictability of early electoral contests, [but] also contributes to the unpredictability and apparent opportunism of party behaviour.'[17] The Czechoslovak case shows that when other areas of conflict (religious, class) are negligible, ethnicity offers fertile ground for political exploitation, with potentially divisive effects. Using their nationalist trump, Czechoslovak elites focused their competition on the institutional structure in order to achieve a distinctive political profile.[18]

The escalation of national conflict commenced with the disintegration of the VPN in 1991, and the subsequent establishment of Vladimir Mečiar's Movement for Democratic Slovakia (HZDS). The popular success of Mečiar's nationalist message made the panorama of Slovak political parties dramatically different from that of the 1990 elections, when consensus on maintaining the Federation prevailed. The Slovak Christian Democrats, led by Ján Čarnogurský, came up with the (in)famous idea of gaining the status of an independent Slovakia within the European Community, a move that shocked not only the Czech political elite, but also the (few) remaining pro-federalists within the VPN-dominated Slovak government. The Party of the Democratic Left (the ex-communists), another major Slovak party, broke away from the

[14] See Petr Kopecký, 'From Velvet Revolution to Velvet Split: Consociational Institutions and the Disintegration of Czechoslovakia', in Kraus and Stanger (eds.), *Irreconcilable Differences?*

[15] See Richard Rose, 'Mobilizing Demobilized Voters', *Party Politics*, 1/4 (1995), 549–63; P. Mair, 'Electoral Markets and Stable States', in Michael Moran and Maurice Wright (eds.), *The Market and the State* (London: Macmillan, 1991), 119–36.

[16] Mair, 'Electoral Markets'.

[17] See Barbara Geddes, 'A Comparative Perspective on the Leninist Legacy in Eastern Europe', *Comparative Political Studies*, 28/2 (1995), 252.

[18] See J. Zielonka, 'New Institutions in the Old East Block', *Journal of Democracy*, 5/2 (1994), 87–104.

Czech party branch, primarily in support of Mečiar's radical stance against the VPN and Prague.

Parties created from the offshoots of the OF, VPN, and other parties modelled their positions concerning visions of the future, constitutional issues, historical issues, evaluations of the communist past, and the fate of Czechoslovakia, around national identity. As the second 1992 elections approached, the campaign rested on the issue of nationalism, pitting Slovaks against Czechs in terms of both individual parties and patterns of competition. Despite occasional links, parties in both republics with similar ideological slants were unable or unwilling to come together. The electoral system, which counted votes for parties separately in each republic, certainly did not generate incentives to forge such links. But the fracture was mainly promoted by divergent political realities in the two republics. The most salient issues for Czechs were the character of the economic reform, decommunization, and solutions for dealing with the country's communist heritage. Meanwhile, almost all Slovak parties focused on the national issue. This paved the way for conflicts; as the constant stream of Slovak demands for greater independence grew more radical, the ad hoc reactions from the Czech political elite grew less conciliatory.

Simply put, given the historical salience of the ethno-national issue and the fact that the issue essentially involved bargaining on institutions, it came as no surprise that the division between Czech and Slovak political leaders, and between Slovak party leaders themselves, gradually manifested itself in the 'velvet split'. In Slovakia, popular mobilization based on new interpretations of Czecho-Slovak relations led to all-too-frequent impasses on pre-existing agreements. Most Czech political parties, while competing on other issues, gradually began seeing the Federation and the ever-shifting positions of Slovak representatives as obstacles to efficient democratic decision-making and economic transformation. In the course of three years, the debate that began as a rather symbolic discussion about the country's name (Czechoslovakia or Czecho-Slovakia) ended in almost total political immobility, adversity, and mistrust between the nations' leaders.

Moreover, the failure to reach a meaningful consensus on the constitutional shape of institutions can be attributed to the fact that the political institutions that were to be regulated by the new Constitution were participating in the constitution-making process. One cannot deny that the Federal Assembly, and the president in particular, both promoted the interests of their own institutions during the constitutional debate. Although federal MPs did not propose a complete constitutional change, they nevertheless tried to make their Assembly the most important institution, by establishing various boards and subjecting other institutions to tight parliamentary control.[19] This was perhaps understandable, given the legacy of communist parliaments that rubber-stamped party-sponsored legislation without any input to the decision-making process. But MPs' attempts to create an all-powerful institution by reserving all important functions for parliament only contributed to the chaos and conflict that dominated the political scene prior to the split of Czechoslovakia.

President Havel attempted several times to strengthen the presidency in his own constitutional drafts (see Table 12.1), claiming that it would ensure efficiency and prevent chaos in the difficult transition period. His ultimate failure to advance his proposals lay in his flawed negotiating strategy. First, he relied too much on his moral authority, justifying his proposals as an impartial common good. Such was the case with a package of constitutional amendments presented to the Federal Assembly in 1992, which included the increase of presidential powers. Without prior debate in parliament Havel submitted his five bills. When the MPs hesitated to pass them, he called on the public for support. Threatened by demonstrators and discredited by the media, the Federal Assembly nevertheless buried the bills. The second flaw lay in the fact that Havel often invited top representatives of major political institutions to talks (such as the prime minister and chairmen of parliaments) but tended to ignore representatives of political parties at a time when not only were the ideological gaps between parties widening but also parties had become the most important actors on the political scene.

The Split of Czechoslovakia and the New Czech Constitution

Unlike Slovakia, where a new constitution was adopted by September 1992, and was considered by many as symbolic of their desire to secede, the process of drafting the Czech Constitution began only after it was clear that the Federation was no longer a viable option. After the winners of the 1992 elections (the ODS in the

---

[19] See Zdeněk Jičínský, 'Československý parlament v letech 1990–1992' (The Czechoslovak Parliament between 1990 and 1992), *Politologická Revue* (June 1995).

Czech Republic and the HZDS in Slovakia) decided to dissolve the Federation, their agreements had to be approved by the national councils and the Federal Assembly. Despite opposition from left-of-centre parties and opinion polls indicating that a majority of Czechs and Slovaks favoured preserving a common state, on 25 November 1992 the Federal Assembly voted to put an end to the seventy-eight-year-old Czechoslovak state.

Constitution drafting was dominated by proposals from the government commission, established in June 1992.[20] This commission included many of the MPs and experts who had been involved in the Federal Assembly's constitution-making process. The Czech parliament established its own commission, including representatives of all parliamentary parties, to present constitutional alternatives to the government commission draft. In practice, though, the government commission took the lead, acting almost like a *de facto* constituent assembly, while the parliamentary commission concentrated on commenting and amending government drafts. Compared to constitution-making under the Federation, this mechanism was marked by cohesion and consistency, and few serious alternatives to the government draft were presented. At the centre of the debate were the issues of the quorum for passing constitutional laws, the scope of the presidential powers, the structure of the parliament, the territorial division of the republic, and whether or not the Charter of Fundamental Rights and Freedoms (passed by the Federal Assembly in January 1991) should be an integral part of the Constitution.

As stated earlier, the past was especially powerful in shaping the Czech Constitution. Whether it was the result of the experiences of the previous three years or due to the democratic traditions and institutions of the First Republic, the past seemed more influential than, for example, constitutional models from democracies abroad. However, the importance of the past—or at least the ghosts of the past—cannot be isolated from the immediate political context. The two distinctive characteristics of the post-communist, post-federal context were the widening gulf between the right-of-centre government coalition and the left-of-centre opposition (creating two relatively cohesive ideological blocs) and the legal and political problems stemming from the dissolution of the Federation. Both

---

[20] See Zdeněk Jičínský and Jan Škaloud, 'Transformace politického systému k demokracii' (The Transformation of the Political System towards Democracy), in Vlasta Šafaříková (ed.), *Transformace české společnosti 1989–1995* (The Transformation of Czech Society 1989–1995) (Prague: Doplněk, 1996), 50–113.

factors raised the stakes of constitutional bargaining. It is against this backdrop that we can understand how Czech parties presented, discussed, and finally adopted the Constitution.

The negotiations on the presidency offer a prime example of how the Constitution was influenced by these two factors. The coalition parties, and in particular Václav Klaus's ODS, betting that Havel would win the first presidential elections, aimed at creating as weak a presidency as possible. The right-of-centre politicians' criticism of Havel's previous attempt to push through his own drafts of the federal Constitution prompted the coalition to contain his charisma through institutional means. Moreover, while making amendments to the commission's proposal, the government was accused of slashing presidential powers as well, presumably fearing that the president could become a strong contender to Klaus's executive power. In the end, only the opposition Social Democrats (ČSSD) favoured the concept of stronger presidency, and managed to secure the president the right to a suspensive veto on legislation. However, the largely ceremonial president finally embodied in the Constitution (see Table 12.2) is a far cry from the strong presidency advocated by Havel, both during his term as the federal president and in his attempts to influence constitution drafting through the media and backroom meetings with the framers themselves.

The debates over the parcelling of Czech territory showed similar cleavages to those that appeared during the debates over presidential powers. The views differed widely from party to party. For example, the representatives of the Movement for Self-Governing Moravia demanded the creation of a small number of self-governing units (e.g. Moravia and Silesia) and linked their support of the entire Constitution to this issue. The coalition parties, and again the ODS in particular, argued strongly against it, motivated by the negative experience with the federal arrangement of Czechoslovakia. The ODS preferred a centralized unitary country, to avoid clashes and squabbles between territorial units and the centre. No robust compromise could be reached on this issue, and the Constitution left the issue to be resolved later. As a result, Moravian MPs were among those who voted against the Constitution, insisting that Moravians constituted a separate nation with the right to assembly and self-government.

The question of the upper house—one of the most controversial issues—bears the hallmarks of the political problems associated with the dissolution of Czechoslovakia and their influence on the Czech Constitution. Debates revolved around two interlinked issues.

First and foremost were the questions of what powers to give the Senate or whether to create the Senate at all. The second issue involved the method by which the Senate would be constituted and, in particular, whether the MPs from the dissolved Federal Assembly should automatically become the first senators. Prior to the dissolution of the Federation, party leaders originally agreed to grant Czech federal deputies automatic seats in the Czech Senate in exchange for their vote for the dissolution of the Federation. However, the deputies of the Czech National Parliament pulled out of the deal only a few days after the vote that ended federation. The federal MPs sent a letter to the MPs of the Czech parliament, mildly advising them to avoid rivalry and to accept their transfer from the Federal Assembly to the newly established Senate. Ultimately, the Senate was included in the institutional structure of the new Czech Constitution, but the problem of how to create the first Senate remained unresolved until 1996 (see below).

Although one would probably not find a strictly comparable example in the legislatures of other countries, this reasoning suggests parallels with the design of bicameral parliaments during the period of extension of universal suffrage and principles of liberal democracy. The European upper houses were said to be 'defended as bulwarks against the rapidly encroaching democracy, an essential limitation upon the power of majority'.[21] The similarity here is that institutional design closely reflected the private interests of its engineers. While the upper houses in Europe protected the interests of aristocracy, the Czech Senate was designed to protect interests of a small group within the political elite. As Elster argues, subscribing to this view, 'the making and implementation of the Czech constitution stands out in this respect, as an example of blatantly self-serving constitutional design'.[22]

On balance, though, one should not overlook two equally important factors in the inclusion of a Senate in the new Constitution. The idea of creating a Senate originally came from the ODA, the small conservative party in the then government coalition. Already by summer 1992, the ODA was pushing for institutionalizing a division between public and private law. Inspired by the work of F. A. Hayek, the party argued that the lower chamber should deal with short-term legislation, such as the budget, whereas the

---

[21] See Vernon Bogdanor, 'The Problem of the Upper House', in Hans W. Blom, Wim P. Blockman, and Hugo de Schepper (eds.), *Bicameralisme: Tweekamerstelsel vroeger en nu* (Bicameralism: Two Chamber Systems in the Past and Now) (The Hague: Sdu Uitgeverij Koninginnegracht, 1992), 411.

[22] See Elster, 'Transition, Constitution-Making', 123.

upper chamber should consider laws of long-term and structural importance, such as property rights. Both chambers should be elected independently, using different electoral systems, to prevent them from becoming too similar in terms of composition. The ODA subsequently became the strongest defender of the Senate, although its rather radical conception gave way in part to more functional considerations. Accordingly, the main functions currently delegated to the Senate are the revision and examination of legislation from the lower house and the introduction of a measure of continuity against sudden electoral swings. The latter was especially important for many right-of-centre politicians who, at that time, could not perceive Czech politics with an alternative to their right-of-centre government. A fear that a sudden swing of electoral mood could produce another (leftist) government made them convinced that the Senate could be useful as an eventual counterbalance to it.

Finally, the debate on the inclusion of the Charter of Fundamental Rights and Freedoms in the Constitution identified the ideological differences between the coalition and opposition. The coalition parties argued that the Charter, as adopted by the Federal Assembly in 1991, was too ambitious and that many of the rights listed could not be guaranteed. Adamant in their liberal-conservative views, the governing coalition argued that a bill of rights should contain only the most fundamental political rights, without specifying any social rights. The left-of-centre opposition parties, which were basically responsible for drafting the Charter in 1991, argued that the full text of the Charter be included in the Constitution. A compromise was eventually reached in which the Constitution ambiguously refers to the Charter as part of the constitutional order, but does not make it an integral part of the Constitution.

The Czech Constitution was the product of a political deal, made under pressing conditions and in a specific context. It was a deal between parties with competing views which were informed as much by rational calculations as by the exigencies of the moment. As stated in the introduction, the Constitution was adopted by a vote in parliament on 16 December 1992, by a remarkably consensual vote of 172 to 6, with 10 abstentions. Prime Minister Klaus's New Year's address to parliament included his interpretation of the new Basic Law: 'We have reached an all sided bearable comprise, and this is why the Constitution was approved in the Czech National Council by a persuasive majority. We reached an important consensus among political parties, and this gives hope for the future that the newborn Czech Republic will carry a minimum of scars and scratches from the initial difficult period.'[23]

Constitutionalism in the Czech Republic

The years that have elapsed since the inauguration of the new Constitution have been a test of its viability, and a reasonably long period to judge the way the Constitution turned out to work in practice. The Czech Republic has been judged as one of the most stable, consolidated, and prosperous of the post-communist countries.[24] As can be seen from Table 12.2, the Constitution establishes a parliamentary system in the Czech Republic, in which the government depends on the support of a majority in the parliament and can be removed from office by a legislative vote of no confidence. The president is indirectly elected and enjoys, on paper, largely ceremonial functions. The principles (not the laws) of election to both chambers of the parliament are anchored in the Constitution, while the judicial system includes the Constitutional Court. The Constitution emphasizes a civic rather than national concept of citizenship, although it notes that the document was adopted by Czech citizens in Bohemia, Moravia, and Silesia.

A comparison of the new Constitution with that of the First Republic is telling, not only because the First Republic was often referred to during 1992 debates, but also because the new Constitution explicitly refers to the traditions of both Czech and Czechoslovak statehood. Nevertheless, it departs significantly from its predecessors, for example, in the inclusion of the right to referendum and the creation of the Senate. An initiative advocated by a handful of Czech politicians in 1989 to readopt the First Republic's Constitution quickly gave way to the more attractive option of creating a constitution that better suited the political goals of a new Czech state. References to the First Republic during constitution-drafting were largely attempts to legitimize particular party proposals, and had little to do with the concepts advocated more than seventy years before.

---

[23] See V. Klaus, 'Novoroční projev v Praze dne 1. ledna 1993' (New Year's Address from 1 January 1993), in Lubomír Brokl et al. (eds.), *Česká Republika v roce 1993* (The Czech Republic in 1993) (Prague: Sociologický ústav, 1994), 71–4.

[24] See Petr Kopecký and Cas Mudde, 'Explaining Different Paths of Democratization: The Czech and Slovak Republics', *Journal of Communist Studies and Transition Politics*, 16/3 (2000), 63–84.

TABLE 12.2. *Structure of institutions as embodied in the 1992 Czech Constitution compared with the First Republic*

Institution	First Republic	Czech Republic
Parliament	National Assembly; supreme organ of legislative authority; bicameral: Chamber of Deputies, consisting of 300 members elected for 6 years and Senate consisting of 150 members elected for 8 years; Chamber of Deputies supreme powers vis-à-vis Senate	parliament of the Czech Republic; supreme organ of legislative authority; bicameral: Chamber of Deputies, consisting of 200 members elected for 4 years, and Senate, consisting of 81 members elected for 6 years; one-third of senators to stand for re-election every two years; Chamber of Deputies supreme powers vis-à-vis Senate
Government	supreme organ of executive authority; responsible to Chamber of Deputies	supreme organ of executive authority; responsible to Chamber of Deputies
President	head of state; elected in joint session of Chamber of Deputies and Senate for 6 years; limited formal powers include suspensive veto on legislation	head of state; elected in joint session of Chamber of Deputies and Senate for 5 years; limited formal powers include suspensive veto on legislation
Judiciary	independent judiciary includes Constitutional Court	independent judiciary includes Constitutional Court
Referendum	yes: could be proposed by the government if National Assembly defeated its bill	no
Electoral system	PR for the election of both houses of the National Assembly; PR principle of the law anchored in the Constitution	PR for the election of Chamber of Deputies; majoritarian system for election of Senate; principles of both laws anchored in the Constitution

There can be no doubt that a relatively stable pattern of executive–legislative relations, especially between 1992 and 1996, contributed to the positive picture of institutional stability in the Czech Republic. In part, this stability appears to stem from a balanced division of powers between the executive and legislative branches (embodied in the Constitution), combined with the significant cohesion of political parties in the parliamentary majority. Formally, the government can be voted down by the Chamber of Deputies, which also casts an investiture vote on any newly appointed cabinet. A vote of no confidence can be proposed by 50 deputies, and passing the proposal requires an absolute majority of all 200 deputies. Deputies have individual rights to interpellate cabinet ministers, to submit written questions, and legislative drafts, as well as collective rights; such as government hearings in parliamentary standing committees. Laws further outlining the relationship between the government and parliament—especially the parliamentary standing orders—supplement the content of the Constitution and favour parliamentary majority and political parties, rather than individual MPs. For example, agenda-setting is done by the parties in close cooperation with the speaker, in the Organizational Committee. MPs without party membership are excluded and have, therefore, little influence. Committee chairmen and members are appointed on the basis of party proposals, which must adhere to the written rule that committee chairmanships belong to the parliamentary majority and committee places are to be distributed on a proportional basis. Significant empowerment of the government lies also in the provisions establishing its collective responsibility and the rules guiding the appointments of individual ministers: the government can be dismissed only en bloc and once appointed by the president (on the suggestion of the prime minister); individual ministers can be dismissed by the president only if requested by the prime minister.

Fortified by the cohesion of parliamentary parties[25] and the strength of the right-of-centre coalition, executive–legislative relations between 1992 and 1996 came to resemble a pattern of strong majority rule and government dominance. The four-party coalition government governed with no major upheavals and it was the opposition that appeared disunited and unable to command significant influence. The available data on the voting distances between individual parties demonstrate that there was an overall congruity between the coalition parties, a strong division between coalition and opposition parties, and divisions amongst opposition parties themselves. Cross-cutting alliances between coalition parties and

---

[25] See Petr Kopecký, 'The Limits of Whips and Watchdogs: Parliamentary Parties in the Czech Republic', in Knut Heidar and Ruud Koole (eds.), *Parliamentary Party Groups in European Democracies: Political Parties behind Closed Doors* (London: Routledge, 2000), 177–94.

opposition parties occurred, but were very rare. Certain opposition parties voted fairly regularly with the coalition, which served to increase the coalition's influence by substituting for the votes lost because of renegade coalition MPs. Despite occasional rifts between the coalition parties, there have been no serious government crises due to the fact that the opposition has usually been too disunited to exploit such conflicts.

Government dominance was challenged in the period after the 1996 elections, when the right-of-centre government that ruled in the previous parliament was maintained, but this time lost its majority status. Three seats short of a majority, the government parties were forced to make a number of important concessions to the Social Democratic Party in order to survive the investiture vote. This development gave way to a more balanced distribution of party influence in terms of electing the parliament chairman and allocating MPs to parliamentary committees. The same situation was repeated after the early 1998 elections, which were conducted after the fall of Klaus's minority cabinet, and after significant upheavals inside the major parties related to their financial scandals.[26] However, this time it was the Social Democrats who formed the new minority cabinet, supported in the investiture vote by their arch-rivals the ODS. These minority cabinets have not significantly changed the party-dominated pattern of executive –legislative relations: in fact, increased competition and the delicate balance of power between the parliamentary parties prompted parties to tow the party line more than in the previous period.

However, maintaining government stability has become complicated for a Czech elite hitherto unaccustomed to the day-to-day bargaining and compromises associated with such a form of government. Minority cabinets might of course become an acceptable form of governing, as they were during the First Republic. Nevertheless, many politicians, particularly from Klaus's ODS, quickly jumped on the relatively easiest (though by no means most predictable) of plans—manufacturing majorities by juggling with the electoral law. The task of electoral engineers is complicated, however. The principle of PR for the election of the lower house is anchored in the Constitution which, given the existence of many smaller parties in and out of parliament, makes it more difficult to undermine proportionality. As a result, the more serious debates have so far focused on rehearsing the various measures,

---

[26] See Petr Kopecký and Cas Mudde, 'The 1998 Parliamentary and Senate Elections in the Czech Republic', *Electoral Studies*, 18/3 (1999), 415–24.

such as the further raising of thresholds or decreasing the number and size of electoral districts, which would create the desired effect without a major constitutional overhaul.

The changed political climate in the country has also changed the role of the president. When Havel was elected president in January 1993, his political role remained a question. Although formally without significant powers (see Table 12.2), Havel was obviously a highly celebrated person, which gave him additional legitimacy to shape—and sometimes overstep—the constitutional limits of the presidency. Havel became known as an advocate for an active presidency, consciously cultivating traditions of influential presidents from the pre-war First Republic. At least initially, his relations with the government were tense. Although Havel did not intervene in the appointment and dismissal of ministers and respected the limited role given to the presidency in the Constitution (Arts. 68 and 74), tension arose in the foreign policy sphere. The Constitution states that the president represents the state in external affairs and, in particular, negotiates and ratifies international treaties (Art. 63). Havel's dissatisfaction with the term 'Czech interests' in the official government foreign policy concept, his long-term open support of military intervention in Bosnia, his (initially) divergent views on Czech–German relations, and official audiences he gave to individuals such as Salman Rushdie and Yasser Arafat inflamed the government and the Ministry of Foreign Affairs.

Havel's insistence on his constitutional right to be involved in certain government policies on the one hand, and the government's attempts to keep him in a ceremonial role on the other, resulted in an institutionalized compromise. The government decided that after cabinet meetings the prime minister would go to the Prague Castle (the official residence of the president) to inform him about the government's activities and coordinate foreign policy activities. In addition to the meetings with the prime minister, Havel regularly meets with politicians from all sides of the political spectrum. These informal gatherings are one way for Havel to remain informed about the political atmosphere and present his views on crucial political issues. Thus, the party leaders, leaders of the trade unions, delegations of parliamentary parties, and individual ministers have all been regular visitors to the Castle. This political practice shows that Havel has evolved from an independent, proactive president to one who hopes to influence policies behind the scenes.

Havel's somewhat secondary role from 1992 to 1996 was no doubt the direct result of the increasing strength of major political parties, which were not interested in the president's intervention in parliamentary and governmental affairs. However, after the 1996 elections the ODS lost crucial parliamentary seats and was in grave need of coalition partners to maintain its dominant position in parliament. Though he was not initially welcomed by many politicians, the president became directly involved in coalition-building, and especially the temporary caretaker cabinet of Josef Tošovský, formed after the fall of Klaus's minority government at the end of 1997, was very much Havel's political creation. After both the 1996 and 1998 elections, Havel adhered to the (informal) rule of nominating as prime minister the leader of the party with the most parliamentary seats. However, his role in mediating between the ODS's, and later the ČSSD's, potential coalition partners, and in negotiations with the opposition, prompted the large players on the Czech political scene to make several constitutional proposals concerning the presidency. Curbing of the right to nominate the prime minister was the major proposal regarding the powers of the president. The representatives of the ODS and ČSSD argued that the Constitution should explicitly state that the president nominates the leader of the (electorally) largest party to form the government, rather than, as under the current Constitution, leave it up to the president's judgement (or the hitherto respected informal rule).

The traditions that assisted Havel in shaping the institution of the president were unavailable to the Constitutional Court, which had no parallel institution in the First Republic. With only the brief experience of the Czechoslovak Constitutional Court (established in 1991), the Czech Constitutional Court was faced with building its role basically from scratch. The Court, composed of fifteen judges appointed by the president (with the consent of the Senate) to a ten-year term, was established in 1993. Since the Senate was not yet elected, consent was given by the Chamber of Deputies, which performed most of the Senate's prerogatives. The Court is regulated by the Constitution, and by a specific law (No. 182/1993) stating who can petition the Court and under what conditions.

Although the Court cannot examine the constitutionality of a law without the existence of an actual lawsuit or complaint, its decisions are binding for all bodies and persons. The Court's jurisdiction is broad (Art. 87). In addition to examining whether laws comply with the Constitution, protecting the fundamental human rights of citizens, and mediating conflicts between various institutions over their jurisdiction, the Court also decides whether electoral laws have been violated, whether the dissolution of a political party is legal, and whether the mandates of deputies and senators are valid. In cases concerning fundamental human rights, the Court can be petitioned by the president, by at least 41 deputies or 17 senators, by the Senate of the Constitutional Court (if the case deals with a constitutional complaint), or by any legal, private entity that has previously filed a claim before a lower court. The Court may be asked to review legal regulations, by the government, 25 deputies, or 10 senators, by an elected body of a higher territorial self-governing unit, or by the Senate of the Constitutional Court (if the case deals with a constitutional complaint).

The Court has not been the most visible of institutions. Its image has been characterized by work designated for the yet-to-be-established Supreme Administrative Court, but it nevertheless has made important rulings concerning the interpretation of fundamental human rights and freedoms. These rights, embodied in the Charter, are directly enforceable in courts, and are divided into several categories: fundamental rights and freedoms; political rights; rights of national and ethnic minorities; economic, social, and cultural rights; and rights to judicial and other legal protection. These categories are specifically defined in the Charter, representing the various battle grounds on which rights are disputed. However, their implementation usually depends upon, and may be limited by, the conditions specified in other laws, and since the Court does not want to challenge the content of legislation, there is little room for manœuvre. In an important ruling concerning the right to (free) protection of health care, for example, the Constitutional Court tried to avoid the direct application of the Charter of Rights and Freedoms. In 1996, at the request of forty-three opposition MPs, the Court was asked to review the constitutionality of the new Medical Treatment Rules, issued by the Ministry of Health and essentially limiting free health care. The Court decided that the Rules were unconstitutional, not because of their content, but rather because they were issued as a ministerial decree instead of by the legislature as specified by the Charter. The identical Rules were later issued as a law, and thus the opposition succeeded only in postponing their implementation.

Eight years since the adoption of the Czech Constitution it is important to note that, in spite of a dramatically changing political situation, there have been few attempts to amend it. The minor amendments made during the first six years after its adoption involve issues either left unresolved during constitution drafting or generated from the heated political clashes after autumn 1992. Perhaps with the exception of electoral reform, the amendments that have been proposed in the aftermath of the 1998 elections, such as specifications of presidential prerogatives during the formation of cabinets, or the proposed transfer of power to nominate the judges from the president to the parliament, do not alter the basic principles of the Constitution. Rather, they aim both at extending the reach of party government, as well as at strengthening the majority rule—something that was an underlying political conception even during the debate on the Czech Constitution at the end of 1992.

Two examples of post-1992 constitutional debates may demonstrate tendencies of constitutional engineering in the contemporary Czech Republic. The Senate remained a major stumbling block for a long time, especially after the Chamber of Deputies reneged on the deal of automatically transferring ex-federal MPs to senatorial benches. As a result, many of its original advocates believed that the Senate lost its *raison d'être*. This in turn provoked a widespread feeling that the Senate was created only to accommodate suddenly irrelevant federal deputies. Moreover, the far-right republicans, far-left communists, and other opposition parties used the unresolved Senate issue as a tool for strengthening their popular appeal, exploiting consistently low public support for the Senate. Four proposals to delete the Senate from the Constitution were tabled between 1993 and 1996—each time by the opposition parties. But despite sceptical notes from former Prime Minister Klaus, who remarked in January 1993 that he could imagine parliament without the Senate, the governing coalition never supported any of the amendment proposals. Instead, the real political battle focused on the electoral formula for the upper chamber which proved an inter-party rather than coalition–opposition issue. The Constitution simply states that the Senate would be created through a majoritarian system. The bigger parties, such as the ODS, favoured a first-past-the-post election in eighty-one constituencies, while smaller parties, especially the ODA and the Christian Democrats (KDU-ČSL), attempted to devise a system that would satisfy the constitutional requirements but would give them a better chance to win senatorial seats. A compromise was reached only in 1995, providing for a two-round formula, identical to that used in France for National Assembly elections. With the electoral law in place, the first Senate elections were held in November 1996. The new senators met in the first plenary session in January 1997, and now that the Senate has been established, new plans to do away with the institution are unlikely to surface in the future.

Political calculations have played an equally important role in the still unresolved debate about the territorial division of the country. A bill tabled in April 1995 by a group of MPs which proposed dividing the country into particular territorial and administrative units caused a spectacular intra- and inter-party division in the Chamber of Deputies. The reluctance of the ODS to decentralize the country clashed with parties that envisioned administrative reform as a way to promote grass-roots local democracy, thereby strengthening civil society. Czech MPs formed various groups supporting proposals that would divide the country in such a way that certain MPs' home towns would be given the status of administrative capitals. The issue caused so much infighting that the coalition conveniently decided to postpone the debate until after the 1996 elections. The most recent proposal, sponsored by the government, aims at dividing the country into thirteen administrative units and was made public in May 1997.

Therefore, on the one hand, there is a reluctance on the large part of political elites to reopen major constitutional issues. Since the prerogatives of each institution were developed to create a balance of power, the Constitution would indeed have to be largely rewritten, even if, for example, the Senate were removed. This, in turn, could destabilize both the political scene and the fragile relationships between political parties—something which the party leaders came to appreciate during constitution-drafting in autumn 1992. It appears that the basic constitutional compromises reached in 1992 turned out to work in favour of all relevant political parties, giving them a fair hope that losing today does not mean losing forever. On the other hand, whenever a constitutional issue appeared on the agenda, constitutional battles were transformed into horse-trading sessions between parties. The gradual stabilization of the Czech party system, in terms of the number of parties and their patterns of competition, has been important in this respect. At least initially, it contributed to a stable pattern of executive–legislative relations, and hence helped avoiding political crises that might have opened a new round of jockeying on institutional rules shortly after they were put into practice. To be sure, this situation neither prevented constitutional squabbles from occurring, nor does it make them completely unlikely in the future, particularly if that future is going to be as politically tense as the aftermath of the 1996 and 1998 elections. Rather, it means both that parties' positions and the nature and conduct of debates have become more predictable, not least because the institutional inertia now created helps to structure political conflict and overcome political uncertainites. Czech (constitutional) politics has shifted from a period of extraordinary and potentially infinite uncertainty to a period of politics as usual.

Conclusion

The ethno-national issue dominated constitutional bargaining between 1989 and 1992 and culminated with the 'Velvet Divorce' and the establishment of the Czech Republic and Slovakia. This first phase of constitution-making highlights the importance of decisions made early in the transition period. In 1989 Czechoslovak elites decided to continue working under the communist Constitution and paid dearly for it. However, to subscribe completely to the arguments that see this particular legacy as the crucial factor behind the Czechslovak split is problematic. Perhaps some kind of quick fix involving a new constitution, possibly drafted by a special constitutional assembly, could have eliminated the constitutional bargaining from the volatile process of post-communist politics. But, it is very unlikely that a new constitution could have evaded the ethno-national problem that had always necessitated compromises in the past. And one wonders how different it would be from the 1968 Constitution which had provided the power-sharing framework for the Czechoslovak Federation.

In this light, the decision to shorten the term of the Federal Assembly to only two years was a blessing rather than a hindrance, for it is not too difficult to imagine what would have happened if the political stalemate which characterized the Czechoslovak political scene before the 1992 elections had continued for another two years. At the very least, the dissolution of Czechoslovakia indicates that without a minimal level of consensus, political institutions themselves cannot produce such large-scale change. Even consociational institutions should embody the will of the elite such that a compromise solution is possible to secure a stable democracy in a segmented society. If the institutions are enforced or, as in the case of the Czechoslovak Federation, inherited, they are more likely to frustrate actors and exacerbate the conflict by providing opportunities for the misconduct of politics.

Debates on the Czech Constitution in 1992 were far less loaded and explosive than in the years immediately preceding them. As I have shown, this does not mean that the legacies of the past were any less influential. Nor does it mean that the particular political context in which the Constitution was drafted was any less important in shaping the final outcome. However, the fact that, at the time the Constitution was debated, the Czech political scene was already reasonably stabilized made a crucial difference. It provided for a relatively stable set of opinions and ideological motivations, conveniently structured into two blocs of political parties, which were interested above all in forging a compromise within which to operate in the future. The 1992 constitutional debates thus produced an institutional structure without a major inbuilt potential for immediate renegotiations. This, together with (at least initially) favourable economic and social conditions, made Czech elites reluctant to engage in ongoing constitutional squabbling, thus allowing institutions to develop their own capacity to structure political conflict and decrease uncertainty. Although the institutional engineering issues on the agenda today (such as the territorial division of the country or electoral reform) partly represent unresolved problems of 1992, they will be debated in a predictable manner, which has been grounded in the Constitution.

Slovakia: From the Ambiguous Constitution to the Dominance of Informal Rules

Darina Malová

The hastily drafted Constitution of Slovakia has proven insufficient to foster the consolidation of democracy, and unsatisfactory to leading political actors. The Constitution's formal rules placed parliament at the centre of power, while informal rules developed since 1994 have allowed the cabinet to take effective control of governance. Because acquiring the parliamentary majority needed to amend the Constitution till 1998 was impossible, these informal rules have expanded to include practices at variance with the Constitution. Since the 1998 elections when a new ruling coalition of four parties emerged, having a required three-fifths majority to change the Constitution, the question of adjusting controversial provisions has been again raised.

The main argument of this chapter is that the preponderance of informal rules has impeded the institutionalization of formal rules and undermined the constitutional government. My attention will be focused on the factors that have contributed to the dominance of informal rules and pushed actors to turn to unconstitutional alternatives.[1] Slovakia's institutional developments are explored in four parts. First, I review institutional traditions and the constitution-making process. Second, I consider the electoral system

This chapter was partially written during my stays at the Wissenschaftskolleg zu Berlin as the East-Central European Research Fellow (sponsored by the Andrew W. Mellon Foundation), and at the Robert Schuman Center of the European University Institute.

[1] In spring 1997 the deputy prime minister for legislation said that the high proportion of unconstitutional bills does not mean the cabinet neglects the legal system, but rather it seeks 'unusual ways in decision-making'.

and its impact on the party system and the composition of political power. Third, I examine the substance of the Constitution, particularly the unclear articles regarding the separation of powers, which have led to institutional conflicts. Fourth, I analyse the durability of the Constitution and attempts made by political actors to balance power through institutional engineering.

Institutional Traditions and Constitution-Making

The history and traditions of previous regimes are often incorporated into the political institutions of successor states. Democracy builders in Slovakia did not have much to gain from the country's legacy, however, since Slovakia's only period of statehood came during the Second World War, when a fascist, puppet regime was established with the assistance of Nazi Germany. Therefore, Slovakia's constitutional history is based mainly on the 1960 socialist Constitution combined with some elements of the 1920 Czechoslovak Constitution.

The institutions of the inter-war Constitution were referred to in the communist constitutions (the preliminary Constitution of 1945, the 'People's Democracy' Constitution of 1948, and the 'Socialist Democracy' Constitution of 1960). Obviously the articles on human rights and private property of the 1920 Constitution were dropped in the communist constitutions, but the basic structure of a strong parliamentary system was preserved. As a result of the 1989 Roundtable Talks in Czechoslovakia, three constitutional articles were abolished: Article 4, which gave the Communist Party a leading role in controlling political institutions; Article 6, which created the National Front, an umbrella organization that monopolized civil society; and Article 16, which constitutionalized Marxist-Leninist ideology. The democratic victory promoted the formal establishment of two anti-communist movements, the Civic Forum (OF) in the Czech Republic and Public against Violence (VPN) in Slovakia. Their claims and demands converged in the broadly defined goals of democratization, liberalization, and market reforms.

The drafting of the Slovak Constitution began soon after the collapse of the communist regime in November 1989. This decision was legitimized and legalized by the provisions of the old constitutional law 'On the Czecho-Slovak Federation' (No. 143/1968, Art. 142), which was passed during the short-lived Prague Spring in 1968. That law stipulated that after passing a new federal constitution, both republics would adopt their own constitutions. For those Slovak politicians and legal experts who drafted the law in the 1960s, this move was a natural step towards democratization and would finally fulfil their original plan to give Slovakia an equal position in the Federation. In March 1990, a group of legal experts led by Professor Juraj Plank prepared the first draft of the Slovak Constitution.

A draft of a new Czechoslovak federal constitution had already been proposed by the Civic Forum in December 1989. On this basis, another group of lawyers, appointed by the federal parliament and cabinet, began drafting a federal constitution during the rule of the 'Government of National Understanding' (December 1989 to June 1990). According to President Václav Havel, the main role of the newly elected federal parliament in June 1990 was to adopt a new constitution.[2] The difficult, controversial, and politicized debates that followed confirmed that giving the new parliaments the double role of drafting constitutions and carrying out regular legislative functions adversely affected the constitution-making process. Soon after the June 1990 elections, the federal parliament established a special Constitutional Commission.[3] At the same time, a commission of legal experts was created by parliamentary parties. The experts' commission was to prepare drafts and proposals for negotiations of the deputies' commission. This division of labour among politicians and experts later proved to be insufficient to prevent ideological, party, and personal biases and conflicts from seeping into the constitution-making process. Moreover, according to the evaluation of Czech legal experts, the federal Constitutional Commission was not active in integrating their work with that of the national-level commissions in both the Czech and Slovak republics.[4]

After the initial solidarity of the anti-communist opposition at the Roundtable Talks, the transition to democracy and a market economy became complicated by the national aspirations of the Slovaks, Czechs, and other ethnic groups. While there was a broad

[2] Václav Havel, *Projevy* (Speeches) (Prague: Vyšehrad, 1990).

[3] The commission was composed of the deputies of all three parliaments; Alexander Dubček (VPN), speaker of the Federal Assembly, was nominated as its chairperson, and Dagmar Burešová (OF) and František Mikloško (VPN), speakers of the Czech and Slovak National Councils, were appointed as vice-chairpersons.

[4] Zdeněk Jičínský and Jan Škaloud, 'Transformace politického systému k demokracii' [Transition of Political System toward Democracy], in Vlasta Šafaříková (ed.), *Transformace české společnosti 1989–1995* (The Transition of Czech Society) (Brno: Doplněk, 1996), 50–113.

consensus on the need to reform political institutions, the problem of rearranging the federal system incited deep political conflicts, which delayed the creation of a new federal constitution. After the June 1990 elections,[5] political institutions were focused on national concerns and other symbolic issues. For example, instead of forging a new democratic framework, debates in the federal parliament were preoccupied with the name of the post-communist federation. The so-called 'hyphen war' erupted when Slovak leaders demanded that the new state be spelled 'Czecho-Slovakia' instead of Czechoslovakia. Prophetically, the conflict was resolved by accepting two different names in March 1990: the hyphen was used in the Slovak language, while the Czech name was 'Czechoslovak Federative Republic'. However, this solution did not really resolve tensions between the Slovak and Czech political elites: Slovak national leaders wished to demonstrate explicitly that there were *two* nations in the Federation, and thus could not be satisfied to use this symbolic name only in the Slovak language and in Slovakia. Therefore, on 20 April 1990 the federal parliament approved 'Czech and Slovak Federative Republic' as a common name for the whole federation.[6]

The issue of Slovak independence dominated the process of drafting the Slovak Republic's Constitution as well. In an effort to garner public support, several political parties and movements drafted their own projects for a Slovak constitution. These proposals concentrated on the position of the Slovak Republic in the Federation, and with respect to other institutional issues they generally followed the constitutional traditions of the First Czechoslovak Republic. The Christian Democratic Movement (KDH) submitted its proposal in February 1991, and was the first to suggest an independent Slovak state.[7] Later, the Slovak National Party (SNS) proposed its own constitution that also favoured an independent Slovakia. Although Public against Violence (VPN) initially supported the draft of the parliamentary and cabinet commission (known as 'Plank's Proposal'), the party split in March

[5] The power of Slovak identity at that time was indicated by the elections results. The newly founded Slovak National Party, campaigning for Slovakia's independence, gained 13.94%, thus becoming the third strongest party after the VPN and Christian Democratic Movement (KDH).

[6] František Mikloško, *Čas stretnutí* (The Time of Meetings) (Bratislava: Kalligram, 1996).

[7] Peter Tatár, 'The Circumstances of the Preparation and Acceptance of the Slovak Constitution', in Irena Grudzińska Gross (ed.), *Constitutionalism and Politics* (Bratislava: European Cultural Foundation, 1994), 318–20.

1991 and its factions took different positions.[8] The pro-federal faction, the Civic Democratic Union (ODÚ), continued to back Plank's draft of the Constitution which favoured a Czech-Slovak federation. Another faction, the Movement for Democratic Slovakia (HZDS), submitted a draft in which Slovakia would became 'a voluntary part of a vaguely defined . . . confederation'.[9] In June 1991, the Slovak parliament decided to form a special parliamentary commission tasked to consolidate the submitted proposals. The commission was composed of one deputy of each parliamentary party club.

After the 1992 elections, constitution-making was fully overshadowed by political conflicts of two main winning parties, the HZDS in Slovakia and the Civic Democratic Party (ODS) in the Czech Republic. Both parties were offshoots of the broad anticommunist movements Civic Forum and Public against Violence. Their controversies originated mainly from completely different priorities. While the HZDS demanded 'subjectivity' for Slovakia in international relations within a confederation, the ODS focused on economic reform, which had already had a negative impact on Slovakia. After two years of negotiations between Czech and Slovak political leaders, the Czecho-Slovak Federative Republic (ČSFR) was finally dissolved on 25 November 1992 by a constitutional law requiring a three-fifths majority vote in both chambers of the Federal Assembly.[10]

At the end of July 1992, the cabinet in Bratislava approved a draft constitution that was then submitted to parliament. Slovakia's speed in approving a constitutional draft was more a question of maintaining national prestige over the Czechs than of their readiness to adopt a constitution. Because the main political forces in

[8] Darina Malová, 'The Relationship between Political Parties and Civil Society in Postcommunist Czecho-Slovakia', in Soňa Szomolányi and Grigorij Mesežnikov (eds.), *The Slovak Path of Transition—to Democracy?* (Bratislava: Slovak Political Science Association, 1994), 111–58.

[9] Tatár, 'The Circumstances of the Preparation', 318.

[10] This law was passed despite the complicated arrangement of the federal parliament, which usually blocked the legislative process. The parliament had a bicameral structure; however, in the case of constitutional amendments it worked as if it were composed of three chambers. Also the bill on the dissolution of the federation required a three-fifths majority in the Chamber of People and also a so-called double majority within the Chamber of Nations, i.e. 60 per cent out of 75 votes had be reached separately in both, i.e. the Czech and Slovak parts of the Chamber of Nations. In the Czech part of the Chamber of Nations the bill gained the required 45 votes out of 75 (7 MPs voted against and 11 abstained) and in the Slovak part the bill received 46 votes (7 deputies were against and 16 abstained). In the Chamber of People 92 votes were for the dissolution, 16 deputies voted against, and 28 refrained from voting.

Slovakia were occupied with drafting institutional structures of a common state which would protect the position of Slovakia, the Slovak Constitution is the unbalanced outcome of two very different institutional traditions: the inter-war Czechoslovak Republic, and the communist Constitution. Its main features are the central position of the legislature in the political system and weak systems of checks and balances. Any legislative majority in Slovakia has a monopoly of authority over both cabinet composition and legislation. Governmental stability and the executive–legislative relations thus depend more on the political context than on the text of the Constitution. Two outcomes are thus possible: either parliament dominates the political process when party discipline and cohesion is weak, or a disciplined and cohesive majority fully controls the political system. Since the formation of the party system depends mainly on the rules that govern elections, the section to follow is devoted to the electoral system.

Electoral System

Since November 1989, Slovakia has held national elections in 1990, 1992, 1994, and 1998. The first post-communist electoral law abolished the majoritarian system of the communist regime and reintroduced the proportional representation system that had existed in the first Czechoslovak Republic. Before the 1990 elections, there was a brief public debate among opponents of the communist regime over the most appropriate electoral system. One group supported the proportional system out of distaste for the majoritarian system imposed by the communist regime. The other group felt a strong anti-party bias, stemming not only from the previous communist legacy, but also from the extreme parliamentary fragmentation and party dominance over the political process characteristic of the First Czechoslovak Republic. Thus, this group preferred a majoritarian system favouring 'well-known personalities'.[11] These political forces tried to reach a compromise, but ultimately abandoned the idea of a mixed system. In the end, a proportional system based on a party list with preferential votes was established. The new electoral law for the Slovak parliament was meant to curb parliamentary fragmentation by adopting the relatively high threshold of 3 per cent for single parties. For elections to the federal and the Czech parliament, the threshold was

---

[11] Havel, *Projevy*.

even higher: 5 per cent. In these conditions, only seven of the thirty-six competing parties entered parliament after the 1990 elections. The 1992 amendment of the electoral law increased the threshold for single parties to 5 per cent in Slovakia also and introduced a new provision regulating the formation of electoral coalitions. It requested 7 per cent for coalitions of two and three parties and 10 per cent for a coalition of more than four parties. In these conditions, after the 1992 elections only five of the twenty-three parties that submitted party lists succeeded in entering the Slovak parliament. Only minor changes to the 1992 electoral law were introduced before the 1994 elections. Although the 1992 threshold requirements were maintained in the 1994 elections, the outcome was quite different. In 1994, parties chose to form electoral coalitions, which resulted in a more fragmented parliament. Though formally only eight parties entered parliament, they actually represented sixteen parties.

The electoral system in Slovakia has had a definite impact on the formation of political parties and coalitions. Once parties gained parliamentary positions, they constantly attempted to change the rules in order to improve their chances of remaining in parliament. However, the example of the 1994 elections shows that the actual outcomes of electoral-law engineering very often differed from desired outcomes. Before the 1994 elections, deputies hoped to decrease the number of political parties in parliament and therefore increased the requirements for parties to receive government funding. Yet by simultaneously increasing the amount of state financial contributions, parliament managed to increase the incentives for coalition formation among numerous small parties which hope to enter parliament through a coalition, so many minor parties are surviving and still emerging in Slovakia.

The attempt by the Slovak parliament to strengthen party leadership was slightly more successful. In 1995, the Slovak National Council passed an amendment to the electoral law regarding the selection of deputy substitutes. According to the previous law, when a deputy gave up her seat in parliament (incompatibility rule, death, etc.), she was replaced by the next candidate on the party list. The amendment gave party leaders the freedom to choose a substitute deputy regardless of the order on the party list, and limited only by the preferential votes given to certain candidates during elections.

The HZDS, the largest party in Slovakia, has been attempting to change the electoral system since 1993, though without much success. Spurred by its loss of a parliamentary majority in March

1994 the HZDS has been searching for a new electoral system that would render an 'efficient majority' of a single party, i.e. the three-fifths necessary to change the Constitution. This plan was included in the Cabinet Programme, proposed in January 1995. At an HZDS party conference in March 1996, Vladimír Mečiar complained that the proportional system resulted in too many political parties gaining seats in parliament and suggested the adoption of a first-past-the-post or a mixed electoral system, with the ultimate goal of creating a two-party system (one of which would be the HZDS).

In April 1996, Mečiar's cabinet proposed an administrative reform plan which changed the country's territorial administration units, creating eight regions and seventy-nine districts, though not defining their areas of administrative competence. It was assumed that this was the first step toward a majoritarian or mixed system. Leaders of Mečiar's coalition partners, the Slovak National Party (SNS) and Association of Workers in Slovakia (ZRS), agreed, however, that the proportional system was more favourable to their small parties, supported by about 5 per cent of voters. Therefore, the HZDS had to modify its plans, because its coalition partners were not willing to sacrifice their own interests.

On 20 May 1998, only four months before the upcoming elections and despite the broad public criticism, parliament adopted the new election act. According to its provisions, Slovakia formed one electoral region. The act required a 5 per cent level for each party for parliamentary entry, including subjects joined in coalitions. The act does not allow for a campaign in the private media.[12] This law aims to improve the position of Mečiar's movement in several respects. First, one electoral district increases the chances of political parties with strong and charismatic leaders. Second, the effective prohibition of electoral coalitions damages the opposition, because the five opposition parties which formed the Slovak Democratic Coalition and the three Hungarian parties grouped in the Hungarian Coalition were forced to create one party. This required difficult and time-consuming negotiations, and the profiles of leading opposition parties may have suffered as a result. Third, the amendment deleted a paragraph according to which

---

[12] By including several unconstitutional provisions in the earlier draft of the act, Mečiar attained his political goals, because the opposition's criticism focused on these parts of the law. At the end, two of the ruling parties, the HZDS and SNS, created an impression that they had made concessions by allowing two provisions of the original draft to be deleted. The first had denied the right to vote of prisoners, and the second had required all candidates to be members of parties.

the Central Electoral Commission (UVK) has a right to govern elections, and its powers were divided between the UVK and electoral commissions (OVK) at district level. This implicitly increases the power of the Ministry of the Interior, because its officials can nominate members of the OVK in cases when political parties do not nominate its members, which may be a rather frequent situation in small districts.

However, Mečiar's attempt to create more favourable conditions for his party failed. Although Mečiar's movement appeared as the strongest party in the 150-seat legislature, with 27 per cent of the vote and 43 seats, he was not able to form a majority government. The only party which wanted to enter into a coalition with the HZDS was the Slovak National Party, which won 14 seats, and therefore their common mandates were insufficient for a parliamentary majority. After the 1998 elections, Slovakia had a new government led by the Slovak Democratic Coalition, which came a strong second to the HZDS. Together with the Party of the Democratic Left, the Hungarian Coalition, and the Party of Civic Understanding, the government commands a 93-seat majority. This means that the opposition acquired the power to change the Constitution and immediately started to prepare an amendment allowing the direct election of the president, as well as other changes.

Constitution: Structure and Performance

The Constitution was passed on 1 September 1992, just a few weeks after the Slovak National Council adopted the declaration of sovereignty on 17 July 1992. Both legal acts demonstrated a commitment by a majority of deputies to build a new national state. The Constitution established a parliamentary government in the tradition of the 1920 Czecho-Slovak Constitution. However, the preamble of the Constitution does not refer to its Czechoslovak roots, but instead invokes remote historical legends, such as 'Great Moravia', linked with 'the spiritual bequest of Cyril and Methodius', and emphasizes 'the natural right of nations to self-determination'. Moreover, the concept of citizenship defined in the Constitution's preamble offers a somewhat unclear combination of two political principles; the concept of individual rights and the right to self-determination of the Slovak nation. The preamble refers to the 'Slovak nation' (sometimes translated as 'people') as the constituent element of the new state and the constitutional order. Only later does the preamble also introduce 'members of national minorities and ethnic groups' as an integral part of the citizenry. This formula is often criticized by Hungarian parties because for its implicit exclusion of inhabitants of Slovakia who do not consider themselves to be ethnically Slovak. The wording of the preamble also reinforces the notion of national unity as opposed to an emphasis on individual rights specified in the main body of the Constitution. Friction between civic and national principles was often felt in debates on determining the leading concept of the new institutional order and especially on installing Slovak as the state language and the use of languages other than Slovak in official communications.

Parliament

The passage of a new constitution for and the arrival of independence in 1993 significantly widened the influence of Slovakia's parliament. The National Council is a unicameral chamber with 150 members, proportionally elected by universal suffrage (over the age of 21) to four-year terms. According to Article 73, clause 2 of the Constitution, Council members 'shall be the representatives of the citizens, and shall be elected to exercise their mandates individually and according to their best conscience and conviction. They are bound by no directives.'

Article 1 states that Slovakia is 'a sovereign, democratic state governed by the rule of law', and thus provides for the separation of powers. Another provision attempts to set up clear separation of executive, judicial, and legislative branches. Article 77 of the Constitution states that a deputy who becomes a minister, the president, a judge, or prosecutor must give up her Council seat. Nevertheless, ministers retain the right to participate in parliamentary proceedings; when a deputy becomes a cabinet member, her mandate is considered to be 'resting'. Therefore, if the minister resigns or the cabinet is dissolved, she may return to her council seat for the duration of her term, according to Article 77 (2).

A review of the powers conferred to the National Council shows that the Slovak parliament carries much more weight than the other institutions. The parliament selects cabinet members and also has the right to hold a vote of no confidence in the cabinet and in individual ministers. Before the 1999 amendment of the constitution, parliament also enjoyed the power to elect and recall the president (Art. 101, clause 2). The parliament also enjoys important powers over the judiciary. Parliament elects the presidents and vice-presidents of the Supreme Court and the Constitutional Court, appoints judges to regular courts (Art. 86, letter j), and proposes twenty candidates to be members of the Constitutional Court (Art. 134, clause 2). The National Council also elects and recalls the chair and vice-chair of the Supreme Auditing Office (Art. 61, clause 1). Moreover ministers, the chairman of the Constitutional Court, and the prosecutor general are obliged to participate in parliamentary sessions if required to do so by a resolution of the National Council. Other powers listed in Article 86 include proposing referendums; establishing government departments and other government bodies; approving the budget; and giving consent to contingents of troops to be sent outside Slovakia. This way of stipulating parliamentary dominance combined with disciplined parties restricts the ability to check the executive, and hence promotes majority rule and a winner-takes-all approach, perhaps even more than in presidential systems. Under these circumstances, the only barrier to the arbitrary exercise of power by a cabinet backed by a disciplined majority in parliament is judicial review.

The Constitution also grants considerable powers to individual members of parliament. Article 80 of the Constitution gives each deputy the right to interpellate the cabinet or one of its members, or the head of another central body of state administration. The MP must receive a formal answer from the subject of interpellation within thirty days. Article 80 also states that this answer may be subject to debate in the National Council and may lead to a vote of confidence. The potential of this instrument to attack the cabinet is increased by the provision that only thirty members are required to move a no-confidence vote. A disciplined majority of seventy-six MPs can, however, prevent the recall of any cabinet member.

Bills may be proposed by deputies, parliamentary committees, and the cabinet. Although the president also had been given this right in a previous constitutional draft, in the final debate this article was deleted by the HZDS, apparently in an effort to limit the powers of other institutions and thus undergird its control of the legislative process. As a result, the president has only a suspensive right of veto, which the parliament can overturn simply by passing the bill again. This provision may strengthen the already powerful position of the parliamentary majority, and, if the cabinet is backed by the majority, the cabinet's power as well.

The Slovak parliament possesses extensive formal powers, and in the first years after the collapse of the communist regime (through 1994) the lack of party discipline and cohesion meant that the governments in Slovakia operated mainly as assembly governments. This was evident from repeated occurrences of: parliament opposing cabinet-proposed legislation; deputies voting down ministers from their own parties; quickly disintegrating coalition cabinets; and unclear accountability. During 1994–8 this situation had completely changed. The coalition cabinet was composed of three members, the HZDS, the SNS, and the ZRS, and gained almost full control over parliament due to the implementation of strong party discipline. Indeed, party discipline allowed this cohesive coalition to change the political system itself to the point where the executive was clearly dominant. Since the 1998 elections, the new governing coalition of four parties has tried to include the current opposition parties the HZDS and the Slovak National Party in the control of government by giving them more seats on parliamentary committees and other bodies. However, these attempts have partially failed, as the HZDS rejected participation in the proposed positions. It seems that the balance of Slovak politics between nationalist and civic parties is not easy to reconcile and will continue to dominate further development.

MPs, Mandates, and Party Discipline

The provisions on 'free mandate' and the lack of formal structures to support party cohesion have led party leaders to develop their own informal internal rules in an effort to promote party loyalty and discipline of MPs. Some parties simply reviewed the voting records of individual MPs and bumped renegade voters from the party list in the next elections, and some tried to change the 'free mandate' provision.

In early 1994, when Mečiar was unable to form a cabinet that the majority in parliament would support, the HZDS initiated a referendum calling for the dismissal of deputies who defect from the party that had nominated them. Mečiar began gathering the required 350,000 signatures (Art. 95 of the Constitution) to hold a referendum. Had the petition drive been successful and legally valid, the president would have had to call a referendum within thirty days. Instead of waiting for the results of the petition drive, President Kováč rejected the initiative on constitutional grounds, arguing that dismissing deputies who had changed their party affiliation after elections would contradict the constitutional prohibition on imperative mandates. The office of the president announced, on 16 March 1994, that the HZDS's petition drive (submitted on 2 March) was invalid, falling short of the required number of signatures. Thus, due to current separation of powers and a fragmented parliament the current formal rules prevented their unconstitutional change.

During the 1994 campaign the HZDS used 'letters of commitment',[13] which were presumed to be symbolic and unenforceable. However, during the December 1996 session, it was proven that these letters could be effectively used, if a majority of deputies is determined to violate the Constitution. In November, František Gaulieder resigned from the HZDS parliamentary party club. The Immunity and Mandate Committee received a letter of resignation from parliament allegedly signed by Gaulieder along with two other letters, also from Gaulieder, which stated that he did not wish to resign. The fact that the date on the letter of resignation was apparently added with a different typewriter seemed to confirm public suspicions that the HZDS forced candidates to sign 'letters of commitment'. Although the validity of this letter remained legally and constitutionally questionable, the Immunity and Mandate Committee—in which the HZDS held an absolute majority—voted to accept Gaulieder's 'resignation' and to remove his mandate. This decision was later confirmed in a floor vote on 4 December, despite Gaulieder's protests, and his vacant seat was promptly filled by another HZDS member.[14] Gaulieder appealed his dismissal to the Constitutional Court, which is ultimate arbiter over such cases (Art. 129 (1)).

The Constitutional Court on 24 July 1997 ruled that the parliament had violated the constitutional rights of Gaulieder.[15] The Court ruled that the fact that the deputy had personally declined to resign was more important than the 'letter of resignation'. However, according to the Court Gaulieder will be able to resume his parliamentary mandate only after the legislature reverses its resolution. The Court argued that parliament's decision cannot be annulled because the parliament only adopted a resolution accepting Gaulieder's 'decision' to give up his mandate. The parliament should act in accordance with the ruling of the Court and cancel its resolution, but the Court has no authority to return the mandate to Gaulieder, and cannot compel the parliament to do so.

[13] Party candidates had to sign a letter of resignation before being put on party lists. In case the MP voted against the party club, party leaders needed only to fill in the date on the letter of resignation.

[14] Gaulieder's dismissal, and the subsequent bombing of his house, have warned HZDS deputies to stay loyal to the party.

[15] The Court ruled that the parliament violated Article 81 (1) of the Constitution, which states that 'Any representative may resign from his or her seat.'

A similar case yielded further evidence of the intransigence of the deputies. The case began after Bartolomej Kunc, a deputy of the Slovak National Party (SNS), passed away on 12 December 1996. According to the electoral law, his place was supposed to be taken by the next candidate on the party's electoral list, Emil Spišák, who received 12.7 per cent of the ballots cast for the party in his electoral district. Since the 1994 elections, however, the relations between Spišák and his party had deteriorated, and he was expelled from the SNS. Soon thereafter the party nominated Ladislav Hruška to replace the late Kunc. In a letter to the chairman of Parliament, Ivan Gašparovič (HZDS), Spišák demanded that he be sworn in as a deputy in accordance with the law. The chairman, however, did not respond.

Following the resolution of the Mandate Committee, seventy-three deputies of the ruling coalition passed a resolution accepting Hruška as a member of parliament. Spišák filed with the Constitutional Court a petition based on Article 30.4, which stipulates that 'All citizens shall have equal access to elected or public offices.' In its decision announced on 8 January 1998, the Court ruled that this constitutional provision had been violated. In addition, the justices held that parliament had violated the electoral law as well an international document on human rights and freedoms.[16] Parliament stood accused of interfering with Spišák's rights and electoral procedures. However, this decision does not mean that Spišák will replace Hruška in the parliament, because the Court cannot cancel the parliamentary resolution. Once again, only the parliament has the authority to cancel its own decision.

The opposition parties (the Christian Democrats, the Hungarian Coalition, and the Party of Democratic Left) have several times attempted to summon a special session of the legislature in order to resolve the Gaulieder and Spišák issues. When sessions were convened the representatives of the ruling coalition either voted

---

[16] The decision also addresses several broader implications of the case. Allowing deputies to rearrange party lists *ex post facto*, the justices held, will inevitably lead to a situation where the legal status of the so-called 'substitutes for members of parliament' (i.e. candidates whose names were next in order on the party lists, immediately after the names of candidates who were actually elected) will be exposed to arbitrary interference by party leaders. Moreover, the Court maintained, if the party leadership are allowed to disqualify 'substitute members', then the right to be elected for a public office will depend on the party affiliation of citizens, a tendency which clearly contravenes fundamental constitutional principles. The citizens' decision to quit a particular party should not result in their dismissal from a public office.

to remove that issue from the agenda, or simply boycotted the session, which had to be cancelled due to lack of quorum. As a result, there were two deputies in the parliament whose mandate was declared invalid by the Constitutional Court.

The Executive: Cabinet and President

Relative to the power of parliament, the position of the executive, as stipulated in the Constitution, is rather weak. The cabinet is constitutionally made responsible to the legislature. Therefore, its 'life' very much depends upon the party in power, and the extent of party discipline. Moreover, Article 86 (letter f) confers on parliament control over setting up government departments and other governmental bodies. The prime minister is appointed and removed by the president (Art. 110, clause 1 of the Constitution). In accordance with this provision, during the period between 1993 and 1996 President Michal Kováč twice appointed the prime minister, once after a vote of no confidence and a second time after the 1994 elections. In both instances, the president's powers turned out to be rather weak. The informal rules accepted by parliamentary parties mandate that the president designate as prime minister the leader of the strongest parliamentary party or coalition. Though this practice was not employed after the 1998 elections as the acting president did not nominate Vladimír Mečiar, who was not able to form a government although his party was the strongest, there is a likelihood that this habit will be accepted later on.

The Constitution is even less specific about the process of appointing and dismissing individual ministers. Article 111 of the Constitution states that the president shall, on the advice of the prime minister, appoint and recall cabinet members. In theory, this should give the prime minister freedom to choose whomever she wants to fill cabinet posts. However, party configuration influences cabinet decisions because an absolute majority of the parliament (seventy-six votes) is required to approve the cabinet. Therefore, if the prime minister's party does not hold an absolute majority in parliament, the prime minister may be under pressure from a coalition partner to appoint ministers from other parties. This dependence on the political context is further complicated by Article 116.4 of the Constitution, which states that a motion for the dismissal of a member of the government may also be presented by the prime minister. This led to a conflict between the president and prime minister in 1993, when Prime Minister Mečiar began dismissing ambassadors and ministers who resisted him. President Kováč petitioned the Constitutional Court to decide whether the president or the prime minister has the power to dismiss ministers. The Court ruled that only the president has the power to appoint or dismiss ministers and ministry officials, while the prime minister may propose dismissals and appointments to the president. The Court has thus maintained the power of the president, in response to an overly wilful prime minister.

The unclear constitutional provisions that define presidential powers create the potential for institutional conflicts. The confusion stems from the fact that this post was a new institution, and constitution drafters were influenced by contradictory institutional legacies. On the one hand, the formal position and powers of the president in the Czechoslovak Republic of the 1920s were quite strong, including the rights to a strong suspensive veto (requiring a two-thirds majority in both chambers), to dissolve parliament, to nominate and dismiss the prime minister and ministers, as well as to convene and chair cabinet meetings. On the other hand, informal political traditions were established by the first Czechoslovak president T. G. Masaryk. Masaryk did not use all of his constitutionally granted powers but respected the decisions made by the leaders of ruling political parties. After the Second World War, the multiple tasks of re-establishing a sovereign Czechoslovak state, punishing war crimes, and rescuing the economy required strong leadership. In the absence of a legitimate parliament, the president obtained the right to rule by decree, as stipulated by the Czechoslovak Constitution of 1945. This decision to institute a strong presidency partly reinforced the influence of Slovakia's authoritarian past in the process of drafting the 1992 Constitution. The 1939 Constitution of Slovakia established the president as a strong autocratic leader. Because the constitutional authority of the Slovak president was crafted according to these controversial institutional and cultural traditions, the office of president includes contradictory elements that have to be solved and balanced in everyday politics.

One criticism of the presidential powers embedded in the Constitution is that while the section on the president falls into chapter 6, as part of the executive,[17] the presidency appears

---

[17] Peter Kresák, *Forma vlády v Slovenskej republike: pokus o porovnávaciu analýzu* (Form of Government in the Slovak Republic: An Attempt for a Comparative Analysis), in *Aktualni problémy parlamentarismu* (The Current Issues of Parliamentarism) (Brno: Nadace Mezinárodního pditikologického ústavu, 1996), 27–47.

nevertheless to be subject to the legislature. Although the Constitution does not explicitly declare that the president is accountable to the parliament, certain provisions implicitly suggest such an interpretation. For instance, Articles 86 (b) and 106 give the parliament the right to recall the president. The rights of the president defined in Article 102 reflect the contradictory and unbalanced traditions and further foster potential discords. One of the shortcomings is connected with the limited right of the president to dissolve the parliament. Article 102 (d) states that the president may dissolve the parliament only if it fails to approve the new cabinet in three subsequent votes of confidence within six months after elections.

Other controversial aspects of presidential powers include the right to participate in parliamentary sessions and deliver reports on 'the state of the Slovak Republic', attend cabinet meetings and preside over them, and require reports from the cabinet and its members (Art. 102 (o), (p), and (r)). While President Michal Kováč has used his right to participate in parliamentary sessions and deliver annual reports there, he has never taken part in cabinet meetings. Kováč may have believed that his intervention in cabinet meetings would increase tensions between the cabinet and the president. His first and last attempt to solicit cabinet reports was in October 1995. The cabinet declined to present these reports, however, interpreting Kováč's decision as an attempt to hand out tasks to the ministers, thus trampling on the power of the prime minister. The cabinet subsequently petitioned the Constitutional Court to investigate the constitutionality of the president's request. Though the Court ruled in favour of Kováč's request, the president did not press the issue and thus never received the reports from the ministers.

Institutional conflict between the prime minister the president escalated in March 1994, when Michal Kováč used his annual report on the Slovak Republic as an opportunity to dismiss Mečiar. After the 1994 pre-term elections, the prime minister had used his party's parliamentary majority to try to discredit President Kováč, limit his powers, and oust him from office. In April 1995, parliament passed an amendment to the law on the Slovak Intelligence Service (SIS), according to which the president lost the right to name and recall the head of the SIS. In July 1995, parliament approved a cabinet bill transferring from the president to the cabinet the power to name the chief of staff of the Slovak army. Formerly, the chief of staff was nominated by the defence minister and approved by the president. Both laws were brought to the Constitutional Court, which, in November 1996, ruled that the first amendment was constitutional while the second was not. Its decision is perceived by the public as inconsistent and politically biased, because according to Article 102 (g) the president has the right to appoint and remove 'the principal officers of national bodies and high officials as defined by law'. Although there is no specific law defining a 'high official', according to the law on 'conflict of interests',[18] the director of the SIS is a high official, whereas general staff are not. In November 1995 parliament passed an amendment to the referendum law that would have shifted the right to screen referendum petitions to parliament.[19] On 2 May 1996, the Constitutional Court rejected this HZDS proposal, based on Article 95 and Article 102 (m) of the Constitution, which stipulate that 'a referendum shall be announced by the president', and that his office is responsible for screening signatures.

The HZDS-led cabinet and parliamentary coalition have tried to discredit the president. For example, in 1995, HZDS interpreted the use of the president's veto power as a 'new type of destructive activity against the parliament and the cabinet'. Moreover, in May 1995, a no-confidence vote in President Michal Kováč was held and passed in parliament. There are no legal consequences of the vote, since the Constitution states that parliament can remove the president only for activities 'against the sovereignty or territorial integrity of Slovakia' or against the country's 'democratic and constitutional system' (Art. 106). Even in these cases, the vote requires a three-fifths majority (90 votes), and the proposal was approved only by 80 of the ruling coalition's MPs. The campaign culminated in August 1995 in the still-unclear case of the abduction of the president's son, Michal Kováč, Jr., who was kidnapped and taken to Austria. Despite these harassment campaigns President Kováč remained in office until the end of his term.

Another weak point of the Constitution is the section regulating presidential elections, which requires a three-fifths majority in parliament to elect the president. This stipulation can be difficult to arrange, particularly in a fragmented parliament. In 1993, the difficult process of political bargaining to find an appropriate presidential candidate led to the nomination of Michal Kováč, and the adoption of more informal rules. The opposition agreed to accept

[18] This law was passed in summer 1995 by a three-fifths majority, which means that the law enjoys constitutional status, and can be amended only by the same majority.

[19] This was clearly in retaliation for the president's decision to forbid the HZDS's 1994 referendum initiative proposing to remove MPs who left their nominating party.

the HZDS's nominee, on the condition that Kováč quit the party. While some post-communist constitutions require the president to cut off party ties, the Slovak Constitution does not impose this restriction. Since his difficult election, Kováč has gained more political clout, autonomy, and respect.

The composition of the president's staff has also helped consolidate party cooperation, and has apparently promoted his independence from the nominating movement HZDS. After Kováč's election, the parliamentary parties that had supporting his nomination profited by being asked to nominate their representatives as officials working in the president's administration office. The result of this composition has been to produce an effective instrument of independent analysis, compromise, and cooperation, which is still lacking in other Slovak institutions. However, it was not possible to implement the informal rules that made Kováč's presidency in the following elections in 1998. On 2 March 1998, Kováč's term expired and no successor has yet been elected, despite five rounds of voting.

On the Edge of Constitutional Crisis?

Fearing the political crisis which would arise if a president could not be elected by the polarized parliament, in December 1996 the opposition initiated a petition calling for a constitutional referendum proposing direct presidential elections. When parliament failed to elect a president, the Constitution stipulated that certain presidential powers were temporarily shifted to the cabinet (Art. 105 (1)). However, since the powers of dissolving parliament, promulgating laws, and appointing the prime minister, cabinet ministers, and other principal officers (Article 102 (d–g)) were not transferred to the cabinet, the opposition feared that the situation could bring on a constitutional crisis.

Prime Minister Mečiar opposed the referendum proposed by the opposition, on the grounds that the possibility of amending the Constitution by referendum is not stipulated by the Constitution. The opposition based its initiative on the provisions declaring citizens as the source of the state power (Art. 2.1 of the Constitution). According to the opposition, these provisions imply that citizens have the right to direct legislation and, consequently, also the right to amend the Constitution. This decision may stabilize the constitutional order in Slovakia by preventing possible frequent plebiscitarian changes of the Constitution, but could not prevent current escalation of political tensions between the ruling coalition and opposition parties. The petition committee collected more than 521,000 signatures, and the president scheduled the referendum for 23 and 24 May 1997.[20]

This move immediately deepened political tensions between President Kováč and Prime Minister Mečiar. Both sides in the conflict appealed to the Constitutional Court to interpret the Constitution (Article 93 (2) of the Constitution).[21] Thus, the Court, which had always been the most publicly trusted institution, was caught in the middle of the conflict. Although the Court suspended the first two petitions for procedural reasons, it had to rule on a third petition, submitted by the group of HZDS members of parliament. On 20 May 1997 the Court ruled that a referendum on direct presidential elections is legal and that a change to the Constitution can be the subject of a referendum. The Court said that a constitutional amendment endorsed by referendum must be confirmed by a three-fifths majority in parliament (Art. 84, clause 3) to gain legal and constitutional validity. Therefore, the result of any referendum amending the Constitution is a simple recommendation to the parliament. The Court, however, decided that the text of a new version of the Constitution concerning direct presidential elections appended to the referendum question by President Kováč contradicted the Act concerning Referenda, and consequently Article 100 of the Constitution, which stipulates that 'the procedures for holding a referendum shall be defined by law'. The Court's decision implied that this constitutional amendment should be a part of the question, not an appendix.

Both the opposition and ruling coalition said that the Court's decision was politically biased. The government took the opportunity provided by the Court's unclear decision to delete the question on direct presidential elections from ballots, and issued ballot papers with only the three questions about NATO membership. Most

[20] The president in his announcement merged two initiatives for referendum. First, the petition calling for direct elections of the president; and second, the HZDS's proposal, passed by parliament, for a referendum on NATO membership. The referendum asked four questions: whether citizens favour Slovakia's entry into NATO; whether they want nuclear weapons to be located on the Slovak Republic's territory; whether they agree to host military bases; and whether they are for direct election of the president.

[21] Art. 93 stipulates: '(1) A constitutional statute on the formation of a union with other states or a secession therefrom shall be confirmed by a public referendum. (2) A referendum may also be used to decide on other crucial issues in the public interest. (3) No issues of fundamental rights, freedoms, taxes, duties or national budgetary matters may be decided by a public referendum.'

voters refused to vote when presented with a ballot of only three questions. Consequently, Slovakia's referendum was marred by confusion over the ballots. The Central Referendum Commission on 26 May 1997 officially announced to the parliament that the referendum was invalidated. According to the Commission, the referendum did not comply with rules because four questions should have been included on the ballots.

The referendum affair continued into 1998. On 9 January, the Constitutional Court ruled that the petition regarding the direct election of the president was still valid. Ivan Šimko, chair of the petition committee, then asked President Kováč once again to call the referendum. The president called the referendum for 19 April, with all four of its original questions. This second referendum was cancelled in March, when Mečiar assumed certain presidential power. His decision further intensified institutional and political conflicts, as it was unclear whether he had the authority to do so.

The whole issue was solved only after the 1998 elections, because the Constitution was amended on 14 January 1999. This change provided for direct elections of the president and carefully addressed the main shortcomings of the previous arrangement. First, presidential candidates can be nominated either by fifteen MPs (previously only one MP was needed), or by popular petition, signed by 15,000 citizens. Presidential elections are held in two rounds. If no presidential candidate draws an absolute majority of the votes in the first round, a second round with the two front runners competing is held within fourteen days. If there is only one candidate in the first round, that person must gain a majority of voters in order to be elected.

Second, the role of president was stripped of some of its prerogatives, but at the same time the president's power was expanded in some respects. On the one hand, the president lost the power to preside over cabinet meetings and to take part in parliamentary meetings without an invitation from the deputies. In the future, delivering a 'state of the republic address' will be the only appearance in parliament to which the president is entitled according to the Constitution. The amendment restricts some of the president's powers: the president may no longer impose a veto on 'constitutional laws' (that is, laws passed by a three-fifths majority in parliament), and will be able to declare amnesty and exercise prerogatives as a commander-in-chief only if those acts are countersigned, respectively, by the minister of justice and the prime minister. The president is no longer able to intervene in the process of forming a government, something previously authorized pursuant to a controversial decision of the Constitutional Court passed in 1993.

On the other hand, the power of the president to dissolve parliament in case of conflict between the legislative and the executive branch has been broadened. According to the new text of the Constitution, the president may dissolve parliament under the following circumstances: if, after a no-confidence vote, the deputies fail to elect a new government on three separate occasions; if parliament does not pass a governmental bill which has been linked to a no-confidence vote; and if parliament fails to pass any laws for a three-month period (a certain indication that there is no working majority in the legislative branch). However, the president cannot exercise this power during the last six months of parliament's term. The amendment to the Constitution also provides for the impeachment of the president, a somewhat unusual provision in a parliamentary system. Compared to the previous arrangement—according to which a three-fifths majority was necessary to impeach a president—the new constitutional amendment renders the removal of a president somewhat harder. First, a three-fifths majority must pass a resolution to the effect that the issue of impeachment should be brought to the electorate; then, a popular vote on the issue is to be held, and the president will be impeached if the impeachment resolution is supported by the majority of voters. Should the president survive the impeachment vote, he or she is entitled to dismiss parliament and automatically begin to serve a new five-year term.

The presidential elections took place in May 1999, and in the divided Slovakia's polity the second round was needed to elect a new president. Rudolf Schuster, the leader of the Party for Civic Understanding, won the elections with 57.18 per cent of the vote. The former Prime Minister Vladimír Mečiar was clearly defeated, receiving only 42.82 per cent. The results indicated that Schuster and also the coalition government still received a solid endorsement from the electorate. Although the Slovak presidency is largely a ceremonial position, the fact that the head of state is directly elected by the people lends it somewhat greater political authority than in countries where the president is elected by the parliament. In particular, the marred referendum on the direct presidential elections in 1997 increased the political weight of this office. As the government-backed candidate, Schuster's main pledge was to ensure that reforms continue unhindered in Slovakia, and that Slovakia's foreign policy would be oriented towards the West. However, the results showed that Mečiar and his party remain a relevant political force in the country.

Executive–Legislative Relations

The nature of the relations between cabinet and parliament cannot be defined merely by studying the Constitution. In Slovakia, as in many other countries, the configuration of the political parties in parliament and their relations with one another is clearly a significant factor in the equation.

Since the fall of the communist regime, four elections have been held in Slovakia, in 1990, 1992, 1994, and 1998. Cabinets and their party compositions have often been changed during the electoral term; each time due to splits in the ruling parties. Twice, new cabinets were formed due to Mečiar's dismissal by parliament. In the autumn of 1991, he was recalled by the parliamentary chairmanship (the collective leadership of parliament, formed by parliamentary parties according to the communist-era Act on Legislative Procedure) because of the ruling party's internal split. In March 1994, Mečiar's cabinet lost its second no-confidence vote in parliament. Political parties which formed the new broad coalition cabinet (the KDH, SDL, and Democratic Union) decided to increase the popular legitimacy of the new government, so they agreed to organize early elections and passed a law on the dissolution of parliament under Article 82 (5) of the Constitution. The period following the early elections of 1994, when Mečiar's HZDS won again, was unusually stable. During this period only eight cabinet reshuffles took place, no ministers were recalled by parliament, no party suffered a major split, and only five deputies defected from their parties.

Since the parliament formally has independent control over legislation and the cabinet, the shift from an assembly government to a strong party government in Slovakia required specific informal rules to create party discipline and cohesion. According to formal constitutional rules, the cabinet and the prime minister have weak positions compared to parliament. Even the prime minister does not have sole control over his ministers, as any of them can be brought down by a vote in the National Council. The one-chambered Slovak parliament has so many constitutional powers over the cabinet that even in a two-party system, it would be difficult to discipline individual deputies. The change in executive–legislative relations during the 1994–8 period can be explained by a sophisticated system of incentives and punishments combining letters of commitment and profits from privatization, which was created by the previous ruling coalition led by Vladimír Mečiar.

The developments following the 1998 elections have proved that to maintain control over one's own MPs is rather difficult. Though only one MP has yet defected from the ruling coalition and set up a new party, it seems that the current government has been holding together its common pro-Western orientation partly by the threat of the possible return of Mečiar, whose party started in February to collect signatures under a petition asking for a referendum on early elections.

This leads us to the preliminary conclusion that the Slovak Constitution set up parliamentary dominance and an unclear division of powers among the branches of government, thus creating the preconditions for unstable governments in general. Parliamentary systems with weak checks on the executive branch and disciplined parties controlling a powerful parliament are not conducive to the survival of democracy. Under these conditions, the only stable barrier for uncontrolled majority rule is the creation of strong powers of judicial review by the Constitutional Court.

The Constitutional Court as a Third Party

The democratic traditions of the First Czechoslovak Republic do not provide a strong framework for constitutionalism. Although a Constitutional Court was established in the First Republic, it did not play an important role in the political system. At that time, democracy was based on concepts like party government and majority rule, instead of constitutional and limited government. Nevertheless, during the Prague Spring in 1968, a group of lawyers hoped to resurrect the institutions of an independent judiciary and the Constitutional Court. Through a 1968 constitutional amendment (No. 143/1968) these hopes were partly realized. However, the Constitutional Court stipulated in the amendment remained on paper for the next twenty-three years. Finally, in 1991 the first Constitutional Court in Czecho-Slovakia was created through another special constitutional amendment (No. 91/1991) and its functioning was regulated by the law which was passed later by the federal parliament (No. 491/1991). In turn, the Slovak National Council passed a constitutional amendment for the creation of a national Constitutional Court (No. 7/1991). But, due to its focus on national issues and economic reform, the Council did not implement this amendment before the Federation split. Though these laws were never implemented as passed, they had a clear impact on the Constitutional Court articles of the 1992 Slovak Constitution, the bulk of which were transcribed from the 1968 and 1991 amendments.

The Slovak Constitutional Court was finally established in March 1993. Ten justices were appointed to seven-year terms by the president, who chose from twenty candidates nominated by parliament. The Court can be petitioned by one-fifth of all deputies (thirty), by the president, the cabinet, any court, and by the attorney general. In cases concerning fundamental human rights and freedoms, any citizen of Slovakia can petition the Court as well. The Court has the power of abstract judicial review, meaning that the Court may examine the constitutionality of any law, statute, or regulation passed by the parliament, Council of Ministers, or local government without the existence of an actual lawsuit (Art. 125). Article 132 states that rules, or parts or clauses thereof, in contradiction of the Court's ruling are null and void, the authorities that passed them being obliged to bring them to conformity with the Constitution and constitutional statutes no later than six months after the ruling of the Constitutional Court. Otherwise these rules, parts, or clauses shall become ineffective after six months following the decision of the Constitutional Court. These two articles explain why the ruling coalition in parliament could ignore the Court's decision in controversial cases concerning mandates, which were treated as resolutions that do not fall under jurisdiction of the Court. These cases were not foreseen by constitution drafters and therefore Court decisions can be enforced only if parliament is more cooperative. The idea of 'limited government' was not fully developed by the Slovak Constitution. Nevertheless, even in such a polarized political context and dominant majority rule, the Court has maintained its independence.

The fact that the Constitutional Court is an untraditional institution is clear from an analysis of petitions submitted to the Court. Citizens are able to petition the Court directly only when their fundamental rights have been violated (Art. 130). Despite this restrictive criterion, since the Court was established in 1993, almost half of all complaints have been citizens' appeals of lower court decisions. The Court declined to deliberate on nearly one-quarter of these petitions, since basic rights had been violated by the lower courts' decisions only in a few instances.[22] The other half of all petitions to the Court were resolved through a written reply (*prípis*). Therefore, the Court actually deliberated on only 2 to 4 per cent of all cases submitted to it. The majority of these cases pertain to the abstract review of legislation, controversies between state institutions, electoral laws, deputies' mandates, and basic rights.

---

[22] See *Collection of Findings and Rulings of the Constitutional Court* (1993–6).

Since its establishment, the Court has enjoyed a reputation as
one of the most trusted institutions in Slovakia. Its public prestige
can be attributed to its success at resolving the many controversies between state institutions, and the general perception that it
is truly independent.

Human Rights in the Constitution

The second part of the Slovak Constitution deals with fundamental
human rights and freedoms. The 1992 Constitution incorporated
a slightly amended version of the Bill of Rights adopted by the
Czecho-Slovak Federal Assembly in 1991. Two factors were dominant in the institutionalization of the Bill of Rights. First, the
communist regime emphasized social rights, while human rights
and basic freedoms were constantly and systematically violated.
Consequently, the main target of the anti-communist opposition's
criticism of the regime was these human rights violations. Therefore, when the dissidents came to power, they immediately adopted
laws guaranteeing and protecting human rights. Second, international organizations, such as the Council of Europe, the Conference
on the Security and Cooperation in Europe, and the European Union,
pressured post-communist countries to adopt human rights protection mechanisms in exchange for possible membership in these
organizations. The fact that a quarter of the Constitution deals
with citizens' rights and freedoms demonstrates how important
they were perceived to be.

The Constitution divides rights into several categories. Articles
14–34 and 46–50 list fundamental rights and freedoms, while
Articles 35–43 enumerate economic, social, and cultural rights. The
latter set of rights was primarily inspired by the former regime's
concept of social rights, including the right to choose a profession,
receive appropriate training, and work; as well as state guarantees for unemployment support, trade union membership, collective bargaining, and the right to strike. Social rights include the
right to free education and health care, and welfare for old age,
disability, or single-parent families. These rights were meant to
ensure that the social security that had been provided by the
previous regime would not disappear completely. Cultural rights
include freedom of scientific research and artistic expression.
Article 44 employs communist-style jargon by affirming not only
the rights but also the 'duties' of citizens 'to protect and improve
the environment and to foster the cultural heritage' (Art. 44.2).

Finally, Articles 33 and 34 preserve the rights of national minorities and ethnic groups through protection from discrimination and
the freedom to use their native languages.

The rights stipulated in the Constitution are directly enforceable
in courts, or through other state authorities as provided by law (Art.
46). Everyone has the right to recover damages for 'a loss caused
by an unlawful decision of a court'. Social and economic rights,
however, 'may be claimed only within the limits of the law' (Art.
51). Consequently, the rights related to social security and welfare
and the right to strike are not only limited, but their application
may be changed through legislation. Furthermore, certain basic
freedoms also can be restricted. Article 13.3 mentions 'restrictions
of constitutional rights and freedoms' and declares that rights
'shall be applied equally and consistently in all similar cases'. Moreover, Article 16 states that the right to integrity and privacy 'may
be limited only in cases specifically provided by law'. Freedom of
movement (Art. 23), freedom of expression and the right to information (Art. 26), and the freedom of assembly (Art. 28) may be
restricted to protect the freedom of others, state security, law and
order, health, and morality. Thus, the Slovak Constitution declares
many rights and freedoms, but almost none of them is absolute.

On several occasions, the Constitutional Court has been petitioned
to elaborate on the extent of socio-economic rights that are broadly
declared by the Constitution. One case, related to the right to work,
was brought to the Court in 1993. The Constitution states that:
'Citizens shall have the right to work. The State shall guarantee,
within reasonable limits, the material welfare of those who cannot
enjoy this right through no fault of their own. The terms thereof
shall be specified by law' (Art. 35.3). The Court's decision elaborated on this article, adding that 'the right to work cannot be
understood as being the right to a specific job for which a citizen
is appropriately qualified'.[23] In similar cases,[24] the Court usually
ruled on the unconstitutionality of legislative procedures. For
example, when the Court deliberated on the Ministry of Health's
'Medical Treatment Order', limiting access to free medical care,
the Court ruled that the decree contravened conclusion of Article
40, which stipulates that the implementation of 'the right to
free medical care will be determined by law', not by ministerial
decree.

[23] See ibid. (1993).

[24] See sections on the constitutional and legislative developments in Slovakia
since 1993 in 'Constitution Watch', *East European Constitutional Review*.

Constitutional Stability and 'Institutional Engineering'

Slovakia's major institutions were crafted according to historical traditions. As a result of the contradictory traditions of inter-war democracy and communism, Slovakia's constitutional structure has created rather unstable institutions. Several factors determined the performance of parliamentary democracy and influenced attempts to alter the constitutional order. First, the inexperience of the main political forces during the constitution-drafting process created the basis for dissatisfaction with the Constitution. Second, the actual institutional performance of parliament was unstable, shifting between government by assembly and strong party government. Third, the Constitution's unclear separation of powers fostered conflicts between the prime minister and the president. Alternative institutional structures were frequently proposed. Although among the most outspoken advocates of change was the former Prime Minister Mečiar, his speculations on constitutional amendments were only pipe dreams given the political context in Slovakia.

After the 1992 elections, with the support of the SDL and SNS, the HZDS secured the required three-fifths majority in parliament needed to pass the Declaration of Sovereignty and the Constitution. In Adam Przeworski's terms, it can be said that the relation of forces was known and uneven in the Slovak parliament. A constitution adopted in this political environment tends to be durable only as long as this power relation lasts.[25] Any substantial political change in the composition of political forces should lead to the amendment of the Constitution. Although the political composition of parliament changed soon after the passage of the Constitution, it took seven years and two elections to form the required majority for the relevant changes to the Constitution. The proportional system has produced a fragmented parliament that limits the possibility of amending the Constitution.

The HZDS had even attempted to change electoral results to secure a three-fifths parliamentary majority after the 1994 elections. Mečiar's party demanded that Democratic Union (DÚ) seats be distributed according to the requirements of the proportional representation system (which would have also surprisingly secured a three-fifths majority between the HZDS, SNS, and ZRS). The

[25] Adam Przeworski, *Democracy and the Market: Political and Economic Reforms in Eastern Europe and Latin America* (Cambridge: Cambridge University Press, 1991).

HZDS and SNS petitioned the Constitutional Court, which dismissed the complaint, arguing that approving party member lists is the responsibility of the Electoral Commission, which had already verified the DÚ list. Controversies over the composition of parliament also continued in spring 1995, when Interior Minister Ľudovít Hudek (HZDS) asked the police to question the 14,929 citizens who signed the DÚ petition lists, in order to ensure that their signatures were valid. However, even this attempt to expel the DÚ from the parliament was unsuccessful, because over 10,000 citizens confirmed their signatures under the DÚ's petition lists. Because of the Constitutional Court's independence and voters' loyalty to their party, the ruling coalition's unconstitutional attempts to secure a parliamentary majority failed.

The increase in party discipline and cohesion after the 1994 elections was striking.[26] No parliamentary party split, and only five deputies quitted their parties. This supports the assumption that parliamentary parties effectively imposed party discipline and promoted party cohesion. Frequent splits within and solidarity among parties have prevented major constitutional changes. Since March 1994, the parliamentary system has evolved into a party government as opposed to an assembly government.[27]

Between 1994 and 1998 the situation in Slovakia was reminiscent of a vicious circle, where the autocratic HZDS tenaciously tried to expand its powers by amending statutory laws, which could not be blocked by the opposition. The opposition could exercise its limited influence only in the case of constitutional amendments. However, this constitutional stability was insufficient for democratic consolidation, because the cabinet used every opportunity to enlarge its power by changing laws that required only a simple majority in parliament. This deadlock was only partially resolved by the 1998 elections that ushered in a more cooperative parliament, because the new government had to reverse previous changes to the legal system and frequent changes of laws are not

[26] Between the elections of 1990 and 1992, 44 parliamentary seats out of 150 changed hands from one PPG to another. Between 1992 and 1994, the number of seats changing hands was 28 out of 150. Between 1994 and mid-1997, only *five* seats changed hands. None of these five joined another PPG and only one attempted to establish a new electoral party, so far with little success. The three-year period without a single major rupture of a PPG is by far the longest such period in Slovakia's post-1989 history.

[27] The only exception was the short period after the formation of the new parliament in November 1994, when the newly formed parliamentary coalition effectively controlled the incumbent cabinet and, moreover, limited some of its powers.

conducive to political and economic stability. Whether the new parliament is substantially able to change the Constitution—especially those rules related to rule of law, separation of powers, judicial review, and limited government—still remains uncertain.

Conclusion

This chapter has analysed the institutional performance of the constitutional system in Slovakia. It has been demonstrated that the formal rules of the Constitution were designed to grant parliament dominance in the political process. However, constitutional rules were often not clearly drafted, and on several occasions have been violated without sanction. As a result, the political process has become dominated by a set of informal rules. Indeed, the predominance of informal rules has emerged as a competing structuring principle shaping the behaviour of the political elite.

The dominance of informal rules over developed institutions was also promoted by political context, in which parties spontaneously appeared and split, creating a political system of unsettled identities, preferences, and interests. Thus, institutional changes were mostly the immediate outcomes of the momentary power configurations rather than that of impartially drafted rules. Ruling political parties in 1994–8 were reluctant to accept formal rules, because they impeded their interest to expand their power. Unconstitutional legislation and violations of the supreme rules of the political game became an inherent feature of Slovak politics in that period.

Although in the Constitution legislative dominance is somewhat weakened by the partial separation of powers between the executive and the legislature, the results of the 1994 elections allowed the HZDS to assume full executive as well as legislative powers. Having designed informal rules to guarantee party discipline, the HZDS (with the help of its coalition partners) reduced parliament to a 'voting' machine. Since the HZDS was usually able to manipulate its junior partners, a single party in fact controls all legislative and executive power. Since 1994, the practices and habits of the ruling elite have further weakened constitutional checks on the executive and prevented the institutionalization of limited government.

Thus, despite the formal incorporation of constitutional rules that are expected to create consensual democracy, the combination of unclear rules and power-maximizing actors led to tyranny by parliamentary majority in Slovakia. The foregoing study of parliamentarism in Slovakia suggests one general conclusion: that systems with dominant unicameral legislatures, weak checks on executive power, and disciplined political parties produce majority rule, polarization, and escalating conflicts within a deeply divided polity. Democratic consolidation under such constitutional arrangements depends more on the political context and skills of the political elite than on the Constitution. Such systems are not conducive to the survival of democracy.

Slovenia: From Elite Consensus to Democratic Consolidation

Miro Cerar

The Slovene transition from communism was characterized by two specific features. First, it was inextricably connected to the process of state-building, since Slovenia's break from communism also meant a break from Yugoslavia. Second, the transition itself did not follow a very radical course since in the 1980s Slovenia had already undergone substantial reforms which brought about a relatively high level of economic development and openness towards the West. Thus, unlike other post-communist countries, which generally began their transition in a state of conflict with radical communism and in poor economic circumstances, Slovenia's elites peacefully arrived at a consensus on almost all of the pressing issues involved in democracy and state-building.

Because Slovenia had no real tradition of statehood or experience with state-building, the establishment of a new constitutional structure was immensely important both as a foundation for a new political and economic system and as the country's 'calling card' for entry into the international community. But the relatively quick and consensual adoption of the new Constitution after independence was followed by a period of slower reform and heightened political tension. Certain unresolved issues were left for the parliament to decide after the Constitution's adoption. As political party competition became greater, issues that were left unresolved during the initial period of transition, such as the structure of local government, privatization, and communist lustration, began to hamper the legislative process. But, at the same time, this development shows that the process of democratic consolidation, which was initiated by a relatively exclusive, elite group, has now widened the scope of political participation. Political parties compete without calling into question the basic constitutional institutions, the interpretation of the Constitution (primarily by the Constitutional

Court and other state bodies) has brought a sufficient level of predictability and certainty to the law, and the democratic principles embodied in the Constitution have been gradually internalized by the society at large, which, over the long term, is clearly the strongest guarantee for democracy.

Simultaneous State Building and Constitution-Making

The process of formulating and implementing the new Slovene Constitution, adopted on 23 December 1991,[1] was inseparably linked to the processes of democratization and the achievement of political independence by Slovenia. The democracy process at the end of the 1980s and the beginning of the 1990s was a precondition for the new constitutional arrangement (indeed, it established the basic framework), while the gaining of national independence was one of the most important aims of this arrangement. But later the independence process 'overtook' the adoption of the new constitution,[2] as a result of the many difficulties that had to be faced in the search for the necessary political consensus over the new constitutional solutions. The adoption of the new Constitution, and a year later the election of the various organs of power (president of the republic, National Assembly, National Council), completed the first and most dramatic phase of the Slovene transition (it should not be forgotten that Slovenia's declaration of independence was followed by a ten-day war and a partial international isolation of Slovenia for several months).[3] While the new Constitution does represent a radical change from the previous arrangement, the elements of continuity reflect the fact that by the end of the 1980s communism in Slovenia had already been reformed to a certain extent and was increasingly pro-Slovene (and anti-Yugoslav), which within Slovenia contributed to what was for the most part a non-conflict transition from the old to the new system.

[1] Constitution of the Republic of Slovenia (*Official Gazette of the Republic of Slovenia*, 33/91).

[2] Slovenia declared independence on 25 June 1991, some six months before the new Constitution was passed.

[3] By the end of 1991 only ten countries had recognized Slovenia as an independent state. The watershed came in January 1992, when a further thirty-three countries recognized Slovenia, including the countries of the European Community. Some ninety-five countries had recognized Slovenia by the end of 1992, and in this same year the new country was accepted as a member of the United Nations. In 1993 Slovenia was conclusively to establish itself internationally, becoming a member of other important European and international organizations, such as the Council of Europe, the IMF, and the World Bank.

Before Slovenia gained its independence, it had been subordinated and adapted its political and legal order to that of Yugoslavia for a period of over seventy years. Following the collapse of the Habsburg Empire at the end of the First World War (October 1918), Slovenia became part of the unified State of Slovenes, Croats, and Serbs, from which soon emerged, after union with the Kingdom of Serbia and Montenegro, the Kingdom of Serbs, Croats, and Slovenes (December 1918). In 1929 King Alexander annulled the 1921 Vidovdan Constitution, dissolved the National Assembly, and brought in a dictatorship. After the Second World War Slovenia became part of socialist (communist) Yugoslavia.

In 1946 the (first) Constitution of the Federal People's Republic of Yugoslavia was adopted, but in 1953 a constitutional statute was passed which marked the beginning of the systematic introduction of self-management and hence a significant intervention in the constitutional arrangement. A new constitution was adopted in 1963, which was subject to a series of amendments by the end of the decade. More change came in 1974 with the adoption of another new constitution, which again was subject to numerous supplements and amendments right up until the collapse of the Socialist Federal Republic of Yugoslavia. Each of these constitutional arrangements brought entirely new elements to the system, although none interfered with the monopoly of the Communist Party. Throughout the post-war period, the changes to the Yugoslav constitutional regime were matched by changes to the Slovene arrangements.

While the new Constitution in many respects marks a complete break from the previous constitutional system (the constitutions of the Socialist Federal Republic of Yugoslavia and the Socialist Republic of Slovenia[4]), the new Constitution emerged principally

[4] For a detailed review of the previous constitutional arrangement, see M. Strobl, I. Kristan, and C. Ribičič, *Ustavno pravo SFR Jugoslavije* (The Constitutional Law of the SFRY) (Ljubljana: CZ Uradni list RS, 1986). On the new constitutional arrangement, see the collection of papers *Nova ustavna ureditev Slovenije* (The New Constitutional Order of Slovenia) (Ljubljana: CZ Uradni list RS, 1992); L. Ude, F. Grad, and M. Cerar, *Ustava Republike Slovenije z uvodnim komentarjem* (The Constitution of the Republic of Slovenia with Introductory Explanations) (Ljubljana: CZ Uradni list RS, 1992); J. Rupnik, R. Cijan and B. Grafenauer, *Ustavno pravo Republike Slovenije* (Constitutional Law of the Republic of Slovenia) (special part), vol. ii (Maribor: Faculty of Law, 1994); F. Grad, I. Kaučič, C. Ribičič, and I. Kristan, *Državna ureditev Slovenije* (Organization of the State of Slovenia) (Ljubljana: CZ Uradni list RS, 1996).

through an evolutionary—not revolutionary—process. This is evidenced on the one hand by the fact that the Constitution emerged gradually, over an extended period (the *formal* draft Constitution took around two years to complete). On the other hand, the continuity between the old and the new constitutional arrangements is reflected by the fact that: (1) the new Constitution has retained certain regulations from the previous constitutional system which are still acceptable under the new constitutional system[5] and (2) the new Constitution was passed by the Slovene Assembly in accordance with the procedure for constitutional review of the 1974 Constitution. Thus, it can be said that continuity exists *substantively* in the sense that some of the provisions under the previous and the present constitutions are partly or wholly identical, and *formally*, in the sense that the constitutions were adopted by the same body[6] and following the same procedure.

Continuity between the old and new constitutions was important primarily as an aid for the transition from communist federalism to an independent liberal-democratic state, with certain characteristics of a welfare state. Despite the questionable legitimacy of the communist Constitution, it served as the basis for regime change by providing the legal framework for initiating economic and political reforms. Furthermore, Slovenia was able to declare its independence on the basis of its recognized separate legal status as a political entity within the Yugoslav framework (Slovenia was a separate federal unit with its own constitution) and its constitutionally guaranteed right as a nation to self-determination.

But there can be no doubt that the 1991 Slovene Constitution is an entirely new constitution and not merely an amended version of the old 1974 Constitution. The extent and importance of the substantive similarity between the old and new Slovene constitutions are significantly less than the numerous and important differences. In particular, the foundations of the new Constitution and the political arrangements they set out represent a complete break with the previous constitutional system.

---

[5] This included primarily some provisions relating to human rights where the previous Constitution had, to a certain extent, already met internationally recognized standards, as well as other provisions such as those relating to the Constitutional Court, which had been established by the 1963 Constitution, and certain other postulates such as the principle of legality and the ban on retroactivity.

[6] The tricameral assembly that adopted the new Constitution was already composed of deputies elected at the democratic elections held in 1990.

Competitive Constitution Drafting

The late 1980s marked the beginning of a period of new openness throughout communist Eastern and Central Europe. In Slovenia, as in most of these countries, groups of dissidents and intellectuals began to organize in the hope of influencing decision-making and effecting social change. Between 1987 and 1991 when the new Slovene Constitution was adopted, the political and other elites in Slovenia succeeded in achieving a relatively high degree of consensus on important constitutional issues.[7] The first influential and organized action taken by the political opposition (led by a core group of intellectuals) occurred in 1987, when the Contributions for the Slovene National Programme were published.[8] The Contributions distinguished the Slovene identity as separate from the rest of Yugoslavia—a position that ran strongly counter to the official stance at the time. Although the authorities categorically rejected the Contributions, the opposition continued to recruit support and polish its strategy. In April 1988 the Constitutional Commission of the board of the Society of Slovene Writers and the Working Group on Constitutional Development at the Slovene Sociology Society published material for a Slovene constitution, in which a special place was occupied by 'Theses for a Constitution of the Republic of Slovenia'. This document was distributed widely and became generally known as the 'sociological' or 'writers' constitution'.

Under mounting domestic public pressure, on 27 September 1989 the Slovene assembly adopted constitutional amendments IX to XC to the 1974 Constitution of the Socialist Republic of Slovenia.[9] Although these amendments were written and adopted by Communist Party members, the 'writers' constitution' highly

---

[7] I will give a brief description of some of the most important events and documents that essentially marked the process of the adoption of the new Constitution. For more detail, see P. Jambrek, *Ustavna demokracija* (Constitutional Democracy) (Ljubljana: Državna založba Slovenije, 1992), 231–94; C. Ribičič, 'Ustavni razvoj Slovenije' (The Constitutional Development of Slovenia), in *Nova ustavna ureditev Slovenije*, 31–41; Rupnik, Cijan, and Grafenauer, *Ustavno pravo Republike Slovenije*, 19–38; R. M. Rizman, 'Between Constitution and Civil Society: The Case of Slovenia', in I. Grudzinska Gross (ed.), *Constitutionalism and Politics* (Bratislava: European Cultural Foundation, Symposium, 1994), 245–6; Miro Cerar, 'Die Verfassungsrechtlichen Grundlagen der Konstituierung des Staates Slowenien', in J. Marko and T. Borić (eds.), Slowenien—Kroatien—Serbien: die neuen Verfassungen (Vienna: Böhlau Verlag, 1991), 100–14; Ude, Grad, and Cerar, *Ustava Republike Slovenije z uvodnim komentarjem*, 8–19.

[8] *Nova Revija* (Ljubljana), 57 (1987).

[9] *Official Gazette of the Socialist Republic of Slovenia*, 32/89.

influenced their work. The amendments reflected the decision of the Slovene Communist Alliance (the Communist Party) to adopt some of the ideas raised by the intellectuals in terms of giving Slovenia a more independent and democratic status within federal Yugoslavia. For instance, Amendment IX stipulated that the Socialist Republic of Slovenia is a state, based on the sovereignty of the Slovene nation and the people of Slovenia. The same amendment introduced the principles of political pluralism and private property. The large number of amendments seems to indicate a dramatic change to the Constitution, but these changes actually did little significantly to alter the foundations of the political system in Slovenia or its status as a federal unit within Yugoslavia. More substantial political changes were promised a few months later when, on 16 December, the Slovene (collective) presidency set up a working group to formulate starting points for an entirely new Slovene and federal constitution. The starting points[10] envisaged a new constitutional system characterized by democracy and the rule of law, pluralism, equality of forms of ownership, and a market economy. They did not, however, envisage an independent and sovereign status for Slovenia.

In response to the government's initiatives, the opposition—now much stronger politically and enjoying greater influence—published a Working Draft of the New Slovene Constitution in its April 1990 journal *Demokracija*.[11] Containing 164 articles, this draft offered a more precisely defined basis for the new Constitution and, compared to the 'writers' constitution', was a more complete concept. The various intellectuals who contributed to this draft grappled with new ideas regarding the political, economic, and socio-cultural options for Slovenia, including the possibility for independence. In March 1990, *Nova revija* (No. 95) published the opinions, professional and otherwise, of more than forty writers on the concept of Slovene independence.

During the initial period of the transformation the Constitution was seen as the central tool for creating political and economic change by both the communists and the opposition. Nevertheless, there was little interaction between the two camps at the time. Its initial exclusion from the constitutional amendment process served further to unify the opposition and to extend their support from a small group of intellectuals to the society at large. Their success in organizing themselves was clear in the results of the April 1990 parliamentary elections.

[10] Published in *Delo* (16 Dec. 1989), 28–9.
[11] *Demokracija* (10 Apr. 1990), 1–8.

Post-electoral Consensus on Independence

The elections held on 8 and 12 April 1990 made possible the decisive transition from a self-managed communist political monopoly to political pluralism.[12] Nine political parties (of the sixteen
parties and one independent list that competed in the elections)
passed the 2.5 per cent threshold to enter parliament. The six-party
Demos coalition received 54.51 per cent of the vote and a majority in two of the three chambers of the assembly. This meant
that the previous power structures (the League of Communists–
Democratic Party of Renewal, the League of Socialist Youth of
Slovenia–Liberal Party, the Socialist Alliance of Slovenia–League
of Socialists) moved into the opposition. Nevertheless, Demos did
not win enough seats to be able to change the Constitution as it
wished. The adoption of a new constitution required a two-thirds
majority of the votes of all the delegates in the assembly of the
Republic of Slovenia (at least 160 out of 240).[13] Despite the optim-
ism expressed by the members of Demos and its intellectual
adherents that a new constitution could nevertheless be adopted
soon after the elections, the constitutional process was impeded not
only by the strong opposition but also by disagreement within the
coalition.

The formal constitution-drafting process began after elections
with the Assembly's creation of a Constitutional Commission on 13
June 1990. The Commission was given the task of formulating a
proposal for a new Slovene constitution to submit to the chambers
of the assembly for adoption.[14] In addition, the newly elected president formulated a Proposal for the Commencement of the Procedure for the Adoption of a New Slovene Constitution on 25 June
1990,[15] which stressed that Slovenia should become an independent

---

[12] D. Zajc, 'Slovenske politične stranke', in id., *Državni zbor Republike Slovenije*
(National Assembly of the Republic of Slovenia) (Ljubljana: National Assembly,
1995), 61.

[13] During the period in which the Constitution was being formulated, there was
no debate on the possibility of setting up a special constitutional assembly. The
idea of a constitutional assembly was already partly implied in the fact that at
the democratic elections in 1990 the voters were, for the most part, aware that
they were authorizing their representatives in the assembly, among other things,
to adopt a new constitution.

[14] See the Decree on the Founding, Tasks, Composition and Number of Members of the Commission of the Assembly of the Republic of Slovenia for Constitutional Issues, *Official Gazette of the Republic of Slovenia*, 25/90.

[15] Published in *Delo* (3 July 1990), 4.

state, and that its future constitution should, above all, embrace the principles of a democratic state governed by the rule of law. Based on the working draft Constitution and referring to numerous public observations and initiatives that had been expressed between August and September 1990, a group of legal experts appointed by the Commission formulated a new constitutional draft.

During this period the new understanding of constitutionality was demonstrated in an *apparently open system*. Whereas during the communist period every constitutional debate was restricted by the single-party system, the principle of unity of power, and other fundamental ideological premises established by the Party, in the constitutional debate prior to the adoption of the new Constitution any proposal for the new constitutional arrangement was legitimate. At the time citizens, various associations, commercial organizations, and, of course, the political parties frequently experimented with constitutional ideas, which they passed on to the Constitutional Commission. But this debate only gave the appearance of being so fully open because in reality a consensus already existed among the leading intellectuals and party leaders regarding some of the most fundamental constitutional solutions (for instance, the principle of the separation of powers, the status of a republic, the parliamentary system, and a market economy), which in fact implied the existence of a rather 'closed system'—albeit democratic and more inclusive than the previous one.

Some of the articles of the text drawn up by the group of experts were recast by the Constitutional Commission, and the text was officially adopted on 12 October 1990 as the draft Constitution of the Republic of Slovenia.[16] The public debate on the draft[17] which followed was officially concluded on 30 November 1990, but in fact lasted much longer, since the Commission continued to accept and debate public initiatives right up until the proposed Constitution was finalized. Within the governing political coalition, the belief still prevailed that the new Constitution would be adopted by the end of December 1990, or (according to the 'pessimistic variant') at the latest by the spring of 1991.[18] Yet both inside the coalition

---

[16] *Poročevalec* [Journal of the Assembly of the Republic of Slovenia], 17/90 (19 Oct. 1990).

[17] Public debates on proposed constitutional amendments were a particular feature of the previous three-stage procedure for amending the Constitution. The new Constitution introduced a two-stage constitutional amendment procedure, without the obligation to hold a public debate (but there is the possibility of holding a constitutional referendum as an optional third phase of the procedure).

[18] See Jambrek, *Ustavna demokracija*, 285–6.

and among the opposition parties objections were raised against this tight deadline. Many politicians and constitutional experts in Slovenia believed more time was needed to adopt the most important legal and political document of the state, so as to allow the constitutional solutions to be properly considered. Moreover, the fact that the adoption of a new constitution would have meant holding new parliamentary elections barely one year after the first pluralist elections drove many parliamentary parties to oppose quick adoption of the draft.

Although the parliamentary parties did not publicly oppose the independence of Slovenia, at the beginning of the formal process of adopting a constitution the opposition parties were initially hesitant to give their clear support for independence. Their hesitation was due, on the one hand, to the continuing ties, political and otherwise, with the other Yugoslav republics and, on the other hand, to the danger of military intervention by the Yugoslav army. Therefore, while constitution-drafting for the Slovene Republic continued, efforts were also under way to come up with a new Yugoslav constitution. On 6 October 1990 a model for a Yugoslav confederation[19] in the form of a draft international treaty was presented to the public by experts from the Slovene and Croatian governments. The Yugoslav confederation of republics envisioned giving sovereignty and the status as international subjects to its members. However, this model was rejected by all the republics— in fact, even Slovenia and Croatia ultimately opposed the idea— and therefore never came to fruition.

The rejection of the confederation model by the Yugoslav republics created an important opportunity for the independence-minded Slovenes to take steps toward secession. However, the slow process of coming to an agreement not only on the specific solutions in the draft Constitution, but also on a suitable date for its adoption stood in the way of quick action on the Slovene independence question. Therefore the original intention of many in the Demos governing coalition to have the Slovene state legally constituted with the adoption of a new constitution failed to materialize towards the end of 1990. Instead Demos agreed to the idea raised by the parliamentary opposition—specifically the Socialist Party of Slovenia—to hold a plebiscite on the issue of independence. The referendum was held on 23 December 1990 and attracted a remarkable turnout of 93.2 per cent of eligible voters. The result was an overwhelming 88.2 per cent in favour of Slovene independence

---

[19] Published in *Delo* (6 Oct. 1990), 20.

and sovereignty, thus revealing the unambiguous legitimacy of the policy of building a sovereign Slovene state.

On 22 February 1991 the Slovene assembly adopted a Resolution on a Proposal for the Break-up of the Socialist Federal Republic of Yugoslavia by Agreement,[20] which first pointed to the decision taken at the Slovene plebiscite and then put forward specific proposals to carry out the process of splitting up Yugoslavia through peaceful agreements. Except for the support given by Croatia, all the other Yugoslav republics either ignored or rejected the resolution. On 25 June 1991 Slovenia embraced statehood with the adoption of the Basic Constitutional Charter on the Independence and Sovereignty of the Republic of Slovenia, the Enabling Statute for the Implementation of the Basic Constitutional Charter on the Independence and Sovereignty of the Republic of Slovenia, and its Declaration of Independence.[21]

The Basic Constitutional Charter only laid down the most urgent matters requiring regulation for the establishment of sovereignty and retained (pending the adoption of a new constitution) the greater part of the 1974 Constitution, including its recent amendments and supplements. This Constitution, now subordinated to the provisions, or the principles, set out in the Basic Constitutional Charter, encompassed the necessary elements for state building, including the institutional construction of state power (assembly, executive council, presidency, etc.), and the appropriate changes to the provisions on the borders of the state. The Basic Constitutional Charter and the enabling statute for its implementation made possible the first decisive legislative changes to the old legal regime, because it was on the basis of these two documents that the assembly of the Republic of Slovenia adopted a collection of independence laws (laws on citizenship, foreigners, passports, border control, foreign affairs, the customs office, international credit transactions, foreign exchange operations, the Bank of Slovenia, etc.).[22]

Fast-track Constitution Drafting

The fact that the national emancipation of Slovenia was a priority had a significant influence on the adoption of the new

---

[20] *Official Gazette of the Republic of Slovenia*, 7/91.
[21] *Official Gazette of the Republic of Slovenia*, 1/91 (after independence).
[22] *Official Gazette of the Republic of Slovenia*, 1/91 (after independence).

Constitution and hence on the establishment of the new state institutions. Once the Slovene authorities had declared independence they were no longer able to afford an unlimited constitutional debate since the international status of Slovenia as a legitimate entity —the country had not yet been internationally recognized—was in essence conditional upon the adoption of a new constitution. Had Slovenia not been forced to push through its new Constitution, the constitutional debate would probably have dragged on for many months, even years. It could be argued in principle that it is better in the East European countries in transition, for example, and especially in the first phase of this process, for new constitutions to have an interim rather than a lasting character;[23] however, the situation in transition countries which have had a longer tradition as a state and which, moreover (because of their size or strategic location, for instance), are more 'interesting' politically or economically for the United States and the countries of Western Europe and which are, indisputably, international subjects, must nevertheless be distinguished from the situation in those countries that do not share these characteristics or which have them to a considerably lesser extent. It was in this second category that Slovenia belonged at the time when it was asserting its independence, and so for Slovenia's existence it was better (vital even) that at the time it should clearly establish, through comprehensive constitutional arrangements, its legitimacy as a relevant political and economic partner in the international community. Because the new Slovene Constitution, as will be demonstrated, is a modern constitution guaranteeing all the essential democratic standards, during the period when Slovenia was most intensively seeking international recognition (the second half of 1991 and the beginning of 1992) this Constitution proved to be a most appropriate 'identity card' and an additional argument in favour of recognition from the international community. Thus, on 4 December 1991 the Constitutional Commission finalized the proposed Constitution of the Republic of Slovenia and the proposed Enabling Statute for the Implementation of the Constitution of the Republic of Slovenia.[24] Both proposals were adopted on 23 December 1991 in all three chambers of the Slovene assembly with (more than) a two-thirds majority of the votes of all the delegates, and were proclaimed at a joint session on the same day.

[23] Jan Zielonka, 'New Institutions in the Old East Bloc', *Journal of Democracy*, 5 (Apr. 1995), 88, 100.

[24] The proposals were published, with an explanation, in *Poročevalec*, 1/92 (17 Jan. 1992).

The absence of a dominant political bloc enjoying a sufficient majority in parliament to adopt the new Constitution had the effect of significantly extending the constitutional debate. This led to greater consideration of possible constitutional solutions and the need to acquire consensus, which helped to stabilize the political situation in Slovenia and prevent any radical settling of scores between the governing coalition and the opposition.[25] Contentious constitutional questions needed to be resolved through political compromise. Some of these compromises led to a number of rather 'unusual' solutions;[26] and in cases where a compromise proved impossible to reach, the writers of the Constitution simply avoided regulation of certain constitutional issues.[27] Such areas were to be

[25] Because of the new governing coalition's inability to make rapid and radical changes to the inherited political and legal structure, in many areas of development Slovenia lagged behind the other East European countries emerging from communism (for instance, in the process of privatization, denationalization, and rectifying post-war injustices committed by the communist regime). Primarily from the economic point of view, but also politically, this period was relatively ineffective. Nevertheless, at the time Slovenia was still a part of federal Yugoslavia and for this reason a great deal of energy was (successfully) expended on the attainment of independence because some of the essential institutional changes were simply not possible in the Yugoslav context (for instance, the Yugoslav army was still stationed in Slovenia and the legal order was still founded on the old Constitution and legislation). It must also be recalled that in this initial period of transition the new and old political elites were endeavouring above all to acquire or retain political and economic ascendancy in Slovenia, and so failed to give sufficiently intensive and consistent attention to a number of the key questions of transition.

[26] I am referring to certain solutions which were not a standard part of most other parliamentary systems; e.g. the provisions relating to the National Council, which introduce elements of corporativism into parliament (Arts. 96 to 101 of the Constitution); the somewhat contradictory regulation of the position of the president of the republic, who has very limited powers (Arts. 102, 107, and 108 of the Constitution) given that the president is directly elected; and the stipulation that ministers of state are appointed by parliament, i.e. the National Assembly (Art. 112 of the Constitution).

[27] For instance, the Constitution does not set out some of the fundamental elements of the electoral system, which in other systems are considered matters for regulation by the Constitution. The Constitution only contains basic provisions on the right to vote (Arts. 43, 80, and 103), but, for example, does not contain any provisions relating to the system of allocating seats. The system under which elections are held for the National Assembly, the National Council, and the president of the republic is currently regulated by several laws. Elections to the National Assembly are based on a proportional system, although there is an important element of the majority system in that in order to enter parliament a party must win at least three seats (for a more detailed analysis of the Slovene electoral system, see F. Grad, *Novi volilni sistem* (New Electoral System) (Ljubljana: Inštitut za javno upravo, 1992).

regulated later by parliament in the form of laws that would be
adopted with a qualified majority. In this way at the symbolic
(constitutional) level, Slovenia could more rapidly establish its
legitimacy as a state with a democratic consensus, which would bring
short-term benefits to, among others, the governing political parties. At the same time, this strategy simply postponed the resolution of many essential constitutional questions.

Initially, it was envisaged in the draft Constitution that constitutional laws and not specific constitutional articles would
regulate primarily the following matters: (*a*) citizenship; (b) the
manner in which the Hungarian and Italian ethnic communities
(minorities) exercise their rights, the areas in which these communities live, and the rights enjoyed by individuals belonging to
either community outside their ethnic area; (*c*) the status and
special rights of the Roma community in Slovenia; (*d*) the conditions under which foreigners may obtain the right to own land;
(*e*) the rights and the conditions under which foreigners may
exploit the natural resources of Slovenia; (*f*) the electoral system;
(*g*) referenda; (*h*) the manner, extent, and organization of the
military defence of Slovene territory; (*i*) the organization and
jurisdictions of courts, the direct participation of citizens in the
exercise of judicial power, the conditions for the election of judges,
and certain other issues related to the judiciary and the holding
of judicial office; and (*j*) the status and function of the office of state
prosecutor. This large set of issues was deemed necessary to be
included in the Constitution, but given that the drafters hoped to
adopt the Constitution quickly, they did not want the process to
be impeded by lengthy debates over these complex or even contentious issues. These constitutional laws would be passed in parliament by a two-thirds majority of deputies present during the
vote. Moreover, the idea to postpone debate over these issues also
stemmed from the fact that constitution drafters (the parliamentary parties) could not accurately predict the outcomes of their
choices. This proposal reflected the high degree of mistrust that
prevailed at the time among the various political parties as well
as the unpredictable nature of further political development.

Ultimately, the majority coalition thought better of postponing debates on these important issues and substantially limited the
number of articles calling for parliament to pass constitutional laws
on the topic. Instead, the drafters opted for a solution in which the
constitutional articles related to the topics mentioned above were
at least basically outlined such that their regulation would not be
wholly transferred to laws. Moreover, where laws were retained in

the draft, in almost all cases, the parliamentary vote required only a simple majority to adopt them. In this way, it was hoped to avoid a situation in which implementation of the constitutional principles would not be further delayed by a parliamentary minority. Two-thirds majority voting was only required for the adoption of electoral laws (Art. 80) and the law on referenda (Art. 90), the organization of national defence (Art. 124), and the standing orders of parliament (Art. 94).

Other important contentious issues were similarly resolved through elite consensus. For instance, some of the right-wing parliamentary parties (such as the Slovene Democratic Alliance) called for the Constitution to set out in principle the national[28] sovereignty of the Slovene state, while the majority advocated the contemporary concept of sovereignty of the people. Under the former position the 'Slovene nation' would have been the constitutive element of the state, while with the latter position the constitutive element was to be the citizens of Slovenia, irrespective of their national or ethnic origin. The latter position advocating sovereignty of the people prevailed convincingly, but nevertheless the Constitution explicitly stipulates that only the Slovene nation as such (the *narod*) has the right of self-determination in Slovenia.[29] Further protection of national minorities was given through a mechanism in which laws, regulations, and general enactments relating exclusively to the constitutionally determined rights and status of the ethnic communities cannot be adopted without the consent of the representatives of the communities[30] (the two deputies representing the Hungarian and the Italian ethnic community have the right of veto over such laws).

In regard to human rights, particular attention was paid in the constitutional debate to the right of workers to participate

[28] The idea of the 'nation' here is understood in the way that is characteristic of Central Europe and the Balkans, where the term denotes a homogeneous ethnic group sharing an identifiable tradition (language, culture), and where such group cannot be identified with the state (remember that Slovenia left a Yugoslav federation composed fundamentally of nation-republics in order to become independent).

[29] Art. 3 of the Constitution, in full, reads as follows: 'Slovenia is a state of all its citizens and is based on the permanent and inalienable right of the Slovene people to self-determination. In Slovenia, supreme power is vested in the people. Citizens exercise that power directly, and at elections, consistently with the principle of the separation of legislative, executive, and judicial powers.'

[30] For instance, the Law on Self-Governing Ethnic Communities (*Official Gazette of the Republic of Slovenia*, 65/94), which was passed in October 1994.

in management, the property rights of foreigners, and the right to freedom of choice in childbearing. Some opposed the right of workers to participate in management because it was reminiscent of the right to self-management under the previous system, which was seen to be an unrealistic and functionally ineffective policy. However, the opposing position prevailed that this was a right which, within certain limits, was established in other modern democracies. In the end, this right is embraced by the Constitution in principle, but its detailed regulation is subject to law.[31]

With regard to the property rights of foreigners, after lengthy debate the solution was adopted and encompassed in Article 68 of the Constitution. This article stipulated that foreigners may only acquire title to property affixed to land under the conditions set out in law. But foreigners may not acquire title to land except by inheritance and on the condition of reciprocity. With this solution the writers of the Constitution sought to prevent the possibility of a 'sell-off' of large parts of Slovene territory, since for a country such as Slovenia with so small a territory (20,256 sq. km), allowing foreigners to buy land was seen to be a major political and security risk. In the past year this inflexible (and uncompromising) solution has proven to be a serious hindrance and could call into question Slovenia's integration into the European Union if the country fails to adapt to the arrangements in place elsewhere and, at least under certain conditions, allow foreigners the possibility of owning land in Slovenia.[32] On 14 July 1997, the National Assembly adopted a constitutional law to amend Article 68 in order to enable legislation to comply with the Association Agreement with

---

[31] Art. 75 of the Constitution stipulates that 'workers may participate in the management of businesses and institutions in such manner and under such conditions as shall be determined by statute'. This area is now regulated in detail by the Law on Workers' Participation in Management (*Official Gazette of the Republic of Slovenia*, 42/93).

[32] In May 1995 the government presented a motion to the National Assembly for the commencement of the procedure to amend the Constitution of the Republic of Slovenia, proposing that the constitutional ban on foreigners acquiring title to land be lifted, and that statutory regulation determine the conditions under which this could take place (*Poročevalec*, 21/95). One of the points the government emphasized in its explanation was that it had given an undertaking that Slovenia, which wishes to become a member of the European Union, would bring its legislation into line with EU legislation by 2001 at the latest, and that the question of changing the arrangements governing the purchase and sale of land was part of this undertaking. Pursuant to the government's proposal, at the end of June 1997 the National Assembly began the procedure to make the relevant amendment to the Constitution.

the European Union. The amended article stipulates that foreigners may acquire the right to real property under conditions set up by law or in any international agreement ratified by the National Assembly, on the condition of reciprocity. Nevertheless, the mentioned law and international agreement must both be adopted by a vote of two-thirds in the Assembly, which is the same qualified majority required for amending the Constitution.

One of the biggest problems in the constitutional debate was the right to abortion. This was a right that had been included in the previous Constitution and its incorporation in the new Constitution was supported primarily by the left-leaning parties and, to a large extent, by public opinion. In 1991 the opposition by some parties (the Slovene Christian Democrats, for example) to the idea of this matter being regulated at the constitutional level even led to public demonstrations, at which women in particular expressed their public support for the constitutional right to abortion. Despite numerous attempts to reach a compromise formulation of the constitutional provision, it remained uncertain right up until the day on which the Constitution was adopted whether the parties which had so decisively opposed this provision would indeed vote to adopt the Constitution (in the end, they did).[33] Interestingly, in the 1996 parliamentary elections none of the political parties raised this constitutional right in their election campaigns.

Debates and Outcomes Concerning the Major Political Institutions

Looking at the political system, the main question that arose at the beginning of the constitutional debate in the Constitutional Commission concerned the position of the president, and, by extension, the relationship between the parliament and the executive branch. To assist in their debate, the Commission's expert group formulated two normative models. The first model envisaged a parliamentary system in which the parliament would have the prevailing influence on the formation of the government. The second model, which we could call semi-presidential or parliamentary

---

[33] Art. 55 of the Constitution states: 'Persons shall be free to decide whether to bear children. The state shall ensure that persons have every opportunity to exercise this freedom and shall create such conditions as enable parents to freely choose whether or not to bear children.'

presidential (modelled primarily after the French system), envisaged a directly elected president[34] who would have influence over the formation of the government. At the very beginning of the constitutional debate the elite already had agreed that the Constitution should establish a parliamentary system along the lines of the first model. But since time was tight and consensus was needed from other political parties, the constitutional arrangement that was adopted has elements of both models. The president is directly elected, although he or she only has, for the most part, powers of a generally representative, initiative, and protocolar nature,[35] which do not provide any real opportunity for strong influence on policy-making. This is something that takes place primarily within the government and parliament, although in practice the president can, of course, have a significant impact on policy through the means of personal authority and informal activities.

It also seems clear that the institution of the president was, to a great extent, adapted to suit the incumbent president, Milan Kučan. Due to his highly successful reformist leadership within the League of Communists in the 1980s, Kučan won enormous popular respect. Thus, in the face of strong popular support for the president, it was clear to all the parliamentary parties that direct election under the new Constitution was almost beyond question. Nevertheless, the parliamentary parties that opposed Kučan's election (and they had a majority in the assembly) sought to reduce his political influence by opting for relatively weak presidential powers.

One of the peculiarities of the Slovene Constitution is the provision contained in Article 112 stipulating that ministers of state are appointed and dismissed by the National Assembly (parliament) upon the proposal of the prime minister. This solution was not adopted until the final phase of the constitutional debate. It was put in without great consideration and was not founded on expert arguments. This is another of those decisions that we can presume was taken with one eye on the specific political situation at the time.

[34] See Jambrek, *Ustavna demokracija*, 316–24.

[35] The relatively weak powers of the president of the republic are set out in Arts. 102, 107, 108, and 111 of the Constitution. For a detailed review of the constitutional position of the president of the republic, see M. Ribarič, 'Predsednik Republike Slovenije in parlament' (The President of the Republic of Slovenia and the Parliament), in M. Brezovšek (ed.), *Slovenski parlament: izkušnje in perspektive* (Slovene Parliament: Experiences and Perspectives), Slovensko politološko društvo (Ljubljana: Slovensko politološko društvo, 1996), 119–36.

The parliamentary parties, unsure of whether or not they would have a part to play in future government coalitions, probably hoped that this stipulation would be a way in which to secure a direct influence on the composition of the government. Yet the current arrangement is reminiscent of the previous 'assembly system' in which, formally, the 'executive council' was more or less subordinated in its implementation of the policies of the assembly, which itself was the formal summit of the system of unity of power (in fact the real summit of the system was of course the League of Communists and its Central Committee).

Thus far, the system under which ministers of state are appointed and dismissed by the National Assembly has not led to any serious problems in practice. During the four-year term of the first parliament, only on a few occasions was the prime minister forced to enter into protracted negotiations with the coalition partners and other parliamentary parties over ministerial candidates. But had the composition of parliament been 'less favourable', that is, more polarized, the appointment and dismissal of ministers could have been rendered practically impossible, and a government crisis would have ensued.[36]

On the issue of the structure of parliament, the required consensus between advocates of a unicameral system and advocates of a bicameral system could not be achieved, and so in the last months of the constitutional debate the chairman of the Constitutional Commission, France Bučar, managed to reach a compromise between the two sides with his proposal concerning the National Council. Under the Constitution, the parliament is bicameral, composed of a National Assembly and a National Council, although the bicameral aspect is extremely limited. Many politicians and some intellectuals even deny that the National Council, which is modelled on the Bavarian Senate (there are, however, certain essential differences between the two), has the status of a house of parliament. What they fail to explain is, among others, quite under which branch of power they would categorize it.[37]

---

[36] Under Art. 11 of the Law on the Government (*Official Gazette of the Republic of Slovenia*, 4/93 and 23/96), if ministers are not appointed, within a specified period, to all ministerial positions, then the prime minister and all other ministers automatically cease to hold office.

[37] See Miro Cerar, 'Status državnega sveta' (The Status of the National Council), *Pravna praksa*, 14 (1993), 5–7; I. Kristan, 'Dvodomnost slovenskega parlamenta' (The Bicamerality of the Slovene Parliament), in Brezovšek (ed.), *Slovenski parlament*, 1–12.

The National Assembly, composed of ninety deputies elected by the citizens in direct and general elections, is a classic example of a representative and legislative body. The National Council, on the other hand, is a corporative body which has forty members representing social, economic, trade and professional, and local interests, where the representatives of local interests form the majority with twenty-two members. Members of the National Council are elected through special voting procedures by representatives of employers, employees, farmers, small business persons, independent professionals, non-profit organizations (schools, universities, cultural and sporting organizations, professional health organizations, etc.) and local communities.[38] The Council may propose the enactment of laws by the National Assembly; transmit to the National Assembly its opinion on matters within the jurisdiction of the National Assembly (generally these opinions relate to bills going through the legislative process); require the calling of a legislative referendum; require that the National Assembly reconsider a law prior to its proclamation (suspensive veto[39]); and require that a parliamentary inquiry be commissioned into matters of public importance.

In its first five-year term, the National Council has had relatively little influence on legislation. It has exercised its suspensive veto in respect to twenty-five laws.[40] In five cases the laws were not passed upon reconsideration by the National Assembly, but all the other laws went through with no changes to the text (taking no account whatsoever of the veto).[41] The National Council has made only one demand for holding a referendum (on a proposal for a new electoral system), which was put to vote and rejected by the electorate in December 1996. In political terms the National Council has played a minimal role so far, which is mainly a reflection of the constitutional definition which gives it no powers to adopt final decisions

---

[38] See I. Lukšič, 'Državni svet Republike Slovenije' (National Council of the Republic of Slovenia), in D. Fink-Hafner and B. Strmčnik (eds.), *Problemi konsolidacije demokracije* (Problems of Democratic Consolidation) (Ljubljana: Slovensko politološko društvo, 1993), 139–50, and I. Lukšič, 'Korporativni Državni svet' (The National Council as Corporative Body), in Brezovšek, *Slovenski parlament*, 13–26.

[39] Under Art. 91 of the Constitution, in its reconsideration the National Assembly must achieve an absolute majority of votes in order to pass the law in question.

[40] During this period the National Assembly has ploughed through a huge workload; it has adopted 1,493 enactments, including 242 completely new laws and 131 laws to amend or supplement existing legislation.

[41] These figures are taken from a report on the work of the National Assembly of the Republic of Slovenia in the period between 23 Dec. 1992 and 16 Oct. 1996.

on anything at all. Its primary role is one of initiative and supervision, as a corrective mechanism to the activities of the National Assembly and an element in a system of checks and balances.

Another of the major problems that had to be confronted in the constitutional debate was the new concept of local self-government, replacing the former 'communal' system based on relatively large municipalities (or 'communes' as they were called) that combined a self-management and a state role.[42] Under the previous system, the state functions of the commune became increasingly stronger at the expense of the self-management functions. In fact, the commune operated more or less as the first level of state administration.[43] The new Constitution establishes an entirely different concept of local self-government, which is founded on the municipalities as exclusively units of self-government and on the possibility of combining municipalities to form wider units of local self-government (such as regions). Local government is regulated in a separate chapter of the Constitution (Arts. 138–44).

In the Constitutional Commission there was a strong split between the advocates of regionalism and the centralists. The former group (mainly members of the left-wing parties) argued Slovenia's regions should be specified in the Constitution and that these clearly defined territories should enjoy a relatively high degree of autonomy. This was partly linked to their idea of a bicameral parliament in which the second house would represent local interests and would have significantly greater powers than the current National Council (in certain matters it would have had the same decision-making power as the National Assembly). Opponents to this idea (mainly members of the Demos parties) considered Slovenia to be too small for such regionalism. Instead, they called for a sharper division between national and local government, with a smaller role for the latter, while also advocating a unicameral parliament. In the end it was the second vision, the centralist concept, which prevailed, but the compromises that were struck when the constitutional articles came to be written are today revealed in the fact that some of the provisions are inadequately formulated and lacking in clarity.

The Constitution defines the municipality as the basic self-governing community but permits the linking of two or more municipalities into a wider self-governing community. In practice,

---

[42] See Strobl, Kristan, and Ribičič, *Ustavno pravo SFR Jugoslavije*, 283–98.
[43] See J. Šmidovnik, *Lokalna samouprava* (Local Self-government) (Ljubljana: Cankarjeva založba, 1995), 153–5.

however, such linking is improbable because as a rule the state does not finance the municipalities,[44] let alone the self-governing activities of wider local communities, thus, there is little incentive for having several municipalities link together to form integral regions. Reform of local government is still an ongoing process. Pursuant to the Constitution and the Law on Local Self-Government,[45] which has by now undergone several major revisions, following the holding of preliminary consultative referenda at the local level initially around 150 municipalities were established in Slovenia (at the referenda only 111 of the 340 proposed 'referendum areas' of municipalities were accepted). Another referendum was organized in 1998 which expanded the number of municipalities to 192. This process has come up against numerous complications and the number of municipalities and their boundaries may well yet change significantly.

As the supreme or ultimate interpreter of the Constitution, the Constitutional Court plays a decisive role in directing constitutional development. It is fair to say that while its constitutional checks and balances role, especially during the period of transition, is extremely significant, in more important cases the Court's decisions have been seen to be overly political, and it is giving too little consideration to the principle of judicial self-restraint.

The basic principles of the Constitution are laid down in its general provisions. These cover primarily the principle of democracy (Art. 1); the principles of the rule of law and a social state (Art. 2); the principles of sovereignty of the people and the separation of powers (Art. 3); the principle of territorial unity and indivisibility (Art. 4); the principle of the protection of human rights and the rights of the Italian and Hungarian ethnic communities, and the principle that the Slovene state shall attend to the welfare of ethnic Slovenes throughout the world (Art. 5); the principle of the separation of the Church and state and the principle that religious groups shall enjoy equal rights (Art. 7); the principle of the supremacy of the generally accepted principles of international law and ratified international agreements over laws and other

---

[44] The state provides certain funds only to municipalities whose poor level of economic development means that they are unable to meet all the expenditures required of them in the performance of their duties and functions (Art. 142 of the Constitution). Obviously the state finances those duties and functions which it has vested in a municipality or wider self-governing community in accordance with the prior consent of the municipality or community (Art. 140 of the Constitution). On the issue of Slovene local government, see ibid. 145–261.

[45] *Official Gazette of the Republic of Slovenia*, 72/93, 57/94, and 14/95.

legislative measures (Art. 8); and the principle of the autonomy of local government (Art. 9). These constitutional principles have a special significance, not least because the Constitutional Court often directly invokes them in its adjudication of the constitutionality and legality of legal acts and in its rulings on constitutional complaints. Hence the Constitutional Court deals with cases involving subject matter not explicitly regulated by the Constitution on the basis of the theory (doctrine) on which these principles are founded. This is an extremely important dynamic aspect of the Constitution whereby it acquires substance through Constitutional Court precedent that is otherwise not directly evident.

If we look at how this applies to the principle of the rule of law, we see that the Constitution explicitly lays down a number of principles and rules falling within this framework, such as the principles of constitutionality, legality, equality before the law, the presumption of innocence, and the prohibition against retrospective legislation. Yet since the adoption of the new Constitution the Constitutional Court has, in several cases, partly based its rulings directly on the principle of the rule of law as such, and on principles derived from it that are not laid down explicitly in the Constitution. Such doctrinal principles, which as an essential part of the practice of the Constitutional Court have now become elements in Slovenia's constitutional order, include primarily the principles of legal certainty, trust in the law, proportionality, the ban on arbitrariness, and the principle of justice.[46]

While the Slovene Constitutional Court has an extremely important constitutional control function, especially during the period of transition, in more important cases the court is applying insufficient judicial self-restraint and is having an overly political effect despite the undoubted professional calibre of its judges. Although the boundaries between the law and politics are of course fluid and often difficult to determine, the approach taken by Slovenia's Constitutional Court is too frequently 'innovative' or 'creative' and hence even from a professional perspective its practice is excessively unpredictable. On the more important rulings there tends to be an internal polarizing among the judges of the Constitutional Court, which heightens the impression of it having a political nature. The nine Constitutional Court judges have passed many of their important rulings 5 to 4, and as a rule have

---

[46] See Miro Cerar, 'Rechtsstaatlichkeit in Slowenien', in R. Hofmann, J. Marko, F. Merli, and E. Wiederin (eds.), *Rechtsstaatlichkeit in Europe* (Heidelberg: C. F. Müller, 1996), 243–5.

been publicly vocal about their professional disagreements, which weakens the coherence and authority of the rulings themselves and frequently causes an even greater polarization among the public (the media, the professional public, the political parties, etc.). In a similar manner to that described above in connection with the principle of the rule of law, in its argumentation the Constitutional Court sometimes makes direct recourse to other highly abstract principles (such as the principle of a social state and the principle of democracy), which give it enormous room for 'free argumentation'.

In general the Slovene Constitutional Court can be described as an 'activist court'[47] in the positive sense, since its rulings do not imply a capitulation to the political sphere (state authorities, political parties) even though the political preferences of some of the Constitutional Court judges are evident. And, moreover, in a situation in which the regular judiciary in Slovenia is only gradually consolidating itself on the basis of the new constitutional arrangements, the Constitutional Court is the one part of the judicial branch of power that has already seized upon the general trend characteristic of Western Europe during the past twenty years where the judiciary has taken on an increasingly significant role in the national decision-making process.[48] From this perspective the Slovene Constitutional Court is also a protagonist in the process of the emancipation of the Slovene judiciary. But in the future the Constitutional Court will need to be more careful to remain within the boundaries of judicial self-restraint.

Looking now at the question of social and economic rights, in the constitutional debate the position prevailed that the Constitution should explicitly guarantee only those social and economic rights whose nature is not so 'programmatic' (that is, policy goals that are very distant from social reality) as to prevent their effective exercise before the courts. Given that even during the constitutional debate it was possible to foresee that in the future Slovenia would be confronted by high unemployment and other economic and social problems, the writers of the Constitution consciously rejected laying down, for example, the right to work and the right

---

[47] According to the definition of Cass R. Sunstein, 'The Legitimacy of Constitutional Courts: Notes on Theory and Practice', *East European Constitutional Review*, 6/1 (1997), 62.

[48] See N. C. Alivizatos, 'Judges as Veto Players', in Herbert Döring (ed.), *Parliaments and Majority Rule in Western Europe* (New York: St Martin Press, 1995), 566 ff.

to adequate housing.[49] One of the characteristics of the previous socialist constitutional system was that the Constitution contained numerous highly 'programmatic' principles and rights which could not be implemented in practice or brought before the courts, and this gradually led to a general undermining of confidence in the legal system. The new Constitution still embraces certain economic and social rights but they are generally dependent upon statutory regulation, which can more easily take account of the real possibility of guaranteeing such rights.[50] Clearly, even a short and abstract definition of a human right or freedom in the Constitution means that a constitutional complaint[51] is possible in proceedings to ensure legal protection of such right, which is not envisaged for the protection of other rights.[52]

---

[49] In these two instances the writers of the Constitution adopted a special approach. They transformed both of these rights into the duty of the state to create the opportunity for their achievement. Thus Art. 66 of the Constitution stipulates that 'the state shall be responsible for the creation of opportunities for employment and for work and shall ensure the protection thereof by law', and Art. 78 'the state shall create the conditions necessary to enable each citizen to obtain suitable housing'. Although both provisions are of a programmatic nature, they clearly do not involve a (fundamental) right of citizens. In other words, there is no legal remedy (e.g. a lawsuit) directly available to citizens in respect of a guarantee of work and housing.

[50] For example, the Constitution explicitly guarantees the basic right to social security (Art. 50) and to health care (Art. 51), but also states that citizens only enjoy these rights under the conditions laid down by statute. Similarly, the Constitution guarantees the right to own property (Art. 33), but adds (in Art. 67) that 'the manner in which property is acquired and enjoyed shall be regulated by statute so as to ensure the economic, social and environmental function of such property'. Under economic rights, the Constitution guarantees, for example, free enterprise, but here again adds that the conditions under which commercial organizations are founded are to be determined by law.

[51] In accordance with the constitution and pursuant to the Law on the Constitutional Court (*Official Gazette of the Republic of Slovenia*, 15/94), any person may bring a constitutional complaint before the Constitutional Court if they believe that their human rights have been violated by an individual act passed by a state body, local authority, or public authority. As a rule, a constitutional complaint may only be lodged after all other legal remedies have been exhausted.

[52] Here we should note that the Constitutional Court has taken the position that certain constitutional rights laid down in the third chapter of the Constitution ('Economic and Social Relations') are not human rights and freedoms in respect of which a constitutional complaint could be lodged (of course, they do enjoy protection before ordinary courts of law). In other words, the right to a healthy living environment (Art. 72 of the Constitution states: 'Everyone shall have the right under the law to a healthy environment in which to live'), for example, is not a 'human right' because it is not laid down in the second chapter of the Constitution, which carries the title 'Human Rights and Fundamental Freedoms'.

This constitutional concept has so far proven to be appropriate because in the past few years numerous problems concerning the protection of the rights of individuals in practice have arisen in the area of economic and social relations. Yet the fact that legal protection in these areas is relatively poor does not directly affect our assessment of the Constitution as such—the focus of the problems remains at the level of social and economic policy, statutory regulation, and judicial practice.

Conclusions

The period since the last parliamentary elections in November 1996 demonstrates that the confrontation with communism is not yet over in Slovenia.[53] Yet this settling of scores is now little more than an *appearance*, for communism in Slovenia actually represents merely an abstract and symbolic point of reference ('communism as a common enemy') against which the citizens can be rallied through manipulation and populism.[54] The right-leaning political

Yet since the Constitution is not particularly systematic in this regard, this is a somewhat questionable position to take (for more detail, see M. Pavčnik, 'Prispevek k razlagi temeljnih pravic' (A Contribution to the Interpretation of Basic Rights), *Podjetje in delo* (Ljubljana), 5–6 (1994), 489–90.

[53] This period was marked by a government crisis which lasted several months, with the ninety-member parliament polarizing symmetrically after the elections into a group of so-called parties of the Slovene spring (forty-five deputies) and another group of parties and deputies (also totalling forty-five) headed by the strongest party, the Liberal Democrats. After several months of impasse, during which time it was impossible even to vote in a new government, a 'solution' was found in the form of a left-right coalition between the Liberal Democrats and the Slovene People's Party. But the subsequent months have demonstrated how very difficult it is for such a coalition to be effective when the basic policy directions of the two parties do not coincide on most issues. The 1992–6 coalition was also a similar type of compromise, with the Liberal Democrats, the Slovene Christian Democrats, and the Associated List (the former communists) in government together throughout most of the period; and this coalition, too, demonstrated the almost inevitable bipolarity of Slovene politics (as in the current government, this bipolarity was carried over into the coalition itself, with the Christian Democrats having essentially different policy directions from the Liberal Democrats and the Associated List).

[54] The fact is that the 'grand themes' such as the gaining of independence and the initial breakthrough into democracy (first democratic elections in 1990) were concluded several years ago. In Slovenia these projects activated and channelled an enormous collective energy against the 'external enemy', i.e. the pro-Serbian federal Yugoslavia, and also against the international community, which at the beginning was strongly disinclined to recognize Slovenia as a state. This led to

parties of the Slovene spring (the Slovene People's Party, Social Democratic Party, and Slovene Christian Democrats) in their political rhetoric are frequently 'leading the battle' against the remnants of the previous regime, that is, against the parties such as the Liberal Democrats and the Associated List of Social Democrats (the latter being the formal successor to the League of Communists). But the fact is that communism as such is now practically non-existent in Slovenia, and that important and less important former members of the League of Communists can now be found in all the parties, although obviously to a greater extent in those parties in which there exists a certain continuity of personnel with the League of Communists and its satellite organizations from the previous regime. And it is also true that because of the non-radical way in which Slovenia broke with communism these parties, the successors to the political organizations of the previous regime, retained possession of numerous levers of economic and political power, with the Liberal Democrats already a permanent and dominant party in each of the governing coalitions. To categorize these parties as 'communist' can really only be justified from the point of view of personnel (and not in any ideological sense), because many politicians and people occupying other key positions who have dominated the economic and political scene in Slovenia already held these or similar positions under the previous regime (as far as politicians are concerned this only applies to the younger individuals, since most of the older communists generally withdrew from politics in the period directly after the transition to a democratic system, that is at the beginning of the 1990s). On this point a general problem remains in Slovenia that a certain totalitarian political mentality is being perpetuated, something which is inevitably inherited from a dictatorship of any sort, including communism. This is the political mentality mentioned earlier, whereby the parties tend towards total predominance in terms of ideas and personnel, something which is most apparent in every new government coalition. Of course, in a democracy this is legitimate in principle and within certain boundaries, but may, particularly in transition countries, become a threat to the very existence of a young democracy if it causes a perpetual discontinuity in the political orientation of the country.

a very high degree of homogenization around the basic common goals. Slovene politics today of course can no longer set such grand and common goals; above all it is the difficult confrontation with oneself that is now having to be faced, and not least with one's own shortcomings.

Obviously in transitions to democracy a general problem is that there always exists an 'uncertainty of democratic outcomes',[55] but it is nevertheless possible to identify some of those constitutional postulates without which democracy would not *a priori* be possible. These are postulates such as the principle of sovereignty of the people, the separation of powers, the protection of basic rights,[56] and, within this framework, in particular the guarantee of free and fair elections, freedoms of association and information, etc. The argument that the architects of the new democratic constitutions were faced with two fundamental choices—the choice between plurality elections and proportional representation, and between parliamentary and presidential forms of government[57]—can only be confirmed with regard to Slovenia; and it is fair to say that the choice of a parliamentary form of government together with a proportional electoral system made a great contribution to the development of democracy and especially to constitutional continuity. In the absence of a single dominant group or strong individual (such as a president with wide-ranging powers), the political, economic, and other processes, while in places being somewhat slow compared with certain other countries in transition (for example, the slow pace of privatization and denationalization in Slovenia), are indeed bringing results over the long term in spite of the difficulties encountered. Currently a political debate is going on in Slovenia on the issue of the radical replacement of the proportional election system by a two-round majority system. This debate follows the contentious decision of the Constitutional Court,[58] which in its adjudication arbitrarily, and in violation of its constitutional competencies, interpreted the results of the so-called 'election referendum', held in

[55] Giuseppe di Palma, *To Craft Democracies: An Essay on Democratic Transition* (Berkeley and Los Angeles: University of California Press, 1990), 44.

[56] In the spirit of Madison and Hamilton it is possible even today in general to question whether declarations of basic rights are a necessary condition of constitutions. G. Sartori, *Comparative Constitutional Engineering* (London: Macmillan, 1994), for example, answers this question by stating that 'in vital matters some redundancy does not hurt'. But I think that in the example of countries in transition from communism to democracy the reply to this question has to be unequivocal: constitutions *must* include a list of basic rights, or these rights must in some other way be elevated to the level of constitutional protection. And it is perhaps even better if too many rather than too few are guaranteed (after all, 'some redundancy does not hurt'), provided this does not make the constitution excessively programmatic.

[57] See A. Lijphart, 'Constitutional Choices for New Democracies', in Larry Diamond and Marc F. Plattner, *The Global Resurgence of Democracy* (Baltimore: Johns Hopkins University Press, 1993), 146.

[58] Decision of the Constitutional Court from 8 Oct. 1998, No. U-I-12/97.

1996, and changed the already proclaimed negative decision of the voters (against any change of the electoral system) into a positive one (that is, in favour of a majority election system). Although most of the parliamentary political parties (but not all of them and not all deputies irrespective of their party affiliations) now declare themselves as being fully committed to the obligatory court's decision, the outcome of the legislative debate is still uncertain because we have already entered the election year (2000) and each solution in the new law on the election system—especially those solutions concerning new electoral units—will be evaluated in a very hot atmosphere of assessment of concrete predictability of the possible election results. If the parliament adopts a majority election system, it will result in further intensive ideological and political (left–right) bipolarization of Slovenes. Nevertheless, the process of integrating Slovenia into the European Union and the prevalent stability and continuity of the Slovene constitutional order are two of the most important factors that should prevent any radical decline from the basic democratic orientation of Slovene politics.

Democratic consolidation, seen as a multifaceted process of ensuring and preserving the basic institutions of the new Slovene Constitution, can thus be regarded as more or less achieved, despite the political turbulence that continues to dominate Slovene politics. And since the constructing of the new Constitution can undoubtedly be classified in the category of 'free and consensual constitution-making',[59] and because its basic principles and individual solutions fully correspond with the democratic spirit of the age, the continuity of these institutions represents a key stabilizing element in the political and other fluctuations, turbulence, and extremes in society, and, inasmuch as they provide the basic democratic rules of the game, also a generator of political stability.

[59] Linz and Stepan propose this category as one of six very different possible constitution-making contexts and/or formulas which highlight the various problems that a specific context can cause for transition and democratic consolidation. See Juan J. Linz and Alfred Stepan, *Problems of Democratic Transition and Consolidation: Southern Europe, South America and Post-communist Europe* (Baltimore: Johns Hopkins University Press, 1996), 81–3.

Hungary's Pliable Constitution

Istvan Szikinger

Hungary is the only country among the emerging democracies in Central and Eastern Europe without a new constitution. This does not mean that constitutional values are absent in Hungary, nor is there a complete vacuum at the top of Hungary's continental-type hierarchical legal system. Indeed, Hungary's 1989 radical institutional reform coupled with free and fair political competition clearly merits the democratic label. Nevertheless, the current Constitution is far from being a product of deliberate institutional engineering. Instead, it is malleable, reflecting rather than framing the dynamic political current. If evolutionary development and institutional engineering could be seen as two models for implementing political and legal transformation,[1] Hungary has followed the first model. The result has been that the parliamentary system created by the 1989 constitutional amendments has been warped by the formation of a parliamentary 'super-majority' which can easily amend the Constitution further (and has) to suit its political goals. Power is somewhat balanced by a proactive Constitutional Court, but since the Constitution can be changed with such ease, most of the political power remains in the hands of the coalition parties.

Before delving into the analysis of the Hungarian Constitution, it is important to consider the central motives behind its design. András Sajó asserts that fear is a determining factor for legal codification at the highest level.[2] To a great extent, the guarantees

[1] See R. J. Lipkin, 'The Quest for the Common Good: Neutrality and Deliberative Democracy in Sunstein's Conception of American Constitutionalism', *Connecticut Law Review*, 26 (Spring 1994), 1039–92, at 1051. Lipkin cites Bruce A. Ackerman who referred to common law judges and lawyers preferring evolution to revolution, slow and unconscious adaptation to self-conscious institutional engineering ('The Common Law Constitution of John Marshall Harlan', 36 *NYL Sch. L. Rev.* 5, 6 (1991).

[2] András Sajó, *Az önkorlátozó hatalom* [Self-Restricting Power], (Budapest: Közgazdasági és Jogi Könyvkiadó, 1995), 17–24.

included in the 1989 amendments to the Constitution were indeed introduced to moderate fears. The opposition feared persecution by the still-powerful Hungarian Socialist Workers Party (HSWP) prior to free elections, while the communists (aware of their inevitable loss of authority) feared retaliation by their successors. Both fears were well founded despite the peacefully negotiated transition. But the safeguards laid down in the amended Constitution could not prevent power-grabbing by both sides. This is not to say that democratic principles were unheeded by the governing forces. Nevertheless, party politics still plays a more important role in preserving the rules of the game than the Constitution itself.

Hungarians did not reject adopting a post-communist constitution deliberately. But while there was some consensus on the final outcome of reforms—democracy—political actors could not agree on how to restrain the branches of power constitutionally. Although the Hungarian Constitution remains officially cited as 'Act No. XX of 1949 (as amended)', practically no provision survived unscathed after the numerous modifications—except the one declaring Budapest as the country's capital. Thus, Hungary has a formally old, substantially new constitution which was the result of the amendments passed by the outgoing communist parliament following the decisions made at the Roundtable Talks. The 1989 amendment (Act No. XXXI) changed not only an overwhelming majority of positive rules in the basic law, but also its spirit. The party-state regime enshrined in the 1949 communist Constitution was thus transformed into one structured along the principles of division of power and the liberal values of human rights and public power. Although the amendments have contributed to the consolidation of democracy in terms of restructuring power and institutions, the regime's legitimacy continues to be challenged. The Roundtable Talks were not intended to be a constitution-drafting body, and the amendments were neither publicly scrutinized or debated, nor approved by referendum. This led to a situation where the declaration of universally accepted constitutional values was codified and institutionalized with dubious political legitimacy.

Another problem with the flexibility of the Hungarian Constitution is that it cannot guarantee protection from majority tyranny, which is the major function of any liberal democratic constitution. Post-communist constitutional development in Hungary has reflected both the strengths and weaknesses of the political leadership. Recognition of major political trends and challenges and a focus on implementing reforms has been accompanied by selfish jockeying for position by political parties and interest groups. Without proper restraints on parliament, the dangers of monopolizing power and passing decisions for electoral gain loom large. Political actors try to reinforce their status within the given framework in which little attention is paid to long-term construction of a system providing a solid basis for exercising public power. In constitutional terms, the political superstructure functions according to popular trends while no real progress is made in the field of human rights apart from some modest results triggered by Constitutional Court decisions (data protection) or internationalized political aspirations (minority rights). However, even here an erosion of the constitutionalized foundational rules can be observed.

Constitutional Traditions

Before 1949, no written constitution had ever existed in Hungary and the communist dictatorship saw the Basic Law as a tool with which the ruling political forces could achieve their goals. And it was not even the most important tool. During the period of modest economic liberalization in the late 1960s, official declarations envisaged shifting the use of legal means for social planning and management in favour of using economic tools. In other words, law was perceived as one of the numerous means by which to pursue political ideals and interests. It is no wonder, then, that the Constitution, which inherently sets limits on political activity, was marginalized and seen simply as an example of communist rhetoric rather than an enforceable law.

By the end of the 1980s, the ruling elite's attitude changed slightly. The political opposition gained a voice in politics by focusing on constitutional issues, since legal reforms were seen as a legitimate tool for effecting lasting political change. In the late 1980s, the growing opposition began challenging the legitimacy of the communist leadership by exposing the contradictions between constitutional provisions and the reality of communist politics. Meanwhile, as the collapse of the totalitarian system became increasingly inevitable, Communist Party leaders and their supporters began crafting survival strategies. One initiative was preparing and adopting a new constitution with all the characteristics of a democratic basic law, built upon the principles of division of power and respect for human rights. To that end, intensive state-sponsored research was conducted which concluded that a new constitution was necessary for the 'reformed' communists to retain as much power as possible. Thus, cooperation towards change was enabled by the fact that both the old guard and the opposition aimed towards the same goal: constitutional reform.

Due to the particular structure of the communist regime, the foremost strategy for implementing Hungary's 'Constitutional Revolution'[3] was to create a constitutional court. Under the communist regime, judicial power had been seen simply as a subsystem of the centralized state, and therefore was substantially neglected. The independence of courts and judges was restricted by the centralized prosecution (*prokuratura*) structure, which was directly managed by the HSWP. Legislation was passed by the standing substitute body of parliament, the presidium, which represented the supreme authority within the state. The executive also played an outstanding role in shaping social relations. Behind these actors stood the determining force of socialist politics: the HSWP. Due to the programmatic, socialism-building character of the regime, legal values and court decisions were secondary to the whims of the party.

Hungary's constitutional revolution meant that the majority of rules enacted under communism and judicial personnel remained basically the same while the spirit of the old Constitution was changed radically. But the expectation that communist judges—accustomed to ignoring the Constitution—would suddenly treat it as the basis of law in the country was unrealistic. Even if judges could, confusion over the different interpretations of the law would lead to practical problems and would further weaken legal authority. Thus, in order to reconcile old provisions within a new constitutional order, the Constitutional Court was seen as the solution because of its separation from the traditional judiciary and its characteristic of having strong, quasi-legislative competence.

The Constitutional Revolution

The deputies voting in the 1989 Assembly were elected in 1985, that is, before perceivable political changes began. But by 1989, the Assembly had a different character from when it was initially elected. This was essential for the democratic transformation to take place, since the Communist Party's power was concentrated in the legislative and executive branches. The catalyst for this change was not only the growing opposition but the HSWP itself, which had simply ceased to exercise its powers as the central governing body, giving deputies a certain amount of freedom. Moreover, a small number of opposition deputies were elected after nascent democratic

---

[3] P. Paczolay, 'Constitutional Transition and Legal Continuity', *Connecticut Journal of International Law*, 8 (Spring 1993), 559–73.

parties and movements passed laws making it possible for constituencies to revoke their representatives and elect substitutes.

Initially, the HSWP charged the minister of justice with the task of drafting a set of constitutional guidelines in 1988–9. Although the draft preserved basic socialist values, it was innovative in its inclusion of human rights and the separation of power principle. The draft was scheduled to be discussed in parliament, but before debates could begin, the opposition attacked the parliament's lack of democratic political legitimacy which, it argued, is essential for adopting a new constitution. Parliament therefore changed its agenda, the government revoked the proposal (together with some accompanying draft laws concerning important political institutions, such as political parties), and the preparations for the Roundtable Talks began.

The Roundtable Talks brought together various political parties and factions that had emerged in the late 1980s to negotiate the transition. The Talks were established by the 10 June 1989 agreement between the Opposition Roundtable,[4] the HSWP, and the so-called 'Third Side', composed of organizations and movements characterized by the opposition as HSWP satellites.[5] Though the

---

[4] Naturally, organizations and movements protesting and fighting against totalitarian system of government were themselves divided as to the perspective on Hungary's post-communist development. However, a compromise could be reached and a strong, temporarily united opposition displayed a very resolute course aiming at removal of all residues of the past regime. The Opposition Roundtable was made up of the following groups, movements, and organizations: Bajcsy Zsilinszky Friends' Association, FIDESZ (Fiatal Demokraták Szövetsége—Union of Young Democrats), FKGP (Független Kisgazdapárt—Independent Smallholders' Party), KNDP (Kereszténydemokrata Néppárt—Christian Democratic People's Party), MDF (Magyar Demokrata Fórum—Hungarian Democratic Forum), MNP (Magyar Néppárt—Hungarian People's Party), MSZDP (Magyar Szociáldemokrata Párt—Hungarian Social Democratic Party), SZDSZ (Szabad Demokraták Szövetsége—Alliance of Free Democrats). The League of Free Trade Unions (Liga) took an observer status. Informally dominant positions within the Opposition Roundtable were occupied by the radically liberal SZDSZ and the moderate nationalist MDF.

[5] Members of the 'Third Side' were the following movements and organizations: the Leftist Alternative Association, the People's Patriotic Front, the Hungarian Democratic Youth Union, the Union of Hungarian Members of Resistance and of Antifascists, the Münnich Ferenc Society, and the National Council of Trade Unions. Some of the listed movements and organizations had actually been created by the ruling party as complements and 'colours' to the political centre in order to show a certain degree of democracy. However, by the time of the talks growing criticism toward and emphasis on independence from the Hungarian Socialist Party characterized many of the entities formerly serving the Party's interests without contradiction. Some of them (the Leftist Alternative, the Münnich

Talks were not meant to be a constituent assembly, certain modifications to the Constitution, a new democratic electoral law, and the depoliticization of institutions proved inevitable in the course of creating a framework for the transition.[6] The Roundtable was organized on three levels. Plenary sessions, composed of the highest-ranking party representatives, were to determine the general direction of negotiations and sanction the agreements reached. Intermediate discussions dealt with the substantial problems and preparations for the plenum's decisions. Finally, six expert committees were delegated the task of negotiating various problems of the transition. Only one was created to debate necessary constitutional amendments, while the others discussed the various problems of transition, such as modifying the criminal code and the electoral law.

The initial agreement to prevent parliament from engaging in constitution-making and legislation on politically crucial issues gradually developed into a mutually accepted situation in which the legal safeguards discussed and adopted during the Talks were not restricted to the period preceding free elections but also included long-term political goals. Thus, despite the carefully worded agreement and clearly defined structure of the Talks which prevented it from becoming a constitution-making body, discussion of constitutional amendments prevailed over all other issues and the Roundtable negotiations turned into a quasi-constitutional assembly. There were, in my opinion,[7] two main reasons behind this development. First of all, due to the natural interdependence between the many provisions of the basic law, it proved extraordinarily difficult to change selected elements of the complex constitution without affecting other sections. As a consequence, changing certain constitutional rules meant adapting related stipulations as well. The second and more important

---

Society) were organized with the open intention to form an opposition from the left. Despite expectation from the other two parties to the Roundtable Talks, the 'Third Side' did not just support the position of the HSWP but represented autonomous views concerning the main topics. Nevertheless, based on political realities, the 'Third Side' played a subordinate role in the course of the negotiations.

[6] András Sajó, 'The Roundtable Talks in Hungary', in Jon Elster (ed.), *The Roundtable Talks and the Breakdown of Communism* (Chicago: University of Chicago Press, 1996), 69–98.

[7] I participated in the Roundtable Talks as a member (representing the Patriotic Front within the 'Third Side' delegation) of probably the most important expert group, the one dealing with possible solutions guaranteeing the peaceful character of the political change.

reason was the temptation offered by the situation. Since no one
knew what the outcome of the democratic elections would be,
parties participating in the Roundtable Talks saw it as a legitimate
means for securing their interests in the new regime. No party to
the Roundtable resisted this temptation, and the Talks became a
de facto constitution-making and legislative forum.

It is ironic, then, that the opposition prevented parliament
from adopting a new constitution by arguing that it lacked political legitimacy, because the same arguments applied to the Roundtable Talks. There was no formal proof for popular support behind
any party participating in the Talks. Thus parliament, with
formal—and actually growing political—legitimacy, transferred
its powers to another decision-making body, which had neither
formal nor proven political authorization from the people to engage
in constitution-making. The agreement signed by participants on
18 September concerned major legislative issues of the transition
including proposals for a comprehensive constitutional amendment.
Parliament accepted the agreement reached at the Roundtable
Talks and sanctioned the proposed amendment without substantial changes to its essence. On 23 October 1989, the Hungarian
Republic replaced the People's Republic and the constitutional
amendment was promulgated.

As might be expected, the interests of the parties participating
in the Talks clashed constantly, not only between the three groups
represented, but even within the groups themselves. Debates
focused on formal institutions and on the sources of political
power. Under the communist regime political power was based,
not in state institutions, but in the Communist Party. Therefore,
distinguishing party politics from direct public power was an issue
of paramount importance during negotiations. While the HSWP
recognized and accepted this, it was still the most organized political force and hoped to preserve as much influence as possible.
Meanwhile, the opposition focused its attack on demolishing the
HSWP's economic dominance and most importantly its control
over workers' unions. It hoped to restructure the legal framework
such that the declining HSWP could not make use of its accumulated resources and all parties could participate in the elections
on an equal footing.

Nevertheless, the compromise reached at the Roundtable
favoured the HSWP. The most dramatic protest came from certain
opposition parties, including the Free Democrats, which refused to
sign the agreement and made their dissent public. After failing
to influence the outcomes of the Talks, this group proposed a

referendum, hoping to garner legitimacy through public support. It is interesting to note that none of the points raised in the referendum represented a conflict of political philosophy with the adopted constitutional amendments. Among the four questions posed by the referendum, the most important related to the method of presidential elections[8] and the institutionalized dominance of the Communist Party. The results of the 16 November 1989 referendum brought a slight victory to the initiators, the Free Democrats. But the dissenters' initiative was quashed by the still communist-dominated parliament, which responded by modifying the Constitution and repealing the result of the referendum. As a consolation, parliament placed further restrictions and obligations on the HSWP to appease the dissenters' claim that the Communist Party maintained clear dominance over all other parties. The issue of presidential elections resurfaced in 1990 with the passage of Act No. XVI, restoring the direct election of the president. But when the new, democratically elected parliament came to power, it changed the rules again by reinstating presidential election by the parliament (Act No. XL of 1990), and the president was finally elected by parliament on 3 August 1990.

Originally, the result of the Roundtable Talks should have represented a 'quick fix' of the Constitution, touching upon only those provisions absolutely necessary for managing the transition. This would have been the only solution possible, since none of the parties to the Talks had a clear mandate to engage in constitution-making. Reforming the electoral law and its constitutional implications was, of course, unavoidable. As Kálmán Kulcsár[9] confirmed, the task of the parliament was strictly limited to passing acts necessary to ensure the peaceful character of the transition.[10] But despite these statements, in the course of negotiations the 'quick fix' turned into an interim constitution, which is still in effect today. Having been in force for so many years, there is a general agreement that even if a new constitution is adopted formally, it will need to rely heavily on the one currently in force.

---

[8] Actually, the question on presidential elections was about the date of the process. However, the Constitution in force stipulated that if the president had been elected before parliamentary elections, he would be authorized by referendum. Following the commencement of the new term of the legislature the power to elect the president belonged to the parliament. The Free Democrats and their supporters wanted to prevent direct election of a popular socialist candidate (Imre Pozsgay) by postponing the date and thus shifting the power to parliament.

[9] Kálmán Kulcsár was minister of justice in 1989.

[10] *Parliamentary Records* (1989), 4901–2.

From a procedural point of view it is true that the Hungarian Constitution lacks evidence of popular support. On the other hand, continuity can also be explained by emphasizing the solid, basically unchallenged authority of the supreme law. There is a piece of truth in both statements. On the one hand, it is possible that the parties participating in the Roundtable Talks succeeded in grasping the *Zeitgeist* and created a lasting political framework. As mentioned earlier, comprehensive research had been conducted before the draft Constitution of the Ministry of Justice was elaborated in 1988; this was used as a basis throughout negotiations, even by the opposition. Another undeniable fact is that the Constitution was the result of an agreement between parties that dominated politics and thus had proven their popular legitimacy. This has led to a situation where interpretation and necessary constitutional modifications can be made without enormous difficulty. On the other hand, the Constitution remained the political tool it was under the communist regime without impacting significantly the relations between government and civil society. As István Kukorelli stated: 'The present-day constitution is the result of a bargain between the old and new humanistic professional elite, and it was sanctioned by the old Parliament. The fact that the subject of the constitution is narrowed down still causes damage to the credibility and social acceptance of the constitution.'[11]

The 1989 Amendments in Force

Changing the Constitution from a government tool to a supreme law constraining public power remains the crucial problem for constitutionalism in Hungary. A flexible constitution reflecting rather than framing politics undermines any institutional engineering conducted by the framers because the determining features of the constitutionalized power structure are disregarded.[12] Stephen Holmes perceives an even greater danger, however, in an overly rigid constitutional framework and actually prescribes vesting more power in parliament to allow flexibility in adapting institutions

[11] *Constitutionalism in East Central Europe* (Bratislava: Czecho-Slovak Committee of the European Cultural Foundation, 1994), 74.

[12] See László Trocsányi, 'Az alkotmanyozas elvi kerdesei' (Questions Related to the Principles of Constitution-Making), in Károly Tóth (ed.), *Alkotmány és Jogtudomány* (Constitution and Jurisprudence) (Szeged: JATE Press, 1996), 167–85.

to the changing political environment.[13] But the Hungarian experience illustrates that problems with consolidating democracy do not arise simply from an 'anti-parliamentary feeling'. Instead, Hungary's overly strong parliament has become supra-constitutional. While not denying that the Hungarian institution designers succeeded in introducing some solid elements into the constitutional system, the fact that eleven modifications to the Basic Law have been adopted since the initial 1989 amendments reflects the fact that parliament possesses constitutional authority, placing political-legislative interests above all other institutions.

Constitution-making is the exclusive power of the Hungarian Parliament. Two-thirds of all MPs can introduce a change into the system of provisions determining the scope, limits, and structure of the exercise of public power. The only restriction on this competence was imposed by the 1989 Act (No. XVII) on Referendum and People's Initiative. Section 7 of the Act requires confirmation of a new constitution by referendum. Of course, even this rule can be repealed at any time by a two-thirds majority.[14] While these regulations are fairly flexible, constitution drafters did not intend to create a system in which constitutional amendments required little effort to adopt. Indeed, the amendment procedure alone would be insufficient to create what some observers have called the parliamentary 'constitutional dictatorship'[15] in Hungary. This situation emerged as a direct result of the electoral law, the party balance it created, and the process of coalition-building which ensued.

The Constitution stipulates that 'parties shall not directly exercise public power and, accordingly, no party shall direct any state organ. With a view to separation of parties from public power, positions and public offices incompatible with party membership shall be specified by law.'[16] The 1989 Act No. XXXIII on Functioning and Finances of Political Parties introduced further guarantees to prevent the return of one-party rule. Nevertheless, separating political parties from state organization has not abolished party dominance over the state. Instead, the one-party system has been

[13] Stephen Holmes, 'Back to the Drawing Board', *East European Constitutional Review*, 2/1 (1993), 21–5.

[14] The Constitutional Court reinforced the perspective on absolute supremacy of parliament in several decisions. One of them forbade implicit modification of the basic law by referendum although such a negative condition has not been listed in the otherwise exhaustive and categorical regulation of the 1989 Referendum Act (2/1993 (I. 22) AB hat).

[15] See Andrew Arato, 'Elections, Coalitions and Constitutionalism in Hungary', *East European Constitutional Review*, 3/3–4 (Summer/Fall 1994), 29.

[16] Constitution as amended 1989, s. 3, para. 3.

replaced by a multi-party structure, in which representatives of the civil society, professional organizations, and other interest groups nevertheless remain outside the decision-making process.[17] This situation exists despite legislation promoting the interaction between state and civil society. Section 27 of the 1987 Act on Legislation (No. XI) is still in force requiring coordination with interested social organizations and representative entities in order to learn their opinion prior to submitting drafts to the government. But this provision is often disregarded in practice.

At the same time, the electoral law makes it difficult for new parties to gain access to parliament. Although the proportions have changed radically, broadly the same parties of the 1990 parliament gained seats after the 1994 and 1998 elections. As most basic institutions, the parliamentary electoral system was a product of the Roundtable Talks. It is a mixed scheme based on a combination of individual constituencies and party lists. In addition, by counting residual votes not resulting in mandates, a compensatory scheme has been introduced to correct certain deficiencies of the system. The electoral system prefers big parties and prevents fragmentation of parliamentary representation. Nevertheless, electoral coalitions and list consolidation are allowed. It is also possible for independent candidates to run in elections, but only in individual constituencies.

The 1990 elections rendered the ex-communist party, the Socialists (MSZP), powerless, but left the splintered opposition to resolve its internal tensions. As a consequence, with the aim of consolidating the nationalist-conservative bloc, a three-party coalition (controlling 241 seats in parliament) was formed between the Hungarian Democratic Forum (MDF), the Independent Smallholders' Party (FKGP), and the Christian Democratic People's Party (KNDP), which became the basis for forming the government. On the one hand, the new establishment had gained unquestionable legitimacy because of the reflection of the public support expressed through the votes. On the other hand, the institutional structure relied on the 1989 constitutional amendment which was

---

[17] Even bodies requiring by nature a high degree of independence, such as supervisory boards of public media, are occupied by representatives of political parties. The fight for and regulation of the mass media was one of the most contentious issues of the transition of power. The Act (No. I) of 1996 on Radio and Television Broadcasting repeatedly declares the freedom of the press, while simultaneously giving the power to nominate members of the board exclusively to parliamentary parties. This was contested by FIDESZ-MPP (now in power) in 1998, but this only led to calls for a fairer balance of political appointees.

elaborated by unelected delegations of self-designated political actors. Had a constitutional assembly been established by the new parliament, there could have been an appropriate forum for legitimizing the basic law. However, the newcomers to power made no serious attempt to limit their power for the sake of legitimacy.

Almost immediately after the new parliament was elected, one of the most important guarantees preventing the arbitrary exercise of power adopted in the 1989 amendments to the Constitution was repealed. First, parliament repealed Article 8, paragraph 2 of the Constitution, which required a two-thirds majority for adopting any law on basic rights and duties of citizens. This move was based on a compromise between the two largest parties, the MDF and SZDSZ, in order to prevent paralysing the legislative process since the government did not have a qualified majority in the house. In exchange for the concession, the SZDSZ was given the right to nominate Arpad Goncz as president, even though it was not technically part of the ruling coalition. With the abolition of the general provision on the required two-thirds majority for amending laws on basic rights specific rules demanding the same have not been repealed. In other words, qualified majority is, as before, needed to enact, modify, and repeal norms on basic rights if so provided by particular sections of the Constitution. The rights of paramount importance (freedom of press, assembly, association, etc.) remained in that protected circle of rules. The possible explanation of any effort to make human rights legislation easier by simplifying the procedure can be dismissed because of the fact that no such law-making has taken place except some acts of parliament passed in response to Constitutional Court decisions or international obligations.

Another safeguard included in the 1989 amendments to the Constitution separated military from law enforcement agents. Accordingly, the first democratically formed government put reorganization of the border guards (who perform simultaneously both military and policing functions) on the agenda. The government's intended policy was to convert the border guards into a purely law-enforcement agency. However, the military lobbied to retain the duality of that agency and a constitutional amendment for the exception was passed by parliament in 1993. The army's interest in preserving border guards within its scope of command can be explained by the natural desire of any power agency not to lose influence frequently identified with importance. In addition to that, a substantial decrease of military personnel preceded the decision on border guard service accompanied by a confidence-building withdrawal of

regular troops from the frontiers. All these were meant to be coun-
terbalanced by keeping the border guard service as an agency not
so explicitly belonging to the army but, at the same time, performing
defence duties in temporary subordination to it if necessary.

Even the Constitutional Court proved to be weak against the
government's efforts to use supreme law to satisfy political and
bureaucratic needs. In one of its early decisions (3/1990 (III. 4) AB
hat), the Court ruled that excluding citizens living abroad from
participating in elections was unconstitutional. In an effort to
avoid difficulties derived from extending suffrage to citizens abroad,
a government-sponsored constitutional amendment was adopted
by parliament amending the Constitution, and finally the discriminatory provision was expressly confirmed by the supreme law,
thus overriding the Constitutional Court decision. This amendment,
actually, was introduced by the previous communist-dominated
parliament but none of the numerous subsequent modifications
has changed its substance. This fact refers to a silent consensus
among all parties regarding avoidance of taking the risk of opening the gates for an unknown and unforeseeably voting group of
the electorate, apart from the obvious convenience of not having
the organizational burden of collecting the ballots from abroad.

Generally speaking, narrow partisan interests dominate parliamentary debates in Hungary excluding any chance for outside actors
to have a significant impact on decision-making. In conformity with
the 'closed circuit' character of high-level state activities, there
are almost no provisions on external channels connecting deputies
with other branches of government or the society at large. National
and ethnic minorities cannot delegate deputies to parliament in spite
of a resolute stipulation of the 1993 Act (No. LXXVII) on Rights of
National and Ethnic Minorities, which expressly prescribes such
representation. Attila Ágh describes the underlying contradiction
of decision-making by political parties in Eastern and Central
Europe, which is clearly illustrated in the case of the Hungarian
legislature:

the weaker the parties are socially, the more they try to prevent the other
social and political actors from entering the decision-making process. But
the more the other actors are missing, the more the parties themselves
are weakened, since it is only the organized meso-system (interest groups)
and micro-system (civil society association) that give them a solid social
background.

Ágh perceives 'overparticization' and 'overparlamentarization', that
is, expropriation of almost all decision-making powers by parties

in parliament, as transitory features of the early democratic institutionalization process.[18] Of course, it was not the parliamentary powers as such which caused problems for the democratic, constitutional development, but rather the lack of proper integration of the legislation into a broader system of expressing and representing non-partisan interests which casts doubts on the fully democratic nature of parliament. With no institution checking its power, the parliament can be dominated by the governing party or parties to the extent of endangering the essence of separation of powers.

In Hungary, the power accumulated by the ruling coalition and the flexibility of institutional design has meant spending countless parliamentary sessions debating problems of secondary importance (such as the mode of electing a relatively weak president) and, more importantly, raises the question of the legitimacy of the regime. Referenda are, of course, not a perfect prescription either. But suppressing lawfully prepared initiatives calling for a referendum[19] is a clear rejection of democratic principles.

Constitutional Court

Complying with constitutional requirements in Hungary today necessarily includes respecting the rulings of the Constitutional Court. Moreover, these rulings are based not only on the actual text of the basic law, but on the interpretation of an 'invisible constitution', that is the general principles of constitutionalism as well.[20] Thus, in addition to the text itself, the actual meaning of the Constitution includes also the jurisprudence of the Constitutional Court. In this way, the Court represents an important check on the parliament's power monopoly. Admittedly, the parliament can amend the Constitution when the Court declares its actions or legislation unconstitutional. But even when that happens, it

---

[18] Attila Ágh, 'The Development of the East Central European Party Systems: From "Movements" to "Cartels"', in Máté Szabó (ed.), *The Challenge of Europeanization in the Region: East Central Europe* (Budapest: Hungarian Political Science Association and the Institute for Political Sciences of the Hungarian Academy of Sciences, 1996), 247.

[19] In addition to the stymied referendum prior to the adoption of the 1989 constitutional amendments, two other important referenda were undermined by parliament, as happened with the one of the Workers' Party on NATO membership aspirations.

[20] L. Sólyom, concurring opinion to the decision of the Constitutional Court on abolition of the death penalty (23/1990 (X. 31) AB hat).

emphasizes the importance of the Court's role in synchronizing state actions and the basic law.

The Court's role in balancing the legislature's power is particularly apparent in how the Court has influenced the application of rights. Wojciech Sadurski presents convincing arguments for rethinking the conventional wisdom that constitutional courts are the almost exclusive guardians of basic rights,[21] and he is right in questioning perspectives that overemphasize the advantages of judicial review as opposed to majoritarian decision-making by parliament.[22] Although the Hungarian experience does not defy his conclusions, certain practical considerations render the situation more complex. The Hungarian state is structured in such a way that formally the president (who is elected by parliament) is not part of the executive power and the government, too, is responsible to the legislature. Therefore, according to the logic of this system, the same political parties are behind all three institutions and legislation often involves simply translating government activity into law. As a result, the Court is the only institution which is left to review and criticize these policies.

The work of the Constitutional Court proved to be especially important in defining and protecting its own interpretation of citizens' rights. The 1989 amendment rewrote the structure and particular provisions on human rights. Individual and political freedoms were given most of the attention and careful safeguarding, while detailed guarantees for socio-economic rights that had existed under the communist regime were replaced by simple declarations, such as protecting the right to work, the right to equal and due compensation for work, and to other goods and values, in the amended text of the Constitution. Undeniable differences between these positive rights and individual or political freedoms have led many experts to the conclusion that, despite the actual wording of the Constitution, economic, social, and cultural rights are better understood as tasks of the state without corresponding enforceable subjective claims of the citizens. As a result, constitutional rights would vary depending on the level and methods of enforceability.[23] But there are also numerous advocates for attributing principally

---

[21] Wojciech Sadurski, 'The Tension between the Division of Power and Constitutional Rights (with Special Emphasis on Socioeconomic Rights)', paper presented at the Conference on Democratic Consolidation in Eastern Europe at the European University Institute, Florence (24–5 Jan. 1997), 24–7.

[22] Ibid. 10–13.

[23] W. Osiatynski, 'Rights in New Constitutions of East Central Europe', *Columbia Human Rights Law Review*, 26/1 (1994), 111–66, at 140.

equal legal force in principle to all constitutional provisions, and therefore opting to exclude economic, social, and cultural rights from constitutions since they cannot be enforced properly by courts.[24] This has been the policy of the Hungarian Constitutional Court, which has contributed to developing the legal character of institutions to promote the delivery of such rights. The Constitutional Court passed several rulings addressing the problem of the right to an income conforming with the quantity and quality of work performed. Decisions usually rely on the connected constitutional provision requiring equal pay for equal work. However, there have been cases where even independent examination of due payment has been deliberated. For example, an initiative was filed to the Constitutional Court against certain provisions of the 1996 Service Relations of Members of Armed Organs Act. The act itself determines a salary system for military and law enforcement officers. The policy is built upon a basic salary unit which is to be defined yearly depending on economic conditions, but the legislature decided to introduce the new, naturally more advantageous, salary system only in 1999. This is clearly a case of violation of the constitutional provision on due payment, whereby a purely legal analysis can lead to a decision. Since there is no deadline for Constitutional Court proceedings, the initiative is one of those on the waiting list. Time seems to be the factor solving the problem, though the Court has the power to decide on retroactive force for its rulings.

Another notorious case involving socio-economic rights was the so-called 'Bokros Package', which was nothing more than a set of financial decisions dictated by the government. No comprehensive social policy discussions had taken place before the Cabinet passed this resolution in March 1995. It was only after the 'Bokros Package' was adopted (and after the minister of welfare resigned in protest at the austerity measures) that the ministers examined the problems of implementing the resolution. Wherever a law was found to contradict the Bokros Package, the cabinet found ways to modify those laws in order to accommodate the new welfare programme. Although their approach was most likely in line with economic principles, they acted in violation of fundamental principles of the rule of law. The Constitutional Court gave a rather prompt response to the government's activity by repealing substantial provisions of the Package (43/1995 (VI. 30) AB hat). The Court acknowledged the right of the state to change social policies even

---

[24] Cass Sunstein, 'Against Positive Rights', *East European Constitutional Review*, 2/1 (1993), 36.

if they negatively impact upon public welfare. But, according to the ruling, the state's activities were unconstitutional though the Court reasoned many points through the concept of legal security rather than citing concrete constitutional provisions.

András Sajó published the deepest analytical criticism against the results of judicial review: 'The Hungarian Constitutional Court, in its early decisions, declared that its mission was to restore the rule of law. Ironically, it ended up propounding a concept of material justice, the sworn enemy of the formal rationality of the rule of law. Material justice will undermine the market economy and limit freedom of contract.'[25] Without discussing the particular arguments raised by Sajó, I would like to point out that the activities of the state challenged by the Court cannot be characterized simply as steps toward market economy. Indeed, it was the government that overstepped its jurisdiction by distributing social benefits based on needs of recipients instead of citizens' equality. Therefore, although it is true that by going too far in search of social goods the Constitutional Court can easily turn into a policy-making body, the Court's application of the Constitution irrespective of its implications for social (or any other) ideology is the most effective means to curb misuse of state power. Thus the Court's action reflects the necessity of maintaining a strong judicial body to counterbalance the powers often misused by executive-operated legislation. On the other hand, there are certainly inherent dangers in authorizing a court 'tainted by an important accountability deficit'[26] to review such a wide scale of decisions made by other branches, but in Hungary this is mitigated by the fact that any constitutional modification can overrule the findings of the Constitutional Court.

Section 70/K of the Constitution stipulates that all public authority decisions that violate basic rights may be challenged before courts. This applies to classical freedoms and political rights as well as to economic, social, and cultural rights. However, there are substantial problems in the field of interpretation and implementation of the constitutional provision to which it refers. Important cases remain outside the scope of judicial review because the legislature failed to pass appropriate procedural and competence regulations.

Following a decision of the Constitutional Court (32/1990 (XII. 12) AB hat), an amendment to the Administrative Procedure Act

[25] András Sajó, 'How the Rule of Law Killed Hungarian Welfare Reform', *East European Constitutional Review*, 5/1 (1996), 41.

[26] Sadurski, 'The Tension between the Division of Power and Constitutional Rights', 26.

(Act No. IV of 1957 as amended) opened the way for the ordinary courts to review administrative acts by a general clause. The Constitutional Court ruled that until specific laws on the review of administrative decisions are passed, the Constitution must be implemented directly. However, the Court used the term 'resolution' referring to the acts open to challenge instead of 'decision' of the relevant constitutional text. This distinction is important because measures as opposed to formal decisions (resolutions) do not fall into the category of acts open to judicial review by virtue of narrowing down the original scope of constitutional protection. At the same time, a great number of measures have an impact on very elementary human rights including the right to life and human dignity. Police, for example, do not issue any formal document on deprivation of liberty for public security purposes. As a consequence, these and many other interventions into rights of paramount importance may not trigger any significant act of revision apart from the complaints procedure, leaving the whole case within the police organization.

The Constitutional Court itself has the power to deal with constitutional complaints on alleged violations of constitutional rights (section 48 of the 1989 Act No. XXXII on the Constitutional Court). However, the decision to be reached has to focus on constitutional conformity of the rules applied instead of the behaviour challenged. Thus, this remedy has a secondary importance taking into consideration that posterior constitutional examination of legal norms can be initiated by anybody without satisfying specific requirements (e.g. exhaustion of all other remedies) attached to constitutional complaint against individual violations of rights. The leading principle of basic rights' protection in the Hungarian Constitution is the provision of section 8, paragraph 2 reflecting and practically repeating the words of the German 'Grundgesetz' by stating that in the Republic of Hungary Acts of Parliament regulate fundamental rights and obligations, but even they must not impose any limitations on the essential contents of fundamental rights. The Hungarian Constitutional Court invoked this principal standard when abolishing the death penalty. Referring to section 54, paragraph 1 of the Constitution, the Court ruled that the death penalty was not compatible with a legal system based on the outstanding importance of human life and dignity. The Court reasoned in its decision on abolishment of capital punishment: 'Legal norms on deprivation of life and human dignity by death penalty do not only restrict the essential contents of fundamental rights to life and human dignity but they permit the total and irreparable destruction of life and human dignity, and thus the right guaranteeing them. Therefore the unconstitutionality of the said regulations is declared by the Court and they are repealed' (23/1990 (X. 31) AB hat). It was underlined in the reasoning that human life and dignity were inseparable and form together an integral basic right which is the source and precondition of numerous other rights. One could expect far-reaching consequences for the complete legal system by the extension of the *ratio decidendi* to other pieces of legislation on activities of state organs involving possible use of lethal violence. Although the Court did not go into comprehensive analyses of the issue as it relates to problems outside the scope of the death penalty, it is clear that any 'official killing' is contrary to the constitutional right to life and human dignity. By declaring the unconstitutionality of the death penalty because of the obvious loss of the essential content of the right to life in case of killing by the representatives of the state, the Court inevitably implied that all actions with a similar possible result were to be refrained from in the course of exercising public power within the framework of the Constitution.

Contentious problems emerged in the field of Church–state relations. On the one hand, representatives of the Church supported the transformation process, especially by establishing good relations with conservative and nationalist parties. It is also true that restoring real freedom of religion needed affirmative action because of the damage caused during its suppression under the totalitarian regime. On the other hand, the principle of separation of Church and state needed to be cautiously approached. The parliament declared and legally guaranteed freedom of religion in the 1990 Act (No. IV) based on the corresponding constitutional stipulation. Another act (No. XXXII from the year 1991) provided for returning expropriated assets or compensating the Church for unconstitutional interference with property rights under communism. These two logical conclusions, however, led to many conflicts in practice. Many local schools had been owned by the Catholic Church prior to communist rule. When they were returned to the Church, freedom of religion became restricted when no alternatives for education existed for atheists and non-Catholics. In the Court's ruling on this issue, it asserted that the state had an obligation to compensate those who suffered from injustice caused by the communist regime, but at the same time, the state also was obliged to ensure not only the theoretical but also the real possibility of providing education according to the belief of those concerned (4/1993 (II. 12) AB hat). The Court ruled that the state had to organize the structure and control the curricula of public schools so that freedom of religion should be respected by conveying relevant information in an objective, critical, and pluralistic manner (4/1993 (II. 12) AB hat). In another decision the Court pointed out that 'Separation of church and state does not mean that the particular features of churches may not be taken into consideration by the state and that the state must regulate the legal status of the "church" in an identical manner with those of other societal organizations' (8/1993 (II. 27) AB hat). That is, distinctive treatment of the Church can be perceived as affirmative action in order to enhance conditions of religious freedom.

Thus, due to the instability of the Constitution, the Hungarian Court necessarily plays a more visible and political role than similar institutions in other countries. By relying on the 'invisible constitution', that is, the principles of constitutionalism, judges actually participate in shaping the real legal foundations of public power. This activist position, despite strong efforts of the Court itself to limit its scope of review, cannot be separated from political functions. Although the judges have no specific party affiliation, their sympathies can be identified through their method of selecting cases from the files, and providing for timely feedback to legislative actions certainly put the body into the position of a quasi-upper house of parliament.

Local Administration

One of the sharpest debates of the transition related to the reorganization of local administration. Since no substantial agreement on the structure of local government had been reached during Roundtable Talks, re-engineering local government became a priority of the new democratic regime. All political forces agreed that it was necessary to discard the inherited Soviet-type system of councils which served the interests of the Communist Party and to create local self-governments relatively independent of the central government. After the 1990 elections, the conservative governing coalition of the first democratic parliament introduced significant decentralizing regulations, but still hoped to maintain centralized control as much as possible. Liberal parties fought for expanded freedom for local governments with powers given mainly to municipal organs, but their relatively small numbers in parliament initially prevented them from influencing policy. But after liberal parties prevailed in the local elections, the legitimacy of their position increased and, in the end, a strong system of local self-government emerged displaying a resolute counterbalance to central administration. The result was that local governments gained broad powers and independence in the field of economic activities. They were entitled to levy taxes according to acts of parliament, and to engage in any business not endangering their actual mission. Section 77, paragraph 1 of the 1990 Act (No. LXV) on Local Governments declared: 'The local government offers public services. It disposes of its own property, and manages its budgetary revenues and expenses independently.'

Nevertheless, since the adoption of the 1990 Act, a gradual but resolute recentralization process can been observed. Many powers granted to local bodies by the original act have not really been transferred from central state control. One example is the responsibility for public security. The 1990 Act declared that municipal authorities were to provide for local public security. However, no efforts have been made to create a legal framework for local policing. The 1994 Police Act (No. XXXIV) confirmed that local authorities did not have the competence to maintain law enforcement agencies. The only powers granted to local governments by the Police Act were to offer opinions concerning the establishment, reorganization, or abolishment of police units in their territory, and ask for a review of the public security situation from the local chief of police. Enquiries into activities can also be initiated by local governments but the final decision must be made by the appropriate police superior. Moreover, police are not obliged and furthermore do not have the right to enforce local statutes. According to section 97, paragraph 1, subparagraph a of the Police Act, local statutes are not normative legal acts in terms of the act.

Although centralization is often considered to run counter to the goal of democratization, the Hungarian case shows that decentralization does not necessarily result in a more open administration. Once example of this is the Constitutional Court's ruling to repeal certain provisions of the Local Government Act which had given local representative bodies the freedom to order closed sessions if necessary. It turned out that a number of municipalities used this power to exclude publicity without proper justification. The Court ruled that: 'data processed by state organs or local governments which are not personal and which may not be declared confidential on the basis of statutory regulations are classified as accessible to everyone. Only this way can the requirement that citizens be given access to all data of public interest be satisfied' (32/1992 (V. 29) AB hat).

Efforts to Adopt a New Constitution

The 1989 amendment reflected the compromise made between communists and the opposition in order to initiate political and economic reforms. Although this agreement stipulated the temporary character of the amended Constitution, further constitutional development proved slow-going. After the first free parliamentary elections, the governing coalition showed little interest in constitution drafting.[27] Following the 1994 elections, attention was again focused on the prospect of adopting a new constitution because the governing coalition that was forged between the Socialists and liberal Free Democrats enjoyed an absolute majority in parliament, with which it could conveniently introduce any amendments to the Constitution it wished, or even adopt an entirely new constitution. Several relatively insignificant constitutional amendments were introduced by the coalition, but questions were continually raised by the opposition regarding the coalition's legitimacy to undertake constitution-drafting unilaterally. In response to political pressure, the coalition ultimately waived its right to modify further the Basic Law. This moratorium placed on constitutional amendments was seen as a chivalrous act on the part of the ruling coalition as a concession to smaller parliamentary parties that would otherwise be left out of the constitution-making process.

In 1995 the Ministry of Justice produced a working paper which proposed three options for adopting a new constitution in an inclusive way in order to avoid a situation in which the government coalition would become a 'constitutional dictator'.[28] Some of the measures proposed required more than one parliament to vote on constitutional amendments and instituted the need to gain support for constitutional amendments through referenda. These suggestions prompted parliament to pass an amendment to the Constitution in the summer of 1995, which increased the quorum required to adopt constitutional amendments from three-quarters of all members of parliament to four-fifths. Next, the parliament created a Constitutional Commission consisting of an equal number of representatives from each parliamentary party. In order approve a constitutional draft, support must be given by five parties (out of the six parliamentary parties) and two-thirds of the delegates

[27] R. R. Ludwikowski, 'Constitution Making in the Countries of Former Soviet Dominance', *Georgia Journal of International and Comparative Law*, 23/2 (1993), 155–267, at 230–6.

[28] See Arato, 'Elections, Coalitions and Constitutionalism in Hungary', 26–32.

of the twenty-five-member Commission.[29] If no agreement is reached on a particular issue, the provision of the amended Constitution will remain. Finally, all the draft provisions must be approved by a plenum of the parliament according to the general rule (two-thirds majority). It was a step towards true democratic maturity when the governing parties decided not to use and politically misuse their qualified majority for adopting a new constitution at will. At the same time, restricting the membership of the Commission to parliamentary parties, instead of opening its doors to representatives of civil society organizations and national minorities for example, reveals the Hungarian state's tendency to favour party-dominated parliamentary rule.

By April 1995 an agreement had been reached by the Commission on the guidelines for a new constitution. All but one party approved the new set of guiding principles for adopting a new democratic Hungarian constitution. The document was published and the Commission allotted forty-five days for the public to make comments on the draft. About 1,000 remarks and proposals arrived at the Commission including those of experts and organizations who were directly requested to communicate their opinions. Of the comments received, the suggestions that were eventually included into the draft were determined on a party-interest basis. That is, proposals that further concentrated power in the parliament (for instance, by decreasing the influence of referenda and other forms of direct democracy) were incorporated into the draft, while other proposals were largely ignored. Parliamentary party preferences often seemed petty and hypocritical of their past actions in the legislature. For instance, the highly publicized controversy surrounding presidential elections emerged only after consensus had been reached that the head of state should play a mainly representative role without real powers to interfere with parliamentary decisions, which makes the method of presidential elections rather superfluous. Another contentious issue that arose was the proposal to reorganize the one-house parliament into two chambers. The upper house would include representatives of civic organizations, religious leaders, and minority representatives, thus balancing the power of political parties in the political process. Advocates of the bicameral legislature argued that the current representative system built exclusively on territorial and party interests was inadequately democratic and pointed to the low quality of legislation. The

---

[29] The chairman of the Commission is the president of the parliament without the right to vote. In the meantime a new party, the Hungarian Democratic People's Party has been formed within parliament and included in the preparatory scheme. However, the process is practically stagnating.

introduction of an upper house, they contended, could serve as a check on the legislative process.[30] Moreover, this option was supported by traditionalists, since an upper house existed in the pre-war regime.[31] Nevertheless, the draft was not changed to accommodate these demands. At the last minute, the Socialist Party blocked constitutional preparation in June 1996 by demanding that social rights and a declaration on social commitment of the state be included in the constitutional draft. Although this demand might seem to correspond with the interests of any socialist-leaning party, the Hungarian Socialist Party had endorsed economic policies of its own government which were not only criticized by the opposition for being socially indifferent, but were also declared unconstitutional by the Constitutional Court which repealed numerous provisions of the legislative package curbing social rights.

On 27 June 1996 the plenary session voted on the draft guidelines. Two hundred and fifty-seven affirmative votes were needed to adopt the draft as a basis for future work. But, to the great surprise and dismay of many (even from within the Socialist Party[32]), a number of Socialist Party ministers and party leaders abstained from voting, which amounted to a wholesale rejection of the draft. With only 252 votes supporting the coordinated proposal, the constitution-drafting process was hamstrung. Although the guidelines were finally passed on 21 December 1996 (Res. No. 119/1996 (XII. 21) OGY), growing disagreements over procedural and substantial issues mean that the hope that a new constitution will be adopted in Hungary is fading again. The government lifted its self-imposed moratorium on constitutional amendment when (after consulting with all the parliamentary parties and gaining their approval) several constitutional amendments were drafted in a bill in May 1997 (No. T/4300). With this decision, the Socialists and Free Democrats wilfully destroyed the fragile structure of constitution-drafting which included all parliamentary parties. None of the proposed amendments included in the bill was absolutely necessary for the functioning of the state. But the amendments reflected the inverse logic of Hungary's parliamentary regime, in which the Constitution is adapted to the needs of planned legislation instead of shaping the latter in compliance with the Basic Law. These

[30] K. Kulcsár, 'Alkotmányozás, politikai pártok, társadalom' [Constitution-Making, Political Parties and Society], *Belügyi Szemle*, 34/6 (1996), 3–12; M. Samu, 'Constitution-Making and the Second Chamber (Senate)', *Belügyi Szemle*, 34/6 (1996), 13–22.

[31] Sajó, *Az önkorlátozó hatalom*, 192–7.

[32] The premier was absent at the time of voting but he indicated support for and agreement with those blocking the progress.

developments also confirm the conclusion prevailing among constitutional lawyers in Hungary that constitution-making is ruled by a small monopoly of political elites.[33]

Conclusion

The real chances for success in adopting a brand new Constitution seem to be very weak. This is not a tragedy with regard to the commonly confessed philosophy of constitution-drafting: indeed, there is no emergency requiring a new constitution in Hungary since the amended Constitution does in fact satisfy the needs for democracy. But emphasizing the positive achievements of the Constitution in force does not exclude, of course, criticism concerning certain provisions and proposing some significant changes within the institutions of public power. Although some of these problems could be solved through Constitutional Court rulings, others are far more problematic. For instance, the current arrangement of representation does not necessarily satisfy the needs of society as a whole. Political parties proved to be unable to integrate, or even to convey and express, legitimate interests of non-partisan organizations, movements, and groups. The poor quality of legislation is just a symptom of this underlying problem. This seems to demonstrate that Hungarian constitutional history resembles the classical constitutional principle of rejecting monopolistic power even if exercised by an elected body. Parliament has to play a major role in democratic transformation but it should do so only embedded in a wider range of constitutional institutions ensuring a high degree of responsibility toward a variety of interests worth taking into consideration during debates on issues of paramount importance for the whole society. Any other endeavour in the field of institutional engineering would continue the erosion of constitutional values. Thus, although the very existence of the Constitution and its particular wording has contributed to democratic consolidation, this document has not reached the level of importance it should have. This article has shown that this is not a problem within the text of the Constitution, but rather a problem of its political environment.

[33] I. Kukorelli, *Az alkotmányozás évtizede* [Decade of Constitution-Making] (Budapest: Korona Kiadó, 1995), 38–44; I. Somogyvári, 'Alkotmányozás Magyarországon 1994–1996' [Constitution-Making in Hungary, 1994–1996], *Társadalmi Szemle*, LI/10 (1996), 30–51, at 35–7; I. Lövétei, 'Alkotmányozás mint legitimáció?' [Constitution-Making as Legitimization?], *Politikatudományi Szemle*, V/2 (1996), 75.

....

16

....

Legitimacy: The Price of a Delayed Constitution in Poland

Mirosław Wyrzykowski

To the outside observer, the fact that Poland has a relatively consolidated democracy and that it was very late in adopting a constitution may seem to indicate that constitutions have been relatively insignificant in the country's democratic history. Indeed Poland's case shows a long and protracted process of constitution-making. Although the Constitution was formally adopted in 1997 it was preceded by years of intense political struggle, which had its origins in the events of August 1980. The story of Poland's constitution-making process is about the ability to reach compromises without which it would have been impossible to have moved that process forward. Issues such as legitimacy, balance of power, and the role of the state which were brought up throughout the constitutional debate were inseparable from the consolidation process as a whole: the processes of democratic consolidation and constitutionalization were intertwined. This chapter will analyse the major stages of both struggles. It will point to significant breakthroughs—such as the interim constitution of 1992—but it will also show the numerous shortfalls that emerged from the constitutional deficit. The chapter will analyse the art of reaching compromises in a conflict-prone political setting. I will also show that the adoption of the Polish Constitution by referendum did not resolve the debate on legitimacy as many have supposed. Finally I will show that despite the contentious adoption of the Constitution, it has had a stabilizing impact on Polish democracy.

The Real Beginning of the End of the Totalitarian System in Poland

In the summer of 1980, as a result of a series of meat price rises, dozens of determined workers in an eastern Polish town blocked the railway line by welding to the rails a wagon carrying meat to the Soviet Union. In another town, workers from several factories proclaimed a strike alert. In Gdańsk, and later in other Baltic cities, public transportation employees and workers from large factories went on strike. In Silesia, miners and workers from heavy industrial enterprises—the pride of the regime—also joined the strike to express their solidarity with the striking workers of north-eastern Poland. Thus, within a few weeks, an avalanche was started through the use of a welding torch, plunging the country into a fundamental political crisis.

The strikes were not the first large-scale protest in the People's Republic of Poland.[1] In 1956, during a political 'thaw' in the party, workers protested in the streets of Poznań, but their protest was brutally put down. Twelve years later, in the autumn of 1968, another political crisis was reflected in the fight for power within the Communist Party and in ethnic purges. Many Polish citizens of Jewish ancestry lost their jobs and many emigrated. The decision to raise food prices ignited another crisis in 1970. But just as in 1956, workers' protests in Gdańsk and Gdynia were quelled with blood. Although the government refused to take responsibility for the deaths, the protest served as a pretext for a shift in power from one Communist Party faction to another. In 1976, yet another protest against the high cost of living was organized, but its course was less dramatic. Thus, the strikes of 1980 were the last in a series of symptoms caused by the ailing socio-economic system introduced by the Yalta agreement, which had placed Poland under Soviet dominance.

Nevertheless, in two ways the strike of 1980 differed substantially from previous protests. First, workers did not limit themselves to making economic demands, but for the first time formulated demands that undermined the foundations of the political system. Second, the course of the strike and its intensity was unparalleled: the strike was observed in almost every Polish town. Initially, the

---

[1] For an account of the history of the People's Republic of Poland, see Arthur R. Rachwald, *Poland between the Superpowers: Security vs. Economic Recovery* (Boulder, Colo.: Westview Press, 1983).

striking workers' demands were economic, namely a reversal of the price increases and financial compensation, including full wages for time spent on strike. Shortly afterwards, however, a list of twenty-one proposals surfaced, which were not restricted to economic demands but included more substantial demands such as the release of political prisoners (in particular the founders of the Workers' Defence Committee after the 1976 protests) and radio transmission of the Catholic mass,[2] the legalization of independent workers' and peasants' trade unions, and greater freedom of speech and press liberalization through the elimination of state intervention and preventive censorship. These last two demands in particular had considerable political consequences, since they undermined the foundations of the Communist Party's monopoly of state power.

In response to these demands the government and party authorities arranged formal negotiations with the striking workers, represented by the Inter-factory Strike Committee headed by Lech Wałęsa. The negotiations lasted almost two weeks and ended on 31 August 1980 with the conclusion of the Gdańsk Agreement. In the next few months, the government and legislature (Sejm) took steps to implement the agreement. Most importantly, an amendment was made to the Act on Trade Unions to enable the registration of the Solidarity Trade Union and the Act on Limitation of Preventive Censorship was adopted. Despite these changes, the fundamental political controversies that surfaced during the strikes surrounding the character of the state not only remained unsolved, but also became more heated. The communists did not want to lose their monopoly of power. At the same time, Solidarity (which had already evolved beyond its functions as a trade union to become a popular social movement) continued to criticize the lack of both internal and external sovereignty in Poland. The escalating conflict between the state and Solidarity on basic political, economic, social, and ethical concepts led to the introduction of martial law on 31 December 1981. Although the measure was unconstitutional, the effects were indisputable. For nearly two years, Solidarity was banned and its activists were detained or interned, a curfew was imposed, borders were closed, and the media were again subject to strict censorship. Further workers' strikes and protests were put down through force and violence.

[2] It is important to remember that this protest occurred soon after the first visit of Pope John Paul II, in June 1979, to his homeland. See Neal Ascherson, *The Polish August: What has Happened in Poland* (Harmondsworth: Penguin Books, 1981), 141–3.

Paradoxically, following the imposition of martial law, the state began to adjust its institutional structure.[3] Two new judicial organs were constitutionally entrenched. First, a State Tribunal was created to take decisions on the constitutional accountability of members of state organs. Second, a Constitutional Tribunal was set up to review the constitutional compatibility of state actions, judicial decisions, and legislation. These two new judicial institutions were regarded as a liberalizing gesture by the regime aimed at satisfying both Polish public opinion and the international community. Undoubtedly, sixteen months of Solidarity activity to promote state reform laid the conceptual basis for the introduction of mechanisms for constitutional accountability and constitutionality of the law. In 1980, even before the conclusion of the Social Contract, administrative courts were re-established following decades of non-existence. Another institution created to promote public involvement in the state was the office of ombudsman, which was set up in 1987.

In light of the institutional changes of the 1980s, one may well argue that the communist regime in Poland was moving towards setting up the basic institutional mechanisms typical of a democratic state ruled by law. Of course, the functioning of these institutions was severely constrained by the fact that the state in which they were operating was neither democratic nor ruled by law. Nevertheless, these institutions had a positive impact in the sense that their very existence created a new perspective from which to view state action. The opposition began to formulate arguments according to the rule of law and constitutional principles, which the state had at least symbolically incorporated into its institutional structure. These new courts facilitated the application of constitutional principles for the creation of sound legislation. They contributed to the legitimacy of state operation, and increased the state's sensitivity to the rights and freedoms of its citizens.

The Real End of Totalitarianism in Poland and a New Beginning

The political and social situation in Poland in the late 1980s might be characterized as follows: Solidarity, although banned, had

---

[3] See Andre W. M. Gerrits, *The Failure of Authoritarian Change: Reform, Opposition and Geo-politics in Poland in the 1980s* (Worcester: Dartmouth Publishing Company, 1991).

popular support which could only be measured through strikes and demonstrations, whereas the authorities had neither formal nor visible political support from any substantial social force.[4] The resultant political deadlock pitted Solidarity against the Communist Party. The communists were unable to rule without the consent of Solidarity, but the Party did not want to grant its consent or even admit to the existence of Solidarity's popular support. Nevertheless, events continued to demonstrate Solidarity's growing public consent and political sway.

These events forced the Communist Party to take action to break the political deadlock. The idea of the Roundtable Talks was conceived, as a forum in which all parties could address the crucial economic and political issues. The representatives from all sides were to take seats at a table which was, in fact, round. The state was represented by members of the government, the Communist Party, and pro-government labour unions. The opposition team was composed of Solidarity members.[5] Playing an intermediary role were representatives of the Catholic Church, who in theory were neutral, but who often ended up siding with Solidarity.[6]

The Roundtable Talks were aimed at reforming the political and economic system to the extent that, on the one hand, it would be possible for the democratic opposition to participate in the political process, and, on the other hand, conditions for economic recovery might be created. After two months of negotiations, an agreement was reached which formed the basis for fundamental reform in Poland. First, the agreement envisaged the restoration of Solidarity as a lawfully functioning political opposition. Second, the constitutional structure of the state was redesigned through the adoption of a new electoral system, which would allow the opposition to participate in parliamentary elections, and the creation of two new state institutions: an upper chamber of parliament—the Senate—and the office of the president. Under the agreement, the elections to the Senate were to be completely free and democratic, while the electoral rules for the Sejm (lower chamber) reserved 65 per cent of seats for the Communist Party coalition, leaving the remaining seats to be contested through free elections. It was

[4] See Jan Zielonka, *Political Ideas in Contemporary Poland* (Aldershot: Arebury, 1989).

[5] Although other relatively significant opposition organizations existed at the time, none of them was formally represented at the Roundtable Talks.

[6] See Wiktor Osiatyński, 'The Roundtable Talks in Poland', in Jon Elster (ed.), *The Roundtable Talks and the Breakdown of Communism* (Chicago: University of Chicago Press, 1996), 33–7.

also agreed that the president would be elected by the National Assembly (the Sejm and the Senate jointly) from a group of candidates comprised of Communist Party representatives. In addition, several statutes of great significance were adopted, including the Act on Trade Unions (legalizing Solidarity), the Act on Associations, the Act on Relations between the State and the Roman Catholic Church, as well as the Act on the Guarantee of the Freedom of Conscience and Religion.[7]

The results of the pre-term parliamentary elections, held on 4 June and 19 June 1989, reflected the population's support for reforms. Solidarity gained a remarkable victory over the incumbent Communist Party. It won all the seats in the Senate that were not reserved for the Communist Party except for one gained by an independent candidate, and all the seats (35 per cent) open to free electoral competition in the Sejm. The political climate changed dramatically. Solidarity's overwhelming victory raised concerns about its willingness to follow through with the Roundtable agreements since the probability that its parliamentary representatives would elect a communist president was low. In the end, General Wojciech Jaruzelski (the architect of martial law) was elected president only because several Solidarity deputies abstained from voting.

Another result of the elections was the further deepening of the schism within the Communist Party itself. Even though the Party enjoyed an artificial majority in the Sejm, it failed to form a government. Ultimately, Solidarity deputies were able to gain the consent of a sufficient number of deputies from the Communist Party and its satellite parties to create the first non-communist government in Central and Eastern Europe, headed by Tadeusz Mazowiecki.

Initially, the new pro-democracy parliament and government limited the scope of their reforms to abolishing the political monopoly of the Communist Party, changing the status of the prosecutor general (an office to be held jointly with that of the minister of justice), and altering the centralized hierarchy of local councils (which were subordinated to the president rather than the previously existing Council of State). But soon it became obvious that radical reforms were needed to solve the political and economic crisis in Poland, and these could not be undertaken without modifying the existing 1952 Constitution. The first step taken toward changing

---

[7] For a description of the significance of the Catholic Church in Poland, see Norbert A. Żmijewski, *The Catholic–Marxist Ideological Dialogue in Poland, 1945–1980* (Worcester: Dartmouth Publishing Company, 1991).

the Basic Law was made on 29 December 1989. The preamble as well as chapter I dealing with the foundations of the political system and chapter II concerning the basis of the economic system were repealed. These sections were replaced by a new chapter I entitled 'The Foundations of the System', in which the official name of the state was changed from the People's Republic of Poland to the Republic of Poland, which was to be a democratic state ruled by law, implementing the principles of social justice, and in which power was vested in the nation. This constitutional amendment guaranteed political pluralism and the freedom to create political parties, the right to own property, and the right of succession, freedom of economic activity, and local self-government. Although these changes were revolutionary and represented a shift in the country's political system, they were still limited in that they failed to address the regulation and structure of state institutions (particularly the principle of separation of powers), and, above all, the rights and freedoms of citizens.

Both the Sejm and the Senate agreed on the need to adopt a completely new constitution, but the procedure for its drafting and adoption became highly contentious. On 7 December 1989, the Sejm appointed a Constitutional Committee to draft a new constitution, chaired by the Solidarity parliamentary leader Bronisław Geremek. Upon being notified about the creation of the Sejm Committee, the Senate appointed its own Constitutional Committee. The rivalry between the two houses of parliament was based first on the newness of the institution of the Senate and, second, on the different levels of legitimacy of the two houses stemming from the method of their election. In the Senate's opinion, the 'contractual' Sejm had no political legitimacy to draft or adopt a new Constitution, since it had been elected on the basis of an electoral law that reserved 65 per cent of its seats for representatives of the Communist Party and its allies. Given Solidarity's overwhelming victory over the communists in the seats that were open to free election, there can be no doubt that few communists would have been left in the Sejm had all seats been open to free electoral competition. The Sejm argued, however, that on the basis of its actions, which reflected the changing political climate, its legitimacy was strong. It had initiated constitutional reforms, such as the adoption of a new chapter I, and it had passed several important laws, which dismantled the centrally planned political and economic structure. Thus, although the Sejm lacked full political legitimacy stemming from free, democratic elections, it argued that it had gained, as a result of the sum of its pro-reform actions, a certain level of legitimacy, which also enabled it to draft and adopt a new constitution. Moreover, the Sejm argued that even if not everyone could accept its legitimacy, the method of adopting the constitutional draft—by putting the draft up for vote in a referendum—could overcome this problem.

Both houses stuck to their arguments and work continued on two constitutional drafts. In the end, both constitutional committees presented their own separate draft constitutions. Moreover, between 1989 and 1992, the Sejm received draft constitutions or constitutional propositions formulated by several political parties (including the Democratic Party, Polish Peasant Party, Confederation for an Independent Poland, and Centre Alliance) and individual authors (the so-called professors' drafts, prepared by A. Mycielski and W. Szyszkowski, J. Zakrzewska and J. Ciemniewski, M. Huchla, as well as a team from the University of Warsaw, led by S. Zawadzki).[8] A preliminary deadline for adopting the new Constitution was set for 3 May 1991, which marked the 200th anniversary of the adoption of the first Polish Constitution. However, squabbles between different factions in Solidarity delayed the process. The question of legitimacy was raised anew with the election of Lech Wałęsa in direct presidential elections in late autumn 1990, further weakening the Sejm. The 'contractual' Sejm passed a resolution on early dissolution and new elections were scheduled for October 1991. Thus, the first deadline for passing a constitution was missed and the constitution-drafting process was prolonged.

The electoral law governing the October 1991 elections eliminated the seat quota for the communists, leaving all seats open to free electoral competition. As a result of this new electoral procedure, the political legitimacy of both chambers of parliament was guaranteed, and the legitimacy question was overcome. But the results of the elections raised new problems. Representatives of more than twenty political parties won seats in the Sejm, making cabinet formation extremely difficult. The Olszewski cabinet lasted barely six months. Although the next government, with Hanna Suchocka as prime minister, was formed with the support of the Solidarity parliamentary faction, it was brought down less than one year later by a vote of no confidence initiated by Solidarity deputies.

In the midst of this turbulent political climate, work continued in the Sejm on the procedure for adopting a constitution. On 23 April 1992 the Constitutional Act was adopted which stipulated that

---

[8] See Leszek Garlicki, *Kometarz do Konstytycji Rzeczypospolitej Polkiej* (Warsaw: Wydawnictwo Sejmowe, 1995).

a draft constitution would be adopted by both chambers of parliament and afterwards would be put to popular vote in a national referendum. A single Constitutional Committee was created, composed of fifty-six Sejm deputies and ten senators. The right to submit constitutional drafts or opinions was given to any group of at least fifty-six members of the National Assembly and to the president. After approval in the Committee, the draft would need to be adopted by an absolute two-thirds majority in both chambers in two readings. A third reading was also envisioned in the event that the president was to propose amendments to the draft passed in the second reading. The draft would finally be adopted after a national referendum was held. The Constitution would be approved if a majority of those participating in the referendum voted for its adoption. No threshold of votes cast in a referendum was introduced, so that its result would reflect activity not passivity. It was also stressed that the introduction of such a threshold would have meant imposing a political obligation to vote, which was viewed as a feature typical of the totalitarian regime, and thus rejected by parliament.

The new Constitutional Committee of the National Assembly received drafts from political parties represented in parliament (namely, the Democratic Left Alliance, the Democratic Union, the Confederation for an Independent Poland, the Centre Alliance, and a joint Polish Peasant Party and Union of Labour draft), a draft signed by President Lech Wałęsa, as well as the draft written by the Constitutional Committee of the preceding Senate, formally submitted by fifty-eight deputies and senators. The Constitutional Committee did not initially receive the task of creating a unified draft with enthusiasm. There was awareness that reaching a sufficient consensus among the parliamentary parties (that is, a qualified two-thirds majority) on a comprehensive, compact constitutional model for the state would be difficult. Before the Committee had time to draw up a uniform draft constitution, the president of the republic dissolved parliament as a consequence of the vote of no confidence passed against the Suchocka government.

But before the dissolution of parliament, efforts had been made to regulate the relationship between the legislative and executive branches of power and, to a lesser extent, the judicial branch and the rights and freedoms of citizens. The need for reform combined with the political divisiveness within parliament led to a strategy of gradual or 'step-by-step' constitution-making. It was argued that the deadlock could be overcome through the creation of variable 'constitutional coalitions' willing to support certain types of arrangements in specific areas. For example one such coalition could be formed to support a certain arrangement of the judicial branch, even though some members of that coalition might have divergent views about, for instance, civil rights and freedoms. It was hoped that such an approach would make it possible to amend individual chapters of the 1952 Constitution, so that in effect a new constitution would be eventually adopted.

Two major efforts were made to implement this strategy in the constitution-making process. The first was made by President Wałęsa when he submitted a draft 'Charter of Rights and Freedoms'. The Charter, drawn up largely in cooperation with lawyers working for the Helsinki Foundation for Human Rights, was a draft of a modern framework for individual and political rights and freedoms. It did not guarantee any enforceable economic or social rights, but only indicated particular economic, social, and cultural duties of the state. The Charter was based, to a large extent, on international instruments governing human rights and freedoms, particularly the European Convention on Human Rights and the Universal Declaration of Human Rights, and established an efficient means for enforcing one's rights before courts, including a right of constitutional complaint. Leftist parties responded to the presidential initiative by submitting their own draft of a 'Social and Economic Charter'. Due to intense political competition neither of these drafts was adopted and it was only after the new Constitution was finally adopted in 1997 that human rights and freedoms were constitutionally regulated in Poland.

The second effort was an attempt to clarify the relationship between the legislature and the executive. One of the main reasons for the political turbulence was the ambiguous division of competencies between president, government, and parliament. This attempt was successful and as a result, on 17 October 1992, the so-called 'Little Constitution' was adopted.

The Little Constitution as a Stage in Shaping a New Constitutional Order

Work on the draft of the Little Constitution began in 1991 in an attempt to regulate the relationship between the branches of power, and in particular the procedures for the appointment and dismissal of the government. The Little Constitution was intended, *inter alia*, to establish conditions to promote the government stability necessary for the introduction and implementation of fundamental economic reforms. The political atomization of a parliament elected on the basis of an extremely proportional electoral law had created a very unstable and competitive political atmosphere.[9] Although there had been previous attempts at stabilizing the political system (a governmental bill on amending the Constitution in September 1991 and a presidential proposal for a constitutional act on the appointment and dismissal of a government introduced in November 1991), neither received sufficient support from parliament. A compromise solution was finally found in the creation of the Little Constitution. A special committee, headed by Tadeusz Mazowiecki, was charged with the task of drafting the Little Constitution. It based its work on the constitutional draft submitted by the Democratic Union. In line with the 'step-by-step' strategy, the scope of the Little Constitution was intentionally limited to the relations between the legislative and executive branches of power, though it also touched on issues concerning local self-government and the judiciary. It was also stipulated that the Little Constitution would stay in effect only until a new, comprehensive constitution was adopted.

Indeed, the preamble of the Little Constitution explicitly stated that it was to be in force only 'pending the passage of a new Constitution'. Although it replaced the 1952 Constitution, some of the old Constitution's provisions and institutions—namely the foundations of the political and economic system, the Constitutional Tribunal, the Tribunal of State, the Supreme Chamber of Control, the commissioner for citizens' rights (ombudsman), National Council for Radio Broadcasting and Television, courts and prosecutors' offices, fundamental rights and freedoms of citizens, electoral principles, the coat of arms, colours, national anthem, and capital of Poland, and procedure for amending the Constitution—remained in force. This paradoxical situation in which the old Constitution was invalidated while certain norms continued to be enforced was due to the symbolic importance of rejecting the previous communist regime. It was deemed to be better to have a situation in which the old constitutional provisions were carried over to complement the new Constitutional Act than to keep the communist-era Constitution which might be easily transgressed due to its obsolete legitimacy.

The first strike against the communist Constitution was to weaken the role of parliament. Article 20 of the 1952 Constitution

---

[9] See Tomasz Żukowski, 'Wybory Parlamentarne '91', *Studia Polityczne*, 1/1 (1992), 35–60.

stated that the Sejm was the central organ of state power, dominating all other institutions. The new arrangement created a 'rationalized parliamentary' model, regulating and distributing power between the parliament, president, and government. Article 1 of the Little Constitution stated that the Sejm and the Senate were the organs of legislative power in Poland, that executive power was vested in the president of the republic and the Council of Ministers, and that judicial power was vested in the independent courts. As had been the case under the Roundtable Agreements, the Senate played a limited role in the legislative process and in appointing officials, such as the ombudsman or the president of the Supreme Chamber of Control. At the same time, a significant change was made in the legislative process. The Little Constitution stipulated that, under certain conditions, the Council of Ministers could issue regulations that had the force of law. In the event that such a regulation was issued by the Council of Ministers, parliament would have no influence on its content. Regulations were not subject to approval by parliament but only had to be signed and published by the president. However, regulations could be issued by the cabinet only on certain issues, and the Little Constitution introduced a so-called 'negative catalogue', which specified the types of laws that required parliamentary adoption. This catalogue included amendments to the Constitution, electoral laws, rights and freedoms of citizens, and the ratification of certain types of international agreements. Although the Council of Ministers never made use of this legislative competence (the Suchocka government having been unable to muster a majority in the Sejm which would grant it this power), the concept of executive legislation reflected the need to curb the powers of the parliament and enact a new system of separation of powers.

The most contentious issue during the drafting of the Little Constitution centred on the role and powers of the president. Like the Senate, the office of the president was entirely new and was part of the compromise reached at the Roundtable Talks. Although the first president was elected indirectly by the National Assembly, a constitutional amendment adopted in 1990 fundamentally changed this procedure. The new electoral law envisaged the direct election of the president. This amendment irredeemably undermined President Jaruzelski's legitimacy, since he did not enjoy a popular mandate, and ultimately forced him to resign as a result of political pressure. In the subsequent elections, Lech Wałęsa announced his candidacy and won the elections in the second round.

The Little Constitution significantly changed some presidential competencies. When the office of the president was created in 1989, the right of the president to dissolve parliament was restricted to instances in which the Sejm had adopted a statute or resolution which impinged upon the president's ability to ensure the observance of the Constitution, the safety and sovereignty of the state, the inviolability and integrity of its territory, or to uphold international political and military alliances. These curious conditions can be understood only in the context in which the amendment was adopted. At the Roundtable Talks, the communist authorities feared that an anti-communist National Assembly might attempt to undermine the power of the communist president. Thus, this rule was seen as a means for the communist president to regain control had an emergency arisen. Apart from this clause, presidential powers in the amended 1952 Constitution were quite limited. The Little Constitution partly extended the powers of the president. Like the Cabinet, the president was also given limited legislative capacity through the right to issue official acts, which could be passed with the countersignature of the prime minister or an appropriate minister in instances where the topic of the act did not fall into the exclusive domain of the president. The president was also given a greater role in the appointment and dismissal of the government. With respect to the so-called 'presidential ministries' (foreign affairs, internal affairs, and national defence), these ministers could be appointed only with the consent of the president. The right of the president to dissolve parliament was also extended to cases in which the National Assembly failed to appoint a government or adopt a budget within the required time-frame.

In the context of a chaotic political climate, in which the legislature was deeply divided and Solidarity had splintered, President Wałęsa endeavoured to extend his powers at the expense of both parliament and government. During his presidency, Lech Wałęsa made full use of the powers granted him under the Little Constitution and also often applied his right to control parliamentary and government action by submitting certain laws and activities to the Constitutional Tribunal to check their constitutionality.

The Little Constitution also changed the procedure for appointing the government, by introducing a complex five-stage mechanism requiring cooperation between the president and parliament. The first stage granted the president the right to nominate the prime minister who would present the president with a list of candidates for ministerial positions for approval. After the president appointed the government, the prime minister would submit the government's programme to the Sejm together with a motion requiring a vote of confidence to be passed by an absolute majority vote. If the Sejm failed to adopt a vote of confidence, a new prime minister and members of the cabinet would be chosen exclusively by the Sejm, by an absolute majority vote. If the Sejm failed to approve a new government according to this procedure, the initiative would return to the president who would repeat the first stage of the process, except that approval by the Sejm would only require the support of a simple majority vote. If this procedure failed, the initiative would return to the Sejm which would choose – again by simple majority vote—the prime minister and a members of the cabinet as indicated by him. The president would then appoint a government chosen by such means. Finally, if all these procedures failed, the president could dissolve the Sejm or appoint a prime minister and government for a period of six months. If, within those six months, the Sejm had not passed a vote of confidence in the government, the president would be obliged to dissolve parliament.

Fortunately, this complex procedure never needed to be fully applied. The drafters were influenced by the difficulties experienced by the Sejm in its first term when the fragmentation of political forces made government formation difficult and resulted in a highly unstable system. Although the electoral law could have been modified to favour larger parties, a broad spectrum of party representation in parliament was seen as an advantage due to the Assembly's dual role of legislation and constitution-making. It was thought that restricting the number of parties represented would lessen the legitimacy of the constitution-making body.

Instead, the Little Constitution attempted to ensure government stability by making its dismissal more difficult through the introduction of a requirement of an absolute majority in the Sejm to pass a no-confidence vote. Moreover, the intention was that the Sejm would only pass a constructive vote of no confidence in the government, i.e. naming the new prime minister at the same time as it passed the vote of no confidence. Unfortunately, the wording of the Little Constitution was rather ambiguous on this point, implicitly providing for the possibility of a simple vote of no confidence, i.e. without a new prime minister being named. Thus the Suchocka government fell in May 1993, following a simple motion of no confidence tabled by the representatives of the ruling coalition (another surprising feature of Polish politics). The government's dismissal was immediately followed by President Wałęsa's decision to dissolve parliament. Deputies were caught by surprise and wondered, 'Why were we not told that such an outcome was possible?' The president would have been unable to dissolve parliament had deputies passed a constructive vote of no confidence. Of course, the president's action was in conformity with the Little Constitution—adopted only a few months before by the very same MPs. The result was that deputies not only shortened their own term of office but after elections many of those same representatives were excluded from political participation since, with the exception of the Democratic Union, the ruling parties failed to gain sufficient support from the electorate to keep their seats in parliament.

In the course of work on the Little Constitution, many different approaches for reworking the institutional structure of the state were examined, including presidential, parliamentary-cabinet, and chancellor systems. However none could gain the support of the parliamentary majority required for the adoption of a constitutional act. The strong parliamentary regime along with the proportional electoral system had created a highly unstable system in Poland. The diffuse and unstable party affiliation of parliamentary deputies made the passage of necessary economic and political reforms difficult. Drafting a new constitution was proving well nigh impossible. Therefore, it was clear that the greatest challenge for the Little Constitution was to create greater stability in the government without sacrificing parliament's high legitimacy. With this aim in mind, the Little Constitution installed a 'rationalized parliamentary system' including unusual procedures such as the multi-stage cabinet formation as well as a distribution of powers typical of parliamentary-cabinet and semi-presidential systems.

Constitution-Making: From Conflict to Compromise

The results of the parliamentary elections held in September 1993 after the dismissal of Hanna Suchocka's centre-right government were surprising. The party previously in the parliamentary opposition, the Party of Social Democracy—the strongest pillar of the Democratic Left Alliance electoral coalition—won a majority of seats, while right-wing parties, which had failed to form electoral coalitions, were overwhelmingly defeated. Only three right-of-centre parties overcame the 5 per cent electoral threshold needed to win seats in parliament. It was paradoxical that the new electoral law, which gave an advantage to electoral coalitions, had been adopted by the right-wing parties. The supremacy of the right in previous elections had left these parties convinced that the public would continue to support them despite the painful shock-therapy reforms recently implemented by the right-of-centre government and despite the petty politics played by the right due to their high levels of competitiveness and mutual animosity. Their defeat was sealed by the mechanism established by the electoral law, which allotted a bonus of seats to the parties that received the highest percentage of votes. Due to the relatively high threshold and the myriad of parties participating in elections, around 30 per cent of votes were wasted, having been cast for parties which failed to reach the electoral thresholds. The seats representing this 'wasted' percentage were subsequently allotted to the two largest parties in the Sejm, Social Democracy of the Republic of Poland and the Polish Peasant Party.

Although the losing parties did not contest the election results, several Solidarity-based parties questioned the legitimacy of the new parliament in drafting a new constitution, due to the limited number of parties represented in the parliament. They argued that although they lost the elections, a significant segment of the population identified itself with the political programme of right-wing parties which had failed to gain representation. They argued that all parties should be represented in the constitution-drafting process since it would create a new basis for political organization. The victorious left-wing parties rejected these arguments and the new Sejm appointed yet another Constitutional Committee.

The new Committee consisted mostly of representatives from both ex-communist parties, the Democratic Left Alliance and the Polish Peasant Party. The position of the chairman of the Constitutional Committee was given to the leader of the Democratic Left Alliance, Aleksander Kwaśniewski. Although the most important positions in the Committee were divided up between the parliamentary majority, the parliamentary opposition had the possibility—though limited—to influence the work on the constitutional draft by directing or co-directing individual subcommittees. The Constitutional Committee started its work sluggishly at the end of 1993. A decision was taken to continue—at least symbolically—the work of the previous parliament's Committee by allowing the drafts from the previous parliament to be resubmitted.

Although initially brushed aside by the left-wing parliamentary majority, the contention that parliament did not have adequate legitimacy for constitution-drafting quickly gained strong public support. On 22 April 1994, in response to mounting pressure, the Sejm amended the act governing the procedure for adopting a new constitution. The amendment opened the possibility for a group of at least 500,000 citizens (eligible voters) to present a draft constitution for consideration in the National Assembly. This allowed parties not represented in parliament to submit their drafts and for their representatives to participate in the Constitutional Committee, although without voting rights. Quite soon afterwards, Solidarity presented its own constitutional draft, supported by over 900,000 citizens. Thus the formal conditions for draft submission were met and it became one of the seven drafts considered by the Constitutional Committee.

By September 1994, all seven draft constitutions had passed through the first reading in the Sejm, during which the parties submitting each draft were able to present the basic premises and ideological foundations used in the construction of their drafts. After all drafts had been considered, the Constitutional Committee's task was to draw up a single draft. In January 1995 a rough version of this draft, containing various elements of the different submitted drafts, was finished, although the subcommittees and the plenary meeting of the Constitutional Committee continued to discuss particularly troublesome sections and elucidate detailed provisions.[10]

The Polish Constitution is one of political and ideological compromise. As political power shifted throughout the transition period, compromise had to be renegotiated and achieved at every stage. At the end of the process, the most crucial compromise was reached between the left-wing parliamentary majority and Solidarity. Yet, despite efforts to make the constitution-drafting process more inclusive, and despite the fact that all drafts were considered and elements of each were included in the final document, the extra-parliamentary opposition continued to oppose the parliamentary majority's draft, calling for voters (with the help of the Catholic Church) to oppose the Constitution in the referendum.

Even at the most basic levels of political organization, unifying divergent interests and concerns was essential throughout the constitution-drafting process. The largest parliamentary club, the Democratic Left Alliance, was a coalition of parties, social organizations, and trade unions representing different ideologies and political programmes. Although they all subscribed to the social democratic programme of the Democratic Left Alliance, the differences between the individual groups became particularly visible during work on the constitutional draft. Compromise within the Alliance had to be reached on issues such as Church–state

---

[10] See Jan Galster, Wacław Szyszkowski, Zofia Wąsik, and Zbigniew Witkowski (eds.), *Prawo Konstytucyjne* (Toruń: TNOiK, 1996).

relations, the rights and freedoms of the citizens, and the role of the state in the economic sphere.

The Democratic Left Alliance's government coalition partner, the Polish Peasant Party, also needed to reach a crucial agreement between two basic groups of Polish farmers. One group, characterized by small, underfinanced farms, was deeply concerned about domestic and international competition, about accessibility to low interest loans, and guaranteed state purchases of their products. The other group was much smaller, but represented large farms, and was open to competition based on free market principles. Thus, not only was compromise necessary between the two parties comprising the governing coalition, but it was also necessary within the individual parties.

Compromise between the Democratic Left Alliance and the Polish Peasant Party was not easy either. In fact, these two parliamentary groups had different ideological and economic visions, which found their expression in their attitudes towards issues such as the Christian character of Polish society, the method of privatization, and state support for agriculture. Moreover, although the governing coalition controlled a majority of seats in parliament, it was not the qualified two-thirds majority necessary to adopt the new Constitution. They needed to find allies among the opposition parties represented in parliament. Thus, although the opposition, and in particular Solidarity, continued to oppose the constitution-drafting process due to its insufficient inclusiveness, the Constitution would not have been passed without compromise and cooperation on the part of all the parties involved in the process.

The two opposition parties most willing to seek a constitutional compromise with the ruling coalition were the Labour Union (which had submitted a constitutional draft together with the Polish Peasant Party prior to the 1993 parliamentary elections) and the Freedom Union (formerly the Democratic Union). From an ideological point of view, the Labour Union was much closer to the Democratic Left Alliance than the Polish Peasant Party. The reason why it had not participated in the governing coalition was its attitude toward the dominant party in the Democratic Left Alliance—the Social Democratic Party. The Labour Union considered itself to be the rightful heir of the Polish democratic left, distancing itself from the communists, which it regarded as politically illegitimate due to their responsibility for the period of communism in Poland.

The Freedom Union had its roots in the Solidarity movement and its representatives, such as Tadeusz Mazowiecki, Hanna Suchocka, and Jacek Kuroń, identified with the democratic intelligentsia. Its decision to participate in the constitutional coalition was preceded by internal constitutional compromises on issues such as Church–state relations, the neutral character of the state, socio-economic rights, and the level of decentralization. The remaining right-wing parties connected with Solidarity refused to participate in the constitutional coalition. Although their representatives participated in the Committee, their activity was limited to demanding that the Citizens' Draft be adopted in its entirety. By rejecting the invitation to compromise, the Solidarity representatives severely limited their ability to influence the constitution-drafting process.

The task of the 'constitutional coalition' to reach agreement amidst such divergent ideological views would have been impossible without compromise and cooperation. Each party prioritized its demands and respected a kind of 'tit-for-tat' policy, in which support for a certain issue that was important to one party on one day would need to be reciprocated in support for the other parties' proposals the next day. This method of compromise had negative effects on the quality of the Constitution. One effect was the excessive number of declarative and vague provisions such as 'Public authorities shall support the development of physical culture, particularly among children and young people.' Another negative effect was the inclusion of multiple solutions for the same problem, for example the issue of incompatibility, which could have been regulated by a single provision, is instead addressed in a separate provision for every type of state official and public function. The entire text is overly complex, repetitive, and includes many superfluous regulations. This is not conducive for enabling clear interpretation or application of the Constitution.

The compromise reached by the constitutional coalition enabled the adoption of the draft Constitution in the National Assembly. The real challenge was to gain the support of citizens participating in the constitutional referendum. Solidarity refused to participate in the constitutional compromise in the Committee and its representatives led a public campaign against the draft. During the second reading of the constitutional draft in the National Assembly on 26 February 1997, Solidarity formed a Public Constitutional Committee in which it voiced its criticisms of the parliamentary draft. The Catholic Church supported Solidarity's position by issuing a statement from the Standing Committee of the Episcopate on 13 February 1997, presenting its own negative criticism of the parliamentary draft as well as offering its own proposals. These proposals related to issues such as: a constitutional reference to God; references to Polish history and the basic elements of national identity; the legal and political continuation of independent Poland prior to 1944;[11] the recognition of private ownership as a constitutional principle; clearly defining the model of the economic system as the social market economy with corporatist elements; guarantees for the protection of human life from the moment of conception; definition of marriage as the union between a man and a woman; and full rights of parents to decide on the religious and moral principles of raising children. It would seem that Solidarity applied the simple and often effective rule of 'the more you demand, the more you get'.

The parliamentary Committee had to make a decision about the extent to which these proposals should be taken into account. It was impossible to disregard the influence of Solidarity and Catholic Church due to their high ratings in pre-electoral opinion polls. To make matters more difficult, Solidarity's proposals were not accompanied by the will to negotiate. In fact, they were presented in the form of an ultimatum. Indeed, the stakes at this stage of constitution drafting were the highest ever: so much time had passed since the 1989 amendments and so much effort had been made to reach a compromise on the draft that failure in the referendum would have been devastating. As a result, the parliamentary constitutional coalition had no choice but to accept the majority of these proposals in the third reading of the draft on 2 April 1997, hoping that by doing so it would gain at least the neutral consent of the opposition for its constitutional draft.

The final draft of the Constitution incorporated the *invocatio Dei*, in its references to citizens 'who believe in God as the source of truth, justice, good and beauty, as well as those not sharing such faith but respecting those universal values as they arise from other sources' and in the preamble which refers to the 'responsibility before God or our own consciences'. The preamble also contains a reference to Polish 'culture rooted in the Christian heritage of the Nation' and the nation is described in Article 4 as sovereign and having the supreme power in the republic. The postulate for defining marriage as the union of man and woman (Art. 18) was also included, with obvious consequences for the rights of same-sex partnerships. A reference was also included to the creation of a social market economy, based on the freedom of economic activity,

---

[11] This would have had troubling international law consequences concerning, for example, the territory gained after the Second World War, which had belonged to Germany, or the land which is now within Lithuanian borders.

private ownership, and solidarity, dialogue, and cooperation between social partners (Art. 20). Finally, Solidarity's demand for a symbolic separation between the communist past and the new democratic regime was also addressed in Article 13, which prohibited political parties and organizations from adopting programmes based upon totalitarian methods or embracing Nazi, fascist, or communist ideologies, as well as programmes or activities sanctioning racial or national hatred or the application of violence for the purpose of obtaining power. Finally on 2 April 1997, the National Assembly adopted the draft Constitution. Of the 560 members of the Sejm and the Senate, 461 voted in favour of the draft, 31 voted against, and 5 abstained.

Solidarity's last-minute strategy aimed at undermining the adoption of the parliamentary constitutional draft was to call for an amendment to the act governing the adoption of the Constitution. Although the act required that the National Assembly's draft be submitted to a vote in a national referendum, there was no quota requirement for participation in the referendum. All parties were fully aware that the turnout for referenda and elections tended to be low: less than 42 per cent of eligible voters participated in the 1993 parliamentary elections. They therefore purposefully avoided specifying requirements for participation. Thus, in a last-ditch effort to stall the constitutionalization process Solidarity raised new demands that the act be changed to require at least 50 per cent turnout for the referendum to be valid. However, the parliamentary majority refused to bow to the demands of Solidarity and did not amend the act.

The second element of Solidarity's strategy was to demand that the 'citizens' draft' submitted by Solidarity with the support of over 900,000 citizens' signatures be added to the constitutional referendum ballot, thus allowing voters to chose between the two drafts. Solidarity representatives argued that by giving voters a chance, not simply to reject the parliamentary draft, but actively to choose one draft over the other, the results of the referendum would be more constructive and democratic. Once again, Solidarity returned to the lack of legitimacy in the National Assembly. Once again, parliament refused to respond to Solidarity's demands.

Throughout the referendum campaign, Solidarity continued to attack the parliamentary draft. Its no-holds-barred strategy included slogans such as 'Poland loses its independence,' 'The state will take away children from their parents,' 'The president will have unlimited powers (tyranny),' 'the Constitution destroys the Polish economy,' and 'Anti-Polish constitution protects swindlers and thieves.' The objections against the draft raised during the second reading were brought up once again.[12]

Although a public survey assessing the level of the public's acquaintance with the draft Constitution prior to the referendum was not conducted, we may nevertheless assume that voting was based on the desire to adopt a constitution—perhaps any constitution—rather than further prolong the arduous constitution-drafting process. Even those well acquainted with the draft and all of its faults voted to adopt the Constitution, even though this had to be done with a 'breaking heart'. Indeed, it would have been difficult to vote against a constitution that satisfied the primary criteria for a liberal regime by creating a democratic institutional structure, guaranteeing human rights and freedoms, including an efficient mechanism to ensure compliance with its provisions, officially stating the principle of division and balance of powers, decentralizing the state, and guaranteeing the normative value of the Constitution as the fundamental act with direct applicability. Thus it was necessary to overlook the draft's faults, resulting from an 'overly narrative' style, numerous unnecessary repetitions, partial inconsistency, and various visible deficiencies in its regulations. In the end, only 42.86 per cent of all eligible voters participated in the referendum, of which 53 per cent voted in favor of the draft. The Constitution was thus accepted in the referendum. However from the point of view of the function of the referendum as a mechanism for social legitimization of the basic law through obtaining the widest possible support for its text, the low voter turnout shows that the new Constitution's legitimacy was quite weak: it was supported by only 22.59 per cent of all eligible voters. Nevertheless, after all the electoral petitions were reviewed and rejected by

---

[12] These included, for example, the Constitution's insufficient reference to the Polish nation as sovereign, weak references to Poland's national traditions and Christian heritage, insufficient protection of human life from the time of conception to a natural death, insufficient guarantee of the rights of parents to raise their children, insufficient protection of the family, the weakness of the constitutional complaint, the possibility of transferring in certain cases the competence of the state authorities to an international organization or body, election to the Sejm by proportional representation, the weak political position of Senate, the overly broad scope of competence of the president of Poland—especially in respect to appointments of state officials—deconstitutionalization of the prosecution office, the prohibition of taking loans or giving financial guarantees by the state as a result of which the public debt of the state would exceed three-fifths of annual GNP, the lack of a separate institution of State Treasury, the overly high position of the Financial Policy Council, and the failure to provide for the finality of Constitutional Tribunal judgments.

the Supreme Court, the new Polish Constitution was signed by President Kwasniewski on 16 July 1997 and promulgated on the very same day in the *Journal of Laws*, No. 78 item 483. The Constitution of the Republic of Poland came into force on 17 October 1997.

Most of the institutional solutions of the 'Little Constitution' were incorporated into the new Constitution. Certain solutions were modified as a result of negative experience (i.e. the obligation of the prime minister to consult on candidates with the president before appointing the ministers of foreign affairs, internal affairs, and national defence, the so-called 'presidential ministries', has been dropped) or as a result of political compromise (lowering the majority required to reject the presidential legislative veto from two-thirds to three-fifths).

Conclusion

It is generally recognized that approval of the Constitution by referendum, though obviously raising the level of its social and political validity, was not a sufficient requirement to ensure the Constitution's legitimacy. The authors of the act on the adoption of the Constitution intended the referendum to legitimize the Constitution, but in the end, the low voter turnout and marginal victory was hardly an unequivocally positive result reflecting an integrated social value system. Instead, the Polish Constitution was adopted through a process of continual compromise and readjustment. Both during the work of the Constitutional Committee and in the period between the enactment of the Constitution by the National Assembly and the referendum, the constitutional debate failed to create—under a slogan of 'constitutional patriotism'—the basis for an active social debate. Instead, it soon became obvious that the constitutional referendum was a pawn in the political game. The constitutional debate was not defined in terms of a new legal basis for the regime, but the debate operated in the sphere of symbols, national identity, and attitudes towards the communist past. Thus the constitutional debate resulted in a polarization of views rather than in social consensus.

Solidarity's negative attitude toward the draft Constitution is quite understandable, because no one (and especially not the authors of the victory over the totalitarian system, including their leader Lech Wałęsa) could have imagined in 1989 that their successors in the constitution-drafting process would be the politically bankrupt ex-communist parties. One could say that history treated the revolutionaries somewhat unfairly, but upon closer inspection, Solidarity's main actors brought this paradoxical situation upon themselves. Nevertheless, Solidarity and its successor parties learned some valuable lessons, which clearly affected the political strategy and organizational structure of these parties. Thus, one cannot say, as Talleyrand said of the Bourbons, that they learned and understood nothing. However, the lesson was learned at a very high political price.

The Polish Constitution is a constitution of compromise. Compromise was necessary at every stage of the process and between all the different participants involved in the creation of the draft. Thus, even the extra-parliamentary opposition, which was seemingly cast out of the constitution-drafting process, was ultimately included, since most of the important proposals offered by Solidarity and the Catholic Church were recognized and taken into account at the last stage of constitution-drafting. As a constitution of compromise, it did not fully satisfy any of the participants involved in the process of its creation. But without compromise the Constitution would not have been adopted at all. Thus it can be asserted that the process of constitution drafting was quite open and inclusive, reflecting the various interests of a diverse society.

The Polish Constitution is—as has been demonstrated by the experience of the first year of its application—a constitution of political pragmatism. The 1997 Constitution permitted the peaceful transfer of power to Solidarity after the parliamentary elections of 1997. It seems that the model of strong powers for the government, and in particular strengthening the powers of the prime minister, designed by the constitutional coalition is fully accepted by this political group which—although it categorically rejected the constitutional draft during the referendum—makes skilful use of constitutional provisions.

The Polish Constitution is a reflection—as in a distorting mirror—of the period directly preceding its enactment. But this is, to some extent, a universal feature. Thus the Constitution reflects the political history of a given country in a nutshell. A bit of political imagination and a minimal knowledge of political conditions of the past period is enough to reconstruct—by studying the norms and the system of institutions—a general outline of the system preceding the enactment of the Constitution.

Conclusions: On the Relevance of Institutions and the Centrality of Constitutions in Post-communist Transitions

Wojciech Sadurski

If there is one conclusion that can be drawn from the impressive variety of arguments, reports, and theories included in this book, it must be that institutions *matter*. While it might sound like a shameful platitude, the apparent banality of this comment is somewhat deceptive. Even if this view has become commonplace in current political and constitutional theory, it is worth restating because, in contrast to political and scholarly *observers*, the truth has not been always self-evident to the *participants* of the remarkable transitions in the post-communist countries with which this volume is concerned. Institutions matter in the sense that they are not neutral; they do not merely channel and organize pre-political forms of collective life. Rather, they crucially affect, influence, and change the way politics develop. They importantly constrain the range of choices available to public actors, they organize patterns of socially constructed norms and roles, and they define the prescribed behaviours that those who occupy those roles are expected to pursue.[1]

It is remarkable how the choice of this or that institution—whether it is a form of presidential, semi-presidential, or parliamentary system of government, or a type of electoral system, or a role of a constitutional court—makes an important change in the way that otherwise similar societies can develop at a point of major transformation. To be sure, no two of the societies discussed in this

---

[1] Robert E. Goodin, 'Institutions and their Design', in Robert E. Goodin (ed.), *The Theory of Institutional Design* (Cambridge: Cambridge University Press, 1996), 19.

book are really similar, and so it is not possible to study the role of a particular institution as a variable in the *ceteris paribus* circumstances. But this is not the point; the point is rather to see whether different institutional choices can be meaningfully attributed to *relevant* differences between these countries. Having read the preceding essays in this volume, I conclude that any such determinism—in other words, any attempt to attribute a particular difference in institutional patterns to a relevant difference in the tradition, forms of civil society, economic development, or any other non-institutional factor within any of the countries—would be extremely risky. Any attempt at a generalization of this sort could be negated by counter-examples. And this, in my view, supports a thesis that institutions often *determine*, rather than *are determined by*, the events of history.

The Relevance of Institutions

There are many different ways in which institutions can affect political life. Among the most important are changing the pattern of incentives for particular action or inaction by particular political actors. The existence of institutions may (*a*) make certain choices more costly (up to the point at which they are prohibitively costly, in which case we consider those choices to be effectively foreclosed), (*b*) make certain choices less costly, or (*c*) provide an opportunity for political actors to engage in various forms of strategic behaviour. A good example, raised by a number of authors in this book, is constitutional judicial review, understood as the authority of a quasi-judicial body (a constitutional court) to assess and invalidate laws enacted by the legislature. Leonardo Morlino talks about 'the unavoidable political distortion caused by giving a strong political role to the magistracy, such as the Constitutional Court'.[2] The existence of such an institution obviously affects the calculus of costs and benefits towards particular choices by a variety of relevant actors: legislatures, governments, political parties, pressure groups, and citizens. Certain choices are being made more difficult: the so-called 'Bokros Package', or the set of socio-economic reforms initiated in Hungary in 1995, as discussed by Istvan Szikinger in this book, is an example. Other choices are rendered easier: the judgments of constitutional courts may exact certain types of statutory provisions from legislators, and thus figure conveniently in

[2] p. 108 above.

the justification for these provisions. The Hungarian Constitutional Court which possesses (and has used) the authority to declare that parliament is acting 'unconstitutionally by omission' is an example.

Furthermore, the fact that legislative and political decisions are being taken in the shadow of judicial review facilitates strategic behaviour. For example, there is a possibility of 'irresponsibility with impunity': legislators can take certain initiatives which might be electorally popular but very costly if implemented, knowing full well that the laws will be struck down by the Constitutional Court. They therefore have the benefits (of making politically popular gestures) without the costs. Actually, what seems to be a case of raising the costs of policy choices (affecting the pattern of incentives) may in fact be a case of a premeditated strategic behaviour. Thus Jeffrey Seitzer suggests that, in the case of the above-mentioned Bokros Package of economic reforms in Hungary, '[b]y striking down the program the Court may have done the government a favor because it could bow to public pressure, all the while appearing to make a good faith effort to comply with requirements of international financial institutions'.[3] On the other hand, the fact that decisions of the legislature can be checked for unconstitutionality by another body may provide legislators with a convenient alibi for inaction. Legislators can use the prospect of invalidation by the Court as an excuse for *not* taking steps that should (from a public interest point of view) be taken, but which it is inconvenient for them to take.

Of course, the stronger, the more independent a constitutional court is, the more room there is for strategic behaviour by other actors, and the larger the impact upon the structure of incentives. There is nothing wrong with strategic behaviour as such; however, in politics it more often than not detracts from the attainment of values such as transparence, candour, and accountability. This may explain why some authors at least express certain misgivings about the power of the constitutional courts (an issue to which we will return, in a different context, below); as Miroslav Cerar suggests, the Slovenian Court 'is applying insufficient self-restraint and is having an overly political effect despite the undoubted professional calibre of its judges'.[4]

[3] Jeffrey Seitzer, 'Experimental Constitutionalism: A Comparative Analysis of the Institutional Bases of Rights Enforcement in Post-communist Hungary', in Sally J. Kenney, William M. Reisinger, and John C. Reitz (eds.), *Constitutional Dialogues in Comparative Perspective* (London: Macmillan, 1999), 52.

[4] p. 399 above.

It is one thing to emphasize the independent role of institutions, as important variables having powerful explanatory power with respect to political developments, and quite another to claim that the *functions* that institutions play are context-independent. The latter is certainly not the case. Consider this conclusion of Darina Malová drawn from the parliamentary experience of Slovakia: 'systems with dominant unicameral legislatures, weak checks on executive power, and disciplined political parties produce majority rule, polarization, and escalating conflicts. . . . Such systems are not conducive to the survival of democracy.' With a single—and largely irrelevant—exception, Malová's description of Slovak institutions applies perfectly to the United Kingdom (the exception is bicameralism but in the UK an upper chamber hardly plays the role of checking the power of the dominant parliamentary chamber, so it is irrelevant in this context), and yet the conclusion obviously does not hold there. This is because the context in which the Westminster system operates—with a set of constitutional conventions constraining the range of parliamentary choices, a traditional respect for the role of parliamentary minorities, a strong press, and a strong, independent judiciary, to mention just a few factors—is worlds apart from that of Slovakia.

This may be a confirmation of 'a theory of second-best' which states that, if we have a ranking of preferred outcomes but a particular factor is necessary in order to accomplish the worth of the most preferred outcome, and that particular factor is missing, an altogether different solution is actually preferable to the top one. In the language of game-theory, it is formulated more elegantly: 'given that one of the Paretian optimum conditions cannot be fulfilled, then an optimum situation can be achieved only by departing from all other Paretian conditions.'[5] In our example: even if, in the ideal circumstances, a parliamentary system would give better effect to the democratic aspirations of a nation recovering from an undemocratic regime, if the value of parliamentarianism is contingent upon some factors, and these factors do not occur, a presidential or semi-presidential system might be optimal.

---

[5] Richard G. Lipsey and Kelvin Lancaster, 'The General Theory of Second Best', *Review of Economic Studies*, 24 (1956), 11–32, at 11; for an application of the theory to institutional design, see Bruce Talbot Coram, 'Second Best Theories and the Implications for Institutional Design', in Goodin (ed.), *The Theory of Institutional Design*, 90–102; for an application to constitutional design, see Robert E. Goodin, 'Designing Constitutions: The Political Constitution of a Mixed Commonwealth', in Richard E. Bellamy and Dario Castiglione (eds.), *Constitutionalism in Transformation: European and Theoretical Perspectives* (Oxford: Blackwell, 1996), 223–34, at 229–30.

The analyses in this book also show the importance of 'path dependency': an explanation of a certain state of affairs by the preceding states of affairs. Sometimes institutions exist in a particular way merely because they had been evolving in that way for some time, or they followed from their predecessors, even though no one would have designed them in such a way if they were now being created from scratch. A nice example of such 'path dependency' is provided by Venelin Ganev who informs us in his chapter that 'Bulgaria is the only East European country with a vice-president, and it is plausible to assume that this institution was preserved in the new Constitution simply because it was already "there"'.[6] A similar point might be plausibly made about the higher chamber of the Polish parliament—the Senate—which, at one point, served a very specific and useful purpose (as an institutional form of an electoral compromise reached in the round table between the Communist government and the opposition) but has been retained even since its rationale has fully expired because no significant political actors have had sufficient incentives to call for an abolition of this arguably costly and purposeless institution.

The Role of Constitutionalization

The chapters of this book show how central *constitutional* design is to the institutional engineering in the societies undergoing transitions to democracy. The importance of constitutional design is another broad conclusion that one can draw from this book. Again, this is banal only in its immediate appearance. In fact, constitutionalism is one of a *number* of devices that institutional engineers have at their disposal, and there are forms of institutionalization which bypass the route of constitutionalization. Constitutionalization is a way of institutionalizing political practices by freezing, so to speak, the norms which regulate procedures, separation of powers, and fundamental rights, in a way which makes them (relatively) immune to the changed views and interests of the community as reflected in current legislative majorities. By constitutionalization I mean, naturally, something more specific than merely enacting an act called 'the Constitution'. Almost all of the authors of the essays in this book assume, at least implicitly, that having a constitution is more than that. At a minimum, it means having a written document which is reasonably strongly entrenched against changes by the legislative majority, and thus of a relative

---

[6] p. 190 above.

longevity (at least, in the intention of its makers). It must also be paramount over other legal acts and therefore serve as a basis for declaring those acts unconstitutional; it must be congruent with the fundamental values of the community and at the same time provide for legal protection for those whose rights are likely to be infringed by an unlimited exercise of legislative and administrative powers.

This is not an exhaustive list of the requirements of 'constitutionalism', in the strict sense of the word, and further development of this point would take us beyond the bounds of the topic of this chapter. However, even to recite those seven criteria stated in the preceding paragraph—writtenness, entrenchment, longevity, paramountcy, availability of constitutional review, congruence with basic community values, and protection of fundamental rights— is sufficient to indicate at least two things. First, that having a constitution in the strict sense of the word is a matter of degree: each of these criteria allows for a dimension of quantity (a constitution may be 'more' or 'less' written—in the sense of consisting of a smaller or larger number of implicit norms and constitutional conventions—'more' or 'less' entrenched—as a function of the ease or difficulty of making amendments—etc). The analyses included in this volume can therefore serve as an excellent basis for a comparison of the degree to which a given society is constitutional. But —and this is my second suggested implication—this judgement is not necessarily equivalent to a positive evaluation, because having a constitution in the strict sense of the word is not always, and not necessarily, an unqualified good. Each of the seven criteria of constitutionalism can be shown to have both good and negative consequences. Writtenness leads to certainty but also to rigidity; entrenchment to stability but also to relative insensitivity to changed situations and views, etc. Even the last criterion—protection of minority rights against majority judgement—might be seen to reflect distrust of the wisdom of majority rule.

It would be a fascinating exercise to trace the positive and the negative consequences of constitutionalization in each of the case studies under discussion in this volume, and to pass judgement about the overall result. I have no doubt that different readers will end up with different verdicts, but at the same time I strongly suspect that, at the end of the day, there will be strong support for the very principle of constitutionalization in transitional democracies. It is also the prevailing view of the authors of chapters in this book: they illustrate mostly positive functions of the constitutionalism of their countries. When constitutionalism fails to deliver its promise to facilitate the transition to democracy, they imply, it is because of a defective design—such as the constitutionally prescribed imbalance of powers between the major branches of government in Russia—rather than due to any intrinsic features of the concept of constitutionalism. The theoretical dilemma of 'constitutionalism versus democracy', discussed at length by some Western writers,[7] does not preoccupy the students and participants of the Central and Eastern European political scene. If there *is* a problem related to constitutionalism in these countries, our authors seem to suggest it is that there is too little of it, not too much.

This brings us to the central issue of the *functions* of constitutions and of constitutionalization in the context of institutional engineering. There are, as all students of constitutional politics know, a number of different taxonomies of the functions of constitutions.[8] But rather than reviewing those traditional classifications, and trying to match the descriptions of this volume with them, I would prefer to invoke a simple but powerful distinction proposed by a political and moral philosopher, Hanna Fenichel Pitkin. Constitutions, Pitkin says, are not only something that we *have*. They are also, importantly, something that we *are*, and something that we *do*. Each of these verbs signifies something quite different. Furthermore, while we usually see constitutions as something that we *have*, we tend to disregard that they are also something that we *are* and something that we *do*.

Constitutions and Identity

First, a constitution is who we *are*. This is perhaps the primary sense of the word 'constitution', where it is seen as a 'composition or fundamental make-up'.[9] With respect to a community, Pitkin says, 'this use of "constitution" suggests a characteristic way of life, the national character of a people, their ethos or fundamental nature as a people, a product of their particular history and social

---

[7] 'Constitutions operate as constraints on the governing ability of majorities; they are naturally taken as antidemocratic'; Cass R. Sunstein, 'Constitutions and Democracies: An Epilogue', in Jon Elster and Rune Slagstad (eds.), *Constitutionalism and Democracy* (Cambridge: Cambridge University Press, 1988), 327.

[8] See, e.g., Dario Castiglione, 'The Political Theory of the Constitution', in Bellamy and Castiglione (eds.), *Constitutionalism in Transformation*, 9–11.

[9] Hanna Fenichel Pitkin, 'The Idea of a Constitution', *Journal of Legal Education*, 37 (1987), 167–9, at 167.

conditions'.[10] Or, in the more down-to-earth language of Robert Goodin, a leading theorist of constitutional design: 'Political constitutions make certain crucial presuppositions about the sociological composition of the polity.'[11]

There are some evident ways in which a constitution is 'who we *are*'. Perhaps the most obvious is that constitutional acts often define who are citizens of a particular state. In this respect, the analyses of authors coming from the Baltic states are particularly revealing. All three Baltic republics inherited from their immediate Soviet pasts the politically sensitive problem of having large Russian minorities (29 per cent in Estonia, 34 per cent in Latvia, and 9 per cent in Lithuania), and in each country there were strong pressures to adopt ethnically restrictive criteria of citizenship. One can see reasons why anti-Soviet sentiments in those countries gave rise to the anti-Russian stance on citizenship, but at the same time it is easy to realize how dangerous the situation became (not to mention issues of fairness) when large proportions of permanent residents became non-citizens in the new states. Adopting an exclusionary frame of mind had clear consequences for institutional engineering and constitutional design. As Vello Pettai suggests in discussing the case of Estonia, this kept the legislators 'from having to think about engineering institutions in, say, a consociational way in order to facilitate power-sharing with the Russians'.[12]

Each of these three countries underwent a slightly different evolution in this regard, but the case of Latvia is perhaps the most telling. Before the first democratic election of the newly independent Latvia, Latvian citizenship—and therefore, a right to vote— was given only to those who were citizens of Latvia on 17 June 1980 and their descendants. The principle of naturalization, while adopted in theory, had not been acted on at that time. The first law adopted by the Saeima—the Latvian parliament—in 1994 was quite restrictive, with substantial limits on eligibility for naturalization. However, the discussions that followed revealed a steady liberalization of the concept of Latvian citizenship. As a result, the system of citizenship was largely liberalized in the amendments of 1998, and these amendments were subsequently upheld (albeit by a narrow margin) in a referendum.

But there is also a more fundamental sense in which a constitution is 'who we *are*'. It is that a constitution attempts to identify

---

[10] Hanna Fenichel Pitkin, 'The Idea of a Constitution', *Journal of Legal Education*, 37 (1987), 167–9, at 167.

[11] Goodin, 'Designing Constitutions', 224.   [12] p. 120 above.

some fundamental values common to all members of its community. This, arguably, is a common aspiration of almost all constitutions (and an aim supported by a great number of constitutional theorists), and yet once an aspiration is formulated in such terms, it immediately becomes clear how difficult and chimerical the aspiration is. All the societies under discussion here are truly pluralistic, heterogeneous societies composed of people of widely diverse perspectives and ideologies, even if not always diverse ethnic and religious traditions. Isn't an attempt to identify 'who we are' in the constitution a truly Procrustean task? Either the values will be too narrowly defined, and as a result they will leave some of the citizens beyond the pale, or they will be formulated at such a broad level of generality that they will be reduced to a set of meaningless platitudes.

Some of the answers can be found in our authors' discussions of the *preambles* to their respective countries' constitutions. Slovakia, for one, provides an interesting example of what Malová calls a 'friction between civic and national principles': there are references to 'Great Moravia' and 'the spirit of Cyril and Methodius' as well as to the 'Slovak nation' in the Slovak Constitution, but at the same time it reminds its people that 'members of national minorities and ethnic groups' are also an integral part of the citizenry.[13] Preambles of most of the countries under review are filled with feel-good references to glorious events from the nations' pasts, but then there are also references to 'civil society' (as in the Lithuanian and Slovenian constitutions). Klaus von Beyme sees the preambles' references to history as a sign of these states' insecurity of their continuity.[14] An equally plausible explanation (not incompatible with that of von Beyme) may be that it is a cheap and easy form of manipulative politics: a piece of public relations meant to placate those who might have some misgivings about this or that specific constitutional provision. Often the broad and vague statements of preambles come as a result of an ingenious compromise: the problem is that they then become meaningless for providing insight into the framers' self-images. Perhaps the most extreme example is the part of the preamble to Poland's Constitution that refers to the Supreme Being. As a result of a compromise between those with a religious outlook and those more concerned with the civic character of the state, 'We, the Polish Nation' is now divided into 'those who believe in God as the source of truth, justice, good and beauty' and those 'not sharing such faith but respecting those universal

---

[13] p. 355 above.   [14] p. 10 above.

values as arising from other sources'. Who could quarrel with truth, justice, good, and beauty?

If the task of expressing a set of principal community values in a constitution is either impossible (because there is no sufficiently broad consensus on substantive moral and political issues) or unattractive (because any attempt to articulate such a consensus will be exclusionary towards those who are left out of it and who cannot recognize themselves in constitutional pronouncements), perhaps the most promising path is one limited to a largely procedural set of values of equal citizenship. As Jürgen Habermas says: 'Discourses for achieving self-understanding require that the cultural traditions formative of one's own identity be dealt with in a manner which is at once anxiety-free, reflexive, and open to learning.'[15] Easier said than done: consider, as an example, some of the constitutional debates in Poland surrounding proposed constitutional references to the role of religion or an invocation of deity in the preamble, and you get *anything but* an 'anxiety-free' discourse about a community's collective self-understanding.

Habermas precedes his proposal with the following remark: 'For political-ethical discourses, [consensus] would ideally require that the conditions of systematically undistorted communication be satisfied, thereby protecting the participants from repression, yet without tearing them from their genuine contexts of experience and interests.'[16] This tension between the quest for 'undistorted communication' and the embeddedness in 'genuine contexts of experience' can be traced in the transitional constitutions' oscillation between the ideals of nationhood and citizenship, between ethnic identity and a pluralistic liberal state, between the constitution as a charter of a historically formed community and the constitution as a charter of free and equal citizens. As Ulrich Preuss observes with some concern: 'It is far from clear whether the post-communist countries of East and Central Europe will succeed in reconciling the universalist principles of the nation state with the simultaneously cohesive and divisive forces of ethnic self-definition and self-identification in their multi-ethnic countries.'[17]

As one example this tension, one might recall the report by Renate Weber about Romanian constitution-making. While there are specific

[15] Jürgen Habermas, *Between Facts and Norms*, trans. William Rehg (Cambridge: Polity Press, 1996), 182.

[16] Ibid.

[17] Ulrich K. Preuss, *Constitutional Aspects of the Making of Democracy in the Post-communist Societies of East Europe* (Bremen: Zentrum für Europäische Rechtspolitik an der Universität Bremen, 1993), 32.

provisions about the rights of national minorities, there are also what Weber calls 'nationalist' articles in the Constitution,[18] such as that which proclaims 'the unity of the Romanian people' (Art. 4 (1)), that announcing that Romania is a 'national state' (Art. 1), and that excluding 'aliens and stateless persons' from the right to acquire real property (Art. 41 (2)). On paper, at least, some of these provisions might sound innocuous enough, but they become much more invidious when one learns from Renate Weber that the text of the Constitution was directly influenced by extreme nationalistic rhetoric hostile to Romania's national minorities, in particular Hungarians.

The discussion so far implicitly accepts a presupposition behind Pitkin's view that a 'constitution' is indeed about 'who we *are*', or in other words, that it does, and should, express common views, beliefs, and ideas salient in the community. This is a view that a constitution is not so much an official document as the people's charter—reflecting their deep ideology. But this idea has not gone unquestioned; in particular, Cass Sunstein expresses an opposing view:

> It is often said that constitutions, as a form of higher law, must be compatible with the culture and mores of those whom they regulate. But in one sense, the opposite is true. Constitutions can be understood as pre-commitment strategies, in which nations use a founding document to protect against the most common problems in their usual processes. Constitutions should therefore work against a nation's most threatening tendencies.[19]

This is not the place to discuss the merits of Sunstein's view of constitutions as pre-commitment strategies,[20] or to evaluate his conclusion that constitutions should be seen as brakes on the society's implementation of its prevailing ideologies (though it can be noted in passing that the conclusion does not necessarily follow from the premiss).[21] But apart from its merits, the proposal seems extremely

---

[18] p. 234 above.

[19] Cass R. Sunstein, 'Against Positive Rights', *East European Constitutional Review* (Winter 1993), 35–9, at 36.

[20] For a powerful critique of the pre-commitment theory, see Jeremy Waldron, 'Precommitment and Disagreement', in Larry Alexander (ed.), *Constitutionalism: Philosophical Foundations* (Cambridge: Cambridge University Press, 1998), 271–99.

[21] It *would* follow if the prevailing ideology were identical with the society's impulsive and emotional behaviour, especially during politically stressful times—the sort of emotions that usually figure in the description of what a pre-commitment constitution should protect the society against.

hard to implement, and the constitutional strategies of Eastern and Central Europe certainly do not suggest that constitution makers there took Sunstein's guidance to heart. The best evidence relates to the very issue that Sunstein addressed in his article, namely socio-economic constitutional rights.

According to Sunstein, precisely because of the regrettable tradition of over-reliance on state protection in the region, and a resultant counter-incentive to individual initiative, positive rights should be absent from the post-communist constitutions. In fact, they are conspicuous by their massive presence. This creates potentially important problems, though not necessarily those envisaged by Sunstein. Rather than discouraging self-reliance and individual initiative, socio-economic constitutional rights may contaminate other, more 'traditional' rights, such as civil and personal freedoms or the right to equal treatment. This is because, if the former are necessarily non-enforceable or under-enforceable, then a cavalier attitude towards the enforceability of rights will affect also the latter. To protect against this pernicious effect, a number of strategies have been used (notably by constitutional courts) in drawing principled lines between the modes of enforcement of rights which *do* give strong and clear claims to individuals and those which describe the goals of state policy without being strictly enforceable in courts. As a result, appeals to socio-economic rights have been used mainly in order to challenge discriminatory or arbitrary distinctions in legislation and policy rather than to address more fundamentally the wisdom, or otherwise, of a government's socio-economic policies.

Constitution as a Process

The second use of the term 'constitution' in Pitkin's list is that it denotes something that we *do*: 'constitution' as a verbal noun, understood by reference 'to the action or activity of constituting—that is, of founding, framing, shaping something anew'.[22] To be sure, constitutions 'constitute' polities only rarely, and to varying degrees. There is an unfortunate tendency among some constitutional theorists to exaggerate the degree to which constitutions set up a form of political life. Some of the classical constitutions are indeed originating acts: they do stand at the point of a creation of a totally new polity. The US Constitution or the Basic Law of the Federal Republic of Germany might be examples of such originating

---

[22] Pitkin, 'The Idea of a Constitution', 168.

constitutions. But it is a very rare moment in the history of humanity when a new society is born with its basic charter. One would need to stretch one's imagination to see anything closely resembling an act of *volonté générale* marking the setting up of a political body among the often laborious efforts of various constitutional bodies discussed in this book.

Constitutions are not written on a clean slate, and they are importantly tainted by their predecessors. This is particularly true about transitional regimes, the specificity of which is that they do not involve a simple and clear rupture with the past. In contrast to truly 'originating constitutions' (let us repeat, phenomena which are few and far between in constitutional history), the constitutions of the transitional political systems have a Janus-like character: they face the future, but they also have unfinished business in the past. They are marked by all the ambiguities, uncertainties, and compromises characteristic of 'self-constraining' revolutions, or 'refolutions',[23] which separate the communist past from today and tomorrow. Hence, the coexistence of continuity with change within a transition process inevitably informs the ambiguous nature of constitutions in the transitional period. 'The velvet revolutions generally lacked clean breaks, and as such did not culminate in constitutional change of a foundational sort,' observes Ruti Teitel, a careful student of transitional constitutionalism.[24]

The understanding of constitutions as something that we *do* is important because it points our attention to the constitutional process itself, regardless of its outcome. It is remarkable that a number of writers of the chapters in this book emphasize the quasi-independent role of the process. Constitutions do not necessarily constitute new polities but constitutional processes certainly contribute to the definition of roles that various societal actors occupy, and can define themselves by reference to the constitution-making process. As Robert Elgie and Jan Zielonka declare, in constitution-building 'the process is at least as important as the product'.[25] Hence the importance of the time factor: the long duration of a constitution-making process need not be an unconditionally bad thing. The process of drafting a new constitution should not be seen as valuable only by reference to the quality of the product: it can also be intrinsically valuable as a way of producing compromise, enhancing the legitimacy of a nation's institutions, and focusing a

---

[23] See Timothy Garton Ash, *The Polish Revolution* (London: Granta, 1989), 276.

[24] Ruti Teitel, 'Transitional Jurisprudence: The Role of Law in Political Transformation', *Yale Law Journal*, 106 (1997), 2009–80, at 2068.

[25] p. 34 above.

community's attention on a debate about the public good. One of the values of a lengthy constitution-making process is that it may favour (though by no means guarantee) a broad social debate and deliberation about values and procedures to be announced in the constitution. This emphasis on the deliberative worth of the process resonates with a recent revival of the republican tradition in constitutional theory. Consider the view of one of its main contemporary proponents that one of the distinctive features of such an approach 'is that the outcome of legislative process becomes secondary. What is important is whether it is deliberation . . . that gave rise to that outcome.'[26]

There are, of course, also some important *content*-sensitive reasons *against* 'quick-fix' constitutions. While the product is not the only criterion by which to judge the worth of the process, it cannot be dismissed as an altogether irrelevant factor. In particular, such content-related causes of difficulties occur when time is seen to be so much of the essence that constitution makers hastily reinstate an old, pre-communist constitution, as in Latvia, for example. As Adolf Sprudzs suggests, 'the quick fix of readopting the 1922 Constitution actually exacerbated institutional engineering and slowed down democratic consolidation'.[27] On the other hand, a prolonged constitutional drafting process may also have its disutility: the value of legitimacy and the depth of public discourse promoted by a lengthy process might be outweighed by the instability that such a process may cause. It might also lead to the excessive 'politicization' of the constitution-making process. By this I mean a state of affairs in which the process of constitution-making becomes so enmeshed with everyday politics that its distinctive character as a space for discourse about the common good is virtually eroded, and down-to-earth interests and sectarian preferences contaminate the process of deliberating about values.

The duality of constitutional politics and ordinary politics—which, for some writers, is the epitome of constitutionalism *per se*[28]—is

[26] Cass R. Sunstein, 'Interest Groups in American Public Law', *Stanford Law Review*, 38 (1985), 29–87, at 58. Note that Sunstein made this observation with regard to legislation as such, not to constitution-making.

[27] p. 140 above.

[28] For Geoffrey Brennan and Alan Hamlin, representatives of the Constitutional Political Economy school of thinking, the very idea of constitutionalism revolves around a general distinction 'between those elements of the social fabric that condition and regulate social and political activity on the one hand and the activities that are so conditioned and regulated on the other'. Geoffrey Brennan and Alan Hamlin, 'Constitutional Political Economy: The Political Philosophy of *Homo Economicus*?', *Journal of Political Philosophy*, 3 (1995), 280–303, at 287.

then undermined, with negative consequences. Constitutionalism ceases to be (relatively) immune from rent-seeking by interest groups that are then capable of capturing the process and tailoring constitutional provisions to suit their sectarian needs and interests. In the words of a leading contemporary constitutional theorist: 'Constitutionalism . . . stands for the rare moments in a nation's history when deep, principled discussion transcends the logrolling and horse-trading of everyday majority politics, the object of these debates being the principles which are to constrain future majority decisions.'[29] This, unfortunately, is not even an approximate description of the reality of constitutional debates in the region discussed in this book, and it may be the case that a very long duration of constitution-making contributes to a dominance of 'horse-trading' over principles. When constitution-making becomes a lengthy process, it inevitably tends to resemble ordinary law-making, and the usual rent-seeking behaviour which accompanies legislation—intended to increase returns to those political agents who control the process—is replicated in the process of making the constitution, except that the stakes are higher. This is the 'politics as usual' picture of the constitution-making process.[30] Szikinger provides an example of the enmeshing of the constitution-making process with everyday politics when he talks about the 'inverse logic of Hungary's parliamentary regime', in which proposed constitutional amendments are meant to serve the purposes of planned legislation, rather than the other way round.[31]

The conclusion that can be drawn in this regard from this book is a plea for caution: there is no abstract prescription of 'the sooner, the better' in constitution-making. The right timing is a context-dependent matter, and is usually known only with the benefit of hindsight. There might be some special circumstances where speed is essential: for example, when new states need constitutions as useful additional devices to assert their sovereignty and independence in the international arena. This is a point noted by Nida Gelazis, and it is perhaps no coincidence that several new states emerging from the collapse of the communist world—all three Baltic states, as well as Slovenia and Slovakia—adopted their constitutions relatively quickly 'as the way to boost [their] legitimacy . . . in the hope of securing themselves from possible reannexation'.[32] But, on

[29] Jon Elster, 'Introduction', in Elster and Slagstad (eds.), *Constitutionalism and Democracy*, 6 (footnote omitted).

[30] See Enrico Colombato and Jonathan Macey, 'A Public-Choice View of Transition in Eastern Europe', *Economia delle scelte pubbliche*, 2/3 (1994), 113–32.

[31] p. 429 above.   [32] p. 165 above.

the other hand, it may plausibly be argued that countries such as Poland (which took eight years to adopt a brand new constitution after embarking upon its democratic path) and Hungary (which has not adopted a new constitution at all so far) have not been, on balance, made particularly worse off by this delay. As Istvan Szikinger states in his chapter, the fact that there is no new constitution is 'not a tragedy' for Hungary.[33] Some make an even stronger judgement: that the package of an old amended constitution plus an 'invisible constitution' construed by the case law of the Constitutional Court serves Hungary's needs better than a brand new constitutional act would.[34]

One should be therefore sceptical of a theory of 'constitutional moments', those allegedly brief and unusual windows of constitutional opportunity which transitional societies are said to miss at their peril. In the words of Bruce Ackerman: 'Neither the privatization of the economy nor the construction of civil society should preoccupy revolutionaries first and foremost. . . . The window of opportunity for constitutionalizing liberal revolutions is open for a shorter time than is generally recognized. Unless the constitutional moment is seized to advantage, it may be missed entirely.'[35] One problem with the concept of 'constitutional moments' is that we usually know about them when they have already passed. Another problem is that it is unclear how short is 'short'. As a commentator noted: 'It took the American revolutionaries/framers five years following the end of the Revolutionary War to adopt a viable constitutional framework for national government. Postcommunist Poland took eight years. In both cases, it was a far from easy process.'[36]

---

[33] p. 430 above.

[34] According to a central figure in Hungarian constitutional politics until very recently, the president of the Constitutional Court László Sólyom (as reported by Andrew Arato), 'the [amended but old] constitution, open to self-revision of course, is a sufficient basis for the fullest possible development of constitutionalism. . . . [A] completely new constitution could only be worse than the present one.' Andrew Arato, 'Constitution and Continuity in the Eastern European Transitions: The Hungarian Case (Part Two)', in Irena Grudzińska Gross (ed.), *Constitutionalism and Politics* (Bratislava: European Cultural Foundation, 1994), 276 (footnote omitted). Sólyom left his position in autumn 1998, and was recently described as 'the widely acknowledged intellectual leader of the [Hungarian Constitutional] Court'. Kim Lane Scheppele, 'The New Hungarian Constitutional Court', *East European Constitutional Review* (Fall 1999), 81–7, at 81.

[35] Bruce A. Ackerman, *The Future of Liberal Revolution* (New Haven: Yale University Press, 1992), 46–7.

[36] Daniel H. Cole, 'From Renaissance Poland to Poland's Renaissance', *Michigan Law Review*, 97 (1999), 2063–102, at 2093.

But there is a more fundamental concern about 'constitutional moments': they are meant to indicate those episodes in a society's history when, as it were, the People itself enters into the public stage and retrieves power from its representatives in order to speak with its own voice. This suggests that, during these unusual moments, the People revokes the authority given to its elected leaders and pronounces the rules of the game, and its fundamental values, as 'We the People'. Regrettably perhaps, no such episodes occurred in the contexts of constitution-making in Eastern and Central Europe during the period of transition. 'We the People' spoke in the Gdańsk shipyard in August 1980 and then during the strikes of summer 1988, and in Prague streets in 1989, and also in Timisoara in 1989—but these were not exercises in constitution-drafting. The true constitutive charters that paved the way to institutionalizing the transition were the agreements forged at round tables and in accompanying, behind-the-scene negotiations. And they were so in Warsaw or Budapest, as they were to be a few years later in South Africa.[37]

The negotiated transitions in these cases owed their success *not* to the depth of public deliberation but, just on the contrary, to the relative secrecy and containment of the breadth of public debate which accompanied it. They carried all the traits of a compromise between the declining and the ascending elites. In his chapter on Hungary, Szikinger reminds us that 'Hungary has a formally old, substantially new constitution which was the result of amendments passed by the outgoing communist parliament following the decisions made at the Roundtable Talks'—amendments which were neither publicly debated nor subjected to referendum. One can perhaps deplore that the specific terms of transition from communism to democracy were not hammered out by the Demos in the streets,[38] but such a romantic nostalgia for People Power would

---

[37] While the meetings of the Convention for a Democratic South Africa (CODESA) which began in December 1991, to be followed by the Multi-party Negotiating Process (MPNP) starting in March 1993, were public, as one of the active participants notes, 'the sessions of the Negotiating Council tended to provide more of a formal stamp of approval to agreements reached elsewhere', i.e., in the bilateral talks between the government and the ANC; see Hugh Corder, 'Towards a South African Constitution', *Modern Law Review*, 57 (1994), 491–528, at 503.

[38] In Andrew Arato's words: 'In a continuous transition, the population is demobilized, does not participate in its own liberation, does not come to think of the democratic republic as its own creation. . . . The new constitution does not emerge as the result of democratic participation.' Andrew Arato, 'Constitution and Continuity in the East European Transitions', in Grudzińska Gross (ed.), *Constitutionalism and Politics*, 164 (footnote omitted).

betray a disregard of historical realities. It would also pass over a fact that any student of institutions knows all too well: that in order to *enable* certain processes, institutions must also *disable* actors from certain choices and types of behaviour. A series of historic compromises of 1989 in Central Europe were made largely possible through the relative insulation of the Roundtable Talks from direct societal pressures.[39]

Constitutionalism and Political Discourse

When we consider a 'constitution' as a process rather than as an act, as something that we *do* rather than something that we *have* or that we *are*, it is important to consider the ways in which the constitution actually affects and transforms the political discourse. A constitution 'lives'—becomes an ongoing process rather than being just a single act—by transforming the way political demands, claims, and arguments are made by political actors. Constitutionalization of politics occurs when certain types of arguments are made as a function of the operation of a constitution—even though they would not have been made in the absence of a constitution —while others are aborted, rejected, or ignored only because the constitution is in place. If constitutional criteria enter into the minds of political actors and affect the claims that they press in the public arena, then we can say that constitution has been absorbed into the ongoing political process of a country.

It is relatively easy to discern such a living constitution with respect to governmental procedures and the separation of powers. While there will be always some actors who try to bypass the constitutionally entrenched procedures and allocation of competencies (President Lukashenka of Belarus is an example), and there will be also borderline cases in which discerning the 'true' meaning of the constitutional norms will not be easy, this is not a major problem of principle. Much more problematic is an attempt to discern the constitutionalization of politics through *general* constitutional pronouncements, especially with regard to the nature of the state (rule of law, democracy, social justice) and also to constitutional rights and freedoms.

So has the political discourse in post-communist countries been significantly transformed by constitutional pronouncements, in particular by constitutional bills of rights? The response will differ

[39] I owe this observation to Dr Adam Czarnota.

from country to country. Most of the authors in this book seem to be rather sceptical about the degree to which this constitution-alization of political discourse has actually occurred. But one conclusion is quite obvious: constitutionalization is not self-implementing, and in order to engage in a constitutional discourse, rather than the routine conversations of day-to-day politics, con-stitutionalization must be mediated by specific institutions which have a mission, a set of incentives, and an appropriate structure. In other words, there must be pertinent institutional devices in place, which will encourage specific actors to reason and argue in terms of constitutional values rather than in terms of current interests, preferences, and short-term benefits.

Constitutional courts are the most obvious candidates for playing this role. There has been much hype by constitutional scholars both inside and outside the region about the value of the constitutional tribunals established in post-communist constitutional systems.[40] Those courts have been often represented as almost the only virtuous points on the otherwise bleak horizon of post-communist politics. They have been described as the defenders of individual rights against oppressive bureaucracies, as the enlightened bodies constraining ignorant legislatures, and as the impartial actors pro-tecting against biased and self-interested political elites. Much of this hype has, of course, been just that: self-congratulatory propa-ganda produced mainly by lawyers for lawyers, and produced in order to strengthen the legitimacy of bodies whose authority to dis-place democratically taken decisions has inevitably been doubtful. But it does not follow that these constitutional courts have *not* contributed to the constitutionalization of politics. A cool analysis suggests that, more often than not, these constitutional courts *have* made a difference, by affecting the political discourse and infus-ing it with constitutional considerations. Whether, on balance, this is a good or a bad thing is a matter that ultimately returns us to a

---

[40] 'The performance of some of [the new East European Constitutional] courts so far shows that . . . men and women who don the robe of constitutional court judges can become courageous and vigorous defenders of constitutional principles and human rights, continuing the patterns shown elsewhere in the world.' Herman Schwartz, 'The New East European Constitutional Courts', in A. E. Dick Howard (ed.), *Con-stitution Making in Eastern Europe* (Washington: Woodrow Wilson Center Press, 1993), 194. Another commentator, Spencer Zifcak, expressed his enthusiasm right in the title of his article 'Hungary's Remarkable, Radical, Constitutional Court', *Journal of Constitutional Law in Eastern and Central Europe*, 3 (1996), 1–56, and concluded his discussion of that Court by saying '[t]here have been few, more dis-tinctive or valuable judicial contributions to emergent democracy anywhere', ibid. at 56.

point made towards the beginning of this essay: that constitutionalism, as one specific form of institutionalization of politics, has both
positive and negative consequences. It is a mixed bag. But it does
not follow that, because constitutionalization has inevitable costs
and benefits, the costs and benefits cancel each other out. Far from
it: the constitutionalization of politics in Central and Eastern
Europe has been a powerful factor in strengthening (though not
initiating) the process of transition to democracy in that region.

Selected Bibliography

Ackerman, B. A., *The Future of Liberal Revolution* (New Haven: Yale University Press, 1992).

Ágh, A. (ed.), *The Emergence of East Central European Parliaments: The First Steps* (Budapest: Hungarian Centre for Democracy Studies, 1994).

Alexander, L. (ed.), *Constitutionalism: Philosophical Foundations* (Cambridge: Cambridge University Press, 1998).

Almond, G. A., and Powell, G. B., *Comparative Politics: System, Process and Policy* (Boston: Little, Brown, 1978).

Ash, T. G., *The Polish Revolution* (London: Granta, 1989).

Baccetti, C., *Il PDS: verso un nuovo modello di partito?* (Bologna: Il Mulino, 1997).

Balcerowicz, L., *Socialism, Capitalism, Transformation* (Budapest: Central University Press, 1995).

Banting, K. G., and Simeon, R. (eds.), *Redesigning the State: The Politics of Constitutional Change in Industrial Nations* (Toronto: University of Toronto Press, 1985).

Barany, Z., and Volgyes, I. (eds.), *The Legacies of Communism in Eastern Europe* (Baltimore: Johns Hopkins University Press, 1995).

Bartole, S., *Riforme costituzionali nell'Europa centro-orientale* (Bologna: Il Mulino, 1993).

—— and di Cortona, P. G. (eds.), *Transizione e consolidamento democratico nell'Europa Centro-Orientale: elites, istituzioni e partiti* (Turin: Giappichelli, 1998).

Bartolini, S., and D'Alimonte, R. (eds.), *Maggioritario ma non troppo* (Bologna: Il Mulino, 1995).

Bebler, A., and Seroca, J. (eds.), *Contemporary Political Systems: Classifications and Typologies* (Boulder, Colo.: Lynne Rienner Publishers, 1990).

Beetham, D. (ed.), *Defining and Measuring Democracy* (Thousand Oaks, Calif.: Sage Publications, 1994).

Bellamy, R. E., and Castiglione, D. (eds.), *Constitutionalism in Transformation: European and Theoretical Perspectives* (Oxford: Blackwell, 1996).

Berglund, S., and Dellenbrant, J. A. (eds.), *The New Democracies in Eastern Europe* (Aldershot: Elgar, 1991).

Beyme, K. von, *Political Parties in Western Democracies* (New York: St Martin's Press, 1985).

—— *Transition to Democracy in Eastern Europe* (London: Macmillan, 1996).

Bialer, S. (ed.), *Politics, Society and Nationality: Inside Gorbachev's Russia* (Boulder, Colo.: Westview, 1989).

Bilmanis, A. (compiler), *Latvian–Russian Relations; Documents* (Washington: The Latvian Legation, 1944).

Blom, H. W., Blockman, W. P., and de Schepper, H. (eds.), *Bicameralisme: Tweekamerstelsel vroeger en nu* (Bicameralism: Two Chamber Systems in the Past and Now) (The Hague: Sdu Uitgeverij Koninginnegracht, 1992).

Bogdanor, V. (ed.), *Constitutions in Democratic Politics* (Aldershot: Gower, 1988).

Bozóki, A. (ed.), *Post-communist Transition: Emerging Pluralism in Hungary* (London: Pinter, 1992).

Brown, A., *The Gorbachev Factor* (Oxford: Oxford University Press, 1996).

—— and Gray, J. (eds.), *Political Culture and Political Change in Communist States* (London: Macmillan, 1977).

Budge, I., and McKay, D. (eds.), *Developing Democracy* (London: Sage, 1994).

—— Newton, K., et al., *The Politics of the New Europe: Atlantic to Urals* (London: Longman, 1997).

Bunce, V., *Subversive Institutions: The Design and the Destruction of Socialism and the State* (Cambridge: Cambridge University Press, 1999).

Carrère d'Encausee, H., *L'Empire éclaté: la révolte des nations en URSS* (Paris: Flammarion, 1978).

Ceccanti, S., *La forma di governo parlamentare in trasformazione* (Bologna: Il Mulino, 1997).

Center for International Relations (ed.), *Law and Practice of Central European Countries in the Field of National Minorities Protection after 1989* (Warsaw: Center for International Relations, 1998).

Cohen, J. L., and Arato, A., *Civil Society and Political Theory* (Cambridge, Mass.: Harvard University Press, 1992).

Cotarelo, R. (ed.), *Transición política y consolidación democrática en España (1975–1986)* (Madrid: Centro de Investigaciones Sociológicas, 1992).

Crampton, R. J., *Eastern Europe in the Twentieth Century* (London: Routledge, 1994).

Crawford, B. (ed.), *Markets, States and Democracy: The Political Economy of Post-communist Transformation* (Boulder, Colo.: Westview Press, 1995).

Dahl, R. A., *A Preface to Democratic Theory* (Chicago: University of Chicago Press, 1956).

—— *Democracy and its Critics* (New Haven: Yale University Press, 1989).

—— *A Preface to Economical Democracy* (Cambridge: Polity, 1985).

Dahrendorf, R., *Reflections on the Revolution in Europe* (London: Chatto & Windus, 1990).

Dawisha, K., and Parrott, B. (eds.), *Democratic Changes and Authoritarian Reactions in Russia, Ukraine, Belarus, and Moldova* (Cambridge: Cambridge University Press, 1997).

—— —— (eds.), *The Consolidation of Democracy in East-Central Europe* (Cambridge: Cambridge University Press, 1997).

de Enterria, E. G., and Predieri, A. (eds.), *La Constitución española de 1978* (Madrid: Editorial Civitas, 1982).

Deleanu, I., *Drept constitutional si institutii politice* [Constitutional Law and Political Institutions] (Bucharest: Europa Nova, 1996).

Diamond, L., Linz, J., and Lipset, S. M. (eds.), *Politics in Developing Countries: Comparing Experiences with Democracy* (Boulder, Colo.: Lynne Rienner, 1995).

—— and Plattner, M. F. (eds.), *The Global Resurgence of Democracy* (Baltimore: Johns Hopkins University Press, 1993).

di Palma, G., *To Craft Democracies: An Essay on Democratic Transition* (Berkeley and Los Angeles: University of California Press, 1990).

Döring, H. (ed.), *Parliaments and Majority Rule in Western Europe* (New York: St Martin Press, 1995).

Dreifelds, J., *Latvia in Transition* (New York: Cambridge University Press, 1996).

Duchacek, I., *Power Maps: Comparative Politics of Constitutions* (Santa Barbara, Calif.: ABC-Clio, 1973).

Elgie, R. (ed.), *Semi-presidentialism in Europe* (Oxford: Oxford University Press, 1999).

Elster, J. (ed.), *The Roundtable Talks and the Breakdown of Communism* (Chicago: Chicago University Press, 1996).

—— Offe, C., and Preuss, U. K., with Boenker, F., Goetting, U., and Rueb, F. W., *Institutional Design in Post-communist Societies: Rebuilding the Ship at Sea* (Cambridge: Cambridge University Press, 1998).

—— and Slagstad, R. (eds.), *Constitutionalism and Democracy* (Cambridge: Cambridge University Press, 1988).

Entin, I. M., *Separation of Powers: Experience of Modern States* (Moscow: Literature of Law, 1995).

Featherstone, K., and Katsoudas, D. K. (eds.), *Political Change in Greece* (London: Croom Helm, 1987).

Finer, S. E., *Five Constitutions* (London: Penguin, 1979).

—— Bogdanor, V., and Rudden, B., *Comparing Constitutions* (Oxford: Clarendon Press, 1995).

Fitzmaurice, J., *Politics and Government in the Visegrad Countries: Poland, Hungary, the Czech Republic and Slovakia* (London: Macmillan Press Ltd., 1998).

Frankowski, S., and Stephan, P. B. (eds.), *Legal Reform in Post-communist Europe: The View from Within* (Dordrecht: Martinus Nijhoff, 1995).

Gallagher, M., Laver, M., and Mair, P. (eds.), *Representative Government in Modern Europe* (New York: McGraw-Hill, Inc., 1995).

Galster, J., Szyszkowski, V., Wąsik, Z., and Witkowski, Z. (eds.), *Prawo Konstytucyjne* (Toruń: TNOiK, 1996).

Garlicki, L., *Kometarz do Konstytycji Rzeczypospolitej Polkiej* (Warsaw: Wydawnictwo Sejmowe, 1995).

Gerrits, A. W. M., *The Failure of Authoritarian Change: Reform, Opposition and Geo-politics in Poland in the 1980s* (Worcester: Dartmouth Publishing Company, 1991).

Gillespie, R., Waller, M., and Nieto, L. L. (eds.), 'Factional Politics and Democratization', *Democratization* (special issue), 2/1 (1995).

Goldwin, R. A., and Kaufman, A. (eds.), *Constitution Makers and Constitution Making: The Experience of Eight Nations* (Washington: American Enterprise Institute for Public Policy Research, 1988).

Goodin, R. E. (ed.), *The Theory of Institutional Design* (Cambridge: Cambridge University Press, 1996).

Grad, F., *Novi volilni sistem* (New Electoral System) (Ljubljana: Inštitut za javno upravo, 1992).

Greenberg, D., et al. (eds.), *Constitutionalism and Democracy: Transitions in the Contemporary World* (Oxford: Oxford University Press, 1993).

Greenstein, F. I., and Polsby, N. W. (eds.), *Handbook of Political Science*, Macropolitical Theory 3 (Reading, Mass.: Addison-Wesley Publishing Co., 1975).

Grimm, D., *Braucht Europa eine Verfassung?* (Munich: Carl Friedrich von Siemens-Stiftung, 1994).

Grudzińska Gross, I. (ed.), *Constitutionalism and Politics* (Bratislava: European Cultural Foundation, 1994).

Guggenberger, B., et al., *Eine Verfassung für Deutschland* (Munich: Hanser, 1991).

Gunther, R. (ed.), *Politics, Society, and Democracy: Comparative Studies: Essays in Honor of Juan J. Linz* (Boulder, Colo.: Westview Press, 1995).

—— Diamandouros, P. N., and Puhle, H., *The Politics of Democratic Consolidation: Southern Europe in Comparative Perspective* (Baltimore: Johns Hopkins University Press, 1995).

Habermas, J., *Between Facts and Norms*, trans. William Rehg (Cambridge: Polity Press, 1996).

—— *Faktizität und Geltung: Beiträge zur Diskurstheorie des Rechts und des demokratistischen Rechtsstaats* (Frankfurt: Suhrkamp, 1992).

Hadenius, A. (ed.), *Democracy's Victory and Crisis* (Cambridge: Cambridge University Press, 1997).

Hankiss, E., *East European Alternatives* (Oxford: Clarendon Press, 1990).

Heidar, K., and Koole, R., *Parliamentary Party Groups in European Democracies: Political Parties behind Closed Doors* (London: Routledge, 2000).

Held, D., *Models of Democracy* (Cambridge: Polity, 1987).

Hesse, J. J., and Johnson, N. (eds.), *Constitutional Policy and Change in Europe* (Oxford: Oxford University Press, 1995).

Heywood, P., *The Government and Politics of Spain* (London: Macmillan, 1995).

Higley, J., Pakulski, J., and Welokowski, W. (eds.), *Postcommunist Elites and Democracy in Eastern Europe* (London: Macmillan, 1998).

Holmes, L., *The End of Communist Power: Anti-corruption Campaigns and Legitimation Crisis* (Cambridge: Polity, 1993).

Howard, A. E. D. (ed.), *Constitution Making in Eastern Europe* (Washington: Woodrow Wilson Center Press, 1993).

Huntington, S. P., *The Third Wave. Democratization in the Late 20th Century* (Norman: University of Oklahoma Press, 1991).

Inglehart, R., *Modernization and Postmodernization: Cultural, Economic and Political Change in 41 Societies* (Princeton: Princeton University Press, 1997).

Jowitt, K., *New World Disorder: The Leninist Extinction* (Berkeley and Los Angeles: University of California Press, 1992).

Karatnycky, A., Motyl, A., and Shor, B. (eds.), *Nations in Transit 1997: Civil Society, Democracy and Markets in East Central Europe and the Newly Independent States* (New Brunswick, NJ: Transaction Publishers, 1997).

Karklins, R., *Ethnopolitics and Transition to Democracy: The Collapse of the USSR and Latvia* (Baltimore: Johns Hopkins University Press, 1994).

Karlsson, S. (ed.), *The Source of Liberty: The Nordic Contribution to Europe* (Stockholm: Nordic Council, 1992).

Kenney, S. J., Reisinger, W. M., and Reitz, J. C. (eds.), *Constitutional Dialogues in Comparative Perspective* (London: Macmillan, 1999).

Kirchner, E. J. (ed.), *Decentralization and Transition in the Visegrad: Poland, Hungary, The Czech Republic and Slovakia* (London: Macmillan Press Ltd., 1999).

Kiris, A. (ed.), *Restoration of the Independence of the Republic of Estonia: Selection of Legal Acts (1988–1991)* (Tallinn: Ministry of Foreign Affairs of the Republic of Estonia and Estonian Institute for Information, 1991).

Klingemann, H.-D., and Fuchs, D. (eds.), *Citizens and the State* (New York: Oxford University Press, 1995).

Konrád, G., *Antipolitik* (Frankfurt: Suhrkamp, 1985).

Kornai, J., *The Road to a Free Economy* (New York: Norton, 1990).

Krupavicius, A. (ed.), *Seimo Rinkimai '96: treciasis 'atmetimas'* (Elections to the Seimas, '96: The Third 'Round') (Vilnius: Tverme, 1998).

—— Gaidys, P., Masiulis, K., et al. (eds.), *Politines Partijos Lietuvoje* (Political Parties in Lithuania) (Vilnius: Litterae Universitatis, 1996).

Krygier, M., and Czarnota, A., *The Rule of Law after Communism: Problems and Prospects in East-Central Europe* (Aldershot: Dartmouth, 1999).

Kuzio, T. (ed.), *Contemporary Ukraine: Dynamics of Post-Soviet Transformation* (London: M. E. Sharpe, 1998).

Landfried, C. (ed.), *Constitutional Review and Legislation: An International Comparison* (Baden-Baden: Nomos, 1988).

Laver, M., and Shepsle, K. A. (eds.), *Cabinet Ministers and Parliamentary Government* (Cambridge: Cambridge University Press, 1994).

Lewis, P. (ed.), *Party Structure and Organization in East-Central Europe* (Cheltenham: Edward Elgar, 1996).

Liebert, U., and Cotta, M. (eds.), *Parliament and Democratic Consolidation in Southern Europe* (London: Pinter, 1990).

Lieven, A., *The Baltic Revolution: Estonia, Latvia, and Lithuania and the Path to Independence* (New Haven: Yale University Press, 1993).

Lijphart, A., *Democracy in Plural Societies: A Comparative Exploration* (New Haven: Yale University Press, 1977).

Lijphart, A., *Parliamentary versus Presidential Government* (Oxford: Oxford University Press, 1992).

—— and Weisman, C. (eds.), *Institutional Design in New Democracies* (Boulder, Colo.: Westview Press, 1996).

Linz, J. J., and Stepan, A., *Problems of Democratic Transition and Consolidation: Southern Europe, South America and Post-communist Europe* (Baltimore: Johns Hopkins University Press, 1996).

—— and Valenzuela, A. (eds.), *The Failure of Presidential Democracy: Comparative Perspectives*, vol. i (Baltimore: Johns Hopkins University Press, 1994).

Lipset, S. M. (ed.), *The Encyclopedia of Democracy* (Washington: Congressional Quarterly, 1995), vol. i.

—— and Rokkan, S. (eds.), *Party Systems and Voter Alignments: Cross-national Perspective* (London: Collier-Macmillan, 1967).

Locke, J., *Two Treatises of Government*, ed. Peter Laslett (New York: Mentor, 1965).

Ludwikowski, R. R., *Constitution-Making in the Region of Former Soviet Dominance* (Durham, NC: Duke University Press, 1996).

McWhinney, E., *Constitution-Making: Principles, Process, Practice* (Toronto: University of Toronto Press, 1981).

Mainwaring, S., O'Donnell, G., and Valenzuela, J. S. (eds.), *Issues in Democratic Consolidation: The New South-American Democracies in Comparative Perspective* (Notre Dame: University of Notre Dame Press, 1992).

Mendelbaum, M. (ed.), *Post-communism: Four Perspectives* (New York: Council on Foreign Relations, 1996).

Maravall, J. M., *The Transition to Democracy in Spain* (London: Croom Helm, 1982).

March, J. G., and Olsen, J. P., *Rediscovering Institutions: The Organizational Basis of Politics* (New York: Free Press, 1989).

Marks, G., and Diamond, L. (eds.), *Reexamining Democracy* (London: Sage, 1992).

Mayntz, R., and Scharpf, F. W. (eds.), *Gesellschaftliche Selbstregelung und politische Steuerung* (Frankfurt: Campus, 1995).

Meer Krok-Paszkowska, A. van der, *Shaping the Democractic Order: The Institutionalisation of Parliament in Poland* (Leuven: Garant, 2000).

Merkel, W., et al. (eds.), *Gesellschaftliche Selbstregelung und politische Steuerung* (Frankfurt: Campus, 1996).

Micgiel, J. S. (ed.), *Perspectives on Political and Economic Transitions after Communism* (New York: Institute on East Central Europe, Columbia University, 1997).

Mikloško, F., *Čas stretnutí* (The Time of Meetings) (Bratislava: Kalligram, 1996).

Moran, M., and Wright, M. (eds.), *The Market and the State* (London: Macmillan, 1991).

Morlino, L., *Democracy between Consolidation and Crisis: Parties, Groups and Citizens in Southern Europe* (Oxford: Oxford University Press, 1998).

Motyl, A. J., *Dilemmas of Independence: Ukraine after Totalitarianism* (New York: Council on Foreign Relations, 1993).

Muraru, I., *Drept constitutional si institutii politice* [Constitutional Law and Political Institutions] (Bucharest: Editura ACTAMI, 1995).

Nohlen, D., *Wahlrecht und Parteiensystem* (Opladen: Leske & Budrich, 1990).

Norton, P. (ed.), *Legislatures* (Oxford: Oxford University Press, 1990).

Oberdoff, H. (ed.), *Les Constitutions de l'Europe des Douze* (Paris: La Documentation Française, 1992).

O'Donnell G., and Schmitter, P. (eds.), *Transitions from Authoritarian Rule* (Baltimore: Johns Hopkins University Press, 1986).

Offe, C., *Varieties of Transition* (Cambridge, Mass.: MIT Press, 1996).

Olson, D. M., *The Legislative Process: A Comparative Approach* (New York: Harper & Row, 1980).

Plakans, A., *The Latvians; A Short History* (Stanford, Calif.: Hoover Institution Press, 1995).

Podgorecki, A., and Olgiati, V. (eds.), *Totalitarian and Post-totalitarian Law* (Aldershot: Dartmouth, 1996).

Pogany, I. (ed.), *Human Rights in Eastern Europe* (Aldershot: E. Elgar, 1995).

Powell, W. W., and DiMaggio, P. J. (eds.), *The New Institutionalism in Organizational Analysis* (Chicago: University of Chicago Press, 1991).

Preuss, U. K., *Constitutional Aspects of the Making of Democracy in the Post-communist Societies of East Europe* (Bremen: Zentrum für Europäische Rechtspolitik an der Universität Bremen, 1993).

Pridham, G., and Lewis, P. G. (eds.), *Stabilizing Fragile Democracies: Comparing New Party Systems in Southern and Eastern Europe* (London: Routledge, 1996).

—— and Vanhanen, T. (eds.), *Democratization in Eastern Europe: Domestic and International Perspective* (London: Routledge, 1994).

Przeworski, A., *Democracy and the Market* (Cambridge: Cambridge University Press, 1991).

Putnam, R. D., with Leonardi, R., and Nanetti, R. Y., *Making Democracy Work* (Princeton: Princeton University Press, 1993).

Ramet, S. P., *Social Currents in Eastern Europe: The Sources and the Meaning of the Great Transformation* (Durham, NC: Duke University Press, 1991).

Rose, R., Mishler, W., and Haerpfer, C., *Democracy and its Alternatives: Understanding Post-communist Societies* (Cambridge: Polity Press, 1998).

Rupnik, J., *The Other Europe* (London: Weidenfeld & Nicolson, 1989).

Sabaliunas, L., *Lithuania in Crisis: Nationalism to Communism 1939–1940* (Bloomington: Indiana University Press, 1972).

Šafaříková, V. (ed.), *Transformace české společnosti 1989–1995* (The Transformation of Czech Society 1989–1995) (Prague: Doplněk, 1996).

Sakwa, R., *Russian Politics and Society* (London: Routledge, 1993).

Sanford, G. (ed.), *Democratization in Poland, 1988–90* (New York: St Martin's Press, 1992).

Sartori, G., *Comparative Constitutional Engineering: An Inquiry into Structures, Incentives, and Outcomes* (London: Macmillan, 1994).

—— *The Theory of Democracy Revisited* (Chatham: Chatham House, 1987).

Schneider, H. (ed.), *Taasvabanenud Eesti põhiseaduse eellugu* (The Antecedent Story behind Re-emancipated Estonia's Constitution) (Tartu: Juura, 1997).

Schöpflin, G., *Politics in Eastern Europe 1945–1992* (Oxford: Blackwell, 1993).

Schumpeter, J., *Capitalism, Socialism and Democracy* (New York: Harper Colophon Books, 1975).

Shugart, M. S., and Carey, J. M., *Presidents and Assemblies: Constitutional Design and Electoral Dynamics* (Cambridge: Cambridge University Press, 1992).

Skocpol, T., et al. (eds.), *Bringing the State Back in* (Cambridge: Cambridge University Press, 1985).

Sprudzs, A. (ed.), *The Baltic Path to Independence: An International Reader of Selected Articles* (Buffalo: William S. Hein & Co., 1994).

Szomolányi, S., and Mesežnikov, G. (eds.), *The Slovak Path of Transition—to Democracy?* (Bratislava: Slovak Political Science Association, 1994).

Taras, R. (ed.), *Post-communist Presidencies* (Cambridge: Cambridge University Press, 1997).

Vahtre, L., *Vabanemine* (Emancipation) (Tallinn: IM Meedia, 1996).

Vanhanen, T., *Prospects of Democracy: A Study of 172 Countries* (London: Routledge, 1997).

Verdery, K., *What Was Socialism and What Comes Next?* (Princeton: Princeton University Press, 1996).

Verheijn, T., *Constitutional Pillars for New Democracies: The Cases of Bulgaria and Romania* (Leiden: Leiden University Press, 1995).

Vile, M. J. C., *Constitutionalism and Separation of Powers* (Oxford: Clarendon Press, 1967).

Weaver, R. K., and Rockmann, B. A. (eds.), *Do Institutions Matter?* (Washington: Bookings, 1991).

Wheare, K. C., *Modern Constitutions* (London: Oxford University Press, 1966).

White, S., Batt, J., and Lewis, P. G. (eds.), *Developments in East European Politics* (Houndmills: Macmillan, 1993).

White, S., *Political Culture and Social Politics* (London: Macmillan, 1979).

Whitehead, L., *The International Dimensions of Democratization: Europe and the Americas* (Oxford: Oxford University Press, 1996).

Zielonka, J., *Political Ideas in Contemporary Poland* (Aldershot: Avebury, 1989).

Index